Painted by Dubuffe

Eng'd by Augustus Robin, N.Y.

ROSA BONI

EMINENT WOMEN OF THE AGE.

Engᵈ by G.E. Perine & Co N.Y.

FLORENCE NIGHTINGALE.

S. M. BETTS & CO. HARTFORD, CONN.

EMINENT

WOMEN OF THE AGE;

BEING NARRATIVES OF

THE LIVES AND DEEDS

OF THE

Most Prominent Women of the Present Generation.

BY

JAMES PARTON, HORACE GREELEY, T. W. HIGGINSON, J. S. C. ABBOTT,
PROF. JAMES M. HOPPIN, WILLIAM WINTER, THEODORE TILTON, FANNY FERN,
GRACE GREENWOOD, MRS. E. C. STANTON, ETC.

Richly Illustrated with Fourteen Steel Engravings.

HARTFORD, CONN.:
S. M. BETTS & COMPANY.
W. H. BOOTHROYD, DETROIT, MICH
GIBBS & NICHOLS, CHICAGO, ILL.
H. H. BANCROFT & CO., SAN FRANCISCO, CAL.
1868.

Manufactured by
CASE, LOCKWOOD & BRAINARD,
HARTFORD, CONN.

LIST OF ENGRAVINGS.

PREFACE.

THE world is full of books that narrate the deeds and utter the praises of men. The lives of eminent men of our own time are made familiar to us in newspapers and magazines, in individual sketches and autobiographies, as well as in histories, dictionaries of biography, cyclopedias and other works of greater or less range of subject and extent of information. But, while many things have been written both by and for women, and much information has been published in one form and another in respect to eminent women of our age, there is not in existence, so far as the publishers are aware, any work, or series of works, which supplies the information contained in this volume, or preoccupies its field.

And it appears to the publishers that there is a demand for this very work. The discussions of the present day in regard to the elevation of woman, her duties, and the position which she is fitted to occupy, seem to call for some authentic and attractive record of the lives and achievements of those women of our time who have distinguished themselves in their various occupations and conditions in life. The knowledge of what has been attempted and accomplished by eminent women of our time is fitted to make an impression for good upon the young women of our land, and upon the whole American public. It will tend to develop and strengthen correct ideas respecting the influence of woman, and her share in the privileges and responsibilities of human life.

In selecting the subjects for the sketches here presented, regard has been had not only to individual excellence or eminence, but also to a proper representation of the various professions in which women have distinguished themselves. For obvious reasons, also, the selection has been confined chiefly to American women.

In selecting the writers for the various sketches, the publishers have chosen those only whom they knew to be thoroughly qualified for the particular tasks assigned them, and so interested in the subjects of their sketches as to be prepared to do them full justice. Great attention has been given to the collection of materials which should be at once interesting and authentic. Variety and freshness of interest are secured by obtaining sketches from a large number of able writers, and by arranging their contributions so that no two consecutive chapters are the production of the same person. As it was impossible, on account of the lack of space, to give extended sketches of all who ought to be noticed in this volume, and in some cases, also, the requisite materials for such sketches could not be procured, briefer notices have been prepared of certain groups, which, it is believed, will be no unacceptable addition to the more elaborate chapters.

This work aims to present in its literary department, as well as in its engravings, an attractive series of accurate and life-like pictures. As a literary production, containing the best essays and finest thoughts of many of the first writers of the day, it must be a source of profit and pleasure to every reader of critical taste. The engravings, like the written sketches, are no creations of fancy, but trustworthy delineations of the features of those whom they profess to represent.

The publishers have spared neither time nor expense, in the preparation of the present work, and they confidently believe that the importance of the field which it occupies, the ability and reputation of its writers, the freshness and reliableness of its facts, and the excellence of its engravings and typography, will justify the praises already bestowed upon its plan and execution by men and women of discernment, and insure to it a wide-spread and lasting popularity.

HARTFORD, July 15, 1868.

TABLE OF CONTENTS.

WOMAN AS PHYSICIAN.

EMINENT WOMEN OF THE AGE.

FLORENCE NIGHTINGALE.

BY JAMES PARTON.

FLORENCE NIGHTINGALE is one of the fortunate of the earth. Inheriting from nature a striking and beneficent talent, she was able to cultivate that talent in circumstances the most favorable that could be imagined, and, finally, to exercise it on the grandest scale in the sight of all mankind. Whatever difficulties may have beset her path, they were placed in it not by untoward fortune; they existed in the nature of her work, or were inseparable from human life itself. She has had the happiness, also, of laboring in a purely disinterested spirit, and has been able to do for love what money could neither procure nor reward.

The felicity of both her names, *Florence* and *Nightingale*, has often been remarked; and it appears that she owes both of them to accident. Her father is William Edward Shore, an English gentleman of an ancient and wealthy Sheffield family, and her mother is a daughter of William Smith, who was for many years a member of Parliament, where he was particularly distinguised for his advocacy of the emancipation of the slaves in the British possessions. In 1815, her father inherited the estates of his grand-uncle, Peter Nightingale, on the condition expressed in his uncle's will, of his assuming the name of Nightingale. It so happened that she first saw the light while the family were residing at the beautiful city of Florence, and to this fact she is indebted for her first name. The family consists of but four members, father, mother, and the two daughters, Parthenope and Florence. The date of the birth of the younger sister, Florence, is variously given in the slight accounts which have been published of her life; but it was said in the public prints, at the time when her name was on every tongue, that she was born in the same year as Queen Victoria, which was 1819.

Her father is a well-informed and intelligent man, and it was under his guidance that she attained a considerable proficiency in the Latin language and in mathematics, as well as in the usual branches and accomplishments of female education. Early in life she was conversant with French, German, and Italian; she became also a respectable performer upon the piano; and she had that general acquaintance with science, and that interest in objects of art, which usually mark the intelligent mind.

Even as a little girl she was observed to have a particular fondness for nursing the sick. She had the true nurse's touch, and that ready sympathy with the afflicted which enables those who possess it to divine their wants before they are expressed. In England, as in most other densely peopled countries, poverty and disease abound on every side, in painful contrast to the elegance and abundance by which persons of the rank of Miss Nightingale are surrounded. One consequence of this is, that the daughters of affluence, unless they are remarkably devoid of good feeling, employ part of their leisure in visiting the cottages of the poor, and ministering to the wants of the infirm and the sick. It was thus that Florence Nightingale began her voluntary apprenticeship to the noble art of mitigating human anguish. Not content with paying the usual round of visits to the cottages near her father's estate, and giving, here a little soup, and there a flannel petticoat, and at another place a poor man's plaster, she seriously studied the art of nursing, visited hospitals in the neighborhood, and read with the utmost eagerness whatever she could find in her father's library relating to the treatment of disease, and the management of asylums.

This was no romantic fancy of her youth. Miss Nightingale is a truly intelligent and gifted woman, — as far as possible removed from the cast of character which is at once described and stigmatized by the word romantic. She earnestly desired to know the best manner of mitigating the sufferings of the sick, the wounded, and the infirm; and she studied this beautiful science as a man studies that which he truly and ardently wishes to understand.

As it is the custom of wealthy families in England to spend part of every year in London, Miss Nightingale was enabled to extend the sphere of her observation to the numberless hospitals and asylums of that metropolis. These institutions are on the grandest scale, and were liberally endowed by the generosity of former ages; but at that time many of them abounded in abuses and defects of every description. Everywhere she saw the need of better nurses, women trained and educated to their work. Excellent surgeons were to be found in most of them; but in many instances the admirable skill of the surgeon was balked and frustrated by the blundering ignorance or the obstinate conceit of the nurse. Those who observed this elegant young lady moving softly about the wards of the hospitals, little imagined, perhaps, that from her was to come the reform of those institutions.

Miss Nightingale may almost be said to have created the art of which she is the most illustrious teacher; but she was yet far from having perfected herself; many years were still to elapse before she was prepared to speak with the authority of a master. Mrs. Gamp still flourished for a while, although her days were numbered.

It must not be supposed that this noble-minded lady denied herself the pleasures proper to her age, sex, and rank. She enjoyed society and the pleasures of society, both in the country and in town. Without being strictly beautiful, her face was singularly pleasing in its expression, and she had a slight, trim, and graceful figure. Her circle of friends and acquaintances was large, and among them she was always welcome; but, like most properly constituted persons of our Saxon blood, the happiest spot to her on earth was her own home. The family connection of the Nightingales in England is numerous, and she had friends enough for all the purposes of life among her own relations.

About 1845, in company with her parents and sister, she made an extensive tour in Germany, France, and Italy, visiting everywhere the hospitals, infirmaries, and asylums, and watching closely the modes of treatment practised in them. The family continued their journey into Egypt, where they resided for a considerable time, and where the gifts of Miss Nightingale in nursing the sick were, for the first time, called into requisition beyond the circle of her own family and dependants. Several sick Arabs, it is said, were healed by her during this journey, which extended as far as the farthest cataracts of the Nile. Her tour was of eminent use to her in many ways. It increased her familiarity with the languages of Europe, and gave her a certain knowledge of the world and of men, as well as of her art, which she turned to such admirable account a few years later. Returning to England, she resumed her ordinary life as the daughter of a country gentleman; but not for a long time.

Miss Nightingale, born into the Church of England, was then, and has ever since remained, a devoted member of it. In her religion, however, there is nothing bigoted nor excessive; she is one of those who manifest it chiefly by cheerfulness, charity, and good-living; nor does her attachment to her own church blind her to the excellences of others. In her travels upon the continent of Europe, she had often met the Sisters of Charity, and members of other Catholic Orders, serving in the hospitals and asylums, and serving, too, with a fidelity, constancy, and skill, which excited in her the highest admiration and the profoundest respect. It was a favorite dream of her youth, that, perhaps, there might one day be among Protestants some kind of Order of Nurses, — a band of women devoted, for a time, or for life, to the holy and arduous work of alleviating the anguish of the sick-bed. About the year 1848, she heard that there was something of the kind in Germany, under the charge of a benevolent lady and a venerable Lutheran pastor. She hastened to enter this school of nurses, and spent six months there, acquiring valuable details of her art. In the hospital attached to it she served as one of the regular corps of nurses, among whom she was greatly distinguished for her skill and thoroughness.

Upon her return to England, an opportunity was speedily furnished her for exercising her improved skill.

A very numerous class in England are family governesses. English people are not so well aware, as we are, how much better it is for children to go to a good school than to pursue their education at home, even under the most skilful private teacher. Consequently, almost every family in liberal circumstances has a resident governess, an unhappy being, who suffers many of the inconveniences attached to the lot of a servant, without enjoying the solid advantages which ought to accompany servitude. Upon salaries of twenty or thirty pounds a year, many of these ladies are required to make a presentable appearance, and associate, upon a sort of equality, with persons possessing a hundred times their revenue. Unable to save anything for their declining years, nothing can be conceived more pitiable than the situation of a friendless English governess whom age or infirmities have deprived of employment and of home. For the benefit of such, an asylum was established in London several years ago, which, however, had but a feeble life and limited means. Miss Nightingale, on her return from Germany, was informed that the institution was on the point of being given up, owing to its improper management and the slenderness of its endowment. Her aid was sought by the friends of the asylum. She accepted the laborious post of its superintendent, and she left her beautiful abode in the country, and took up her residence in the establishment in London, to which she gave both her services and a large part of her income. For many months she was seldom seen at the entertainments, public and private, which she was formerly in the habit of enjoying; for she was in her place by the bedside of sick, infirm, or dying inmates of the governesses' hospital. She restored order to its finances; she increased the number of its friends; she improved the arrangements of the interior; and when her health gave way under the excessive labors of her position, and she was compelled to retire to the country, she had the satisfaction of leaving the institution firmly established and well regulated.

But the time was at hand when her talents were to be employed upon a grander scale, and when her country was to reap the full result of her study and observation. The war with Russia occurred. In February and March, 1854, shiploads of troops were leaving England for the seat of war, and the heart of England went with them.

In all the melancholy history of warlike expeditions, there is no record of one which was managed with such cruel inefficiency as this. Everything like foresight, the adaptation of means to ends, knowledge of the climate, knowledge of the human constitution, seemed utterly wanting in those who had charge of sending these twenty-five thousand British troops to the shores of the Black Sea. The first rendezvous was at Malta, an island within easy reach of many of the most productive parts of two continents; but even there privation and trouble began. One regiment would find itself destitute of fuel, but overwhelmed with candles. In one part of the island there was a superfluity of meat, and no biscuit; while, elsewhere, there was an abundant supply of food for men, but none for horses. It afterwards appeared that no one had received anything like exact or timely information, either as to the number of troops expected to land upon the island, or as to the time when they would arrive. A curious example of the iron rigidity of routine in the British service was this: In the old wars it took eight weeks for a transport to sail from England to Malta; but although these troops were all conveyed in steamers, every steamer carried the old allowance of eight weeks' supply of medicines and wines. The chief physician of the force had been forty years in service, and the whole machinery of war worked stiffly from long inaction.

When the troops reached Gallipoli, on the coast of the Sea of Marmora, their sufferings really began. No one had thought to provide interpreters; there were neither carts nor draught animals; so that it frequently happened that a regiment would be on shore several days without having any meat. It does not appear to have occurred to any one that men could ever suffer from cold in a latitude so much more southern than that of England. The climate of that region is, in fact, very similar to that of New York or Philadelphia. There are the same intense heats in summer, the same occasional deep snows, excessive cold, and fierce, freezing rains of winter; — one of those climates which possess many of the inconveniences both of the torrid and the frigid zones, and demand a systematic provision against both. In the middle of April, at Gallipoli, the men began to suffer much from cold. Many of them had no beds, and not a soldier in the army had more than the one regulation blanket. Instead of undressing to go to bed, they put on all the clothes they had, and wrapped themselves in anything they could find. There was a small supply of blankets, but there was no one at hand who was authorized to serve them out, and it was thought a wonderful degree of courage in a senior staff-surgeon when he actually took the responsibility of appropriating some of these blankets for the use of the sick in the temporary hospital. The very honesty of the English stood in their way.

"These French Zouaves," wrote Dr. Russell, the celebrated correspondent of the London Times, "are first-rate foragers. You may see them in all directions laden with eggs, meat, fish, vegetables (onions), and other good things, while our fellows can get nothing. Sometimes, our servant is sent out to cater for breakfast or dinner; he returns with the usual 'Me and the Colonel's servant has been all over the town, and can get nothing but eggs and onions, sir;' and lo! round the corner appears a red-breeched Zouave or Chasseur, a bottle of wine under his left arm, half a lamb under the other, and poultry, fish, and other luxuries dangling round him. 'I'm sure, I don't know how these French manages it, sir,' says the crestfallen Mercury, and retires to cook the eggs."

Some of the general officers, instead of directing their energies to remedying this state of things, appear to have been chiefly concerned in compelling men to shave every day, and to wear their leathern stocks on parade. One of the generals, it is said, hated hair on the heads and faces of soldiers with a kind of mania. "Where there is much hair," said he, "there is dirt, and where there is dirt there will be disease;" forgetting that hair was placed upon the human head and face to protect it against winds and weather such as these soldiers were experiencing. It was not until the army had been ten weeks in the field, and were exposed to the blazing heat of summer, that the Queen's own guards were permitted to leave off those terrible stocks, and they celebrated the joyful event by three as thundering cheers as ever issued from the emancipated throats of men. After six months' service, the great boon was granted of permitting the men to wear a mustache, but not a beard. It was not until almost all order was lost and stamped out of sight in the mire and snow of the following winter, that the general in command allowed his troops to enjoy the protection of the full beard. Nor were the private habits of the men conducive to the preservation of their health. Twenty soldiers of one regiment were in the guard-house on the same day for drunkenness, at Gallipoli. As late as the middle of April there was still a lamentable scarcity of everything required for the hospital. "There were no blankets for the sick," wrote Dr. Russell, "no beds, no mattresses, no medical comforts of any kind; and the invalid soldiers had to lie for several days on the bare boards, in a wooden house, with nothing but a single blanket as bed and covering."

Every time the army moved it seemed to get into worse quarters, and to be more wanting in necessary supplies. The camp at Aladyn, where the army was posted at the end of June, was a melancholy example of this truth. The camp was ten miles from the sea, in the midst of a country utterly deserted, and the only communication between the camp and the post was furnished by heavy carts, drawn by buffaloes, at the rate of a mile and a half an hour; and by this kind of transportation an army of twenty-five thousand men, and thirteen thousand horses, had to be fed. The scene can be imagined, as well as the results upon the comfort and health of the troops.

In July the cholera broke out, and carried off officers and men of both armies in considerable numbers. July the 24th, it suddenly appeared in the camp of the light division, and twenty men died in twenty-four hours. A sergeant attacked at seven, A. M., was dead at noon. What was, at once, remarkable and terrible in this disease, it was often quite painless. And yet, in the midst of all this horror and death, the soldiers of both armies exhibited a wonderful recklessness. "You find them," wrote Dr. Russell, "lying drunk in the kennels, or in the ditches by the roadsides, under the blazing rays of the sun, covered with swarms of flies. You see them in stupid sobriety, gravely paring the rind off cucumbers of portentous dimensions, and eating the deadly cylinders one after another, to the number of six or eight, — all the while sitting in groups, in the open streets; or, frequently, three or four of them will make a happy bargain with a Greek, for a large basketful of apricots, water-melons, wooden pears, and green gages, and then they retire beneath the shades of a tree, where they divide and eat the luscious food till nought remains but a heap of peels, rind, and stones. They dilute the mass of fruit with peach brandy, and then straggle home, or go to sleep as best they can."

Think of the military discipline which could compel the wearing of stocks, forbid the growth of a beard, and *permit* such heedless suicide as this, of men appointed to maintain the honor of their country's flag on foreign soil! How incredible it would be, if we had not abundant proof of the fact, that, at this very time, a lieutenant-general issued an order directing cavalry officers *to lay in a stock of yellow ochre and pipe clay*, for the use of the men in rubbing up their uniforms and accoutrements!

On the 13th of September, 1854, twenty-seven thousand British troops were landed upon the shores of the Crimea, and marched six miles into the country. There was not so much as a tree for shelter on that bleak and destitute coast. The French troops who landed on the same day had small shelter tents with them; but in all the English host there was but one tent. Towards night the wind rose, and it began to rain. At midnight, the rain fell in torrents, and continued to do so all the rest of the night, penetrating the blankets and overcoats of the troops, and beating pitilessly down upon the aged generals, the young dandies, the steady-going gentlemen, as well as upon the private soldiers of the English army, who slept in puddles, ditches, and water-courses, without fire, without grog, and without any certain prospect of breakfast. One general slept under a cart, and the Duke of Cambridge himself was no better accommodated. This was but the beginning of misery. On the following day, signals were made on the admiral's ship for all the vessels of the great fleet to send their sick men on board the Kangaroo. Thoughtless order! In the course of the day, this vessel was surrounded by hundreds of boats filled with sick soldiers and sailors, and it was soon crowded to suffocation. Before night closed in, there were fifteen hundred sick on board of her, and the scene was so full of horror that the details were deemed unfit for publication. The design was that these sick men should be conveyed on the Kangaroo to the neighborhood of Constantinople, to be placed in hospital. But when she had been crammed with her miserable freight, she was ascertained to be unseaworthy, and all the fifteen hundred had to be transferred to other vessels. Many deaths occurred during the process of removal. On the same day men were dying on the beach, and did actually die, without any medical assistance whatever. When the hospital was about to be established at Balaklava, some days after, sick men were sent thither before the slightest preparation for them had been made, and many of them remained in the open street for several hours in the rain.

Winter came on, — such a winter as we are accustomed to in and near the city of New York. It began with that terrible hurricane, which many doubtless remember reading of at the time. The whole army were still living in tents. No adequate preparation had been made, of any kind, for protecting the troops against such snows, and cold, and rain, as they were certain to experience. This hurricane broke upon the camp early in the morning of November the fourteenth, an hour before daylight, the wind bringing with it torrents of rain. The air was filled with blankets, coats, hats, jackets, quilts, bedclothes, tents, and even with tables and chairs. Wagons and ambulances were overturned by the force of the wind. Almost every tent was laid prostrate. The cavalry horses, terrified at the noise, broke loose, and the whole country, as far as the eye could reach, was covered with galloping horses. During the day the storm continued to rage, while not a fire could be lighted, nor any beginning made of repairing the damage. Towards night it began to snow, and a driving storm of snow and sleet tormented the army during the night. This storm proved more deadly on sea than on shore, and many a ship, stored with warm clothing, of which these troops were in perishing need, went to the bottom of the Black Sea.

A few days after, Doctor Russell wrote: "It is now pouring rain, — the skies are black as ink, — the wind is howling over the staggering tents, — the trenches are turned into dykes, — in the tents the water is sometimes a foot deep, — our men have not either warm or water-proof clothing, — they are out for twelve hours at a time in the trenches, — they are plunged into the inevitable miseries of a winter campaign, — and not a soul seems to care for their comfort, or even for their lives. These are hard truths, but the people of England must hear them. They must know that the wretched beggar, who wanders about the streets of London in the rain, leads the life of a prince compared with the British soldiers who are fighting out here for their country, and who, we are complacently assured by the home authorities, are the best appointed army in Europe. They are well fed, indeed, but they have no shelter, no rest, and no defence against the weather. The tents, so long exposed to the blaze of a Bulgarian sun, and now continually drenched by torrents of rain, let the wet through 'like sieves,' and are perfectly useless as protections against the weather."

Never was there such mismanagement. While the army were in this condition they suddenly found themselves reduced to a short allowance of food, and for nine days there was no tea or coffee. The reason was, that the country roads, by which the provisions were brought from the seaside, seven miles distant, had become almost impassable. Every one could have foreseen that this would be the case during the rainy season. Every one could also see that the whole country was covered with small stones, just fit for making good roads; but nothing was done, and, for many miserable weeks, it was all that the commissary officers could do to keep the army alive. As for the port itself, — Balaklava, — it was such a scene of filth and horror as the earth has seldom exhibited. Indeed, it was said, at the time, that all the pictures ever drawn of plague and pestilence, whether in works of fact or of fiction, fell far short of the scenes of disease and death which abounded in this place. In the hospitals the dead lay side by side with the living, and both were objects appalling to look upon. There was not the least attention paid to cleanliness or decency, and men died without the least effort being made to save or help them. "There they lie," records a writer, "just as they were let gently down on the ground by their comrades, who brought them on their backs from the camp with the greatest tenderness, but who are not allowed to remain with them. The sick appear to be tended by the sick, and the dying by the dying." The four-footed creatures suffered not less than their masters. "Two hundred of your horses have died," said a Turk one morning to a British officer. "Behold! what I have said is the truth;" and, as he said these words, he emptied a sack upon the floor, and there were four hundred horses' ears heaped up before the eyes of the wondering officer.

In January deep snows came to aggravate all this misery. At one time there were *three feet of snow* upon the ground. On the 8th of January, 1855, one regiment could only muster seven men fit for duty; another had thirty; a freshly landed company was reduced from fifty-six to fourteen in a few days; and a regiment of Guards, which had had in all fifteen hundred and sixty-two men, could muster but two hundred and ten. What wonder! On that same eighth day of January some of Queen Victoria's own Household Guards were walking about in the snow, and going into action at night, without soles to their shoes! Many men were frozen stiff in their tents; and as late as January the 19th, when there were drifts of snow six feet deep, sick men were lying in wet tents with only one blanket! No one, therefore, will be surprised at the statement that on the 10th of February, out of a total of 44,948 British troops, 18,177 were in hospital.

The word hospital, when used in reference to the Crimean war, only conjures up scenes of horror. Two scenes, selected from many such, will suffice to convey to the reader a vivid idea of the hospitals of the Crimea before an Angel went from England to reform them. January the 25th the surgeon of a ship, appointed to convey the sick to the general hospital at Scutari, went on shore at Balaklava and applied to an officer in charge of stores for two or three stoves to put on board his ship to warm the sick and dying troops. "Three of my men," said he, "died last night from choleraic symptoms brought on by the extreme cold of the ship, and I fear more will follow them from the same cause." "Oh," said the storekeeper, "you must make your requisition in due form, send it up to head-quarters, and get it signed properly, and returned, and then I will let you have the stoves." "But my men may die meantime." "I can't help that; I must have the requisition." "It is my firm belief that there are men now in a dangerous state whom another night will certainly kill." "I really can do nothing; I must have a requisition properly signed before I can give one of those stoves away." "For God's sake, then, *lend* me some; I'll be responsible for their safety." "I really can do nothing of the kind." "But, consider, this requisition will take time to be filled up and signed, and meantime these poor fellows will go." "I cannot help that." "I'll be responsible for any thing you do." "Oh, no, that can't be done." "Will a requisition signed by the post medical officer of this place be of any use?" "No." "Will it answer if he takes on himself the responsibility?" "Certainly not." The surgeon went off in sorrow and disgust, knowing well that brave men were doomed to death by the obstinacy of this keeper of her Majesty's stores.

Another fact: In the middle of this terrible winter there was a period of three weeks when the hospitals nearest the main body of the army were totally destitute of medicines for the three most frequent diseases of an army in winter quarters; namely, fever, rheumatism, and diarrhœa. The most agonizing circumstance was, that the government had provided everything in superabundance. But one hospital would have a prodigious superfluity of fuel, and no mattresses. Another would have tons of pork, and no rice. Another would have plenty of the materials for making soup, but no vessels to make it in. Here, there would be an abundance of coffee, but no means of roasting it; and, there, a hundred chests of tea, and not a pound of sugar to put in it. Again, there would be a house full of some needed article, and no officer within miles who had authority to serve it out. The surgeons did their best; but what could the few surgeons of fifty regiments do with twenty thousand sick men? As for nurses, there was hardly a creature worthy of the name in the Crimea. In view of such facts as these no one can be surprised that the great hospitals at Scutari were in such a condition, that, probably, they were the direct means of killing ten men for every one whom they saved from death. It had perhaps been better if the poor fellows had been wrapped in blankets and laid upon a sheet of India-rubber on the snow in the open air, fed now and then, and left to take their chance.

England heard of all this with amazement and consternation. It was the "Times" newspaper through which it learned the details, and people began spontaneously to send sums of money to the editor of that journal for the relief of the soldiers. The proprietors of the "Times" consented, at length, to receive and appropriate money for this object, and in thirteen days the sum of fifteen thousand pounds sterling was sent in. With this money thousands of shirts, sheets, stockings, overcoats, flannels, and tons of sugar, soap, arrow-root, and tea, and great quantities of wine and brandy, were purchased, and a commissioner was sent out to superintend their distribution. But the great horror was, the neglect of the sick in the hospitals, and a cry arose for a corps of skilful, educated nurses.

There was but one woman in England fitted by character, position, and education, to head such a band. Sidney Herbert, a member of the British cabinet, was an old friend of Florence Nightingale's father. Mr. Herbert was thus acquainted with the peculiar bent of Miss Nightingale's disposition, and the nature of her training. By a curious coincidence, and yet not an unnatural one, she wrote to him offering her services, and he wrote to her asking her aid, on the same day. Other ladies of birth and fortune volunteered to accompany her, to whom were added some superior professional nurses. October the 24th, 1854, Florence Nightingale, accompanied by a clerical friend and his wife, and by a corps of thirty-seven nurses, left England for the Crimea, followed by the benedictions of millions of their countrymen.

They travelled through France to Marseilles. On their journey the ladies were treated with more than the usual politeness of Frenchmen; the inn-keepers and even the servants would not take payment for their accommodation, and all ranks of people appeared to be in most cordial sympathy with their mission. Among other compliments paid Miss Nightingale by the press, one of the newspapers informed the public that her dress was charming, and that she was almost as graceful as the ladies of Paris.

From Marseilles they were conveyed in a steamer to Scutari, where the principal hospitals were placed, which they reached on the 5th of November. In all the town, crowded with misery in every form, there were but five unoccupied rooms, which had been reserved for wounded officers of high rank; these were assigned to the nurses, and they at once entered upon the performance of their duty. They came none too soon. In a few hours wounded men in great numbers began to be brought in from the action of Balaklava, and, ere long, thousands more arrived from the bloody field of Inkermann. Fortunately, the "Times" commissioner was present to supply Miss Nightingale's first demands. Some days elapsed, however, before men ceased to die for want of stores, which had been supplied, which were present in the town, but which could not be obtained at the place and moment required. One of the nurses reported that, during the first night of her attendance, eleven men died before her eyes, whom a little wine or arrow-root would almost certainly have saved.

Miss Nightingale at once comprehended that it was no time to stand upon trifles. On the second day after her arrival six hundred wounded men were brought in, and the number increased until there were three thousand patients under her immediate charge. Miss Nightingale, one of the gentlest and tenderest of women, surveyed the scene of confusion and anguish with unruffled mind, and issued her orders with the calmness that comes of certain knowledge of what is best to be done. If red tape interposed, she quietly cut it. If there was no one near who was authorized to unlock a storehouse, she took a few Turks with her, and stood by while they broke it open. During the first week her labors were arduous beyond what would have been thought possible for any one; she was known to stand for twenty hours directing the labors of men and women. Yet, however fatigued she might be, her manner was always serene, and she had a smile or a compassionate word for the suffering as she passed them by.

As soon as the first needs of the men were supplied, she established a washing-house, which she found time herself to superintend. Before that was done, there had been a washing contract in existence, the conditions of which were so totally neglected by the contractor, that the linen of the whole hospital was foul and rotten. She established a kitchen, which she also managed to inspect, in which hundreds of gallons of beef-tea, and other liquid food, were prepared every day. She knew precisely how all these things should be done; she was acquainted with the best apparatus for doing them; and she was thus enabled, out of the rough material around her,—that is to say, out of boards, camp-kettles, camp-stores, and blundering Turks,—to create laundries and kitchens, which answered the purpose well, until better could be provided. She also well understood the art of husbanding skilful labor. When a few nurses could be spared from the wards of the hospital, she set them to preparing padding for amputated limbs, and other surgical appliances; so that when a thousand wounded suddenly arrived from the battle-field, men no longer perished for the want of some trifling but indispensable article, which foresight could have provided.

The "Times" commissioner wrote: "She is a ministering angel in these hospitals; and, as her slender form glides quietly along each corridor, every poor fellow's face softens with gratitude at the sight of her. When all the medical officers have retired for the night, and silence and darkness have settled down upon those miles of prostrate sick, she may be observed alone, with a little lamp in her hand, making her solitary rounds."

What a picture is this!

The same writer continues: "The popular instinct was not mistaken which, when she set out from England on her mission of mercy, hailed her as a heroine. I trust that she may not earn her title to a higher though sadder appellation. No one who has observed her fragile figure and delicate health can avoid misgivings lest these should fail. With the heart of a true woman, and the manners of a lady, accomplished and refined beyond most of her sex, she combines a surprising calmness of judgment, and promptitude, and decision of character."

Incredible as it now seems, the arrival of these ladies was far from being welcomed either by the medical or military officers, and it required all the firmness and tact of a Florence Nightingale to overcome the obstacles which were placed or left in her way. Several weeks passed before the hospital authorities cordially co-operated with her. Still more incredible is it, that some cruel bigots in England severely criticised her conduct in accepting the services of some of the Sisters of Charity from Dublin. There was much discussion as to whether she was herself a Catholic or a Protestant; which led a witty clergyman to remark: "She belongs to a sect which unfortunately is a very rare one, — the sect of the Good Samaritans." One of the chaplains who labored with her, added, with reference to another charge equally heartless and absurd: "If there is any blame in looking for a Roman Catholic priest to attend a dying Catholic, — let me share it with her, for I did it again and again."

The same excellent and liberal-minded chaplain, the Rev. S. G. Osborne, in his work on the Hospitals of Scutari, describes, in the most interesting manner, the appearance and demeanor of Miss Nightingale. "In appearance," he says, "she is just what you would expect in any other well-bred woman who may have seen, perhaps, rather more than thirty years of life; her manner and countenance are prepossessing, and this without the possession of positive beauty; it is a face not easily forgotten, pleasing in its smile, with an eye betokening great self-possession, and giving, when she pleases, a quiet look of firm determination to every feature. Her general demeanor is quiet and rather reserved; still, I am much mistaken if she is not gifted with a very lively sense of the ridiculous. In conversation, she speaks on matters of business with a grave earnestness one would not expect from her appearance. She has evidently a mind disciplined to restrain, under the pressure of the action of the moment, every feeling which would interfere with it. She has trained herself to command, and learned the value of conciliation towards others and constraint over herself. I can conceive her to be a strict disciplinarian; she throws herself into a work as its head, — as such she knows well how much success must depend upon literal obedience to her every order. She seems to understand business thoroughly. Her nerve is wonderful! I have been with her at very severe operations: she was more than equal to the trial. She has an utter disregard of contagion. I have known her spend hours over men dying of cholera or fever. The more awful to every sense any particular case, especially if it was that of a dying man, her slight form would be seen bending over him, administer ing to his ease in every way in her power, and seldom quitting his side till death released him."

What wonder that the troops idolized her! One of the soldiers said: "She would speak to one and to another, and nod and smile to as many more; but she couldn't do it to all, you know; we lay there by hundreds; but we could kiss her shadow as it fell, and lay our heads on the pillow again content." Another soldier said: "Before she came, there was such cussin' and swearin'; and after that it was as holy as a church."

All through that winter she toiled at her post, and all through the spring until the middle of May. Then she was taken down with the camp fever, and for four or five days her condition excited much alarm. She passed the crisis, however, and the whole army was soon rejoiced by hearing that she was convalescent. In her little book, published since her return home, upon nursing, there are but two allusions to her services in the Crimea. One is, that she had seen death in more forms than any other woman in Europe. The other is a touching reference to this convalescence. Speaking of the delight which the sick take in flowers, she says: "I have seen in fevers (and felt when I was a fever patient myself) the most acute suffering produced, from the patient (in a hut) not being able to see out of window, and the knots in the wood being the only view. I shall never forget the rapture of fever patients over a bunch of bright-colored flowers. I remember (in my own case) a nosegay of wild flowers being sent me, and from that moment recovery becoming more rapid."

By this time, excursionists and yachtsmen began to arrive at the Crimea, one of whom lent her a yacht, the use of which much aided her recovery. When she first sailed in it, she had to be carried to the vessel in the arms of men.

She remained in the Crimea a year and ten months, and

reached home again in safety, but an invalid for life, on the 8th of September, 1856. All England felt that something must be done to mark the national gratitude, and perpetuate the memory of it forever. Fifty thousand pounds were raised, almost without an effort, and it was concluded at length, to employ this fund in enabling Miss Nightingale to establish an institution for the training of nurses. She sanctioned and accepted this trust, and has been chiefly employed ever since in labors connected with it. The Sultan of Turkey sent her a magnificent bracelet. The Queen of England gave her a cross beautifully formed, and blazing with gems. The queen invited her also to visit her in her retreat at Balmoral, and Miss Nightingale spent some days there, receiving the homage of the royal family.

Not the least service which this noble lady has rendered the suffering sons of men has been the publication of the work just referred to, entitled "Notes on Nursing; what it is, and what it is not,"— one of the very few little books of which it can be truly said that a copy ought to be in every house. In this work she gives the world, in a lively, vigorous manner, the substance of all that knowledge of nursing, which she has so laboriously acquired. Her directions are admirably simple, and still more admirably wise. "The chief duty of a nurse," she says, "is simply this: *to keep the air which the patient breathes as pure as the external air, but without chilling him.*" This, she insists, is the main point, and is so important that if you attend properly to that you may leave almost all the rest to nature. She dwells most forcibly upon the absolute necessity, and wonderfully curative power, of perfect cleanliness and bright light. Her little chapter upon Noise in the Sick Room, in which she shows how necessary it is for a patient never to be startled, disturbed, or fidgeted, is most admirable and affecting. She seems to have entered into the very soul of sick people, and to have as lively a sense of how they feel, what they like, what gives them pain, what hinders or retards their recovery, as though she were herself the wretch whose case she is describing. If she had done nothing else in her life but produce this wise, kind, and pointed little work, she would deserve the gratitude of suffering man.

The book, too, although remarkably free from direct allusions to herself, contains much biographical material. We see the woman on every page, — the woman who takes nothing for granted, whom sophistry cannot deceive, who looks at things with her own honest eyes, reflects upon them with her own fearless mind, and speaks of them in good, downright, Nightingale English. She ever returns to her grand, fundamental position, the curative power of fresh, pure air. Disease, she remarks, is not an evil, but a blessing; it is *a reparative process*, — an effort of nature to get rid of something hostile to life. That being the case, it is of the first importance to remove what she considers the *chief* cause of disease, — the inhaling of poisonous air. She laughs to scorn the impious cant, so often employed to console bereaved parents, that the death of children is a "mysterious dispensation of Providence." No such thing. Children perish, she tells us, because they are packed into unventilated school-rooms, and sleep at night in unventilated dormitories.

"An extraordinary fallacy," she says, "is the dread of night air. What air can we breathe at night but night air? The choice is between pure night air from without and foul night air from within. Most people prefer the latter. An unaccountable choice! An open window, most nights in the year, can never hurt any one." Better, she remarks, shut the windows all day than all night. She maintains, too, that the reason why people now-a-days, especially ladies, are less robust than they were formerly, is because they pass the greater part of their lives in breathing poison. Upon this point she expresses herself with great force: —

"The houses of the grandmothers and great grandmothers of this generation (at least, the country houses), with front door and back door always standing open, winter and summer, and a thorough draft always blowing through, — with all the scrubbing, and cleaning, and polishing, and scouring, which used to go on, — the grandmothers, and, still more, the great-grandmothers, always out of doors, and never with a bonnet on except to go to church; these things entirely account for a fact so often seen of a great-grandmother who was a tower of physical vigor, descending into a grandmother, perhaps a little less vigorous, but still sound as a bell, and healthy to the core, into a mother languid and confined to her carriage and her house, and lastly into a daughter sickly and confined to her bed. For, remember, even with a general decrease of mortality, you may often find a race thus degenerating, and still oftener a family. You may see poor, little, feeble, washed-out rags, children of a noble stock, suffering, morally and physically, throughout their useless, degenerate lives; and yet people who are going to marry and to bring more such into the world, will consult nothing but their own convenience as to where they are to live or how they are to live."

On the subject of contagion she has decided and important opinions. "I was brought up," she says, "both by scientific men and ignorant women, distinctly to believe that small-pox, for instance, was a thing of which there was once a first specimen in the world, which went on propagating itself in a perpetual chain of descent, just as much as that there was a first dog (or a first pair of dogs), and that small-pox would not begin itself any more than a new dog would begin without there having been a parent dog. Since then, I have seen with my eyes, and smelt with my nose, *small-pox growing up in first specimens*, either in close rooms or in overcrowded wards, where it could not by any possibility have been caught, but *must* have begun! Nay, more. I have seen diseases begin, grow up, and pass into one another. Now, dogs do not pass into cats. I have seen, for instance, with a little overcrowding, continued fever grow up; and, with a little more, typhoid fever; and, with a little more, typhus; and all in the same ward or hut. Would it not be far better, truer, and more practical, if we looked upon disease in this light?"

"Again," she says, addressing parents, "why must a child have measles? If you believed in and observed the laws for preserving the health of houses, which inculcate cleanliness, ventilation, whitewashing, and other means (and which, by the way, *are laws*) as implicitly as you believe in the popular opinion (for it is nothing more than an opinion) that your child *must* have children's epidemics, don't you think that, upon the whole, your child would be more likely to escape altogether?"

Miss Nightingale is an enemy of crinoline, the wearing of which she styles "an absurd and hideous custom." "The dress of women," she adds, "is daily more and more unfitting them for any mission or usefulness at all. It is equally unfitted for all poetic and all domestic purposes. A man is now a more handy and far less objectionable being in a sick-room than a woman. Compelled by her dress, every woman now either shuffles or waddles; only a man can cross the floor of a sick-room without shaking it! What has become of woman's light step, — the firm, light, quick step we have been asking for?"

She has a very pleasing and suggestive passage upon the kind of conversation which is most beneficial to the sick. "A sick person," she observes, "does so enjoy hearing good news; for instance, of a love and courtship while in progress to a good ending. If you tell him only when the marriage takes place, he loses half the pleasure, which, God knows, he has little enough of; and, ten to one, but you have told him of some love-making with a bad ending. A sick person also intensely enjoys hearing of any material good, any positive or practical success of the right. He has so much of books and fiction, of principles, and precepts, and theories! Do, instead of advising him with advice he has heard at least fifty times before, tell him of one benevolent act which has really succeeded practically; it is like a day's health to him. You have no idea what the craving of the sick, with undiminished power of thinking, but little power of doing, is to hear of good practical action, when they can no longer partake in it. Do observe these things with the sick. Do remember how their life is to them disappointed and incomplete. You see them lying there with miserable disappointments, from which they can have no escape but death, and you can't remember to tell them of what would give them so much pleasure, or at least an hour's variety. They don't want you to be lachrymose and whining with them; they like you to be fresh, and active, and interesting; but they cannot bear absence of mind; and they are so tired of the advice and preaching they receive from everybody, no matter whom it is, they see. There is no better society than babies and sick people for one another. Of course you must manage this so that neither shall suffer from it, which is perfectly possible. If you think the air of the sick-room bad for the baby, why it is bad for the invalid, too, and therefore you will of course correct it for both. It freshens up the sick person's whole mental atmosphere to see 'the baby.' And a very young child, if unspoiled, will generally adapt itself wonderfully to the ways of a sick person, if the time they spend together is not too long."

These passages give us a more correct conception of the

mind and character of Florence Nightingale than any narrative of her life which has yet been given to the public. There has been nothing of chance in her career. She gained her knowledge, as it is always gained, by faithful and laborious study, and she acquired skill in applying her knowledge by careful practice.

There can be no doubt that the example of Miss Nightingale had much to do in calling forth the exertions of American women during our late war. As soon as we had wounded soldiers to heal, and military hospitals to serve, the patriotic and benevolent ladies of America thought of Florence Nightingale, and hastened to offer their assistance; and, doubtless, it was the magic of her name which assisted to open a way for them, and broke down the prejudices which might have proved insurmountable. When Florence Nightingale overcame the silent opposition of ancient surgeons and obstinate old sergeants in the Crimea, she was also smoothing the path of American women on the banks of the Potomac and the Mississippi. Her name and example belong to the race which she has honored; but to us, whom she served in the crisis of our fate, and thus associated her name with the benevolent and heroic ladies of our land, she will ever be peculiarly dear.

LYDIA MARIA CHILD.

BY T. W. HIGGINSON.

To those of us who are by twenty years or more the juniors of Mrs. Child, she presents herself rather as an object of love than of cool criticism, even if we have rarely met her face to face. In our earliest recollections she comes before us less as author or philanthropist than as some kindly and omnipresent aunt, beloved forever by the heart of childhood, — some one gifted with all lore, and furnished with unfathomable resources, — some one discoursing equal delight to all members of the household. In those days she seemed to supply a sufficient literature for any family through her own unaided pen. Thence came novels for the parlor, cookery-books for the kitchen, and the "Juvenile Miscellany" for the nursery. In later years the intellectual provision still continued. We learned, from her anti-slavery writings, where to find our duties; from her "Letters from New York," where to seek our purest pleasures; while her "Progress of Religious Ideas" introduced us to those profounder truths on which pleasures and duties alike rest. It is needless to debate whether she has done the greatest or most permanent work in any especial department of literature, she has done work so valuable in many. She has shown memorable independence in repeatedly leaving beaten paths to strike out for herself new literary directions, and has combined the authorship of more than thirty books and pamphlets with a singular devotion both to public and private philanthropies, and with almost too exacting a faithfulness to the humblest domestic duties. *Sero in cœlum.* May it be long before her full and final eulogy is written; but meanwhile it would be wrong to attempt even a sketch of her career without letting sympathy and love retain a large share in the service.

Lydia Maria Francis was born at Medford, Mass., February 11th, 1802. Her ancestor, Richard Francis, came from England in 1636, and settled in Cambridge, where his tombstone may still be seen in the burial-ground. Her paternal grandfather, a weaver by trade, was in the Concord fight, and is said to have killed five of the enemy. Her father, Convers Francis, was a baker, first in West Cambridge, then in Medford, where he first introduced what are still called "Medford crackers." He was a man of strong character and great industry. Though without much cultivation, he had uncommon love of reading; and his anti-slavery convictions were peculiarly zealous, and must have influenced his children's later career. He married Susannah Rand, of whom it is only recorded that "she had a simple, loving heart, and a spirit busy in doing good."

They had six children, of whom Lydia Maria was the youngest, and Convers the next in age. Convers Francis was afterwards eminent among the most advanced thinkers and scholars of the Unitarian body, at a time when it probably surpassed all other American denominations in the intellectual culture of its clergy. He had less ideality than his sister, less enthusiasm, and far less moral courage; but he surpassed most of his profession in all these traits. He was Theodore Parker's first learned friend, and directed his studies in preparation for the theological school. Long after, Mr. Parker used still to head certain pages of his journal, "Questions to ask Dr. Francis." The modest "study" at Watertown was a favorite head-quarters of what were called "the transcendentalists" of those days. Emerson, Margaret Fuller, Ripley, and the rest came often thither, in the days when the "Dial" was just emancipating American thought from old-world traditions. Afterwards, when Dr. Francis was appointed to the rather responsible and conservative post of professor in the Cambridge Theological School, he still remained faithful to the spirit of those days, never repressing free inquiry, but always rejoicing to encourage it. He was a man of rare attainments in a variety of directions, and though his great reading gave a desultory habit to his mind, and his thinking was not quite in proportion to his receptive power, he still was a most valuable instructor, as he was a most delightful friend. In face and figure he resembled the pictures of Martin Luther, and his habits and ways always seemed to me like those of some genial German professor. With the utmost frugality in other respects, he spent money almost profusely on books, and his library — part of which he bequeathed to Harvard College — was to me the most attractive I have ever seen, — more so than even Theodore Parker's. His sister had undoubtedly the superior mind of the two; but he who influenced others so much must have influenced her still more.

"A dear good sister has she been to me; would that I had been half as good a brother to her!" This he wrote, in self-depreciation, long after. While he was fitting for college, a process which took but one year, she was his favorite companion, though more than six years younger. They read together, and she was constantly bringing him Milton and Shakespeare to explain. He sometimes mystified her, — as brothers will, in dealing with maidens nine years old, — and once told her that "the raven down of darkness," which was made to smile, was but the fur of a black cat that sparkled when stroked; though it still perplexed her small brain.

why *fur* should be called *down*. This bit of levity from the future Professor of Theology I find in the excellent sketch of Dr. Francis, by Rev. John Weiss, his successor, — a little book which gives a good impression of the atmosphere in which the brother and sister were reared.

Their earliest teacher was a maiden lady, named Elizabeth Francis, — but not a relative, — and known universally as "Ma'am Betty." She is described as "a spinster of supernatural shyness, the never-forgotten calamity of whose life was that Dr. Brooks once saw her drinking water from the nose of her tea-kettle." She kept school in her bedroom; it was never tidy, and she chewed a great deal of tobacco; but the children were fond of her, and always carried her a Sunday dinner. Such simple kindnesses went forth often from that thrifty home. Mrs. Child once told me that always, on the night before Thanksgiving, all the humble friends of the household, — "Ma'am Betty," the washerwoman, the berry-woman, the wood-sawyer, the journeymen-bakers, and so on, — some twenty or thirty in all, were summoned to a preliminary entertainment. They there partook of an immense chicken-pie, pumpkin-pies (made in milk-pans), and heaps of doughnuts. They feasted in the large old-fashioned kitchen, and went away loaded with crackers and bread by the father, and with pies by the mother, not forgetting "turn-overs" for their children. Such plain applications of the doctrine "It is more blessed to give than to receive" may have done more to mould the Lydia Maria Child of maturer years than all the faithful labors of good Dr. Osgood, to whom she and her brother used to repeat the Westminster Assembly's Catechism once a month.

Apart from her brother's companionship the young girl had, as usual, a very unequal share of educational opportunities; attending only the public schools, with one year at the private seminary of Miss Swan, in Medford. Her mother died in 1814, after which the family removed for a time to the State of Maine. In 1819, Convers Francis was ordained over the First Parish in Watertown, and there occurred in his study, in 1824, an incident which was to determine the whole life of his sister.

Dr. J. G. Palfrey had written in the "North American Review" for April, 1821, a review of the now forgotten poem of "Yamoyden," in which he ably pointed out the use that might be made of early American history for the purposes of fictitious writing. Miss Francis read this article, at her brother's house, one summer Sunday noon. Before attending the afternoon service, she wrote the first chapter of a novel. It was soon finished, and was published that year, — a thin volume of two hundred pages, without her name, under the title of "Hobomok; a Tale of Early Times. By an American."

In judging of this little book, it is to be remembered that it appeared in the very dawn of American literature. Irving had printed only his "Sketch Book" and "Bracebridge Hall;" Cooper only "Precaution," "The Spy," "The Pioneers," and "The Pilot;" Miss Sedgwick only "The New England Tale," and possibly "Redwood." This new production was the hasty work of a young woman of twenty-two, inspired by these few examples. When one thinks how little an American author finds in the influences around him, even now, to chasten his style or keep him up to any high literary standard, it is plain how very little she could then have found. Accordingly "Hobomok" seems very crude in execution, very improbable in plot, and is redeemed only by a certain earnestness which carries the reader along, and by a sincere attempt after local coloring. It is an Indian "Enoch Arden," with important modifications, which unfortunately all tend away from probability. Instead of the original lover who heroically yields his place, it is to him that the place is given up. The hero of this self-sacrifice is an Indian, a man of high and noble character, whose wife the heroine had consented to become, when almost stunned with the false tidings of her lover's death. The least artistic things in the book are these sudden nuptials, and the equally sudden resolution of Hobomok to abandon his wife and child on the reappearance of the original betrothed. As the first work whose scene was laid in Puritan days, "Hobomok" will always have a historic interest; but it must be read in very early youth to give it any other attraction.

The success of this first effort was at any rate such as to encourage the publication of a second tale in the following year. This was "The Rebels; or, Boston before the Revolution. By the author of Hobomok." It was a great advance on its predecessor, with more vigor, more variety, more picturesque grouping, and more animation of style. The historical point was well chosen, and the series of public and private events well combined, with something of that tendency to the over-tragic which is common with young authors, — it is so much easier to kill off superfluous characters than to do anything else with them. It compared not unfavorably with Cooper's revolutionary novels, and had in one respect a remarkable success. It contained an imaginary sermon by Whitefield and an imaginary speech by James Otis. Both of these were soon transplanted into "School Readers" and books of declamation, and the latter, at least, soon passed for a piece of genuine revolutionary eloquence. I remember learning it by heart, under that impression, and was really astonished, on recently reading "The Rebels" for the first time, to discover that the high-sounding periods which I had always attributed to Otis were really to be found in a young lady's romance.

This book has a motto from Bryant, and is "most respectfully inscribed" to George Ticknor. The closing paragraph states with some terseness the author's modest anxieties: —

"Many will complain that I have dwelt too much on political scenes, familiar to every one who reads our history; and others, on the contrary, will say that the character of the book is quite too tranquil for its title. I might mention many doubts and fears still more important; but I prefer silently to trust this humble volume to that futurity which no one can foresee and every one can read."

The fears must soon have seemed useless, for the young novelist soon became almost a fashionable lion. She was an American Fanny Barney, with rather reduced copies of Burke and Johnson around her. Her personal qualities soon cemented some friendships, which lasted her life long, except where her later anti-slavery action interfered. She opened a private school in Watertown, which lasted from 1825 to 1828. She established, in 1827, the "Juvenile Miscellany," that delightful pioneer among children's magazines in America; and it was continued for eight years. In October, 1828, she was married to David Lee Child, a lawyer of Boston.

In those days it seemed to be held necessary for American women to work their passage into literature by first compiling a cookery-book. They must be perfect in that preliminary requisite before they could proceed to advanced standing. It was not quite as in Marvell's satire on Holland, "Invent a shovel and be a magistrate," but, Give us our dinner and then, if you please, what is called the intellectual feast. Any career you choose, let it only begin from the kitchen. As Charlotte Hawes has since written, "First this steak and then that stake." So Mrs. Child published in 1829 her "Frugal Housewife," a book which proved so popular that in 1836 it had reached its twentieth edition, and in 1855 its thirty-third.

The "Frugal Housewife" now lies before me, after thirty years of abstinence from its appetizing pages. The words seem as familiar as when we children used to study them beside the kitchen fire, poring over them as if their very descriptions had power to allay an unquenched appetite or prolong the delights of one satiated. There were the animals in the frontispiece, sternly divided by a dissecting-knife of printer's ink, into sections whose culinary names seemed as complicated as those of surgical science, — chump and spring, sirloin and sperib, — for I faithfully follow the original spelling. There we read with profound acquiescence that "hard gingerbread is good to have in the family," but demurred at the reason given, "it keeps so well." It never kept well in ours! There we all learned that one should be governed in cookery by higher considerations than mere worldly vanity, knowing that "many people buy the upper part of the sparerib of pork, thinking it the most genteel; but the lower part is more sweet and juicy, and there is more meat in proportion to the bone."

Going beyond mere carnal desires, we read also the wholesome directions "to those who are not ashamed of economy." We were informed that "children could early learn to take care of their own clothes," — a responsibility at which we shuddered; and also that it was a good thing for children to pick blackberries, — in which we heartily concurred. There, too, we were taught to pick up twine and paper, to write on the backs of old letters, like paper-sparing Pope, and if we had a dollar a day, which seemed a wild supposition, to live on seventy-five cents. We all read, too, with interest, the hints on the polishing of furniture and the education of daughters, and got our first glimpses of political economy from the "Reasons for Hard Times." So varied and comprehensive was the good sense of the book that it surely would have seemed to our childish minds infallible, but for one fatal admission, which through life I have recalled with dismay, — the assertion, namely, that "economical people will seldom use preserves." "They are unhealthy, expensive, and useless to those who are well." This was a sumptuary law, against which the soul of youth revolted. Really the line of asceticism must be drawn somewhere. If preserves were to be voted extravagant, economy had lost its charms; let us immediately become spendthrifts, and have a short life and a merry one.

The wise counsels thus conveyed in this more-than-cookery-book may naturally have led the way to a "Mother's Book," of more direct exhortation. This was published in 1831, and had a great success, reaching its eighth American edition in 1845, besides twelve English editions and a German translation. Probably it is now out of print, but one may still find at the bookstores the "Girl's Own Book," published during the same year. This is a capital manual of indoor games, and is worth owning by any one who has a houseful of children, or is liable to serve as a Lord of Misrule at Christmas parties. It is illustrated with vignettes by that wayward child of genius, Francis Graeter, a German, whom Mrs. Child afterwards described in the "Letters from New York." He was a personal friend of hers, and his pencil is also traceable in some of her later books. Indeed the drollest games which he has delineated in the "Girl's Own Book" are not so amusing as the unintentional comedy of his attempt at a "Ladies' Sewing Circle," which illustrates American life in the "History of Woman." The fair laborers sit about a small round table, with a smirk of mistimed levity on their faces, and one feels an irresistible impulse to insert in their very curly hair the twisted papers employed in the game of "Genteel lady, always genteel," in the "Girl's Own Book."

The "History of Woman" appeared in 1832, as one of a series projected by Carter & Hendee, of which Mrs. Child was to be the editor, but which was interrupted at the fifth volume by the failure of the publishers. She compiled for this the "Biographies of Good Wives," the "Memoirs" of

Madame De Stael and Madame Roland, those of Lady Russell and Madame Guion, and the two volumes of "Woman." All these aimed at a popular, not a profound, treatment. She was, perhaps, too good a compiler, showing in such work the traits of her brother's mind, and carefully excluding all those airy flights and bold speculations which afterwards seemed her favorite element. The "History of Woman," for instance, was a mere assemblage of facts, beginning and ending abruptly, and with no glimpse of any leading thought or general philosophy. It was, however, the first American storehouse of information upon that whole question, and no doubt helped the agitation along. Its author evidently looked with distrust, however, on that rising movement for the equality of the sexes, of which Frances Wright was then the rather formidable leader.

The "Biographies of Good Wives" reached a fifth edition in the course of time, as did the "History of Woman." I have a vague, childish recollection of her next book, "The Coronal," published in 1833, which was of rather a fugitive description. The same year brought her to one of those bold steps which made successive eras in her literary life, the publication of her "Appeal for that Class of Americans called Africans."

The name was rather cumbrous, like all attempts to include an epigram in a title-page, — but the theme and the word "Appeal" were enough. It was under the form of an "Appeal" that the colored man, Alexander Walker, had thrown a firebrand into Southern society which had been followed by Nat Turner's insurrection; and now a literary lady, amid the cultivated circles of Boston, dared also to "appeal." Only two years before (1831) Garrison had begun the "Liberator," and only two years later (1835) he was destined to be dragged through Boston streeets, with a rope round his neck, by "gentlemen of property and standing," as the newspapers said next day. It was just at the most dangerous moment of the rising storm that Mrs. Child appealed.

Miss Martineau in her article, "The Martyr Age in America,"—published in the "London and Westminster Review" in 1839, and at once reprinted in America,—gives by far the most graphic picture yet drawn of that perilous time. She describes Mrs. Child as "a lady of whom society was exceedingly proud before she published her Appeal, and to whom society has been extremely contemptuous ever since." She adds: "Her works were bought with avidity before, but fell into sudden oblivion as soon as she had done a greater deed than writing any of them."

It is evident that this result was not unexpected, for the preface to the book explicitly recognizes the probable dissatisfaction of the public. She says: —

"I am fully aware of the unpopularity of the task I have undertaken; but though I expect ridicule and censure, I cannot fear them. A few years hence, the opinion of the world will be a matter in which I have not even the most transient interest; but this book will be abroad on its mission of humanity long after the hand that wrote it is mingling with the dust. Should it be the means of advancing, even one single hour, the inevitable progress of truth and justice, I would not exchange the consciousness for all Rothschild's wealth, or Sir Walter's fame."

These words have in them a genuine ring; and the book is really worthy of them. In looking over its pages, after the lapse of thirty years, it seems incredible that it should have drawn upon her such hostility. The tone is calm and strong, the treatment systematic, the points well put, the statements well guarded. The successive chapters treat of the history of slavery, its comparative aspect in different ages and nations, its influence on politics, the profitableness of emancipation, the evils of the colonization scheme, the intellect of negroes, their morals, the feeling against them, and the duties of the community in their behalf. As it was the first anti-slavery work ever printed in America in book form, so I have always thought it the ablest; that is, it covered the whole ground better than any other. I know that, on reading it for the first time, nearly ten years after its first appearance, it had more formative influence on my mind, in that direction, than any other, although of course the eloquence of public meetings was a more exciting stimulus. It never surprised me to hear that even Dr. Channing attributed a part of his own anti-slavery awakening to this admirable book. He took pains to seek out its author immediately on its appearance, and there is in his biography an interesting account of the meeting. His own work on slavery did not appear until 1835.

Undaunted and perhaps stimulated by opposition, Mrs. Child followed up her self-appointed task. During the next year she published the "Oasis," a sort of anti-slavery annual, the precursor of Mrs. Chapman's "Liberty Bell," of later years. She also published, about this time, an "Anti-slavery Catechism," and a small book called "Authentic Anecdotes of American Slavery." These I have never seen, but find them advertised on the cover of a third pamphlet, which, with them, went to a second edition in 1839. "The Evils of Slavery and the Cure of Slavery; the first proved by the opinions of Southerners themselves, the last shown by historical evidence." This is a compact and sensible little work.

While thus seemingly absorbed in reformatory work she still kept an outlet in the direction of pure literature, and was employed for several years on her "Philothea," which appeared in 1833. The scene of this novel was laid in ancient Greece. It appeared with her name on the title-page, was inscribed to her brother, and the copyright was taken out by Park Benjamin, a literary friend residing in New York. The preface to the book has so much the character of autobiography, that it must be inserted without abridgment.

"This volume is purely romance; and most readers will consider it romance of the wildest kind. A few kindred spirits, prone to people space 'with life and mystical predominance,' will perceive a light *within* the Grecian Temple.

"For such I have written it. To minds of different mould, who may think an apology necessary for what they will deem so utterly useless, I have nothing better to offer than the simple fact that I found delight in doing it.

"The work has been four or five years in its progress; for the practical tendencies of the age, and particularly of the country in which I lived, have so continually forced me into the actual, that my mind has seldom obtained freedom to rise into the ideal.

"The hope of extended usefulness has hitherto induced a strong effort to throw myself into the spirit of the times; which is prone to neglect beautiful and fragrant flowers, unless their roots answer for vegetables, and their leaves for herbs. But there have been seasons when my soul felt restless in this bondage, — like the Pegasus, of German fable, chained to a plodding ox, and offered in the market; and as that rash steed when he caught a glimpse of the far blue sky, snapped the chain that bound him, spread his wings, and left the earth beneath him, — so I, for awhile, bid adieu to the substantial fields of utility, to float on the clouds of romance.

"The state of mind produced by the alternation of thoughts, in their nature so opposite, was oddly pictured by the following dream, which came before me in my sleep, with all the distinctness of reality, soon after I began to write this work.

"I dreamed that I arose early in the morning and went into my garden, eager to see if the crocus had yet ventured to peep above the ground. To my astonishment, that little spot, which, the day before, had worn the dreary aspect of winter, was now filled with flowers of every form and hue. With enthusiastic joy I clapped my hands, and called aloud to my husband to come and view the wonders of the garden. He came; and we passed from flower to flower, admiring their marvellous beauty. Then, with a sudden bound, I said, 'Now come and see the sunshine on the water!'

"We passed to the side of the house, where the full sea presented itself in all the radiance of the morning. And as we looked, lo, there appeared a multitude of boats with sails like the wings of butterflies, which now opened wide and reposed on the surface of the water; and now closed like the motions of weary insects in July; and ever as they moved, the gorgeous colors glittered in the sunshine.

"I exclaimed, 'These must have come from fairy land!' As I spoke, suddenly we saw among the boats, a multitude of statues, that seemed to be endowed with life; some large and majestic, some of beautiful feminine proportions, and an almost infinite variety of lovely little cherubs. Some were diving, some floating, and some undulating on the surface of the sea; and ever as they rose up, the water-drops glittered like gems on the pure white marble.

"We could find no words to express our rapture while gazing on a scene thus clothed with the beauty of other worlds. As we stood absorbed in the intensity of delight, I heard a noise behind me, and, turning round, saw an old woman with a checked apron, who made an awkward courtesy, and said, 'Ma'am, I can't afford to let you have that brisket for eight pence a pound.'

"When I related this dream to my husband, he smiled and said, 'The first part of it was dreamed by Philothea; the last, by the Frugal Housewife.'"

I well remember the admiration with which this romance was hailed; and for me personally it was one of those delights of boyhood which the criticism of maturity cannot disturb. What mattered it if she brought Anaxagoras and Plato on the stage together, whereas in truth the one died about the year when the other was born? What mattered it if in her book the classic themes were treated in a romantic spirit? That is the fate of almost all such attempts; compare for instance the choruses of Swinburne's "Atalanta," which might have been written on the banks of the Rhine, and very likely were. But childhood never wishes to discriminate, only to combine; a period of life which likes to sugar its bread-and-butter prefers also to have its classic and romantic in one.

"Philothea" was Mrs. Child's first attempt to return, with her anti-slavery cross still upon her, into the ranks of literature. Mrs. S. J. Hale, who, in her "Woman's Record," reproves her sister writer for "wasting her soul's wealth" in this radicalism, and "doing incalculable injury to humanity," seems to take a stern satisfaction in the fact that "the bitter feelings engendered by the strife have prevented the merits of this remarkable book from being appreciated as they deserve." This was perhaps true; nevertheless it went through three editions, and Mrs. Child, still keeping up the full circle of her labors, printed nothing but a rather short-lived "Family Nurse" (in 1837) before entering the anti-slavery arena again.

In 1841, Mr. and Mrs. Child were engaged by the American Anti-slavery Society to edit the "Anti-slavery Standard," a weekly newspaper then and now published in New York. Mr. Child's health being impaired, his wife undertook the task alone, and conducted the newspaper in that manner for two years, after which she aided her husband in the work, remaining there for eight years in all. She was very successful as an editor, her management being brave and efficient, while her cultivated taste made the "Standard" attractive to many who were not attracted by the plainer fare of the "Liberator." The good judgment shown in her poetical and literary selections was always acknowledged with especial gratitude by those who read the "Standard" at that time.

During all this period she was a member of the family of the well-known Quaker philanthropist, Isaac T. Hopper, whose biographer she afterwards became. This must have been the most important and satisfactory time in Mrs. Child's whole life. She was placed where her sympathetic nature found abundant outlet, and plenty of co-operation. Dwelling in a home where disinterestedness and noble labor were as daily breath, she had great opportunities. There was no mere almsgiving there, no mere secretaryship of benevolent societies; but sin and sorrow must be brought home to the fireside and to the heart; the fugitive slave, the drunkard, the outcast woman, must be the chosen guest of the abode, — must be taken and held and loved into reformation or hope. Since the stern tragedy of city life began, it has seen no more efficient organization for relief, than when dear old Isaac Hopper and Mrs. Child took up their abode beneath one roof in New York.

For a time she did no regular work in the cause of permanent literature, — though she edited an anti-slavery Almanac in 1843, — but she found an opening for her best eloquence in writing letters to the "Boston Courier," then under the charge of Joseph T. Buckingham. This was the series of "Letters from New York" that afterwards became famous. They were the precursors of that modern school of newspaper correspondence, in which women have so large a share, and which has something of the charm of women's private letters, — a style of writing where description preponderates over argument, and statistics make way for fancy and enthusiasm.

Many have since followed in this path, and perhaps Mrs. Child's letters would not now be hailed as they then were. Others may have equalled her, but she gave us a new sensation, and that epoch was perhaps the climax even of her purely literary career.

Their tone also did much to promote the tendency, which was showing itself in those days, towards a fresh inquiry into the foundations of social science. The "Brook Farm" experiment was then at its height; and though she did not call herself an "Associationist," yet she quoted Fourier and Swedenborg, and other authors who were thought to mean mischief; and her highest rhapsodies about poetry and music were apt to end in some fervent appeal for some increase of harmony in daily life. She seemed always to be talking radicalism in a greenhouse; and there were many good people who held her all the more dangerous for her perfumes. There were young men and maidens, also, who looked to her as a teacher, and were influenced for life, perhaps, by what she wrote. I knew, for instance, a young lawyer, just entering on the practice of his profession under the most flattering auspices, who withdrew from the courts forever, — wisely or unwisely, — because Mrs. Child's book had taught him to hate their contests and their injustice.

It was not long after this that James Russell Lowell, in his "Fable for Critics," — that strange medley of true wit and feeling intermingled with sketches of celebrities that are forgotten, and of personal hostilities that ought to be, — gave himself up to one impulse of pure poetry in describing Mrs. Child. It is by so many degrees the most charming sketch ever made of her, that the best part of it must be inserted here.

"There comes Philothea, her face all aglow,
She has just been dividing some poor creature's woe,

And can't tell which pleases her most, to relieve
His want, or his story to hear and believe;
. . . .
"The pole, science tells us, the magnet controls,
But she is a magnet to emigrant Poles,
And folks with a mission that nobody knows
Throng thickly about her, as bees round a rose;
She can fill up the *carets* in such, make their scope
Converge to some focus of rational hope,
And with sympathies fresh as the morning, their gall
Can transmute into honey, — but this is not all;
Not only for these she has solace, oh, say,
Vice's desperate nursling adrift in Broadway,
Who clingest with all that is left of thee human
To the last slender spar from the wreck of the woman,
Hast thou not found one shore where those tired drooping feet
Could reach firm mother earth, one full heart on whose beat
The soothed head in silence reposing could hear
The chimes of far childhood throb thick on the ear?
Ah, there's many a beam from the fountain of day
That to reach us unclouded, must pass on its way,
Through the soul of a woman, and hers is wide ope
To the influence of Heaven as the blue eyes of Hope;
Yes, a great soul is hers, one that dares to go in
To the prison, the slave-hut, the alleys of sin,
And to bring into each, or to find there, some line
Of the never completely out-trampled divine;
If her heart at high floods swamps her brain now and then,
'Tis but richer for that when the tide ebbs again,
As after old Nile has subsided, his plain
Overflows with a second broad deluge of grain;
What a wealth would it bring to the narrow and sour,
Could they be as a Child but for one little hour!"

The two series of "Letters" appeared in 1843 and 1845, and went through seven or more editions. They were followed in 1846 by a collection of Tales, mostly reprinted, entitled "Fact and Fiction." The book was dedicated to "Anna Loring, the child of my heart," and was a series of powerful and well-told narratives, some purely ideal, but mostly based upon the sins of great cities, especially those of man against woman. She might have sought more joyous themes, but none which at that time lay so near her heart. There was more sunshine in her next literary task, for, in 1852, she collected three small volumes of her stories from the "Juvenile Miscellany," and elsewhere, under the title of "Flowers for Children."

In 1853 she published her next book, entitled "Isaac T. Hopper; a True Life." This gave another new sensation to the public, for her books never seemed to repeat each other, and belonged to almost as many different departments as there were volumes. The critics complained that this memoir was a little fragmentary, a series of interesting stories without sufficient method or unity of conception. Perhaps it would have been hard to make it otherwise. Certainly, as the book stands, it seems like the department of "Benevolence" in the "Percy Anecdotes," and serves as an encyclopædia of daring and noble charities.

Her next book was the most arduous intellectual labor of her life, and, as often happens in such cases, the least profitable in the way of money. "The Progress of Religious Ideas through successive Ages" was published in three large volumes, in 1855. She had begun it long before, in New York, with the aid of the Mercantile Library and the Commercial Library, then the best in the city. It was finished in Wayland, with the aid of her brother's store of books, and with his and Theodore Parker's counsel as to her course of reading. It seems, from the preface, that more than eight years elapsed between the planning and the printing, and for six years it was her main pursuit. For this great labor she had absolutely no pecuniary reward; the book paid its expenses and nothing more. It is now out of print, and not easy to obtain.

This disappointment was no doubt due partly to the fact that the book set itself in decided opposition, unequivocal though gentle, to the prevailing religious impressions of the community. It may have been, also, that it was too learned for a popular book, and too popular for a learned one. Learning, indeed, she distinctly disavowed. "If readers complain of want of profoundness, they may perchance be willing to accept simplicity and clearness in exchange for depth." "Doubtless a learned person would have performed the task far better, in many respects; but, on some accounts, my want of learning is an advantage. Thoughts do not range so freely, when the store-room of the brain is overloaded with furniture." And she gives at the end, with her usual frankness, a list of works consulted, all being in English, except seven, which are in French. It was a bold thing to base a history of religious ideas on such books as Enfield's Philosophy and Taylor's Plato. The trouble was not so much that the learning was second-hand, — for such is most learning, — as that the authorities were second-rate. The stream could hardly go higher than its source; and a book based on such very inadequate researches could hardly be accepted, even when tried by that very accommodating standard, American scholarship.

Apart from this, the plan and spirit of the work deserve much praise. It is perhaps the best attempt in our language to bring together in a popular form, or indeed in any form, the religious symbols and utterances of different ages, pointing out their analogies and treating all with respect. Recognizing all religions as expressions of one universal and ennobling instinct, it was impossible that she should not give dissatisfaction to many sincere minds; had it been possible to avoid this, she would have succeeded. Not only is there no irreverence, but the author is of almost too sympathetic a nature to be called even a rationalist. The candor is perfect, and if she has apparently no prejudice in favor of the Christian religion, she has certainly what is rare among polemics who tend in her direction, — no prejudice against it. She takes pains — some readers would say exaggerated pains — to point out its superiority to all others.

In 1857, Mrs. Child published a volume entitled "Autumnal Leaves; Tales and Sketches in Prose and Rhyme." It might seem from this title that she regarded her career of action as drawing to a close. If so, she was soon undeceived, and the attack of Captain John Brown upon Harper's Ferry aroused her, like many others, from a dream of peace.

Immediately on the arrest of Captain Brown she wrote him a brief letter, asking permission to go and nurse him, as he was wounded and among enemies, and as his wife was supposed to be beyond immediate reach. This letter she enclosed in one to Governor Wise. She then went home and packed her trunk, with her husband's full approval, but decided not to go until she heard from Captain Brown, not knowing what his precise wishes might be. She had heard that he had expressed a wish to have the aid of some lawyer not identified with the anti-slavery movement, and she thought he was entitled to the same considerations of policy in regard to a nurse. Meantime Mrs. Brown was sent for, and promptly arrived; while Captain Brown wrote Mrs. Child one of his plain and characteristic letters, declining her offer, and asking her kind aid for his family, which was faithfully given.

But with his letter came one from Governor Wise, — courteous, but rather diplomatic, — and containing some reproof of her expressions of sympathy for the prisoner. To this she wrote an answer, well-worded, and quite effective, which, to her great surprise, soon appeared in the "New York Tribune." She wrote to the editor (Nov. 10, 1859): "I was much surprised to see my correspondence with Governor Wise published in your columns. As I have never given any person a copy, I presume you must have obtained it from Virginia."

This correspondence soon led to another. Mrs. M. J. C. Mason, wrote from "Alto, King George's County, Virginia," a formidable demonstration, beginning thus: "Do you read your Bible, Mrs. Child? If you do, read there, 'Woe unto you hypocrites,' and take to yourself, with twofold damnation, that terrible sentence; for, rest assured, in the day of judgment, it shall be more tolerable for those thus scathed by the awful denunciations of the Son of God than for you." This startling commencement — of which it must be calmly asserted that it comes very near swearing, for a lady — leads to something like bathos at the end, where Mrs. Mason adds in conclusion, "no Southerner ought, after your letters to Governor Wise, to read a line of your composition, or to touch a magazine which bears your name in its list of contributors." To begin with doubly-dyed future torments, and come gradually to the climax of "Stop my paper," admits of no other explanation than that Mrs. Mason had dabbled in literature herself, and knew how to pierce the soul of a sister in the trade.

But the great excitement of that period, and the general loss of temper that prevailed, may plead a little in vindication of Mrs. Mason's vehemence, and must certainly enhance the dignity of Mrs. Child's reply. It is one of the best things she ever wrote. She refuses to dwell on the invectives of her assailant, and only "wishes her well, both in this world and the next." Nor will she even debate the specific case of John Brown, whose body was in charge of the courts, and his reputation sure to be in charge of posterity. "Men, however great they may be," she says, "are of small consequence in comparison with principles, and the principle for which John Brown died is the question at issue between us."

She accordingly proceeds to discuss this question, first scripturally (following the lead of her assailant), then on general principles; and gives one of her usual clear summaries of the whole argument. Now that the excitements of the hour have passed, the spirit of her whole statement must claim just praise. The series of letters was published in pamphlet form in 1860, and secured a wider circulation than anything she ever wrote, embracing some three hundred thousand copies. In return she received many private letters from the slave States, mostly anonymous, and often grossly insulting.

Having gained so good a hearing, she followed up her opportunity. During the same year she printed two small tracts, "The Patriarchal Institution," and "The Duty of Disobedience to the Fugitive Slave Law;" and then one of her most elaborate compilations, entitled "The Right Way the Safe Way, proved by Emancipation in the British West Indies and elsewhere." This shows the same systematic and thorough habit of mind with its predecessors; and this business-like way of dealing with facts is hard to reconcile with the dreamy and almost uncontrolled idealism which she elsewhere shows. In action, too, she has usually shown the same practical thoroughness, and in case of this very book, forwarded copies at her own expense to fifteen hundred persons in the slave States.

In 1864 she published "Looking towards Sunset,"—a very agreeable collection of prose and verse, by various authors, all bearing upon the aspects of old age. This was another of those new directions of literary activity with which she so often surprised her friends. The next year brought still another in the "Freedmen's Book,"—a collection of short tales and sketches suited to the mental condition of the Southern freedmen, and published for their benefit. It was sold for that purpose at cost (sixty cents), and a good many copies are still being distributed through teachers and missionaries.

Her latest publication, and perhaps (if one might venture to guess) her favorite among the whole series, appeared in 1867, — "A Romance of the Republic." It was received with great cordiality, and is in some respects her best fictitious work. The scenes are laid chiefly at the South, where she has given the local coloring in a way really remarkable for one who never visited that region, — while the results of slavery are painted with the thorough knowledge of one who had devoted a lifetime to their study. The leading characters are of that type which is now becoming rather common in fiction, because American society affords none whose situation is so dramatic, — young quadroons educated to a high grade of culture, and sold as slaves after all. All the scenes are handled in a broad spirit of humanity, and betray no trace of that subtle sentiment of caste which runs through and through some novels written ostensibly to oppose caste. The characterization is good, and the events interesting and vigorously handled. The defect of the book is a common one, — too large a framework, too many *vertebræ* to the plot. Even the established climax of a wedding is a safer experiment than to prolong the history into the second generation, as here. The first two-thirds of the story would have been more effective without the conclusion. But it will always possess value as one of the few really able delineations of slavery in fiction, and the author may well look back with pride on this final offering at that altar of liberty where so much of her life had been already laid.

I have now enumerated all of Mrs. Child's writings, so far as I can ascertain them, — some having been attributed to her which she did not write, — and have mentioned such of her public acts as are inseparable from her literary career. Beyond this it is not now right to go. It is now nearly twenty years since she left not only the busy world of New York, but almost the world of society, and took up her abode (after a short residence at West Newton), in the house bequeathed to her by her father, at Wayland, Massachusetts. In that quiet village she and her husband have peacefully dwelt, avoiding even friendship's intrusions. Into the privacy of that home I have no right to enter. Times of peace have no historians, and the later career of Mrs. Child has had few of what the world calls events. Her domestic labors, her studies, her flowers, and her few guests keep her ever busy. She has no children of her own, — though, as some one has said, a great many of other people's, — but more than one whom she has befriended has dwelt with her since her retirement, and she comes forth sometimes to find new beneficiaries. But for many of her kindnesses she needs not to leave home, since they are given in the form least to be expected from a literary woman, — that of pecuniary bounty. If those who labor for the freedmen, in especial, were to testify, they could prove that few households in the country have contributed on a scale so very liberal, in proportion to their means. During the war this munificence was still farther enhanced in the direction of the soldiers. But it is not yet time for the left hand to know what these right hands have done, and I forbear.

One published letter, however, may serve as a sample of many. It was addressed to the last Anti-slavery Festival at Boston, and not only shows the mode of action adopted by Mr. and Mrs. Child, but their latest opinions as to public affairs: —

"WAYLAND, Jan. 1st, 1868.

"DEAR FRIEND PHILLIPS:—We enclose $50 as our subscription to the Anti-slavery Society. If our means equalled our wishes, we would send a sum as large as the legacy FRANCIS JACKSON intended for that purpose, and of which the society was deprived, as we think, by an unjust legal decision. If our sensible and judicious friend could speak to us from the other side of Jordan, we doubt not he would say that the vigilance of the Anti-slavery Society was never more needed than at the present crisis, and that, consequently, he was never more disposed to aid it liberally.

"Of course the rancorous pride and prejudice of this country cannot be cured by any short process, not even by lessons so sternly impressive as those of our recent bloody conflict. There is cause for great thankfulness that 'war Abolitionists' were driven to perform so important a part in the great programme of Providence; but their recognition of human brotherhood is rarely of a kind to be trusted in emergencies. In most cases, it is not '*skin* deep.' Those who were Abolitionists in the teeth of popular opposition are the only ones who really made the case of the colored people their own; therefore they are the ones least likely to be hoodwinked by sophistry and false pretences now.

"To us the present crisis of the country seems more dangreous than that of '61. The insidiousness of oppressors is always more to be dreaded than their open violence. There can be no reasonable doubt that a murderous feeling toward the colored people prevails extensively at the South; and we are far from feeling very sure that a large party could not be rallied at the North in favor of restoring slavery. We have no idea that it ever *can* be restored; but if we would avert the horrors of another war, more dreadful than the last, we must rouse up and keep awake a public sentiment that will compel politicians to do their duty. This we consider the appropriate and all-important work of the old Anti-slavery Society.

"The British Anti-slavery Society deserted their post too soon. If they had been as watchful to protect the freed people of the West Indies as they were zealous to emancipate them, that horrid catastrophe in Jamaica might have been avoided. The state of things in those islands warns us how dangerous it is to trust those who have been slaveholders, and those who habitually sympathize with slaveholders, to frame laws and regulations for liberated slaves. As well might wolves be trusted to guard a sheepfold.

"We thank God, friend Phillips, that you are preserved and strengthened to be a wakeful sentinel on the watch-tower, ever ready to warn a drowsy nation against selfish, timid politicians, and dawdling legislators, who manifest no trust either in God or the people.

"Yours faithfully,

"DAVID L. CHILD,
"L. MARIA CHILD."

This is all of Mrs. Child's biography that can now be written; and it is far more than her sensitive nature — shrinking from publicity even when she brings it on herself — would approve. She is one of those prominent instances in our literature, of persons born for the pursuits of pure intellect, whose intellects were yet balanced by their hearts, and both absorbed in the great moral agitations of the age. "My natural inclinations," she once wrote to me, "drew me much more strongly towards literature and the arts than towards reform, and the weight of conscience was needed to turn the scale." She has doubtless gained in earnestness far more than she has lost in popularity, in wealth, or even in artistic culture; the first two losses count for little, and the last may not be due to her advocacy of reforms alone, but to the crude condition, as respects even literary art, which yet marks us all. In a community of artists, she would have belonged to that class, for she had that instinct in her soul. But she was placed where there was as yet no exacting literary standard; she wrote better than most of her contemporaries, and well enough for her public. She did not, therefore, win that intellectual immortality which only the very best writers command, and which few Americans have attained. But she won a meed which she would value more highly, — that warmth of sympathy, that mingled gratitude of intellect and heart which men give to those who have faithfully served their day and generation. No rural retirement can hide her from the prayers of those who were ready to perish, when they first knew her; and the love of those whose lives she has enriched from childhood will follow her fading eyes as they look towards sunset, and, after her departing, will keep her memory green.

FANNY FERN—MRS. PARTON.

BY GRACE GREENWOOD.

Sara Payson Willis, daughter of Nathaniel and Sara Willis, was born in Portland, Maine, in midsummer of the year of our Lord 1811. In that fine old town, in that fine old State, where as she says, "the timber and the human beings are sound," she spent the first six years of her life. During those years, our country passed through a troublous time, — a supplementary grapple with the old country, — final, let us hope, and eminently satisfactory in its results, to one party at least. But it is not probable that the shock and tumult of war seriously disturbed the little Sara, sphered apart from its encounters, sieges, conflagrations, and unnatural griefs, in the fairy realm of a happy childhood. Whether we made a cowardly surrender at Detroit, or incarnadined Lake Erie with British blood, — whether we conquered at Chippewa, or rehearsed Bull Run at Bladensburg, — whether our enemy burned the Capitol at Washington, or was soundly thrashed at New Orleans, — it was all the same to her. However the heart of the noble mother may have been pained by the tragedies, privations and mournings of that time, it brooded over the little baby-life in sheltering peace and love; — as the robin, when her nest rocks in the tempest, shields her unfledged darlings with jealous care.

I have a theory, flanked by whole columns of biographical history, that no man or woman of genius was ever born of an inferior, or common-place woman. The mother of Nathaniel, Richard, and Sara Willis was a large-brained, as well as great-hearted woman. The beautiful tributes of her poet-son made all the world aware of her most lovable qualities — her faithful, maternal tenderness and broad, sweet charity; but to these were added rare mental power and character of singular nobility and weight.

From a private letter, addressed by the subject of this biographical sketch to a friend, in answer to some questions concerning this noble mother, I am permitted to take the following touching tribute: "All my brother's poetry, all the capability for writing which I possess — be it little, or much — came from her. She had correspondence with many clergymen of the time and others, and, had she lived at this day, would have been a writer worthy of mention. In those days women had nine children — her number and stifled their souls under baskets of stockings to mend and aprons to make. She made every one who came near her better and happier for having seen her. She had a heart as wide as the world, and charity to match. Oh, the times I have thrown my arms wildly about me and sobbed 'Mother!' till it seemed she *must* come! I shall never be 'weaned,' never! *She* understood me. Even now, I *want* her, every day and hour. Blessed be eternity and immortality! *That* is what my mother was to me. God bless her!"

In 1817 Mr. Willis removed to Boston, where he for many years edited the "Recorder," a religious journal, and "The Youth's Companion," a juvenile paper, of blessed memory. In Boston, Sara spent the remainder of her childhood; and a grand old town it is to be reared in, notwithstanding the east wind, its crooked, cow-path streets, and general promiscuousness, — notwithstanding its exceeding self-satisfaction, its social frigidity, its critical narrowness and its contagious *isms;* among the most undesirable of which count conventionalism and dilettanteism; and it is an admirable town to emigrate from, because of these notwithstandings.

The stern Puritan traditions and social prejudices of the place seem not to have entered very strongly into the character of Sara Willis. She probably chased butterflies on Boston Common, or picked wild strawberries (if they grew there) on Bunker Hill, without much musing on the grand and heroic associations of those places. She doubtless tripped by Faneuil Hall occasionally, without doing honor to it, as the august cradle of liberty. She must have been an eminently happy and merry child; indulging in her own glad fancies in the bright present, with little reverence for the past, or apprehension for the future, — much given to mischief and mad little pranks of fun and adventure.

Sara was educated at Hartford, in the far-famed Seminary of Miss Catharine Beecher. At that time, Harriet Beecher, Mrs. Stowe, was a teacher in this school. She was amiable and endearing in her ways, and was recognized as a decidedly clever young lady, with a vein of quiet humor, a sleepy sort of wit, that woke up and flashed out when least expected; but of a careless, unpractical turn of mind. She was not thought by any means the equal in mental power and weight of her elder sister, whose character was full of manly energy, who was a clear thinker, an excellent theologian, a good, great, high-hearted woman, with a strong will and remarkable executive abilities. Of all his children, Dr. Beecher is said to have most highly respected Catharine.

Sara Willis must here have laid an excellent foundation for successful authorship, though probably nothing was farther from her thoughts at the time than such a profession. It would have seemed too quiet and thought-compelling a career for her, with her heart as full of frolic as a lark's breast is of singing. There are yet traditions in that staid old town of Hartford, of her merry school-girl escapades, her "tricks and her manners," that draw forth as hearty laughter as the witty sallies, humorous fancies, and sharp strokes of satire that give to her writings their peculiar sparkle and dash.

If she grappled with the exact sciences it is not probable that they suffered much in the encounter. For Geometry she is said to have had an especial and inveterate dislike. Indeed, her teacher, Mrs. Stowe, still tells a story of her having torn out the leaves of her Euclid to curl her hair with. So she laid herself down to mathematical dreams, her fair head bristling with acute angles, in parallelogrammatic and paralellopipedonic *papillotes*, — in short, with more Geometry outside than in. A novel way of getting over "the dunce bridge," by taking that distasteful Fifth Proposition not only inwardly, but as an outward application; so that it might have read thus: "The angles at the base of an isosceles triangle are equal to one another; and if the equal sides be produced in curl papers, the angles on the other side of the *os frontis* are also equal."

But in the laughing, high-spirited girl there must have existed unsuspected by those about her, almost unsuspected by herself, the courage and energy, the tenderness, the large sympathy, the reverence for the divine and the human, which love and sorrow, the trials and stress of misfortune, were to evolve from her nature, and which her genius was to reveal. A seer that might have perceived towering above the ringleted head of her absent-minded young teacher, a dark attendant spirit, benignant, but mournful, — poor, grand, old world-bewept, polyglotted Uncle Tom, — might also have seen in the few shadowy recesses of her young pupil's sunny character, the germs of those graceful "Fern Leaves" that were to bring to the literature of the people new vigor and verdure, the odors of woodlands, and exceeding pleasant pictures of nature.

It must have been while Sara was at school in Hartford,

that her brother Nathaniel began to be famous as a poet. In that unlikely place, Yale College, he seems to have had a period of religious enthusiasm, or sentiment, and his scriptural poems were the result. They have always continued to be his most popular productions, but they are far from being his best. They are Scripture diluted, though diluted with rose-water. The young school-girl must have had a sister's pride in this handsome, brilliant brother, in the golden dawn of his fame. And here, let one whom he once befriended add this slight tribute to the poet's memory: What though his life did not wholly fulfil the promise of its fair morning? It was a life marked by many a generous act, though beset by more than ordinary temptations to utter worldliness and egotism, — a life that gladdened with its best thoughts and most brilliant fancies lives less fortunate, and yet perhaps less sad. His genius delighted us long; for his faults, who, standing over his grave, feels true and earnest and blameless enough to sternly condemn him?

Miss Willis, soon after leaving school, married Mr. Eldridge, of Boston, and for several years lived in ease and comfort, and, what was far better, in domestic happiness. Three daughters were born to her, and the wondrous experience of motherhood must have come to her to exalt, yet subdue the passionate impulses and the undisciplined forces of her nature. Doubtless life with the new gladness, put on new solemnity; with the new riches, must have come humility.

Love had done much for Sara Eldridge, maternity more; but she needed yet another heavenly teacher and helper, — one no less benignant than they, but stern of aspect, mysterious, relentless, — Death. He descended on that happy little household, "the angel with the amaranthine wreath," and the husband and father "was not." Again he descended and bore away the first born, — a lovely, spiritual little girl, who in numbering over her bright, blameless years, could only say, "Seven times one are seven."

Then came a weary beating out against the heavy sea of sorrow, of that dismantled pleasure-boat of a life, with one poor, grieving, inexperienced soul at the oars, and still such a precious freight of helpless love and childish dependence! Behind was the lee-shore of despair; beneath cold, bitter, merciless want, and very faintly in the horizon shone the fair, firm land.

It is not for me to paint the cruel anxieties and perplexities of the widowed mother, — of a proud, independent woman, who could not ask for the help, withheld with what seemed to her unnatural indifference. The experience doubtless infused into a nature generous and frank, but strongly passionate in both its loves and resentments, an element of defiant, almost fierce, bitterness and hate, which caused it to be condemned by some whose good opinion would have been worth the gaining, and applauded by others whose praise brought no honor. But such an infusion of deadly night-shade juice as misanthropy and estrangement from friends once held most dear, could not long poison a mental organization so healthy as hers; it had a quick, fiery run through her blood, struck, once or twice, with deadly effect, and was gone. It must be that her clear reasonable mind, seeing the swift, stern flight of the unrecallable days, must soon have felt that "Life is too short for such things as these," as poor Douglas Jerrold said, when extending his hand to a friend from whom he had been for some time separated by a misunderstanding, — "an estrangement for which," said that noble friend, Charles Dickens, with generous tenderness, "*I* was the one to blame."

In 1851 "Fanny Fern" was born into literary life. An essay was penned by the widowed mother, on whose heart lay a great burden of loving care. That care was her inspiration, her desperate hope. Her muses were a couple of curly-haired little maidens, in short frocks, who, in that gay unconsciousness of young girlhood, so charming, yet so exasperating, called innocently for new frocks, cloaks, and hats, kid gloves, slippers, ribbons, and French candies. So an essay was penned, — a little essay it was, I believe, measured by paragraphs and lines, but it was in reality "big with the fate" of Fanny and her girls. It was a venture quite as important to its author as was the first "Boz" sketch to Charles Dickens, or as was "Jane Eyre" to Charlotte Bronté. After a patient trial and many rebuffs, she found, in a great city, an editor enterprising, or charitable, enough, to publish this essay, and to pay for it, — for he was a just man, who held that verily "the laborer is worthy of his hire," — to pay for it — *fifty cents!* It is to be hoped this Mæcenas found himself none the poorer for his liberality at the end of the year.

The essay proved a hit, "a palpable hit," and was widely copied and commented on. It was followed by others, written in the same original, fearless style, which were gladly received by the public, and a little better paid for by publishers. A few months more of patient perseverance and earnest effort in her new field, and Fanny Fern could command her own price for her labor. Her head was above water, never again to be submerged, let us trust.

The winds of good fortune scattered those first "Fern Leaves" far and wide, till the country was green with them everywhere. Their peculiar dash and electrical vitality made for the unknown author thousands of eager, questioning admirers, and literary curiosity almost mobbed the publication office from which they emanated. Critics were not wanted, — oh, not by any means! — critics who charged the new story-writer and essayist with eccentricity, flippancy, cynicism, irreverence, masculinity, — with every conceivable sin of authorship except sentimentality, pharisaism, and prosiness. There was an unprofessional freedom and fearlessness in her style that made her very faults acceptable to that indefinite individual, "the general reader,"—an honest easy-going fellow, who is little inclined to raise fine points in regard to an author's manner of expression, provided the feeling be all right.

I remember thinking that this bold rival was poaching a little on my own "merrie" Greenwood preserves; but as I watched her cool proceedings, saw how unerring was her aim, and with what an air of proprietorship she bagged her game, I declined to prosecute, and went to Europe. When I returned I found she had the whole domain to herself, and she has kept it to this day. So mote it be!

A most astonishing instance of literary success was the first book of "Fern Leaves," of which no less than seventy thousand copies were sold in this country alone! I would not seem to detract in the slightest degree from the genius of our author,—I would not rob her chaplet of one Fern Leaf,—but I must say she was extremely fortunate in her publisher. Had she made choice of some aristocratic houses, for instance, her books would have borne the envied Athenian stamp, but then, regarding copies sold, the reader of this veracious biography would have read for thousands—hundreds. But Fanny Fern, with her rare business sagacity and practical good sense, did not choose her publisher as young Toots chose his tailor,—"Burgess & Co., fash'nable, but very dear."

Then followed "Little Ferns, for Fanny's Little Friends,"—whose names seem to have been Legion, for there were no less than thirty-two thousand of these young Fern gatherers. Then came a "Second Series of Fern Leaves," in number thirty thousand. Total,—*one hundred and thirty-two thousand!* I write it out carefully, for not having a head for figures, I am almost sure to make some mistake if I meddle with them. Moreover, these American Ferns, fresh and odorous with the freedom and spirit of the New World, took quick root in England, and spread and flourished like the

American rhododendron. The mother country took for British home consumption forty-eight thousand copies, and much good did they do our little cousins, I doubt not.

In 1854 "Ruth Hall" (I had almost said Ruth-less Hall) was published. In 1857 "Rose Clarke," — a kindlier book. These are, I believe, the only novels of Fanny Fern. They were eagerly read, much commented upon, and had, like the "Leaves," a large sale. They were translated into French and German.

In 1856 Fanny Fern was married to Mr. James Parton, of New York; a man of brilliant, but eminently practical, ability as a writer. It was a marriage that seemed to the world to promise, if not happiness of the most romantic type, much hearty good fellowship, with mutual aid and comfort. Both were authors whose provinces bordered on Bohemia. They had apparently many tastes and characteristics in common; they were both acute, independent thinkers, rather than students or philosophers; they were rather special pleaders than reasoners, — rather wits than logicians. The style of each writer has decidedly improved of late years; yet neither has lost in individuality by this happy consolidation of provinces. Mr. Parton's style has gained much in nerve and terseness, and even more in polish. Mrs. Parton's has more softness than of old, with no less vigor; it shows a surer grasp on, yet a more delicate handling of, thought; she does not startle as frequently as in her first essays, but she oftener pleases.

Five years ago sorrow came again to this brightened and prosperous life. It came like a relentless ploughshare, and every smiling hope and ripe ambition went under for a time. It came like a volcanic sea-rise on a fair day, sweeping over the firm land of assured good fortune. A beloved daughter, a young wife and mother, died suddenly, leaving an infant child, for whose dear sake that brave soul gathered up all its forces and staggered up, and on. To this young life, "bought with a price," this frail flower, born in anguish and nurtured with tears, Fanny Fern has since devoted herself with more than a mother's tender solicitude. In this work, as in household duties, she has been efficiently aided and supported by her sole remaining daughter.

Mrs. Parton has been from the first a most acceptable writer for children. Her motherhood, a true motherhood of the heart, has given her the clue to the most mysterious, angel-guarded labyrinths of a child's soul. She is the faithful interpreter of children, from the poor "tormented baby," on its nurse's knee, trotted, and tickled, and rubbed, and smothered, and physicked, — all the way up through the perils, difficulties, and exceeding bitter sorrows of childhood, out of short frocks and roundabouts, into the rosy estate of young womanhood and the downy-lipped dignity of young manhood. Having a heart of perennial freshness, full of spontaneous sympathies and enthusiasms, she never gets so far away from her own youth that she cannot feel a thrill of kindred delight in looking on the pleasures of the young, — on their bright, glad, eager faces. Bulwer says, "Young girls are very charming creatures, except when they get together and fall a-giggling." Now I will venture to say this is just the time when Fanny Fern likes them best, — unless, indeed, the giggling is ill-timed, and therefore ill-mannered. In a scene of festal light, bloom, and music, of glancing and dancing young figures, she would never stand aside in the gloom of dark shrubbery, hard and cold and solemnly envious, like the tomb in a certain landscape of Poussin, bearing the inscription, "I also once lived amid the delights of Arcadia."

Yet, while ready to rejoice in the innocent mirth and exultant hopes of youth, this true woman can also feel a tender charity for its follies, and a yearning pity for its errors. No poor unfortunate in her utmost extremity of shame and mad abandonment, need fear from her lips a word of harsh rebuke, from her eyes a look of lofty scorn or merciless condemnation. But for the heartless wrong-doer, for the betrayer of an innocent, though ever so foolish, trust,—for the despoiler of hearts and homes, she has rebukes that scathe like flame, and scorn that bites like frost.

With a healthy reverence for all truly devout souls, all earnest, humble, practical Christians,—for all things essentially pure and venerable,—Fanny Fern has an almost fierce hatred of cant, of empty pomp and formalism, assuming the name of religion. She valiantly takes sides with God's poor against the most powerful and refined pharisaism. She would evidently rather sit down to worship with the "old salts," in Father Taylor's Seaman's Chapel, than in the most gorgeously upholstered pew, under the most resplendent stained windows, in the highest high church on Fifth Avenue. Not that she is wanting in a poet's sensuous delight in bright colors, rich textures, beautiful, refined faces, grand music and noble church-architecture, but that in the lives of the poor, colorless, homely, ungraceful, almost blindly aspiring and devout, there is something that moves her heart more tenderly and yet more solemnly. In "the low, sad music of humanity" there is something that touches a higher than the poetic sense; and to her the humblest Christian soul, simple and ignorant, but trusting and loving, is a grander temple of God than the Cathedral of Milan, with its wondrous Alp-like peaks of snowy architecture, sentinelled with sculptured saints.

Another noticeable characteristic of Fanny Fern is her hearty contempt for all pretensions, affectations, and dainty sillinesses; be they social, literary, or artistic. She is eminently a woman "with no nonsense about her." She detests shams of all sorts, and sentimentality, French novels and French phrases. Almost as fiercely as she hates cant, she hates snobbery. Her honest American blood boils at the sight of a snob, and she never fails soundly to "chastise him with the valor of her tongue." For that unnatural little monster, that anomaly and anachronism, an American flunkey, even her broadest charity can entertain no hope, either for here, or hereafter.

Though whole-hearted in her patriotism, Fanny Fern is not a political bigot. She probably does not aver that she was born in New England at her "own particular request;" she has found that life is endurable out of Boston; she would doubtless admit that it can be borne with Christian philosophy out of Gotham, — even in small provincial towns, in which the "Atlantic Monthly" and "New York Ledger" are largely subscribed for. When here, she was enough of a cosmopolitan to praise our great city market, — uttering among some pleasant things, this rather dubious compliment: "What have these Philadelphians done, that they should have such butter?" Done? — lived virtuously, dear Fanny, — refused to naturalize the "Black Crook," or to send prize-fighters to Congress.

But to return. Not because of the happy accident of her birth, does Fanny Fern stand gallantly up for our America; but because it is what it is, — the hope, the refuge, the sure rock of defence for the poor and oppressed of all nations, — their true *El Dorado*, their promised land.

Mrs. Parton is now, if parish registers, family records, and biographers do not lie, fifty-seven years old. But time which has done "its spiriting gently" with the style of the writer, softening and refining it, cannot have touched the woman roughly, or drawn very heavy drafts on her energy and vitality; for they who have seen her within a late period, speak of her as yet retaining all the spirit and wit of what are called "a woman's best days," but which were, to her, days of care, trial, and toil, that would have borne down a heart less brave, and prostrated an organization less healthful. She must have had from the first a rare amount of "muscular Christianity" — must have been a conscientious self-care-taker — must have lived wisely and prudently, — in short, must have kept herself well "in hand," or she would have gone down in some of the ugly ditches, or stuck in some of the hurdles she has had to leap in this desperate race of a quarter of a century. Some New York paragraphist tells of having encountered her on Broadway, a short time since, — not as usual, walking with a hurried and haughty tread, the elastic step of an Indian princess, of the school of Cooper, — but pausing, after a manner quite as characteristic, to talk to a lovely baby in its nurse's arms; and, our amiable Jenkins relates, her face then and there shone with the very rapture of admiration and unforgotten maternal tenderness, melting through its mask of belligerent pride and harshness, and in that wonderful transfiguring glow,seemed to wear the very look of the time when it first hung over a little cradle, or nestled down against a little baby-face, in the happy long ago. Yet it had looked on many a dear coffined face since then.

Fanny Fern has been the subject of many piquant and amusing anecdotes, some of them, perhaps most of them, having a foundation in fact, — for she is a person of too much spirit and character not to have noteworthy things happening to her and round about her rather frequently. Hers is a stirring, breezy life, to which anything like a dead calm is impossible. She is too swift and well freighted a craft not to leave a considerable wake behind her. She sails with all her canvas spread, by a chart of her own, so occasionally dashes saucily athwart the bows of steady-going old ships of the line, or right under the guns of a heavy man-of-war. As an author and woman, she consults neither authority, nor precedent, fashion, nor policy. As woman and author, she has always defied and despised that petty personal criticism, that paltry gossip which is the disgrace of American journalism; which insists on discussing the author's or artist's most private and intimate life,—his domestic relations, his holiest affections, his most sacred human weaknesses and virtues,—on unveiling every sanctuary of sorrow, and following a poor wounded soul into its last fastnesses of decent reserve.

Among the most spicy anecdotes of my subject ever set floating about the country, is one of her having smashed, with her own vengeful hand, the china-set in her room, at the Girard House in Philadelphia,—because, after honorably reporting the accidental breaking of a bowl, she found herself charged a round sum for the entire toilet-set. This story we of a fun-loving and justice-loving household, have laughed over many times; but, as poor Beatrice Cenci says, "We shall not do it any more;" for alas, the story isn't true!—that is, as to the grand dramatic denouement. Wishing to chronicle only the exact truth in a matter of so much importance, I addressed to Mrs. Parton a letter of inquiry, and received in reply the following succinct statement:—

"Mr. Parton and I had been stopping at the Girard House, and just as we were about starting for the cars, I said, 'Wait till I wash my hands.' As I did so, the bowl slipped from my soapy fingers, and was broken. I said, 'Report that when you pay the bill, lest the blame should come upon the poor chambermaid;' whereupon, to my intense disgust, the landlord charged for the whole toilet-set! Then, in my indignation, I did say to Mr. Parton, 'I have a good mind to send all the rest of the set flying out of the window!' His less impetuous hand stayed me. I assure you it was no virtue of mine. My blood is quick and warm."

This frank account spoils an excellent story, and shows us how meanness and injustice again went unpunished, after the manner of this miserable, mismanaged world, which it will take many a Fanny Fern and much crockery-smashing to set right.

Fourteen years ago Fanny Fern made an engagement with Mr. Bonner, of the "New York Ledger," to furnish an article every week for his journal, — that giant among literary weeklies, but by no means a weakly giant, of the Pickleson order, with a "defective circulation," nor even of the style of the seven league-booter, and freebooter of fairy lore; but rather of the type of the Arabian genii, who were anywhere and everywhere at once.

Fourteen years ago, Fanny Fern made an engagement with Mr. Bonner, to furnish an article every week for the "Ledger," and "thereby hangs a tale," the most wonderful fact in this veracious biography: Behold! *from that time to this, she has never failed one week to produce the stipulated article, on time!* Think, my reader, what this fact proves! what habits of industry, what system, what thoughtfulness, what business integrity, what super-woman punctuality, and O Minerva — Hygeia! what health!

Aspasia was, Plato says, the preceptress of Socrates; she formed the rhetoric of Pericles, and was said to have composed some of his finest orations; but *she* never furnished an article every week for the "Ledger" for fourteen years.

Hypatia taught mathematics and the Philosophy of Plato, in the great school of Alexandria, through most learned and eloquent discourses; but *she* never furnished an article for the "Ledger" every week for fourteen years.

Elena Lucrezia Comoso Piscopia, — eminently a woman of *letters*, — manfully mastered the Greek, Latin, Arabic, Hebrew, Spanish, and French; wrote astronomical and mathematical dissertations, and received a doctor's degree from the University of Padua; Laura Bassi, Novella d'Andrea, and Matelda Tambroni were honored with degrees, and filled professors' chairs in the University of Bologna; but as far as I have been able to ascertain, by the most careful researches, not one of these learned ladies ever furnished an article for the "Ledger" every week for fourteen years. Corinna, for her improvisations, was crowned at the Capitol in Rome with the sacred laurel of Petrarch and Tasso; but *she* never furnished an article every week for the "Ledger" for fourteen years.

Miss Burney, Miss Porter, Mrs. Radcliffe, Miss Austin, Miss Baillie, Miss Mitford, Miss Landon, Mrs. Hemans, Mrs. Marsh, Mrs. Gaskell, and the Brontés did themselves and their sex great honor by their literary labors; but not one of them ever furnished an article for the "Ledger" every week for fourteen years. Neither Mrs. Lewes nor Mrs. Stowe could do it, George Sand wouldn't do it, and Heaven forbid that Miss Braddon should do it!

Why, to the present writer, who is given to undertaking a good deal more than she can ever accomplish; who is always surprised by publication-day; who postpones every literary work till the last hour of grace, and then, a little longer; who requires so much of self-coaxing and backing, to get into the traces, after a week or so of freedom and grass, — all this systematic purpose, this routine, and rigid exactitude, is simply amazing, — it verges on the marvellous, — it is *Ledger-de-main.*

Ah, Fanny, is then your Pegasus *always* saddled, and bridled, and whinnying in the court? Is the steam always up in that tug-boat of a busy brain? Is the wine of your fancy never on the lees? Are there no house-cleaning days in your calendar? Don't your country friends ever come to town and drop in on your golden working-hours? Are there no autograph-hunters about your doors? Do not fond mammas ever send in their babies to deliciously distract you on a "Ledger" day? Do your dear five hundred friends always respect it, and postpone their weddings, musical *matinées* and other mournful occasions? Does the paper-hanger never put you to rout? Do you never have a bout with your sewing-machine and get your temper *ruffled?* Does not that "wonderful wean," that darling grandchild, dainty little Effie, ever have a fit of naughtiness, or whooping-cough, or a tumble downstairs, on that day? Don't you ever long, on just that day, to lie on the sofa and read Thackeray? Ah, do not wars and influenzas, national crises and kitchen imbroglios, disappointed hopes and misfitting dresses, an instinctive rebellion against regulations and resolutions, even of your own making, *ever* interfere with your writing for the "Ledger"? Doubtless you have been tempted, in times of hurry, or languor, in journeyings and dog-day heats, to break your agreement; but an honest fealty to a generous publisher has hitherto constrained you to stand by; and we like you for it. Other publishers may be *bon*, but he is *Bonner*. So you do not demean yourself by following the triumphal chariot of his fortunes (Dexter's trotting wagon) like Zenobia in chains, — since the chains are of gold.

As a writer of brief essays and slight sketches, Fanny Fern excels. She seems always to have plenty of small change in the way of thoughts and themes. She knows well how to begin without verbiage, and to end without abruptness. She starts her game without much beating about the bush. She seems to measure accurately the subject and the occasion, and wastes no words, — or, as poor Artemus Ward used to say, never "slops over." As a novelist, she is somewhat open to the charge of exaggeration, and she is not sufficiently impersonal to be always artistic. Her own fortunes, loves, and hates live again in her creations, — her heroines are her doubles. As a moralist, she is liable to a sort of uncharitable charity and benevolent injustice. In her stout championship of the poor, of the depressed and toil-worn many, she seems to harden her heart against the small, but intelligent, rich but respectable, portion of our population, known as "Upper-tendom." Can any good thing come out of Fifth

Avenue? is the spirit of many of her touching little sketches. She seems to think that the scriptural comparison of the difficult passage of the camel through the eye of the needle settled the case of Mr. Crœsus. Her tone is sometimes a little severe and cynical when treating of the shortcomings of the world of fashion. It is so easy to criticise from the safe position of a philosopher or poet; but how many of us would dare to answer for our Spartan simplicity and moderation, and our Christian charity and benevolence,—virtues which of course we all now possess in abundance,—should fortune take a sudden turn, open for us her halls of dazzling light, provide for us ample changes of purple and fine linen, of the fashionable cut, wine and strong drink, and terrapin suppers, chariots, and horses, yachts, opera-boxes, diamonds, and French bonnets?

Fanny Fern herself regrets that she has not been able to give more careful study to her writing,—to concentrate here, and elaborate there,—to be, in short, always the artist. She has done many things well,—she might have done a few things surpassingly well. But she has, I doubt not, written out of an honest heart always, earnestly and fearlessly,—written tales, sketches, letters, essays spiced with odd fancies, satire, and humor,—some exquisitely tender and pitiful, some defiant and belligerent in tone; but none with a doubtful moral ring about them. She has chosen to feed the multitude on the plain with simple, wholesome food, rather than to pour nectar for the Olympians. Her genius is practical and democratic, and so has served the people well, and received a generous reward in hearty popular favor. She has probably not accomplished the highest of which she is capable, but all that the peculiar exigencies of her life have permitted her to accomplish. In faithfully doing the work nearest to her hand she may be consoled by the consciousness that art has been shouldered aside by duty alone. Speaking of her little grand-daughter, in a private letter, she says: "Our little Effie has never been left with a servant, and, although to carry out such a plan has involved a sacrifice of much literary work, or its unsatisfactory incompleteness, I am not and never shall be sorry. *She* is my poem."

By these things we may see that whatever masks of manly independence, pride, or mocking mischief Fanny Fern may put on, she is, at the core of her nature, "pure womanly."

I have written this article with little more personal knowledge of Mrs. Parton than I have been able to obtain from brief biographical sketches, and the recollections and impressions of friends. Not from choice have I so done, after the manner of the critic, who made it a rule not to read a book before reviewing it, for fear of being "prejudiced;" but because I have never been so fortunate as to cross orbits with my brilliant, but somewhat erratic subject. Her life has been attempted many times; indeed, literary biographers seem to be under the impression that "the oftener this wonderful woman is repeated the better," to quote from the immortal Toots. May that life have years enough and fame and prosperity enough to justify many other sketches, worthier than this, before the coming of that

> "Last scene of all,
> That ends this strange eventful history."

And may that scene come with tender gradations of purple twilight shades, deepening into a night, star-lit with hope, and sweet with love — all balm, and rest, and peace; "the peace of God which passeth all understanding."

H. B. Hall Jr

Mrs. SIGOURNEY.

LYDIA H. SIGOURNEY.

BY REV. E. B. HUNTINGTON.

WERE any intelligent American citizen now asked to name the American woman, who, for a quarter of a century before 1855, held a higher place in the respect and affections of the American people than any other woman of the times had secured, it can hardly be questioned that the prompt reply would be, MRS. LYDIA HUNTLEY SIGOURNEY.

And this would be the answer, not simply on the ground of her varied and extensive learning; nor on that of her acknowledged poetic gifts; nor on that of her voluminous contributions to our current literature, both in prose and verse; but rather, because with these gifts and this success, she had with singular kindliness of heart made her very life-work itself a constant source of blessing and joy to others. Her very goodness had made her great. Her genial good-will had given her power. Her loving friendliness had made herself and her name everywhere a charm. So that, granted that other women could be named, more gifted in some endowments, more learned in certain branches, and even more ably represented in the literature of the times; still, no one of them, by universal consent, had succeeded in winning so largely the esteem and admiration of her age.

It is of this woman that we need not hesitate to write, when we would make up our list of the representative women of our times. She was a woman so rare, we need not hesitate to claim it, for her native gifts, and still more, so genial and lovable, in deed and spirit, that her very life seemed a sort of divine benediction upon our age. And who, more worthily than she, can represent to us the best and highest type of cultivated womanhood?

LYDIA HOWARD HUNTLEY, the only child of Ezekiel and Sophia (Wentworth) Huntley, was born in Norwich, Connecticut, Sept. 1, 1791. In her parentage and birthplace we have no indistinct prophecy of her future life. Their lessons, wrought into the very texture of her sensitive soul, served as the good genius of her long and bright career. She could never forget or deny them. Their precious memory was to her a perpetual and exceeding joy.

Witness this sweet picture of her early home, drawn by her own child-hand, yet, even so early, foreshowing the lifelong brightness of her loving spirit: —

> "My gentle kitten at my footstool sings
> Her song, monotonous and full of joy.
> Close by my side, my tender mother sits,
> Industriously bent — her brow still bright
> With beams of lingering youth, while he, the sire,
> The faithful guide, indulgently doth smile."

What but a blessed influence over her could such a home have had? And we shall not wonder, when, fifty years later, we find her filial hand sketching, so exquisitely, the "beaming smile," and "the love and patience sweet," with which those dear names were embalmed. Few, very few, have borne with them through life, so freshly and so lovingly, the forms and the affections of their home-friends. The impression they made upon her must have been exceedingly precious to her heart; and so her affectionate love kept faithful vigil over these dearest treasures of her memory.

Hardly less forceful than these home-influences, must have been the beautiful and romantic sceneries, and the genial social life of her native town. It could but have stirred and educated such a soul as hers to have spent her childhood amid such scenes: —

> "Rocks, gray rocks, with their caverns dark,
> Leaping rills, like the diamond spark,
> Torrent voices, thundering by,
> Where the pride of the vernal floods swelled high."

It is her own testimony which reveals to us the power of these home-charms over her life, — a testimony given, when, to use her own felicitous figure, she was now "journeying towards the gates of the West": —

"Yet came there forth from its beauty a silent, secret influence, moulding the heart to happiness, and love of the beneficent Creator."

And still again she records their power: —

> "We have garnered those charms and attractions that bring
> A spell o'er our souls when existence was young."

So nurtured, we can understand the secret of that love for Norwich and its scenery which she never failed to show to her latest day. It only needed an invitation to her to revisit the "dear old places" of her childhood, to kindle anew the fervors of more than her childhood joy: —

> "We accept, we will come, wheresoever we rove,
> And wreathe round thy birthday our honor and love.
> We love thee, we love thee; thy smile, like a star,
> Hath gleamed in our skies, though our homes were afar."

Added to the affection of her parents, and to these sweet charms of her native town, was still another, and a very marked home-influence, which was destined to prove educational to her. Madame Lathrop, one of the noblest of the many worthy Norwich matrons of that day, a daughter of Governor Talcott, of Hartford, and widow of Daniel Lathrop, a wealthy and accomplished citizen of Norwich, had made her own elegant and hospitable home that also of the Huntley family. She took great interest in Lydia, and drew strongly to her own the heart of the sensitive girl. And did she not, in the daily communing of their souls, leave somewhat of her own noble spirit of self-denial and rich charity as fruitful seed in that young heart? What other proof do we need than that which comes from the oft-repeated testimony of the child herself, even down to her latest years? Let her sketch for us, in her own sweet way, the record of this blessed influence over her character and life: —

"A fair countenance, a clear blue eye, and a voice of music return to me as I recall the image of that venerated lady over whom more than threescore and ten years had passed ere I saw the light. Her tall, graceful form, moving with elastic step through the parterres whose numerous flowers she superintended, and her brow raised in calm meditation from the sacred volume she was reading, were to me beautiful. The sorrowful came to be enlightened by the sunbeam that dwelt in her spirit, and the children of want to find bread and a garment. The beauty of the soul was hers that waxeth not old. Love was in her heart to all whom God had made. At her grave I learned my first lesson of a bursting grief that has never been forgotten. Let none say that the aged die unloved or unmourned by the young."

It must have been an influence of great power which such a character wielded over such a nature; and we cannot wonder that, long years after that hallowed intimacy, we find the grateful child thus recording her remembrance of it: "The cream of all my happiness was a loving intercourse with venerable old age." Nor can we deny her the dutiful joy of dedicating one of her earliest publications, as "an offering of gratitude to her whose influence, like a golden thread, had run through the whole woof of my life."

It was under influences like these that her life had its dawning. Exceedingly sensitive and impressible, she readily responded to their power. They found her a keen observer, and a very rapid learner. Her infancy seems to have been like the later childhood of most girls, and her girlhood wore the thoughtfulness and reached the attainments of ordinary womanhood.

The insight into this earliest period of her life, which her "Letters of Life" so artlessly give us, is one of the most curious pages in our autobiographic literature. We have here, perhaps, the most unaffected and childlike prattle about child-life, in the language of doting old age. Possibly there may be something excessive in the coloring given to the whole picture; but surely we can afford to let the pen of old age use the freedom which a warm heart, warming anew amid the scenes and play-places of its young life, might dictate. Let the venerated authoress, if in her deep joy she recalls the events which seemed so important to her young fancy, tell the whole story, which once she might have hesitated to do, and which other authors, more careful to prune their thoughts to the accepted proprieties, would not assuredly have done. It certainly cannot harm us to be made, once in our lives, familiar in letters with the very precocities, if you will, which are so often seen in bright children, yet which we do not usually elevate to the dignity of the printed page.

If she speaks of the little attempts at conversation made in the first year of her life, have we not all heard and been charmed with hearing the same thing in our own little ones? If she details even the prattle, and the occasional wise and over-scholarly sayings or fancies of her third summer among the flowers, why not give her credit for what, though perhaps not very common, is still plainly possible to a child of gifts, especially if she has spent her first three years under the most helpful of influences? It need not be counted an offence if she tell us over what nobody else will be likely to tell us, — the whole story of her doll-teaching and training. It is a pretty picture which that same scene makes when acted in all of our homes, and why should not its sketch, whether by the pencil of the artist or the pen of the writer, charm us too?

But is there not, also, in this the very best of sense? How it aids us to understand the woman, to see the little one with her dolls around her, and hear her begin there her work of persuasion and authority! It instructs as well as charms us to visit the artless child in her "spacious garret;" to note her curious search among its gathered household treasures; to find her settling herself down like the bee to its flower-food, as she finds an old hymn-book there; to see her hearty love for the "large black horse," "the red-coat cows," "the crowing, brooding, and peeping poultry," and the "pliant pussy" which sat in her lap or sported by her side, and which was "as a sister" to her. It will instruct us, where we shall need light, to roam awhile with the laughing babe and child, "from garden to garden;" to run with her "at full speed through the alleys;" to recline by her side, "when wearied, in some shaded recess," or even on the "mow of hay in the large, lofty barn," where we can together "watch the quiet cows over their fragrant food;" and then to sit down with her at the family table, and taste with her of the bread so sweet, "made in capacious iron basins." Suppose, in this way, we learn how early and how regular her meals were; how uniform and simple the diet on which she was reared; and how exact and respectful and decorous the behavior of that hour. Do not all of these lessons explain the character which they so certainly help to form? And so we may well thank the authoress of seventy years that she allowed herself to recall, for our delight and instruction, those germinal forces of her favored childhood.

Let us now follow this child, as she prepares herself for the life-work before her. At four years of age we find her in the school nearest to the house of her parents; and we only learn of that first school, that its "spelling-classes" were the chief delight of the child. Trivial as this fact is, it gives us no unmeaning hint. Her second teacher, a gentleman, perhaps the teacher of the winter school, won the child to the use of the pen, and laid the foundation of that distinct, print-like chirography which was so serviceable to her whole future career. Next, the teacher of needle-work does her good service by starting her well in this feminine art, of which she made later the best of use. And now comes the young ladies' school, under an English lady of varied accomplishment; and here she makes a good beginning in music and painting and embroidery. And here, too, we get valuable hints, and it would well repay us, had we time, to watch the child in the beginning of her art-life. It was full of meaning,—that extemporized studio at home, that "piece of gamboge," that "fragment of indigo, begged of the washer-woman," those coffee-grounds to give the ambered brown, and those child-experiments, again and again repeated, to secure desired tints. We may note, too, about this time, how the literary taste and enthusiasm of the child was aroused. How life-like was its beginning! She started a story, which the record does not finish; for they all said it was too much for her. She was "only just eight years old."

Next we find her in the school of a graduate of Dublin, and here she makes rapid progress in mathematics. Her next step forward, in the school on the Green, under an educated and veteran teacher, places her at the head of the reading-classes. Then, under the training of Mr. Pelatiah Perit, who became so eminent among the business men of the country, she spent another year of successful study. Pursuing still the English classics and Latin, she finished in her fourteenth year her school-life at home. Then followed a course of domestic training in the duties of house-keeping, yet not so pressingly as to hinder the private study of the Latin. For the higher ornamental branches she spent parts of two years in Hartford; and, with more than ordinary mental activity and attainment, she takes leave of her school-life. Yet, such was her thirst for learning, that nothing could hinder her studies; and we find her, with the enthusiasm of a scholar, devoting her later girlhood to the study of even the original Hebrew of the Christian Scriptures.

And now begins her career as teacher, — a life which she seems to have chosen scarcely more for want of something to do than from love of teaching itself. Her first experiment had been made in her father's house, and the result confirmed her purpose to make it her life-work. In her nineteenth year, in company with Miss Nancy M. Hyde, a very intimate friend, she opened a select school for girls in Chelsea, now Norwich City. Her interest in the work was very great, and her success no less so. We can readily accept her later testimony that she found her daily employment "less a toil than privilege." But, through the influence of Mr. Daniel Wadsworth, of Hartford, she was induced to establish for herself a private school for girls in that city; and, in 1814, she entered upon its duties.

During the five years she remained in this school she won a twofold reputation. Her success as teacher was well-nigh unparalleled for the times, and deservingly so; while her influence over the social circles of the city had become no less marked. Her influence over her pupils was something wonderful. They loved her with a love which nothing could repress; and their devotion was as true and lasting as their love. What testimony to the strength of her hold upon them those annual reunions on their commencement day furnishes! Even long years after they had become scattered over the land, those days were held sacred in their hearts. And when their little ones began to gather about them, they, too, were taken to the hallowed place, that on them also might fall the sweet influence which had so long blessed their mothers.

But, from the very beginning of her life in Hartford, she made for herself a place in the confidence and affections of the people, which every successive year only served to confirm. She became, in the just language of as high authority as the venerable S. G. Goodrich, "the presiding genius of its young social circle," and she was never called in her long career to vacate that post of honor.

It was while thus winning her way as teacher that she also began her public literary life. At the urgent request of her friend, Mr. Wadsworth, she consented to issue her first volume, entitled, "Pieces in Prose and Verse." This work was printed in 1815, at the expense of Mr. Wadsworth. And the list of subscribers, which was also printed, indicates thus early the reputation which newspaper publicity had given her.

But another event soon interrupts her career as teacher. Charles Sigourney, a merchant of the city, a gentleman of wealth and literary culture and high social position, solicits and wins her hand. Their marriage was celebrated in the Episcopal church of her native town, in the early summer of 1819. Mr. Sigourney, of Huguenot descent, was already a communicant in the Episcopal church; and, on her marriage, Mrs. Sigourney, who, since 1809, had been a devoted Christian and a member of the Congregational church, felt it to be her privilege and duty to transfer her membership to the church to which her husband belonged.

This marriage threw upon Mrs. Sigourney the care of the

three children of her husband by a former wife; and that care was assumed with a singular devotion to their comfort and welfare; and in this field only did she find room henceforth for her gifts as teacher. But both her position at the head of the first circle in the leading metropolis of the State, and her means, and the culture of her husband, conspired to encourage her in the literary field in which she was now winning such a triumph. Besides the volume printed in 1815, in 1816 she had published her "Life and Writings of Nancy Maria Hyde," an interesting tribute to the memory of her most intimate friend and fellow-teacher; and during the year of her marriage appeared, also, "The Square Table," a pamphlet designed as a corrective of what were deemed the harmful tendencies of "Arthur's Round Table," which was then exciting considerable attention in the community.

From this date to that of her death our record must be that of an earnest woman, filling up every hour of her day with its allotted duty, cheerfully and nobly done. Few women have been so diligent workers, few have maintained such fervency of spirit, and few have, in all their working, so faithfully served the Lord.

Her position, that of second wife and step-mother, has not always been found an easy one to fill; yet, even with the temptations which her literary tastes might be supposed to offer, she could never be justly reproached for neglecting any home-duty. Bound to her friends with no ordinary ties of affection, she lived, first of all, for them. Even her literary life is most crowded with its witnesses to her home-love, and indeed was largely its result. She worked, and wrote, and prayed, that she might faithfully meet this prime claim upon her heart and life.

We cannot follow, in detail, this busy and painstaking career. We find her at the head of her household, which at times was large, shrinking from no burden or self-denial needed in her work, — living to see her two step-daughters educated and settled in life, and their brother, at the age of forty-five, consigned to a consumptive's grave; to educate her own daughter and son, and then, just on the verge of a promising manhood, to follow him, too, to his grave; to care for both her own parents, until, in a good old age, she might tenderly hand them down to their last rest; to follow her beloved and honored husband to his grave; to give her own only daughter away in acceptable marriage; and then to settle herself down, joyful and trustful yet, in her own home, vacated indeed of her loved ones, but filled still with precious mementos of their love, until her own change should come. These forty-six years, between her marriage and her death, were mainly spent at her home in Hartford. Her travels were chiefly those of brief journeys through the Eastern and Middle States. Once she visited Virginia, and once crossed the Atlantic, visiting within the year the chief points of attraction in England, Scotland, and France. The rest of those forty-six years were most industriously employed in her own loved home, filled up with domestic duties or with literary and benevolent work; and it is safe to say that few women have ever worked to better account. She won universal respect and love. The poor and the rich, the ignorant and the educated, alike found in her that which delighted and charmed them; and so she came to occupy a place in their affections which they accorded to no other.

But, doubtless, it will be as a literary woman that she will be most widely known. And no estimate of her career which leaves out of the account the character and value of her writings can do justice to her memory. Beginning in 1815, and closing with her posthumous "Letters of Life" in 1866, her published writings numbered fifty-seven volumes. Besides these, our newspaper and magazine literature must have furnished nearly as much more. Her correspondence, not published, amounting to nearly one thousand seven hundred letters annually for several years, must have exceeded largely these printed writings; so that she must have been one of the most voluminous writers of her age.

We have not space for a critical analysis of her writings. We would simply indicate their aim and success. Whatever may be said of their artistic execution, of one thing we are sure, that their spirit and aim are as noble as ever inspired human literature; and the world has already accepted them as a worthy offering. A sharp critical judgment must agree with Mrs. Sigourney's own decision, that she wrote too much for highest success, both in invention and style. But when we stop to ask why she wrote so much, we shall find our answer in the very elements of her character, which contributed most to her eminence. Her first published volume reveals with great clearness at least these two qualities of the writer: the strength of her affections, and her equally strong sense of duty to others. We feel that she wrote what her kind heart prompted, that she might please or aid those who seemed to her to have just claims upon her. Instead of using the precious moments on the mere style of her expression, she was ever hurrying along on some urgent call of affection or duty. She could not stop to think of her literary reputation when some dear friend was pleading at her heart, or some sorrowing soul needed to be comforted. More than almost any other writer of the day, she wrote not for herself, but for others. And it is precisely here that we find the real key, both to whatever faults of style her writings may betray, and to the very best success of her life. For, while she greatly blessed the multitudes for whom she so rapidly wrote, we cannot but notice, also, how in her successive works, she is gaining both in the force and beauty of her style.

We see on almost every page of her writings how tender

her spirit, how sensitive her sympathy was. From the beginning, her affections, sanctified by a Christian purpose, took the lead. We know that it was her greatest

> . . . . "joy to raise
> The trembler from the shade,
> To bind the broken, and to heal
> The wounds she never made."

But we must not dwell on these charming witnesses to the tenderness of her loving heart. It is easy to see that one so ruled, would not regard the mere style of her expression of highest value. And yet it would do injustice to Mrs. Sigourney, to leave out of the account the care and painstaking, with which she sought to make her writings most effective. We know she must have sought ease and fluency as well as exactness and vigor of expression. Her writings abound in witnesses innumerable to these graces. The call made upon her pen from the first magazines of the day, and from the more solid works issuing from our best publishing-houses, of itself testifies to the great merit even of her style.

No critic can read that beautiful poem on the "Death of an Infant," commencing with

> "Death found strange beauty on that polished brow,
> And dashed it out,"

without feeling that none but a true poet, practised in the art, could have written it. We might instance her "Scottish Weaver," "Breakfast," "Birthday of Longfellow," "My Stuffed Owl," "Niagara," and hundreds of other poems, in all of which may be found passages of great beauty and power. We are sure we cannot afford, these many years, to let those graceful, and at times exquisite, gems, drop out of our literature; nor can we doubt that their author will continue to rank high even among the poets of her age.

Without space for repeating the entire list, even of her poetic works, it is due to our readers to indicate those which shall best exhibit the merits and the extent of her poetic writings, and we believe we shall do this by naming the eight following volumes, with their dates:—

Her Poems, 1827, pp. 228; Zinzendorf, and other Poems, 1835, 2d edition, pp. 300; Pocahontas, and other Poems, 1841, pp. 284; London edition, 1841, pp. 348; Select Poems, 1842, pp. 324, fourth edition, of which eight thousand copies had been already sold; Illustrated edition, 1848, pp. 408; Western Home, and other Poems, 1854, pp. 360; and Gleanings, 1860, pp. 264.

Of her prose works we can only indicate that which most clearly establishes the writer's rank among our very best prose-writers of the age. Her "Past Meridian," given to the world in her sixty-fifth year, which has now reached its fourth edition, is one of our most charming classics. One cannot read those delightful pages, without gratitude that the gifted author was spared to give us such a coronal of her useful authorship. It were easy to collect quite a volume of the most enthusiastic commendations of this charming work; but we must leave it, with the assurance that it gives a new title to its beloved author to a perpetual fame in English literature.

And what a testimony we also have in the reception our authoress has received among even our best critics! It certainly was no mean praise, which Hart, in his selections from the Female Prose Writers gives us, when he so graphically and truthfully says of her writings, that they "are more like the dew than the lightning." Peter Parley pronounced her, "next to Willis, the most successful and liberal contributor to the Token." Professor Cleveland, in his Compend of English Literature, could not more truthfully have characterized her writings than he did, as "pure, lofty, and holy in tendency and influence." C. W. Everest, in his Connecticut

Poets, only repeats the common judgment in his decision, "Love and religion are the unvarying elements of her song." E. P. Whipple, the very Nestor of our critics, was obliged to bear testimony to the popularity of her works. He speaks of her facility in versification, and her fluency both in thought and language; and only claims, what all critics will easily allow, that from the very quantity of her writing, she "hardly does justice to her real powers."

But we need not pursue our citations of critical approval further.

We acknowledge the skill with which Mrs. Sigourney used our flexible English tongue; but we still more admire, and would never fail to honor, the deep undertone of "the still, sad music of humanity," which hallowed all her song. We will let her, though unwittingly, while describing the noble devotion of the pleading Queen Philippa, sketch herself: —

> "THE ADVOCATE OF SORROW, AND THE FRIEND
> OF THOSE WHOM ALL FORSAKE."

We cannot but return to this ruling spirit of her life, equally unaffected and controlling in her girlhood and her latest years. Her gifts of charity and love often exceeded the allowance of her income which she saved for herself.

What monuments she thus built for herself in grateful hearts! Witness her frequent visits to the Reform School in Meriden. Those delighted boys cannot soon forget that beautiful orchard, whose thrifty trees she gave as her blessing to them; nor that last gift, the generous Easter cake, which made that festival so joyous to them; nor, most of all, that beautiful smile of hers, always so radiant with her hearty good-will and hope. Oh, there was a blessing in that presence, even for young lives that have been tempted down into the dark shadows of a premature disgrace!

Or who shall make her presence good to the pupils of the

Deaf and Dumb Asylum in her own city, on whose mute joy her very looks beamed a more eloquent sympathy than our best words can express? Or when will the poor orphans of the asylums she so loved to visit forget her tenderness and love?

Hear this good woman, even amid the pain and exhaustion of her last sickness, thoughtful still of the suffering ones who might miss her timely charity, tenderly asking, morning after morning, "Is there any gift for me to send to-day?" More touchingly still, as you stand over her on the very last night of her stay on earth, you will hear this faintly, yet clearly uttered wish of the dying woman, "I would that I might live until morning, that I may, with my own hand, do up that little lace cap for that dear little babe." And so she left us, with her thought of love still on those whom she was to leave behind. Blessed departure, that! And did she not find how true her own sweet verse proved: —

> "And thy good-morning shall be spoke
> By sweet-voiced angels, that shall bear thee home
> To the divine Redeemer"?

And how appropriate the last lines of the last poem that she was permitted to write on earth, — the beautiful image of her soul to leave for us to look on forever: —

> "Heaven's peace be with you all!
> Farewell! Farewell!"

Saturday morning, June 10, 1866, was the date of her death. Her funeral was itself a witness to us of all that we have claimed for her in the city where she lived and died. Specially fitting was it, that those "children of silence" to whom she had loved to minister, and those now doubly orphaned little ones from the asylum, should have their place in that mourning throng.

And after the funeral, when the papers of the city attempted to sum up the city's loss, it was specially fitting that from the pen of a neighbor we should have this testimony: "For fifty years this good lady has blessed our city."

To these abundant witnesses to Mrs. Sigourney's noble goodness, we can only add that of her personal friend, S. G. Goodrich, who was, also, extensively acquainted with the best characters of the generation to which she belonged: "No one whom I know can look back upon a long and earnest career of such unblemished beneficence."

And how can we better close this too brief sketch of this honored woman, than in the words in which she so well has announced the imperishable fame of the gifted Mrs. Hemans: —

"Therefore, we will not say
Farewell to thee; for every unborn age
Shall mix thee with its household charities.
The sage shall greet thee with his benison,
And woman shrine thee as a vestal flame
In all the temples of her sanctity;
And the young child shall take thee by the hand
And travel with a surer step to heaven."

MRS. FRANCES ANNE KEMBLE.

BY JAMES PARTON.

THERE was excitement and expectation among the play-goers of New York, in the early days of September, 1832. Stars, new to the firmament of America, were about to appear, — a great event in those simple days, when Europe supplied us with almost all we ever had of public pleasure. Charles Kemble, brother of Mrs. Siddons the peerless, and of John Kemble the magnificent, was coming to America, accompanied by his daughter, "Fanny Kemble," the most brilliant of the recent acquisitions to the London stage. Charles Kemble was then an exceedingly stout gentleman, of fifty-seven, fitter to shine in Falstaff than in Hamlet; yet such is the power of genuine talent to overcome the obstacles which nature herself puts in its way, that he still played with fine effect some of the lightest and most graceful characters of the drama. He played Hamlet well, and Benedick better, when he must have weighed two hundred and fifty pounds; and people forgot, in admiring the charm of his manner, and the noble beauty of his face, that he had passed his prime. His daughter, at this period, was just twenty-one years of age, and stood midway in her brief and splendid theatrical career, which had begun two years before, and was to end two years after.

The play selected for the first appearance of the young actress in America was Fazio. The old Park theatre was the place. It was the evening of Tuesday, September the 18th, 1832. Charles Kemble had appeared the night before to a crowded house in his favorite part of Hamlet, which he performed with that finish and thoroughness characteristic of all the family of the Kembles. On this evening the house was still more crowded, and the weather was oppressively warm. At half past six Miss Kemble went to the theatre to prepare for the ordeal before her. To give time for the audience to assemble and settle in their seats, the farce of Popping the Question was first performed. It was a night of mishaps. When she reached the theatre, she discovered that the actor (a novice from London) who was to play the principal male part in the tragedy of Fazio was so completely terror-stricken at the prospect before him that he gasped for breath, and he excited the pity, even more than the alarm, of the lady whose performance he was about to mar. She did her best to reassure him, but with small success. When they were about to take their place upon the stage just before the curtain rose, he was in an absolute panic, and appeared to be choking with mere fright. She hastily brought him some lemonade to swallow, and was immediately obliged to take her place with him in the scene.

According to the custom of actresses who play the chief part in Fazio, she sat with her back to the audience. The curtain rose. As the back of one young lady bears a striking resemblance to that of another, and as she was dressed with perfect plainness, the audience did not recognize her, and remained silent. The actor supporting her, who had calculated upon the usual noisy reception, and was still in the last extremity of terror, stood stock still gazing at the heroine, evidently waiting for the audience to do *their* part before he began his. The hint was taken at length, or, probably, some friends of the lady recognized her, and then the whole assembly clapped their hands and used their voices, according to the established custom on such occasions. Her reception, indeed, was in the highest degree cordial, — such as New York has ever delighted to bestow upon distinguished talent, from whatever part of the world it may have come.

The play began. The frightened actor broke down in his second speech. Miss Kemble prompted him, but he was too completely terrified to understand her, and he spoiled the situation. This happened so frequently that the great actress was prevented, not merely from exerting her powers, but from fixing her mind upon her part at all; for, what with prompting her distracted Fazio, and his total obliviousness of what actors call "the business" of the scene, she became at length almost as much frightened as he was, and she thought that her total and ignominious failure was inevitable. It is a curious thing, however, that a performer upon the stage may be enduring a martyrdom of this kind, and scarcely a soul in the audience suspect it. I remember once being close to the stage when Edwin Booth was playing Hamlet, and the king was so intoxicated that it was with real difficulty that he kept himself upright upon his throne, and he had to be prompted at every other word. Mr. Booth was on the rack during the whole of the first scene in which he appears, and kept up a running fire of the most emphatic observations upon the conduct of his royal uncle. It was with the greatest difficulty that the scene was carried on; and yet, I was informed by persons in front of the house, that they had not observed anything extraordinary, except that the king was a very bad actor, which in *that* part is as far as possible from being extraordinary.

And so it was with Miss Kemble. She struggled through the first two acts with her miserable Fazio. She was rid of him at the beginning of the third act, and from that time began to play with freedom and effect. Her success was complete. Every point of that intense and passionate performance was heartily applauded, and when the curtain went down at the close of the fifth act, she was summoned to reappear as vociferously as heart could wish. This was the beginning of a most brilliant and successful engagement in New York. Here, as everywhere, her crowning triumph was in the part of Julia, in Sheridan Knowles' play of the Hunchback, a play which was written expressly for her, and in which she gained her greatest London success. Most of those telling "points," which are repeated by every actress whenever this play is performed, were originated by Miss Kemble, and never failed, or can fail, to produce a powerful effect upon an audience whenever they are respectably made.

This young lady came rightly by her dramatic talent. She was a member of a family which, for three generations, had contributed to the English stage its brightest ornaments. Roger Kemble, the first of the family who is known to fame, born in 1721, himself an actor and manager, was the father of twelve children, five of whom embraced his profession and became eminent in it. His eldest child, Sarah Kemble, married at the age of eighteen an actor of a country company, named Siddons, and became the greatest actress that ever lived. John Philip Kemble, the eldest son of Roger, was perhaps, upon the whole, the greatest actor of modern times. George Stephen Kemble, another son of the country manager, was also an excellent actor, and is now remembered chiefly for his performance of Falstaff, which he was fat enough to play without stuffing. Elizabeth Kemble, a sister of Mrs. Siddons, married an actor named Whitlock, with whom she came to the United States, where she rose to the first position on the stage, and had the honor of performing before General Washington and the other great men of that day. She made a fortune in America, and retired to England in 1807 to enjoy it. Finally, there was Charles Kemble, the youngest child of Roger except one, an actor of great note on the English stage for many years.

It was by no means the intention of Roger Kemble that all his children should pursue his own laborious vocation. On the contrary he was much opposed to their going upon the stage, and in some instances took particular pains to prevent it. This was the case with Charles, who received an excellent education, and for whom a place was procured in the London post-office. But it seemed as natural for a Kemble to act, as it is for an eagle to soar. They all appear to have possessed just that combination of form, feature, voice, presence, and temperament, which are fitted to charm and impress an audience. Charles Kemble was soon led to try the stage, upon which he rose gradually to a high, but never to the highest, position. He was the best light comedian of his time, and has perhaps never been surpassed in such characters as Benedick, Petruchio, Charles Surface, Cassio, Faulconbridge, Edgar, and Marc Antony. He was also an excellent, though not a great, Hamlet. In due time he married a popular actress, Miss De Camp, who began her dramatic career as a member of the ballet troupe of the Italian Opera House in London. Two daughters were the fruit of this union, — Frances Anne Kemble, the subject of this memoir, and Adelaide Kemble, — both of whom, after a short but striking career upon the stage, married gentlemen of fortune and retired to private life.

Six weeks before the evening on which Miss Kemble made her first appearance in London, neither she nor her parents had ever thought of her attempting the stage. Charles Kemble was then manager of Covent Garden Theatre, one of the two great theatres of London. The plays which he presented did not prove attractive; the season threatened to end in disaster; and he looked anxiously about him for the means of restoring to the theatre its former prestige. His eldest daughter, Frances, was then eighteen years of age. Except that she had frequently heard her aunt, Mrs. Siddons, read the plays of Shakespeare, and had lived from her infancy in a family of actors, she had made no special preparation for the stage. She inherited, however, that fine presence, that admirable self-possession, that magnificent and flexible voice, for which the Kembles were distinguished. It suddenly occurred to the family that this brilliant and saucy girl, perhaps a little spoiled by parental fondness, might prove a great actress and save the failing fortunes of the family. The experiment was tried. In October, 1829, she made her first appearance. The play selected for the occasion was Romeo and Juliet, in which her father played the part of Romeo, her mother that of the nurse, and herself, Juliet. Her success was so remarkable, it was so evident that she possessed in an eminent degree the talent of the family, that, when the curtain descended at the close of the evening, she was felt to be, both before and behind the curtain, an established favorite. Her first success was followed by other triumphs. As Portia, in the Merchant of Venice, as Bianca, in the tragedy of Fazio, as Lady Teazle, in the School for Scandal, and in other parts of similar calibre, she shone without a rival; since, whatever may have been wanting in the artist was amply atoned for, in the public mind, by the youthful grace and beauty of the woman. The house was nightly filled to overflowing. Her father was saved from bankruptcy, and the old popularity of the theatre was fully restored. A play which she had written in her seventeenth year, entitled Francis the First, was produced, and attained a certain success. Sheridan Knowles, then at the height of his renown as a dramatist, and in the full vigor of his powers, wrote for her his master-piece, the Hunchback, in which her popularity was almost beyond precedent.

It was after two years of such a life as this, when she was

twenty-one years of age, that her father and herself crossed the Atlantic to make the usual tour of the American theatres. New York, as we have seen, gave her a cordial welcome, and sent her forth to the other cities relieved of all anxiety, to continue a career which was nothing but triumph.

Fortunately for our present purpose, she kept a diary of this tour, the publication of which, in 1835, was one of the agreeable literary events of the year. Thirty-five years ago! The lifetime of but a single generation! And yet, what a different country does this diary reveal to us from the United States of to-day! What a different person, too, was the dashing, vivacious, and spoiled child of the public of 1832, from the patient, mature, and lofty character which Mrs. Kemble has since attained!

Her diary was amusing when it was published, but it is to-day a lesson in history. She lived, during her first engagement in New York, at the American Hotel, on the corner of Barclay Street and Broadway, which was then considered the most elegant hotel in the city. She gives nevertheless a sorry account of it: The rooms were "a mixture of French finery and Irish disorder and dirt," and there was a scarcity, not only of servants, food, and space, but even of such common articles as knives and forks. "The servants," she adds, "who were just a quarter as many as the house required, *had no bedrooms allotted to them*, but slept about anywhere in the public rooms, or on sofas, in drawing-rooms let to private families. In short, nothing can exceed the want of order, propriety, and comfort in this establishment, except the enormity of the tribute it levies upon pilgrims and wayfarers through the land."

To give the reader an idea, at once, of the character of Miss Kemble's style at the time, and of the startling changes which time has wrought in the country, I will here transcribe the account she gives of her first journey from New York to

Philadelphia, which occurred on the 8th of October, 1832. The steamboat started from the foot of Barclay Street at half-past six in the morning, which obliged the young lady and her father to get up long before daylight. This steamboat, which excited the special wonder of the party from its magnitude and splendor, conveyed them as far as Perth Amboy.

"At about half-past ten," she continues, "we reached the place where we leave the river, to proceed across a part of the State of New Jersey, to the Delaware. The landing was beyond measure wretched; the shore shelved down to the water's edge; and its marshy, clayey, sticky soil, rendered doubly soft and squashy by the damp weather, was strown over with broken potsherds, stones, and bricks, by way of pathway; these, however, presently failed, and some slippery planks, half immersed in mud, were the only roads to the coaches that stood ready to receive the passengers of the steamboat. Oh, these coaches! English eye hath not seen, English ear hath not heard, nor hath it entered into the heart of Englishmen to conceive, the surpassing clumsiness and wretchedness of these leathern inconveniences! They are shaped something like boats, the sides being merely leathern pieces removable at pleasure, but which in bad weather are buttoned down to protect the inmates from the wet. There are three seats in this machine; the middle one having a movable leather strap, by way of a *dossier*, which runs between the carriage doors, and lifts away, to permit the egress and ingress of the occupants of the other seats. Into the one facing the horses D—— and I put ourselves; presently, two young ladies occupied the opposite one; a third lady and a gentleman of the same party sat in the middle seat, into which my father's huge bulk was also squeezed; finally, another man belonging to the same party ensconced himself between the two young ladies. Thus the two seats were filled each with three persons, and there should by rights have been a third on ours; for this nefarious black hole on wheels is intended to carry nine. However, we profited little by the space; for, letting alone that there is not really and truly room for more than two human beings of common growth and proportions on each of these seats, the third place was amply filled up with baskets and packages of ours, and huge *un-double-up* coats and cloaks of my father's.

"For the first few minutes I thought I must have fainted from the intolerable sensation of smothering which I experienced. However, the leathers having been removed, and a little more air obtained, I took heart of grace and resigned myself to my fate. Away walloped the four horses, trotting with their front and galloping with their hind legs; and away went we after them, bumping, jumping, thumping, jolting, shaking, tossing, and tumbling, over the wickedest road, I do think, the cruelest, heard-heartedest road that ever wheel rumbled upon. Through bog, and marsh, and ruts, wider and deeper than any Christian ruts I ever saw, with the roots of trees protruding across our path, their boughs every now and then giving us an affectionate scratch through the windows; and, more than once, a half-demolished trunk or stump lying in the middle of the road lifting us up, and letting us down again, with most awful variations of our poor coach-body from its natural position. Bones of me! what a road! Even my father's solid proportions could not keep their level, but were jerked up to the roof and down again every three minutes.

"Our companions seemed nothing dismayed by these wondrous performances of a coach and four, but laughed and talked incessantly, the young ladies at the very top of their voices and with the national nasal twang. The conversation was much of the *genteel* shopkeeper kind, the wit of the ladies and the gallantry savoring strongly of tapes and yard measures, and the shrieks of laughter of the whole set enough to drive one into a frenzy. The ladies were all pretty; two of them particularly so, with delicate, fair complexions, and beautiful gray eyes. How I wish they could have held their tongues for two minutes! We had not long been in the coach before one of them complained of being dreadfully sick. This, in such a place and with seven near neighbors! Fortunately, she was near the window, and, during our whole fourteen miles of purgatory, she alternately leaned from it, overcome with sickness, then reclined languishingly in the arms of her next neighbor, and then starting up with amazing vivacity, joined her voice to the treble duet of her two pretty companions, with a superiority of shrillness that might have been the envy and pride of Billingsgate. 'Twas enough to bother a rookery!

"The country through which we passed was woodland; flat and without variety, save what it derived from the wondrous richness and brilliancy of the autumnal foliage. Here, indeed, decay is beautiful; and nature appears more gorgeously clad in this her fading mantle, than in all the summer's flush of bloom in our less favored climates. I noted several beautiful wild-flowers growing among the underwood, some of which I have seen adorning with great dignity our most cultivated gardens. None of the trees had any size or appearance of age; they are the second growth, which have sprung from the soil once possessed by a mightier race of vegetables. The quantity of mere underwood, and the number of huge black stumps, rising in every direction a foot or two from the soil, bear witness to the existence of fine forest timber. The few cottages and farm-houses which we passed reminded me of similar dwellings in France and Ireland; yet the peasantry here have not the same excuse for disorder and dilapidation as either the Irish or French. The farms had the same desolate, untidy, untended look; the gates broken, the fences carelessly put up or ill-repaired; the farming utensils sluttishly scattered about a littered yard, where the pigs seem to preside by undisputed right; house-windows broken and stuffed with paper or clothes; dishevelled women and barefooted, anomalous-looking human young things. None of the stirring life and activity which such places present in England and Scotland; above all, none of the enchanting mixture of neatness, order, and rustic elegance and comfort, which render so picturesque the surroundings of a farm, and the various belongings of agricultural labor in my own dear country. The fences struck me as peculiar. I never saw any such in England. They are made of rails of wood placed horizontally, and meeting at obtuse angles, so forming a zigzag wall of wood, which runs over the country like the herring-bone seams of a flannel petticoat. At each of the angles, two slanting stakes, considerably higher than the rest of the fence were driven into the ground, crossing each other at the top so as to secure the horizontal rails in their position. There was every now and then a soft, vivid strip of turf along the roadside that made me long for a horse. Indeed, the whole road would have been a delightful ride, and was a most bitter drive.

"At the end of fourteen miles, we turned into a swampy field, the whole fourteen coachfuls of us, and by the help of heaven, bag and baggage were packed into the coaches that stood on the railway ready to receive us. The carriages were not drawn by steam, like those on the Liverpool railway, but by horses, with the mere advantage in speed afforded by the iron ledges, which, to be sure, compared with our previous progress through the ruts, was considerable. Our coachful got into the first carriage of the train, escaping, by way of especial grace, the dust which one's predecessors occasion. This vehicle had but two seats in the usual fashion, each of which held four of us. The whole inside was lined with blazing, scarlet leather, and the windows shaded with stuff curtains of the same refreshing color; which, with full complement of passengers, on a fine, sunny, American summer's day, must make as pretty a little miniature hell as may be, I should think. The baggage-wagon, which went before us a little, obstructed the view. The road was neither pretty nor picturesque, but still fringed on each side with the many-colored woods, whose rich tints made variety even in sameness. This railroad is an infinite blessing; 'tis not yet finished, but shortly will be so, and then the whole of that horrible fourteen miles will be performed in comfort and decency in less than half the time.

"In about an hour and a half, we reached the end of our railroad part of the journey, and found another steamboat waiting for us, when we all embarked on the Delaware. Again, the enormous width of the river, struck me with astonishment and admiration. Such huge bodies of water mark out the country through which they run as the future abode of the most extensive commerce and greatest maritime power in the universe. The banks presented much the same features as those of the Raritan, though they were not quite so flat, and more diversified with scattered dwellings, villages, and towns. We passed Bristol and Burlington, stopping at each of them to take up passengers. I sat working, having finished my book, not a little discomfited by the pertinacious staring of some of my fellow-travellers. One woman in particular, after wandering round me in every direction, at last came and sat down opposite me, and literally gazed me out of countenance.

"One improvement they have adopted on board these boats is, to forbid smoking, except in the forepart of the vessel. I wish they would suggest that if the gentlemen would refrain from spitting about, too, it would be highly agreeable to the female part of the community. The universal practice here of this disgusting trick makes me absolutely sick; every place is made a perfect piggery of, — street, stairs, steamboat, everywhere, — and behind the scenes, and on the stage at rehearsal. I have been shocked and annoyed beyond expression by this horrible custom. To-day, on board the boat, it was a perfect shower of saliva all the time; and I longed to be relieved from my fellowship with these very obnoxious chewers of tobacco. At about four o'clock we reached Philadelphia, having performed the journey between that and New York (a distance of a hundred miles), in less than ten hours, in spite of bogs, ruts, and all other impediments. The manager came to look after us and our goods, and we were presently stowed into a coach which conveyed us to the Mansion House, the best reputed inn in Philadelphia."

Such was travelling in the United States, between our two largest cities, only thirty-five years ago! Such was Miss Kemble in the twenty-second year of her age!

Some of the incidents of her tour in America were very amusing. Being exceedingly fond of riding on horseback, she gave a great impetus to the fashion of ladies' indulging in that pleasure. Particularly at Philadelphia, there was great hunting for good saddle-horses, which, Miss Kemble assures us in her diary, scarcely existed in the country at that time. A particular cap which she wore when riding was imitated and sold as "the Kemble cap." She appears, at that time, to have had a contempt for the beautiful art which she practised, and by which her family had become so distinguished. "How I do loathe the stage!" she exclaims. "These wretched, tawdry, glittering rags flung over the breathing forms of ideal loveliness; these miserable, poor, and pitiful substitutes for the glories with which poetry has invested her magnificent and fair creations. What a mass of wretched, mumming mimicry acting is! Pasteboard and paint, for the thick breathing orange-groves of the south; green silk and oiled parchment, for the solemn splendor of her noon of night; wooden platforms and canvas curtains, for the solid marble balconies and rich dark draperies of Juliet's sleeping chamber, that shrine of love and beauty; rouge, for the startled life-blood in the cheek of that young passionate woman; an actress, a mimicker, a sham creature, *me*, in fact, or any other one, for that loveliest and most wonderful conception, in which all that is true in nature and all that is exquisite in fancy are moulded into a living form! To *act* this! To *act* Romeo and Juliet! Horror! horror! How I do loathe my most impotent and unpoetical craft!"

Ah! how necessary it is to know precisely in what mood, and in what circumstances, a passage was written, before we can tell how far it expresses the author's real and habitual sentiment. The sentences just quoted signify, chiefly, that she had been just playing Juliet to a most awkward and abominable Romeo. In the last scene of the play, she tells us, she was so mad with the mode in which all the other scenes had been performed, that, lying over Romeo's dead body, and fumbling for his dagger, which she could not find, she thus addressed her dead lover: —

"Why, where *the* devil *is* your dagger, Mr. ——."

In truth, she was not a little proud of her honorable and arduous vocation. She was not insensible to the magic of that art which enables an audience to forget that they are looking upon pasteboard and rouge, and to forget, also, that it is not the veritable Juliet who is moving them to rapture and to tears. Some of the best passages in Miss Kemble's diary are subtle disquisitions upon the art of acting.

She had another mishap with her Romeo at Baltimore. The play went off pretty well on this occasion, she says in her humorous way, "except that they broke one man's collar bone, and nearly dislocated a woman's shoulder, by flinging the scenery about." She gives the following absurd account of the conclusion of the play: —

"My bed was not made in time, and when the scene drew, half a dozen carpenters, in patched trowsers and tattered shirt-sleeves, were discovered smoothing down my pillows and adjusting my draperies. The last scene is too good not to be given verbatim: —

"'*Romeo.* Rise, rise, my Juliet,
And from this care of death, this house of horror,
Quick let me snatch thee to thy Romeo's arms.'

"Here he pounced upon me, plucked me up in his arms like an uncomfortable bundle, and staggered down the stage with me.

"Juliet (*aside*). Oh, you've got me up horridly! that'll never do; let me down, pray let me down!

"'*Romeo.* There, breathe a vital spirit on thy lips,
And call thee back, my soul, to life and love!'

"Juliet (*aside*). Pray put me down; you'll certainly throw me down if you don't set me on the ground directly.

"In the midst of 'cruel, cursed fate,' his dagger fell out of his dress; I, embracing him tenderly, crammed it back again, because I knew I should want it at the end.

"*Romeo.* 'Tear not our heart-strings thus!
They crack! they break! Juliet! Juliet! (*dies*).'

"Juliet (*to corpse*). Am I smothering you?

"Corpse (to Juliet). Not at all; could you be so kind, do you think, as to put my wig on for me? it has fallen off.

"Juliet (*to corpse*). I'm afraid I can't, but I'll throw my muslin veil over it. You've broken the phial, haven't you?

"(*Corpse nodded*).

"Juliet (*to corpse*). Where's your dagger?
"Corpse (*to Juliet*). 'Pon my soul, I don't know."

It is curious to notice how prompt this young lady, who sometimes affected such a horror of the stage, was to defend it when attacked by another. She had a long conversation once with Dr. Channing on this subject, who thought that detached scenes and passages well declaimed could serve as a good substitute for the stage. The young actress at once took fire. "My horror," she says, "was so unutterable at this proposition, and my amazement so extreme that he should make it, that I believe my replies were all but incoherent. What! take one of Shakespeare's plays bit by bit, break it piecemeal, in order to make recitals of it! Destroy the marvellous unity of one of his magnificent works to make patches of declamation! . . . I remember hearing my Aunt Siddons read the scenes of the witches in Macbeth, and while doing so was obliged to cover my eyes, that her velvet gown, modern cap, and spectacles might not disturb the wild and sublime images that her magnificent voice and recitation were conjuring up around me."

Miss Kemble's dramatic career in the United States was troubled by only one disagreeable incident, which occurred while she was playing an engagement at Washington. On returning to her hotel, one evening, from her usual ride, she found a man sitting with her father, and her father in a towering passion.

"There, sir," said Mr. Kemble, when she came in, "there is the young lady to speak for herself."

And truly the young lady did so in a highly spirited manner.

"Fanny," continued her father, "something particularly disagreeable has occurred; pray can you call to mind anything you said during the course of your Thursday's ride which was likely to be offensive to Mr. ——, or anything abusive of this country?"

Miss Kemble, who comprehended the situation at a glance, untied her bonnet, and replied, with haughty nonchalance, that she did not recollect a word she had said during her whole ride, and should certainly not give herself any trouble to do so.

"Now, my dear," said her father, his own eyes flashing fire, "don't put yourself into a passion; compose yourself and recollect. Here is a letter I have just received."

He read the letter, which proved to be a ridiculous and dastardly anonymous one, to the effect, that Miss Kemble had said during the ride in question, that she did not choose to ride an American gentleman's horse, and had offered the owner two dollars for the hire of it, and had otherwise spoken most disrespectfully of the American people. The letter proceeded to state that, unless something was done in the way of explanation or apology, she should be hissed off the stage that night the moment she appeared.

The evening came. The pit was littered with handbills from the same malicious and cowardly hand. The only effect was, that every time she appeared during the play the audience received her with a perfect uproar of applause. At the end of the second act, one of the handbills was brought to Mr. Kemble, who immediately went with it before the audience, and denounced it as an infamous falsehood. The play proceeded, and, when Miss Kemble next came upon the scene, the audience rose to their feet, waved their hats, and gave a succession of such thundering cheers, that she burst into tears, and had extreme difficulty in going on with her part. Nor was this all. The public, justly indignant at this contemptible act of inhospitality to eminent artists from a foreign land, crowded the theatre during the rest of their engagement, and gave them two benefits of such an overwhelming character, that a smart Yankee remarked, "He shouldn't wonder if Mr. Kemble had got up the whole thing himself."

This visit to America had more important and lasting consequences than Miss Kemble had anticipated. Among the most ardent of her American admirers was a young gentleman of large fortune and ancient family, residing in a spacious mansion in Philadelphia. Pierce Butler was his name. He was a descendant of the famous Pierce Butler of South Carolina, whose history was so familiar to the public seventy years ago, but has long since been forgotten. Major Pierce Butler came to America before the Revolutionary war with one of the regiments sent over by the tory government to overawe rebellious Boston. He was an Irishman by descent, a scion of the ancient family, the head of which was the Duke of Ormond. Instead of assisting an obstinate and ignorant king to subdue the most loyal of his subjects, he had the good sense to embrace their cause. He resigned his commission, sold his property in Great Britain, and settled in South Carolina, where he purchased a very large estate in lands suited to the culture of rice and cotton. There he lived and flourished, a leading planter and politician, from about the year 1780 until the time of his death in 1822. He was a democrat of the most decided type, a warm adherer of Jefferson, and a main stay of successive democratic administrations.

It was the son of this distinguished man, the heir of his name and his estates, who was captivated by Miss Kemble's talents. His admiration of the actress became, at length, a passion for the woman, and he offered her his hand. According to the usual English view of such matters, it was a brilliant offer; for, in England, no splendor of talent or fame, no worth of character, no extent of learning, *nothing*, is considered to place an individual on a par with one who possesses a large quantity of inherited land. This young man was at the head of society at Philadelphia. His estates in South

Carolina he visited but seldom, and he lived at the Quaker capital the life of elegant and inglorious ease which is so captivating to the imagination of the toiling and anxious multitude. Miss Kemble was so little acquainted with him and his affairs that she did not know the nature of his property. She did not know that he derived his whole income from the unrequited toil of slaves, extorted from them by the lash. She did not know that he owned one slave.

It so happened that she had brought with her from her English home a *particular* abhorrence of slavery, and the feeling was increased in America by what she casually heard of the condition and treatment of the negroes. Several passages in her diary, written before she ever saw the face of this Pierce Butler, prove her utter detestation of slavery. But who can avoid his destiny? In an evil hour, she turned her back upon her noble art, upon the public that admired and honored her, upon her country, too, and gave her hand to this democratic lord of seven hundred slaves. All the world congratulated her. She was thought to have made a most brilliant match,—*she*, the woman of genius and feeling, the heir of an illustrious name, which she had proved herself worthy to bear!

For a time, all went well. Children were born. Women of a certain calibre are not long in discovering the quality of their husbands; and it is highly probable, that Frances Anne Kemble had taken the measure of Pierce Butler before the events occurred which led to their estrangement. In the fourth year of their marriage, in December, 1838, the family, for the first time since the marriage, went together to spend the winter upon the Butler plantations in South Carolina. She recorded her impressions at the time in a diary, according to her custom, which diary has been recently published.

What a contrast between this work, written in 1839, and her other diary written in 1832 and 1833! In the first, there is a good deal of immaturity, a little affectation, perhaps, and, occasionally, a certain lack of the refinement and dignity which belong to the well-bred woman. We see the favorite actress a little spoiled by her sudden and great celebrity, though full of the elements of all that is high and great in the character of woman. In the second diary, we find those elements developed. Disappointment, — the greatest a woman can know, — the discovery that her mate is not her equal, had imparted a premature maturity and an unusual depth of reflection to the matron of twenty-seven. Her record of this winter's residence in South Carolina, among her husband's slaves, is the best contribution ever made by an individual, to our knowledge, of the practical working of the slave system in the United States. One of her friends cautioned her not to go down to her husband's plantation "prejudiced" against what she was to find there.

"Assuredly," she replied, "I *am* going prejudiced against slavery, for I am an Englishwoman, in whom the absence of such a prejudice would be disgraceful. Nevertheless, I go prepared to find many mitigations in the practice to the general injustice and cruelty of the system, — much kindness on the part of the masters, much content on that of the slaves."

She was disappointed. She discovered that slavery was *all* cruelty. The very kindness shown to slaves did but aggravate their sufferings, because that kindness was necessarily fitful and capricious, and was liable at any moment to terminate. With those fresh and honest eyes of hers she looked through all the sophistry of the masters, and saw the system exactly as it was. They told her, for example, that the large families of the slaves were a proof of their good treatment and welfare.

"No such thing," she replied. "If you will reflect for a moment upon the overgrown families of the half-starved Irish peasantry and English manufacturers, you will agree with me that these prolific shoots by no means necessarily spring from a rich or healthy soil. Peace and plenty are certainly causes of human increase, and so is recklessness; and this, I take it, is the impulse in the instance of the English manufacturer, the Irish peasant, and the negro slave. . . None of the cares, — those noble cares, that holy thoughtfulness which lifts the human above the brute parent, — are ever incurred here by either father or mother. The relation indeed resembles, as far as circumstances can possibly make it do so, the short-lived connection between the animal and its young. The father, having neither authority, power, responsibility, nor charge in his children, is, of course, as among brutes, the least attached to his offspring; the mother, by the natural law which renders the infant dependent on her for its first year's nourishment, is more so; but, as neither of them is bound to educate or to support their children, all the unspeakable tenderness and solemnity, all the rational, and all the spiritual grace and glory of the connection is lost, and it becomes mere breeding, bearing, suckling, and there an end. But it is not only the absence of the conditions which God has affixed to the relation which tends to encourage the reckless increase of the race; they enjoy, by means of numerous children, certain positive advantages. In the first place, every woman who is pregnant, as soon as she chooses to make the fact known to the overseer, is relieved of a certain portion of her work in the field, which lightening of labor continues, of course, as long as she is so burdened. On the birth of a child certain additions of clothing and an additional weekly ration are bestowed on the family; and these matters, small as they may seem, act as powerful inducements to creatures who have none of the restraining influences actuating them which belong to the parental relation among all other people, whether civilized or savage. Moreover, they have all of them a most distinct and perfect knowledge of their value to their owners as property; and a woman *thinks*, and not much amiss, that the more frequently she adds to the number of her master's live-stock by bringing new slaves into the world, the more claims she will have upon his consideration and good-will. This was perfectly evident to me from the meritorious air with which the women always made haste to inform me of the number of children they had borne, and the frequent occasions on which the older slaves would direct my attention to their children, exclaiming, 'Look, missis! Little niggers for you and massa; plenty little niggers for you and little missis!' A very agreeable apostrophe to me, indeed, as you will believe."

Of the cruelty committed upon this estate she gives ample details, which need not be repeated here. Her husband's negroes were considered fortunate by those upon surrounding plantations, and yet almost everything that she saw and heard during her residence among them filled her with grief and horror. What surprised her very much was, the low *physical* condition of the colored people, and the great mortality among the children. This was partly owing to insufficient and innutritious food, but chiefly to the incessant child-bearing of the women. She found mothers who were fifteen years of age, and grandmothers who were thirty. She found women in middle life who had borne from twelve to sixteen children. One cause of intense misery was compelling the women to return to their labor in the field three weeks after confinement. In short, the whole system, and all its details and circumstances, excited in her nothing but the most profound and passionate repugnance.

Out of the abundance of the heart the mouth will speak, and, especially, a woman's mouth! She remonstrated with her husband upon the cruelties practised almost in his very presence. She might as well have addressed her remonstrances to one of his own palmetto-trees. Once, when she had related to him a peculiarly aggravated atrocity committed upon the mother of a family, he replied, that, no doubt, the punishment inflicted upon the woman was "*disagreeable.*" At other times, he would say, "Why do you listen to such stuff? Why do you believe such trash? Don't you know the niggers are all d——d liars?" At length, he commanded her never to speak to him upon the subject again, never to try to stand between a defenceless female slave and the overseer's withering lash.

This was almost beyond bearing. Read one passage from her diary: —

"I have had an uninterrupted stream of women and children flowing in the whole morning to say, 'Ha, de missis.' Among others, a poor woman called Mile, who could hardly stand for pain and swelling in her limbs; she had had fifteen children; nine of her children had died; for the last three years she had become almost a cripple with chronic rheumatism, yet she is driven every day to work in the field. She held my hands, and stroked them in the most appealing way, while she exclaimed, 'O my missis! my missis! me neber sleep till day for de pain,' and with the day her labor must again be resumed. I gave her flannel and sal-volatile to rub her poor swelled limbs with; rest I could not give her, — rest from her labor and her pain, — this mother of fifteen children.

"I went out to try and walk off some of the weight of horror and depression which I am beginning to feel daily more and more, surrounded by all this misery and degradation that I can neither help nor hinder."

In addition to all this, she could not be ignorant that her young husband degraded himself and dishonored her, as the young planters of the South were accustomed to degrade themselves, and dishonor their wives.

I shall not dwell here upon what followed. The difference of opinion, or rather of feeling, upon this subject of slavery — so vital to them as slave-owners — ended at last in complete and bitter estrangement. A separation followed. Mrs. Kemble retired to the beautiful village of Lennox in Massachusetts, where she occasionally had the pleasure of associating with her children, and where she was the delight and ornament of a large circle. Nor was the public entirely deprived of the benefit of her talents. Inheriting from her father an amplitude of person which time did not diminish, she was no longer fitted to resume her place upon the stage. She has given, however, as every one knows, series of readings from Shakespeare and other authors, in the principal cities of the United States and Great Britain. One happy year she spent in Italy, and, according to her habit, made her residence there the subject of a volume of poetry and prose, which she entitled "A year of Consolation." During our late civil war she resided in England. She was true to the country of her adoption, and rendered to it the most timely and valuable services. In the midst of the hostility against the North which prevailed among the educated classes in England, she wrote a most eloquent and powerful vindication of the United States for the "London Times;" and, about the period when the question of Emancipation was agitating all minds, she gave to the public her Southern diary, which had been in manuscript more than twenty years. The last two sentences of this work will serve to show that at the darkest period of the war, when all but the stoutest hearts felt some misgivings as to the final result, this brave and high-minded woman had undiminished faith in the final triumph of the right. They are these: —

"Admonished by its terrible experience, I believe the nation will reunite itself under one government, remodel the

Constitution, and again address itself to fulfil its glorious destiny. I believe that the country sprung from ours — of all our just subjects of national pride the greatest — will resume its career of prosperity and power, and become the noblest as well as the mightiest that has existed among the nations of the earth."

Mrs. Kemble is now fifty-seven years of age, but neither the vigor of her body nor the brilliancy of her talents has undergone any perceptible diminution. Her readings have been, for nearly twenty years, among the most refined and instructive pleasures accessible to the public, and they still attract audiences of the highest character. I had the pleasure of hearing her read in the city of New York, in March, 1868. It was the coldest night of the year; the streets were heaped high with snow, and a cutting north-west wind was blowing. Notwithstanding these adverse circumstances, which thinned every place of amusement in the city, more than a thousand people assembled in Steinway Hall to listen once more to this last and best of the Kembles. The play was Coriolanus, one of the most effective for her purpose, in the whole range of the drama. When she presented herself upon the platform and took her usual seat behind a small low table, she looked the very picture of one of the noble Roman matrons whose grand and passionate words she was about to utter. As she sat, she appeared to be above the usual stature of women, although in fact she is not. Her person, although finely developed, has in no degree the appearance of corpulence. Her hair, naturally dark, has been so delicately touched by time, that the frost of years looks like a sprinkling of the powder which has lately been in fashion again. Her face is full and ruddy, indicating high health, and her features are upon that large and grand scale for which her family have been always remarkable, and which call to mind the fact that the Romans once ruled in England. Her voice is exceedingly fine, being ample in quantity as well as harmonious and flexible. On this occasion, she was attired in a dress of plain black silk, relieved only by a narrow lace collar around the neck, which was fastened by a small plain gold pin. Nothing can exceed the force, beauty, and variety of her reading; she is perhaps the only person, who has yet practised this art, that can hold a large audience attentive and satisfied during the reading of a play.

Like all genuine artists, Mrs. Kemble marks an habitual respect for the public whom she serves. Her low courtesy to the audience, and her pleasant, respectful way of addressing them when she has occasion to do so, are in striking contrast with the ridiculous and insolent airs which some of the spoiled children of the opera sometimes give themselves. Her dress varies with the play she is to read. When the Midsummer Night's Dream is the play, she wears a bridal dress of white silk adorned with lace. Her self-possession in the presence of an audience is complete, and although she exerts herself to please them with far more than the energy of a novice, no one is aware of the fact, and she seems to enchant us without an effort.

EUGENIE, EMPRESS OF THE FRENCH.

BY JOHN S. C. ABBOTT.

The city of Malaga, in Spain, was the birthplace of Eugénie, the Empress of the French. This quaint old Moorish town, containing about sixty thousand inhabitants, is situated on the shores of the Mediterranean, at the head of a bay which constitutes so fine a harbor that the city has been, for centuries, one of the most important seaports of the Spanish peninsula. Bleak, barren, rugged mountains encircle the city, approaching so near to the sea that there is scarcely room for the streets of massive, lofty stone houses, which are spread along the shore. These streets, as in all the old Moorish towns, are very narrow, many of them being not more than six or eight feet wide. The houses are large and high, and are built around a court-yard. The ruins of ancient fortifications and the battlements of a fine old Moorish castle add to the picturesque beauties of the crags, which rise sublimely in the rear of the town.

The climate is almost tropical, and the market abounds with all the fruits and vegetables which ripen beneath an equatorial sun. Though most of the city presents but a labyrinth of intricate and narrow streets, there is one square around which the buildings are truly magnificent. This square, or public walk, called the Alameda, is the favorite resort of all the fashion and gayety and pleasure-seeking of the city.

Engd. by G.E. Perine & Co. N.Y.

EUGENIE.

In the street of St. Juan de Dios, of Malaga, there was, in the early part of the present century, a wealthy, intelligent, and very attractive family residing in one of the most stately mansions. The master of the house was an opulent merchant from England, William Kirkpatrick, a Scotchman by birth. He had been the English consul at Malaga, and had married a young lady of Malaga, of remarkable beauty both of form and feature, Francisca Gravisne, the daughter of one of the ancient Spanish families.

They had three daughters, all of whom inherited the beauty, grace, and vivacity of their mother, blended with the strong sense and solid virtues of the father. The eldest of these daughters, Maria, was a young lady of extraordinary beauty. She was tall, with features as if chiselled by a Grecian sculptor, beaming with animation, with brilliant eyes, ready wit, and possessing perfect command of all the graces of language and the attractions of manner. Blended Saxon and Spanish blood circled in her veins and glowed in her cheeks. Her exquisitely moulded form is represented to have been perfect.

Her two younger sisters, Carlotta and Henriquetta, were also far-famed for beauty, grace, intelligence, and all those virtues which give attractions to the social circle. Mr. Kirkpatrick was engaged in extensive commerce with England and America. His circle of acquaintance was consequently very extensive. All foreigners of distinction were welcomed to his hospitable board; and it was also the resort of the most refined and aristocratic native society of Malaga.

Among the guests who visited in this attractive family there was a Spanish noble, alike illustrious for his exalted birth, his large fortune, and his military prowess. A scar upon his face and a crippled limb were honorable wounds, which gave him additional claims to pre-eminence. He had joined the army of Napoleon, in the endeavor to liberate Spain from the despotism of the Bourbons. He was then known by the name of Cipriano Palafox, Count of Theba. A strong attachment sprang up between this member of one of the old Spanish families and Senorita Maria Kirkpatrick, the daughter of the wealthy English merchant. They were married in 1819.

This marriage secured for the beautiful and highly accomplished Maria all the advantages which wealth and rank could confer. The count took his young and lovely bride, who was some years younger than himself, to Madrid, and presented her at court. She had enjoyed the advantages of both a Spanish and an English education. Her beauty, intelligence, and varied accomplishments rendered her a great favorite with the queen, Maria Christina, and she was elevated to the most influential post among the feminine offices,—that of first lady of honor.

Her husband, Count Theba, soon received additional wealth and honor, inheriting from a deceased brother the title and estates of the Count of Montijo. Maria's sister, Carlotta, soon after married an English gentleman, her cousin Thomas, the son of her father's brother, John Kirkpatrick. This gentleman had accompanied Wellington to Spain, and had served as paymaster to the English army until 1814. As Maria's husband had espoused the cause of Napoleon, and had shed his blood in fighting against Wellington, the two extremes of political antagonism were represented in the family; and yet, so far as we can learn, harmoniously represented, for the passions which had inflamed that deadly conflict yielded to the ties of family affection. Both Thomas and his wife are now dead.

The third daughter, Henriquetta, married Count Cabarras, a very wealthy Spanish sugar-planter, residing near Velez Malaga. Her lot has been peculiarly tranquil and happy. She is probably, at the time of this writing, residing in pleasant retirement, with her husband, on their beautiful estate in the south of sunny Spain, in the enjoyment of opulence and high position.

The Empress Eugénie is the daughter of the elder sister, Maria Kirkpatrick, and of Cipriano Palafox, double Count of Theba and of Montijo. She was born the 5th of May, 1826. English and Spanish blood are mingled in her veins. She has enjoyed all the advantages of an English, a French, and a Spanish education. She is familiar with the literature and the best society of the three realms, and in her person and features there are blended, in a remarkable degree, the grace and beauty of the highest specimens of the Spanish and Saxon races.

The death of her father, a few weeks before her birth, left Eugénie an orphan in her earliest infancy. But she was blest with the training of a very excellent and highly educated mother. It is said that a part of her education was acquired in England, and that she has enjoyed the advantages of the best schools in France. Thus she speaks English, Spanish, and French with equal fluency. There is no court in Europe where the claims of etiquette are more rigidly observed than in the royal palaces of Madrid. Eugénie, from childhood, has been so accustomed to all these forms, that she moves through the splendors of the Tuileries with ease and grace which charm every beholder.

John Kirkpatrick, who had married Eugénie's aunt, Carlotta, became subsequently a banker in Paris. In the year 1851, Maria the Countess of Montijo, with her daughter Eugénie, the Countess of Theba, visited Paris. The marvellous loveliness of Eugénie, the ease, grace, and perfect polish of her address, and her vivacity and wide intelligence, surrounded her with admirers. The classical regularity of her features, her exquisitely moulded form, her rich, soft auburn hair, and her large, expressive black eyes, arrested the attention of every observer. Equally at home in several languages, and endowed with great powers of conversation and of fascination, the most distinguished, of all lands, gathered around her, rendering her that homage which genius everywhere yields to the perfection of feminine charms. One familiar with her has said: —

"Her beauty was delicate and fair, from her English ancestry; while her grace was all Spanish, and her wit all French. These made her one of the most remarkable women in the French capital, though her independence of character and her English habits imparted to her more liberty of action than the restraints imposed on French *demoiselles* allow, and therefore exposed her to remark. There is not one well authenticated adventure which can be told to her disadvantage. The empress, besides her brilliant qualities, which make her the most lovely sovereign in Europe, is kind and generous; and in the few opportunities to test her higher qualities has displayed great courage and sense."

The emperor did not escape the fascination which all alike felt. The countess became the most brilliant ornament of the gay assemblies of the Tuileries; and when she rode along the Boulevards or the Champs Elysée, all eyes were riveted upon her. It is to the present day alike the testimony of all, who are favored with her acquaintance, that she is as amiable and as lovely in character as she is beautiful in person. No one can behold her countenance, beaming with intelligence, and witness her sweet smile, without the assurance that Eugénie is richly endowed with the most attractive graces which can adorn humanity.

The Countess of Theba, Eugénie, had been educated a Catholic, and was reputed an earnest Christian of the Fenelon type. God only can judge the heart; but externally she manifested the utmost devotion to the claims of religion, and was scrupulous in the observance of the rites of the church. The cavillers said, "she is a very rigid Catholic." The devout said, "she is a very earnest Christian." All alike acknowledged that she was the foe of irreligion in every form, and that the prosperity of the Church, in that great branch of Christianity to which she belonged, was dear to her heart.

It is reported that the Emperor of the French had previously met Eugénie, and admired her in the court circles of London, when he was an exile from his native land. He gave her a cordial welcome at the palace of the Tuileries, and friendship soon ripened into love. The marked religious character of Eugénie awakened sympathy in the bosom of the emperor. He had often taken occasion to say, in his public addresses, that while others had sustained Christianity as a "measure of state," as a "political necessity," he supported Christianity from a full conviction of its *divine origin*, and as thus indispensable to the welfare of nations and of men.

It is probable that the emperor, more familiar with the world, and having studied the workings of Protestant forms of Christianity in England and America, is more liberal in his denominational views. Still he regards Catholicism as the religion of France, and, while advocating the most perfect freedom of conscience, recognizes the papal church as the denomination to which he belongs, and to which he should give his fostering care. Thus the emperor and Eugénie found a bond of union in their religious convictions.

On the 22d of January, 1853, the emperor, in the following communication to the Senate, announced that Eugénie, the Countess of Theba, had consented to share with him the throne, in becoming his partner for life: —

"GENTLEMEN: — I yield myself to the wish so often manifested by the country in announcing to you my marriage. The union I contract is not in accord with the traditions of the ancient policy. In that is its advantage. France, by her successive revolutions, is always rudely separated from the rest of Europe. Every sensible government should seek to introduce her to the bosom of the old monarchies. But this result will be much more surely attained by a policy just and frank, and by loyalty of transactions, than by royal alliances which create false security and often substitute the interest of families for the national interest. Moreover the examples of the past have left upon the minds of the people superstitious impressions. They have not forgotten that, for seventy years, foreign princes have ascended the steps of the throne, only to see their race dispersed or proscribed by war or by revolution. One woman only has seemed to bring happiness to France, and to live, more than others, in the memory of the people; and that woman, Josephine, the modest and excellent wife of General Bonaparte, was not of royal blood.

"We must, however, admit that the marriage, in 1810, of Napoleon Bonaparte with Maria Louisa was a great event. It was a pledge for the future, a true satisfaction to the national pride, since the ancient and illustrious house of Austria, with which we had so long waged war, was seen to solicit an alliance with the elected chief of a new empire. Under the last reign, on the contrary, did not the self-love of the country suffer when the heir of the crown solicited, in vain, during many years, the alliance of a royal house, and obtained, at last, a princess, accomplished, undoubtedly, but only in the secondary ranks, and of another religion?

"When, in the face of ancient Europe, one is borne, by the force of a new principle, to the height of the ancient dynasties, it is not in endeavoring to give antiquity to his heraldry, and in seeking to introduce himself, at whatever cost, into the family of kings, that one can make himself accepted. It is much more, in ever remembering his origin, in maintaining his appropriate character, and in taking, frankly, in the face of Europe, the position of a *parvenu*, — a glorious title when one attains it by the free suffrage of a great people.

"Thus obliged to turn aside from the precedents, followed until this day, my marriage becomes but a private affair. There remains only the choice of the person. The one who has become the object of my preference is of elevated birth. French in heart, and by the recollection of the blood shed by her father in the cause of the empire, she has, as a Spaniard, the advantage of not having, in France, a family to whom it might be necessary to give honors and dignities. Endowed with all the qualities of the mind, she will be the ornament of the throne, as, in the day of danger, she will become one of its most courageous supports. Catholic and pious, she will address the same prayers to Heaven with me for the happiness of France. By her grace and her goodness she will, I firmly hope, endeavor to revive, in the same position, the virtues of the Empress Josephine.

"I come then, gentlemen, to say to France, that I have preferred the woman whom I love, and whom I respect, to one who is unknown, whose alliance would have advantages mingled with sacrifices. Without testifying disdain for any one, I yield to my inclinations, after having consulted my reason and my convictions. In fine, by placing independence, the qualities of the heart, domestic happiness, above dynastic prejudices and the calculations of ambition, I shall not be less strong because I shall be more free.

"Soon, in repairing to Notre Dame, I shall present the empress to the people and to the army. The confidence they have in me assures me of their sympathy. And you, gentlemen, on knowing her whom I have chosen, will agree that, on this occasion again, I have been guided by Providence."

In France, marriage is regarded both as a civil and a religious rite, and both ceremonies are often accompanied with great solemnity and pomp. The marriage of the Emperor and Eugénie, the Countess of Theba, was celebrated at the Tuileries, on the 27th of January, 1853. The next day, which was Sunday, the religious ceremonies took place, with great splendor, at the Cathedral of Notre Dame. The Archbishop of Paris officiated. Probably a more brilliant assembly was never convened in France, or in the world, than the throng which then filled, to its utmost capacity, that venerable and capacious edifice. All the courts of Europe were represented, and nothing was wanting which wealth and rank and power and taste could give to contribute to the attractions of the spectacle.

"All the pomp of the Catholic service, all the opulence of the capital, all the beauty and brilliance of the court, all the grim majesty of the military, whatever was illustrious in science and art, every resource of celebrity, fascination, and lavish luxury were exhausted on the incidents and displays of this felicitous day. The imperial couple sat on two thrones erected in front of the high altar. Sublime and heavenly melody resounded beneath the lofty arches of the ancient pile. A numerous and gorgeous array of priests assisted. The great representatives of the army, of the senate, of the municipal authorities, of the diplomatic corps, delegations from the great cities of France, and the most brilliant and beautiful female leaders of fashion in the capital, — all were there. The agitation of the young empress, the focus of so many inquisitive eyes, during the ceremony, was extreme. It was necessary for the emperor to soothe and allay her emotions. All passed off happily and favorably; and everybody, except the fierce and implacable leaders of the dark and desperate factions, rejoiced at the consummation of the imperial nuptials."

These were nuptials inspired on both sides by affection and

esteem, and they have been followed, apparently, with far more happiness than has usually been found in a palace.

The union of the emperor and Eugénie was a union of hearts. The emperor signalized his marriage by granting amnesty to nearly five thousand persons who were in banishment for political offences. The empress has proved herself all that France could desire in one occupying her exalted position. The nation is proud of the grace, beauty, and accomplishments which have now for fifteen years rendered Eugénie not only the brightest ornament of the Tuileries, but the most conspicuous queen of Europe. A sincere Christian, devotedly attached to the recognized Christian faith of France, — the faith in which she was born and educated, — she secures the homage of all the millions who bow before the supremacy of the Catholic religion; and her influence, in the court, has ever been ennobling and purifying.

In more than one scene of danger Eugénie has proved herself the possessor of that heroism which sheds such an additional lustre upon one destined to the highest walks of earthly life. As a wife, as a mother, and as an empress, history must award to Eugénie a very high position of merit. The city of Paris voted the empress, upon the occasion of her marriage, a large sum — we think about six hundred thousand dollars — for the purchase of diamonds. It was a matter even of national pride that the Empress of France, the bride of the *people's* emperor, should be splendidly arrayed. But there was no one who could more easily forego these adornings than Eugénie. The glitter of gems could add but little to that loveliness which captivated all beholders. Eugénie had ample wealth of her own. The emperor had a well-filled purse. There was no danger that her jewel caskets would be empty.

Gratefully Eugénie accepted the munificent gift, having first obtained the consent of the donors that she should devote it to founding a charitable institution for the education of young girls belonging to the working classes. Here she watches over her sisters of humbler birth, with heartfelt sympathy, alike interested in their physical, mental, and religious culture.

In the year 1855 the emperor and Eugénie visited the court of Queen Victoria. They were received with every possible demonstration of enthusiasm. England seemed to wish to blot out the memory of Waterloo, and to atone for the wrongs she had inflicted upon the first Napoleon, by the cordiality with which she greeted and the hospitality with which she entertained his successor and heir. There was English blood in the veins of Eugénie, and English traits adorned her character. It is not too much to say that she was universally admired in the court of St. James. The London journals of that day were full of expressions of admiration. It was said that Buckingham Palace and Windsor Castle were never honored with the presence of a guest more truly queenly. In purity of character, in sincerity of Christian faith, Eugénie and Victoria must have found mutual sympathy, though one was a communicant of the Church of England, and the other of the Church of Rome.

Eugénie loved England. Her grandfather was an Englishman. Many of her dearest relatives were English; much of her education was English. The emperor, a man of warm affections, could not forget the hospitable welcome he had received in London, when an exile, banished by Bourbon law from his own country, simply because his name was Napoleon Bonaparte. The emperor has also ever been ready to render the tribute of his admiration to the institutions of England.

Thus both Louis Napoleon and Eugénie could be happy as the guests of Queen Victoria. There was moral sublimity in the event itself. It constituted a new era in the history of the rival nations. The Emperor of France and the Queen of England met in the palaces of the British kings, and France left a kiss upon the cheek of England. The kiss was given and received in perfect sincerity. On both sides it expressed the hope that war should be no more,—that henceforth France and England should live in peace, in co-operation, in friendship.

This visit of the emperor and empress to the court of England's queen is said to have been the first instance in the world in which a reigning French monarch set foot upon the soil of his hereditary foes. Not long after this Queen Victoria and Prince Albert returned the compliment, and England's queen became the guest of Eugénie at the Tuileries, St. Cloud, and Fontainebleau. Victoria was received by the Parisian population, in the Champs Elysée and along the Boulevards, with the same enthusiasm, with the same tumultuous and joyful acclaim with which Eugénie had been received in the streets of London. There is no city in the world so well adapted to festal occasions as Paris. All the resources of that brilliant capital were called into requisition to invest the scene with splendor. The pageant summoned multitudes to Paris from all the courts of Europe.

On the 16th of March, 1856, the Empress Eugénie gave birth to her first and only child. The young prince received the baptismal name of Napoleon Eugéne Louis Jean Joseph. His birth caused great joy throughout France, as it would leave the line of succession undisputed. This gave increasing assurance that France, upon the decease of the emperor, would be saved from insurrection and the conflict of parties. From all parts of France congratulations were addressed to the emperor. In the emperor's reply to the Senate he said:—

"The Senate has shared my joy on learning that Heaven has given me a son; and you have hailed, as a propitious event, the birth of a *child of France*. It is intentionally that

I use that expression. It is because, gentlemen, when an heir is born, who is destined to perpetuate a national system, that child is not only the scion of a family, but he is, also, in truth, the son of the whole country, and that name indicates his duties. If this were true under the ancient monarchy, which represented more exclusively the privileged classes, how much more is it so now, when the sovereign is the elect of the nation, the first citizen of the country, and the representative of the interests of all. I thank you for the prayers you have offered for the child of France and for the empress."

To the congratulations of the Legislative Corps the emperor responded: —

"I have been much affected by the manifestation of your feelings at the birth of the son whom Providence has so kindly granted me. You have hailed in him the hope, so eagerly entertained, of the perpetuity of a system which is regarded as the surest guaranty of the general interests of the country. But the unanimous acclamations which surround his cradle do not prevent me from reflecting on the destiny of those who have been in the same place, and under similar circumstances. If I hope that his lot may be more happy, it is, in the first place, because, confiding in Providence, I cannot doubt its protection, when, seeing it raise up, by a concurrence of extraordinary circumstance, all that which Providence was pleased to cast down forty years ago; as if it had wished to strengthen, by martyrdom and by suffering, a new dynasty springing from the ranks of the people.

"This child, consecrated in its cradle by the peace now at hand, and by the benedictions of the Holy Father, brought by telegraph an hour after his birth; in fine, by the acclamations of the French people, whom the emperor *loved so well*, — this child I hope will prove worthy of the destinies which await him."

No man can be in power without having bitter enemies. There have been a few attempts at the assassination of Louis Napoleon. The most desperate was that of Orsini, an Italian refugee. This wretch and his two confederates, with their murderous hand-grenades, hesitated not to strike down in bloody death scores of gentlemen and ladies crowding the avenues to the opera, if they could thus reach the single victim at whom they aimed. On the evening of the 14th of January, 1858, as the emperor and empress were approaching the Grand Opera in their carriage, accompanied by many of the dignitaries of the court, and followed and preceded by a crowd of carriages, just as they drew near the opera house, where the throng was greatest and the speed of the horses was checked into a slow walk, these assassins threw beneath the imperial carriage several bombs, or hand-grenades of terrific power. These balls, each about the size of an ostrich's egg, were ingeniously constructed so as to burst by the concussion of their fall.

The explosion was dreadful in power and deadly in its effects. The street was immediately strown for quite a distance with the dead and the mutilated bodies of men and horses. The imperial carriage was tossed and rocked as if upon the billows of a stormy sea. The glasses were shivered and the wood-work splintered; and yet, as by a miracle, both the emperor and empress escaped without any serious injury. The Empress Eugénie manifested, in the midst of this tumult, a spirit of calmness and heroism worthy of her exalted position. Shrieks and groans resounded all around her. She knew not but that the emperor was mortally wounded. But without any outcry, without any fainting, she seemed to forget herself entirely, in anxiety for her spouse. When some persons attempted to break open the door of the shattered vehicle, Eugénie, supposing them to be the assassins, with their poniards in their hands, thew herself before the emperor, that with her own body she might protect him from the dagger-thrusts.

Before this attempt at assassination Eugénie was greatly beloved by all France. But the heroism which she manifested on this occasion added to that love emotions of profound homage and admiration. Even the imperial throne was strengthened by the conviction that the empress was equal to any emergency; and that, should disaster darken upon the empire, as in the past, Eugénie, unlike Maria Louisa, the "daughter of the Cæsars," would develop the imperial nature with which God had endowed her, and would be equal to her responsibilities, however weighty they might be.

On the 3d of May, 1859, the emperor announced to the French people that he was about to leave France, to take command of the army of Italy. In the announcement he said: —

"The object of this war is to restore Italy to herself, and not to cause her to change masters. We shall then have, upon our frontiers, a friendly people who will also owe to us their independence."

On the 10th of May the emperor, after having appointed the Empress Eugénie regent during his absence, and having solemnly confided her and also their son to the valor of the army, the patriotism of the national guard, and to the love and devotion of the entire nation, was prepared to leave the Tuileries for his Italian campaign.

It was five o'clock in the afternoon of a beautiful May day. The carriage of the emperor, an open barouche, stood before the grand entrance of the palace. A brilliant retinue of carriages, filled with the military household of the emperor, was also in line in the court-yard. A mounted squadron of the guards, glittering with burnished helmets and coats of mail, was gathered there, in military array, to escort the cortége through the Rue Rivoli, the Place de la Bastile, and the Rue de Lyon to the railway station for Marseilles. An immense crowd of the populace was gathered in the court-yard to witness the departure of the emperor.

A few minutes after five o'clock several officers of the emperor's household descended the stairs, followed immediately by the emperor, with the empress leaning upon his arm. They were followed by several ladies and gentlemen of the court. As soon as the emperor and empress appeared the air was rent with shouts of "Vive l'Empereur," which burst from the lips of the crowd. The emperor uncovered his head and waved his hat in response to this cordial greeting. Then, bidding them adieu, and shaking hands with several of the ladies, he handed the empress into the carriage and took a seat by her side. The imperial cortége then left the court-yard, passing out through the triumphal arch. The emperor was in a simple travelling dress, and wore a cap which permitted every expression of his countenance to be distinctly seen. He was apparently calm, and a smile was upon his lips as he met the ever-increasing enthusiasm of the crowd. But the eyes of Eugénie were red and swollen, and she could not conceal the tears which rolled down her cheeks. With one hand she lovingly clasped the hand of the emperor, while with the other she frequently wiped away the tears which *would* gush from her eyes.

The guards followed the carriage, but did not surround it. The crowd was so great that the horses could only advance on the slow walk. Consequently the people came up to the very steps of the carriage and many addressed words to the emperor, of sympathy and affection. It was a very touching scene. The crowd was immense. The windows of all the houses, the balconies, the roofs even, along the whole line of the route were filled with spectators. The streets were hung with flags and decorated with garlands of flowers; while on all sides shouts ascended of "Vive l'Empereur!" "Victoire!" "Dieu vous garde!"

At the Place de la Bastile the populace, in their enthusiasm, began to take the horses from the carriage that they might triumphantly draw the emperor themselves. For a moment the emperor was quite overcome with emotion in view of these proofs of confidence and love. Standing up in the carriage, he addressed the multitude, saying, "My friends, do not delay me; time is precious." Instantly they desisted, with renewed shouts of "Vive l'Empereur!" The crowd now gathered so closely around the carriage that the emperor reached out both hands and cordially grasped all the hands which were extended towards him. The affecting and the ludicrous were singularly blended in the remarks which were addressed to the emperor and the empress. One said, "Sire, you have victory in your eyes." Another said, "If you want more soldiers, don't forget us." A woman, noticing the tears streaming down the cheeks of the empress, exclaimed, soothingly, "Don't cry, don't cry; he will soon come back again." A sturdy man endeavored to add to the words of solace as he leaned his head into the carriage, saying tenderly to the empress, "Don't cry; we will take care of you and the boy."

At the station of the Lyons railroad many of the cabinet ministers and a large number of distinguished members of the court, gentlemen and ladies, were present. Prince Napoleon, son of Jerome, was there with his young bride, Princess Clotilde, daughter of Victor Emanuel. The Princess Matilda, Prince and Princess Murat were also there.

"It was a touching scene," writes Julie de Marguerittes; "the waiting-room crowded with mothers, wives, sisters, and friends, — tears and sobs making their way spite of imperial example, spite of court etiquette. At length the moment of departure arrived. The emperor again embraced the empress and entered the car amidst the deafening shouts of enthusiasm. All was ready. The chief director went up to the imperial car and asked if he might give the signal to depart. The emperor answered in the affirmative. And so amidst the shouts of the multitude, which echoed far along the road, the car bearing the fortunes of France, left the capital."

The empress returned to the palace, where she reigned as Regent of France until the return of the emperor. The following was the form of the Imperial announcement of the regency: —

"Napoleon, by the grace of God and the national will, Emperor of the French,

"To all present and to come, greeting.

"Wishing to give to our well-beloved wife, the empress, marks of the great confidence we repose in her, and, seeing that we intend to take the head of the army of Italy, we have resolved to confer, as we do confer, by these presents, on our well-beloved wife, the empress, the title of Regent, that she may exercise its functions during our absence, in conformity with our instructions and orders, such as we shall have made known in the general order of the service that we shall have established, which will be copied into the book of state.

"We desire that the empress shall preside, in our name, over the Privy Council and the Council of Ministers," etc.

All the decrees and state papers were presented to Eugénie, who appended to them her signature in these terms: —

"For the emperor, and in virtue of the power by him conferred. "EUGENIE."

The emperor entered Genoa on the 12th. No language can do justice to the enthusiasm with which he was received. On the day of his arrival at Genoa, the wife of the Sardinian minister, at Paris, presented Eugénie with a magnificent bouquet, which had arrived, in perfect preservation, from the ladies in Genoa. It came from the most distinguished ladies of the city. In the accompanying address they said: —

"The ladies of Genoa entreat your Majesty, who so nobly partakes in the magnanimous feelings of the emperor, to accept these flowers, which they would have strowed on your path had you accompanied your august husband on the entrance into Genoa. May these flowers be the symbols of the immortal wreaths of victory which history will twine round the brow of Napoleon III., and will bequeath to his son as the most precious ornaments of the imperial diadem."

Our brief sketch of the empress must here terminate. We would gladly speak of her devotion to institutions of learning and benevolence; of her visits to the hospitals where the sick languish, and to the asylums where the deaf gaze lovingly upon her smiles, and where the blind listen almost entranced to the melody of her loving voice. France has had two empresses who will ever be gratefully remembered by the nation, Josephine and Eugénie. Neither of them were of royal blood, but both of them were endowed, richly endowed, with that nobility which comes from God alone. Both were crowned by mortal hands on earth; we cannot doubt that one has already received, and that the other will yet receive, that diadem of immortality which God places upon the victor's brow.

GRACE GREENWOOD—MRS. LIPPINCOTT.

BY JOSEPH B. LYMAN.

About thirty years ago, when Andrew Jackson and Martin Van Buren lived in the White House; when questions of a national bank and a protective tariff interested without arousing the popular mind; when the great and glorious valley of the Mississippi still gave homes to the red man and haunts to wild beasts; when Bryant was fresh from those native hills, broad, round, and green, where he dreamed the Thanatopsis; when visions of Absalom and Jephthah's daughter were floating fresh and sacred before the eyes of Willis, —a traveller through Pompey, one of the youthful towns of western New York, might have turned in his saddle to take a second look at the lithe figure and the glowing face of a village romp. Could such tourist have known that, in the bright-eyed school-girl with rustic dress and touseled hair, he saw one of the rising lights of the coming age; a letter-writer who should charm a million readers by the piquant dash and spicy flavor of her style; a delightful magazinist; a poetess, the melody and ring of whose stanzas should remind us of the most famous lyres of the world; a woman who, standing calm, graceful, and self-poised before great audiences, and thrilling them by noble aud earnest words spoken in the deep gloom of national disaster, should call up rich memories of the Roman matron in her noblest form, or of the brightest figures that move on the storied page of France,—

could he have foreseen all *that* as in the future of this village beauty, the traveller would have done more than turn for a second look. He would have halted, and talked with the young Corinne; he would have lingered to hear her speak of wild flowers, and birds' nests, of rills and rocks and cascades; he might have gone with her to her father's door, and caught a glimpse of silvered hair and a noble forehead, and he would have observed upon that face lineaments that have for two hundred years been found in all the high places of American thought and character. For the father of this little Sara was Dr. Thaddeus Clarke, a grandson of President Edwards. Fortunate it is, and a blessing to the race, when a man so rarely and royally gifted as was this great theologian, with everything that makes a human character noble, is so wisely mated that he can transmit to the coming age, not only the most valuable thinking of his time, but a family of children, blessed with sound constitutions, developed by harmonious fireside influences, and endowed with vigorous understandings. In doing *that*, Jonathan Edwards did more to stir thought than when he wrote the history of the Great Awakening; he did more to establish the grooves of religious and moral thinking, and to fix the model of fine character, than he could ever accomplish by his Treatise on the Will. In mature life, the great-grand-daughter has shown many of the traits of the Edwards family. She has rejected the iron-hooped Calvinism of her ancestor, but she is indebted to him for an unflagging and ever-fresh interest in nature; for ceaseless mental fecundity, that finds no bottom to its cruse of oil, and for a toughness of intellectual fibre that fits her for a life of perpetual mental activity.

There was not a gayer or more active girl in Onondaga County than Sara Clarke. The bright Alfarata was not fonder of wild roving. No young gipsy ever took more naturally to the fields. She loved the forests, the open pastures, the strawberry-lots, and the spicy knolls, where the scarlet leaves of the wintergreen nestle under the dainty sprigs of ground pine and the breezy hill-sides, where the purple fingers and painted lips attest the joy of huckleberrying. She says of herself that she was a mighty hunter of wild fruits. At this early age, she developed a taste which, at a later age, gave her name a piquant flavor of romance; the taste for horseback riding, and the ability to manage with fearless grace the most spirited steeds. Her figure was lithe and wiry, her step elastic, her eye cool, and her nerves firm. At ten years of age she was given to escapades, in which she found few boys hardy and fearless enough to rival her. She would go into an open pasture with a nub of corn, call up a frolicsome young horse, halter him, and then jump on his back. No saddle or bridle wants the little Amazon. She had seen bold riding at the circus, and in the retirement of the woods she could surpass it. So she would toss off her shoes, and stand upright on the creature's back, with a foot on each side of the spine. At first she was content to let the animal walk with his spirited little burden; then she would venture into a gentle amble, and finally into full gallop. As she grew older, the deep woods had a perpetual charm for her. She loved to wander afar into dim shades, and listen to the wild, sweet song of the wood-lark, and to watch the squirrels gambolling on the tops of beech-trees, or leaping from one oak to the other. It is not possible to say how much she, and every other active and finely tempered genius, gains by such a childhood. A love of nature and a habit of enjoying nature is thus rooted in the spirit, so deeply that no flush of city life can destroy it. The glare of palaces and the roar of paved streets seem, for a lifetime, tiresome and false; the world-weary spirit evermore longs for the music of the west wind blowing through the tree-tops, the melodies of the forest, the splash of waterfalls, the ring of the mower's steel, the swaying of the golden wheat fields, the songs of the whippoorwills, and the glancing of the fireflies. Such a childhood gives a firmness of health, a vigor and a hardihood, a power of recovering from fatigue, and a capacity for constant labor without exhaustion, that are a greater blessing than the wealth of a Girard or a Stewart.

At the age of twelve Sara Clarke went to Rochester to attend school. Her home was with an elder brother, and she entered with zeal and with success on the studies of a regular education. Like many others who, in after life, have written that which the world will not willingly let die, she did not excel in mathematical studies. The multiplication table was no labor of love. The Rule of Three was a hopeless conundrum. Interest had no interest for her. But whatever related to the graceful expression of fine thought, whatever unsealed the ancient fountains of song and of story, was easy, harmonious, and attractive; this was native air.

Nothing is harder than to say just what faculty or grouping of faculties makes the writer. One may be witty, vivacious, charming in the parlor, or at the dinner-table, yet no writer. Many have the faculty of expressing a valuable thought in appropriate language; but that does not endow one with the rights, the honors, and the fame of authorship. Give Edward Lytton Bulwer three hours of leisure daily, and in a year he will give the world three hundred and sixty-five chapters of unequalled story-telling, in a style that never grows dull, never palls upon the taste, that is perpetually fresh, clear-cut, and brilliant.

Charles Dickens will sit down by any window in London, or lounge through any street in London, and describe the characters that pass before him, in a way that will charm the reading public of two continents, in paragraphs for every one of which his publishers will gladly pay him a guinea before the ink is dry. Sara Clarke was not three years in her teens before the Rochester papers were glad to get her compositions. They were fresh, piquant, racy. It was impossible to guess whether she had read either Whately or Blair, but it was clear that she had a rhetoric trimmed by no pedantic rules. It was nature's own child talking of nature's charms, her pen, like a mountain rill, neither running between walls of chiselled stone, nor roofed with Roman arches, but wandering between clumps of willows, and meandering at its own sweet will through beds of daisies and fields of blooming clover. There was nothing remarkable about her education. When she left school in 1843, at the age of nineteen, she knew rather more Italian and less algebra, more of English and French history, and less of differential and integral calculus, than some recent graduates of Oberlin and Vassar; but perhaps she was none the worse for that. Indeed, austere, pale-faced Science would have chilled the blood of this free, bounding, elastic, glorious girl. Meantime, Dr. Clarke had removed from Onondaga County to New Brighton, in Western Pennsylvania. This village is nestled between the hills among which the young Ohio, fresh from the shaded springs and the stony brooks of the Alleghanies, gathers up its bright waters for a long journey to the far-off Southern Gulf.

Not long after she went home, in 1845 and 1846, the literary world experienced a sensation. A new writer was abroad. A fresh pen was moving along the pages of the Monthlies. Who might it be? Did Willis know? Could General Morris say? Whittier was in the secret; but he told no tales. And her nom de plume, so appropriate and elegant! This charming Grace Greenwood, so natural, so chatty, so easy, chanting her wood-notes wild. Ah me! those were jocund days. We Americans were not then in such grim earnest as we are now. The inimitable, much imitated pen, that in the early part of the century had given us "Knickerbocker" and the "Sketch Book," was still cheerfully busy at

Sunny Side. Willis, beginning with the sacred and nibbling at the profane, was in the middle of his genial, lounging, graceful career. Poe's Raven was pouring out those weird, melodious croakings. Ik Marvel was a dreaming bachelor, gliding about the picture-galleries of Europe. Bryant was a hard-working editor, but when he lifted up those poet eyes above the smoke of the great city, he saw the water-fowl, and addressed it in lines that our great-grandchildren will know by heart. William Lloyd Garrison was sometimes pelted with bad eggs. Horace Greeley had just started the "New York Tribune." Neither Clay, Calhoun, nor Webster had grown tired of scheming forty years for the presidency. That great thunder-cloud of civil war, that we have seen covering the whole heavens, was but a dark patch on the glowing sky of the South. In these times, and among these people, Grace Greenwood now began to live and move, and have a part, and win a glowing fame. For six or eight years her summer home was New Brighton. In winter she was in Philadelphia, in Washington, in New York, writing for Whittier or for Willis and Morris, or for "Neal's Gazette," or for "Godey." She was the most copious and brilliant lady correspondent of that day, wielding the gracefullest quill, giving the brightest and most attractive column. It is impossible, without full extracts, to give the reader a full idea of these earlier writings of Grace Greenwood. They had the dew of youth, the purple light of love, the bloom of young desire. As well think of culling a handful of moist clover-heads, in the hope of reproducing the sheen and fragrance, the luxuriance and the odor of a meadow, fresh bathed in the Paphian wells of a June morning! In 1850 many of these sketches and letters were collected and republished by Ticknor & Fields, under the name of Greenwood Leaves. The cotemporary estimate given to these writings by Rev. Mr. Mayo is so just and so tasteful that no reader will regret its insertion here: —

"The authoress is the heroine of the book; not that she writes about herself always, or often, or in a way that can offend. But her personality gets entangled with every word she utters, and her generous heart cannot be satisfied without a response to all its loves, and hopes, and misgivings, and aspirations. There is extravagance in the rhetoric, yet the delicious extravagance in which a bounding spirit loves to vindicate its freedom from the rules laid down in the 'Aids of Composition,' and the 'Polite Letter Writer.' There is a delightful absurdity about her wit, into which only a genuine woman could fall. And one page of her admiring criticism of books and men, with all its exaggerations, is worth a hundred volumes of the intellectual dissection of the critical professors.

"Yet the most striking thing in her book is the spirit of joyous health that springs and frolics through it. Grace Greenwood is not the woman to be the president of a society for the suppression of men, and the elevation of female political rights. She knows what her sisters need, as well as those who spoil their voices and temper in shrieking it into the ears of the world; but that knowledge does not cover the sun with a black cloud, or spoil her interest in her cousin's love affair, or make her sit on her horse as if she were riding to a public execution. She can love as deeply as any daughter of Eve. Yet she would laugh in the face of a sentimental young gentleman till he wished her at the other side of the world. She loves intensely, but not with that silent, brooding intensity which takes the color out of the cheeks and the joy out of the soul. Hers is the effervescence, not the corrosion, of the heart. And it is no small thing, this health of which I now speak. In an age when to think is to run the risk of scepticism, and to feel is to invite sentimentalism, it is charming to meet a girl who is not ashamed to laugh and cry, and scold and joke, and love and worship, as her grandmother did before her."

But this is not a review of Grace Greenwood's writings. *Litera scripta manet.* Those who wish to see the cream of our magazine writings from 1845 to 1852, will find it in "Greenwood Leaves," first and second series. About this time, her Poems were published. To say that they are beautiful is not enough. Though redolent of the open country, where most of them were written; though composed while doing housework, as was "Ariadne;" or in the saddle, like the "Horseback Ride,"—the best element in them is the frank, generous, cordial, winning personality which pervades them all. We find, too, evidences, that below the dashing and piquant exterior there was growing up an intense sympathy with the most earnest and strenuous spirits. Already the mutterings of the distant thunder were heard, mellowed by distance, but clear enough to hush the chattering of the bobolinks, and the scream of the blue-jays. Thus the lines "To One Afar" close with the following admirable stanzas: —

"Truth's earnest seeker thou, I fancy's rover;
Thy life is like a river, deep and wide;
I but the light-winged wild bird passing over,
One moment mirrored in the rushing tide.

"Thus are we parted; thou still onward hasting,
Pouring the great flood of that life along;
While I on sunny slopes am careless, wasting
The little summer of my time of song."

But before this gay creature of the elements becomes an earnest woman, as we foresee she must, let us picture in outline the New Brighton life; let us see our heroine, not as a magazinist, or a correspondent, but in a character more admirable and charming than either, — as a fine, handsome, brilliant, fearless young lady. No whit spoiled by a winter of adulation, by the gracefullest of letters from Mr. Willis, by the warmest and the truest appreciation from Whittier, by a colonnade of kindliest notices from the great dailies, the braider of Greenwood chaplets has come back to her cottage-home amid the swelling hills, and beside the glancing river. As plain Sara Clarke, she had helped her mother through the morning work, sweeping, dusting, watering flowers, feeding chickens, sitting down for a few moments to read two stanzas to that white-haired father of hers, his head as clear and cool as ever it was, and as able to give his daughter the soundest judgments and the most valuable criticisms she ever enjoyed. In the heat of midday she seeks her chamber, gazes for a few moments with the look of a lover upon the glorious landscape, then dashes off a column for the "Home Journal" or the "National Press." Now, as the shadows of the hills are beginning to stretch eastward, we hear a quick, elastic step on the stair, and the responsive neigh from the hitching-post in the yard tells us that the "Horseback Ride" is to be rehearsed; and horse and heroine alike feel that

> "Nor the swift regatta, nor merry chase,
> Nor rural dance on the moonlight shore,
> Can the wild and thrilling joy exceed
> Of a fearless leap on a fiery steed."

She must tell, as nobody else can, how quick and marvellous is the change, when she feels the bounding and exuberant animal life of the steed rejoicing in the burden; exulting in the free rein, devouring the long reach of the grassy lane with his gladsome leaps: —

> "As I spring to his back, as I seize the strong rein,
> The strength to my spirit returneth again!
> The bonds are all broken that fettered my mind,
> And my cares borne away on the wings of the wind;
> My pride lifts its head, for a season bowed down,
> And the queen in my nature now puts on her crown."

Now our gentle and poetic Penthesilea has gained the woodland cool and dim. On they press, horse and rider alike enthused, till they reach some retired valley, a sequestered nook, where no profane eyes may look. Lady and pony are going to have a grand equestrian frolic. Pony likes it as well as lady. What prancing and pawing! what rearing and backing! Now a swift gallop, as if in the ring of some fairy circus. But this is no vulgar horse-opera; no saw-dust or tan-bark here; nothing for show, since the blue-jays have no eye for horse-flesh, nor can squirrels be made envious by such exploits. At length pony acts as though the game had been carried as far as he cared to have it; and Grace leaps to the greensward and lets him breathe, and get a drink, and bite the sod. Will he not start for home? Not he. His fetters are silken; but his mistress has that rare gift, unusual among men, and very uncommon with the softer sex, the faculty of controlling animals. He obeys her word like a spaniel; goes and comes at her bidding; stands on his hind feet, if she tells him to; lies down; gets up again; follows her up the steps of the piazza. In fact, if such a thing could be, he would carry out the nursery rhyme and go after her "upstairs, downstairs, in the lady's chamber."

The ride home is somewhat more gentle; for, in the cool of the evening dusk, our heroine has turned poetess again, and is chiselling out Pygmalion word by word, or indulging in such spirit-longings as this: —

"I look upon life's glorious things,
The deathless themes of song,
The grand, the proud, the beautiful,
The wild, the free, the strong;
And wish that I might take a part
Of what to them belong."

After the evening meal, and an hour of quiet chat, while

flecks of moonbeam dance on the gallery floor, we might suppose the day ended, and these hours of beautiful life would now be rounded by a sleep. Not yet. This fearless and ardent lover of nature delights in every rich sensation that earth, or air, or water can impart.

She glides away across the pasture to have a glorious swim in

"Yon lake of heavenly blue;
The long hair, unconfined,
Is flung, like some young Nereid's now
To tossing wave and wind."

This is no timid, frightened bather. Had she been Hero on the shores of Hellespont, she would have plunged in and met Leander half-way between the continents. None but an assured swimmer could have written this stanza: —

"And now when none are nigh to save,
While earth grows dim behind;
I lay my cheek to the kissing wave,
And laugh with the frolicsome wind.

"On the billowy swell I lean my breast,
And he fondly beareth me;
I dash the foam from his sparkling crest,
In my wild and careless glee."

What a pity her bathing-place was not the fountain of perpetual youth! No matter how ably a woman writes, or how eloquently she speaks, — and there are very few of her sex so able or so eloquent to-day as Grace Greenwood, — we can but endorse this sentiment of one of her earliest admirers. In a letter to Morris, written when Miss Clarke was living this life, and writing these lines, he says: "Save her from meriting the approbation of dignified critics. Leave this fairest blossom on the rose-tree of woman for my worship, and the admiration of the few who, like me, can appreciate the value of an elegant uselessness, and perceive the fascination of splendid gayety and brilliant trifling. Adieu, and send me more Grace Greenwoods."

But no woman, with an acute brain and a warm heart, could live in such a land as ours, and in the nineteenth century, and remain long a writer of splendid gayeties. The times called for earnest thinking and vigorous writing. The age of rose-tinted album-leaves, covered with graceful impromptus, was past. Willis, and his elegant "Home Journal," went into the mild oblivion of June roses. Great questions agitated the public mind; and we heard hoarse voices and blasts of brazen trumpets on the slopes of Parnassus.

Meantime Miss Clarke went to Europe. This was in 1853. She spent a little over a year abroad, which, in the dedication to her daughter of one of her juvenile books, she calls "the golden year of her life." Perhaps America has never sent to the shores of the Old World a young lady traveller, who was a better specimen of what the New World can do in the way of producing a fine woman. She was a flower from a virgin soil, and a new form of civilization; but rivalling, in the delicacy of its tints, and the richness of its perfume, anything from older and longer cultivated parterres. With one of those felicitous memories that has its treasures ever at command, and can always remember the right thing at the right time and place; fully stored by wide readings in belles-lettres; with the spirit of an enthusiast for everything beautiful, or good, or famous; in the joyous overflow of unbroken health and unflagging spirits, the trip was to her one long gala-day, crowded with memorable sights, with sensations which enrich the whole of one's after-life.

Harriet Beecher Stowe has written as well in her "Sunny Memories of Other Lands," but no lady tourist from America has surpassed Grace Greenwood in the warm tinting and gorgeous rhetoric of her descriptions, and in the vivacious interest which she felt herself, and which she conveys to others in her letters. This correspondence was collected immediately after her return, and published under the title of "Haps and Mishaps of a Tour in Europe."

Nobody has described the marble wonders of the Vatican with finer appreciation than can be seen in the following passage: —

"Of all the antique statues I have yet seen, I have been by far the most impressed by the Apollo Belvidere, and the Dying Gladiator, — the one the striking embodiment of the pride, and fire, and power, and joy of life; the other of the mournful majesty, the proud resignation, the 'conquered agony' of death. In all his triumphant beauty and rejoicing strength, the Apollo stands forth as a pure type of immortality — every inch a god. There is an Olympian spring in the foot which seems to spurn the earth, a secure disdain of death in the very curve of his nostrils, — a sunborn light on his brow; while the absolute perfection of grace, the supernal majesty of the figure, now, as in the olden time, seem to lift it above the human and the perishing, into the region of the divine and the eternal. Scarcely can it be said that the worship of this god has ceased. The indestructible glory of the lost divinity lingers about him still; and the deep, almost solemn emotion, the sigh of unutterable admiration, with which the pilgrims of art behold him now, differ little, perhaps from the hushed adoration of his early worshippers. I have never seen any work of art which I had such difficulty to realize as a mere human creation, born in an artist's struggling brain, moulded in dull clay, and from thence transferred, by the usual slow and laborious process, to marble. Nor can I ever think of it as having according to old poetic fancy, pre-existed in the stone, till the divinely directed chisel of the sculptor cut down to it. Ah, so methinks, the very marble must have groaned, in prescience of the god it held. To me it rather seems a glowing, divine conception, struck instantly into stone. It surely embodies the very soul and glory of the ancient mythology, and, with kindred works, forms, if not a fair justification of, at least a noble apology for, a religion which revelled in ideas of beauty and grace, which had ever something lofty and pure even in its refined sensuality; and for the splendid arrogance of that genius which boldly chiselled out its own grand conceptions, and named them gods. The Apollo I should like to see every day of my life. I would have it near me; and every morning, as the darkness is lifted before the sun, and the miracle of creation is renewed, I would wish to lift a curtain, and gaze on that transcendent image of life and light, — to receive into my own being somewhat of the energy and joy of existence with which it so abounds, — to catch some gleams of the glory of the fresh and golden morning of poetry and art yet raying from its brow. One could drink in strength, as from a fountain, from gazing on that attitude of pride and grace, so light, yet firm, and renew one's wasted vigor by the mere sight of that exulting and effortless action."

What a gem of description we have here at the end of a letter, written from Naples on the 18th of April: —

"We drove to Naples this morning over a road, which, for its varied scenery and picturesque views, seems to me only comparable with the Cornice leading to Genoa. It was with heartfelt reluctance that we left Sorrento, which must ever seem to me one of the loveliest places on earth. O pride and darling of this delicious shore, — like a young festive queen, rose-crowned, sitting in the shade of oranges and myrtles, watched over with visible tenderness by the olive-clad hills, gently caressed and sung to by the capricious sea, — bright, balmy, bewitching Sorrento, adieu!"

But the finest piece of writing in the volume is a bravura on the Roman Catholic Religion. It occurs in a long and splendid description of High Mass, at St. Peter's on Christ mas morning: —

"To my eyes, the beauty and gorgeousness of the scene grew most fitting and holy; with the incense floating to me from the altar, I seemed to breathe in a subtile, subduing spirit; and to that music my heart hushed itself in my breast, my very pulses grew still, and my brain swam in a new, half-sensuous, half-spiritual emotion. For a moment I believe I understood the faith of the Roman Catholic, — for a moment I seemed to taste the ecstasy of the mystic, to burn with the fervor of the devotee, and felt in wonder, and in fear, all the poetry, mystery, and power of the Church. Suddenly rose before my mind vivid wayside and seaside scenes, — pictures of humblest Judean life, when the 'meek and lowly' Author of our faith walked, ministering, and teaching, and comforting among the people, — humblest among the humble, poorest among the poor, most sorrowful among the sorrowful, preaching peace, good-will, purity, humility, and freedom, — and then, all this magnificent mockery of the divine truths he taught, this armed and arrogant spiritual despotism, in the place of the peace and liberty of the gospel, faded from before my disenchanted eyes, and even my ear grew dull to that pomp of sound, swelling up as though to charm his ear against the sighs of the poor, and the groanings of the captive.

"O Cleopatra of religions, throned in power, glowing and gorgeous in all imaginable splendors and luxuries, — proud victor of victors, — in the 'infinite variety' of thy resources and enchantments more attractive than glory, resistless as fate; now terrible in the dusky splendors of thy imperious beauty; now softening and subtile as moonlight, and music, and poet dreams; insolent and humble, stormy though tender! alluring tyranny, beautiful falsehood, fair and fatal enchantress, sovereign sorceress of the world! the end is not yet, and the day may not be far distant when thou shalt lay the asp to thine own bosom, and die."

Since her marriage to Leander K. Lippincott, Grace Greenwood's pen has been employed chiefly in writings for the young. She edits the "Little Pilgrim," a monthly devoted to the amusement, the instruction, and the well-being of little folks. Its best articles are her contributions. These have been collected from time to time, and published by Ticknor & Fields, and make a juvenile library, numbering nearly a dozen volumes. Though intended for children, none of these books but will charm older readers, with the elegance and freshness of their style, their abounding vivacity and harmless wit, and the hopeful and sunny spirit which they breathe. They are remarkable for the felicitous manner in which they convey historical information. No child can fail to be drawn on to wider readings of the storied past, and to know more of old heroes, ancient cities, and famous lands.

Soon after its establishment, Mrs. Lippincott became a contributor to the "Independent," and during the war a lecturer to soldiers and at sanitary fairs. Her last book is made up from articles in the "Independent," and passages from lectures. It shows the fire of her youthful zeal, and the glowing rhetoric of twenty-five no whit abated. On the contrary, there are evidences in her later productions of a full grasping of the significance of the heroic and stormy times in which we live.

There appear in the writings of Grace Greenwood three phases of development, three epochs of a literary career. The first lasted from the days of the boarding-school till marriage, — from the first merry chit-chat and fragrant Greenwood Leaves beyond the Alleghanies, to the full-rounded, mellow, golden prime, as displayed in the letters from Europe. Then follows a decade, during which story-writing for children has principally occupied her pen. With the war commences the third period, — years "vexed with the drums and tramplings," the storms and dust-clouds of middle life; a great republic convulsed by a giant struggle; woman gliding from the sanctity of the fireside, going out to do, to dare, and to suffer at the side of her war-worn brother, attacking social wrongs, doing all that woman can do to cheer, to adorn, to raise the downfallen, to proclaim liberty to the captive, to open the prison to those that are bound. Up to the full summit level of such a time her spirit rises. She brings to the requirements of this epoch faculties polished by long and diligent culture; a heart throbbing with every fine sensibility, and every generous emotion; a large, warm, exuberant nature; a ripe and glorious womanhood.

For such a character in such a wondrous mother age, there lies open a long career of strenuous exertion, worthy achievement, and lasting fame.

ALICE AND PHEBE CARY.

BY HORACE GREELEY.

YEARS ago — a full score, at least — the readers of some religious, and those of many rural, newspapers first noted the fitful appearance, in the poet's corner of their respective gazettes, of verses by ALICE CARY. Two or three years later, other such — like, and yet different — also irradiated, from time to time, the aforesaid corner, purporting to be from the pen of PHEBE CARY. Inquiry at length elicited the fact that the writers were young sisters, the daughters of a plain, substantial farmer, who lived on and cultivated his own goodly but not superabundant acres, a few miles out of Cincinnati, Ohio. He was a Universalist in faith, and they grew up the same, — writing oftener for the periodicals of their own denomination, though their effusions obtained wide currency through others, into which they were copied. I do not know, but presume, that Alice had written extensively, and Phebe occasionally, for ten years, before either had asked or been proffered any other consideration therefor than the privilege of being read and heard.

This family of Carys claim kindred with Sir Robert Cary, a stout English knight, who, in the reign of Henry V., vanquished, after a long and bloody struggle, a haughty chevalier of Arragon, who challenged any Englishman of gentle blood to a passage-at-arms, which took place in Smithfield, London, as is chronicled in "Burke's Heraldry." Henry authorized the victor to bear the arms of his vanquished antagonist, and the crest is still worn by certain branches of the family. The genealogy is at best unverified, nor does it matter. From *Walter* Cary — a French Huguenot, compelled to flee his country, upon the revocation by Louis XIV. of the great Henry's Edict of Nantes, and who, with his wife and son, settled in England, where his son, likewise named Walter, was educated at Cambridge — the descent of the Ohio Carys is unquestioned. The younger Walter migrated to America, very soon after the landing of the "Mayflower" pilgrims, and settled at Bridgewater, Mass., only sixteen miles from Plymouth Rock, where he opened a "grammar school," claimed to have been the earliest in America. Walter was duly blest with seven sons, whereof John settled in Windham, Connecticut; and of *his* five sons, the youngest, Samuel, was great-grandfather to the Alice and Phebe Cary of our day.

Samuel, educated at Yale, becoming a physician, settled and practised at Lyme, where was born, in 1763, his son Christopher, who, at eighteen years of age, entered the armies of the Revolution. Peace was soon achieved; when, in default of cash, the young soldier received a land grant or warrant, and located therewith the homestead in Hamilton County, Ohio, whereon was born his son Robert, who in due time married the wife who bore him a son, who died young, as did one daughter. Two more daughters have since passed away, and three remain, of whom the two who have not married are the subjects of this sketch. Their surviving sister, Mrs. Carnahan, is a widow, and lives in Cincinnati. Two brothers, sturdy, thrifty farmers, live near the spot where they first saw the light.

Alice Cary was born in 1820, and was early called to mourn the loss of her mother, of whom she has written: "My mother was of English descent, — a woman of superior intellect, and of a good, well-ordered life. In my memory, she stands apart from all others, — wiser, purer, doing more, and living better, than any other woman." Phebe was born in 1825; and there were two younger sisters, of whom one died in youth, greatly beloved and lamented. A few weeks before her departure, and while she was still in fair health, she appeared for some minutes to be plainly visible in broad daylight to the whole family, across a little ravine from their residence, standing on the stoop of a new house they were then building, though she was actually asleep, at that moment, in a chamber of their old house, and utterly unconscious of this "counterfeit presentment" at some distance from her bodily presence. This appearance naturally connected itself with her death, when that occurred soon afterward; and thenceforth the family have lent a ready ear to narrations of spiritual (as distinguished from material) presence, which to many, if not most, persons are simply incredible.

The youngest of the family, named Elmina, was a woman of signal beauty of mind and person, whose poetic as well as her general capacities were of great promise; but she married, while yet young, Mr. Swift, a Cincinnati merchant, and thenceforward, absorbed in other cares, gave little attention to literature. She was early marked for its victim by Consumption, — the scourge of this, with so many other families, — and yielded up her life while still in the bloom of early womanhood, three or four years since. I believe her marriage, and the consequent loss of her society, had a share in determining the elder sisters to remove to New York, which they did in 1850.

Alice had begun to write verses at eighteen, Phebe at seventeen, years of age. Their father married a second time, and thence lived apart from, though near, the cottage wherein I first greeted the sisters in 1849; and, when the number was reduced to two by the secession of Elmina, Alice and Phebe meditated, and finally resolved on, a removal to the great emporium.

Let none rashly conclude to follow their example who have not their securities against adverse fortune. They were in the flush of youth and strength; they were thoroughly, inalienably devoted to each other; they had property to the value, I think, of some thousands of dollars; they had been trained to habits of industry and frugality; and they had not merely the knack of writing for the press (which so many mistakenly imagine sufficient), but they had, through the last ten or twelve years, been slowly but steadily winning attention and appreciation by their voluntary contributions to the journals. These, though uncompensated in money, had won for them what was now money's worth. It would *pay* to buy their effusions, though others of equal intrinsic merit, but whose writers had hitherto won no place in the regard of the reading public, might pass unread and unconsidered.

Being already an acquaintance, I called on the sisters soon after they had set up their household gods among us, and met them at intervals thereafter at their home, or at the houses of mutual friends. Their parlor was not so large as some others, but quite as neat and cheerful; and the few literary persons or artists who occasionally met, at their informal invitation, to discuss with them a cup of tea and the newest books, poems, and events, might have found many more pretentious, but few more enjoyable, gatherings. I have a dim recollection that the first of these little tea-parties was held up two flights of stairs, in one of the less fashionable sections of the city; but good things were said there, that I recall with pleasure even yet; while of some of the company, on whom I have not since set eyes, I cherish a pleasant and grateful remembrance. As their circumstances gradually though slowly improved, by dint of diligent industry and judicious economy, they occupied more eligible quarters; and the modest dwelling they have for some years owned and improved, in the very heart of this emporium, has long been known to the literary guild as combining one of the best private libraries, with the sunniest drawing-room (even by gaslight) to be found between King's Bridge and the Battery.

Their first decided literary venture — a joint volume of poems, most of which had already appeared in sundry journals — was published in Philadelphia early in 1850, before they had abandoned "Clovernook," their rural Western home, for the brick-and-mortar whirl of the American Babel. Probably the heartiness of its welcome fortified, it did not stimulate, their resolve to migrate eastward; though it is a safe guess that no direct pecuniary advantage accrued to them from its publication. But the next year witnessed the "coming out" of Alice's first series of "Clovernook Papers;" prose sketches of characters and incidents drawn from observation and experience, which won immediate and decided popularity. The press heartily recognized their fresh simplicity and originality, while the public bought, read, and admired. Several goodly editions were sold in this country, and at least one in Great Britain, where their merits were generously appreciated by the critics. A second series, published in 1853, was equally successful. "The Clovernook Children" — issued in 1854 by Ticknor & Fields, and addressed more especially to the tastes and wants of younger readers — has been hardly less commended or less popular.

"Lyra and other Poems," published by Redfield in 1853, was the first volume of verse wherein Miss Cary challenged the judgment of critics independently of her sister. That it was a decided success is sufficiently indicated by the fact that a more complete edition, including all the contents of

Redfield's, with much more, was issued by Ticknor & Fields in 1855. "The Maiden of Tlascala," a narrative poem of seventy-two pages, was first given to the public in this Boston edition.

Her first novel — "Hagar; a Story of To-Day" — was written for and appeared in "The Cincinnati Commercial," appearing in a book form in 1852. "Married, not Mated," followed in 1856, and "The Bishop's Son," her last, was issued by Carleton, in 1867. Each of these have had a good reception, alike from critics and readers; though their pecuniary success has, perhaps, been less decided than that of her poems and shorter sketches.

Of her "Pictures of Country Life," brought out by Derby & Jackson in 1859, "The Literary Gazette" (London), which is not accustomed to flatter American authors, said: —

"Every tale in this book might be selected as evidence of some new beauty or unhackneyed grace. There is nothing feeble, nothing vulgar, and, above all, nothing unnatural or melodramatic. To the analytical subtlety and marvellous naturalness of the French school of romance she has added the purity and idealization of the home affections and home life belonging to the English; giving to both the American richness of color and vigor of outline, and her own individual power and loveliness."

Except her later novels, Miss Cary's works have in good part appeared first in periodicals, — "The Atlantic Magazine," "Harpers'," "The New York Ledger," and "The Independent;" but many, if not most of them, have generally been afterward issued in her successive volumes, along with others not previously published. "Lyrics and Hymns," issued in 1866 by Hurd & Houghton, "The Lover's Diary," admirably brought out by Ticknor & Fields in 1867, and "Snow Berries; a

Book for Young Folks," by the same house, are her latest volumes. Nearly all of her prose works have been reprinted in London, and have there, as well as here, received a cordial and intelligent welcome.

Few American women have written more than Miss Cary, and still fewer have written more successfully. Yet she does not write rapidly nor recklessly, and her works evince conscientious, painstaking effort, rather than transcendent genius or fitful inspiration. Ill-health has of late interrupted, if not arrested, her labors; but, in the intervals of relative exemption from weakness and suffering, her pen is still busy, and her large circle of admiring readers may still confidently hope that her melody will not cease to flow till song and singer are together hushed in the silence of the grave.

From her many poems that I would gladly quote, I choose this as the shortest, not the best: —

> " We are the mariners, and God the sea;
> And, though we make false reckonings, and run
> Wide of a righteous course, and are undone,
> Out of his deeps of love we cannot be.
>
> " For, by those heavy strokes we misname ill,
> Through the fierce fire of sin, through tempering doubt,
> Our natures more and more are beaten out
> To perfecter reflections of his will! "

Phebe has written far less copiously than Alice; in fact, she has for years chosen to bear alone the burden of domestic cares, in order that her more distinguished sister should feel entirely at liberty to devote all her time and strength to literature. And, though she had been widely known as the author of good newspaper prose, as well as far more verse, I think the critical public was agreeably surprised by the quality of her "Poems of Faith, Hope, and Love," recently issued by Hurd & Houghton. There are one hundred pieces in all, covering two hundred and forty-nine pages; and hardly one of the hundred could well be spared, while there surely is no one of them which a friend would wish she had omitted from the collection. There are a buoyant faith, a sunny philosophy evinced throughout, with a hearty independence of thought and manner, which no one ever succeeded in affecting, and no one who possesses them could afford to barter for wealth or fame. The following verses, already widely copied and relished, are here given, as affording a fair chapter of wholesome, bracing autobiography:-

"A WOMAN'S CONCLUSIONS.

"I said, if I might go back again
To the very hour and place of my birth;
Might have my life whatever I chose,
And live it in any part of the earth;—

"Put perfect sunshine into my sky,
Banish the shadow of sorrow and doubt;
Have all my happiness multiplied,
And all my suffering stricken out;

"If I could have known, in the years now gone,
The best that a woman comes to know;
Could have had whatever will make her blest,
Or whatever she thinks will make her so;

"Have found the highest and purest bliss
That the bridal wreath and ring enclose;
And gained the one out of all the world
That my heart as well as my reason chose;

"And if this had been, and I stood to-night
By my children, lying asleep in their beds,
And could count in my prayers, for a rosary,
The shining row of their golden heads;—

"Yea! I said, if a miracle such as this
Could be wrought for me, at my bidding, still
I would choose to have my past as it is,
And to let my future come as it will!

"I would not make the path I have trod
More pleasant or even, more straight or wide;
Nor change my course the breadth of a hair,
This way or that way, to either side.

"My past is mine, and I take it all;
Its weakness—its folly, if you please;
Nay, even my sins, if you come to that,
May have been my helps, not hindrances!

"If I saved my body from the flames
Because that once I had burned my hand;
Or kept myself from a greater sin
By doing a less—you will understand;

"It was better I suffered a little pain,
Better I sinned for a little time,
If the smarting warned me back from death,
And the sting of sin withheld from crime.

"Who knows its strength by trial, will know
What strength must be set against a sin;
And how temptation is overcome
He has learned, who has felt its power within!

"And who knows how a life at the last may show?
Why, look at the moon from where we stand!
Opaque, uneven, you say; yet it shines,
A luminous sphere, complete and grand!

"So let my past stand, just as it stands,
And let me now, as I may, grow old;
I am what I am, and my life for me
Is the best—or it had not been, I hold."

If I have written aright this hasty sketch, there are hope and comfort therein for those who are just entering upon responsible life with no more than average opportunities and advantages. If I have not shown this, read the works of Alice and Phebe Cary, and find it there!

Engᵈ by H.B. Hall Jr. N.Y.

MARGARET FULLER.

MARGARET FULLER OSSOLI.

BY T. W. HIGGINSON.

Travelling by rail in Michigan, some ten years ago, I found myself seated next to a young Western girl, with a very intelligent face, who soon began to talk with me about literary subjects. She afterwards gave me, as a reason for her confidence, that I "looked like one who would enjoy Margaret Fuller's writings," — these being, as I found, the object of her special admiration. I certainly took the remark for a compliment; and it was, at any rate, a touching tribute to the woman whose intellectual influence thus brought strangers together.

Margaret Fuller is connected, slightly but firmly, with my earliest recollections. We were born and bred in the same town (Cambridge, Massachusetts), and I was the playmate of her younger brothers. Their family then lived at the old "Brattle House," which still stands behind its beautiful lindens, though the great buildings of the University Press now cover the site of the old-fashioned garden, whose formal fish-ponds and stone spring-house wore an air of European stateliness to our home-bred eyes. There I dimly remember the discreet elder sister, book in hand, watching over the gambols of the lovely little Ellen, who became, long after, the wife of my near kinsman, Ellery Channing. This later connection cemented a new tie, and led to a few interviews in maturer years with Margaret Fuller, and to much intercourse with others of the family. It is well to mention even such slight ties of association as these, for they unconsciously influence one's impressions; and, after all, it is the personal glimpses which make the best part of biography, great or small, and indeed of all literature. How refreshing it is, amid the chaff of Aulus Gellius, to come upon a reference to Virgil's own copy of the Æneid, which the writer had once seen, "*quem ipsius Virgilii fuisse credebat;*" and nothing in all Lord Bacon's works ever stirred me like that one magic sentence, "When I was a child, and Queen Elizabeth was in the flower of her years." I can say that when I was a child, Margaret Fuller was the queen of Cambridge, though troubled with a large minority of rather unwilling and insurrectionary subjects.

Her mother I well remember as one of the sweetest and most sympathetic of women; she was tall and not unattractive in person, refined and gentle, but with a certain physical awkwardness, proceeding in part from extreme nearsightedness. Of the father I have no recollection, save that he was mentioned with a sort of respect, as being a lawyer and having been a congressman. But his daughter has described him, in her fragment of autobiography, with her accustomed frankness and precision: —

"My father was a lawyer and a politician. He was a man largely endowed with that sagacious energy which the state of New England society for the last half century has been so well fitted to develop. His father was a clergyman, settled as pastor in Princeton, Massachusetts, within the bounds of whose parish farm was Wachusett. His means were small, and the great object of his ambition was to send his sons to college. As a boy, my father was taught to think only of preparing himself for Harvard University, and, when there, of preparing himself for the profession of law. As a lawyer, again, the ends constantly presented were to work for distinction in the community, and for the means of supporting a family. To be an honored citizen and to have a home on earth were made the great aims of existence. To open the deeper fountains of the soul, to regard life here as the prophetic entrance to immortality, to develop his spirit to perfection, — motives like these had never been suggested to him, either by fellow-beings or by outward circumstances. The result was a character, in its social aspect, of quite the common sort. A good son and brother, a kind neighbor, an active man of business, — in all these outward relations, he was but one of a class which surrounding conditions have made the majority among us. In the more delicate and individual relations he never approached but two mortals, my mother and myself.

"His love for my mother was the green spot on which he stood apart from the commonplaces of a mere bread-winning, bread-bestowing existence. She was one of those fair and flower-like natures which sometimes spring up even beside the most dusty highways of life, — a creature not to be shaped into a merely useful instrument, but bound by one law with the blue sky, the dew, and the frolic birds. Of all persons whom I have known she had in her most of the angelic, — of that spontaneous love for every living thing, for man, and beast, and tree, which restores the golden age."

Sarah Margaret Fuller was born May 23, 1810; the eldest child of Timothy Fuller and Margaret Crane. Her birthplace was a house on Cherry Street, in Cambridge, before whose door still stand the trees planted by her father on the year when she saw the light. The family afterwards removed to the "Dana House," which then crowned, in a stately way, the hill between Old Cambridge and Cambridgeport. It was later still that they resided in the "Brattle House," as I have described. This was Margaret Fuller's home until 1833, exept that she spent a year or more at the school of the Misses Prescott, in Groton, Mass., where she went through that remarkable experience described by herself, under the assumed character of Mariana, in "Summer on the Lakes." In 1826 she returned to Cambridge.

The society of that University town had then, as it still has, great attractions for young people of talent. It offers something of that atmosphere of culture for which such persons yearn, — tinged, perhaps, with a little narrowness and constraint. She met there in girlhood the same persons who were afterwards to be her literary friends, colaborers, and even biographers. It was a stimulating and rather perilous position, for she found herself among a circle of highly cultivated young men, with no equal female companion; although she read Locke and Madame de Stael with Lydia Maria Francis, afterwards better known as Mrs. Child. Carlyle had just called attention to the rich stores of German literature; all her friends were exploring them, and some had just returned from the German universities. She had the college library at command, and she had that vast and omnivorous appetite for books which is the most common sign of literary talent in men, but is for some reason exceedingly rare among women. At least I have known but two young girls whose zeal in this respect was at all comparable to that reported of Margaret Fuller, these two being Harriet Prescott and the late Charlotte Hawes.

In 1833 her father removed to Groton, Mass., much to her regret. Yet her life there was probably a good change in training for one who had been living for several years in an atmosphere of mental excitement. In March, 1834, she wrote thus of her mode of life: —

"*March*, 1834. — Four pupils are a serious and fatiguing

charge for one of my somewhat ardent and impatient disposition. Five days in the week I have given daily lessons in three languages, in geography and history, besides many other exercises on alternate days. This has consumed often eight, always five hours of my day. There has been also a great deal of needle-work to do, which is now nearly finished, so that I shall not be obliged to pass my time about it when everything looks beautiful, as I did last summer. We have had very poor servants, and, for some time past, only one. My mother has been often ill. My grandmother, who passed the winter with us, has been ill. Thus you may imagine, as I am the only grown-up daughter, that my time has been considerably taxed.

"But as, sad or merry, I must always be learning, I laid down a course of study at the beginning of winter, comprising certain subjects, about which I had always felt deficient. These were the History and Geography of modern Europe, beginning the former in the fourteenth century; the Elements of Architecture; the works of Alfieri, with his opinions on them; the historical and critical works of Goethe and Schiller, and the outlines of history of our own country.

"I chose this time as one when I should have nothing to distract or dissipate my mind. I have nearly completed this course, in the style I proposed, — not minute or thorough, I confess, — though I have had only three evenings in the week, and chance hours in the day for it. I am very glad I have undertaken it, and feel the good effects already. Occasionally I try my hand at composition, but have not completed anything to my own satisfaction."

On September 23, 1835, her father was attacked by cholera, and died within three days. Great as must have been the blow to the whole family, it was greatest of all to Margaret. The tie between them had been very close, and this sudden death threw the weight of the whole household upon the eldest child. It came at what had seemed to her the golden moment of her whole life; for she was about to visit Europe with her constant friends, Professor and Mrs. Farrar, and with their friend Harriet Martineau, who was just returning home. But all this must be at once abandoned. Mr. Fuller had left barely property enough to support his widow, and to educate the younger children, with the aid of their elder sister. Mrs. Fuller was in delicate health, and of a more yielding nature than Margaret, who became virtually head of the house. Under her strong supervision, two out of the five boys went honorably through Harvard College, — a third having previously graduated, — while the young sister was sent to the best schools, where she showed the family talent.

In the autumn of 1836, Margaret Fuller went to Boston, where she taught Latin and French in Mr. Alcott's school, and had classes of young ladies in French, German, and Italian. She also devoted one evening in every week to translating German authors into English, for the gratification of Dr. Channing, — their chief reading being in De Wette and Herder. The following extract will show how absorbing were her occupations: —

"And now let me try to tell you what has been done. To one class I taught the German language, and thought it good success, when, at the end of three months, they could read twenty pages of German at a lesson, and very well. This class, of course, was not interesting, except in the way of observation and analysis of language.

"With more advanced pupils I read, in twenty-four weeks, Schiller's Don Carlos, Artists, and Song of the Bell, besides giving a sort of general lecture on Schiller; Goethe's Hermann and Dorothea; Goetz von Berlichingen; Iphigenia;

first part of Faust, — three weeks of thorough study this, as valuable to me as to them; and Clavigo, — thus comprehending samples of all his efforts in poetry, and bringing forward some of his prominent opinions; Lessing's Nathan, Minna, Emilia Galeotti; parts of Tieck's Phantasus, and nearly the whole first volume of Richter's Titan.

"With the Italian class, I read parts of Tasso, Petrarch, — whom they came to almost adore, — Ariosto, Alfieri, and the whole hundred cantos of the Divina Commedia, with the aid of the fine Athenæum copy, Flaxman's designs, and all the best commentaries. This last piece of work was and will be truly valuable to myself."

She was invited, in 1837, to become a teacher in a private school just organized, on Mr. Alcott's plan, in Providence, R. I. "The proposal is," she wrote, "that I shall teach the elder girls my favorite branches for four hours a day, — choosing my own hours and arranging the course, — for a thousand dollars a year, if upon trial I am well pleased enough to stay." This was a flattering offer, and certainly shows the intellectual reputation she had won. She accepted it, for the sake of her family, though it involved the necessity of leaving the friends and advantages which Boston had given. She had also to abandon her favorite literary project, the preparation of a Life of Goethe for Mr. Ripley's series of translations from foreign literature. It was perhaps as a substitute for this that she translated "Eckermann's Conversations with Goethe," though it did not appear till after her removal to Jamaica Plain, in 1839. It is an admirable version, and there is after all no book in English from which one has so vivid and familiar impression of Goethe. Her preface is clear, moderate, and full of good points, though less elaborate than her subsequent essay on the same subject. No one, I fancy, has ever compressed into one sentence a sharper analysis of this great writer than when she says of him in the preface, "I think he had the artist's eye and the artist's hand, but not the artist's love of structure."

She took a house in Jamaica Plain, on her own responsibility, in the spring of 1839, and removed thither the family, of which she was practically the head. The next year they returned once more to Cambridge, living in a small house near her birthplace.

In the autumn of 1839, she instituted that remarkable conversational class, which so stimulated the minds of the more cultivated women of Boston, that even now the leaders of thought and intellectual society date back their first enlightenment to her, and wish that their daughters might have such guidance. The very aim and motive of these meetings showed her clear judgment. She held that women were at a disadvantage as compared with men, because the former were not called on to test, apply, or reproduce what they learned; while the pursuits of life supplied this want to men. Systematic conversations, controlled by a leading mind, would train women to definite statement, and continuous thought; they would make blunders and gain by their mortification; they would seriously compare notes with each other, and discover where vague impression ended and clear knowledge began. She thus states, in her informal prospectus, her three especial aims: —

"To pass in review the departments of thought and knowledge, and endeavor to place them in due relation to one another in our minds. To systematize thought, and give a precision and clearness, in which our sex are so deficient, — chiefly, I think, because they have so few inducements to test and classify what they receive. To ascertain what pursuits are best suited to us, in our time and state of society, and how we may make best use of our means for building up the life of thought upon the life of action."

These conversations lasted during several successive winters, with much the same participants, numbering from twenty to thirty. These were all ladies. During one brief series, the experiment of admitting gentlemen was tried, and it seems singular that this should have failed, since many of her personal friends were of the other sex, and certainly men and women are apt to talk best when together. In this exceptional course, the subject was mythology, and it was thought that the presence of those trained in classical studies might be useful. But an exceedingly able historian of the enterprise adds, "All that depended on others entirely failed. . . . Even in the point of erudition on the subject, which Margaret did not profess, she proved the best informed of the party, while no one brought an idea, except herself. Take her as a whole," adds this lady, "she has the most to bestow upon others by conversation of any person I have ever known. I cannot conceive of any species of vanity living in her presence. She distances all who talk with her."

It is said by all her friends that no record of her conversation does it any justice. I have always fancied that the best impression now to be obtained of the way she talked when her classes called her "inspired," must be got by reading her sketch of the Roman and Greek characters, in her autobiographic fragment. That was written when her conversations most flourished, in 1840, and a marvellous thing it is. It is something to read and re-read, year after year, with ever new delight. Where else is there a statement, so vivid, so brilliant, so profound, of the total influence exerted on a thoughtful child by those two mighty teachers? No attempted report of her conversation gives such an impression of what it must have been, as this self-recorded reverie. If on the tritest of all subjects, she could so easily write something admirable, what must it have been when the restraints of the pen — to her most distasteful — were removed?

On the last day of these meetings — which were closed only by her departure for New York — she wrote thus: —

"*April* 28, 1844. It was the last day with my class. How noble has been my experience of such relation now for six years, and with so many and so various minds! Life is worth living, — is it not? We had a most animated meeting. On bidding me good-by, they all and always show so much good-will and love that I feel I must really have become a friend to them. I was then loaded with beautiful gifts, accompanied with those little delicate poetic traits, which I should delight to tell you of, if you were near."

While thus serving women, she aided men also, by her editorship of the "Dial." This remarkable quarterly, established in 1840, by a circle of her friends, was under her exclusive charge for two years, and these the most characteristic years of its existence. It was a time of great seething in thought and many people had their one thing to say, which being said, they retired into the ranks of common men. The less instructed found their outlet in the radical conventions, then so abundant; the more cultivated uttered themselves in the "Dial." The contributors, who then thronged around Margaret Fuller, — Emerson, Alcott, Parker, Thoreau, Ripley, Hedge, Clarke, W. H. Channing, — were the true founders of American literature. They emancipated the thought of the nation, and also its culture, though their mode of utterance was often crude and cumbrous from excess of material. These writers are all now well known, and some are famous; but at that time not one of them was popular, save Theodore Parker, whose vigorous common-sense soon created for itself a wide public. It was his articles, as Mr. Emerson has since told me, that sold the numbers; that is, as far as they did sell, which was not very far. The editor was to have had two hundred dollars as her annual salary, but it hardly reached that sum, and I believe that the whole edition was but five hundred copies.

I can testify to the vast influence produced by this periodical, even upon those who came to it a year or two after its first appearance, and it seems to me, even now, that in spite of its obvious defects, no later periodical has had so fresh an aroma, or smacked so of the soil of spring. When the unwearied Theodore Parker attempted, half a dozen years after, to embody the maturer expression of the same phase of thought in the "Massachusetts Quarterly Review," he predicted that the new periodical would be "The Dial, with a beard." But the result was disappointment. It was all beard, and no "Dial."

During the first year of the "Dial's" existence, it contained but little from the editor, — four short articles, the "Essay on Critics," "Dialogue between Poet and Critic," "The Allston Exhibition," and "Menzel's View of Goethe," — and two of what may be called fantasy-pieces, "Leila," and "The Magnolia of Lake Pontchartrain." The second volume was richer, containing four of her most elaborate critical articles, — "Goethe," "Lives of the Great Composers," "Festus," and "Bettine Brentano." Few American writers have ever published in one year so much of good criticism as is to be found in these four essays. She wrote also, during this period, the shorter critical notices, which were good, though unequal. She was one of the first to do hearty justice to Hawthorne, of whom she wrote, in 1840, "No one of all our imaginative writers has indicated a genius at once so fine and so rich." Hawthorne was at that time scarcely known, and it is singular to read in her diary, four years earlier, her account of reading one of his "Twice-told Tales," under the impression that it was written by "somebody in Salem," whom she took to be a lady.

I find that I underscored in my copy of the "Dial," with the zeal of eighteen, her sympathetic and wise remark on Lowell's first volume. "The proper critic of this book would be some youthful friend to whom it has been of real value as a stimulus. The exaggerated praise of such an one would be truer to the spiritual fact of its promise than accurate measure of its performance." This was received with delight by us ardent Lowellites in those days, and it still seems to me admirable.

In the third volume of the "Dial," she wrote of "Beethoven," "Sterling," "Romaic and Rhine Ballads," and other themes. In the fourth volume she published a remarkable article, entitled, "The Great Lawsuit; Man versus Men, Woman versus Women." It was a cumbrous name, for which even the vague title, "Woman in the Nineteenth Century," was hailed as a desirable substitute, when the essay was reprinted in book-form. In its original shape, it attracted so much attention that the number was soon out of print; and it is not uncommon to see sets of the "Dial" bound up without it.

She printed, in 1841, another small translation from the German, — a portion of that delightful book, the correspondence between Bettine Brentano and her friend Günderode. One-fourth of this was published in pamphlet form, by way of experiment; and it proved an unsuccessful one. Long after, her version was reprinted, the work being completed by a far inferior hand. Margaret Fuller was one of the best of translators, whether in reproducing the wise oracles of Goethe, or the girlish grace and daring originality of Bettine and her friend. She says of this last work, in a spirit worthy the subject: "I have followed as much as possible the idiom of the writer as well as her truly girlish punctuation. Commas and dashes are the only stops natural to girls; their sentences flow on in little minim ripples, unbroken as the brook in a green field unless by some slight waterfall or jet of Ohs and Ahs." I know of no other critic who has ever done exact justice to the wonderful Bettine, recognizing fully her genius and her charms, yet sternly pointing out the inevitable failure of such self-abandonment and the way in which the tree which defies the law mars its own growth.

During the summer of 1843, she made a tour to the West with her friends James Freeman Clarke and his artist-sister. The result of this was her first original work, "Summer on the Lakes," — a book which, with all artistic defects upon its head, will yet always remain delightful to those who first read it in its freshness. To this day it is almost the only work which presents Western life in any thoughtful or ideal treatment, — which is anything more than a statistical almanac or a treatise on arithmetical progression. Though most of its statements of fact are long since superseded, it yet presents something which is truer than statistics, — the real aroma and spirit of Western life. It is almost the only book which makes that great region look attractive to any but the energetic and executive side of man's nature. In this point of view even her literary episodes seem in place; it is pleasant to think that such books as she describes could be read upon the prairies. In the narrative of most travellers it would seem inappropriate to say that they stopped in Chicago and read a poem. It would seem like being offered a New York "Tribune" at Pæstum. But when Margaret Fuller reads "Philip Van Artevelde," by the lake shore, just in the suburbs of the busy city, all seems appropriate and harmonized, and the moral that it yields her is fit to be remembered for years.

"In Chicago I read again 'Philip Van Artevelde,' and

certain passages in it will always be in my mind associated with the deep sound of the lake, as heard in the night. I used to read a short time at night, and then open the blind to look out. The moon would be full upon the lake, and the calm breath, pure light, and the deep voice harmonized well with the thought of the Flemish hero. When will this country have such a man? *It is what she needs; no thin idealist, no coarse realist, but a man whose eye reads the heavens, while his feet step firmly on the ground, and his hands are strong and dexterous for the use of human implements.*"

What was that power in Margaret Fuller which made her words barbed arrows, to remain in the hearts of young people forever? For one I know that for twenty years that sentence has haunted me, as being, more than any other, the true formula for the American man, the standard by which each should train himself in self-education. I fancy that the secret of my allegiance to this woman lies in the shaping influence of that one sentence. Others have acknowledged the same debt to other stray phrases she uses, — her "lyric glimpses," as Emerson called them. Thus William Hunt, the artist, acknowledged that a wholly new impulse of aspiration was aroused in him by a few stray words she had pencilled on the margin of a passage in Mrs. Jameson's "Italian Painters."

Even the narrative in this book, and its recorded conversations, show that she exerted on travelling acquaintances this stimulating and unlocking power. This showed itself with the Illinois farmers, "the large first product of the soil," and especially with that vanishing race, who can only be known through the sympathy of the imagination, the Indians. There is no book of travels, except, perhaps, Mrs. Jameson's, which gives more access to those finer traits of Indian character that are disappearing so fast amid persecution and demoralization. But the book as a whole, is very fragmentary and episodical, and in this respect, as well as in the wide range of merit and demerit in the verses here and there interspersed, it reminds one of Thoreau's "Week on the Concord and Merrimack Rivers." It is hardly possible, however, to regret these episodes, since one of them contains that rare piece of childish autobiography, "Mariana;" which is however separated from its context in her collected works.

In 1844 she removed to New York. It is not the least of Horace Greeley's services to the nation, that he was willing to entrust the literary criticisms of the "Tribune" to one whose standard of culture was so far above that of his readers or his own. Nevertheless, there she remained for nearly two years, making fearless use of her great opportunity of influence. She was dogmatic, egotistic, and liable to err; but in this she did not differ from her fellow-critics. The point of difference was in the thoroughness of training to which she had submitted, — at least in certain directions, — the elevation of her demands, her perfect independence, and her ready sympathy. With authors who demanded flattery on the one side, and a public on the other which demanded only intellectual substance, and was almost indifferent to literary form, she bravely asserted that literature was to be regarded as an art. Viewing it thus, she demanded the highest; reputations, popularity, cliques, to her were nothing; she might be whimsical, but she was always independent, and sought to try all by the loftiest standard. If she was ever biased by personal considerations, — and this rarely happened, — it was always on the chivalrous side.

Of all Americans thus far, she seems to me to have been born for a literary critic. One of her early associates said well "that she was no artist; she could never have written an epic, or romance, or drama; yet no one knew better the qualities which go to the making of these; and, though catholic as to kind, no one was more rigidly exacting as to quality." She puts this still better in her own journal: "How can I ever write, with this impatience of detail? I shall never be an artist. I have no patient love of execution. I am delighted with my sketch, but if I try to finish it, I am chilled. Never was there a great sculptor who did not love to chip the marble."

But the very fact that she was able to make this discrimination shows her critical discernment. There are not a dozen prose-writers in America who "love to chip the marble;" but so long as we do not discover the defect, we can neither do good work ourselves nor appreciate that of another. All Margaret Fuller's books are very defective as to form; but because she saw the fault, she was able to criticise the books of others.

She had also the rare quality of discerning both needs of the American mind, — originality and culture, — and no one, except Emerson, has done so much to bridge the passage from a tame and imitative epoch to a truly indigenous literature. Most of us are either effeminated by education, or are left crude and rough by the want of it. She who so exquisitely delineated the Greek and Roman culture in her fragment of autobiography, had yet the discernment to write in an essay, "It was a melancholy praise bestowed on the German Iphigenia, that it was an echo of the Greek mind. Oh, give us something rather than Greece more Grecian, so new, so universal, so individual!"

It was, therefore, an event in the history of our literature, when a woman thus eminently gifted became the literary critic of the New York "Tribune," — then, and perhaps still, the journal possessing the most formative influence over the most active class of American minds. There were, of course, drawbacks upon her fitness. She was sometimes fantastic in her likings; so are most fastidious people; so is Emerson. She might be egotistical and overbearing. But she was honest and true. It was apt to be the strong, not the weak, whom she assailed. Her greatest errors were committed in vindicating those whom others attacked, or in dethroning popular favorites to make room for obscurer merit. A different course would have made her life smoother and her memory less noble.

In her day, as now, there were few well-trained writers in the country, and they had little leisure for criticism; so that work was chiefly left to boys. The few exceptions were cynics, like Poe, or universal flatterers, like Willis and Griswold. Into the midst of these came a woman with no gifts for conciliation, with no personal attractions, with a habit of saying things very explicitly and of using the first person singular a good deal too much. In her volume of "Papers on Literature and Art," published in 1846, there is a preface of three pages in which this unpleasant grammatical form occurs just fifty times. This is very characteristic; she puts the worst side foremost. The preface once ended, the rest of the book seems wise and gentle, and only egotistic here and there.

Or at least, nothing need be excepted from this claim, except the article on "American Literature" — the only essay in the book which had not been previously published. Gentle this was not always, nor could it be; and she furthermore apologized for it in the preface (wisely or unwisely), as prepared too hastily for a theme so difficult, and claimed only that it was "written with sincere and earnest feelings, and from a mind that cares for nothing but what is permanent and essential." "It should, then," she adds, "have some merit, if only in the power of suggestion." It certainly has such merit. It is remarkable, after twenty years, to see how many of her judgments have been confirmed by the public mind. How well, for instance, she brought forth from obscurity the then forgotten genius of Charles Brockden Brown; how just were her delineations of Bryant, Willis, Dana, Halleck; how well she described Prescott, then at his culmination, —his industry, his wealth of material, his clear and elegant arrangement, and his polished tameness! So much the public could endure. It was when she touched Longfellow and Lowell that her audience, or that portion of it which dwelt round Boston, grew clamorously indignant.

In reverting, after twenty years, to these criticisms, one perceives that the community must have grown more frank or less sensitive. There seems no good reason why they should have made so much stir. There is no improper personality in them, and, though they may be incorrect, they are not unfair. She frankly confesses to "a coolness towards Mr. Longfellow, in consequence of the exaggerated praise bestowed upon him. When we see a person of moderate powers receive honors which should be reserved for the highest, we feel somewhat like assailing him and taking from him the crown which should be reserved for grander brows. *And yet this is perhaps ungenerous.*" She then goes on to point out the atmosphere of overpraise which has always surrounded this poet, — says that this is not justly chargeable on himself, but on his admirers, publishers, and portrait-painters; and adds in illustration that the likeness of him in the illustrated edition of his works suggests the impression of a "dandy Pindar." This phrase, I remember, gave great offence at the time; yet, on inspection of that rather smirking portrait, it proves to be a fair description; and she expressly disclaims all application of the phrase to the poet himself. She defends him from Poe's charges of specific plagiarism, and points out, very justly, that these accusations only proceed from something imitative and foreign in many of his images and in the atmosphere of much of his verse. She says, as many have felt, that he sees nature, whether human or external, too much through the windows of literature, and finally assigns him his place as "a man of cultivated taste, delicate though not deep feeling, and some, though not much, poetic force." This may not be an adequate statement of the literary claims of Longfellow; but it certainly does not differ so widely from the probable final award as to give just ground for complaint against the critic. It is also recorded by Mr. Greeley that she only consented to review Longfellow's poems with the greatest reluctance, and at the editor's particular request, "assigning the wide divergence of her views of poetry from those of the author and his school as the reason."

Towards Lowell she showed more asperity. Yet there was nothing personal in her remarks, even here; there was simply an adverse literary criticism, conveyed with a slight air of arrogance. To preface an opinion with "We must declare it, though to the grief of some friends and the disgust of more," was undoubtedly meant for a deprecatory and regretful expression; but it had a sort of pompous effect that did not soften the subsequent brief verdict. She declared him "absolutely wanting in the true spirit and tone of poesy," with the addition that "his interest in the moral questions of the day had supplied the want of vitality in himself." Even this last statement was far too strong, no doubt. Yet it will now be admitted by Lowell's warmest admirers that his poetic phases have been singularly coincident with his phases of moral enthusiasm. His early development of genius was united with extreme radicalism of position; then followed many years, comprising the prime of his life, when both his genius and his enthusiasm seemed quiescent. It was the unforeseen stimulus of the war which made him again put on his singing robes, for that "Commemoration

Ode," which is incomparably the greatest of his poems. All this vindicated in some degree the discernment, though it could not justify the sweeping manner of Margaret Fuller's criticism; and her tone of arrogance is more than counterbalanced by the fierce personalities with which the poet retaliated upon her in the "Fable for Critics."

The criticisms on English poets in this collection seem to me singularly admirable; they take rank with those of Elizabeth Barrett Browning, in her "Essays on the Poets." There are many single phrases that are unsurpassed in insight and expression, as where she speaks of the "strange, bleak fidelity of Crabbe." "Give Coleridge a canvas," she says, "and he will paint a picture as if his colors were made of the mind's own atoms." "The rush, the flow, the delicacy of vibration in Shelley's verse can only be paralleled by the waterfall, the rivulet, the notes of the bird and of the insect world." "It is as yet impossible to estimate duly the effect which the balm of his [Wordsworth's] meditations has had in allaying the fever of the public heart, as exhibited in Byron and Shelley." This is a rare series of condensed criticisms, on authors about whom so much has been written, and her remarks on the new men — Sterling, Henry Taylor, and Browning — were almost as good. She was one of the first in America to recognize the genius of Browning, and, while his "Bells and Pomegranates" was yet in course of publication, she placed him at the head of contemporary English poets.

There is much beside, in these rich volumes; a brief criticism on "Hamlet," for instance, in one of the dialogues, which is worthy to take rank with those of Mrs. Jameson; and an essay on "Sir James Mackintosh," which, in calm completeness and thorough workmanship, was her best work, as it was one of her latest. Indeed, the "Papers on Literature and Art" always seemed to me her best book; far superior to the

"Woman in the Nineteenth Century" (published two years previously), which was perhaps framed on too large a scale for one who had so little constructive power. It was noble in tone, enlightened in its statements, and full of suggestion; yet after all it was crude and disconnected in its execution. But the "Papers" have been delightful reading, to me at least, for twenty years, and I could quote many a sentence which has passed into my bone and marrow, as have those of Emerson. "Tragedy is always a mistake." "The difference between heartlessness and the want of a deep heart." "We need to hear the excuses men make to themselves for their worthlessness." "It needs not that one of deeply thoughtful mind be passionate, to divine all the secrets of passion. Thought is a bee that cannot miss those flowers." And so on.

The only complaint I should make in regard to this book is founded on its title," Papers on Literature and Art." With art, save as included in literature, she should not have meddled. At least, she should have dealt only with the biography and personal traits of artists,—not with their work. One of her early friends said that the god Terminus presided over her intellect; but to me it seems that she did not always recognize her own limits. A French wit said that there were three things he had loved very much, without knowing anything about them,—music, painting, and women. Margaret Fuller loved all three, and understood the last.

If, however, she was thus tempted beyond her sphere, it was less perhaps from vanity than because she yielded to the demand popularly made on all our intellectual laborers, that they should scatter themselves as much as possible. Literary work being as yet crude and unorganized in America, the public takes a vague delight in seeing one person do a great many different things. It is like hearing a street musician perform on six instruments at once; he plays them all ill, but it is so remarkable that he should play them together. If we have a stirring pulpit orator, he must try his hand on a novel; if a popular editor, he must write a history of the rebellion. Margaret Fuller, under the same influence, wrote on painting and music, and of course wrote badly.

As to this whole charge of vanity, indeed, there have certainly been great exaggerations. She had by inheritance certain unpleasant tricks of manner, which gave the impression, as Emerson said, of "a rather mountainous Me." She was accustomed to finding herself among inferiors, and lorded it a little in her talk. She was also obliged, as a woman, to fight harder than others, first for an education and then for a career. All these influences marred her, in some degree; and those whom her criticisms wounded, made the most of the result. But though her most private diaries and letters have been set before the public, I do not see that anything has been produced which shows a petty or conceited disposition, while she has certainly left on record many noble disclaimers. A woman who could calmly set aside all the applauses she received for her wonderful conversation by pointing out to herself that this faculty "bespoke a second-rate mind," could not have had her head turned by vanity. At another time she wrote in her diary, "When I look at my papers, I feel as if I had never had a thought that was worthy the attention of any but myself; and 'tis only when, on talking with people, I find I tell them what they did not know, that my confidence at all returns."

In truth, she was not made of pure intellect; if that quality marks men (which I have never discovered), then she was essentially a woman. "Of all whom I have known," wrote one of her female friends, "she was the largest woman, and not a woman who wished to be a man." And one of her friends of the other sex wrote of her, "The *dry light* which Lord Bacon loved she never knew; her light was life, was love, was warm with sympathy, and a boundless energy of affection and hope." The self-devotion of her closing years brought no surprise to those who remembered how she had sacrificed her most cherished plans for the sake of educating her brothers; and how she had through all her life been ready to spend money and toil for those around her, when she had little money and no health. She gave to the community, also, the better boon of moral courage; it showed itself most conspicuously in the telling of unwelcome truth; but it was manifested also in heroic endurance, since she was, as Mr. Emerson has testified, "all her life the victim of disease and pain."

Her life thus did more for the intellectual enfranchisement of American women than was done by even her book on the subject, though that doubtless did much, exerting a permanent influence on many minds. No one has ever given so compact a formula for the requirements of woman. She claims for her sex "not only equal power with man, — for of that omnipotent nature will never permit her to be defrauded, — but a *chartered* power, too fully recognized to be abused." Never were there ten words which put the whole principle of impartial suffrage so plainly as these. And even where her statements are less clear, they always rest on wise reflection, not on any one-sided view. Thus, for instance, she showed better than most her faith in the eternal laws which make woman unlike man, — for she was ready to trust these laws instead of legislating to sustain them. She knew that there was no fear of woman's unsexing herself. "Nature has pointed out her ordinary sphere by the circumstances of her physical existence. She cannot wander far. . . . Achilles had long plied the distaff as a princess, yet at first sight of a sword, he seized it. So with woman, — one hour of love would teach her more of her proper relations than all your formulas."

After twenty months of happy life and labor in New York,

she sailed for Europe, thus fulfilling the design abandoned eleven years before, when her home duties demanded the sacrifice. She published in the "Tribune" (Aug. 1, 1846), a cordial and almost enthusiastic "Farewell to New York," thanking the great city for all it had been to her. She had found no more of evil there than elsewhere, she said, and more of sympathy, and there was at least nothing petty or provincial. Perhaps, after visiting Europe, she thought differently. New York does not at first seem provincial to a Bostonian, nor Paris to a New Yorker; but all great cities soon show themselves provincial, by their disproportioned self-estimate, their tiresome local gossip, and their inability to tolerate real independence. Still it was good for one, who lived her life as strongly as Margaret Fuller, to seek the largest atmosphere she could find, and win her own emancipation at last.

Over the tragic remainder of her life I shall pass but lightly, for I have preferred to reverse the proverb and be the historian of her times of peace alone. It is because they were not really her times of peace, but only her training for final action; besides, it was during those years that she was most misconstrued and maligned; and it is more interesting to dwell on this period than to add a garland where all men praise. Enough to say that in that later epoch all the undue self-culture of her earlier life was corrected, and all its self-devotion found a surer outlet. That "hour of love" of which she had written came to her, and all succeeding hours were enriched and ennobled. Throwing herself into the struggle for a nation's life, blending this great interest with the devotion due to her Italian husband, she lived a career that then seemed unexampled for an American woman, though our war has since afforded many parallels. During the siege of Rome, in 1848, the greater part of her time was passed in the hospital "*dei Pellegrini,*" which was put under her special direction. "The weather was intensely hot; her health was feeble and delicate; the dead and dying were around her in every stage of pain and horror; but she never shrank from the duty she had assumed." "I have seen," wrote the American consul, Mr. Cass, "the eyes of the dying, as she moved among them, extended on opposite beds, meet in commendation of her universal kindness."

She was married in Italy, during the year 1847, to Giovanni Angelo, Marquis Ossoli, — a man younger than herself, and of less intellectual culture, but of simple and noble nature. He had given up rank and station in the cause of the Roman Republic, while all the rest of his family had espoused the other side; and it was this bond of sympathy which first united them. Their child, Angelo Philip Eugene Ossoli, was born at Rieti, September 5th, 1848. After the fall of the republic it was necessary for them to leave Rome, and this fact, joined with her desire to print in America her history of the Italian struggle, formed the main reasons for their return to this country. They sailed from Leghorn, May 17th, 1850, in the barque Elizabeth, Captain Hasty.

Singular anticipations of danger seem to have hung over their departure. "Beware of the sea" had been a warning given Ossoli by a fortune-teller, in his youth, and he had never before been on board a ship. "Various omens have combined," wrote his wife, "to give me a dark feeling." "In case of mishap, however, I shall perish with my husband and child." Again she wrote, "It seems to me that my future on earth will soon close." "I have a vague expectation of some crisis, I know not what. But it has long seemed that in the year 1850 I should stand on a plateau in the ascent of life, where I should be allowed to pause for a while and take a more clear and commanding view than ever before. Yet my life proceeds as regularly as the fates of a Greek tragedy, and I can but accept the pages as they turn."

As they were leaving Florence at the last moment, letters arrived which would probably have led them to remain in Italy, had not all preparations been made. And on the very day of sailing, in Leghorn, Margaret lingered for a final hour on shore, almost unable to force herself to embark. It seemed as if there were conflicting currents in their destiny, which held them back while they urged them forward.

Their voyage was very long, and the same shadow still appeared to hang over them. The captain of the barque, in whom they had placed the greatest confidence, soon sickened and died of malignant small-pox, and was buried off Gibraltar. They sailed thence on June 9th. Two days after, the little Angelo was attacked with the same fearful disease, and only recovered after an illness that long seemed hopeless. On July 15th, they made the New Jersey coast at noon, and stood to the north-east, the weather being thick, and the wind south-east. The passengers packed their trunks, assured that they should be landed at New York the next morning. By nine o'clock the wind had risen to a gale, and this, with the current, swept them much farther to the north than was supposed. At two and a half, A. M., the mate in command took soundings, found twenty-one fathoms of water, pronounced all safe, and retired to his berth. One hour afterwards, the bark struck on Fire Island beach, just off Long Island.

The main and mizen masts were at once cut away, but the ship held by the bow, and careened towards the land, every wave sweeping over her, and carrying away every boat. She was heavily laden with marble and soon bilged. The passengers hastily left their berths and collected in the cabin, which was already half full of water. They braced themselves as well as they could, against the windward side. Little Angelo cried, the survivors say, until his mother sang him to sleep, while Ossoli quieted the rest with prayer.

The crew were at the forward end of the vessel; and when the wreck seemed ready to go to pieces, the second mate, Mr. Davis, came aft to the cabin with two sailors, and helped the passengers to a safer place. This transfer was made terribly dangerous by the breaking surf. The captain's wife, who went first, was once swept away, and was caught only by her hair. Little Angelo was carried in a canvas bag, hung round the neck of a sailor.

Passengers and crew were now crowded round the foremast, as the part likely to last longest. Here they remained for several hours. Men were seen collecting on the beach, but there was no life-boat. After a time, two sailors succeeded in reaching the shore, the one with a life-preserver, the other with a spar. Then Mr. Davis, the courageous mate, bound the captain's wife to a plank, and swam with her to the shore, where she arrived almost lifeless. The distance was less than a hundred yards, but the surf was fearful. Madame Ossoli was urged to attempt the passage as Mrs. Hasty had done, but steadily refused to be separated from her husband and child. Time was passing; the tide was out; the sea grew for the time a little calmer. It was impossible to built a raft, and there was but this one chance of escape before the tide returned. Still the husband and wife declined to be parted; and, seeing them resolute, the first mate ordered the crew to save themselves, and most of them leaped overboard. It was now past three o'clock; they had been there twelve hours. At length the tide turned, and the gale rose higher.

The after part of the vessel broke away, and the foremast shook with every wave. From this point the accounts vary, as is inevitable. It seems however to be agreed, that the few remaining sailors had again advised the Ossolis to leave the wreck; and that the steward had just taken little Angelo in his arms to try to bear him ashore, when a more powerful sea swept over, and the mast fell, carrying with it the deck, and all on board. Ossoli was seen to catch for a moment at the rigging, and then to sink. The last recorded glimpse of Margaret was when she was seated at the foot of the mast, in her white night-dress, with her hair fallen loose about her shoulders.

Their bodies were never found; but that of the little Angelo was cast upon the beach twenty minutes after, and was reverently buried among the sand-hills by the sailors, one of whom gave his chest for a coffin. The remains were afterwards transferred to Mount Auburn cemetery, near Boston, and there reinterred in presence of weeping kinsfolk, who had never looked upon the living beauty of the child.

It was the expressed opinion of one who visited the scene, a few days after, that seven resolute men could have saved all on board the "Elizabeth." The life-boat from Fire Island light-house, three miles off, was not brought to the beach till noon, and was not launched at all. For a time the journals were full of the tragedy that had taken away a life whose preciousness had not been fully felt till then. But now, looking through the vista of nearly twenty years, even this great grief appears softened by time. The very forebodings which preceded it seem now to sanctify that doom of a household, and take from its remembrance the sting. Three months before, in planning her departure, this wife and mother had thus unconsciously accepted her coming fate: "Safety is not to be secured by the wisest foresight. I shall embark more composedly in our merchant-ship, praying fervently, indeed, that it may not be my lot to lose my boy at sea, either by unsolaced illness or amid the howling waves; or, if so, that Ossoli, Angelo, and I may go together, and that the anguish may be brief." Her prayer was fulfilled.

The precious manuscript, for whose publication her friends and the friends of Italy had looked with eagerness, was lost in the shipwreck. Her remaining works were reprinted in Boston, a few years later, under the careful editorship of her brother Arthur; — that "Chaplain Fuller," who had been educated by her self-sacrifice, and who afterwards gained a place beside hers, in the heart of the nation, by his heroic death at Fredericksburg, during the late rebellion. Her biography has also been amply written by the friends whom she would most readily have selected for the task, Messrs. Emerson, Clarke, and Channing.

Since her day, American literature has greatly widened its base, but has raised its summit no higher. There is a multiplicity of books and magazines, and a vast increase of untrained literary activity. Yet, not only has she had no successor among women, but we still miss throughout our criticism her culture, her insight, her fearlessness, her generous sympathies, and her resolute purpose to apply the highest artistic standard to the facts of American life. It is this sense of loss that is her true epitaph. It was said to have been Fontenelle's funeral oration, when the most brilliant woman in France, having uttered after his death a witticism too delicate for her audience, exclaimed sadly, "Fontenelle! where are you?" And so every American author, who has a higher aim than to amuse, or a nobler test of merit than his publishers' account, must feel that something is wanting while Margaret Fuller's place remains unfilled.

GAIL HAMILTON—MISS DODGE.

BY FANNY FERN.

"Will I write a sketch of Gail Hamilton?" Will I touch off a Parrott gun? I thought, and will it "kick" if I do? However, I ventured to send the following missive:—

"My dear Miss Dodge, otherwise Gail Hamilton:—A book is in prospect. Many of our well-known literary people are to write for it. Its title is to be 'Eminent Women of the Time.' You and I are to be in it. I am to do *you*. Who is to serve me up, the gods only know. Will you be good enough to inform me at your earliest convenience, when and where you cut your first tooth, whether you had the measles before the mumps, or the mumps before the measles; also, any other interesting items about yourself.

"Writing about you will be a labor of love with me; for although a stranger to you, save through your writings, I rejoice every day in your existence.

"Please send an early answer.

"Yours, etc.,
"Fanny Fern."

In a few days I received the following reply:—

"My dear Mrs. Fern:—The coolness of you New Yorkers is astonishing. You are about to burn me at the stake, and will I have the goodness to send on shavings and dry wood by the next mail?

"Thank you, ma'am, I will.

"LIFE AND SUFFERINGS OF
"GAIL HAMILTON.

"WRITTEN BY ITSELF. AND WITH FORMER TRANSLATIONS DILIGENTLY COMPARED AND REVISED.

"To the best of my knowledge and belief, I was born in the 'New York Independent,' some time during the latter half of the present century, and before the 'Independent' had been annexed to the domains of Theodore, King of Abyssinia, against whom the great powers have just advanced an expedition. Simultaneously, or thereabouts, I was also born in the 'National Era.' So I must be twins. On that ground it has never been satisfactorily settled, whether I am myself or Mrs. Simpson, of Washington. If I am Mrs. Simpson, I am the wife of an officer, who, to his infinite regret, was not killed in the late unpleasantness, and am a lineal descendant of that Simple Simon, who once went a-fishing for to catch a whale, though all the water that he had was in his mother's pail. If I am not Launcelot, nor another, but only my own self, I am like Melchisedec, without father, without mother, without descent, and my enemies fear, also, I have no end of life. On one point commentators are agreed, — that I am not an 'Eminent Woman' of my time, and therefore have no part nor lot in your book. In fact I am

"Neither man nor woman,
I am neither brute nor human,
I'm a ghoul!

"And all that I ask is to be let alone. From the 'Independent' I graduated into the 'Congregationalist,' of blessed memory; and from the 'Era' I paddled over into the 'Atlantic.' I flourish in immortal vigor on the cover of 'Our

Young Folks,' and at sundry times, and in divers other manners and places, have, I fear, contributed to the deterioration of our youth. I sadly confess, also, that I am guilty of as many books as Mrs. Rogers had small children; but being written in love, and in the spirit of meekness, they are held in high esteem, especially of men. Whereunto I also add, like St. Paul, that which cometh upon me daily, the care of all the churches.

"Such, unhappy fellow-sufferer, is my thrilling story. If any one shall add unto these things, let him tremble lest I imprecate upon him all the plagues of the Apocalypse; and if any person shall dare saddle any other man or woman with the sins which I alone have perpetrated, I say prophetically to such saddler, 'Lord Angus, thou hast' ——

"Thanking you for your friendly words, and rejoicing, like King David in his great strait, that I am not to fall into the hands of *man*,

"I am very respectfully,

"GAIL HAMILTON.

"Respectfully, that is, if you respect my rights; but I shall have a lifelong quarrel even with you, if you spread before the public anything which I myself have not given to the public. I have really very strong opinions on that point; and, notwithstanding its commonness, I consider no crime more radically heinous than the violation of privacy. You must have suffered from it too severely yourself to be surprised at any abhorrence of it on my part. I most heartily wish you could find it in your plan to leave me out in the cold. Of course, if you judge from my writings that I am a woman, you can say what you please about that woman, that writer, and I have neither the wish nor the right to say you nay. So much of the woman as appears in an author's writings is public property by her own free will. All the rest belongs to her reserved rights. I pray you speak, if speak you must, so wisely as to make this clear. Launch thunderbolts, or sing songs, as you find fit; but read the preface of my first book, 'Country Living and Country Thinking,' and govern yourself accordingly; and I shall be, without any condition, and positively the last time,

"Yours very truly,

"Gail Hamilton."

Upon the receipt of this I wrote again, requesting permission to give the public the above characteristic epistle; which I told her was altogether too good to be buried in my desk; adding that, if she wanted me to behave prettily, she should not threaten me, as a threat always made me "balky;" that it was quite useless also, because I wished and intended to handle her as tenderly as would her own "mammy." I received a reply, of which this is a part: —

"Dear Fanny: — Do whatever you like with the letter; I don't care, and don't think you 'must handle me tenderly.' Say anything and everything you like; storm or shine within your 'sphere.' You don't like threats: strange, — but I will give you one more. If you do write a paper on me, and do not put in any of those impertinences which are so common in newspapers, but confine yourself to that which is common and lawful plunder, I shall not only put you a notch higher than the general run of people, but I shall keep a select corner for you in my private regard and gratitude, where you can come and take a nap by yourself, any time. Now 'balk' if you dare!

"Gail Hamilton."

This, dear reader, by way of preface. Now allow me to say that there are only two things in this world I am afraid of, —

one is a mouse, the other is a woman. My first impulse on being brought face to face with either, is to jump upon the nearest chair or table. Judge, then, how dear the public must seem, in my eyes, when, ignoring this my chronic terror, I boldly march up to the indomitable lady, whose name graces the head of this article, and attempt to sketch her: A lady, at whose mention stalwart men have been known to tremble, and hide in corners; who "keeps a private graveyard" for the burial of those whom she has mercilessly slain; who respects neither the spectacles of the judge, nor the surplice of the priest; who holds the mirror up to men's failings till they hate their wives merely because they belong to her sex; this lady who blushes not to own that she is "a Ghoul,"—who lately impaled the Rev. Dr. Todd on the point of her lance, and left him writhing without so much as pouring a drop of oil on to his wounds, or bathing his very soft head; this lady who keeps defiantly doing it, although she has been told that notwithstanding she has amassed several pennies, the fruits of these wicked promulgations, and deposited the same in banks for a rainy day, the sex whom she defies may, contrary to their usual custom in such cases, refuse even to nibble at *that* bait, and doom her to die, without a chance to sew on shirt-buttons, or "seat" a pair of trowsers.

One naturally inquires how such a female monster came to exist? In other and more elegant phrase, "*what did it?*" Was she, like Romulus and Remus, suckled by a she-wolf in her infancy? Were vipers her cherished toys in childhood? Was her youth defrauded of the usual sugar-plums that she keeps on making mouths at her fellow-creatures in this way? Or, what is still more important to ascertain, is there any way she could be pacified, or bought off, or "shut up," from this infernal attempt to set women upon their feet, and to trip men from off theirs.

To convince you how pertinent is my question, I will

quote in this connection a few of her most incendiary passages: —

"It costs a woman just as much to live as it does a man. If men were willing to practise the small economies that women practise, they could live at no greater expense."

"Man is a thief, and holds the bag, and if women do not like what they get, so much the better. They will be all the more willing to become household drudges."

"Make a man understand that he shall eat his dinner like a gentleman, or he shall have no dinner to eat. If he will be crabbed and gulp, let him go down into the coal-bin and have it out alone; but do not let him bring his Feejee-ism into the dining-room, to defile the presence of his wife, and corrupt the manners of his children."

"A woman should dress so as to be grateful to her husband's eye, I grant; nay, I enjoin; and he is under equally strong obligations to dress so as to be grateful to her eye. I have heard a woman say variety in dress is necessary in order that her husband may not be wearied. But does a man ever think of having several winter coats, or summer waistcoats, so that his wife may not weary of him? And if a man buys his clothes, and wears them according to his needs, why shall not a woman do the same? Is there any law or gospel forcing a woman to be pleasant to her husband, while the husband is left to do that which is right in his own eye? Or are the visual organs of a man so much more exquisitely arranged than those of a woman, that special adaptations must be made to them, while a woman may see whatever happens to be *à la mode?* Or has a man's dress intrinsically so much more beauty and character than a woman's that less pains need be taken to make it charming?"

"Take example from the toad," Gail says to her sisters; "swallow your dress, not precisely in the same sense, but as effectually. Overpower, subordinate your dress, till it shall be only a second cuticle, not to be distinguished from yourself, but a natural element of your universal harmony."

"Women's work is a round of endless detail. Little insignificant, provoking items, that she gets no credit for doing, but fatal discredit for leaving undone. Nobody notices that things are as they should be; but if things are not as they should be, it were better for her that a millstone were hanged about her neck."

"The best women, the brightest women, the noblest women, are the very ones to whom house-keeping is the most irksome. I do not mean house-keeping with well-trained servants; for that is general enough to admit 'a brother near the throne,' but that alas! is almost unknown in the world wherein I have lived; and a woman who is satisfied with the small economies, the small interests, the constant contemplation of small things which a household demands, is a very small sort of woman. I make the assertion both as an inference and as an observation. A noble discontent, not a peevish complaining, but a universal and a spontaneous protest, is a woman's safeguard against the deterioration which such a life threatens, and her proof of capacity, and her note of preparation for a higher. Such a woman does not do her work less well, but she rises superior to her work."

"Men do not believe, so much as they profess to, this menial gravitation. If they did they would never lecture women so much about it. *The very frenzy and frequency of their exhortations are suspicious.*"

"Some men dole out money to their wives as if it were a gift, a charity, something to which the latter have no right, but which they must receive as a favor, and for which they must be thankful. Now a man has no more right to his earnings than his wife has; they belong to her as much as to him. As a general rule the fate and fortunes of the family lie in her hands as much as in his. What absurdity to *pay* him his *wages* and to *give* her money to go shopping with!

"The money should be regularly and mechanically supplied to her as the dinner, exciting no more comment, and needing no more argument. Whether it is kept in her pocket or his may be of small moment; but as she does not lock up the dinner in the cupboard, and then stand at the door and dole it out to him by the plateful, but sets it on the table for him to help himself, so it is better and more pacific that he should deposit the money in an equally neutral and accessible locality. I portray to myself the flutter which such a proposition would raise in many marital bosoms. Would that they might be soothed. It is well known among farmers that hens will not eat so much if you set a measure of corn where they can pick whenever they choose, as they will if you only fling a handful now and then, and keep them continually half-starved. At the same time they will be in better condition. So, looking at the matter from the very lowest stand-point, a woman who has free access to the money will not be half so likely to lavish it, as the woman who is put off with scanty and infrequent sums.

"It is marvellous to see the insensibility with which men manage these delicate matters. It is impossible for a man to be too scrupulous, too chivalrous, too refined, in his bearing towards his wife. The very act of receiving money from him puts her in a position so equivocal that the utmost affection and attention should be brought into play to reassure her. Yet men will deliberately, in the presence of their wives, *to* their wives, groan over the cost of living. They do not mean extravagant purchases of silk and velvet which might be a wife's fault or thoughtlessness, and furnish an excuse for rebuke; but the butcher's bill, and the grocer's bill, and the joiner's bill. Man, when a woman is married, do you think she loses all personal feeling? Do you think your glum look over the expenses of house-keeping is a fulfilment of your promise to love and cherish? Does it bring sunshine, and lighten toil, and bless her with knightly grace? Do you not know that it is only a way of regretting that you married her? *You* go out to your shop, or sit down to your newspaper, and forget all about it. She sits down to her sewing, or stands over her cooking-stove, and meditates upon it with indescribable pain. These very men, who complain because it costs so much to live, will lose by bad debts more than their wives spend; they will, by sheer negligence, by a selfish reluctance to present a bill to a disagreeable person, by a cowardly fear lest insisting on what is due should alienate a customer,—by indorsing a note, or lending money, through mere want of courage to say No, — lose money enough to foot up a dozen bills. They waste money in cigars; in sending packages by express, rather than have the trouble to take them themselves; in buying luxuries which they were better without. A man is persistently, perversely, and with malice aforethought, extravagant. He is so, in spite of admonition and remonstrance. Where his personal comfort or interest is concerned, he scorns a sacrifice. He laughs at the suggestion that such a little thing makes any difference one way or another."

This is a long extract from Miss Hamilton, but every word is solid gold, and should be printed and framed and hung up in every husband's —— well, wheresoever he keeps his cigars, so that he would be *sure* to see it. I myself have heard a man ask a wife who had borne them twelve children, and who was an economical, painstaking, thrifty house-keeper, "What she *did* with the *last* dollar he gave her?" True, men do not like to see this unpleasant reflection of themselves in our author's glass; but that is no reason why she should smash it. And as she once remarked to a married lady, who told her that her husband was greatly incensed at her mention of such things: "Well, — let him rasp, — he is no husband of mine!"

At this safe distance, this Parrott gun of a woman explodes the following, for which I confess a hearty relish: —

"A father goes into the nursery, and has a merry romp with his children; but when he is tired, or they take too many liberties, he goes out, and thinks his children very charming. When papa comes in, the children are often hurried out of sight and sound, for they will 'disturb papa.' This kind woman shuts them up carefully within her own precincts. They may overrun her without stint. They may climb her chair, pull her work about, upset her basket, scratch the bureau, cut the sofa, turn to her for healing in every little heartache; but no matter. They are kept from 'disturbing papa!' I am amazed at the folly of women! Kept from disturbing papa! Rather hound them on! Put the crying baby in his arms the moment he enters the house, and be sure to run away at once beyond reach, or, with true masculine ingenuity, he will be sure at the end of five minutes to find some pretext for delivering the young orator back into your care. *He ought to experience their obviousness, their inconvenience, their distraction. Let him come into close contact with his children, and see what they are, and what they do, and he will have far more just ideas of the whole subject than if he stands far off, and from old theories on the one side, and ten minutes of clean apron and bright faces on the other, pronounces his euphonious generalizations. His children will elicit as much love and interest, together with a great deal more knowledge, and a great deal less silly, mannish sentimentalism.*"

I italicize the last sentence, as one of the choicest and most sensible verses in Miss Gail's new gospel. I really think I couldn't have done better myself!

Read this, too: —

"Men often have too much confidence in their measuring-lines. They fancy they have fathomed a soul's depths when they have but sounded its shallows. They think they have circumnavigated the globe, when they have only paddled in a cove. They trim their sails for other seas, leaving the priceless gems of their own undiscovered. Many a wife is wearied and neglected into moral shabbiness, who, rightly entreated, would have walked sister and wife of the gods."

As our author's books are for sale, perhaps I should remember the fact, and curb my desire to copy all her very just and very intrepid sayings; but here is one which every husband should pin into the crown of his hat: —

"Men, — you to whose keeping a woman's heart is entrusted, — can you heed this simple prayer, Love me, and *tell me so sometimes?*"

Our author has probably heard husbands reply to this: "Why, *that* is of course understood; it is childish to wish or expect such a thing put into words." Now, without stopping to discuss the "childishness" of it, if it makes a wife happier, is it wise, or best, for a husband to overlook that fact? And sure I am, many a wife loses all heart for her monotonous round of duties for the want of it; beside, when men the world over have promulgated the fact that women are but "grown-up children," where's the harm of being "childish?"

Does not Gail Hamilton see anything commendable, or virtuous, or honorable, or manly in men? is the question some times propounded by them; after which follows this slung-shot: "She must have been very unfortunate in her selection of male acquaintances."

Leaving this last unworthy slur in the kennel where it belongs, listen to the following from the lady in question: —

"Every-day occurrences reveal in men traits of disinterestedness, consideration, all Christian virtues and graces. My heart misgives me when I think of it all, — their loving kindness, their forbearance, their unstinted service, their integrity, and of the not sufficiently unfrequent instances in which women, by fretfulness, folly, or selfishness, irritate and alienate the noble heart which they ought to prize above rubies. Considering the few good husbands there are in the world, and how many good women there are, who would have been to them a crown of glory had the coronation been effected, but who instead are losing all their pure gems down the dark, unfathomed caves of some bad man's heart; considering this, I account that woman to whom has been allotted a *good* husband, and who can do no better than to spoil him and his happiness by her misbehavior, guilty, if not of the unpardonable sin, at least of unpardonable stupidity. I could make out a long list of charges against women, and of excellences to be set down to the credit of men. But women have been stoned to death, or at least to coma, with charges already; *and when you would extricate a wagon from a slough, you put your shoulder first and heaviest to the wheel that is the deepest in the mud; especially if the other wheel would hardly be in at all unless this one had pulled it in!*"

There — after this who shall speak? Not I. It is a fitting finale to the whole subject. Gail Hamilton needs no lawyer when her case appears in court. But there may exist benighted human beings who have not read her summings up;

or have declined reading them, because it is so much easier to decide upon a question when you only look at *one* side of it.

For their benefit I have culled a few nettles, whose wholesome pricking may let out some bad blood, and prepare for them a more healthful mental and moral condition. There is no necessity for thanks on their part, as the work has really been its own reward.

Now, if my readers suppose that there is "no fun" in our author, or that she looks only at the shady side of every subject, let them read the following extract from her "Gala-Days": —

"I don't know how it is, but in all the novels that I have read, the heroines always have delicate, spotless, exquisite gloves, which are continually lying about in the garden paths, and which lovers are constantly picking up, and pressing to their hearts and lips, and treasuring in little golden boxes or something, and saying how like that soft glove, pure and sweet, is to the beloved owner; and it is all very pretty, — but I cannot think how they manage it. I am sure I should be very sorry to have my lovers go about picking up my gloves. I don't have them a week before they change color; the thumb gapes at the base, the little finger rips away from the next one, and they all burst out at the ends; a stitch drops in the back, and slides down to the wrist before you know it is started. You can mend, to be sure, but for every darn you've twenty holes. I admire a dainty glove as much as any one; I look with enthusiasm not unmingled with despair, at these gloves of romance; but such things do not depend entirely upon taste, as male writers seem to think. A pair of gloves cost a dollar and a half, or two dollars, and when you have them, your lovers do not find them in the summer-house. Why not? Because they are lying snugly wrapped in oiled silk in the upper bureau-drawer, only to be taken out on great occasions. You would as soon think of wearing Victoria's crown for a head-dress as those gloves on a picnic. So it happens that the gloves your lovers find will be sure to be Lisle thread, and dingy and battered at that; for how can you pluck flowers, and pull vines, and tear away mosses, without getting them dingy and battered? And the most fastidious lover in the world cannot expect you to buy a new pair every time. For me, I keep my gloves as long as the backs hold together, and go around for forty-five weeks of the fifty-two with my hands clenched into fists to cover omissions."

And now you will naturally say to me, — This is all very well; but tell us something about *her* personally. Where does she live; and how? Is she single or wedded? Is she tall or short? Plain or pretty? Has she made money as well as made mouths? In short, let us have a little gossip. That's what we are after.

Don't I know it? I should think I had been laid on the gridiron times enough myself to understand your appetite. Well — here goes. "Gail Hamilton's" real name is Mary Abigail Dodge. Her birthplace is in Hamilton, Massachusetts. She is unmarried, a Calvinist, and an authoress from choice. Her father was a farmer. Her mother produced Gail Hamilton; that is sufficient as far as she is concerned. She had a brother, who Mrs. Grundy declares is the "Halicarnassus" mentioned in her books, and whom the men she has flagellated in her writings call "poor devil!" supposing him to be her *husband!*

She was brought up as New England girls are generally brought up in the country —, simply, healthfully, purely; with plenty of fences for gymnastics; with plenty of berries, and birds, and flowers, and mosses, and clover-blossoms, and fruit, in the sweet, odorous summers; with plenty of romping companions, not subjects for early tombstones and obituary notices, but with broad chests, sun-kissed faces, and nimble limbs and tongues, — children who behaved naturally for their age; who twitched away books and balls from their owners, and pouted, and sometimes struck, and often got mad, and strutted when they wore fine clothes, and told lies, — "real whoppers,"— and took the biggest half of the apple, and were generally aggravating, as exuberant, healthy childhood always is.

Then little Mary had other companions less aggressive in the birds, the bees, and the grasshoppers. She went Maying, too, on May mornings, as every true-born New England child should, as I myself have done, whether the sky were blue or black; whether she shivered or was warm in a white gown; whether the May-flowers were in blossom for May-day wreaths, or the snow-flakes were coming down instead. She had chickens, too, and when they first came, she fed them with soaked and sweetened cracker; later, she made fricassees of them, and omelets of their eggs. She had three cats; one, named Molly after herself; another, a hideous, saffron-colored, forlorn, little wretch, that was abandoned by an Irish family, and which she felicitously baptized Rory O'More. This cat one day crept into the oven. Mary, ignorant of the fact, shut the door, wishing to retain the heat. Hearing a stifled "mew," she opened it, and out flew the cat and plunged through the house outside into the nearest snow-bank, from whence she emerged, with true Irish elasticity, right-end up, and as good as new. The third cat little Mary housed was a perfect savage; her mistress never being able to catch sight of her save in her fierce and lightning-like transits through the house. These cats fought each other, scratched, and made the fur fly, stole chickens, and gave that zest and excitement to her childish days which might well astonish our city-prisoned urchins, — shut up with a cross French nurse, to keep their silk dresses clean, in a nursery, from whose windows the only view is a dead brick wall.

Then she rode to mill in an old wagon, with mammoth wheels, painted green outside and drab within, with a movable seat, on which was placed a buffalo-robe for a cushion. After little Mary had taken her seat, the wagon was backed up to the gate, the "tailboard" let down, and huge bags of tow-cloth filled with shelled corn were placed in the cart to be ground, then transformed into Johnny-cakes, brown bread, and Indian pudding. As they were put beside her, this imaginative little girl fancied that they might resemble those of Joseph's brethren, mentioned in the Bible, which were carried down into Egypt, with plenty of room in every sack's mouth for a silver cup and corn-money.

When all these bags were safely deposited in the mill, and little Mary and the old horse started for home, who happier than she? The rough gates, which opened to let them through, seemed to turn on golden hinges. Her quick eye noted the branches of feathery fern, the panting cows, standing knee-deep in the cool water, and even the stagnant pool which she knew would by and by blossom forth with pure white lilies; while the yellow blossoms of the barberry hedge would ripen to crimson clusters in the crisp days of the coming autumn; this barberry bush, around which she joined hands with her little romping companions, and sang: —

"As we go round the barberry bush,
The barberry, barberry, barberry bush;
As we go round the barberry bush,
So early in the morning;
This is the way we wash our clothes,
We wash, we wash, we wash our clothes;
This is the way we wash our clothes,
So early in the morning.

Then Mary and her companions would imitate the washing of clothes and the ironing, and woe to her who should first lose breath in doing it.

Then there were the lovely New England country Sundays, heralded by the song of birds, and odor of blossoms, and creeping away of mist from valley and mountain, as the warm sun gladdened every living thing. Every New Englander knows what that is without farther preface.

Sundays to little Mary, under these conditions, were not prisons or chains. They were best clothes, with a pleasant, clovery smell in them when they were taken out of the drawer to be worn. Sunday was baked beans, and a big, red Bible with the tower of Babel in it full of little bells, and a lovely walk two miles through a lane full of sweetness and bird-singing; over the bars, through ten acres, over another pair of bars, through a meadow, over another pair of bars, by a hill, over a wall, through another meadow, through the woods, over the ridge, by Black Pond, over a fence, across a railroad, over another fence, through a pasture, through the long woods, through another gate, out upon the high road at last.

Then, as our little girl was no diseased, embryo saint, during the long service, which she could not understand, she looked at the people and the fine bonnets around her, and never was she willing to stay at home, be the service ever so long. Then she went to Sunday school, where the children on coming out used to say, "I think your ribbon is prettier than mine." "Is your veil like Susy's?" "Why don't you wear your blue dress to meeting?" "Do you know Joe got fourteen perch yesterday?" And she read the library-books and ate gingerbread in the interim, and then came the afternoon service, and then the long, pleasant ride home, and then the catechism in the evening, and the unfailing big red

Bible. And this is the brilliant tribute of her maturer years to the New England, much-reviled Sabbaths: —

"O Puritan Sabbaths! doubtless you were sometimes stormy without and stormy within; but, looking back upon you from afar, I see no clouds, no snow, but perpetual sunshine and blue sky, and ever eager interest and delight; wild roses blooming under the old stone wall; wild bees humming among the blackberry bushes; tremulous, sweet columbines skirting the vocal woods; wild geraniums startling their shadowy depths; and I hear now the rustle of dry leaves, bravely stirred by childish feet, just as they used to rustle in the October afternoons of long ago. Sweet Puritan Sabbaths! breathe upon a restless world your calm, still breath, and keep us from the evil!"

To-day, Gail Hamilton is not only independent in thought and expression, but I am happy to say, in *pocket*. She is also a living, breathing, brilliant refutation of the absurd notion that a woman with brains must necessarily be ignorant of, or disdain, the every-day domestic virtues. When she writes of house-keeping and kindred matters, she knows what she is talking about. All the New England virtues of thrift, executiveness, thoroughness — in short, "*faculty*" — are exemplified in her daily practice. Well may there be sunshine inside her house; well may the flowers in her garden bloom, and the fruits ripen, skilfully tended by *such* fingers!

One piece of advice before I close I will volunteer to the male sex who "desire to keep clear of a woman like that." Let them consider it a heaven-sent impulse; as several rash gentlemen, who, to my personal knowledge, disregarded it, have with base ingratitude towards the tame of her species, who fully endorsed their seraphic qualities, not only upon personal acquaintance with her, forgiven her for smiting them on one cheek, but voluntarily and lovingly have turned the other. Forewarned—forearmed!

Eng^d by G.E. Perine & Co N.Y.

MRS. E. BARRETT BROWNING.

ELIZABETH BARRETT BROWNING.

BY EDWARD Y. HINCKS.

THERE has probably lived within the past century no woman whose genius, character, and position are more full of interest than Mrs. Browning's. She was not only far above all the female poets of her age, but ranked with the first poets. She was not only a great poet, but a greater woman. She loved and honored art, but she loved and honored humanity more. Born and reared in England, her best affections were given to Italy, and her warmest friends and most enthusiastic admirers are found in America. And when to her rare personal endowments is added the fact that she was the wife of a still greater poet than herself, what is needed to make her the most remarkable woman of this, perhaps of any, age?

And, as there is no woman in whose life and character we may naturally take a greater interest, so there is none whom we have better facilities of knowing. Of the ordinary materials out of which biographies are made, her life indeed furnishes few. Its external incidents were not many nor marked. The details of her family life have been very properly kept from the public. The publication of her letters has been deferred until after her husband's death. But what Mrs. Browning thought, felt, and was, is revealed with almost unexampled clearness in her writings. With all her genius she possessed in full measure the artlessness of her sex. Her theory of poetry, too, was that it was but the expression of the poet's inner nature. Hence, as might be expected, her poems are but transparent media for the revelation of herself. Her queenly soul shines through them as wine through a crystal vase. Her friendships, her love, her grief, her patriotism, her philanthropy, her religion—all are in them simply and unaffectedly revealed to us. To obtain a correct conception of Mrs. Browning, therefore, we must study her character as revealed in her poems, aided, of course, by the light which our scanty knowledge of the events of her outward life will afford. As the result of our study we shall find that whatever fault we may be compelled to find with the artist, we cannot withhold our entire and hearty admiration for the character of the woman. We shall find that her genius, far from marring, exalted and ennobled her womanhood. We shall feel that the poet was greater than her poems.

Elizabeth Barrett Barrett was born in London, in 1809. Her father was a private gentleman in opulent circumstances. Her early life was passed partly in London, partly in the county of Herefordshire, in sight of the Malvern Hills. One of her minor poems, "The Lost Bower," describes with her peculiar power of graphic picturing the scenery surrounding her early home.

"Green the land is where my daily
Steps in jocund childhood played,
Dimpled close with hill and valley,
Dappled very close with shade;
Summer snow of apple blossoms running up from glade to glade.

"Far out, kindled by each other,
Shining hills on hills arise,
Close as brother leans to brother,
When they press beneath the eyes
Of some father praying blessings
From the gifts of Paradise."

The whole poem, which is one of its author's simplest and sweetest, is well worthy of study for its autobiographical interest. It gives us the picture of a dreamy and thoughtful, but not morbid child, loving to ramble in the wild woods, which her fancy peopled with the heroes and heroines of old.

Mrs. Browning was a child of remarkable precocity. She wrote verses at ten, and appeared in print at the age of fifteen. In the dedication to her father of the edition of her poems which appeared in 1844, she pleasantly speaks "of the time far off when I was a child and wrote verses, and when I dedicated them to you who were my public and my critic." This childish precocity was not an indication of early ripening genius. Her powers matured slowly. She wrote very crudely when past thirty. She never attained her full maturity. Miss Barrett's education was such as a woman rarely receives. She was taught in classics, philosophy, and science. Her acquaintance with Greek literature was very extensive. It embraced, not only the great classic authors, but also many of the fathers, and the Greek Christian poets. She studied Greek under the instruction of her blind friend, the Rev. Hugh Stuart Boyd, to whom she afterward dedicated the poem entitled "The Wine of Cyprus," in which she thus pleasantly alludes to the hours they had spent together:—

"And I think of those long mornings
  Which my thought goes far to seek,
When, betwixt the folio's turnings,
  Solemn flowed the rhythmic Greek.
Past the pane the mountain spreading
  Swept the sheep-bell's tinkling noise,
While a girlish voice was reading,
  Somewhat low for αιs and οιs."

And then she goes on to give in a word or two, with that happy facility in hitting off the leading features of a great genius in a single phrase, which is one of her most noticeable characteristics, the impression made upon teacher and pupil by each author as they read.

But she was not merely a passive recipient of knowledge;

"For we sometimes gently wrangled,
Very gently, be it said,
Since our thoughts were disentangled
By no breaking of the thread!
And I charged you with extortions
On the nobler fames of old;
Ay, and sometimes thought your Porsons
Stained the purple they would fold."

But it may be doubted whether Mrs. Browning was a thorough and scientific student of the Greek language. If she had been so, the effect of such study would have been to correct her taste, and render much of her language less obscure. Indeed, in spite of her wide reading, one can but form the impression from perusing her writings that she did not receive a thorough and systematic mental training. Had she been able to receive the drill of the grammar school and university she might have used her extraordinary natural gifts to far greater advantage.

Miss Barrett's first published volume was a small book entitled "An Essay upon Mind and other Poems," published in 1826. The "Essay on Mind" was an ambitious and immature production, in heroic verse, which the author omitted from the collection of her poems which she afterward made, and which is in consequence rarely to be found. A critic in the "Edinburgh Review" speaks of it as neither possessing much intrinsic merit nor giving great promise of originality, but as "remarkable for the precocious audacity with which it deals with the greatest names in literature and science."

In 1833 she published a translation of the "Prometheus Bound" of Æschylus. This translation was severely criticised at the time of its publication, and Miss Barrett herself was so dissatisfied with it that she executed an entirely new version, which was included in a subsequent collection of her poems.

In 1835 she formed an acquaintance with Mary Russell Mitford, which soon ripened into intimacy. To this intimacy the public are indebted for Mrs. Browning's charming little poem, addressed "To Flush, my Dog" (Flush was a gift from Miss Mitford), and for the oft-quoted description of Miss Barrett as a young lady in her friend's "Recollections of a Literary Life."

This sketch is so graphic, and gives so much information not elsewhere to be found, that we must quote from it a few extracts.

Miss Mitford thus describes her friend as she appeared at the age of twenty-six: —

> "Of a slight, delicate figure, with a shower of dark curls falling on either side of a most expressive face, large, tender eyes, richly fringed by dark eyelashes, a smile like a sunbeam, and such a look of youthfulness that I had some difficulty in persuading a friend that the translatress of the 'Prometheus' of Æschylus, the authoress of the 'Essay on Mind,' was old enough to be introduced into company."

The next year Mrs. Browning met with that unfortunate accident which, with the yet sadder casualty of which it was the indistinct occasion, cast a dark shadow over her life. A blood-vessel was ruptured in one of her lungs. A milder climate being deemed necessary for her recovery, she went, in company with her eldest and favorite brother, to Torquay. There she remained nearly a year, and was rapidly gaining in vigor, when that sad event occurred which nearly killed her by its shock, and saddened much of her future life. Her brother was drowned while on a sailing excursion, within sight of the windows of the house in which she lived. Even his body was never found.

"This tragedy," writes her friend, "nearly killed Elizabeth Barrett. She was utterly prostrated by the horror and the grief, and by a natural but most unjust feeling that she had been in some sort the cause of this great misery. . . . . She told me herself that, during the whole winter, the sounds of the waves rang in her ears like the moans of one dying." The depth of her anguish may be imagined from the fact that, as another friend tells us, when about to be married ten years after, she exacted from her husband a promise never to refer to her brother's death. So prostrated in body was she by this calamity that a year elapsed before she could be removed by slow stages to her father's house in London. There she lived for seven years, confined to a darkened room, at times so feeble that life seemed almost extinct, but struggling against debility and suffering with almost unexampled heroism. There she continued her studies, having a Plato bound like a novel to deceive her physician, who feared that mental application would react injuriously upon her enfeebled frame. There she wrote, while lying on a couch, unable to sit erect, the poem of "Lady Geraldine's Courtship" in twelve hours, in order that the volume of her poems to be published in this country might be completed in season to catch the steamer. From that sick chamber went forth poems sufficient in quantity to be the result of industrious application on the part of one in good health. And though these poems bear marks of the peculiar circumstances in which they were written, in a somewhat morbid tone, they show no trace of debility in thought or imagination. Mrs. Browning has written no "In Memoriam" to tell in melodious notes the story of her grief. No direct allusion to it is made, if we mistake not, in her poems. She does not, like most of the poets of her sex, brood plaintively over her woes, and sing over and over again, in slightly altered form, the melancholy strain, "I am bereft, and life is dark." Her nature was too strong thus to allow grief to take possession of it. Sorrow deepened and elevated her nature, instead of mastering it. There was in her none of the egotism of grief. She threw her whole soul with redoubled ardor into her high vocation, finding consolation where great souls have always found it — in noble work. And yet, though there is not the least trace in her writings of an egotistical brooding over grief, there is abundant evidence in them of the deep suffering through which she passed. It would be difficult to find a nobler expression of great sorrow, bravely endured, than is afforded by her sonnets on "Comfort," "Substitution," "Bereavement," and "Consolation." These simple but majestic records of her grief are far more affecting, because they are far less labored and artistic, and seem to come more directly from the heart, than the mournful beauty of the "In Memoriam."

In 1838 Mrs. Browning published "The Seraphim and other Poems," and in 1844 a collection of her Poems in two volumes, including the "Drama of Exile." The reception with which these poems met in England was, though not highly flattering, certainly very far from discouraging. Their faults were severely but not unjustly criticised, and full recognition was given to their merits. The "Quarterly Review" for 1840 concludes an article in which are criticised the works of nine female poets, who are now nearly or quite all forgotten, except Mrs. Browning, in these words: "In a word, we consider Miss Barrett to be a woman of undoubted genius and most unusual learning, but that she has indulged her inclination for themes of sublime mystery, not certainly without great power, yet at the expense of that clearness, truth, and proportion which are essential to beauty.

At about this time Leigh Hunt speaks of her in the following language: —

"Miss Barrett, whom we take to be the most imaginative poetess that has appeared in England, perhaps in Europe, and who will grow to great eminence if the fineness of her vein can but outgrow a certain morbidity."

In our own country Mr. E. P. Whipple wrote, that, —

"Probably the greatest female poet that England has ever produced, and one of the most unreadable, is Elizabeth B. Barrett. In the works of no woman have we ever observed so much grandeur of imagination, disguised as it is in an elaborately infelicitous style. She has a large heart and a large brain, but many of her thoughts are hooded eagles."

It seems to us that these critics dealt very justly with Mrs. Browning. The faults of the two largest poems which she had published were glaring and extremely offensive to a correct taste. "The Seraphim" is a dialogue between two angels who are witnessing the crucifixion, and giving utterance to their emotion as they gaze upon the awful spectacle.

The very theme of the poem is enough to show that it must be a failure. The task of depicting the feelings which that stupendous sacrifice awakened in seraphic souls, is one which no one of our race should attempt. What do we know of the workings of angelic natures? If, as Mrs. Browning so often tells us, truth is an essential quality of poetry, how can we look for poetry where there is no basis on which truth can rest? A poet of imperial imagination, like Milton or Dante, may successfully introduce angels as actors in an epic poem, where the interest centres in what is done, and in which there is a groundwork of human action, and the most prominent actors are men; but is not this far different from attempting to depict *dramatically* the working of angelic natures?

As might naturally be expected, therefore, the "Seraphim" is a failure. It is extravagant, mystical, and, in some places, very unpleasant, by reason of its efforts to depict what should be forever left unattempted by human pencil.

To speak plainly, the freedom with which Mrs. Browning in these earlier poems attempts to describe the Deity is exceedingly shocking to a reverent soul. Of course this freedom is merely an error of taste, and is rather the attempt of a vivid faith and ardent love to realize their object, than of a self-confident spirit to win praises for itself by vividly setting forth the glories of its Maker; but good taste and a true reverence alike protest against it.

The "Drama of Exile" shows greater imaginative power and deals with a more approachable subject than the "Seraphim," but is hardly less open to criticism. It is based upon the expulsion of Adam and Eve from the garden of Eden. The following is an outline of its plot: The poem opens with an exulting soliloquy by Lucifer, which is interrupted by the entrance of Gabriel. In the colloquy which ensues between them the fallen angel exults over his success, and Gabriel meets his taunts with pitying scorn, and bids him depart and "leave earth to God." The scene then changes. Adam and Eve appear in the distance, flying across the glare made by the flaming sword, and are followed in their flight by a lamentation and farewell, chanted by a chorus of Eden spirits; the spirits of the trees, the rivers, the birds and the flowers each in turn taking up the song. The scene now changes to the outer extremity of the light cast by the flaming sword. There Adam and Eve stand and look forward into the gloom. Eve, in an agony of remorse, throws herself upon the ground, and begs her husband to spurn her, his seducer, from him forever. Adam raises and comforts her, and assures her of his forgiveness and continued love. A chorus of invisible angels, who had ministered to their pleasure in Eden, then chant the exiles a "faint and tender" farewell. Lucifer now appears upon the scene, and taunts his victims upon their ruin, until he is interrupted and driven away by a lament coming from his lost love, the morning star.

In the next scene Adam and Eve have advanced farther into a wild, open country. As they stand lamenting their fate, they are confronted by twelve shadowy creatures, which are the projections of the signs of the Zodiac, — the ram, the bull, the crab, the scorpion, etc. To let the poet state her own obscure conception: —

> "Not a star pricketh the flat gloom of heaven;
> But girdling close our nether wilderness,
> The zodiac figures of the earth loom slow,
> Drawn out as suiteth with the place and time
> In twelve colossal shapes instead of stars."

Their attention is drawn from these by two spirits, of whom one calls itself "the spirit of the harmless earth," and the other "the spirit of the harmless beasts," who mourn the ruin that man has brought upon them, and, joined and assisted by Lucifer, revile the wretched pair for the curse they have brought upon God's fair creation. When they have driven Adam and Eve to a frenzy of agony, Christ appears, rebukes the earth-spirits and commands them to become man's comforters and ministers, foretells the redemption which He will accomplish for the race, and bids our first parents, —

> "In which hope move on,
> First sinners and first mourners; love and live,
> Doing both nobly because lowlily."

The earth-spirits promise obedience and disappear. A chorus of angels then chants the promise of immortal life to mortals, and thus the drama ends.

We have given the plot of the "Drama of Exile" at some length, that the reader may judge for himself of the justice of our criticism when we say that, as a whole, the poem is strained, extravagant, and unequal to its theme.

There are some subjects which are set apart for the great creative intellects of the race, and with which it is useless for any others of lesser grasp, however brilliant their powers may be within their own range, to attempt to grapple. Anything short of complete success in their treatment is failure. Their successful handling requires a sustained and steady elevation of imagination, as well as an occasional lofty flight; it requires also the power of construction and arrangement, as well as of originating single great conceptions. Neither of these was given to Mrs. Browning. Her imagination could soar very high, but it could not, like Milton's, float tranquilly, supported by its strong pinion, in the clear upper air. Her genius seemed rather to emit brilliant flashes than to shed a steady radiance. The "Drama of Exile" contains many noble passages. Some of its conceptions give evidence of great originality and power. But passages in a poem written upon such a subject, which excite a reader's laughter by their extravagance, are fatal to its claims to be considered a great work of the imagination. Homer sometimes nods, but he never rants. It has been the unanimous voice of criticism, and cannot fail to be the opinion of every candid and intelligent reader, that in the "Drama of Exile" Mrs. Browning very often and very laughably rants.

But those seven years of solitude and illness bore other and better fruit than the "Drama of Exile." Many of those beautiful short poems, on which Mrs. Browning's claims to our gratitude chiefly rest, are the fruit of that stern and protracted contest with extreme physical weakness and mental suffering. Then was written "Lady Isobel's Child;" a poem which combines more of Mrs. Browning's peculiar powers, — her tenderness, her clear vision into the spiritual world, her ability to describe with wonderful vividness the appearances of nature, and her skill in using the pictures which she paints to heighten emotional effect, — with fewer faults than almost any of her other poems. Then, also, was written "Bertha in the Lane," — the simplest and sweetest of her poems; and the "Rime of the Duchess May," — a poem whose vigor of movement and graphic picturing no woman has equalled and few men have surpassed.

Then was written the "Cry of the Children," which will rank with those few noble poems, in which genius utters, in its own thrilling tones, the cry of a humble and neglected class for relief.

Then was written "The Dead Pan," — a poem full of noble truth as well as beauty; a poem which gladly bids farewell to the old classic fables in which beauty was once enshrined, because a higher beauty is found in the truth and spiritual illumination of to-day.

What nobler creed for a poet than this: —

> "What is true and just and honest,
> What is lovely, what is pure, —
> All of praise that hath admonished
> All of virtue, shall endure;
> These are themes for poets' uses,
> Stirring nobler than the muses,
> Ere Pan was dead."

We cannot find a more suitable place than this in which to speak of a prose work of Mrs. Browning's, published after her death, but originally printed in the "London Athenæum" in 1842, entitled "Essays on the Greek Christian Poets and the English Poets." It is written in a terse and vigorous style, disfigured here and there by a harsh or unpleasant figure or strained metaphor, but possessing sufficient merit to show that their author might have attained a high rank as a prose writer. Their most noticeable merit is a certain felicity in putting subtle spiritual thought into language. They are of especial interest to the student of Mrs. Browning's poetry, as giving, in connection with her judgment upon most English poets, her theory of the true nature of the poetic art. This theory, which is closely allied to the theory of the realists in painting, may be stated as follows: There is poetry wherever God is and the works of God are. There is as true poetry in man and whatever pertains to man, of whatsoever grade of society or degree of cultivation, as in the grandest objects of nature. The poet must delineate what he sees and express what he feels.

As Mrs. Browning herself afterward finely says in "Aurora Leigh": —

"Never flinch,
But still, unscrupulously epic, catch
Upon the burning lava of a song,
The full-veined, heaving, double-breasted age,
That when the next shall come the men of that
May touch the impress with reverent hand and say,
Behold, — behold the paps we all have sucked.
. . . .
This is living art,
Which thus presents and thus records true life."

And again, with reference to that part of the poet's office which has to do with the expression of his inner nature, she says: —

"The artist's part is both to be and do,
Transfixing with a special, central power
The flat experience of the common man,
And turning outward with a sudden wrench,
Half agony, half ecstasy, the thing
He feels the inmost."

Describe what you see and tell what you feel, is, then, the sum of Mrs. Browning's poetic creed. We can but think that this theory of the poetic art leaves out of view one of its most important features, which is the elaborating thoughts and conceptions into symmetrical form; using them as the plastic material out of which to construct a polished, perfect work of art. The old Greek conception is right: the poet is the maker, not the reflector. We have a right to demand more of the poet than a faithful record of the impressions made upon any or all of his sensibilities. We have a right to demand melody, clearness, symmetry of design, proper joining of parts, — all the results of the severest taste guided by unremitting diligence. A poem should not be an incoherent and rugged rhapsody; it should join to all the freshness of nature the smoothness of the highest art.

In 1846 Mrs. Browning left her sick-room (she was literally assisted from her couch) to become the wife of Robert Browning. We have not the space to enter into any discussion of Mr. Browning's rank as a poet. It is sufficient for our purpose to say that, though his poems find a much narrower circle of readers than those of his wife, the most cultivated and appreciative critics pronounce them to be of a higher order of merit than hers, and in many of the rarer and finer qualities of poetry superior to the works of any living poet. It is enough for those who have learned to love Mrs. Browning through her writings to know that those who have known and loved both husband and wife pronounce the husband not unworthy in nobility of soul as well as in depth of intellect of such a wife. And not to be unworthy of such a woman's love is indeed to be great!

In a series of sonnets, slightly disguised by their title, "Sonnets from the Portuguese," written to her husband before their marriage, she has poured out the wealth of her love, and at the same time displayed the loftiness and delicacy of her nature. Whoever wishes to know Mrs. Browning should study carefully these beautiful and artless poems, which tell the most sacred feelings of a woman's heart with such simplicity and truthfulness and freedom from false shame that the most fastidious taste cannot be offended by their recital. Nor are they interesting alone from the insight which they give us into the heart of their author. They are of unique interest, because they give us the revelation of a great woman's love. They set before us an affection which combines, with the passionate fervor of man's devotion, a clinging, self-renouncing tenderness which is peculiar to woman. They reveal to us a love unselfish in its essence, distrusting only its own worthiness and sufficiency to satisfy its object, and longing to be swallowed up in his larger nature. How false in the presence of such desire for self-renunciation on the part of so highly-gifted a nature appears the common cant that culture and genius and strong thought injure the finer qualities of a woman's soul! What better refutation to this theory than such lines as these: —

> "A heavy heart, belovéd, have I worn,
> From year to year, until I saw thy face,
> And sorrow after sorrow took the place
> Of all those natural joys as lightly worn
> As the stringéd pearls, — each lifted in its turn
> By a beating heart at dance-time. Hopes apace
> Were changed to long despairs, till God's own grace
> Could scarcely lift above the world forlorn
> My heavy heart. Then thou didst bid me bring
> And let it drop adown thy calmly great
> Deep being! Fast it sinketh, as a thing
> Which its own nature doth precipitate,
> While thine doth close above it, mediating
> Betwixt the stars and the unaccomplished fate."

"From their wedding day," writes a friend, "Mrs. Browning seemed to be endowed with new life. Her health visibly improved, and she was enabled to make excursions in England prior to her departure for the land of her adoption, — Italy, — where she found a second and a dearer home."

She lived some time at Pisa, and thence removed to Florence, where the remainder of her life was passed.

"For nearly fifteen years," says the writer from whom we have quoted above, "Florence and the Brownings were *one* in the thoughts of many English and Americans."

Mrs. Browning's poems, for many years before her death, were more widely and heartily admired by American than by English readers. Her love of liberty and generous sympathy with all efforts to elevate the race made America dear and Americans welcome to her. Her conversational powers were of the highest order. It was but natural, therefore, that her house should attract many American travellers to discuss with this little broad-browed woman those "great questions of the day," which we are told "were foremost in her thoughts and, therefore, oftenest on her lips."

Mrs. Browning's affections soon took root in Italy. The depth and fervor of the love which she bore her adopted country was such as man or woman have rarely borne for native land. It had the intensity of a personal attachment with a moral elevation such as love for a single person never has. It glows like fire through all her later poems. Would that we had had a poet who had sung the heroism and suffering of the late war in strains of such power and pathos as those in which "she sang the song of Italy." Her love for her adopted country was not a mere romantic attachment to its beauty and treasures of art and historic associations. It was a practical love for its men and women. She longed to see them elevated, and therefore she longed to see them free.

Her affection for Italy found its first expression in "Casa Guidi Windows," which was published in 1851. "This poem," says the preface, "contains the impressions of the writer upon events in Tuscany of which she was a witness. . . . . . It is a simple story of personal impressions whose only value is in the intensity with which they were received, as proving her warm affection for a beautiful and unfortunate country, and the sincerity with which they were related, as indicating her own good faith and freedom from partisanship."

The poem consists of two parts, the former of which (written in 1848) describes the popular demonstrations in Florence occasioned by the promise of Duke Leopold II. to grant a constitution to Padua. It goes on from this to call upon Italy to free her conscience from priestly domination, and her person from Austrian rule. It calls for a deliverer to break the fetters of priestcraft and tyranny. It asks the sympathy of all European nations, each of which is so deeply indebted to Italy for literature and art: —

"To this great cause of southern men, who strive
In God's name for man's rights, and shall not fail."

The second part of the poem, written three years afterward, when Leopold had proved false, and the constitutional party had been crushed, describes the return of the Duke to Florence under the protection of Austrian bayonets, and gives utterance to the execrations of the despairing patriots of Italy against "false Leopold," a treacherous pope, and a lying priesthood. The poet then goes on in a magnificent strain to accuse the nations who were then flocking to the "World's Fair" in London of gross materialism and insensibility to the sufferings of their own oppressed and miserable, and the wrongs of outraged Italy. She concludes thus: —

"Let us go.
We will trust God. The blank interstices
Men take for ruins he will build into

With pillared marble rare, or knit across
With generous arches, till the fane's complete."

In 1848 Mrs. Browning's son and only child was born. As before, she had thrown the sorrow of her early life, and the love which had followed and superseded it into her poetry, so this new and crowning affection found its fit and full expression in her verse. Before, it was the wife who wrote; now, it is the wife and mother. Her love for her child deepened and intensified her love for humanity. It strengthened her faith in God. It made her love him with that love which only mothers know. And as her poetry was the expression of what was noblest and deepest in her nature, it could but follow that it should be full of the evidences of this its best affection.

In the "Casa Guidi Windows," speaking of perjured Duke Leopold, she says: —

"I saw the man among his little sons;
His lips were warm with kisses while he swore;
And I, because I am a woman, I,
Who felt my own child's coming life before
The prescience of my soul, and held faith high, —
I could not bear to think, whoever bore,
That lips, so warmed, could shape so cold a lie."

The world has seen many greater poets, but it has never seen one who thus clothed noble womanhood in noble verse. And in the same strain is the apostrophe to her little son in the last part of the poem, of which we would gladly quote the whole, but are obliged to content ourselves with these few lines: —

"Stand out my blue-eyed prophet, thou, to whom
The earliest world-daylight that ever flowed
Through Casa Guidi windows chanced to come!
And be God's witness that the elemental

New springs of life are gushing everywhere,
  To cleanse the water-courses and prevent all
Concrete obstructions which infest the air!"

Had Mrs. Browning died childless, she never could have written that noble poem entitled "Mother and Poet," in which she has expressed so powerfully the anguish of that Italian poetess, whose two sons fell fighting for Italian liberty. Nor could she have written "Only a Curl," that touching, exquisite poem written to console two bereaved friends in America. Those who are fond of making comparisons will find a good opportunity for the exercise of their ingenuity in comparing this little poem with that of Tennyson entitled "To J. S.," likewise written to comfort an afflicted friend. That of the laureate is a far more beautiful work of art; after reading its melodious lines Mrs. Browning's verses sound rugged and harsh. Its writer's sympathy and love are expressed with exquisite delicacy and pathos. Its metaphors are full of beauty. Under ordinary circumstances one would read it with far more pleasure than "Only a Curl." But the latter poem, if it gratifies less the sense of beauty, is more richly fraught with consolation to a sorrowing soul. Its sympathy seems the more heartfelt for being less graceful. It does more than express sympathy. It carries the bereaved to the source of all comfort. It inspires him with the writer's lofty faith. It lets a ray of heavenly light into his soul. The contrast between the two poems can be best exhibited by quoting a verse of each. One of the concluding verses of Tennyson's poem is this: —

"Sleep sweetly, tender heart, in peace,
  Sleep, holy spirit, blessed soul;
While the stars burn the winds increase,
  And the great ages onward roll."

That of Mrs. Browning: —

"So look up, friends! you who indeed
Have possessed in your house a sweet piece
Of the Heaven which men strive for, must need
Be more earnest than others are, speed
Where they loiter, persist where they cease."

It is easy to decide which of the two stanzas is more beautiful; and it is not difficult to determine which is in its essential contents the nobler.

In 1856 "Aurora Leigh" was published. This poem, which Mrs. Browning calls "the most mature of my works, and that into which my highest convictions upon life and art have entered," was finished in England, under the roof of the writer's cousin and friend, John Kenyon, — to whom it is dedicated. Mr. Kenyon was a genial and cultivated gentleman, the author of several graceful poems. He died in 1858, leaving his cousin a considerable addition to her fortune.

"Aurora Leigh" is a social epic, — a sort of novel in blank verse. The following is a brief outline of its plot: Aurora Leigh, the heroine, who is represented as telling the story of her life, is a lady of Italian birth, the daughter of an English gentleman, who, while making a brief visit to Florence, fell in love with and married a beautiful Italian woman.

Aurora lived in Italy until thirteen years old, when, her parents having both died, she was taken to England, to live with her father's sister. This aunt, a prim, rigid, and stony person, endeavors, by subjecting Aurora to rigid discipline and the orthodox young lady's education, to eradicate the Italian nature which she had inherited from her mother, and mould her into a correct, accomplished, and commonplace Englishwoman. Aurora, though outwardly submissive, is secretly rebellious, and determines that her aunt shall neither crush out her life, nor make of her the flat, tame woman she designs her niece to become.

Having found in a garret a box of her father's books, she studies them secretly with great zeal. Fired by reading the poets, she determines to become one of their number. Leading thus a double life, outwardly submissive and demure, but secretly enjoying intellectual and spiritual freedom, she reaches the age of twenty.

Then her cousin, Romney Leigh, a young man of talent and worth, whose soul is bent upon schemes for improving the physical condition of the poor, asks her to become his wife. Suspecting that a desire for an assistant in his philanthropic labors, rather than love, has caused him to make this offer, she declines his hand. At this point, her aunt, who is determined that she shall marry Romney, suddenly dies. Romney renews the offer of his hand, and, this being refused, generously and delicately offers a large part of his fortune to his cousin, whom her father's foreign marriage has prevented from inheriting his estates. She refuses this also, and goes to London to write poems and live by their sale. In course of time she obtains celebrity. She has no direct communication with Romney, but learns, by occasional information derived from their common friends, that he is devoting himself with great zeal to lessening the sum of human misery. At length she is told that her cousin is about to marry a young girl of the lowest origin, whom he has met with while carrying on his philanthropic labors.

She visits this young lady, and finds her to be, in spite of her low origin, winning and refined. At her rooms she meets with Romney. He explains to her his design in marrying this Marian Erle, which is to protest against the insuperable barrier which custom has raised between the different classes of society. To increase the effect of this strange union, Romney gives public notice that the marriage will take place in a London church. At the appointed hour the church is crowded with a mixed assemblage, composed of curious people of fashion, and a large and foul delegation from the class to which the bride belongs. The hour arrives, but no bridal party appears. After some delay, Romney enters alone, and announces that his intended bride has fled. The mob swear that she has been abducted by Romney's friends, to prevent the marriage, and a riot ensues, which is quelled by the police.

Some time after Marian's flight, a report is circulated and generally believed by his friends that Romney has formed an engagement of marriage with Lady Waldemar, — a lady of wealth, rank, and beauty, but whose character is utterly devoid of moral principle.

In the full belief of this report, Aurora Leigh, having published a poem which contains the full expression of her genius, starts for Italy. Stopping at Paris on the way, she meets upon the street Marian Erle. Accompanying her home she hears her story. Lady Waldemar (who had long cherished a secret love for Romney Leigh) had persuaded Marian that her affianced husband entertained no real affection for her, but was, in marrying her, sacrificing his own happiness on the altar of his social theories; and that it was her duty to prevent him from performing this rash act by flight. Accordingly she fled the country, under the care of a servant of Lady Waldemar, who conveyed her to a vile den in some French seaport, where she was drugged and outraged. Escaping them, she made her way to Paris, where a child is born to her.

Aurora, after writing this story in a letter to a common friend of Romney and herself in England, taking Marian and her child with her, continues her journey to Italy. The party make their home in Florence. After some months had passed, Romney unexpectedly appears at their house. He tells Aurora what had happened in her absence. He had turned his country-seat into a phalanstery. It had been set on fire and burned to the ground. In rescuing one of his patients, he had been stricken down by a falling beam. The injury had made him hopelessly blind. On hearing the story of Marian's innocence and betrayal, he has hastened to Italy, — come to fulfil his former contract of marriage with Marian. But Marian's love has been killed by the sorrow and shame through which she has passed, and she refuses to marry him. And so, as Romney has loved Aurora with unabated affection since his former offer of marriage, and as Aurora discovers that she has all the time unconsciously loved her cousin, they are married.

Of course a very imperfect conception of the poem can be obtained from this meagre outline of the plot. This is the mere skeleton, which is to be covered with flesh and blood, and into which the breath of life is to be breathed. But a symmetrical body cannot be built upon a deformed skeleton. A great poem cannot be constructed upon an absurd and improbable plot. Its characters must act as human beings in the same circumstances might naturally be expected to do. They must talk like men and women, making allowance for the limitations under which the artist works. They must not be used as puppets, to express the thoughts of the writer, but whatever they say must be the natural expression of their own personality. And especially should this be the case when the scene of the poem is laid, not in the mythical past, but in the broad, clear light of to-day. An epic of the social life of our own time should faithfully reflect that life, by making probable characters talk and act in a natural manner. Almost its first requisite is that the story should be naturally put together, and pleasingly told; that the characters should produce an impression of reality; that the interest and power of the narrative should increase as the poem advances; and that the whole story should tend toward one consummation, and leave upon the mind, when its perusal has been finished, the effect of a connected and symmetrical whole.

Judged by this standard, Aurora Leigh cannot be pronounced a great poem. The plot is awkward and improbable. The author trifles with her readers by making Aurora declare in the early part of the poem:—

> "I attest
> The conscious skies and all their daily suns,
> I think I loved him not; nor then; nor since;
> Nor ever."

And at the close of the poem:—

> "Now I know
> I loved you always, Romney."

The events of the story are improbable and clumsily connected. They do not seem to flow out of each other, as do the occurrences of real life. They have not the semblance of probability. The adventures of Marian Erle, after her flight from England, are as absurd as they are disgusting. Romney Leigh, with his sublime disregard of self, his willingness to contract engagements of marriage to further his noble schemes, his ugly Juggernaut of philanthropy, under which he would crush the nobler affections of his own and other people's lives,—is a very absurd character, if he can be called a character and not a walking abstraction.

It is not too much to say that the story and characters of Aurora Leigh seem like a very clumsy and ill-contrived piece of mechanism intended to serve as a vehicle to convey the writer's impressions of the social life of to-day. But the poem only fails of the accomplishment of what is or should be its main design,—it is full of sins against taste. Disagreeable conceits abound in it. Much of it is but distorted and quaintly expressed prose.

It tells of disgusting crimes with offensive frankness. There is a class of crime upon which even philanthropy cannot gaze too closely. We have certainly a right to ask that crime of this sort, if introduced into a work of the imagination, shall be so veiled as neither to shock our taste nor wound our sensibilities.

But, notwithstanding all the faults which disfigure "Aurora Leigh," it is full of genius and power. It is not a great poem, but many of its passages are great. It contains much vigorous thought; many profound spiritual truths delicately and forcibly expressed; much noble description of natural scenery. It is a book to be read by detached passages rather than as a single work of art; and to one reading it thus it is full of interest and profit. Though not worthy of being the great work of Mrs. Browning's life, it must hold a high rank among the poems which the present century has produced.

In 1859 Mrs. Browning published a little book entitled "Poems before Congress." These poems, which contained eulogies upon Louis Napoleon for the assistance which he had rendered to Italy in her struggle for independence, and blamed England for lukewarmness toward the new nation struggling into freedom, were severely criticised by the English press. She was called disloyal to her native land, and was said to have prostituted her genius to eulogizing a tyrant and usurper. How far her opinions as to Napoleon's character and motives in assisting Italy to freedom were correct is a question into which we will not enter here. Had she been living in the fall of 1867, she would probably have found occasion to modify her opinion. But of the nobility of the motives which actuated her to write as she did, the following extract from a letter which she wrote to a friend affords ample evidence:—

"My book," she wrote, "has had a very angry reception in my native country, as you probably observe; but I shall be forgiven one day; and meanwhile, forgiven or unforgiven, it is satisfactory to one's own soul to have spoken the truth as one apprehends the truth."

It may readily be supposed that Mrs. Browning's deep love of liberty would have led her to take a deep interest in America. That this was indeed the case, her own writings and the testimony of her friends give us abundant evidence. "Her interest in the American anti-slavery struggle," says Mr. Tilton, "was deep and earnest. She was a watcher of its progress, and afar off mingled her soul with its struggles. She corresponded with its leaders, and entered into the fellowship of their thoughts."

She wrote for a little book, which the Abolitionists published in 1848, called the "Liberty Bell," a poem entitled "A Curse for a Nation." Of this we will quote a single verse as a specimen: —

> "Because yourselves are standing straight
> In the state
> Of Freedom's foremost acolyte,
> Yet keep calm footing all the time
> On writhing bond-slaves — for this crime
> This is the curse — write."

Many years after she wrote to an American friend concerning this poem: —

"Never say that I have cursed your country. I only declared the *consequences of the evil* in her, and which has since developed itself in thunder and flame. I feel with more pain than many Americans do the sorrow of this transition time; but I do know that it is transition; that it *is* crisis, and that you will come out of the fire purified, stainless, having had the angel of a great cause walking with you in the furnace."

But she did not live to see her prophecy verified. The disease against which she had so long struggled, broke out with new violence in the spring of 1861. So rapid was its progress that her friends did not realize her danger until death was near. She wasted away in rapid consumption, and died on the morning of the 29th of June. Her last words, or rather her first words when the heavenly glory burst upon her vision, were, "It is beautiful."

Twenty-three days after Cavour's death plunged Italy in mourning, and saddened the friends of liberty through the world. The impassioned poet and the heroic statesman of the new nation were both taken from it while it was on the very threshold of its life. Had they both lived, the one would, by his resistless energy and far-sighted wisdom, have given the land so dearly loved by both a far nobler history for the other to sing. The death of both was hastened, their friends tell us, by their grief at the peace of Villafranca. Such a poet and such a statesman were worthy of a nobler people.

Mrs. Browning was buried in the English burying-ground at Florence. The *municipio* have placed over the doorway of Casa Guidi a white marble tablet, on which is inscribed the following beautiful tribute to her memory: —

"Here wrote and died E. B. Browning, who in the heart of a woman united the science of a sage and the spirit of a poet, and made with her verse a golden ring binding Italy and England.

"Grateful Florence placed this memorial, 1861."

"To those who loved Mrs. Browning," says a friend in a letter published in the "Atlantic Monthly" for September, 1861, "(and to know her was to love her), she was singularly attractive. Hers was not the beauty of feature; it was the loftier beauty of expression. Her slight figure seemed hardly to contain the great heart that beat so powerfully within, and the soul that expanded more and more as one year gave place to another. It was difficult to believe that such a fairy hand could pen thoughts of such a ponderous weight, or that such a 'still, small voice' could utter them with equal force. But it was Mrs. Browning's face upon which one loved to gaze, — that face and head which almost lost themselves in the thick curls of her dark-brown hair. That jealous hair could not hide the broad, fair forehead, 'royal with the truth,' as smooth as any girl's, and

"'Too large for wreath of modern wont.'

"Her large brown eyes were beautiful, and were, in truth, the windows of her soul. They combined the confidingness of a child with the poet-passion of heart and of intellect, and in gazing into them it was easy to see *why* Mrs. Browning wrote. God's inspiration was her motive-power, and in her eyes was the reflection of this higher light."

The same friend continues: —

"Mrs. Browning's conversation was most interesting. . . . All that she said was *always* worth hearing; a greater compliment could not be paid her. She was a most conscientious listener, giving you her mind and heart, as well as her magnetic eyes. Though the latter spoke an eager language of her own, she conversed slowly, with a conciseness and point, which, added to a matchless earnestness that was the predominant trait of her conversation as it was of her character, made her a most delightful companion. *Persons* were never her theme, unless public characters were under discussion, or friends who were to be praised, which kind office she frequently took upon herself. One never dreamed of frivolities in Mrs. Browning's presence, and gossip felt itself out of place. *Your*self, not *her*self, was always a pleasant subject to her, calling out her best sympathies in joy, and yet more in sorrow. Books and humanity, great deeds, and, above all, politics, which include all the grand questions of the day, were foremost in her thoughts, and therefore oftenest on her lips I speak not of religion, for with her everything was religion."

We have expressed our opinion so fully regarding the merits and defects of Mrs. Browning's poetry, in the progress of this sketch, that we need do no more at its close than briefly sum up what has been said. Rarely have so rich a genius, such an affluent and powerful imagination, such an acute and original mind, such a passionate devotion to the poetic art, been so withheld from producing their worthy fruit, by want of suitable elaboration and chaste and simple expression. Had Mrs. Browning's constructive faculty been equal to the wealth of her originating powers, and had she studied luminous expression, she might have given to the world one of those poems which are its perennial delight and inspiration. As it is, though she has written much that is full of beauty and power, her longest poems are least successful, and her fame must rest chiefly on her humbler efforts. But in many respects she is the noblest poet of our time. In her poems as in no other does an intense love for God and man throb and palpitate. They glow as do no others with the "enthusiasm of humanity." Whether they sing of Italian patriots, or the ragged children of London, or the fugitive slaves of America, they have an intense moral earnestness, springing from an intense love of the race. And as we lament that the author's genius is inadequately expressed in her works, we thank God for the woman's soul whose greatness no poems can express.

JENNY LIND GOLDSCHMIDT.

BY JAMES PARTON.

THERE are those who think it unjust that we should bestow upon the children of song honors such as are seldom given to the most illustrious servants of their kind.

What a scene does the interior of an opera-house present when a great singer comes upon the stage, or leaves it after a brilliant display of her talent! In Italy the whole audience spring to their feet, and give cheer upon cheer, continuing their vociferation for several minutes; and it has occasionally happened that a great crowd has rushed round to the stage door and drawn home the vocalist in her own carriage. In these colder climes we bestow less applause, but more money. The favorite of the public who enchants us upon the operatic stage receives a larger income in the northern nations of Europe and America than England bestowed upon Wellington for maintaining her honor in the field, and larger than any nation has ever bestowed upon its savior.

There may be some injustice in this. It is not, however, a part of the general scheme that the greatest sum of money shall be the reward of the greatest merit; and we are generally inclined to pay a far higher price for pleasure than for more substantial benefits. Life needs cheering. Among the thousands of our countrymen who gave three dollars, or five, or ten, to hear Jenny Lind sing four songs, who does not now feel that he received the worth of his money? and who would not gladly pay the sum again to enjoy that rapture once more? These song birds, too, are among the rarest of nature's rarities, and rarities are ever costly. Before a great singer can be produced, there must exist a combination of gifts and circumstances. A fine voice is only one of the requisites. The possessor of that voice must have received from nature an extraordinary physical stamina and a great power of sustained effort, as well as a considerable degree of taste and intelligence. The training of a great vocalist is one of the severest trials of human endurance, — so severe that no creature would submit to it unless compelled to do so by necessity or an overmastering ambition.

I have heard young ladies try their powers upon the operatic stage, who had had what is called in New York a thorough musical education, and who had received from nature a sufficient voice. Before they had been three minutes upon the stage their incapacity would become so apparent as to be painful to the listener. They had every requisite for success except a five years' drill from some crabbed and unrelenting old Italian master. When, therefore, we burst into wild applause after the execution of a fine aria, and when we pay for its execution a thousand dollars, it is not the mere accidental possession of a voice which we so bountifully compensate; it is culture, toil, years of self-denial, as well. The singers may be reaping the late reward of the greater part of a lifetime of most arduous exertion.

To no singer who has ever delighted the public are these remarks more applicable than to the subject of this memoir. The gift that nature bestowed upon her was beautiful, but imperfect, and a culture which we may well style heroic was necessary to perfect it.

Jenny Lind is a native of Sweden. She was born at Stockholm, October 6, 1821. Her parents were respectable, laborious, and poor — her father a teacher of languages, her mother a school-mistress. Jenny was the first child of their marriage, and there was afterwards born to them a son named John. There is a great difference in children as to the age when they can first sing a tune; some children being unable to sing a bar of one until they are six or seven years of age. Jenny Lind, it need scarcely be said, was not one of these. She could sing the airs of her native land with correctness, and even with some expression, when she was but twenty months old. By the time she was three years of age singing was her delight; she was always singing; and she had the faculty of catching every song she heard, and repeating it with remarkable exactness. She was a lonely and timorous child. The absence of her father, who was abroad all day pursuing his vocation, and the constant occupation of her mother in her school, left her very much alone; and during her solitary hours, her voice and her music were the unfailing solace of her existence. The first nine years of her life were marked by no particular event. The Swedes are a musical people, and many children in Stockholm, besides Jenny Lind, were fond of singing.

When she was about nine years of age the silvery tones of her voice chanced to catch the ear of an actress, named Lundberg, who at once discerned its capabilities. Madame Lundberg went to the parents and told them how delighted she had been with the singing of their child, and advised them to have her educated for the opera. It so happened that the mother of the child, being a rather strict Lutheran, had a prejudice against the drama, and regarded going upon the stage as something dishonorable, if not disreputable. The talents of the child, however, were so remarkable that her scruples were in part overcome, and she consented to leave the matter to the decision of Jenny herself. The child was more than willing, and very soon Madame Lundberg had the pleasure of conducting her to one of the most noted music-masters of Stockholm. M. Croelius—for such was the name of this teacher—was an old man; and nothing delights a good old music-teacher more than to have a docile and gifted pupil. He soon became an enthusiast respecting his new acquisition, and at length he resolved to present her to Count Pücke, manager of the King's Theatre.

It is a custom in Europe for the conductors of royal opera-houses to educate and train promising pupils, and there is sometimes a school attached to the theatre for the purpose. When the opera-house in New York was built, something of the same kind was contemplated, and consequently the edifice was named "Academy of Music,"—a title which it retains without having done anything to merit it.

When the enthusiastic Croelius presented Jenny Lind to the manager of the royal opera, that potentate saw before him a pale, shrinking, slender, under-sized child, between nine and ten years of age, attired with Sunday stiffness in a dress of black bombazine. The count, we are told, gazed upon her with astonishment and contempt.

"You ask a foolish thing," said he. "What shall we do with that ugly creature? See what feet she has! and then her face! She will never be presentable. No, we cannot take her. Certainly not!"

The old music-teacher was too confident of the value of the talent which the child possessed to be abashed by this ungracious reception.

"Well," said he, with some warmth, "if you will not take her, I, poor as I am, will take her myself, and have her educated for the stage."

The old man's enthusiasm piqued the curiosity of the noble manager, and he consented at length to hear her sing. Undeveloped as her voice then was, it already had some of that rapture-giving power which it afterwards possessed in such an eminent degree. The count changed his mind, and Jenny was at once admitted to the training-school attached to the royal opera.* There she had the benefit of highly competent instructors, as well as the inspiring companionship of children engaged in the same pursuits.

The pupils of the training-school were required, now and then during the season, to perform in little plays written and arranged expressly for them. It was in one of these, in the eleventh year of her age, that Jenny Lind made her first appearance in public. The part assigned her was that of a beggar-girl, —a character which her pallid countenance and slight person fitted her to represent. She acted with so much simplicity and truth, and sang her songs with such intelligent expression, as to secure the favor of the audience in a high degree. She made what we now call a hit. Other children's plays were written for her, in which for two winters she delighted the people of Stockholm, who regarded her as a prodigy. At the height of her transient celebrity, her brilliant prospects clouded over. She observed with alarm that her upper notes grew weaker, and that her other tones were losing their pleasure-giving quality. By the time she was thirteen years of age her upper notes had almost ceased to exist, and no efforts of her teachers could restore them. It was as though the heiress of a great estate were suddenly informed that her guardian had squandered it, and that she must prepare to earn her livelihood by ordinary labor. The scheme of educating her for the opera was given up, though she continued for four years longer to be an assiduous member of the school, studying instrumental music, and the theory of composition. One of the severest of her trials was being forbidden to use her voice, except for a very short time every day in very simple music.

Her seventeenth birthday came round. The master of the

* This anecdote and some other particulars are derived from "Queens of Song," by Ellen Creathorne Clayton: London and New York, 1865.

training-school was about to give at the theatre a grand concert, in order to display the talents and improvement of his pupils. The chief part of this concert was to consist of the celebrated fourth act of "Robert le Diable," in which *Alice* has but one solo assigned to her, and that is not a favorite with singers. When all the parts had been distributed except that of the undesirable *Alice*, the director thought of poor Jenny Lind, and offered it to her. She accepted it and began to study the music. She had become a woman since she had last looked the terrible public in the face, and she became so anxious as the time approached for her reappearance, that she began to fear the total suspension of her powers. A strange thing happened to her that night. When the moment came for her to sing the solo attached to her part, she rose superior to the fright under which she had been suffering, and began the air with a degree of assurance which surprised herself. Wonderful to relate, her upper notes suddenly returned to her in all their former brilliancy, and every note in her voice seemed at the same moment to recover its long-lost sweetness and power. No one had anticipated anything from the *Alice* of that evening, and thunders of applause greeted the unexpected triumph. Except herself no one was so much surprised as the director of the school, whose pupil she had been for six years. Besides warmly congratulating her that evening, he told her on the following morning that she was cast for the important part of *Agatha* in "Der Frieschütz." Great was the joy of the modest girl, conscious of her powers, upon learning that *Agatha*, the very character towards which she had long felt herself secretly drawn, but to which of late she had hardly dared to aspire, was the one appointed for her first appearance at the royal opera. At the last rehearsal, it is said, she sang the music with so much power and expression that the musicians laid down their instruments to give her a round of applause.

The evening came. We have an account of her début from the pen of her friend and kindred genius, Frederika Bremer: —

"I saw her at the evening representation. She was then in the spring of life, fresh, bright, and serene as a morning in May; perfect in form; her hands and her arms peculiarly graceful, and lovely in her whole appearance. She seemed to move, speak, and sing without effort or art. All was nature and harmony. Her singing was distinguished especially by its purity, and the power of soul which seemed to swell in her tones. Her 'mezzo voice' was delightful. In the night scene, where *Agatha*, seeing her lover coming, breathes out her joy in rapturous song, our young singer, on turning from the window at the back of the stage to the spectators again, was pale for joy; and in that pale joyousness she sang with a burst of outflowing love and life, that called forth, not the mirth, but the tears of the auditors."

But her probation was not yet finished. After this dazzling success, she remained for a while the favorite of the Stockholm public, adding new characters to her list and striving in every way known to her to remedy certain serious defects in her voice and vocalization. Miss Clayton informs us that her voice was originally wanting in elasticity, which prevented her from holding a note, and made it difficult for her to execute those rapid passages and those brilliant effects upon which the reputation of an operatic singer so much depends. Who could imagine this when hearing that wonderful execution of her later years? In her efforts to improve her voice while performing at the opera she overstrained it, and the public of Stockholm, limited in number and fastidious in taste, left her to sing to empty boxes. She felt the necessity of better instruction than her native city afforded. Garcia was then living at Paris, at the height of his reputation as a trainer of vocalists. She desired to place herself under his instruction; but although she had been a leading performer at the Stockholm opera for a year and a half, she was still unable to afford the expense of a residence in Paris. To raise the money she gave concerts, accompanied by her father, in the principal towns of Sweden and Norway. Her concerts were successful, according to the standard of Sweden; nevertheless, she was compelled to make the journey alone, while her parents pursued their ordinary labors at home. Her first interview with Garcia was disheartening in the extreme.

"My good girl," said he, after hearing her sing, "you have no voice; or, I should rather say, that you *had* a voice, but are now on the point of losing it. Your organ is strained and worn out; and the only advice I can offer you is to recommend you not to sing a note for three months. At the end of that time, come to me again, and I will do my best for you."

Few readers can conceive of the dejection and tedium of such a period spent by this lonely girl, far from her home and country, and denied the consolation of exercising her talent.

"I lived," said she once, "on my tears and my thoughts of home."

At the appointed time she stood again in the master's presence. He told her that her voice was improved by rest and capable of culture. She placed herself under his instruction, and profited by it; but, strange to say, Garcia never predicted for her a striking success, either because her voice had not yet regained its freshness, or the old master's ear had lost its acuteness. He used to say that if she had as much voice as she had intelligence, she would become the greatest singer in Europe, and that she would have to sing second to many who had not half her ability.

During her residence at Paris, she had the honor of singing before Meyerbeer, who instantly perceived the peerless quality of her voice. He arranged a grand rehearsal for her, with a full orchestra, when she sang the three most difficult scenes from three favorite operas. She delighted the company of musicians and the great master who heard her, and she narrowly escaped being engaged at once for the Grand Opera of Paris.

Her musical education was now complete. Returning home, she gave a series of performances at Stockholm, which enraptured the public, carried her local reputation to the highest point, and secured for her a pressing invitation to sing at Copenhagen. It seems that she was still distrustful of her powers, and shrank from the ordeal of appearing in a country not her own. Her scruples at length gave way, and she appeared before the Danes in the part of Alice, in "Robert le Diable." We have an interesting account of her success at Copenhagen, in the autobiography of Hans Christian Andersen, who not only heard her sing, but became acquainted with her. He says: —

"It was like a new revelation in the realms of art. The youthful, fresh voice forced itself into every heart; here reigned truth and nature, and everything was full of meaning and intelligence. At one concert she sang her Swedish songs. There was something so peculiar in this, so bewitching, people thought nothing about the concert-room; popular melodies, executed by a being so purely feminine, and bearing the universal stamp of genius, exercised an omnipotent sway. All Copenhagen was in raptures."

The students of the university gave her a serenade by torchlight, and she was the first to whom such a compliment was paid. Her success incited her to fresh exertions. Andersen, who was with her when this serenade was given, records, that after it was over she said, while her cheek was still wet with tears: —

"Yes! yes! I will exert myself; I will endeavor; I will be better qualified when I again come to Copenhagen!"

It was at Copenhagen that she began to taste the noblest fruit of her exertions, — the delight of doing good. Andersen relates the first occasion of her singing for a benevolent object: —

"On one occasion, only," he says, "did I hear her express her joy in her talent and her self-consciousness. It was during her residence in Copenhagen. Almost every evening she appeared either in the opera or at concerts; every hour was in requisition. She heard of a society, the object of which was to assist unfortunate children, and to take them out of the hands of their parents, by whom they were misused and compelled to beg or steal, and to place them in other and better circumstances. Benevolent people subscribed annually a small sum each for their support; nevertheless, the means for this excellent purpose were very limited. 'But have I not still a disengaged evening?' said she; 'let me give a night's performance for the benefit of those poor children: but we will have double prices!' Such a performance was given, and returned large proceeds. When she was informed of this, and that, by this means, a number of poor children would be benefited for several years, her countenance beamed, and the tears filled her eyes.

"'It is, however, beautiful,' said she, 'that I can sing so!'"

From this time forward, she knew little but triumph. When she left Stockholm again to enter upon an engagement at Berlin, the streets were crowded with people to bid her farewell. At Berlin, the Countess Rossi (Madame Sontag) pronounced her "the best singer in Europe." At Hamburg, a silver wreath was presented to her at the end of a most brilliant engagement. At Vienna, her success was beyond all precedent, and when she reappeared at Berlin the enthusiasm was such that it became a matter of great difficulty to procure admission to the theatre. We have heard much ourselves lately of speculation in tickets. After she had performed a hundred nights in Berlin, the manager found it necessary to issue the following notice:—

"Tickets must be applied for on the day preceding that for which they are required, by letter, signed by the applicant's proper and Christian name, profession, and place of abode, and sealed with wax, bearing the writer's initials with his arms. No more than one ticket can be granted to the same person; and no person is entitled to apply for two consecutive nights of the enchantress's performance."

After four years of such success as this, her popularity ever increasing, she accepted an engagement to sing in London. Her departure from her native city was attended by most extraordinary demonstrations. Her last concert in Stockholm was given in aid of a charitable institution founded by herself, and the tickets were sold at auction at prices unheard of before in frugal Sweden. Many thousand persons, it is said, were upon the wharf when she sailed, and she went on board the steamer amid the cheers of the people and the music of military bands. She reached London in April, 1847, and soon began her rehearsals at the Queen's Theatre. When her voice was first heard in that spacious edifice at a rehearsal, no one was so enchanted as Lablache, the celebrated basso.

"Every note," he exclaimed, "is like a pearl!"

She was pleased with the simile, and when they had become better acquainted, she reminded him of it in a very agreeable manner. She came up to him one morning at rehearsal, and said to him: —

"Will you do me the favor, Signor Lablache, to lend me your hat?"

Much surprised, he nevertheless handed her his hat, which she took with a deep courtesy, and, tripping away with it to the back part of the stage, began to sing an air into it. She then brought back the hat to Lablache, and, ordering that portly personage to kneel, she returned it to him with the remark: —

"I have now made you a rich man, signor, for I have given you a hat full of pearls!"

Everything which a favorite does seems graceful and pleasant. This trifling act delighted the whole company.

Three weeks elapsed before she appeared in London, during which the excitement of the public rose to fever heat, and when the eventful evening came the theatre was crammed to its utmost capacity. The Queen, Prince Albert, and many of the leading personages in England were present. She sang the part of Alice, in "Robert le Diable." Nervous, as she really was, she succeeded so completely in controlling herself, that she appeared to the audience remarkably self-possessed, and by the time she had completed her first aria every one present felt that the greatest singer of the time, if not of any time, was this stranger from Stockholm.

"At its conclusion," said one of the critics, "she gave the 'Roulade' in full voice, limpid and deliciously sweet, and finished with a shake so delicate, so softly executed, that each one held his breath to listen, and the torrent of applause at the end baffled description."

Every succeeding effort was a new triumph, and when the

performance closed the audience were in such raptures that they behaved more like Italians than Englishmen. Her acting, too, at this time was greatly admired, and there was an air of simplicity and goodness about her which won every heart.

It is not necessary for us to dwell upon her career in England, because there is nothing to say of it except that, everywhere and in every character, she appeared to have all the success and glory which the stage affords. Such was the struggle for tickets that persons were known to come hundreds of miles to London on purpose to hear her sing, and, after spending several days in fruitless attempts to gain admission to the opera house, return home without having heard her. At Edinburgh a concert was given, for performing in which she received a thousand pounds sterling, Lablache two hundred, and another singer one hundred and fifty, and yet the managers cleared twelve hundred pounds. Her charities constantly increased in number and amount. In almost every place she gave a part of her gains to charitable institutions. After two years of continual triumph, she resolved to take her leave of the stage, and to sing thenceforth only in the concert-room. Her last performance was in May, 1849, when she played the part of Alice, in the presence of the Queen of England and an immense multitude of the most distinguished personages in England.

Her fame had long ago crossed the Atlantic. In October, 1849, Mr. P. T. Barnum, who had recently returned home after a three years' tour with the famous General Tom Thumb, conceived the happy idea of bestowing upon his countrymen the delight of hearing the voice of the Swedish Nightingale. "I had never heard her sing," he tells us. "Her reputation was sufficient for me." He cast about him at once for a fit person to send to Europe to engage the songstress, and soon pitched upon the right person, Mr. John Hall Wilton, who had had some experience in the business of entertaining the public. He was instructed to engage Jenny Lind on shares, if he could; but he was authorized, if he could do no better, to offer her a thousand dollars a night for one hundred and fifty nights. Besides this, all her expenses were to be paid, including servants, carriages, and secretary, and she was to have the privilege of selecting three professional persons to accompany her. Mr. Barnum further agreed to place the whole amount of money for the hundred and fifty nights in the hands of a London banker before she sailed. When Mr. Wilton reached Europe he discovered that four persons were negotiating with her for an American tour. All of these individuals, however, merely proposed to divide with her the profits, and none of them were in a position to guarantee her against loss. She frankly said to Wilton, after she had satisfied herself respecting Mr. Barnum's character: —

"As those who are trying to treat with me are all anxious that I should participate in the profits or losses of the enterprise, I much prefer treating with you, since your principal is willing to assume all the responsibility, and take the entire management and chances of the result upon himself."

The negotiation did not linger. Mr. Barnum gives a ludicrous account of the manner in which he received the news that Jenny Lind had signed the desired agreement. He received the telegraphic dispatch in Philadelphia which announced Wilton's arrival in New York with the agreement in his pocket, and that Mademoiselle Lind was to begin her concerts in the following September.

"I was somewhat startled," he tells us, "by this sudden announcement, and feeling that the time to elapse before her arrival was so long that it would be policy to keep the engagement private for a few months, I immediately telegraphed Wilton not to mention it to any person, and that I would meet him the next day in New York. The next day I started for that city. On arriving at Princeton we met the cars, and, purchasing the morning papers I was overwhelmed with surprise and dismay to find in them a full account of my engagement with Jenny. However, this premature announcement could not be recalled, and I put the best face upon the matter. Being anxious to learn how this communication would strike the public mind, I informed the gentlemanly conductor (whom I well knew) that I had made an engagement with Jenny Lind, and that she would surely visit this country in the following August.

"'Jenny Lind! Is she a dancer?' asked the conductor.

"I informed the conductor who and what she was, but his question had chilled me as if his words were ice! Really, thought I, if this is all that a man in the capacity of a railroad conductor between Philadelphia and New York knows of the greatest songstress in the world, I am not sure that six months will be too long a time for me to occupy in enlightening the entire public in regard to her merits."

How well Mr. Barnum employed that time, most of us remember. Long before the great songstress landed all America was on the *qui vive*. On Sunday, September 1, 1850, at twelve o'clock, the steamer "Atlantic," with Jenny Lind on board, came to opposite the quarantine ground, and Mr. Barnum, who had been on the island since the evening before, was soon on board.

"But where did you hear me sing?" Jenny Lind asked him, as soon as the first compliments had been exchanged.

"I never had the pleasure of hearing you before in my life," said the manager.

"How is it possible," she rejoined, "that you dared risk so much money on a person you never heard sing?"

"I risked it on your reputation," he replied, "which in

musical matters I would much rather trust than my own judgment."

Mr. Barnum had made ample provision for her landing. The wharves and ships were covered with thousands of people on that pleasant Sunday afternoon to see her step on shore. A large bower of green trees and two triumphal arches covered with flags and streamers, were seen upon the wharf, — the work of Mr. Barnum's agents. The carriage of that enterprising person conveyed her to the Irving House, which was surrounded all that afternoon and evening with crowds of people. Mr. Barnum tells us that he had the pleasure of dining with her that afternoon, and that during the meal she invited him to take a glass of wine with her. He replied: —

"Miss Lind, I do not think you can ask any other favor on earth which I would not gladly grant; but I am a teetotaler, and must beg to be permitted to drink your health and happiness in a glass of cold water."

Nineteen days elapsed before her first appearance in public, during which she was the centre of attraction, and the theme of every tongue. The acute and experienced Barnum, perceiving that his enterprise was an assured success, endeavored to guard against the only danger which could threaten it. Two days after the arrival of the nightingale he told her that he wished to make a little alteration in their agreement.

"What is it?" she asked, much surprised.

"I am convinced," replied he, "that our enterprise will be much more successful than either of us anticipated. I wish, therefore, to stipulate that you shall always receive a thousand dollars for each concert, besides all the expenses, and that after taking fifty-five hundred dollars per night, for expenses and my services, the balance shall be equally divided between us."

Jenny Lind was astonished; and supposing that the proposition was dictated by a sense of justice, she grasped the manager by the hand, and exclaimed: —

"Mr. Barnum, you are a gentleman of honor! You are generous. I will sing for you as long as you please. I will sing for you in America, — in Europe, — anywhere!"

Mr. Barnum hastens to let us know that the change in the agreement was not the dictate of pure generosity. He feared that envious persons would create discontent in her mind, and he thought "it would be a stroke of policy to prevent the possibility of such an occurrence."

The tickets for the first concert were sold at auction, and produced the astonishing sum of $17,864. Jenny Lind instantly resolved to give her portion of the proceeds to the charitable institutions of the city.

The eventful evening came. Five thousand persons assembled at Castle Garden, who had paid for the privilege sums which varied from two dollars to two hundred and twenty-five. It was the largest audience before which she had ever appeared, and she was considerably agitated. When the conductor of the concert led her forward, attired in white, with a rose in her hair, the audience rose and gave her three thundering cheers, and continued for several seconds to clap their hands and wave their hats and handkerchiefs. She had a singularly pleasing way of acknowledging the applause of an audience. She had a timid, shrinking look, which appealed powerfully to popular sympathy, and inflamed the enthusiasm of the spectators to the highest degree. The orchestra began to play the prelude to "Casta Diva," — a piece which displayed all the power, all the thrilling sweetness, and some of the defects of her wonderful organ. Never had an assembly come together with such high-wrought expectations. Nevertheless, those expectations seemed to be more than realized, and the last notes of the song were lost in the irrepressible acclamations of the people.

This success was the beginning of a splendid career in America. Under Mr. Barnum's management, she gave ninety-five concerts. The total receipts were $712,161. The average receipts of each concert were $7,496. The sum received by Jenny Lind was $176,675. Mr. Barnum's receipts, after paying her, were $535,486. Some of the tickets brought remarkable prices. The highest price paid for a ticket in New York was $225; in Boston, $625; in Providence, $650; in Philadelphia, $625; in New Orleans, $240; in St. Louis, $150; in Baltimore, $100. The price of seats, not sold by auction, ranged from three dollars to seven dollars.

After enchanting the United States it remained for Jenny Lind to conquer the fastidious and difficult public of Havana. A striking scene occurred on the occasion of her first appearance in Havana. The people, it seems, were much offended by the unusual prices charged for admission, and came to the concert determined not to be pleased, — a circumstance of which Jenny Lind was ignorant. The scene was thus described at the time in the New York Tribune: —

"Jenny Lind appeared, led on by Signor Belletti. Some three or four hundred persons clapped their hands at her appearance; but this token of approbation was instantly silenced by at least two thousand five hundred decided hisses. Thus, having settled the matter that there should be no *forestalling* of public opinion, and that if applause was given to Jenny Lind in that house it should first be incontestably *earned*, the most solemn silence prevailed. I have heard the Swedish nightingale often in Europe as well as America, and have ever noticed a distinct tremulousness attending her first appearance in any city. Indeed, this feeling was plainly manifested in her countenance as she neared the foot-lights; but when she witnessed the kind of reception in store for her, —

so different from anything she had reason to expect, — her countenance changed in an instant to a haughty self-possession, her eye flashed defiance, and, becoming immovable as a statue, she stood there, perfectly calm and beautiful. She was satisfied that she now had an ordeal to pass and a victory to gain worthy of her powers. In a moment her eye scanned the immense audience, the music began, and then followed — how can I describe it? — such heavenly strains as I verily believe mortal never breathed except Jenny Lind, and mortal never heard except from her lips. Some of the oldest Castilians kept a frown upon their brow and a curling sneer upon their lip; their ladies, however, and most of the audience began to look surprised. The gushing melody flowed on, increasing in beauty and glory. The *caballeros*, the *señoras*, and *señoritas* began to look at each other; nearly all, however, kept their teeth clenched and their lips closed, evidently determined to resist to the last. The torrent flowed faster and faster, the lark flew higher and higher, the melody grew richer and richer; still every lip was compressed. By and by, as the rich notes came dashing in rivers upon our enraptured ears, one poor critic involuntarily whispered a 'brava.' This outbursting of the soul was instantly hissed down. The stream of harmony rolled on till, at the close, it made a clean sweep of every obstacle, and carried all before it. Not a vestige of opposition remained, but such a tremendous shout of applause as went up was never before heard.

"The triumph was most complete. And how was Jenny Lind affected? She, who stood a few moments previous like adamant, now trembled like a reed in the wind before the storm of enthusiasm which her own simple notes had produced. Tremblingly, slowly, and almost bowing her face to the ground, she withdrew. The roar and applause of victory increased. *Encore! encore! encore!* came from every lip. She again appeared, and, courtesying low, again withdrew; but again, again, and again did they call her forth, and at every appearance the thunders of applause rang louder and louder. Thus *five* times was Jenny Lind called out to receive their unanimous and deafening plaudits."

Mr. Barnum gives his version of the story:—

"I cannot express," he says, "what my feelings were as I watched this scene from the dress circle. When I witnessed her triumph, I could not restrain the tears of joy that rolled down my cheeks; and, rushing through a private box, I reached the stage just as she was withdrawing after the fifth encore.

"'God bless you! Jenny, you have settled them,' I exclaimed.

"'Are you satisfied?' said she, throwing her arms around my neck. She, too, was crying with joy, and never before did she look so beautiful in my eyes as on that evening."

In Havana, as in every other large city in America, she bestowed immense sums in charity, and gave charity concerts which produced still larger benefactions. During her residence in America, she gave away, in all, about fifty-eight thousand dollars.

The precaution which Mr. Barnum had taken against the intermeddling of envious persons proved to be insufficient, and, after the ninety-fifth concert, Jenny Lind desired the contract to be annulled, and to give concerts on her own account. The manager gladly assented, and they separated excellent friends.

Mr. Horace Greeley, in one of his recent contributions to the "New York Ledger," adds an anecdote of Mademoiselle

Lind's stay among us. It was at the time when the "Rochester Knockings" were a topic of interest.

"I called," said Mr. Greeley, " on Mademoiselle Jenny Lind, then a new-comer among us, and was conversing about the current marvel with the late N. P. Willis, while Mademoiselle Lind was devoting herself more especially to some other callers. Our conversation caught Mademoiselle L.'s ear and arrested her attention; so, after making some inquiries, she asked if she could witness the so-called 'Manifestations.' I answered that she could do so by coming to my house in the heart of the city, as Katy Fox was then staying with us. She assented, and a time was fixed for her call; at which time she appeared, with a considerable retinue of total strangers. All were soon seated around a table, and the 'rappings' were soon audible and abundant. 'Take your hands from under the table!' Mademoiselle Jenny called across to me in the tone and manner of an indifferently bold archduchess. 'What?' I asked, not distinctly comprehending her. 'Take your hands from under the table!' she imperiously repeated; and I now understood that she suspected me of causing, by some legerdemain, the puzzling concussions. I instantly clasped my hands over my head, and there kept them until the sitting closed, as it did very soon. I need not add, this made not the smallest differences with the 'rappings;' but I was thoroughly and finally cured of any desire to exhibit or commend them to strangers."

Jenny Lind, like Miss Kemble, met her destiny in America. Among the performers at her concerts was Mr. Otto Goldschmidt, a pianist and composer, whom she had formerly known in Germany, and with whom she had pursued her musical studies. Her friendship for this gentleman ripened into a warmer attachment, and ended in their marriage at

Boston, in 1851. After residing some time at Northampton, in Massachusetts, they returned to Europe, where they have ever since resided. Occasionally, Madame Goldschmidt has appeared in public concerts, accompanied by her husband. She is now forty-seven years of age, and her voice is said to retain a considerable degree of its former brilliancy and power. Living, as she does, in great privacy, little is known of her way of life; but that little is honorable to her. Her charities, it is said, are still bountiful and continuous, and she is as estimable a member of society as she is a shining ornament to it. The great secret of her success as an artist was well expressed by her friend, Jules Benedict: —

"Jenny Lind makes a conscience of her art."

OUR PIONEER EDUCATORS.

BY REV. E. B. HUNTINGTON.

To woman rather than to man, and to woman in this century rather than in any former one, belongs the credit of preparing the way for the future liberal education of women. Heretofore the aids to her education have been few and defective. A really liberal education for her has hardly been possible. Collegiate and University courses have been closed against her; so that if occasionally a woman has succeeded in gaining the reputation of a scholar, it has been mainly due to her own unaided exertions, — a triumph of her personal genius and will. We have reached a state of public sentiment now, however, which, partially, at least, accords to woman the right to enter any field of literature or art, which she may choose; and, to a certain extent, we are furnishing her with such aids as for generations have been furnished for her brothers.

Already we are gathering excellent fruits from this advance made in our theory and system of woman's culture. Our multiplied young ladies' seminaries and collegiate institutions, and still more our colleges and professional schools in which the two sexes are, to their mutual benefit, prosecuting together the studies which were formerly confined to only one of them, are important results already attained. Still maturer fruit we have, in the increasing numbers of

EMMA WILLARD.

thoroughly educated women who are now prepared to occupy chairs of instruction, once filled only by the most honored alumni of our best universities. We are coming to welcome woman's taste, and tact, and power, into every department of our educational work, and we have much to hope from the new element thus introduced. Without attempting to name, even, the many eminent women whose personal attainments and services have contributed largely towards this result, we shall, in this chapter, briefly sketch the career of only two of them, who, by common consent, must be held to rank as pioneers in this most excellent work.

MRS. EMMA WILLARD.

First among the women, still living, who have attained high rank as professional educators, must stand the name at the head of this sketch. And this position Mrs. Willard deserves, whether we regard her as a pioneer, creating for herself, and her sex, a new place and rank among educators, or simply as an earnest and skilful worker, rendering eminent service in this field. That she is fairly entitled to this eminence among the gifted women of our day, a very brief sketch of her career will fully show. The story itself is a true epic, needing only the simplest recital, — its main facts being more exciting than any fiction we should dare to invent.

HER BIRTH AND CHILDHOOD.

February 23, 1787, is the date of her birth; Samuel and Lydia (Hinsdale) Hart, her parents; and a quiet country farmhouse in the parish of Worthington, in Berlin, Connecticut, her birthplace. Born of the best New England stock, she inherited the noblest qualities of her parentage. Her father, a man of unusual strength of intellect and will, was self-reliant, and well-read, in, at least, the English literature of the times; and her mother a quiet and practical woman, gifted with native tact and shrewdness, gentle, firm, and efficient. The home they made for their children was just the home in which gifted children would like to be reared. And this home, more than anything else determined the character and success of Emma, their sixteenth child, whose record we are now to trace. Being one of seventeen of her father's children, and one of the ten whom her own mother had borne him, she early found in this large circle one important means of her training.

Let us enter that rural home. We will take an early evening hour, about mid-winter, and for the date it may be anywhere between her birthday and the year 1804, the date of her first attempt to teach. The scene we shall witness will best prepare us for what we are to learn of the great work of her future life.

The children have already spent their six hours in their school. They have severally done up the chores which, in those primitive times, our children were supposed able to do. They had just finished with thanksgiving their relishful supper. The youngest of them have already dropped away into the sweet sleep of their night's rest. The huge wood fire glows warmly upon that happy home-circle gathering around it. The older children, all aglow with a joyful interest, finish the little story of their day's fun, and frolic, and work, and successively test their skill in reading aloud a few well-chosen passages from the selectest authors of the day. Then father and mother, no less joyful, add the benediction of their few words of approval, and their timely hints for correction. And now, for another half hour, or hour, if this be deemed needed, the father and mother — blessed mentors they! — read, in their turn, aloud, and with the skill which long practice has given them, their lessons for themselves and their little flock. Milton chances, it may be, to be the classic now in hand; and, as the magnificent word-picture opens before them, the very youngest of the group is stirred with fancies and thoughts which shall be to them the germs of thought for many a year to come.

Happy, blessed group, for whose early years such a home is furnished! What child of gifts could fail of largest fruitage, whose bloom is amid such home sunshine and warmth?

Let us take one more lesson from that Worthington home; and let the mother of the family be our teacher. Notice with what womanly ingenuity she makes their slender resources ample for all their home wants, and even for the gratification of a cultivated home taste. Notice how thoughtfully she provides for the poor family out under the hill, to whom the warm breakfast she sends them, makes the only glad hour of their poverty-stricken home. And then, when all these home and neighborhood duties are so skilfully discharged, she is not satisfied until she has given her children a lesson of thoughtful kindness to the little birds that are to sing for them. The refuse wool, which can be of no use to the family, she teaches her little ones how to leave about on the bushes for a hint to the charming warblers to build their fleece-lined nests near to the human home which she would have blest by their sweet singing.

And thus, this admirable home-training, with some two years of study in the village academy, then just opened under a skilful teacher, brought Emma forward to the beginning of her life-work. She had used her opportunities well. She had been required to think and plan for herself. Her powers of observation and her practical judgment had been equally taxed and improved; and it is not too much to say, that, in literary attainment, and still more, in ability to learn, she had exceeded her years. A young lady of fourteen, who, on a cold night in mid-winter, wrapping herself in her cloak, with the horse-block for her observatory, could there by moonlight master the lesson of astronomy, which the merry song-singers in the house would leave her no opportunity there to learn, has already some elements of character which are the best pledges of success.

HER EXPERIMENTAL CAREER.

She has now just passed her seventeenth birthday. Through the friendly solicitation of a neighbor, an intelligent lady, who, though more than twice her age, had found in her an equal, she was installed as teacher of one of the village schools. Her first day's experience here settled many a principle for her future course. The tact with which she began would well have crowned the end of another teacher's professional career. With her, a difficulty once encountered was mastered forever. Discarding the rod as a means of discipline, after the second day's trial, she sought and found her way so directly to the hearts of her pupils; she so skilfully planned their exercises and their sports; she so soon and so thoroughly excited their interest in their school duties, and so made this interest itself the only needed discipline, that her first school soon reported itself in all the neighborhood as a marvel of the times. She found herself, even thus early in her mere girlhood, crowned with the laurels of her first success. And now, for three years, in learning and teaching, a part of which time was spent in the excellent schools of Mrs. Royce and the Misses Patten, in Hartford, she was fast preparing herself for entering upon the great work of her life. And what was of especial value to her was the habit, then established, of prosecuting her own advanced studies while engaged in teaching those already mastered.

Such success soon attracted attention. The spring of 1807 brings to her calls from three important schools, in Westfield, Massachusetts; Middlebury, Vermont; and Hudson,

New York. She accepted the Westfield call; and as assistant teacher in the excellent academy of that town, she at once won for herself a good name. But Miss Hart was not the person to fill long a subordinate place. Before her first season was over, she had decided to accept the call from Middlebury; and midsummer of the same year finds her at the head of her new school there. A year of "brilliant success" crowns this third experiment, and settles the question of her fitness for the work she had chosen. Local jealousies soon spring up, and the school, in spite of her great popularity, suffers; yet even this opposition had its influence in training and disciplining her for a better and stronger work.

While in this struggle, a new call is made upon her. Dr. John Willard, of Middlebury, a physician of good repute, and a man of solid political merit, had discovered the gifts and graces of the young teacher. Nor was he long in winning his way to her heart and hand. They were happily married in August, 1809, when, for a few years, her work of teaching was interrupted.

Pecuniary reverses soon came upon them; and to aid in retrieving their fortune, Mrs. Willard, in 1814, proposed to return to her chosen profession. She opened in Middlebury a boarding-school for girls. But she was also preparing for something more. She had, even then, detected how low and unworthy were the aims and results of that class of schools. She was especially struck with the difference between the collegiate course of a young man, and the highest culture which the best schools of the day furnished for young women; and the discovery had been to her a summons to a new work.

With what enthusiasm she entered upon that work! Carefully reviewing the whole subject of woman's education, she drew up her plan for an enlarged course of study, corresponding, as nearly as the different sexes would indicate, with the collegiate course for young men. But she found herself in advance of the age. The leaders in public opinion were not yet ready for such a change. She fortunately finds her husband in full sympathy with her, and so takes heart again, as she goes on testing its feasibility. Working daily, ten, twelve, or even fifteen hours in her school duties, she still takes time to master new studies herself that she may in due time carry her pupils through them. And so, by exploring new fields of science and literature herself; by teaching and drilling her classes, as few classes of young ladies had ever before been drilled; by adding to the old course new studies, and submitting the proficiency of her pupils to the criticism of the most learned men of the day; and by skilfully winning over to her new ideas a few leading minds, she was preparing the way for a new era in woman's education; making possible the establishment and support of the great collegiate institutions in which women may take rank in all literature with their most scholarly brothers.

Some four years were spent in this preparation. Meanwhile the unwonted stimulus thus furnished to her own boarding-school had worked greatly in her favor. The fame of her experiment had gone far and wide; and she was now prepared to take the first steps towards a permanent institution in which her enlarged views and hopes could be more fully realized. The very location of the institution was a matter of careful thought; and for it, the State of New York, and of that State, the neighborhood of the head-waters of the Hudson, was chosen.

HER GREAT WORK.

And now, in 1818, she is prepared for her work. She has matured her plans, and secured strength for their execution.

She submits her proposals to the large-minded Governor Clinton, of New York, with a special plea that he would lay the matter in due form, and with the weight of his approval, before the legislature. The very plan, which in 1814 had begun to shape itself to her eager search, sketched and resketched even to the seventh time, was thus, in 1818, submitted to the judgment of those who make and sustain the institutions of their age. Of the details of that plan we have not space to treat. It is due, however, to say, that down to this day, nothing has been contributed to our educational literature which exceeds either the wisdom of its details or the eloquence of its plea. The governor heartily approved the measures which it recommended. The legislature so far endorsed them as to incorporate an academy at Waterford, New York, in which the founder might still more clearly show their feasibility.

A still more important end secured by this movement was an acknowledgment, on the part of the legislature, that the academies in the State, designed for the education of women, were entitled to the same pecuniary aid as institutions of learning for the other sex; and a vote was accordingly passed appropriating their proportion of the literature fund to academies for girls.

We cannot but feel that it was most fortunate for Mrs. Willard that such a man as Governor Clinton was ready to second her aims. And yet, it is very certain, we think, that but for Mrs. Willard herself, her years of patient and zealous and skilful working, we have no reasons for believing, that for at least another quarter of a century, such concessions would have been made, even to so just a demand.

In the spring of 1819, thus encouraged by the legislature, Doctor and Mrs. Willard opened their new school in a rented building in Waterford, New York. Their success was such as to justify Governor Clinton, in his message of 1820, to allude to it in these terms: —

"I cannot omit to call your attention to the Academy for Female Education, which was incorporated last session at Waterford, and which, under the superintendence of distinguished teachers, has already attained great usefulness and prosperity. As this is the only attempt ever made in this country to promote the education of the female sex by the patronage of government; as our first and best impressions are derived from maternal affections; and as the elevation of the female character is inseparably connected with happiness at home, and respectability abroad; I trust that you will not be deterred, by commonplace ridicule, from extending your munificence to this meritorious institution."

The citizens of Troy, attracted by the success of the Waterford school, proposed to furnish a building with suitable grounds for a larger institution there, if Mrs. Willard would consent to a removal. On the expiration of their lease in Waterford, this proposal from Troy was accepted, and in May, 1821, they took possession of the Troy property, which since that date has been used for the Troy Seminary thus established.

The same industry and zeal in her profession, and the same progress in her personal culture marked the course of Mrs. Willard here as in her former schools. To the studies she had already added to the ordinary curriculum of the schools for young ladies of that day, she now, after thoroughly mastering them herself, adds the higher mathematics, geometry, including trigonometry, algebra, conic sections, and Enfield's natural philosophy. With all this working she still found time for remodelling the science of geography and history; and the results of this painstaking to furnish herself suitable implements of her profession we had in Willard and Woodbridge's popular Geography in 1821, and Mrs. Willard's "Temple of Time and Chronographer of Ancient History." This ingenious design received a medal at the World's Fair in 1851. The certificate of testimonial, signed by Prince Albert, was no empty tribute to the eminent author, but rather a tribute to the substantial contribution to our aids in learning and teaching what ought to be the most fascinating, yet what had notoriously become the most uninteresting, of all our studies.

In entering upon her enlarged sphere of labors in Troy, Mrs. Willard found the gain of her preceding work. The young ladies whom she had taught, and who had caught something of the inspiration of her aims and zeal, were now already trained for her help. Her experience and practice had made the work of classification and management easy to her, and her great reputation, of itself, would go far towards making her success a certainty.

She had scarcely settled herself to her work when an unforeseen trial came upon her. Her husband, who, as head of the family, as physician and financial manager of the large household, and as her constant and intelligent adviser, had been a real partner and sharer of her work, after a painful sickness, died in 1825. On her rested now the great burden which he had borne for her.

Yet, with a resolution more than we look for in woman, she did not hesitate. Rearranging her school terms, simplifying and methodizing her work, she could even add to her former duties the financial management of her school. She neither neglected the claim of the humblest pupil under her charge, nor any important item of business in managing the large establishment. Down to 1838, she thus continued the motive power and main spring of that first of American schools for young women.

And her reward was not long delayed. It came in the triumph of her own school. It came in the increased stimulus she had given to the cause of woman's education. It came in the readier facilities accorded to young women in our collegiate institutions; and still more signally in those large institutions expressly for women which her success had made possible. We can now readily see how much South Hadley, Oberlin, Antioch, Packer, and Vassar are indebted to her pioneer work.

While achieving this success at home, she had not been unmindful of the claims of woman abroad. In 1830 she had sought abroad the rest and health which her home duties required, and the relief from her professional work gave her the opportunity to examine the educational condition of women in other lands. Her womanly heart was touched with the report which came to her of the degraded condition of woman in classic Greece, and on her return she organized a society in Troy to aid in establishing a school in Athens for educating native teachers. She prepared a volume of her European tour, giving the benefit of its profits to the Greek school.

But the time at length came when it was necessary for her to retire from the pressure of these great burdens upon her. Her son, Mr. John H. Willard, who had grown up under a training which had specially fitted him for it, and his wife, who for nineteen years had been with her as pupil, or teacher, or vice-principal, now accepted the trust, and relieved her of its further care.

But Mrs. Willard all these years had been not simply the practical teacher, but also a most unwearied student, and the opportunity is now afforded her of prosecuting her studies with new zeal. She had been testing Dr. William Harvey's theory of the circulation of the blood, in which the heart is made the motive power, and she soon detected its fallacy.

She now sets herself to the more careful study of this interesting problem. With all the enthusiasm of a professional anatomist and physiologist, she explores thoroughly the entire field, and the result was a work on the "Motive Powers which produce the Circulation of the Blood." This treatise, published in 1846, arrested the attention of the medical faculty, and won for its author the reputation of a successful discoverer.

At the same time these investigations were going on, her feelings became deeply interested in the public schools of her native State. While on a visit to Berlin, she was asked to furnish her views on the subject of common-school education, to be submitted to the citizens of her native town assembled in an educational meeting. The paper she submitted showed so much wisdom, and indicated so true an interest in the common schools, that the parish, by vote, put their schools for the year under her care. Her success in managing them was a marvel, and the schools, thus skilfully superintended, were referred to by Mr. Barnard, then as now, a prince among educators, as witnesses to what skilful management will do for schools.

And so, by study and writing, even to twelve and fourteen hours daily; by stirring up educators and schools to more skilful and earnest working, both in Connecticut and New York; by suggesting new plans and methods of teaching; by projecting normal schools before the day of normal schools had come, — this woman, thoroughly alive to all that promised to advance her race, used more diligently her years of rest than most workers do the hours of their busiest working. And if the question is raised, how could one with only a woman's strength sustain such efforts, the answer will only lead us to still another field of her unwearied and painstaking labor. She worked for it. She studied carefully the condition and wants of her physical nature, and provided for both. She trained even her muscles to their healthful and self-sustaining work. She wishes a clear, vigorous, lifeful brain, and she uses the only methods she could discover that promised it. See her, early in the morning, at her honest, earnest, muscular work. And when she has entered upon the mental labor of the day, see her, at the end of each two hours through the day, resting her toiling brain by vigorous physical exercise, until the equilibrium is restored. You need not fear for her, as she drops the sash of her study window, and facing the fresh cold breeze stands there exercising the muscles of her chest until her lungs have been satisfied with their needed food, and her blood freshly pours its health-tides throughout her now reinvigorated frame. She has now worked her whole system up to working trim, and you need not wonder if, when she seats herself at her papers, she should record a thought or a theory which shall henceforth change and rule the thoughts and theories of men. It is really no marvel that one with such a physical and mental constitution as she inherited, with such skilful training as her very necessities had imposed on her younger life, and with the care which her maturer years had exercised over both her body and brain, should at fifty years of age give to the world her Troy Seminary; at sixty, her original demonstration on the "Motive Powers in the Circulation of the Blood;" at sixty-two, her treatise on "Respiration and its Effects;" and at sixty-five, a work on astronomy, which even the masters in the science were ready to endorse. It is no marvel, that, after having had an important part in the training of more than five thousand young ladies, she still found time and strength to become the teacher of the teachers of men. It is no marvel that at fifty-eight she could, in a journey of eight thousand miles, traverse a continent, rejoicing everywhere equally in the joy of her pupils and in the prosperity of the schools for young ladies which her influence had contributed to found; nor that at sixty-seven she could cross the ocean, and mingle in the exercises and enjoy the honors of the World's Educational Convention, and thence make the tour of France, Switzerland, Germany, and Belgium tributary still to her zeal for observation and learning.

But not alone in these literary and educational works has Mrs. Willard used her great powers. Her religious character has been also as carefully educated, and an effective Christian culture has been a constant aim and triumph in her work. Uniting with the Episcopal church in Burlington, she has ever since been a devout and worthy communicant. In all her study and work, her appeal has been to God's word for her standard and law. She spoke with great deliberation in her weighty charge to those whom she would commission with the solemn trust of teachers, when she said to them, in all the seriousness of her earnest convictions: "So far, however, from depending on set times for the whole discharge of the duty of training the young to piety and virtue, you are, during all your exercises, to regard it as the grand object of your labors."

Of her active and wide-reaching benevolence the record has been a private one. Yet many and timely have been her benefactions which the angel has recorded on high. We know this much, that scores of the young women whom she has aided to secure the education, which, without such aid, they could not have secured, are still grateful for her quick sympathies and generous aid. It is safe to say that twenty thousand dollars would not now make Mrs. Willard's exchequer good for these offerings to the cause of woman's education.

But we cannot linger longer on these lessons of her useful and honored life. Mrs. Willard is still living, and as we might, from all we have learned of her former life, expect, her latest years are not without their rich and worthy fruits. The serene dignity of age well befits now the form which forty years ago was radiant with womanly beauty. Under the shadow in her own dear seminary, she can but rejoice in this proud monument of her life.

Here, surrounded with the trophies of her life-work, embosomed in the love of those whose young affections she drew to herself, and cheered by that precious religious hope which has purified her life, long may she yet enjoy with us the rewards of her long life, so nobly and worthily spent for her sex and race!

MRS. MARIANNE P. DASCOMB.

Hardly less positive need we be in assigning the second place on our list of educational pioneers to the excellent and popular principal of the Ladies' Department of Oberlin College. Since 1835, she has held, in this Western institution, a place of great responsibility, and during all those years she has shown herself every way worthy the confidence she has inspired. True she has never presumed to claim for herself any such position; yet for this very reason she is all the worthier of it. True she may not have arrested the gaze of the world, like many another woman whose life has been a glittering show, yet we shall find her to be one of those quiet and silent forces, which are noiselessly working out the most useful and even the grandest problems of the age and race.

Who has not noticed how men and women of exceedingly defective character, and even of very limited ability, are often lifted, in spite of themselves, into notoriety, and, for a while at least, enjoy a reputation for goodness and power, for which the unthinking world do not fail to honor them? Or who has failed to see how others, of great native ability and of rarest excellence of character, have been so retiring and modest, or so overshadowed by showier presumers, as scarcely during their lifetime to attract our attention? Has not noisy and blaring pretence always seemed at least to win its way more readily than highest merit? — even as the lightning's flash is more sure of winning your attention than the most genial sunbeam of the loveliest morning. And, still, who has not also seen how certainly Providence at length reverses all this seeming experience of life ? He lifts the lowliest to the loftiest place. He makes the weakest the strongest. He confounds what men call wisdom, by establishing what they have pronounced folly. He, at length, brings worthy merit out of its obscurity into the clearest light; and, over the dazzle and glory of all mere gilded radiance, sooner or later spreads the pall which covers all its empty shams. And when this rectification comes, who does not see how real was the merit before undiscovered, and how exceedingly thin and worthless the gilding which so dazzled the eye?

Possibly the sketch we here attempt may justify these reflections. We shall have to speak of a character which has never courted the world's notice, yet one to which the world is certainly under no small obligation. With no brilliant display of personal charms, no parade of talents, no exciting incidents to kindle to an impassioned glow our admiration, we shall still find, at every step in our review, ample reason for the place we have assigned to one of the world's true and faithful and successful workers. As a pioneer in establishing and sustaining the fullest curriculum of studies for woman yet reached, embracing a mental discipline as severe and thorough as that which has been required of young men,— especially, as pioneer in a movement which has done so much towards supplying our broad West with their great and efficient institutions for the advanced culture of woman, — she certainly deserves well of her sex and her race. Very competent authority, Mrs. Caroline H. Dall, of Boston, has well characterized her fitness for the post of lady principal at Oberlin. "The splendid endowment of Vassar College," she says, "could not give to Oberlin a woman better suited to this purpose than Mrs. Dascomb."

Let us, then, briefly trace the educational career of this gifted and successful woman. We must do this, in full knowledge of two special hindrances to our attempt, — the extreme modesty of Mrs. Dascomb's character, which shrinks sensitively from all public exhibition and criticism ; and the fact that her entire educational life has been so intimately associated with that of so many other educators, so that it may be difficult to decide of any particular result, how much of it is due to her agency, or what part of it she should share with her associates.

Marianne Parker, a child of Christian parents, of good New England stock, which itself was of best English puritan blood, was born in Dunbarton, N. H., in 1810. She was the seventh of eight children, five daughters and three sons, whom her mother, Martha Tenney, had borne to her father, William Parker. At the early age of four she became fatherless; and with a large family of children, and but a small patrimony, was left to such care and culture as her mother, who was an excellent woman, could supply. The children were therefore, of necessity, early taught the lessons of economy and mutual helpfulness. The elder members of the family cheerfully fitted themselves to aid their mother in caring for the younger; and these in their turn were trained in habits of thoughtful and helpful industry. It was thus that that interesting group were best disciplined and trained to lives of great usefulness. Those days of preparation were well and wisely spent. The physical and social culture then furnished was of incalculable value to them all. The necessities which imposed such burdens may have been trying to both the mother and her young charge; but its fruits in after years even until now have proved an exceeding reward.

We cannot wonder when, in later years, we find how all of that group have worked themselves up into positions of honored usefulness, such as only earnest and intelligent workers can fill. How like the story of how many New England families of fifty years ago it reads!

Three of the sisters in due time became the wives of three ministers, and the fourth that of a professional and useful teacher. Of the brothers, the eldest, after graduating at college, became a successful teacher; the second, on whom the care of the home and widowed mother fell, has done good service in the church and world; and the third is still, as for the last quarter of a century, an approved minister of Christ. A whole family thus given to the cause of learning and religion is just the source from which we might expect a pioneer and leader, or at any rate an efficient promoter, of some needed movement in education or in ethics.

And such a character we believe we have in the subject of this sketch. From the first she gave indications of possessing large native ability. To her natural inquisitiveness was added clear and quick perception, with a corresponding fulness of the reasoning faculty; and so, under the stimulus of the home and early school culture which she enjoyed, she made rapid progress in acquiring knowledge. Nor was she deficient in such social and affectional qualities as are needed to constitute one the best and most serviceable of friends; or to give one the firmest hold on the confidence and affections of others, and so the most efficient power for good or evil over them.

In early girlhood she is reported to us as "one of the best of playmates," and in maturer years we find her as sympathetic and affectionate and persuasive as then; while to these merely companionable qualities she has added the power and authority of a dignified and matronly grace.

Her early school education was much like that of the majority of girls of that day. Specially favorable to her progress was the influence over her of Miss Chase, a sister of our present Chief Justice Chase, who was in her thirteenth year her teacher; and also that of her brother-in-law, Rev. Thomas Tenney, who had charge of the Hampton Academy. After leaving the Hampton Academy, she prosecuted her education in various schools as pupil or teacher, until, anxious to lay deeper and broader foundations for what she was coming to look upon as her future profession,—teaching,—she entered the Ipswich Academy, then in charge of Miss Grant, one of the ablest of our lady teachers of that day. Here she graduated in 1833, ranking high in her class, and ready for any good service in almost any field of woman's work which might open before her. Nor had she long to wait. She entered with enthusiasm the first field open to her,—a school in Boscawen, New Hampshire, and was there making full proof of the wisdom of her choice of pursuits, when another call was made upon her.

Dr. James Dascomb, a young physician, well fitted for his profession,—a Christian gentleman, longing to find the field in which he might do best service for his race,—had then just offered himself to the American Board of Commissioners for Foreign Missions, as a missionary physician to some heathen field. While looking forward to such service, he became acquainted with Miss Parker. He was not long in detecting, in the spirit and character of the young and ardent teacher, the qualities which would be most fitting for one who should be his helpmeet in such a life-work. Nor was she long in reciprocating his confidence and affection.

Pending his negotiation with the American Board, Providence was preparing for him another field and service. A movement had been started to establish at the West a school of collegiate rank for both sexes, in which, by manual labor, the students could at once promote their health and contribute towards their support. In the forests of Northern Ohio a site had been found for the attempt, and the earnest and large-hearted men who had projected the movement commenced their work, naming both the institution and the town, of which it was to be the beginning and life, from Oberlin, the Christian pastor and teacher, and civilizer of the rude peasantry of the Ban de la Roche, in Switzerland. In this novel movement, started in the interests of literature, religion, and humanity, the young physician was now invited to take part; and, after a consultation with Miss Parker, they mutually and heartily accepted the post. Resigning the school she had just opened in Canajoharie, New York, into other hands, Miss Parker was married in the spring of 1834; and with her husband entered at once upon the work which has never yet been intermitted. For thirty-four years they have wrought together on that field, apparently so forbidding, — the husband rising step by step in scholarship and professional popularity, until now, and the wife to a post of responsibility and usefulness, second, perhaps, to none in the country, which woman has been called to fill. They have lived to see the old forest give way to an institution which more than any other in the West has made itself a power among the noblest movements of the age.

On connecting herself with the young college, Mrs. Dascomb was appointed the principal of the ladies' department. Her strength then proving unequal to the burden, at the end of the year she resigned, not, however, without having made full proof of her many admirable qualifications for the post. She was immediately transferred to the Ladies' Board of Managers, where, for years, her good sense was of incalculable service to the board. In 1852 she was urged to resume the post of principal of the ladies' department, and again, though hesitatingly, she accepted the charge. In this post she has remained until now. Her office, calling as it does for large executive and administrative ability, has been most worthily and acceptably filled. The trustees of the college are unanimous in their admiration of her signal success. They cheerfully accept her counsel, in all matters relating to her department, as law; and they never find her counsels or her plans to fail. Under her judicious management, and, owing to this perhaps as much as to any one agency, the college at Oberlin has practically shown the safety and wisdom of educating, even through the college course, the two sexes together. It has, also, proved the ability of woman to prosecute creditably all the studies of the college course, and to compete successfully with men in any field of literature.

But precisely how much of the success at Oberlin has been due to any one of the agencies employed, it may be difficult to decide. There have been in the work some of the ablest men our country has produced. Certainly, no more earnest workers have anywhere used to the utmost all their resources to sustain and build up any institution of the age. The enterprise, itself, was hopeless to any but a strong faith and resolute heart. And they who took the work in hand worked on together with good heart and hope. Its three presidents — Mahan, Finney, and Fairchild — have all done the work of strong and fearless men. Their associates in the Faculty, of their own sex, have worked with them, under the glow and inspiration of the same enthusiasm. Nor could the institution have been established and sustained without such agency. With it, Oberlin has attained a good rank among the literary institutions of the land.

But for the successful attainment of its special aim, that of the co-education of the two sexes, even through the entire college course, another style of educational agency was needed. If young women were to be admitted and carried through the course, the presence of woman would be indispensable in the faculty. Her intelligence and tact, her sympathy and taste, and her quick sense of social proprieties would all be a necessity. Her control and authority would reach and regulate, as man's could not, these new college relations.

Especially also, was the aid of woman needed, to secure another leading idea of the Oberlin movement. The founders wished to organize a community, as well as establish a college, — a community in thorough sympathy with their own Christian work. The town itself was to be the home for their college, and its families were to feel themselves, in some sort, identified with the aims and interests of the college. It must be a community in which young men and women could be Christianly educated, and from whose nurture they should be thoroughly prepared to go forth to their own earnestly aggressive Christian work. But to aid in organizing such a community, the presence and culture and grace of Christian women would be requisite.

Most fortunate, was it, then, that, when such a movement was projected, this needed agency was not wanting. To make no mention of other gifted Christian women, who were counted worthy to engage in such a work, — though such names as those of Mrs. Shipherd, and Mahan, and Finney, and Cowles, may well claim no small share in this noble enterprise, — it was peculiarly providential that such a woman as Mrs. Dascomb was then ready, both in literary attainment, and in every most needed social quality, to give herself to the work. And it is not saying too much that she was ready also for the consecration. Without reservation she entered the service, which, with no abatement of zeal, she has pursued and honored until now.

Nor is it claiming too much to say that her reward has been great. Of about five hundred young ladies who are annually under her instruction or influence, very few can be found who do not regard her with a feeling akin to filial affection. Of the thousands who have gone out from Oberlin, of both sexes, we have but one uniform testimony to the high esteem with which they regard her. Her associates in the work tell us the same story of their dependence upon her, and their great indebtedness to her influence.

Nor is it difficult to detect the secret of her power. It lies both in her temperament and character. She is lifeful and cheerful. She shows good sense and judgment. She abounds in hopefulness, which gives her confidence and courage. She has no misgivings lest duty should prove inexpedient; and so her faith in the results of duty never fails her. She is self-sacrificing, — doing cheerfully for others, what she would gladly be excused from doing on her own account. She is conscientious, anxious only to do the right thing herself, and solicitous only to aid others in seeing what is right, and doing it. One of the most sensitively gentle of women, she has still the firmest strength of will, holding herself and holding others, as by inevitable law, to truth and duty. She could not compromise principle, though a world were to be won. With her the first question and the last is, not, Will it pay? not, Is it fashionable? not, Will it please the world? but, Is it right? She has the courage to face sneers and danger even, if in the path of duty. In the day when to befriend a fugitive negro was to arouse a storm of popular rage and vengeance, she never hesitated to recognize the fugitive's claim. She acknowledged no misnamed patriotism, which required her to prove faithless to the plain call of humanity. Higher than all human enactments, she held and holds the claims and the law of the only God.

And so, by her gentle and patient kindness; by her fervent zeal in duty; by her disinterested love and service for others; by her uncompromising devotion to what is true and right, — she has made for herself a place of power in the community where she has lived, and especially in the hearts and minds she has aided in educating for the service of the church and world. And still, as for so many years, she is prosecuting the same good work, with the same success. Without denying the claims of her own family and home, — in which she has reared to womanhood the two adopted, the only children given to her to rear, — she is still laboriously employed in the duties of her great charge at the college. In her daily work of personal interview and consultation with pupils and teachers, and the matrons of the homes in which the pupils reside; in assigning daily exercises and studies; in familiar lectures to the young ladies on all topics, outside of the general course of instruction in the classes, on which they need instruction and advice, — Mrs. Dascomb is still adding to the reputation she has already won, as a woman of eminent ability and service. But, pre-eminently, her best record is yet to be written. It must be traced in the career of the many gifted young women whom she has aided in fitting for service, good and great, like her own. Their success, when its causes are fully known, will add new lustre to the crown, which she now so unconsciously wears.

HARRIET BEECHER STOWE.

BY REV. E. P. PARKER.

Harriet Beecher, daughter of Rev. Lyman Beecher, D.D., was born in the town of Litchfield, in the State of Connecticut, on the 14th day of June, in the year of our Lord 1812. Her father, than whom no man of his generation is more reverently and affectionately remembered, was one of the sturdiest and grandest men that New England has produced. Among American divines his position as a theologian was one of distinction, and as a pulpit orator he stood full abreast with the most eloquent. There have been no more powerful preachers in our country than he.

In the year 1799 he married Roxana Foote, whose father, Eli Foote, was a genial and cultivated man, and, notwithstanding he was a royalist and churchman, was universally respected and honored. She was also the grand-daughter of General Ward, who served under Washington in the Revolutionary war. This union was blessed with eight children: — Catharine, William, Edward, Mary, George, Harriet, Henry Ward, and Charles. Dr. Beecher had sworn never to marry a weak woman; nor, in marrying Roxana Foote, did he forswear himself. In one of the Mayflower sketches, in the character of Aunt Mary, and later, in a letter contributed to the "Autobiography of Lyman Beecher" (vol. I., page 301), Mrs. Stowe herself describes her mother. She was a woman of extraordinary talents, rare culture, fine taste, sweet and gentle temper; full of the Holy Ghost and of that power which comes not with observation, but whose exercise is alike unconscious and irresistible.

She died when Harriet was not quite four years old, but "her memory and example had more influence in moulding her family, in deterring from evil and exciting to good, than the living presence of many mothers."

Mrs. Stowe relates that when, in her eighth year, she lay dangerously ill of scarlet fever, she was awakened one evening just at sunset by the voice of her father praying at her bedside, and heard him speaking of "her blessed mother, who is a saint in heaven!" The passage in Uncle Tom, where St. Clair describes his mother's influence, is simply a reproduction of the influence of Mrs. Stowe's own mother, as it had always been in her family.

All who have read the "Minister's Wooing" must remember the beautiful letter which Mary wrote to the Doctor. That letter is one which, years before, Mrs. Beecher had written, and was copied by Mrs. Stowe into the pages of her story. Immediately after her mother's death, Harriet was taken to live with her mother's sister, in whose well-ordered house the little girl found a happy home, the tenderest care, and the benefits of an unusually wholesome moral discipline and intellectual companionship. Her mother had been a quiet but devout churchwoman who, at her marriage with Dr. Beecher, conformed herself to the simpler manners of the Congregational churches, and bent her steps to the ways in which her husband walked, but not without cherishing an ineradicable love of the better way in which her fathers walked and worshipped. Something of this feeling Harriet may have inherited. Having had such a mother, she found herself, in the circle of her mother's relatives, surrounded by those who believed in the Church, and walked after its ordinances only, with all their hearts. Nor is it unlikely that these facts furnish a sufficient explanation of that preference for the mode of divine worship which obtains in the Episcopalian Church, which, in these later years, Mrs. Stowe has publicly manifested.

Of her pleasant life in the farm-house at Nutplains; of the good old grandma with bright white hair, who took her — the little motherless — into her arms, and held her close, and wept over her; who read the evening service, after supper, from a great prayer-book, with such impressiveness as touched the child's heart with a feeling of its intrinsic simplicity and beauty which she never outgrew; and who also, in the sincerity of her toryism, often read over, with trembling voice, the old prayers for king, queen, and royal family, grieving that they should have been omitted in all the churches; of her energetic, precise, smart, orderly Aunt Harriet, who was one of the women who contrive to bring all their plans to pass and to have their ways perfectly, — a splendid specimen of the best kind of a genuine Yankee woman, believing in the Church with a faith in which disdain of all Meeting-house religion was so far mingled that, when on a visit to Litchfield, she could not bring herself to listen to Dr. Beecher, of whom she was very proud and fond, but must needs go to Church, where all things were "done decently and in order," — who did more than encourage little Harriet to "move gently, to speak softly and prettily, to say 'yes, ma'am' and 'no, ma'am,'" to keep her clothes clean, and knit and sew at regular hours, to go to Church on Sundays and make all the responses, and come home and be thoroughly drilled in the catechism; of her Uncle George who was a great reader, and full of poetry, and had Burns and Scott at his tongue's end, and whose recitations of Scott's ballads were the first poems she ever heard; of the house stored with all manner of family relics, and also with all manner of strange and wonderful things brought by a sea-faring uncle, from the uttermost parts of the earth, — supplied moreover with what were exceedingly rare things in those days, a well-selected library, and a portfolio of fine engravings, — of all these things Mrs. Stowe tells us in one of her pleasantest letters, and adds, "The little white farm-house under the hill was a Paradise to us, and the sight of its chimneys after a day's ride was like a vision of Eden!"

Nearly two years passed by, and Harriet, now again in her father's house, wonders at "a beautiful lady, very fair, with bright-blue eyes, and soft auburn hair," who comes into the nursery where she with her younger brothers are in bed, and kisses them, and tells them she loves them and will be their mother. This fair stranger was Dr. Beecher's second wife, Harriet Porter, of Portland, Maine; and of little Harriet she writes to her friends very handsomely: "Harriet and Henry . . . . are as lovely children as I ever saw, amiable, affectionate, and very bright." She speaks also of "the great familiarity and great respect subsisting between parent and children," and of the household as "one of great cheerfulness and comfort." "Our domestic worship is very delightful. We sing a good deal, and have reading aloud as much as we can. It seems the highest happiness of the children to have a reading circle." These observations afford us glimpses of that inner domestic life amid whose healthful and quickening influences Mrs. Stowe's child-life developed itself. Her sister Catharine writes of her when she was five years of age: "Harriet is a very good girl. She has been to school all this summer, and has learned to read very fluently. She has committed to memory twenty-seven hymns and two long chapters in the Bible. She has a remarkably retentive memory, and will make a good scholar." She very early manifested a great eagerness for books, and "read everything she could lay hands on." Her young mind drank eagerly at every available literary spring, and such was the inspiration of Dr. Beecher's presence among his children, that they daily lived and breathed in a bracing intellectual atmosphere, and their wits were kept constantly in exercise.

One incident from Mrs. Stowe's "Early Remembrances" of Litchfield well illustrates his "inspiring talent," and not only that, but the unusual degree of intellectual activity which characterized the whole domestic life. One of the famous occasions in the course of the year was the apple-cutting season, in the autumn, when a barrel of cider apple-sauce had to be made. "The work was done in the kitchen, — an immense brass kettle hanging over the deep fire-place, a bright fire blazing and snapping, and all hands, children and servants, employed on the full baskets of apples and quinces which stood around. I have the image of my father still, as he sat working the apple-peeler. 'Come, George,' he said, 'I'll tell you what we'll do to make the evening go off. You and I'll take turns, and see who'll tell the most out of Scott's novels'! And so they took them, novel by novel, reciting scenes and incidents, which kept the eyes of the children wide open, and made the work go on without flagging." Dr. Beecher was very fond, too, of setting all manner of discussions on foot, into which he would draw the children, arguing with them, correcting them in their logical slips, and so not only putting them in the way of acquiring new knowledge, but what was far better, arousing their minds, sharpening their wits, and teaching them how to think and reason. Allusion has been made to Harriet's eagerness to read. But the light literature which, in our days, is to be found in such abundance even in parsonages, to say nothing of Sunday-school libraries, was wanting in her father's library, and she was hardly ready to satisfy her hunger as one young lady of our acquaintance once attempted to do, by beginning at one end of the library and reading it through, book by book. She had found, and for a while had revelled in, a copy of the "Arabian Nights;" and afterward, in her desperate search among sermons, tracts, treatises, and essays, she turned up a dissertation or commentary on Solomon's Song, which she read with avidity, "because it told about the same sort of things she had read of in the "Arabian Nights." She was again rewarded for her several hours' toil in what she calls "a weltering ocean of pamphlets," by bringing to light a fragment of "Don Quixote," which seemed to her like an "enchanted island rising out of an ocean of mud"!

This was the time when the names of Scott, Byron, Moore, and Irving were comparatively new, and yet not so new as not to be in the mouths of all intelligent people. The Salmagundi papers were recent publications. Byron had not quite finished his course. Scott had written his best poems, and the "Lay of the Last Minstrel," and "Marmion," were familiar to people of intelligence, the world over; but the "Tales of my Landlord," and "Ivanhoe," had just made their appearance. Now the novel, in those days, was regarded, by all pious people at least, as an unclean thing. It was not tolerated, and, indeed, it had become really unclean and intolerable in the hands of the previous generation of writers of fiction.

Great was the joy in that household when an exception was made to the prohibitory law under which all works of fiction were excluded from well-ordered households, as only so much trash and abomination, and Dr. Beecher said, "George, you may read Scott's novels. I have always disapproved of novels as trash, but in these are real genius and real culture, and you may read them"! This generous license was improved, for in one summer Harriet and George "went through 'Ivanhoe' seven times," so that they could recite several of the scenes from beginning to end! In the next house to the one in which Dr. Beecher lived, and but a few steps distant, dwelt "Aunt Esther,"—a woman of strong mind, ready wit, and large information, to whose keen criticism Dr. Beecher frequently submitted his sermons and articles, and whose geniality and inexhaustible fund of entertaining information made her room a favorite resort of the children. From her hands Harriet one day received a volume of Byron's poems containing the "Corsair." This she read with wonder and delight, and thenceforth listened eagerly to whatever was said in the house concerning Byron. Not long after, she heard her father say sorrowfully, "Byron is dead,—*gone*"*!* "I remember," she says, "taking my basket for strawberries that afternoon, and going over to a strawberry field on Chestnut Hill. But I was too dispirited to do anything; so I lay down among the daisies, and looked up into the blue sky, and thought of that great eternity into which Byron had entered, and wondered how it might be with his soul"! Harriet was then eleven years old, but was sufficiently precocious to appreciate the genius that was exhibited in Byron's passionate poetry, and to share in the enthusiasm which that genius has everywhere created.

Not only in her father's house, and in the family circle, but in the society and schools of Litchfield as well, was her mind enriched and stimulated to independent thought. The town of Litchfield was celebrated in those days for the unusual number of cultivated, scholarly, and professional men who resided there, and for the high literary character of its society. "A delightful village, on a fruitful hill, richly endowed with schools both professional and scientific, with its venerable governors and judges, with its learned lawyers, and senators, and representatives both in the national and state departments, and with a population enlightened and respectable, Litchfield," says Mrs. Stowe, "was now in its glory."

The high reputation of Miss Pierce's school for young ladies brought a goodly number of fair women into the town, while the excellent law-school of Judge Reeve attracted thither brave young men from all quarters.

Miss Catharine Beecher relates that when Mrs. Stowe was at Paris, she was repeatedly visited by an aged French gentleman of distinction, who in youth had spent some years in Litchfield as a student at the law school, and, in his conversations with Mrs. Stowe, he frequently referred to, and dwelt with enthusiasm upon, the society of Litchfield, which he declared was the most charming in the world. In such a home, and in such a society, Harriet Beecher passed the first twelve years of her life. She was a pupil in the school taught by Miss Pierce and Mr. Brace. Of Mr. Brace, Mrs. Stowe speaks in terms of the highest praise, as a gentleman of wide information, well-read in the English classics, of singular conversational powers, and a most "stimulating and inspiring instructor." Her own simpler lessons were neglected and forgotten as she sat listening intently, hour after hour, to the recitations of the older classes, and to the conversations of Mr. Brace with them, in moral philosophy, rhetoric, and history. In this school particular attention was given to the writing of compositions. An ambition was kindled in the minds of the scholars to excel in this exercise.

Harriet was but nine years old, when, roused by Mr. Brace's inspiration, she volunteered to write a composition every week. The theme for the first week was sufficiently formidable, — The Difference between the Natural and the Moral Sublime. But so great was the interest which the preparatory discussions had awakened in her mind, that she found herself in labor with the subject, felt sure that she had some clear distinctions in mind, and, although she could hardly write legibly or spell correctly, brought forth her first composition upon that question. Persevering in her efforts, she was soon publicly commended for her progress, and two years later received the honor of an appointment to be one of the writers at the annual exhibition of the school. On that distinguished occasion she argued the negative of the following question: Can the Immortality of the Soul be proved by the Light of Nature? We may smile at the idea of an argument on such a topic by a girl in her twelfth year, but she shall describe the scene of her first public triumph: —

"I remember the scene at that exhibition, — to me so eventful. The hall was crowded with the *literati* of Litchfield. Before them all our compositions were read aloud. When mine was read, I noticed that father, who was sitting on high by Mr. Brace, brightened and looked interested; and, at the close, I heard him say, 'Who wrote that composition?' '*Your daughter, sir!*' was the answer. It was the proudest moment of my life."

The conditions and circumstances of Mrs. Stowe's early life, the scenes and surroundings of her childhood, and the nature of that domestic and social life in which her own life was rooted, and from which some, at least, of its peculiar qualities must have been derived, deserve a much more careful and complete representation than the limits of this sketch will allow; for they reveal where and how the solid foundations of her future fame were laid, and by what subtile but potent influences her intellectual powers were quickened, her character moulded, and her whole history happily predetermined in its course of development.

At about twelve years of age, Harriet went to Hartford, where her sister Catharine had opened a school for young ladies. She was one of a brilliant class which numbered among its members several ladies whose names are well and widely known. She was known as an absent-minded, introspective, reticent, and somewhat moody young lady, odd in her manners and habits, but a fine scholar, a great reader, and exceedingly clever in her compositions, whether of poetry or of prose. Even then she displayed something of that fondness and aptitude for delineating the peculiarities of New England manners and character, for which, in later years, both she and her brother Henry Ward have been distinguished. Children of New England, born and reared under its clearest skies, and amid its loveliest scenes, perfectly familiar with every phase of its social life, full of its native spirit of independence, — whose home, also, and family relations were such as were sufficient to inspire them with an ardent enthusiasm for the land of their fathers, they have revelled in charming reminiscences and descriptions of it; and have never written more graphically, and as if under a genuine inspiration, than in those pages of the "Mayflower," of "The Minister's Wooing," of "The Pearl of Orr's Island," and of "Norwood," where they have led their readers to and fro over its peaceful hills, and among its peculiar people of long ago.

For a season Harriet was an associate teacher in the Hartford Seminary; but, on the failure of Miss Beecher's health, both she and her sister sought rest in their father's house, which, since the year 1832, had been located in the environs of Cincinnati. Here, also, after a brief respite, they opened a school, of which — and particularly of the religious influence of which, and of a Bible class in Old Testament history which Harriet Beecher conducted — we have heard one of the pupils speak in terms of high praise.

Miss Beecher at length gave herself up to the organization of larger educational enterprises, — to the furtherance of which her whole life has been nobly devoted. And on the 5th day of January, in the year 1836, Harriet married Professor Calvin E. Stowe, a man of learning and distinction, and, at that time, Professor of Biblical Literature in Lane Theological Seminary.

For several years previous to her marriage, however, Mrs. Stowe had occasionally made her appearance, both in private circles and in the periodical literature of the day, as a writer of no little promise. Some of her productions of that period have not yet passed out of public notice.

It now becomes necessary to refer to certain literary associations into which Mrs. Stowe was happily drawn, and which had no little influence in awakening in her a consciousness of her powers, and furnished her with opportunities, motives, and encouragements to make trial of those powers. Out of the good fellowship which prevailed among many of the literary men and women of that vicinity, — a fellowship which was fostered by the hospitality of several gentlemen of culture and property, — a remarkable series of social and literary reunions were established under the name of the "Semicolon Club." At the meetings of the club, which were under just enough of regulation to prevent confusion and dissipation of time, without hindering perfect freedom of discussion and intercourse, essays, sketches, reviews, stories, and poems were read, discussions and conversations were carried on, and music came in to enliven and diversify the exercises.

Many of those who were accustomed to participate in these reunions have since distinguished themselves in their respective vocations. Among these we may mention Judge Hall, editor of the "Western Monthly Magazine," and a critic of no little reputation; Miss Catharine Beecher, and her sister Harriet; Prof. Hentz and his wife, Caroline Lee Hentz, a novelist of popularity, and a woman of distinguished grace; E. P. Cranch, whose exquisite humor flowed from either pen or pencil with equal facility; James H. Perkins, a man of extraordinary talents; Col. E. D. Mansfield;

Prof. J. W. Ward; Charles W. Elliot, the New England historian; Daniel Drake, a medical professor and author of celebrity; William Greene; three Misses Blackwell, two of whom have gained distinction as physicians; Prof. C. E. Stowe, widely known, both in Europe and America, as a scholar and author; and Professor, and subsequently Major-General O. M. Mitchell, whom the nation remembers as one of its most accomplished scientific men, and mourns as one of its noblest martyrs in the cause of liberty.

In this brilliant circle Mrs. Stowe's genius soon began to shine conspicuously. Some of her contributions to these reunions were received with unaffected wonder and delight. The portraiture of old Father Mills, of Torringford, Conn., which appears in the "Mayflower" under the title of "Father Morris," was greeted with uproarious applause. But her "Uncle Tim," written in 1834 for the "Semicolon Club," and read at one of its sessions, made the deepest impression. And this same sketch, which is still one of the most charming and characteristic productions of her pen, published first in Judge Hall's Magazine, and afterward in the "Mayflower," first attracted public attention to her as a writer of great versatility and promise.

In this "Semicolon Club" the woman of genius seems to have first become really conscious of her powers; in it she received also recognition, sympathy, and an impulse, and by it found a way for herself out beyond the circle of private fellowships into the wider circles of the great world. Meanwhile she was an occasional contributor to the Western Magazine, to Godey's Magazine, and perchance to other periodicals. And not long after her marriage the "Mayflower" was published, which contained, beside some of the best of her "Semicolon" papers, several new sketches of New England life and character. Thenceforward her life flowed on in purely domestic channels for several years, without putting forth any decided signs of its future fruitfulness. And now we are brought to the threshold of that great arena on which her mightiest works were done, and her great triumph was achieved, while the whole world looked on and applauded. Uneventful as the next few years of her life seemed then to be, they were years of peculiar trial and discipline, wherein God himself was secretly preparing and furnishing her for the fulfilment of his great purposes.

She had always felt a deep interest in the slaves, and, whenever opportunities occurred, had always manifested a practical benevolence towards them. By journeys into the adjoining State of Kentucky, by visits at the homes of her pupils from that State, she had made herself perfectly familiar with the different aspects of plantation life. For years she had enjoyed and improved excellent opportunities of studying the negro character, and also the operations of the slavery system. Fearful examples of the evils and miseries, of the unspeakable wrongs and crimes and shames of slavery, were ever and anon laid at her very door. She was at the very point where the great anti-slavery conflict raged most fiercely, — in the midst of the border warfare of abolitionism. Fugitive slaves were frequently concealed in her house. Children of fugitives were harbored and instructed there. Hard by was the Walnut Hills under-ground railroad, of which her husband had the credit of being an active director. One day her two little children were going to the barn to play. The elder, to frighten his sister into some submission, cried, "The black man will catch you!" whereupon four burly fugitives, who were resting and hiding in the hay till nightfall, thinking themselves discovered, started up and ran away, to the infinite terror of both children. Sometimes quite a family would be secreted in the house, and the great difficulty, says Prof. Stowe, "was to keep the little pickaninnies from sticking their heads out of the windows, and so betraying their retreat."

Often at dead of night the rattle of wagons bearing escaped slaves onward to the land of promise, and afterwards the ominous tramp of hard-ridden horses were heard, telling of rapid flight and hot pursuit.

The actual spiriting away from her pursuers of a poor colored girl by Mrs. Stowe's husband and her brother Charles, who, trusting first to God, and secondly to a sagacious old black horse, carried the fugitive away under cover of a starless night and over a perilous road to a place of safety in honest old Van Zandt's cabin, needed only a little disguising in the description to fit it for the pages of "Uncle Tom." Amid all the anti-slavery discussions and tumults,—amid all the excitements and outrages and sufferings of which she had personal knowledge, and when mob-violence threatened the safety of the roof that sheltered her, Mrs. Stowe manifested no unusual intensity of feeling on the subject. Amid the earnest voices that argued and described and denounced the iniquities of slavery her voice was not heard. She was a silent but close observer of passing events. Materials for her future work were unconsciously accumulating as she watched, and waited, and hoped, and prayed.

The seminary in which her husband was a prominent instructor became at length the scene of a painful and disastrous struggle between the two great forces of the age. Conservatism triumphed, but in its blind zeal pulled down some of the strongest columns on which the institution rested. The seminary was seriously crippled, and, after protracted labors to restore its prosperity, finding his health failing, Prof. Stowe retired to accept a professorship in Bowdoin College, in Brunswick, Maine, and in the year 1850 he entered upon his duties there. Just at this time the fugitive slave law was passed, and Mrs. Stowe was one of those whose souls were kindled with indignation at this infamous piece of legislation. In the light of that political act which converted the people of a great and free nation into so many compulsory negro-catchers, she saw clearly that the policy of inaction was no longer right nor safe, and that slavery was an insatiable monster that threatened not simply the dishonor, but the utter ruin, of the country. One single, definite purpose arose out of her deep convictions, and took possession of her mind. The whole system of slavery must be shown up as it really was! This simple and all-controlling conviction was the corner-stone of "Uncle Tom's Cabin"!

Mrs. Stowe herself says: —

"For many years the author avoided all reading upon, and all allusion to, the subject of slavery, considering it too painful to be inquired into, and one which advancing light and civilization would certainly live down. But since the act of 1850, when she heard with consternation Christian and humane people actually recommending the remanding escaped fugitives into slavery, as a duty binding on all good citizens; when she heard, on all sides, from kind, compassionate, and estimable people, in the free States of the North, deliberations and discussions as to what Christian duty could be on this head, she could only think, *these men and Christians do not know what slavery is;* and from that arose a desire *to exhibit it in a living, dramatic reality"!*

Mrs. Stowe had, then, a perfectly clear idea of what was necessary to be done, and also a just appreciation of the most effective literary instruments and the best artistic methods for the accomplishment of the work.

But as yet there was no definite plan of proceeding. Indeed, "Uncle Tom's Cabin" was not so much put together and built up, like a house, according to a complete, preexistent design, as developed, like a tree, from one high, holy, and controlling idea.

Topsy's solution of the problem of her own personal existence is the most satisfactory explanation of the production of this story. It grew! While as yet the form and plan of the work lay undeveloped in her mind, she made a beginning, which, instead of a beginning, was a stroke at the very heart of her whole story.

One day, on entering his wife's room in Brunswick, Prof. Stowe saw several sheets of paper lying loosely here and there, which were covered with her handwriting. He took them up in curiosity and read them. The death of *Uncle Tom* was what he read. That was first written, and it was all that had then been written. "You can make something out of this," said he. "I mean to do so," was the reply. Soon after, Mr. Bailey, who was then publishing an anti-slavery paper in Washington, solicited Mrs. Stowe to write a series of articles for its columns.

The way was open, and she was ready, and, being called of God, by faith she went forth, not knowing whither she went! Her *Uncle Tom* should have a history, of which his death-scene should be the logical consequence and culmination. As she mused the fire burned. The true starting-point was readily found, and gradually a most felicitous story-form was conceived, in which a picture of slavery as it is might be exhibited, — a web was laid, into which she might weave, with threads of gold and silver and purple, her brave designs. "Uncle Tom" began to be published in the "National Era," as a serial, in the summer of 1851, and was continued from week to week until its conclusion in March, 1852.

It was not a product of leisure hours. She

"Wrought with a sad sincerity,"

and under most grievous burdens and disadvantages. Her

health was delicate. Her cares were great. In charge of a large family, and compelled by the sternest of all necessities to make the most of very little and poor help in her household labors, much of this wonderful book was actually written by Mrs. Stowe, as she sat, with her portfolio upon her knee, by the kitchen fire, in moments snatched from her domestic cares. We may be pardoned for saying that if the *cuisine* was half as well managed as the composition, those who sat at Mrs. Stowe's table, as well as those other innumerable ones who have feasted upon the fruits of her literary toil, were fortunate indeed. "The book," as Prof. Stowe finely says, "was written in sorrow, in sadness, and obscurity, with no expectation of reward save in the prayers of the poor, and with a heart almost broken in view of the sufferings which it described, and the still greater sufferings which it dared not describe."

Our older readers need not to be told with what avidity the weekly instalments of this serial were caught up and devoured by the readers of the "National Era." The writer of this article was then a little boy in one of the remoter villages of Maine, but remembers how "Uncle Tom's Cabin" was the theme of universal discussion, and how those in his own home, and all through the village too, who, had never before bowed down to any idols of fiction, nor served them, were so completely demoralized by this novel, that they not only read it, but read it to their children; and how the papers which contained it, after being nearly worn out in going through so many hands in so many different homes, were as carefully folded up and laid away as if the tear-stains on them were sacred, as indeed they were. We were all, from the baby upward, converted into the most earnest kind of abolitionists. Strangely enough, however, when, after its publication in the "Era," Mrs. Stowe proposed its republication in book-form to Messrs. Phillips and Sampson of Boston, the proposition was respectfully declined. That, she thought, was the end of it. A woman's shrewdness had something to do with securing its publication. The wife of Mr. Jewett, of Boston, had read the story, and advised her husband to publish it, if possible. It was offered to him, and he remarked to Prof. Stowe that it would bring his wife "something handsome!" On returning home, his success and the remark of Mr. Jewett were reported to Mrs. Stowe, who, with an eye-twinkle, and a tone in which a little hope, more joy, and still more incredulity were expressed, replied, that she hoped it would bring her enough to purchase what she had not possessed for a long time, — *a new silk dress!*

She was not obliged to wait long for that very desirable article, nor to limit herself very rigidly in the gratification of so legitimate a desire; for only a few months after its republication, Mr. Jewett made his first settlement with Prof. Stowe, and placed the sum of ten thousand dollars in his hands; — "More money," says the professor, "than I had ever seen in my life!" Large as were these first fruits, and enormous as was the sale of the book, for some reasons which do not require to be set forth here, the enterprise was far more remunerative to the publishers than to the author, and Mrs. Stowe was not made rich by her story.

The popularity of the book was unbounded, and its circulation was unprecedented. No work of fiction in the English language was ever so widely sold. Within six months, over one hundred and fifty thousand copies were sold in America, and within a few years it reached a sale of nearly five hundred thousand copies. The first London edition was published in May, 1852. The next September, the publishers furnished to one house alone, ten thousand copies each day for four weeks; making a sale of two hundred and forty thousand copies in one month. Before the end of the year 1852, the book had been translated into the Spanish, Italian, French, Danish, Swedish,

Dutch, Flemish, German, Polish, and Magyar languages. Ere long it was translated into every European language, and also into Arabic and Armenian. There is a bookcase in the British Museum, filled with its various translations, editions, and versions. In Italy, the "powers that be" published an edition in which all allusions to Christ were changed to the Virgin Mary,—a piece of craftiness that argues better for the book than for its mutilators.

But remarkable as was the literary popularity of the book, its political and moral influence was hardly less so. Said Lord Palmerston to one from whose lips the remark was taken as it here stands, "I have not read a novel for thirty years; but I have read that book three times, not only for the story, but *for the statesmanship of it!*" Lord Cockburn said, "She has done more for humanity than was ever before accomplished by any single book of fiction." No political pamphlet or discussion directed against the Fugitive Slave Law could have dealt that sacred iniquity so deadly a blow as did this book. Not only the reading, but the acting of "Uncle Tom,"—and particularly the thrilling scene of *Eliza's* passage of the Ohio River,—in New York, for one hundred and fifty successful nights, operated mightily to awaken popular sympathy for the fugitive, and to make negro-hunting contemptible. The friends of slavery instinctively felt the danger, and arose in all their wrath and cunning to hinder the operation of the power that was going forth in that book among all people. They ridiculed its pretensions, denied its statements, abused the author as a malevolent caricaturist and wilful disturber of the peace; and, reinforced by time-servers from the North, among whom many Doctors of Divinity were not ashamed to be seen, they went forth, a great multitude, terrible with banners and eager for the labor, armed and equipped also with brooms, and mops, and sundry other such suitable implements, to sweep back from all our coasts the rising tide of abolitionism, to which Mrs. Stowe's book had given such an irresistible impulse. Everywhere there was heard the noise of endless splashings, and an infinite confusion, but the tide had its way, — the same tide, which, a few years later, broke over all barriers, swept over the whole country, and washed it clean of its old defilement and curse. "Uncle Tom's Cabin" was the honored instrument of that new and noble impulse which was given to public opinion and feeling throughout all Christendom against the infamous slavery system. It was an indirect but most powerful cause of the great political revolution which soon after culminated in the organization of the great anti-slavery party of the country, at whose triumph, slavery, in the recklessness of its wrath, and in the haughtiness of its pride, rose up in rebellion, only to be utterly cast down and destroyed. Mrs. Stowe was violently assailed as the author of an anti-Christian book, and as herself an infidel disorganizer and agitator; and even religious newspapers joined in the assault. True, her gospel brought not peace but a sword, because it was *the old Gospel of Jesus Christ!* She was an agitator, as are the great winds that blow all abroad, and give us a pure atmosphere to breathe; — as every power is, whether it be of earth or of heaven. But she was an agitator, not like the woman of heathen fable, who flung the apple of discord down into an harmonious company, so wantonly provoking strife; but like that other woman of Christian parable, who took a little leaven and hid it in three measures of meal until the whole was leavened.

Aside from its political influence, "Uncle Tom" was a mighty power in the world as a witness for Christ, and was no less a contribution to the cause of Christianity than to the cause of emancipation and to American literature. One peculiarity of it is, that the inevitable pair of lovers, the history of whose crooked love-courses forms the staple of most novel writing, are hardly to be found in it. It is a picture of social life, in which the development of individual fortunes and the history of personal relations are included, but subordinated.

Again, it confuted the oft-repeated calumny, that none but infidels, and lawless, godless people, were abolitionists. On every page of "Uncle Tom," there are the breathings of a tender, earnest piety, and the manifestations of an ardent loyalty to the Christian faith. What wonderful use of the Scriptures is made in it! Mrs. Stowe's quiver is full of arrows, drawn from the word of God, not one of which fails her. Not only with the facility of perfect acquaintance, but with equal felicity and legitimacy, she quotes and applies the Scriptures to prove, or illustrate, or emphasize her positions. In Paris, the reading of "Uncle Tom" created a great demand among the people for Bibles; and purchasers eagerly inquired if they were buying the *real Bible — Uncle Tom's Bible!* The same result was produced in Belgium, and elsewhere. Could the most eloquent preacher do better than this? What more triumphant vindication of its Christian character and influence could the book have than these facts furnish?

It was a perfectly natural, thoroughly honest, truly religious story, with nothing unwholesome in its marvellous fascinations, but contrariwise, fairly throbbing in every part with a genuine Christian feeling. No wonder that ministers, and deacons, and quiet Quakers too, and all the godly folk who had always been accustomed to frown with holy horror upon novels, did unbend themselves to read, and diligently to circulate the words of this woman whom the Lord had so evidently anointed to "preach deliverance unto the captives, to set at liberty them that are bruised, to preach the acceptable year of the Lord."

To search out the causes of this remarkable literary success would take us too far, in several directions, from the main road in which this sketch must travel. To meet a great popular necessity, to serve the cause of truth and humanity in a time when good men's minds were darkened, and when the powers of evil were coming in upon the nation like a flood, a story was written.

The writer thoroughly understood her subject; was perfect master of the literary instruments she employed; was a Christian woman of genius, and not only brought all the powers of a splendid intellect to the task, but poured out her whole heart in the work. This book was written, as we have said, "in sorrow, in sadness, in obscurity, and with the *heart almost broken* in view of the sufferings it describes!" Here, surely, is one secret of its power. David long ago revealed it. "He that goeth forth, weeping, bearing precious seed, shall doubtless return again with songs, bringing his sheaves with him." So she went forth, and so returned.

Charles Dickens said, "*A noble book with a noble purpose!*"

In "Uncle Tom" we have a charming story, and an unanswerable argument. And the artistic idea, and the moral purpose are coördinately developed and finally fulfilled in perfect harmony.

With no other theme, even had it been treated with equal ability, would Mrs. Stowe have attained equal success. On the other hand, the subject of slavery could never have commanded the attention of the world as this book has done, had it been treated in some undramatic method and with less artistic skill. There is a tremendous *movement* (argument is too cold a word) in the book which, to one who only suffers himself to be once caught in it, is perfectly fascinating and irresistible. And such is the consummate art by which this movement is set on foot, and guided, and led on, that all the while one is being swept along by it, whether or no, his keenest interest is awakened in every change of scene and circumstance, and in every one of the many persons with whom he is made acquainted. Great statesmen like Mr. Seward and Mr. Sumner had argued the question of slavery.

Able divines had given the testimony of the Scriptures upon it. Eloquent platform orators, and vigorous writers had discussed all its aspects and relations. And still a mist of romance, and an atmosphere of sanctity, or at least of privilege, enveloped and concealed its real features. Mrs. Stowe treated the subject, not as a question of law, or of logic, or of political economy, or of biblical interpretation, but as a simple question of humanity; not as an "abstract theory of social relations, but as a concrete reality of human life." She does not *tell*, but *shows* us what it is. She does not analyze, or demonstrate, or describe, but, by a skilful manner of indirection, takes us over the plantation, into the master's house, into the slave's cabin, into the fields,—through the whole Southern country in fact,—and shows us not only the worst but the best phases of the slavery system, and allows us to see it as it really is. And all the while the power of her own intense sympathy for the oppressed millions whose cause she pleads, is felt throbbing in every line of the narrative.

In the year 1852, Mrs. Stowe took up her residence in Andover, Massachusetts, her husband having already accepted a call to the Professorship of Sacred Literature in the Theological Seminary there located. Soon after she published the "Key to Uncle Tom's Cabin," wherein the accuracy of the statements, and the substantial truth of the representations she had made in her recent story, were fully vindicated.

For a long while her health had been delicate, but now it was very seriously impaired. Her severe toil and the great excitement under which her labor had been performed had exhausted her strength, and she was almost prostrated. This fact determined her to accept the very urgent and flattering invitations she had received, from various parts of England and Scotland, to cross the sea and visit the mother country;

and, accordingly, she embarked with her husband, her brother, and one or two personal friends, and arrived in Liverpool on the 11th day of April. She was everywhere welcomed with surprising enthusiasm and cordiality. Great assemblies gathered about her, at almost every step in her journey, to do her honor. One and the same feeling was everywhere expressed. The same enthusiasm pervaded all ranks of society. On the third day after her arrival in England, at a public meeting in Liverpool, the chairman, in the name of the associated ladies of Liverpool, presented Mrs. Stowe with a most signal testimonial of the esteem in which she was universally held, both as a woman of genius who had written a story of world-wide renown, and as an instrument in the hands of God of arousing the slumbering sympathies of England in behalf of the suffering slave. Great public meetings were held in Glasgow, in Edinburgh, in Aberdeen, and in Dundee; there were receptions, and dinners, and addresses, and scarcely an end to the public manifestations of affectionate enthusiasm towards her.

Perhaps the general feeling that prompted and found expression in all these outward demonstrations may be most satisfactorily described by a few extracts from an address which was presented to Mrs. Stowe at a public meeting in Dundee, by Mr. Gilfillan, in behalf of the Ladies' Anti-Slavery Association: —

"We beg permission to lay before you the expressions of a gratitude and an enthusiasm in some measure commensurate with your transcendent literary merit and moral worth. We congratulate you on the success of the *chef-d'œuvre* of your genius, — a success altogether unparalleled in the history of literature. We congratulate you in having, in that tale, supported with matchless eloquence and pathos the cause of the crushed, the forgotten, and the injured. We recognize, too, with delight, the spirit of enlightened and evangelical piety which breathes through your work, and serves to confute the calumny that none but infidels are interested in the cause of abolition."

These three points were made and emphasized in almost every speech or address that was offered in her honor. She had given the world a most charming and wonderful work of fiction. She had shot, with her own tender hand, the arrow that had pierced the joints of the armor wherewith the system of slavery was clad, and had given the monstrous evil a mortal wound. She had furnished, in her "Uncle Tom," "one of the most beautiful embodiments of the Christian religion that was ever presented to the world." And if these last words, which were uttered by no other than the well-known Rev. John Angell James, seem extravagant praise, we have only to remind the reader that the celebrated critic, Heinrich Heine, whom no one can suspect of partiality in such a matter, after describing his gropings and flounderings amid the uncertain and unsatisfactory speculations of German philosophy, tells us how at length he came to quit Hegel, and to quote the Bible with *Uncle Tom,* — came, too, to see that there was a higher wisdom in the poor slave's simple faith than in the great philosopher's dialectics, and found peace and satisfaction in "kneeling with his praying brother," *Uncle Tom.*

After various excursions, to Paris, to Switzerland, to Germany, Mrs. Stowe returned to England and re-embarked for America on the 7th of September. In the following year she published an account of these European experiences, in the form of letters written to friends at home, under the title of "Sunny Memories of Foreign Lands," to which her husband contributed an introduction, in which some account is given of the public meetings which were held in her honor during the tour through England and Scotland. About this time a new and enlarged edition of the "Mayflower" was also published.

Established in her home once more, and restored in health, Mrs. Stowe's literary labors were resumed; and in the year 1856, shortly after another foreign tour, her second anti-slavery novel was published, under the title of "Dred; a Tale of the Dismal Swamp." In the preface, the author declares her great purpose to be the same as that of her previous story. Once more she endeavors to do something towards revealing to the people the true character of the system of slavery. The book inevitably comes into comparison with its predecessor; and whatever may be truly said in its praise, it cannot be questioned that, both as a work of art and as an effective revelation of slavery, it falls far below "Uncle Tom." The chief defects of the book, and those which hindered the completest fulfilment of its noble purpose, are its lack of unity, and ever and anon a departure from the simplicity of a narrative or representation, into the disenchantments of discussion and argument, by which the reader is disturbed in his pleasant dream and vision, and the reality of the scenes that move before him is explained away. The panorama does not move on without an interruption and in silence, as in the case of "Uncle Tom," interpreting itself, and silently but powerfully unfolding its purpose or moral, but stops now and then to give place to the voice of the delineator in explanations or vindications.

In writing "Uncle Tom," the author seems never to have thought that her representations would be called in question, and accordingly she did not so much as think of fortifying herself as she advanced, or of throwing in justifications and arguments, or of going aside for facts to substantiate her narrative, but kept faithfully to the simplicity of her purpose to exhibit slavery as she had seen and known it. But, in writing "Dred," she seems to have labored under the embarrassment of feeling that her exhibitions needed to be explained, or justified and substantiated here and there; and as often as the artist ceased painting, and began declaiming or defining; or, in other words, by as much as Mrs. Stowe attempted to give us, with "Dred," a "Key" to it also, she violated the most fundamental artistic conditions of success. Thus, also, the whole exposition of slavery was more positive, and formal, and dogmatic than in "Uncle Tom." The story did not grow like "Uncle Tom," but was put together, and is rather a series of sketches than one, organic, indivisible story.

Dred himself, if not imperfectly conceived, is a conception so difficult of realization, and, in fact, so imperfectly created, that he fails to excite our sympathies. He is an unreal presence, — a dark, gloomy, ghostly being, at whose apparitions we wonder, at whose sufferings we are not very much moved, and over whose fate it is impossible to fetch a tear, — hardly a sigh, and that of relief. The fact that in a recent edition of this story the title is changed from "Dred" to "Nina Gordon," is suggestive. But there are unsurpassable passages and characters in "Dred." *Tiff*, *Aunt Milly*, *Nina Gordon*, *Jekyl*, and *Aunt Nesbit* are personages that demonstrate Mrs. Stowe's matchless power in delineating and differentiating individual characters. *Uncle Tiff*, so perfectly devoted to "dese y'er chil'en," so noble and simple of heart, and yet so irresistibly droll in his manners; — who wants to be "ordered round 'fore folks," to maintain the family dignity; who, when his fire goes out immediately after it was kindled, exclaims, "Bress de Lord, *got all de wood left!*" — who sits by the bed of his dying mistress, with his big spectacles on his upturned nose, and a red handkerchief pinned about his shoulders, comforting the sick, darning a stocking, rocking the cradle, singing to himself, and talking to the baby, all at once, — is a character in which the earnestness of *Uncle Tom* and the jollity of *Mark Tapley* are blended. That scene at the bedside of his mistress, and his dialogue with *Fanny*, wherein revival preaching is so finely criticised, and his famous lecture to the young ladies on their manners, are passages in which the relationship of pathos and humor is made manifest in the happiest possible manner. And what more powerful chapter has Mrs. Stowe ever written than that in which *Aunt Milly* tells to *Nina Gordon* the tragic, the terrible story of her life?

Not long after the publication of "Dred," Mrs. Stowe began to write another story, which was published as a serial in the columns of the "Atlantic Monthly," in the year 1859. The "Minister's Wooing," a tale of New England life in the latter part of the eighteenth century, has not unfrequently been pronounced by literary men to be the ablest of all the books which Mrs. Stowe has written. This opinion was expressed by so competent a critic as the Rev. Henry Alford, D.D., Dean of Canterbury. In it the author quits the subject of her previous stories, and returns again to that New England life, of which she has so genuine an appreciation, and is so fond and admirable an interpreter. But while this story was universally acknowledged to be one of great ability, and one in which the author gained new reputation, it was somewhat bitterly criticised on several grounds. Many very proper people professed the utmost disgust at the treatment which the celebrated Dr. Hopkins received at the hands of the author. It was declared to be an unpardonable sin to have brought so dignified, august, and venerable a divine down to the common level of lovers in a love story. Dr. Hopkins, or any other orthodox and exemplary doctor of divinity, should unquestionably have been far above any such worldliness and weakness as falling in love, especially with a young and pretty woman. He certainly should have chosen some elderly, thin, angular, solemn, uncomfortable Calvinistic spinster, and so manifested his willingness to be damned for the glory of God. But, unfortunately, in a moment of inexplicable weakness, Dr. Hopkins did allow his affections to fix upon and twine about a young and beautiful maiden, and with him as he was, and not as he undoubtedly ought to have been, Mrs. Stowe dealt, — not without causing the great divine to appear somewhat diviner, to carnal eyes, at least, by her revelation of human feelings (frailties, if you please) that still remained uncrucified in his bosom. Indeed, after having read his ponderous treatises, and also an exhaustive biography of him, written by able hands, we had regarded him somewhat as we might have regarded a statue, by Michael Angelo, of the ideal theologian. That he had "parts" seemed probable; but that he had "passions" we hardly dreamed. Mrs. Stowe told us that this cold, hard, colossal theological image was, after all, a great, simple-minded, honest, powerful, tender-hearted man, clad in Calvinism as in a cumbrous coat of mail, and armed therewith as with a weaver's beam, but loving and lovable withal as a little child. We felt grateful to the image-breaker, and thanked her for showing us the man underneath the theologian, — the Christian underneath and more glorious than the Calvinist; but as between those who were gratified and those who were horrified, who could judge, save the great reading public; and has not their judgment been rendered?

Moreover the book was supposed by many watchmen on the walls of Zion to be heterodox in its tendencies, and to be well adapted, if not expressly designed, to bring what is called New England theology into contempt. That a woman of strong will, and of quick and ardent temperament, who had put her convictions under the rigid theology of that age and region, — on receiving the news of the sudden death at sea of the son of her love, who had never given evidence of the effectual calling of God, and was therefore to be given over as among the lost, — should rise up, in the intensity of her anguish, in a momentary rebellion against the God of her creed, and utter wild and even wicked cries, and show herself intractable to the common arts, and insensible to the ordinary platitudes of consolation, and be quite beside herself in fact, seemed strange to these suspicious watchmen. Had they never read of Job, or of Peter? Is it then an easy thing for a mother to give up her only God, or her only son? And is it not quite enough to drive an earnest soul into temporary madness to be shut up to such a dreadful alternative? It seemed strange also to these watchmen that poor old *Candace*, an ignorant but Christian colored woman, should have been brought forward, rather than *Dr. Hopkins*, to soothe and quiet and comfort and bring back to reason this distracted mother. But *Candace* had tact, and a woman's instinctive comprehension of the case in hand, neither of which the theologian possessed. Did they never read that "God hath chosen the weak things of this world to confound the things that are mighty, and base things of the world, and things that are despised, hath God chosen . . to bring to naught things that are; that no flesh should glory in his presence"?

The critical watchmen took it very hardly that *Miss Prissy* should free her mind in such a shockingly latitudinarian manner. That estimable but garrulous young lady ventured to say, "We don't ever know what God's grace has done for folks;" and that she hoped that the Lord made "*Jim* one of the elect;" and proceeded to quote what a certain woman once said to a certain other woman whose wild son had fallen from the mast-head of a vessel, to the effect that "from the mast-head to the deck was time enough for divine grace to do its work." But *Miss Prissy* is certainly a very pure and consistent Calvinist in all she says. Taking into account the doctrines of an unconditional and absolute personal election, and together with it that of an instantaneous regeneration by a divine power that descends irresistibly upon each elect individual at the predestinated moment, it seems as though *Miss Prissy* was simply making a practical application of the Hopkinsian theology, and giving poor *Jim* the benefit of it.

The twenty-third chapter, entitled "Views of Divine Government," is the heart of the book. Her description of New England, at the date of her story, "as one vast sea, surging from depths to heights with thought and discussion on the most insoluble of mysteries;" her noble characterization of the early ministry of New England; her representation of the preaching of that time, and of the current views both of human existence and of religious doctrines; her vivid statement of the fearful issues which the theological systems presented to the mind, and of the different effects produced thereby, so that "while strong spirits walked, palm-crowned, with victorious hymns, along these sublime paths, feebler and more sensitive ones lay along the track, bleeding away in life-long despair," — all this is set forth with great clearness and power.

Mrs. Marvyn, whose probably unregenerate son had been lost at sea, as was reported, was bound up in the logical consequences of her rigorous creed. Her brave, beautiful boy was lost! She broke out in a strain of wild despair to *Mary*. She could not be reconciled, simply because, according to her theology, there was nothing in God or in his government to attract or comfort.

The poor woman was well-nigh crazy, and no wonder, with nothing but the sharp points of her unsuspected conceptions of divine sovereignty to fall back upon.

"I am a lost spirit," she cried; "leave me alone!"

At that moment poor old *Candace*, who had never been able to understand theology at all, but knew the God and the

Saviour of the gospel, having anxiously overheard the dreadful monologue, burst into the room.

"Come, ye poor little lamb," she said, walking straight up to Mrs. Marvyn, "come to old Candace!" — and with that she gathered the pale form to her bosom, and sat down and began rocking her, as if she had been a babe. "Honey, darlin', ye a'n't right, — dar's a dreadful mistake somewhar. Why, de Lord a'n't like what ye tink. — He *loves* ye, honey! why, jes' feel how *I* loves ye, — poor ole black Candace, — an' I a'n't better'n Him as made me! Who was it wore de crown o' thorns, lamb? — who was it sweat great drops o' blood? — who was it said, 'Father forgive dem'? Say, honey, wasn't it de Lord dat made ye? Dar, dar, now ye'r cryin'! — cry away, and ease yer poor little heart. He died for Mass'r Jim, — loved him and *died* for him, — jes' give up his sweet, precious body and soul for him on de cross! Laws, jes' *leave* him in Jesus' hands! Why, honey, dar's de very print o' de nails in his hands now!"

The flood-gates were rent; and healing sobs and tears shook the frail form, as a faded lily shakes under the soft rains of summer. All in the room wept together.

"Now, honey," said Candace, "I know our Doctor's a mighty good man, an' larned, — an' in fair weather I ha'n't no 'bjection to yer hearin' all about dese yer great an' mighty tings he's got to say. But, honey, dey won't do for yer now. Sick folks mus'n't hab strong meat; an' times like dese, dar jes' a'n't but one ting to come to, an' dat ar's *Jesus*. *Look right at Jesus!* Tell ye, honey, ye can't live no other way now. Don't ye 'member how He looked on his mother, when she stood faintin' an' tremblin' under de cross, jes' like you? He knows all about mothers' hearts. He won't break yours.

It was jes' 'cause He know'd we'd come into straits like dis yer, dat He went through all dese tings, — Him, de Lord o' Glory! Is dis Him you was a-talkin' about? Him you can't love? Look at Him, an' see if you can't! Look an' see what He is! — don't ask no questions, an' don't go to no reasonin's, — jes' look at *Him*, hangin' dar, so sweet and patient on de cross! All dey could do couldn't stop his lovin' 'em; he prayed for 'em wid all de breath he had. Dar's a God you can love, a'n't dar? Candace loves Him, — poor, old, foolish, black, wicked Candace, — and she knows He loves her."

And here *Candace* broke down into torrents of weeping.

"They laid the mother, faint and weary, on her bed, and beneath the shadow of that suffering cross came down a healing sleep on those weary eyelids."

Could anything be more beautiful than the irrepressible outburst of this simple woman's Christian sympathy and love, as she took her mistress into her arms, and offered her up to God on the altar of her own heart, and bore her griefs and carried her sorrows, and drew her gently away from her theories of the divine purposes and government, and laid her tenderly down beneath the cross, in the shelter of the central fact of Christianity, where she might *feel* the love of God, and weep her madness away, and find comfort and peace?

It is perfectly clear that Mrs. Stowe is no blind believer in the old New England theology. She believes in the theology of the feelings as well as in that of the intellect. Poor old *Candace*, with her tender, sympathetic representations of the love of Jesus, is needed quite as much as the strong divine with his theory of underived virtue and his metaphysical subtleties concerning it. And while "The Minister's Wooing" is precisely what its name indicates, a love-story, and both a charming and powerful one, it contains also a free and bold handling of the traditional orthodoxy of New England, and a masterly exhibition of both its strong and its weak points, its wholesome and its pernicious effects. We are led to think of it somewhat as *James Marvyn* thought of *Dr. Hopkins* himself: "He is a great, grand, large pattern of a man, — a man who isn't afraid to think, and to speak anything he does think; but then I do believe, if he would take a voyage round the world in the forecastle of a whaler, he would know more about what to say to people than he does now; it would certainly give him several new points to be considered!" It is not unlikely that many of the systems and bodies of divinity that have been compacted and elaborated with wonderful skill in the secluded work-shops of our great theologians, might have been modified in some of their parts, and on the whole greatly improved by such a voyage as young *Marvyn* suggests. "The Minister's Wooing," apart from the mere story which is told in it, was rightly regarded as a subtle and masterly piece of theological criticism. As such it was no less warmly welcomed than bitterly assailed. But whatever may be thought of its soundness and merit, there can be no doubt of its great influence. Few books that have been published within the last twenty years have done more to confirm the popular suspicion that the most perfectly compacted dogmatic systems of theology are of all things the most imperfect, inadequate, and unsatisfactory, and to strengthen what may be called the liberal evangelical party of New England.

Immediately after the publication of "The Minister's Wooing" in book-form, Mrs. Stowe visited Europe again, sojourning for the most part in Italy, where she wrote her next story, "Agnes of Sorrento," which also appeared as a serial in the "Atlantic Monthly," during the year 1862.

For many years Mrs. Stowe had been an occasional contributor to the "New York Independent," — a religious newspaper of great reputation and large circulation throughout the country. In the year 1862 she began to write for its columns "The Pearl of Orr's Island," — a pleasant story, whose scene is laid on the beautiful coast of Maine, at Harpswell, not far from Brunswick, where she formerly resided, and whose plan turns upon certain traditions of that seaside community. Summer tourists still visit Orr's Island, and inspect the shell of a house in which the pretty *Pearl* grew. For many years Mrs. Stowe has been one of the able corps of writers whose articles have enriched the columns of the "Atlantic Monthly," and no one of them has done more to give that magazine its large circulation and high reputation than she. "Little Foxes" and "Chimney Corner" papers were written for it, and both these series of piquant essays have had a large sale at home and abroad. The "Queer Little People," whom Mrs. Stowe described to the readers of "Our Young Folks," were people of so much interest that her papers concerning them were gathered into a volume and scattered through the land to the delight of thousands of people both big and little.

Throughout her literary career Mrs. Stowe has been known by her friends, and in later years has become known to the public, as a poet whose songs, in certain tender and plaintive keys, have a peculiar charm and power. Within a few years a goodly number and a judicious selection of her poems have been published. They are chiefly of a religious character, and are the rhythmical breathings of a deep and almost mystic piety. Their music is like the sounds that come up out of the heart of the sea in peaceful summer days when one is by himself on the shore, — sadly sweet and sweetly sad. One of the most beautiful of all these poems is the following which has found a place in many of the hymnologies of our churches, and has gone out, indeed, through all the world :—

"When winds are raging o'er the upper ocean,
  And billows wild contend with angry roar,
'Tis said, far down beneath its wild commotion,
  That peaceful stillness reigneth evermore.

"Far, far beneath, the noise of tempests dieth,
  And silver waves chime ever peacefully,
And no rude storm, how fierce soe'er it flieth,
  Disturbs the Sabbath of that deeper sea.

"So, to the heart that knows thy love, O Purest,
  There is a temple, sacred evermore,
And all the babble of life's angry voices
  Dies in hushed stillness at its peaceful door.

"Far, far away the roar of passion dieth,
  And loving thoughts rise calm and peacefully,
And no rude storm how fierce soe'er it flieth,
  Disturbs the soul that dwells, O Lord, in thee.

"O rest of rest! O peace, serene, eternal!
  Thou ever livest, and thou changest never;
And in the secret of thy presence dwelleth
  Fulness of joy, forever and forever."

In the year 1864 Mrs. Stowe built a beautiful house in the city of Hartford, where she has since resided, surrounded by a large circle of family friends, and both admired and loved by all who enjoy the honor of her acquaintance.

In the midst of whatever can minister to comfort, or invite to leisure and repose, her years are still years of literary labors, and also of rich fruits in their season. Late may she rest from those labors!

MRS. ELIZABETH CADY STANTON.

BY THEODORE TILTON.

I ONCE watched an artist while he tried to transfer to his canvas the lustre of a precious stone. His picture, after his utmost skill, was dull. A radiant and sparkling woman, full of wit, reason, and fancy, is a whole crown of jewels. A poor, opaque copy of her is the most that one can render in a biographical sketch.

Elizabeth Cady, daughter of Judge Daniel Cady and Margaret Livingston, was born November 12th, 1816, in Johnstown, New York, — forty miles north of Albany.

Birthplace is a secondary parentage, and transmits character. Elizabeth's birthplace was more famous half a century ago than since; for then, though small, it was a marked intellectual centre; and now, though large, it is an unmarked manufacturing town. Before her birth, it was the vice-ducal seat of Sir William Johnson, the famous English negotiator with the Indians. During her girlhood, it was an arena for the intellectual wrestlings of Kent, Tompkins, Spencer, Elisha Williams, and Abraham Van Vechten, who, as lawyers, were among the chiefest of their time. It is now devoted mainly to the fabrication of steel springs and buckskin gloves. So, like Wordsworth's early star, "it has faded into the light of common day."

A Yankee said that his chief ambition was to become more

Eng.d by H.B. Hall, Jr. N.Y.

E. CADY STANTON.

famous than his native town: Mrs. Stanton has lived to see her historic birthplace shrink into a mere local repute, while she herself has been quoted, ridiculed, and abused into a national fame.

But Johnstown still retains one of its ancient splendors,—a glory still as fresh as at the foundation of the world. Standing on its hills, one looks off upon a country of enamelled meadow lands, that melt away southward toward the Mohawk, and northward to the base of those grand mountains which are God's monument over the grave of John Brown. In sight of six different counties in clear weather, Elizabeth Cady, a child of free winds and flowing brooks, roamed at will, frolicking with lambs, chasing butterflies, or, like Proserpine, gathering flowers, "herself a fairer flower." As Hanson Cox, standing under the pine tree at Dartmouth College, and gazing upon the outlying landscape, exclaimed, "This is a liberal education!" so Elizabeth Cady, in addition to her books, her globes, her water-colors, and her guitar, was an apt pupil to skies and fields, gardens and meadows, flocks and herds. Happy the child whose foster-parents are God and Nature!

The one person who, more than any other, gave an intellectual bent to her early life, even more than her father and mother, was her minister. This was the Rev. Simon Hosack,—a good old Scotchman, pastor for forty years of a Presbyterian church in which the Cady family had always been members, and of which Mrs. Stanton (though she has long resided elsewhere) is a member to this very day;—a fact which her present biographer takes special pains to chronicle, lest, otherwise, the world might be slow to believe that this brilliant, audacious, and iconoclastic woman is actually an Old School Presbyterian. The venerable Scotch parson—snowy-haired, heavy-browed, and bony-cheeked — was generally cold to most of his parishioners, but always cordial to Elizabeth. A great affection existed between this shepherd and his lamb. What she could not say to either father or mother, she unbosomed to him. Full of the sorrows which all imaginative natures suffer keenly in childhood, she found in this patriarch a fatherly confessor, who tenderly taught her how to bear her little burdens of great weight, or, still better, how to suffer them and be strong. Riding his parish rounds, he would take Elizabeth into his buggy, give the reins into her hands, and, while his fair charioteer vainly whipped the mild-mannered mare, the good man would put on his spectacles, and read aloud from some book or foreign review, or, when not reading, would talk. The favorite subject, both for reading and talking, was religion, — never the dark, but always the bright side of it. Indeed, religion has no dark side. The fancied shadow is not in the thing seen, but in the eye seeing. "If the light that is in thee be darkness, how great is that darkness!" Seeking to fill the girl's mind with sunshine and glory, her minister kept always painting, to her young fancy, fair pictures of paradise and happy saints. Peregrinating in his antique vehicle, the childless old man, fathering this soulful child, taught her that the way to heaven was as lovely as a country road fringed with wild roses and arched with summer blue.

"My father," she says in one of her letters, "was truly great and good, — an ideal judge; and to his sober, taciturn, and majestic bearing, he added the tenderness, purity, and refinement of a true woman. My mother was the soul of independence and self-reliance, — cool in the hour of danger, and never knowing fear. She was inclined to a stern military rule of the household, — a queenly and magnificent sway; but my father's great sense of justice, and the superior weight of his greater age (for he was many years her senior), so modified the domestic government that the children had, in the main, a pleasant childhood."

The child is not only father of the man, but also mother of the woman. This large-brained, inquisitive, and ambitious girl, who early manifested a meditative tendency, soon found her whole nature sensibly jarred with the first inward and prophetic stirrings toward the great problem to which she has devoted her after years, — the elevation and enfranchisement of woman.

"In my earliest girlhood," she says, "I spent much time in my father's office. There, before I could understand much of the talk of the older people, I heard many sad complaints, made by women, of the injustice of the laws. We lived in a Scotch neighborhood, where many of the men still retained the old feudal ideas of women and property. Thus, at a man's death his property would descend to his eldest son, and the mother would be left with nothing in her own right. It was not unusual, therefore, for the mother, who had probably brought all the property into the family, to be made an unhappy dependent on the bounty of a dissipated son. The tears and complaints of these women, who came to my father for legal advice, touched my heart; and I would often childishly inquire into all the particulars of their sorrow, and would appeal to my father for some prompt remedy. On one occasion, he took down a law-book, and tried to show me that something called 'the laws' prevented him from putting a stop to these cruel and unjust things. In this way, my head was filled with a great anger against those cruel and atrocious laws. After which the students in the office, to amuse themselves by exciting my feelings, would always tell me of any unjust laws which they found during their studies. My mind was thus so aroused against the barbarism of the laws thus pointed out, that I one day marked them with a pencil, and decided to take a pair of scissors and cut them out of the book, — supposing that my father and his library were the beginning and end of the law! I thought that if I could only destroy those laws, those poor women would have no further trouble. But when the students informed my father of my proposed mutilation of his volumes, he explained to me how fruitless my childish vengeance would have been, and taught me that bad laws were to be abolished in quite a different way. As soon as I fairly understood how the thing could be accomplished, I vowed that, when I became old enough, I would have such abominable laws changed. And I have kept my vow."

After the failure of Elizabeth's novel and original plan of amending the laws with her scissors, another equally strange ambition took possession of her mind.

"I was about ten years old," she says, "when my only brother, who had just graduated at Union College with high honors, came home to die. He was my father's pride and joy. It was easily seen that, while my father was kind to us all, the one son filled a larger place in his affections and future plans than the five daughters together. Well do I remember how tenderly he watched the boy in that last sickness; how he sighed, and wiped the tears from his eyes, as he slowly walked up and down the hall; and how, when the last sad moment came, and all was silent in the chamber of death, he knelt and prayed for comfort and support. I well remember, too, going into the large, dark parlor to look at my brother's corpse, and finding my father there, pale and immovable, sitting in a great arm-chair by his side. For a long time my father took no notice of *me*. At last I slowly approached him and climbed upon his knee. He mechanically put his arm about me, and, with my head resting against his beating heart, we sat a long, long time in silence, — he, thinking of the wreck of all his hopes in the loss of his dear son, and I fully feeling the awful void death had made. At length, he heaved a deep sigh and said, 'O my daughter, I wish you were a boy!' '*Then I will be a boy*,' said I, 'and will do all that my brother did.'

"All that day, and far into the night, I pondered the problem of boyhood. I thought the chief thing was, to be learned and courageous, as I fancied all boys were. So I decided to learn Greek, and to manage a horse. Having come to that conclusion, I fell asleep. My resolutions, unlike most made at night, did not vanish in the morning. I rose early, and hastened to put them into execution. They were resolutions never to be forgotten,—destined to mould my whole future character. As soon as I was dressed, I hastened to meet our good pastor in his garden, which joined our own. Finding him at work there as usual, I said, 'Doctor, will you teach me Greek?' 'Yes,' he replied. 'Will you give me a lesson now?' 'Yes, to be sure,' he added. Laying down his hoe, and taking my hand, 'Come into my study,' said he, 'and we will begin at once.' As we walked along, I told him all my thoughts and plans. Having no children, he loved me very much, entered at once into the sorrow which I had felt on discovering that a girl was less in the scale of being than a boy, and praised my determination to prove the contrary. The old grammar which he had studied in the University of Glasgow, was soon in my hand, and the Greek article learned before breakfast.

"Then came the sad pageantry of death,—the weeping friends, the dark rooms, the ghostly stillness, the funeral cortege, the prayer, the warning exhortation, the mournful chant, the solemn tolling bell, the burial. How my flesh crawled during those three sad days! What strange, undefined fears of the unknown took possession of me!

"For months afterward, at the twilight hour, I went with my father to the new-made grave. Near it stood a tall poplar, against which I leaned, while my father threw himself upon the grave with outstretched arms, as if to embrace his child. At last the frosts and storms of November came, and made a chilling barrier between the living and the dead, and we went there no more.

"During all this time, the good doctor and I kept up our lessons; and I learned, also, how to drive and ride a horse, and how (on horseback) to leap a fence and ditch. I taxed every power, in hope some day to make my father say, 'Well, a girl is as good as a boy, after all!' But he never said it. When the doctor would come to spend the evening with us, I would whisper in his ear, 'Tell my father how fast I get on.' And he would tell him all, and praise me too. But my father would only pace the room and sigh, 'Ah, she should have been a boy!' And I, not knowing why, would hide my head on the doctor's shoulder, and often weep with vexation.

"At length, I entered the academy, and, in a class mainly of boys, studied Mathematics, Latin, and Greek. As two prizes were offered in Greek, I strove for one, and got it. How well I remember my joy as I received that prize! There was no feeling of ambition, rivalry, or triumph over my companions, nor any feeling of satisfaction in winning my honors in presence of all the persons assembled in the academy on the day of exhibition. One thought alone occupied my mind. 'Now,' said I, 'my father will be happy, — he will be satisfied.' As soon as we were dismissed, I hastened home, rushed into his office, laid the new Greek Testament (which was my prize) on his lap, and exclaimed, 'There, I have got it!' He took the book, looked through it, asked me some questions about the class, the teachers, and the spectators, appeared to be pleased, handed the book back to me, and, when I was aching to have him say something which would show that he recognized the equality of the daughter with the son, kissed me on the forehead, and exclaimed with a sigh, 'Ah, you should have been a boy!'

That ended my pleasure. I hastened to my room, flung the book across the floor, and wept tears of bitterness.

"But the good doctor, to whom I then went, gave me hope and courage. What a debt of gratitude I owe to that dear old man! I used to visit him every day, tell him the news, comb his hair, read to him, talk with him, and listen with rapture to his holy words. Oh, how often the memory of many things he has said has given me comfort and strength in the hour of darkness and struggle! One day, as we sat alone, and I held his hand, and he was ill, he said, 'Dear child, it is your mission to help mould the world anew. May good angels give you thoughts, and move you to do the work which they want done on earth. You must promise me one thing, and that is, that you will always say what you think. Your thoughts are given you to utter, not to conceal; and if you are true to yourself, and give to others all you see and know, God will pour more light and truth into your own soul. My old Greek lexicon, testament, and grammar, which I studied forty years ago, and which you and I have thumbed so often together, I shall leave to you when I die; and, whenever you see them, remember that I am watching you from heaven, and that you can still come to me with all your sorrows, just as you have always done. I shall be ever near you.'

"When the last sad scene was over, and his will was opened, sure enough, there was a clause in it, saying, 'My Greek lexicon, testament, and grammar, I give to Elizabeth Cady.'

"Great was the void which the doctor's death made in my heart. But I slowly transferred my love to the books. When I first received them they were all falling to pieces. So I had them newly bound in black morocco and gilt. Dear are they to me to this day, and dear will continue to be as long as I live. I never look at them without thanking God that he gave me, in my childhood, so noble a friend."

At the time of Dr. Hosack's death, which was in Elizabeth's fifteenth year, her term at the Johnstown Academy was drawing to a close. Among the scholars, whether girls or boys, none could recite better, or run faster, than herself; none missed fewer lessons, or frolics; none were oftener at the head of recitations, or mischiefs. If she was detained from the class, the teacher felt the loss of her cheery company; if she was absent from the out-door games, the boys said that half the sport was gone. She who had been the loved companion of a sedate theologian had, at the same time, remained the ringleader of a bevy of mad romps. A school-house is a kingdom; and Elizabeth was a school-house queen.

After graduating at the head of her class, a sudden blow fell upon her heart, and left a grievous wound. She had secretly cherished the hope, that as she had kept ahead of the boys, and thus shown at least her equality with the domineering sex, she would be sent (as Johnstown boys were then usually sent) to Union College at Schenectady.

The thought never occurred to her, that this institution, like most other colleges, was not so wise and liberal as to educate both sexes instead of one. There will come a time when any institution that proposes to educate the sexes separately, will be voted too ignorant of human nature to be trusted with moulding the minds of the sons and daughters of the republic. To shut girls and boys out of each other's sight during the four most impressible years of life is one of the many conventional interferences with natural law which society unwittingly ordains to its own great harm. It is a happiness to see that most of the new colleges, particularly in the Western States, have been based on a more sensible theory.

Just when Elizabeth Cady's heart was most set on Union College, — whither she would have gone had she pleased her father by being a boy, — she was told that she must go instead to Mrs. Willard's Female Seminary in Troy because she had disappointed him by being a girl. Great was her indignation at this announcement, impetuous her protest against this plan. The stigma of inferiority thus cast upon her on account of her sex, and on account of her sex alone, was galling to a maiden who had already distanced all her competitors of the opposite sex. At every step of her journey to Troy she seemed to herself to be treading on her pride, and crushing out her life. Exasperated, mortified, and humbled, she began, in a sad frame of mind, a boarding-school career. "If there is any one thing on earth," she says, "from which I pray God to save my daughters, it is a girls' seminary. The two years which I spent in a girls' seminary were the dreariest years of my whole life." Nevertheless, nothing remained for the disappointed child but to make the best of a bad situation. So she beguiled her melancholy by playing mischievous pranks. For instance, in the seminary, a big hand-bell was rung downstairs every morning, as a call to prayer, and upstairs every night, as a call to bed. After the nightly ringing, the bell was set down on the upper floor in an angle of the wall. One night, at eleven o'clock, after the inmates had been an hour in bed, Elizabeth furtively rose, stole out of her dormitory in the drapery of a ghost, and solemnly kicked the bell step by step down every flight of stairs to the ground floor! Although everybody in the house was wakened by the noise, and many of the doors were opened, she glided past all the peeping eyes like a phantom, to the general terror of the whole house, and was never afterwards suspected as the author of the mischief.

Soon, however, the merry frightener of others was solemnly frightened herself. The Rev. Charles G. Finney, — a pulpit orator who, as a terrifier of human souls, has proved himself the equal of Savonarola, — made a visit to Troy, and preached in the Rev. Dr. Beman's Presbyterian church, where Elizabeth and her school-mates attended. "I can see him now," she says (describing Mr. Finney's preaching), "his great eyes rolling round the congregation, and his arms flying in the air like a windmill. One evening he described Hell and the Devil so vividly, that the picture glowed before my eyes in the dark for months afterwards. On another occasion, when describing the damned as wandering in the Inferno, and inquiring their way through its avenues, he suddenly pointed with his finger, exclaiming, "There! do you not see them?" and I actually jumped up in church and looked round, — his description had been such a reality.

In quoting this allusion to Mr. Finney, I cannot forbear saying that, although high respect is due to the intellectual, moral, and spiritual gifts of the venerable ex-president of Oberlin College, such preaching works incalculable harm to the very souls which it seeks to save. It worked harm to Elizabeth. The strong man struck the child as with a lion's paw. Fear of the judgment seized her soul. Mental anguish prostrated her health. Visions of the lost haunted her dreams. Dethronement of her reason was apprehended by her friends. Flinging down her books, she suddenly fled home.

The good minister of Johnstown, her revered counsellor, was in his grave. His successor was a stranger whom she could not approach. In her despair, she turned to her father. "Often," said she, "I would rise out of my bed, hasten to his chamber, kneel at his side, and ask him to pray for my soul's salvation, lest I should be cast into hell before morning." At last, she regained her wonted composure of spirits, and joined the Johnstown church. "But I was never happy," she writes, "in that gloomy faith which dooms to eternal misery the greater part of the human family. It was no comfort to me to be saved with a chosen few, while the multitude, and those too who had suffered most on earth, were to have no part in heaven."

The next seven years of her life she spent at Johnstown, dividing her time between book-delving and horse-taming, and, having an almost equal relish for each, she conquered the books in her father's library, and the horses in her father's stable. In fact, she would sometimes ride half the day over hill and meadow, like a fox-hunter, and then study law-books half the night, like a jurist. When she was busy at her embroidery or water-colors, her father, who had a poor opinion of such accomplishments, would bring to her the "Revised Statutes," and say, "My daughter, here is a book which, if you read it, will give you something sensible to say to Mr. Spencer and Mr. Williams when they next make us a visit." Mr. Spencer and Mr. Williams were legal magnates, who made Judge Cady's dinner-table a frequent arena for the discussion of nice points of law. So Elizabeth, with a fine determination to make herself the peer of the whole table, diligently began and pursued that study of the laws of her country, which has since armed and equipped her, as from an arsenal of weapons, for her struggle against all oppressive legislation concerning woman. As to her horse-riding, she has of late years discontinued it, for the reason — if I may be so ungallant as to hint it — that a lady of very elegant but also very solid proportions is somewhat more at her ease in a carriage than on a saddle.

In 1839, in her twenty-fourth year, while on a visit to her distinguished cousin, Gerrit Smith, at Peterboro', in the central part of New York State, she made the acquaintance of Mr. Henry B. Stanton, then a young and fervid orator, who had won distinction in the anti-slavery movement. The acquaintances speedily became friends; the friends grew into lovers; and the lovers, after a short courtship, married, and immediately set sail for Europe.

This voyage was undertaken, not merely for pleasure and sight-seeing, but that Mr. Stanton might fulfil the mission of a delegate to the "World's Anti-slavery Convention," to be held in London in 1840. Many well-known American women were delegates, but, on presenting their credentials, were denied membership on account of their sex. Lucretia Mott, Sarah Pugh, Emily Winslow, Abby Kimber, Mary Grew, and Anne Greene Phillips, — who had no superiors in all England for moral worth, — found, to their astonishment, that, after having devoted their lives to the anti-slavery cause, they were repulsed from an anti-slavery convention which they had gone three thousand miles to attend. Wendell Phillips argued manfully for their admission, but in vain. William Lloyd Garrison — who, having crossed in a tardy ship, did not arrive till after the question had been decided, and decided unjustly — refused to present his credentials, took no part in the proceedings, and sat a silent spectator in the gallery, — one of the most chivalrous acts of his life. Beaten in the committee, the ladies transferred the question to the social circles. Every dinner-table at which they were present grew lively with the theme. At a dinner-table in Queen Street, Mrs. Lucretia Mott — then in the prime of her intellectual powers, and with a head which Combe, the phrenologist, pronounced the finest he had ever seen on a woman — replied so skilfully to the arguments of a dozen friendly opponents, chiefly clergymen, that she was the acknowledged victor in the debate. It was then and there that Mrs. Stanton, for the first time, saw, heard, and became acquainted with Lucretia Mott. Often and often, during her maidenly years, Elizabeth Cady had pondered the many-sided question of woman's relations to society, to the State, to the industrial arts, and particularly to the laws of property,

But, in thinking these thoughts, she had hitherto supposed herself to be alone in the world. Now, however, during a six weeks' constant and familiar companionship with Mrs. Mott, she wonderingly heard the whole cyclopedia of her own hidden and secretly cherished convictions openly confessed by another's lips. All the women with whom Mrs. Stanton had ever associated in America had, without exception, belonged to the circle of conservative opinion. Mrs. Mott was the first liberal thinker on womanhood whom she had ever encountered. Elizabeth's delight at thus finding a woman who had thought farther than herself, on some of the most vital questions affecting the human soul, was as glowing and enchanting as if she had suddenly discovered a cavern of hid treasures. It is not too much to say that the influence of the elder of these women on the younger was greater than the combined influence of everything else which that younger saw and heard during her foreign tour. This is not an exaggerated statement. I once asked her the question, "What most impressed you in Europe?" and she instantly replied, "Lucretia Mott!" One day, as a party of a dozen or more friends were visiting the British Museum, Mrs. Mott and Mrs. Stanton, who were of the company, had hardly entered the building when they sat down and began to talk to each other. The rest went forward, made the circuit of the curiosities, and came back to the entrance, to find that the two talkers still sat with their heads together, never having stirred from their places. The sympathetic twain had found more in each other than either cared to look for in the whole British Museum. Mrs. Stanton's enthusiasm for Mrs. Mott continues still as fresh and warm as then. And no wonder! For, in the same sense in which the greatest man ever produced in this country was Benjamin Franklin, the greatest woman ever produced in this country is Lucretia Mott.

On returning to America, Mr. Stanton began the practice of law in Boston, where, with his wife and family, he resided for five years. The east winds, always unfriendly to his throat, at last drove him to take shelter in the greater kindliness of an inland climate. Accordingly he transferred his household and business. to Seneca Falls, in the State of New York.

The first "Woman's Rights Convention" (known to history by that name) was held July 19th and 20th, 1848, in the Wesleyan Chapel at Seneca Falls. Copies of the official report of the proceedings are now rare, and will one day be hunted for by antiquarians, — a petite pamphlet, about the size of a man's hand, resembling in letter (though hardly in spirit) an evangelical tract by the American Tract Society. My own copy has become yellow-tinted by time. With a reverential interest I look back on this modest chronicle of a great event. That convention little thought it would be historic. But it was the first of a chain of similar conventions which, like the links round a Leyden jar, have since girdled half the world with the brightness of a new idea. The chief agent in calling the convention was Mrs. Stanton. It met in the town of her residence. Its resolutions and declarations of sentiment were the offspring of her pen. Its one great leading idea — the elective franchise — was a suggestion of her brain. I do not know of any public demand for woman's suffrage, made by any organized convention, previous to Mrs. Stanton's demand for it in the following resolution: "Resolved, that it is the duty of the women of this country to secure to themselves their sacred right to the elective franchise." I am aware that women long before had voted (for a short time) in New Jersey. But woman's political rights had already been slumbering for years when Mrs. Stanton jarred them into sudden wakefulness. This she did to the consternation of her best friends. The convention at

Seneca Falls was called, as the advertisement phrased it, "to discuss the social, civil, and religious condition of woman." Nothing was here said of woman's political condition, except so far as that might be ambiguously included in her civil. Probably very few of the delegates, on going to the meeting, carried to it any such idea as woman's suffrage. When Mrs. Stanton privately proposed to introduce the resolution which I have quoted, even Lucretia Mott — who (as the report characterizes her) was "the ruling spirit of the occasion" — attempted to dissuade the bold innovator. But the innovator would not be dissuaded. She offered her resolution, and, in support of it, made, for the first time in her life, a public speech. Not a natural orator, she at first shrank from taking the floor. But a sense of duty impelling her to utter her thought, she conquered her bewilderment, stated her views, answered the convention's objections, fought a courageous battle, and carried her proposition. No American woman ever rendered a more signal service to her country than was, on that day, bashfully, yet gracefully and triumphantly, performed by Mrs. Stanton.

That convention, and, above all, its demand for woman's suffrage, excited the universal laughter of the nation. Wonder-stricken people asked each other the question, "What sort of creatures could those women at Seneca Falls have been?" It was never suspected by the general public that they were among the finest ladies in the land. Even their own relatives and friends, who knew their personal virtues, lamented their public eccentricities and joined the general crowd of critics and satirists. Judge Cady, on hearing of what his daughter had done, fancied her crazy, and immediately journeyed from Johnstown to Seneca Falls to learn for himself whether or not that brilliant brain had been turned. "After my father's arrival," says she, "he talked with me a whole evening till one o'clock in the morning, trying to reason me out of my position. At length, kissing me good-night, he said, 'My child, I wish you had waited till I was under the sod, before you had done this foolish thing!' But I replied, laughing, 'Ah, sir, don't you remember how you used to give me law-books to read in order that I might have something sensible to say to your friends, Mr. Spencer and Mr. Williams, when they came to dine with us? It was by reading those law-books that I found out the injustice of our American laws toward women. I might never have known anything on the subject except for yourself.'" The good man before his death (which occurred several years afterward), although he had never relaxed his opposition to his daughter's views, nevertheless had come to cherish a secret pride at the skill, vigor, and eloquence with which she maintained them against all antagonists.

From the day of the Seneca Falls Convention to the present, Mrs. Stanton has been one of the representative women of America. At a similar convention, held at Cleveland, Ohio, in 1853, Lucretia Mott proposed the adoption of the declaration of sentiments put forth at Seneca Falls in 1848. "She thought," says the official report, "that this would be but a fitting honor to her who initiated these movements in behalf of the women of our country, Elizabeth Cady Stanton."

I have seen the old and tattered manuscript of the first "set speech" which Mrs. Stanton ever delivered. It was a lyceum lecture, ably and elaborately written; and was repeated at several places in the interior of the State of New York, during the first months that followed the first convention. The manuscript, unaccountably slipping out of the author's hands, was passed from friend to friend, from town to town, and from State to State, until she not only lost sight of it for the time, but gave up all hope of ever seeing it again. Eighteen years afterward, it was returned to her, somewhat the worse for wear. It had, meanwhile, travelled I know not how many hundreds of miles, and been read by I know not how many hundreds of persons. On recovering the lost scroll, she penned on its margin this inscription, addressed to her daughters: —

"Dear Maggie and Hattie, this is my first speech. It was delivered several times immediately after the first Woman's Rights Convention. It contains all I knew at that time. I did not speak again for several years. The manuscript has, ever since, been a wanderer through the land. Now, after a separation of nearly eighteen years, I press my first-born to my heart once more. As I recall my younger days, I weep over the apathy and indifference of women concerning their own degradation. I give this manuscript to my precious daughters, in the hope that they will finish the work which I have begun."

Miss Susan B. Anthony — a well-known, indefatigable and life-long advocate of temperance, anti-slavery, and woman's rights — has been, since 1850, Mrs. Stanton's intimate associate in reformatory labors. These celebrated women are of about equal ages, but of the most opposite characteristics, and illustrate the theory of counterparts in affection by entertaining for each other a friendship of extraordinary strength. Mrs. Stanton is a fine writer, but poor executant; Miss Anthony is no writer at all, but a thorough manager. Both have large brains and great hearts; neither has any selfish ambition for celebrity; but each vies with the other in a noble enthusiasm for the cause to which they are devoting their lives. Nevertheless, to describe them critically, I ought to say that, opposites though they be, each does not so much supplement the other's deficiencies as augment the other's eccentricities. Thus, they often stimulate each other's aggressiveness, and at the same time diminish each other's discretion. But whatever may be the imprudent utterances of the one, or the impolitic methods of the other, the animating motives of both, judged by the highest moral standards, are evermore as white as the light. The good which they do is by design; the harm, by accident. These two women, sitting together in their parlor, have, for the last fifteen years, been diligent forgers of all manner of projectiles, from fireworks to thunderbolts, and have hurled them, with unexpected explosion, into the midst of all manner of educational, reformatory, and religious conventions — sometimes to the pleasant surprise and half-welcome of the members; more often to the bewilderment and prostration of numerous victims; and, in a few signal instances, to the gnashing of angry men's teeth. I know of no two more pertinacious incendiaries in the whole country! Nor will they themselves deny the charge. In fact, this noise-making twain are the two sticks of a drum for keeping up what Daniel Webster called "the rub-a-dub of agitation."

The practice of going before a legislature to present the claims of an unpopular cause has been more common in many other States than in New York; most common, perhaps, in Massachusetts. With the single exception of Mrs. Lucy Stone, — a noble and gifted woman, to whom her sisterhood owe an affectionate gratitude, not merely for an eloquence that has charmed thousands of ears, but for practical efforts in abolishing laws oppressive to their sex, — I believe that Mrs. Stanton has appeared oftener before a State legislature than can be said of any of her co-laborers. She has repeatedly addressed the Legislature of New York at Albany, and, on these occasions, has always been honored by the presence of a brilliant audience, and has always spoken with dignity and ability. Her chief topics have been the needful changes in the laws relating to intemperance, education, divorce, slavery, and suffrage. "Yes, gentlemen," said she, in her address of 1854, "we, the daughters of the revolutionary heroes of '76, demand at your hands the redress of our grievances, — a revision of your State constitution, — a new code of laws."

At the close of that grand and glowing argument, a lawyer who had listened to it, and who knew and revered Mrs. Stanton's father, shook hands with the orator and said, "Madam, it was as fine a production as if it had been made and pronounced by Judge Cady himself." This, to the daughter's ears, was sufficiently high praise.

I have carefully read several of Mrs. Stanton's other addresses before the New York Legislature, and have felt, in reading them, that so able a woman ought long ago to have been eligible to membership in a body whom she thus so admirably addressed. But there will come a day — and Heaven speed it! — when a legislature, or a congress, will not be considered as representing the whole people of a State, or of a nation, until women as well as men shall sit as its duly chosen members, — until women as well as men shall be expected to make, as they now are to obey, the laws of the land, — until women as well as men shall be held politically responsible for the moral and Christian government of the republic. "Ye are members one of another," says the wise book; and the saying is no more true of the family than of society, — no more true of the church than of the state. It has taken a terrific contest (and not yet completed) to achieve the political rights of American citizens without distinction of color. But from this point onward — without an appeal to arms, and without a testimony of blood — a more peaceful but not less victorious struggle is in due time to achieve the political rights of American citizens without distinction of sex.

In a cabinet of curiosities, I have laid away, as an interesting relic, a little white ballot, two inches square, and inscribed:

> For Representative in Congress,
>
> ELIZABETH CADY STANTON.

Mrs. Stanton is the only woman in the United States who, as yet, has been a candidate for Congress. In conformity with a practice prevalent in some parts of this country, and very prevalent in England, she nominated herself. The public letter in which she proclaimed herself a candidate was as follows:—

"TO THE ELECTORS OF THE EIGHTH CONGRESSIONAL DISTRICT.

"Although, by the Constitution of the State of New York, woman is denied the elective franchise, yet she is eligible to office; therefore I present myself to you as a candidate for Representative to Congress. Belonging to a disfranchised class, I have no political antecedents to recommend me to your support, but my creed is *free speech, free press, free men, and free trade,*—the cardinal points of Democracy. Viewing all questions from the stand-point of principle rather than expediency, there is a fixed uniform law, as yet unrecognized by either of the leading parties, governing alike the social and political life of men and nations. The Republican party has occasionally a clear vision of personal rights, though in its protective policy it seems wholly blind to the rights of property and interests of commerce. While it recognizes the duty of benevolence between man and man, it teaches the narrowest selfishness in trade between nations. The Democrats, on the contrary, while holding sound and liberal principles in trade and commerce, have ever in their political affiliations maintained the idea of class and caste among men, — an idea wholly at variance with the genius of our free institutions and fatal to a high civilization. One party fails at one point and one at another. In asking your suffrages — believing alike in free men and free trade — I could not represent either party as now constituted.

"Nevertheless, as an Independent Candidate, I desire an election at this time, as a rebuke to the dominant party for its retrogressive legislation in so amending the Constitution as to make invidious distinctions on the ground of sex.

"That instrument recognizes as persons all citizens who obey the laws and support the State, and if the Constitutions of the several States were brought into harmony with the broad principles of the Federal Constitution, the women of the nation would no longer be taxed without representation, or governed without their consent. One word should not be added to that great charter of rights to the insult or injury of the humblest of our citizens. I would gladly have a voice and vote in the Fortieth Congress to demand *universal suffrage*, that thus a republican form of government might be secured to every State in the Union.

"If the party now in the ascendency makes its demand for 'negro suffrage' in good faith, on the ground of natural right, and because the highest good of the State demands that the republican idea be vindicated, on no principle of justice or safety can the women of the nation be ignored.

"In view of the fact that the Freedmen of the South and the millions of foreigners now crowding our Western shores, most of whom represent neither property, education, nor civilization, are all, in the progress of events, to be enfranchised, the best interests of the nation demand that we outweigh this incoming pauperism, ignorance, and degradation, with the wealth, education, and refinement of the women of the republic. On the high ground of safety to the nation and justice to its citizens, I ask your support in the coming election.

"ELIZABETH CADY STANTON.

"NEW YORK, *October* 10, 1866."

The "New York Herald"—though, of course, with no sincerity, since that journal is never sincere in anything—warmly advocated Mrs. Stanton's election. "A lady of fine presence and accomplishments in the House of Representatives," it said (and said truly), "would wield a wholesome influence over the rough and disorderly elements of that body." The "Anti-slavery Standard," with genuine commendation, said, "The electors of the Eighth District would honor themselves and do well by the country in giving her a triumphant election." The other candidates in the same district were Mr. James Brooks, Democrat, and Mr. LeGrand B. Cannon, Republican. The result of the election was as follows: Mr. Brooks received thirteen thousand eight hundred and sixteen votes, Mr. Cannon eight thousand two hundred and ten, and Mrs. Stanton twenty-four. It will be seen that the number of sensible people in the district was limited! The excellent lady, in looking back upon her successful defeat, regrets only that she did not, before it became too late, procure the photographs of her two dozen unknown friends.

In the summer of 1867, the people of Kansas were to debate, and in the autumn to decide, the most novel, noble, and beautiful question ever put to a popular vote in the United States,—the question of adopting a new Constitution whose peculiarity was that it extended the elective franchise not merely to "white male citizens," but to those of what Frederick Douglass calls "the less fashionable color," and to those also of what Horace Greeley calls "the less muscular sex." Mrs. Lucy Stone and Miss Olympia Brown—helped by other ladies less famous, and by several earnest men, including the Hon. Samuel C. Pomeroy, Senator of the United States—

made public speeches at prominent places in that State, urging the people to give the new idea a hospitable welcome at the polls. This canvass was as chivalrous as a tournament, and abounded, from beginning to end, with romantic incidents. To hear from the lips of Mrs. Stone (in that delightful eloquence of conversation which she has never surpassed on the platform), a recital of the most serious or the most comical of these, is as pleasant an entertainment as a supper-table chat can well afford. Toward the close of that memorable campaign, Mrs. Stanton and Miss Anthony, like a reserved force, joined themselves to the general battle. Accidentally associated with them (first with Miss Anthony and afterwards with Mrs. Stanton) was Mr. George Francis Train, — soldier of fortune, hero of Fenianism, martyr to creditors, guest of jails, and candidate for the presidency. The "Tribune" has admiringly called Mr. Train "a charlatan and blatherskite." Ampler justice compels me to add that he is, nevertheless, of all mountebanks the most amiable, and of all clowns the most innocent. These women of substance and this man of froth formed in Kansas a coalition which provoked their opponents to smiles, and their friends to regrets. Anxious watchers of the progress of the good cause were apprehensive that the flightiness of Mr. Train's speeches would bring the new question into disrepute. But the history of reforms in all countries, and especially in this, has shown that neither the wildest friends nor the fiercest enemies of a great idea can any more trample it under their feet than if they had trodden on a sunbeam. The result of the vote on the new Constitution was flattering beyond the most sanguine expectation. No wise observer of the signs of the times had looked for the adoption of that radical instrument, but only for a generous minority in its support. The figures stood nine thousand for, and nineteen thousand against. I have never met any student of American politics who was not greatly sur prised thus to find that one-third of the voters in any State of the Union were sufficiently advanced in opinion to demand at the ballot-box the political equality of the sexes. If the anti-slavery party in Massachusetts, like the woman's suffrage party in Kansas, had received, on a first trial at the polls, one-third of the votes cast, the early abolitionists would have shouted for joy, and have rung their church-bells for a jubilee. Whether the vote in Kansas was increased or diminished by Mr. Train's harangues, I am unable to say. But it is proper to say that the anti-slavery movement, gathering, as it did, to its annual platforms, many of the greatest as well as some of the shallowest of human brains; and the woman's suffrage movement, constantly repeating, as it does, these same phenomena, thereby furnish to the world a magnificent proof of the universality of those great ideas which thus make known their power upon all classes of human beings, great and small, wise and simple, sane and crazy. God has ordained that the noble army of reformers, while marshalled by the choicest spirits of the age, should give honorable rank also to Tag, Rag, and Bobtail. I can see no reason why the gifted and anointed leaders of great movements should decline to make common cause with any and all who are willing to work for the common end.

After the election in Kansas, Mrs. Stanton, Miss Anthony, and Mr. Train made a slow progress eastward, stopping at the chief cities on their way, and addressing public meetings on woman's rights. These meetings provoked merited criticism on account of the performances of Mr. Train, who amused his audiences with the capers of a harlequin. The previous substantial reputation of the two ladies, as earnest reformers, was, on this account, greatly shaken. And yet their own speeches, on all these occasions, were grave, earnest, and impressive, — always worthy of their authors and of the cause. It was, therefore, supposed that the grotesque partnership would be only temporary, but it proved to be permanent. By the time the three travellers had reached New York, they had projected a weekly journal, which made its appearance at the beginning of 1868, under the topsy-turvying title of "The Revolution;" edited by Elizabeth Cady Stanton and Parker Pillsbury, and published by Susan B. Anthony. Like Jupiter Tonans in the rainy season, this sheet always thunders. It is the stormiest of journals. Its pages, as one turns them over, seem to crinkle, flutter, and snap with electric heats. Examine almost any number of "The Revolution," and it will be found the strangest mixture of sense and nonsense known anywhere in American journalism, — a rag-bag of the most incongruous topics. The articles signed "E. C. S." and "P. P." are full of force and fire, — seldom commonplace or tame. Mr. Pillsbury has a gorgeous and sombre imagination, which, when it plays about any subject that can bear its strong colors, makes some of his best essays truly magnificent. Mrs. Stanton, who is always in high animal spirits, and who, like a ripe grape, carries a whole summer's sunshine in her blood, fills her most serious articles with fun, frolic, and satire, and, even in her most humorous escapades, shows a rare vein of tenderness, pathos, and eloquence. She so abounds in metaphors and pithy phrases that a characteristic article from her pen is like a Chinese jar of chow-chow, — filled with little lumps of citron, apricot, and ginger, all swimming in a sweet and biting syrup. The political disquisitions of this co-working yet non-assimilating pair are sometimes grand and just, sometimes visionary and absurd, and sometimes outrageous and wicked. Mr. Train and his money-writers dance up and down through one-third of each week's space in the paper, and hold a high carnival of balderdash. One particular contribution, kept up every week, is made so to coruscate with outlandish notions, comments, and criticisms, that it reminds one of an old barn-door in a dark night, scrawled over, in phosphorus, with "gorgons, hydras, and chimeras dire." But in speaking thus freely of this conglomerate sheet, — a journal, which, on its present plan, can never take a respectable rank among the influential presses of the country, — I must honorably say, on the other hand, that some of the noblest thoughts and utterances pertinent to this day and generation, — ringing words for liberty, justice, and womanhood, — glowing rebukes of false customs, social tyrannies, and degrading conventionalities, — eloquent appeals for a more liberal civil polity, and a more equitable social order, — fervid aspirations toward whatever dignifies human nature and purifies the immortal soul, — these, too, "thoughts that breathe and words that burn," — are spread week by week upon the pages of "The Revolution," and from no brain oftener than from the fiery, wayward, scornful, sympathetic, and Christian soul of Elizabeth Cady Stanton.

I may now paint her features, and sum up her character.

Mrs. Stanton's face is thought to resemble Martha Washington's, but is less regular and more animated; her hair — early gray, and now frosty white — falls about her head in thick clusters of curls; her eyes twinkle with amiable mischief; her voice, though hardly musical, is mellow and agreeable; her figure is of the middle height, and just stout enough to suggest a preference for short walks rather than for long. In reality, however, she can walk like an Englishwoman, — though, if, during a stroll in the street, some jest sets her to laughing, she is forced to halt, cover her countenance with her veil, and shake contagiously till the spasm be past. The costume that most becomes her (and in which her historic portrait ought to be garmented) is a blue silk dress and a red India shawl, — an array, which, topped with her magnificent white hair, makes her a patriotic embodiment of "red, white, and blue."

Her gift of gifts is conversation. Her throne of queenship is not the official chair of the Woman's Rights Convention (though she always presides with dignity and ease), but is rather a seat at the social board, where the company are elderly conservative gentlemen, who combine to argue her down. I think she was never argued down in her life. Go into a fruit-orchard, jar the ripe and laden trees one after another, and not a greater shower of plums, cherries, and pomegranates will fall about your head, than the witticisms, anecdotes, and repartees which this bounteous woman sheds down in her table-talk. House-keeping and babies, free trade and temperance, woman's suffrage and the "white male citizen,"— these are her favorite themes. Many a person, on spending a delightful evening in her society, has gone away, saying, "Well, that is Madam de Staël alive again."

Never a human being had a kindlier nature than Mrs. Stanton's. Pity is her chief vice; charity, her besetting sin. She has not the heart to see a chicken killed, or a child punished. If robbed of all her property, she could not endure to have sentence passed on the thief. When a wretch does wrong, she is apt to think his act not so much his own fault, as the fault of the law under which he lives. A judge punishes the offender, and lets the law go uncondemned; but this judge of judges lets the offender go free, and condemns the law instead. On the one hand, her sense of justice is so sensitive, and, on the other, her tender-heartedness is so excessive, that she compounds for pardoning the criminal by attacking all those usages of society which have conspired to lure him to his crime. Thus, seeing a man drunken in the streets, she does not chide the culprit so much as she denounces the sale of liquor; seeing a seamstress underpaid, she does not denounce the meanness of the employer so much as the narrow range of women's employments; seeing a widow cheated out of her inheritance, she would not so eagerly seek to punish the scoundrel as to secure woman's suffrage for woman's self protection.

"It is a settled maxim with me," she says, "that the existing public sentiment on any subject is wrong." Accordingly, as against the customary, stringent laws of divorce, she holds to the doctrine of John Milton; as against the prevailing tariffs, she argues vehemently for free trade; as against old-fashioned religious opinions, she inclines to an unchecked free-thinking; and as against the common notion of what constitutes woman's sphere, she holds that woman's sphere is to be widened unto equal greatness with man's.

If it be supposed that, in all this, she desires to make woman less womanly, such a supposition is unjust. It is because, under the present canons of society, woman's nature is denied its true growth, defrauded of its true liberty, and defeated of its true end and aim, that Mrs. Stanton, being a woman herself, so earnestly tries to take woman's feet out of the Chinese shoes of dwarfing custom, — to rescue her from her present constrained position in a restrictive social order, — to inspire her toward a fairer ideal of womanhood, — to restore her to her own truer self, — and to present her back once more to God.

Mrs. Stanton's knowledge of human nature in its various ranges, and of human life in its various experiences, has been as rich, varied, and profound as often falls to the lot of any human being. The sacred lore of motherhood is to her a familiar study. Five sons and two daughters sit around her table, all as proud of their mother as if she were a queen of Fairyland, and they her pages in waiting. Drinking not seldom at the fountain of sorrow, she has found, in its bitter waters, strength for her soul. Religious and worshipful by constitution, she has cast off in her later life the superstitions of her earlier, but has never lost her childhood's faith in God. Society being (as she looks at it) full of hollowness and falsity, she sometimes yearns for its reformation as if her heart would break, — the cause of woman's elevation being with her not merely a passion but a religion. She would willingly give her body to be burned, for the sake of seeing her sex enfranchised. But over all this aching and restless earnestness of her inward life nature has kindly drawn a countenance of sunny smiles, a perpetual good-humor, and an irresistible flow of spirits; so that, as she faces the world, she is one of the most fascinating, exhaustless, and perennial of companions; and, as she turns away from it, and faces God alone, she offers to him a soul whose very sorrows, disappointments, and hopes deferred have long ago wrought within her a solemn, cheerful, and immortal peace. Nothing in her outward career — nothing in her representative position — nothing in her gayety and wit — nothing in the whole cluster of those fine intellectual faculties that make her one of the ablest women of our day — nothing in any part of her mind, character, or life is so truly admirable as the one, central characteristic quality of moral energy, which, like a hidden and glowing ember, ignites within her a fiery indignation against all forms of oppression, a sacred love of liberty and justice, a proud reverence for human nature, even in its lowliest fortunes, and a perpetual and defiant appeal from the falseness of society to the justice of God.

THE WOMAN'S RIGHTS MOVEMENT AND ITS CHAMPIONS IN THE UNITED STATES.

BY ELIZABETH CADY STANTON.

We may date the Woman's Rights cause proper, from the division in the anti-slavery organization in 1840; though before that time, Frances Wright, an Englishwoman of rare gifts both as a writer and speaker, had visited this country, and addressed large audiences, demanding at that early day all that the champions of woman's rights now claim.

She was followed by Ernestine L. Rose, a native of Poland, — a woman of great beauty, refinement, and cultivation, — of generous impulses, liberal views, and oratorical power. She came to this country in 1836, addressed large audiences in Charleston, South Carolina, and in Detroit, Michigan, on "The Science of Government." When it was announced in those cities, that *a woman* was to speak on such a theme, men made themselves merry at her presumption; but, after listening to her able exposition of the republican idea, leading men came to her, and, with marked respect, complimented her successful effort. She was among the first who agitated the property rights of married women in the State of New York. As early as 1838 she circulated petitions on that subject, which were presented by Judge Hertell in the Legislature. She has been one of the leaders in the Woman's Rights movement since that time, and spoken at all the annual conventions. The active part the women of this country had taken in the anti-slavery cause, beginning in 1830, had prepared them for this new demand.

In those early organizations woman had an equal voice with man. She did more than sew pincushions, and ask alms; she proclaimed the living truths of the gospel of freedom, in public assemblies, as well as at the hearthstone, — to grave and reverend seniors in halls of legislation, as well as to her husband at home.

SARAH AND ANGELINA GRIMKE.

In 1836 Sarah and Angelina Grimké, daughters of a wealthy planter in South Carolina, emancipated their slaves, and came North to lecture on the evils of slavery. They were high-toned, noble women, well educated, of keen moral perceptions, and deeply religious natures. The one desire in their childhood and youth had been to escape the daily torture of witnessing the cruelties inflicted upon the slave; to get beyond the abominations they saw no way to end.

Angelina, the younger sister, was a natural orator. Fresh from the land of bondage, there was a fervor in her speech that electrified her listeners, and drew crowds wherever she went. She was tall, delicately organized, with a sad, thoughtful face, dark hair and eyes, with great depth of expression. Her voice was rich, clear, and strong, and could easily fill any hall.

Both sisters were ready writers, and, while lecturing through the North, wrote for the press, on slavery and woman's rights. Sarah published a book reviewing the Bible arguments, which the clergy were then making in all our pulpits, to prove that the degradation of the slave and woman were alike in harmony with the expressed will of God. In May, 1837, a National Woman's Anti-slavery Convention was called in New York, in which eight States were represented by seventy-one delegates. The meetings were ably sustained through two days. The different sessions were opened by prayer and reading of the Scriptures, by the women themselves, and a devout, earnest, and Christian spirit pervaded all the proceedings. The debates, resolutions, speeches, and appeals were fully equal to those in any conventions held by the men of that period.

Angelina Grimké was appointed in this convention to prepare an appeal for the slaves to the people of the free States, and a letter to John Quincy Adams, thanking him for his services in defending the right of petition for women and slaves, qualified with the regret that, by expressing himself "adverse to the abolition of slavery in the District of Columbia," he did not sustain the cause of freedom and of God. What man has done as the result of war, women asked to prevent war thirty years ago. In 1838 she was married to Theodore D. Weld, and settled in New Jersey. She is the mother of one daughter and two sons. Among those who took part in the debates of that convention, we find the names of Lydia Maria Child, Mary Grew, Henrietta Sargent, Sarah Pugh, Abby Kelley, Mary S. Parker, of Boston, who was president of the convention, Anne Weston, Deborah Shaw, Martha Storrs, Mrs. A. L. Cox, Rebecca B. Spring, and *Abigail Hopper Gibbons*, a daughter of that noble Quaker, Isaac T. Hopper. Though early married, and the mother of several children, her life has been one of constant activity and self-denial for the public good. Those who know her best can testify to her many acts of benevolence and mercy, working alike for the unhappy slave, the unfortunate of her own sex, the children on Randall's Island, and the suffering soldiers in our late war.

ABBY KELLEY,

A young Quakeress, made her first appearance on the anti-slavery platform. She was a tall, fine-looking girl, with a large, well-shaped head, regular features, dark hair, blue eyes, and a sweet, expressive countenance. She was a person of clear moral perceptions, and deep feeling. She spoke extemporaneously, always well, at times with great eloquence and power. As soon as the rare gifts as orators, that both she and Angelina Grimké displayed in the women's meetings, were noised abroad, the men, one by one, asked permission to come into their meetings, and thus, through man's curiosity, they soon found themselves speaking to promiscuous audiences. For a period of thirty years Abby Kelley has spoken on the subject of slavery. She has travelled up and down the length and breadth of this land, — alike in winter's cold and summer's heat, mid scorn, ridicule, violence, and mobs, suffering all kinds of persecution, — still speaking, whenever and wherever she gained audience, in the open air, in school-house, barn, depot, church, or public hall, on week-day, or Sunday, as she found opportunity.

In 1845 she married Stephen S. Foster, and soon after, they purchased a farm in Worcester, Massachusetts, where, with an only daughter, she has lived several years in retirement. Having lost her voice by constant and severe use, she gave up lecturing while still in her prime.

MARY GREW,

The daughter of Rev. Henry Grew, of Philadelphia, has been for thirty years one of the ablest and most faithful workers both in the anti-slavery and woman's rights cause. She is a cousin of Wendell Phillips. Being a woman of sound judgment, and great general information, she has been one of his most reliable friends and counsellors, in planning and executing his lifelong work. She is one of the most terse and finished writers of the age. Her anti-slavery reports made out annually, and published in "The Anti-slavery Standard," are concise and comprehensive statements of facts and principles governing them. She is a woman of vigorous thought, and high moral principle. Gentle, refined, unobtrusive in manner, she is still a woman of great independence, and self-reliance of character. Being one of the delegates to the World's Anti-slavery Convention, I met her for the first time in London in 1840. I remember how charmed I was to hear her laud our republican institutions, in the presence of boasting Englishmen, and, in her keen, sarcastic way, express the utmost contempt for the sham and tinsel, the pomp and ceremony of the Old World. I was especially pleased with a little incident that occurred one day, at a large dinner party, at Samuel Gurney's, — a wealthy banker who had a beautiful country-seat near London. Lord Morpeth and the Duchess of Sutherland had been invited to meet a party of Americans there, as they had expressed a wish to see the American abolitionists. As it was a warm, pleasant afternoon in June, we went out on the smooth green lawn, under the shade of some majestic old trees, to hear Lord Morpeth read the reports to the British government from Jamaica. Most of us had been formally presented to the Lord and Lady, but Mr. Grew, having come late, had not yet had the honor of an introduction. Having formed ourselves into a semicircle round his lordship during the reading, at the close Miss Grew took her father's arm, and, in a cool, self-possessed manner, walked across the intervening space, and introduced her father to the Duchess of Sutherland, then mistress of the robes, with the same air as she would have presented two plain republicans in her own country. Standing near the daughter of Sir Fowell Buxton, she said to me, "What are you American girls made of? Not a girl in all England would have presumed to introduce a commoner, to one of such rank as her Grace." "Ah! madam," I replied, "you forget that in our country we are all of noble blood, all heirs apparent to the throne."

The women who devoted themselves to the anti-slavery cause in the early days, endured the double odium of being abolitionists, and "women out of their sphere;" hence the men who were engaged in the same cause little knew all the peculiar aggravations and trials of their position. The admiration such women as Angeline Grimké, Abby Kelley, and Lucretia Mott, commanded by their presence and eloquence, was well tempered by ridicule and denunciation. The press and the pulpit exhausted the English language to find adjectives to express their detestation of so horrible a revelation as "a woman out of her sphere." A clerical appeal was issued and sent to all the clergymen in New England, calling on them to denounce in their pulpits this unwomanly and unchristian proceeding. Sermons were preached portraying in the darkest colors the fearful results to the church, the State, and the home, in thus encouraging women to enter public life. It was the opposition of the clergy to woman's speaking and voting in their meetings, that occasioned the first division in "The American Anti-slavery Society."

The reports of the meeting held in New York, May, 1840, are worthy the perusal of every philosophical thinker, to see how ridiculously even good common-sense men can talk and act when moved by prejudice rather than principle.

The question under debate on that occasion was, whether woman should speak and vote in all business matters in their meetings. Men opposed to this went through the audience *urging every woman who agreed with them* to vote against it, thus calling on them to do then and there what, with fervid eloquence, on that very occasion, they had declared a sin against nature and Scripture for them to do anywhere. It was a stormy meeting held that day by the friends of the slave, and, though he still groaned in bondage, it was urged by many that woman's voice should not be heard in his behalf. Whilst with one hand they strove to loose the chains that clanked on the rice plantations in Georgia, with the other they tried to force woman back into the narrow niche where barbarism had found her. So partially does truth illumine some minds that even the colored man was found voting to exclude woman from an anti-slavery organization. History, however, records that William Lloyd Garrison, ever sound on questions of human rights, carried the resolution by one hundred majority in favor of woman's right to speak and vote in their meetings. At this crisis a World's Anti-slavery Convention was called to meet in London. Several American organizations saw fit to send women as delegates to represent them in that august assembly. But, after going three thousand miles to attend a World's Convention, it was discovered that woman formed no part of the constituent elements of the moral world.

In summoning the friends of the slave from all parts of the two hemispheres, to meet in London, John Bull never dreamed that woman, too, would answer to his call, though the idea of immediate emancipation was first published by Elizabeth Herrick, an English woman, in a well-reasoned pamphlet in 1824.

Accordingly, on the opening of the convention in London, June 12th, 1840, the delegates from the Massachusetts and Pennsylvania societies were denied their seats. The delegation consisted of Lucretia Mott, Mary Grew, Abby Kimber, Elizabeth Neale, Sarah Pugh, from Pennsylvania; Emily Winslow, Abby Southwick, and Anne Greene Phillips, from Massachusetts. This sacrifice of human rights, by men who had assembled from all quarters of the globe to proclaim universal emancipation, was offered up in the presence of such women as Lady Noel Byron, Harriet Martineau, Elizabeth Fry, Mary Howitt, and Anna Jamieson. The delegates had been persuasively asked to waive their claims that the harmony of the convention might not be disturbed by a question of such *minor importance.* But through their champion, Wendell Phillips (who was then a young man, and brave too, I thought, to advocate so unpopular an idea almost alone in such an assembly), they maintained that as they had been delegated by large and influential organizations, they must press their claims and thus discharge their duty, not only to those whom they represented, but to the speechless victims of American slavery. Thus the debate on this question was forced upon them, and many distinguished gentlemen of France, England, and America took part in the discussion, which lasted through one entire day.

ANNE GREENE PHILLIPS.

As we stood in the vestibule of Freemason's Hall that morning, talking over the coming event, I saw the wife of Wendell Phillips for the first time. Her earnest, impressive manner arrested my attention at once. She had just returned from her bridal tour on the continent, and was in the zenith of her beauty. She had a profusion of dark-brown hair, large, loving blue eyes, and regular features. She was tall, graceful, and talked with great fluency and force. Her whole soul seemed to be in the pending issue. As we were about to enter the convention she laid her hand most emphatically on her husband's shoulder and said, "Now, Wendell, don't be simmy-sammy to-day, but brave as a lion;" and he obeyed the injunction. Most of the speeches that day were narrow and bigoted, setting forth men's prejudices without touching the principle under consideration, and, when the vote was taken, among the few who stood by principle, were Daniel O'Connell, Dr. Bowring, Henry B. Stanton, George Thompson, and Wendell Phillips. William Lloyd Garrison did not reach England until the third day of the convention, having been unfortunately becalmed at sea. When he learned that Massachusetts women had been denied their rights in the convention he declined to take his seat as a member of that body. His anti-slavery principles being too broad to restrict human rights to color or sex, he took his seat in the gallery, and through all those days looked down on the convention. Thomas Clarkson was chosen president, but he being too old and feeble to endure the fatigue, Joseph Sturge, the celebrated Quaker merchant, presided over the deliberations. Sitting near Mrs. Mott in the convention, I mischievously suggested to her one day a dangerous contingency. "With a Quaker in the chair," said I, "suppose, in spite of the vote of excommunication, the spirit should move you to speak, what could the chairman do, and which would you obey, — the spirit, or the convention?" She promptly replied, "Where the spirit of God is, there is liberty." The general indignation felt by the advanced minds among the women of England, France, and America, and the puerile tone of the debates on this question, gave birth to what is called the Woman's Rights movement on both continents. The women of England soon after established a Woman's Rights journal, and petitioned Parliament for their rights of property. Their demands were ably maintained by Lord Brougham in the House of Peers. The French women, too, soon after established a journal, so liberal and republican in its sentiments, that they were compelled to publish it in Italy, though it was clandestinely circulated in France. At the same time Frederika Bremer, in her popular novels, was ridiculing the creeds and codes and customs of her country, and thus undermining the laws of Sweden in regard to women, which, in many particulars, were soon after essentially modified.

Engd by G.E. Perine & Co. N.Y.

Lucretia Mott

LUCRETIA MOTT.

It was in London that I first met Lucretia Mott. We chanced to stop at the same house, with a party of Americans, who had come to attend the "World's Convention." Seated by her at the dinner-table I was soon oblivious to everything but the lovely Quakeress, though a bride, with my husband by my side. She was then in her prime, small in stature, slightly built, with a large head, high, square forehead, remarkably fine face, regular features, dark hair and eyes. She was gentle and refined in her manners, and conversed with earnestness and ease. There were several clergymen at the table that day, who, in the course of conversation, rallied Mrs. Mott on her views of woman. She calmly parried all their attacks, — now by her quiet humor turning the laugh on them, and then by her earnestness and dignity silencing their ridicule and sneers. Though a stranger, I could not resist saying all the good things I thought on her side of the question, and I shall never forget the look of recognition she gave me when she saw that I already comprehended the problem of woman's rights and wrongs. She was the first liberal-minded woman I had ever met, and nothing in all Europe interested me as she did. We were soon fast friends, and were often rallied on our seeming devotion to each other. I was never weary listening to her conversation. On one occasion, with a large party, we visited the British Museum, where it is supposed all people go to see the wonders of the world. On entering, Mrs. Mott and myself sat down near the door to rest for a few moments, telling the party to go on, that we would follow. They accordingly explored all the departments of curiosities, supposing we were slowly following at a distance; but when they returned to the entrance, after an absence of three hours, there we sat in the same spot, having seen nothing but each other, wholly absorbed in questions of theology and social life. She had told me of the doctrines and divisions among Quakers, of the inward light, of Elias Hicks, of Channing, of a religion of life, and of Mary Wollstonecraft and her social theories. I had been reading Combe's Constitution of Man, and Moral Philosophy, and Channing's Works, and had already thought on all these questions; but I had never heard a woman talk what, as a Scotch Presbyterian, I had scarcely dared to think. On the following Sunday I went to hear Mrs. Mott preach in a Unitarian church. Though I had never heard a woman speak, yet I had long believed she had the right to do so, and had often expressed the idea in private circles; but when at last I saw a woman rise up in the pulpit and preach as earnestly and impressively as Mrs. Mott always does, it seemed to me like the realization of an oft-repeated happy dream.

The day we visited the Zoölogical Gardens, as we were admiring the gorgeous plumage of some beautiful birds, one of the gentlemen remarked: —

"You see, Mrs. Mott, our Heavenly Father believes in bright colors. How much it would take from our pleasure if all the birds were dressed in drab!"

"Yes," said she, "but immortal beings do not depend on their feathers for their attractions. With the infinite variety of the human face and form, of thought, feeling, and affection, we do not need gorgeous apparel to distinguish us. Moreover, if it is fitting that woman should dress in every color of the rainbow, why not man also? Clergymen with their black clothes and white cravats are quite as monotonous as the Quakers."

Owing to her liberal views, Mrs. Mott was shunned by the Orthodox Quakers of England, though courted by the literati and nobility. I have seen her by the side of the Duchess of Sutherland, conversing on the political questions of the time with a grace and eloquence that proved her in manners the peer of the first woman in England, though educated in Quaker austerity, under our plain republican institutions. From the following extracts from Mrs. Mott's memoranda, the reader will get an insight into the moving and governing principles of her calm, consistent, and beautiful life.

EXTRACTS FROM MEMORANDA, BY LUCRETIA MOTT.

"A native of the Island of Nantucket, — of the Coffins and Macys on the father's side, and of the Folgers on the mother's; through them related to Dr. Franklin.

"Born in 1793. During childhood was made actively useful to my mother, who, in the absence of my father, on a long voyage, was engaged in mercantile business, often going to Boston and purchasing goods in exchange for oil and candles, the staple of the island. The exercise of women's talents in this line, as well as the general care which devolved upon them in the absence of their husbands, tended to develop their intellectual powers and strengthen them mentally and physically.

"In 1804 my father's family removed to Boston, and in the public and private schools of that city I mingled with all classes without distinction. My parents were of the religious society of Friends, and endeavored to preserve in their children the peculiarities of that sect, as well as to instil its more important principles. My father had a desire to make his daughters useful. At fourteen years of age I was placed with a younger sister, at the Friends' Boarding-School, in DutchessCounty, State of New York, and continued there for more than two years without returning home. At fifteen, one of the teachers leaving the school, I was chosen as an assistant, in her place. Pleased with the promotion, I strove hard to give satisfaction, and was gratified, on leaving the school, to have an offer of a situation as teacher, if I was disposed to remain, and informed that my services should entitle another sister to her education without charge. My father was, at that time, in successful business in Boston; but with his views of the importance of training a woman to usefulness, he and my mother gave their consent to another year being devoted to that institution. In the spring of 1809, I joined our family in Philadelphia, after their removal there. At the early age of eighteen, I married James Mott, of New York, — an attachment formed while at the boarding-school. He came to Philadelphia and entered into business with my father. The fluctuation in the commercial world for several years following our marriage, owing to the embargo, and the war of 1812, the death of my father, and the support of a family of five children devolving on my mother, surrounded us with difficulties. We resorted to various modes of obtaining a comfortable living; at one time engaged in the retail dry goods business, then resumed the charge of a school, and for another year was engaged in teaching. These trials, in early life, were not without their good effect in disciplining the mind, and leading it to set a just estimate on worldly pleasures. I, however, always loved the good, in childhood desired to do the right, and had no faith in the generally received idea of human depravity. My sympathy was early enlisted for the poor slave, by the class-books read in our schools, and the pictures of the slave-ship, as published by Clarkson. The ministry of Elias Hicks and others, on the subject of the unrequited labor of slaves, and their example in refusing the products of slave labor, all had their effect in awakening a strong feeling in their behalf. The unequal condition of woman in society also early impressed my mind. Learning, while at school, that the charge for the education of girls was the same as that for boys, and that when they became teachers, women received but half as much as men for their services, the injustice of this was so apparent, that I early resolved to claim for my sex all that an impartial Creator had bestowed. At twenty-five years of age, surrounded with a little family and many cares, I felt called to a more public life of devotion to duty, and engaged in the ministry in our Society, receiving every encouragement from those in authority, until a separation among us, in 1827, when my convictions led me to adhere to the sufficiency of the light within us, resting on truth as authority, rather than 'taking authority for truth.' The popular doctrine of human depravity never commended itself to my reason or conscience. I 'searched the Scriptures daily,' finding a construction of the text wholly different from that which was pressed upon our acceptance. The highest evidence of a sound faith being the practical life of the Christian, I have felt a far greater interest in the moral movements of our age than in any theological discussion.

"The temperance reform early engaged my attention, and for more than twenty years I have practised total abstinence from all intoxicating drinks. The cause of peace has had a share of my efforts, leading to the ultra non-resistance ground, — that no Christian can consistently uphold, and actively engage in and support a government based on the sword, or relying on that as an ultimate resort. The oppression of the working-classes by existing monopolies, and the lowness of wages, often engaged my attention; and I have held many meetings with them, and heard their appeals with compassion, and a great desire for a radical change in the system which makes the rich richer and the poor poorer. The various associations and communities tending to greater equality of condition have had from me a hearty God-speed. But the millions of down-trodden slaves in our land being the greatest sufferers, the most oppressed class, I have felt bound to plead their cause, in season and out of season, to endeavor to put my soul in their souls' stead, and to aid, all in my power, in every right effort for their immediate emancipation. This duty was impressed upon me at the time I consecrated myself to that gospel which anoints 'to preach deliverance to the captive,' 'to set at liberty them that are bruised.' From that time the duty of abstinence as far as practicable from slave-grown products was so clear, that I resolved to make the effort 'to provide things honest' in this respect. Since then our family has been supplied with free-labor groceries, and, to some extent, with cotton goods unstained by slavery. The labors of the devoted Benjamin Lundy, and his 'Genius of Universal Emancipation' published in Baltimore, added to the untiring exertions of Clarkson, Wilberforce, and others in England, including Elizabeth Heyrick, whose work on slavery aroused them to a change in their mode of action, and of William Lloyd Garrison, in Boston, prepared the way for a convention in Philadelphia, in 1833, to take the ground of immediate, not gradual, emancipation, and to impress the duty of unconditional liberty, without expatriation. In 1834 the Philadelphia Female A. S. Society was formed, and, being actively associated in the efforts for the slaves' redemption, I have travelled thousands of miles in this country, holding meetings in some of the slave States, have been in the midst of mobs and violence, and have shared abundantly in the odium attached to the name of an uncompromising *modern* abolitionist, as well as partaken richly of the sweet return of peace attendant on those who would 'undo the heavy burdens and let the oppressed go free, and break every yoke.'

"In 1840, a World's Anti-slavery Convention was called in London. Women from Boston, New York, and Philadelphia, were delegates to that convention. I was one of the number; but, on our arrival in England, our credentials were not accepted because we were women. We were, however, treated with great courtesy and attention, as strangers, and as women, were admitted to chosen seats as spectators and listeners, while our right of membership was denied, — we were voted out. This brought the Woman question more into view, and an increase of interest in the subject has been the result. In this work, too, I have engaged heart and hand, as my labors, travels, and public discourses evince. The misrepresentation, ridicule, and abuse heaped upon this, as well as other reforms, do not, in the least, deter me from my duty. To those, whose name is cast out as evil for the truth's sake, it is a small thing to be judged of man's judgment.

"This imperfect sketch may give some idea of the mode of life of one who has found it 'good to be always zealously affected in a good thing.'

"My life, in the domestic sphere, has passed much as that of other wives and mothers in this country. I have had six children. Not accustomed to resigning them to the care of a nurse, I was much confined to them during their infancy and childhood. Being fond of reading, I omitted much unnecessary stitching and ornamental work, in the sewing for my family, so that I might have more time for this indulgence, and for the improvement of the mind. For novels and light reading I never had much taste. The 'Ladies Department,' in the periodicals of the day, had no attraction for me."

While walking in the streets of London, Mrs. Mott and I resolved on a Woman's Convention, as soon as we returned to America. Accordingly, in the summer of 1848, while she was on a visit to her sister, Martha Wright, of Auburn, I proposed to her, to call a Woman's Rights Convention, at

Seneca Falls, where I then lived. She consented, and the call was immediately issued in the county papers, and we at once prepared resolutions, speeches, and a declaration of sentiments. After much consultation over the declaration, finding that our fathers had similar grievances to our own, and the same number, we decided to adopt the immortal declaration of '76 as our model. James Mott — one of nature's noblemen, both in character and appearance, the husband of Lucretia — presided at this first convention. Among those who took part in the discussions were Frederick Douglass, Thomas and Mary Ann McClintock, and their two daughters, Ansel Bascom, Catharine Stebbins, Amy Post, and Martha Wright. It continued through two days, was well attended, and extensively reported. The declaration was published in nearly every paper in the country, and the nation was convulsed with laughter, from Maine to Louisiana, though our demands for suffrage, the right to property, work, and wages were the same that wise men accept to-day, the same that Henry Ward Beecher preaches in his pulpit, and John Stuart Mill presses on the consideration of the British Parliament. Martha Wright, the sister of Lucretia, took an active part in this convention, and has presided over nearly every convention that has been held in later days. She is a woman of fine presence, much general information, and rare common sense. Though not a public speaker, she has been a most efficient worker in our cause. In a recent letter to me, speaking of her sister, soon after the death of Mr. Mott, she says, "The striking traits of Lucretia's character are remarkable energy, that defies even time, unswerving conscientiousness, and all those characteristics that are summed up in the few words, love to man, and love to God." "Though much broken by the heavy affliction, that has come to her so unexpectedly, for, frail as she is, she never thought she should survive her strong and vigorous husband, she has borne it better than we anticipated." Our next convention was held in Rochester, a few weeks later. Mrs. Amy Post and Mrs. Abigail Bush made the arrangements, and Mrs. Bush presided on the occasion. Mrs. Mott and I were opposed to a woman as president,—this was a step we were not quite prepared for, to have a woman call a promiscuous assembly to order. However, we were out-voted, and we were compelled to admit, at the close, that Mrs. Bush did us all great credit. The meetings were held in the Unitarian church, and created much interest in the city. One very interesting incident occurred during the morning session. A newly married couple, soon after the convention opened, walked slowly up the aisle to the altar, when the groom stepped forward, and asked the president, in a low tone, if the lady with him might have the opportunity to speak. "Passing through the city," he said, "they heard of the convention, and having but an hour before leaving town, she would like to add her voice in favor of woman's rights." She was accordingly introduced at once, and made a most eloquent and finished speech of twenty minutes. Whilst she was speaking, the groom remained standing near the altar, hat and cane in hand, reverently gazing on his beautiful bride. When she finished, a profound silence reigned, and they disappeared as quietly and suddenly as they came. Who they were, whence they came, or whither going, we never knew.

In 1850 and 1851 several State Conventions were held in Indiana and Ohio. At the convention held at Indianapolis, the moving spirits were Frances D. Gage, and Caroline M. Severance. In a brief sketch of

CAROLINE M. SEVERANCE

I cannot do better, than to give the reader, what, in her easy, playful way, she writes in a letter to me of herself. I wrote to her asking for facts of her life, telling her there was no escape, that *nolens volens* she was to be sketched, and it rested with her, whether it should be based wholly on such an objective view, as one could take hundreds of miles away, or on a subjective view, such as I could get in being *en rapport* with herself. She chose the latter, as the least of two evils, and frankly tells me what she knows of herself.

"DEAR FRIEND, — Isn't this an interesting dilemma to find one's self in? — to be exhibited whether we will or no! One who has arrived at years of discretion, surely, in our free land, to have no chance of a choice, whether to remain incog., or be set on high for all the daws to peck at! 'But to this it seems we have come at last,' and, in my extremity, if I may choose nothing else, I surely shall snatch at the chance to say by whom this most undesirable service shall be performed, and I gladly submit to you.'

"I have done so little to justify my years, that I might shrink from such a sketch as you propose, with better reason than could influence many of our sex. But lest you should think my humility affectation, I frankly avow that I was born in Canandaigua, N. Y., in January, 1820, if you consider date and birthplace important to the sketch, of neither "poor or pious parents," although cultivated, conscientious persons. My father's name was Orson Seymour, a banker, my mother's name was Caroline M. Clark. I was married in 1840, at Auburn, New York, to T. C. Severance, a banker of Cleveland, Ohio. Neither the world nor my historian would have any particular interest in what I said, or did, after that remarkable event of January 20th, and the good sense of choosing so beautiful a portion of the earth's surface for a birthplace, until the mother of five children, with little experience in life, and less in society, having devoted myself to home and books, I was chosen, in 1853, to read before the Mercantile Library Association, the first lecture ever delivered by a woman, in Cleveland, Ohio, where I had resided since marriage. I had been already identified with the Woman's Rights movement, having attended conventions in Indiana, Ohio, and New York; and this accounts for my invitation on this occasion. I cannot tell you how long I hesitated to accept this invitation; the more I plead my unfitness, the more I was pressed with a sense of my duty, and at last I wrote the most exhaustive essay I could on the subject, to make sure, for once, that my city should have all that could be said on the subject. An immense audience listened, through an hour and three quarters, with becoming silence and respect. This lecture I repeated several times, in different parts of the State. After that, the Woman's Rights Association asked me to prepare a tract for their circulation. Later I was appointed to present a memorial to the Legislature, asking suffrage, and such amendments to the State laws of Ohio as should place woman on a civil equality with man. In 1855 we came to Massachusetts, the home of my heart always, and here I have done nothing, deserving the punishment of public exposure, that I now remember against myself, until, as one of the lecture committee of the Fraternity Association, it became my duty to assist in securing lecturers for the course. We invited Mrs. Stanton, but, she failing us at the last moment, I was not able to resist the entreaties of the committee, and the obligation I felt myself under, to make good her place, so far as in me lay. That was, I believe, the first lecture ever delivered in Boston before a Lyceum Association by a woman. I will not tell you how prosy and dull I fear it was, but I know it was earnest, and well considered, and dear Mrs. Follen's, and Miss Peabody's beaming eyes, kept me in heart all through, as they glowed with interest before me from below the platform of Tremont Temple Hall. Since then, from want of health and voice, I have not spoken much in public, though I have given soul service, in many directions, standing as corresponding secretary for the Anti-slavery Society, one of the Board of Managers to the New England Female Medical College, and reading a course of private lectures on practical ethics, before Dio Lewis' school of girls. These lectures cover the relations of the young woman to the school, the State, the home, and her own complete development. As a mother, I am happy to say that my sons and daughters have never disgraced, and I see no reason to believe, ever will disgrace, my name, or bring in question, my influence over them, or my fidelity to them. Pure in heart, noble in all their tastes and tendencies, they are my joy in the present, my hope in the future, and my best legacy to it. Here you have me, my good friend, in a nutshell. Not *multum in parvo*, it must be confessed.

"Yours, sincerely, C. M. S."

Mrs. Severance now resides in West Newton, Massachusetts, where she is living a quiet life, in a beautiful home. She is using her pen in a way she hopes will some day prove a means of broader influence. In manners and appearance, Mrs. Severance is very attractive. She has a handsome face and figure, dignified carriage, and fine conversational powers. She is an amiable, affectionate, conscientious woman, faithful alike in her private and public duties.

FRANCES D. GAGE.

Born October 12th, 1808, in Marietta, Washington County, on the banks of the Muskingum, Ohio. Her father, Joseph Barker, was a native of New Hampshire, and an early pioneer to the western wilds. Through her mother, Elizabeth Dana, she was allied to the distinguished Massachusetts families of Dana and Bancroft. A log cabin in the woods, was the seminary where Frances Barker acquired the rudiments of education. And, though she had few early advantages, she became a sound thinker, a good writer of both prose and verse, and one of the most effective speakers in the country. She was born with a sound mind in a sound body. Her large, well-balanced head, and strong physical development made learning and hardships alike easy for her to surmount. Her father was a farmer and cooper, and the duties of a farmer's daughter, in a new country, were all cheerfully and easily disposed of by her. She assisted her father in making barrels, and I have heard her often tell that, as she would roll out a well-made barrel, her father would pat her on the head, and say, "Ah, Fanny, you should have been a boy!" Fanny had a kind and loving nature, and early felt the most intense sympathy for the fugitives from slavery. Her tenderness and charity for these despised people often subjected her to the ridicule of her young companions. She became familiarized with their sufferings and wants, in her frequent visits to her grandmother, Mrs. Mary Bancroft Dana, whose home was on the Ohio River, opposite Blennerhasset's Island.

At the age of twenty-one she married James L. Gage, a lawyer of McConnellsville, Ohio,— a man of great humanity and moral integrity. With a family of eight children, and all the hardships of that Western life, Mrs. Gage still found time, through all those years, to read, and write for leading journals, and often to speak, too, on temperance, slavery, and woman's rights. As she stood almost alone on these questions, she was often subject to ridicule and persecution. Those who have never advocated an unpopular idea — who have not made principle, rather than policy, their guiding star — cannot appreciate the peculiar trials of those who are true in word and action to their enlightened conscientious opinions.

In 1851, Mrs. Gage attended a "Woman's Rights Convention," in Akron, Ohio, and was chosen president of the meeting. Her opening speech, on that occasion, is remarkable for its common sense, and a pathos peculiarly her own. In 1853 she moved to St. Louis. Those who fought the anti-slavery battle in Massachusetts cannot realize the danger of such a warfare in a slave-holding State. With her usual frank utterances of opinions, she was soon branded as an abolitionist, her articles excluded from the journals, and she from "good society," with daily threats of violence to her person and the destruction of her property. Three disastrous fires — the work of incendiaries, no doubt — greatly reduced the resources of the family. Owing to her husband's ill health, and failure in business, she took the post of assistant editor of an agricultural paper in Columbus, Ohio; but as the breaking out of the war soon destroyed the circulation of the paper, and four of her sons had gone into the army, her thoughts turned to the scenes of conflict in the Southern States. The "suffering freedmen" and the "boys in blue" appealed alike to her loving heart for kindness and help; and, without appointment or salary, she went to Port Royal in 1862. She remained in Beaufort, Paris, and Fernandina thirteen months, ministering alike to the soldiers and freedmen, as opportunity offered. Pages might be written on the heroism of Mrs. Gage and her daughter Mary during this period. Oppressed with the magnitude of the work to be accomplished there, she returned North, to give her experiences acquired among the freedmen, hoping to rouse others, younger and stronger than herself, to go down and teach those neglected people the A B C of learning and social life.

During this year she travelled through many of the northern States, speaking nearly every evening to Soldiers' Aid Societies. She worked without pay, only asking enough to defray her expenses. When the summer days made lecturing impossible, she went as an unsalaried agent of the Sanitary Commission down the Mississippi, to Memphis, Vicksburg, and Natchez. In the month of September she was overturned in a carriage at Galesburg, Illinois, which crippled her for that year. As soon as she recovered she was employed and well paid by various temperance organizations to lecture for that cause; and she was thus occupied, when her plans for future activity and usefulness were suddenly terminated by a stroke of paralysis, in August, 1867. She has since been confined to her room, though able to walk about, read, and write. A visit to her sick-room is always pleasant and profitable, and everything from her pen breathes a sweet spirit of love to man and trust in God. In appearance, Mrs. Gage is large and vigorous, has a good, benevolent face, easy manners, and a varied fund of conversation. She is capable, as her life shows, of great self-denial and heroism. She is an extemporaneous speaker, — a talker rather than an orator, — and never fails to interest and hold an audience. There is no woman in the country who can speak so readily, without preparation, on so many different subjects, as Mrs. Gage. She has taken a prominent part in most of the National Woman's Rights Conventions, and, but for her illness, would have spoken all through Kansas in the last campaign.

In reply to my letter, asking her for some facts relating to our Woman's Rights movement, she writes me from her sick-room: —

"459 Sixth Avenue, New York.

"Dear Mrs. S., — Your letter is before me. . . . . I have little to say; yet I remember the first convention. I was travelling East, with my husband, and was at Buffalo that very day, and longed to be with you. The next conventions were held in Indiana and in Ohio in 1850. I remember, too, emanating from the Salem Convention was a memorial, drawn up by Mary Ann Johnson, asking that the words 'white male' should be omitted from the constitution, which was that year to be given to the State. I also drew up a memorial, asking for the equal rights of woman before the law, and that the words 'white male' should be stricken from the constitution. I did not know Mrs. Johnson, and we had no communication with each other. Those memorials were presented by the member from my district; the subject was vehemently discussed, and voted upon. Nine votes were given for striking out the word 'male' and eleven for striking out 'white.' I think this was the first memorial ever presented in any State asking suffrage for woman. From 1849 to 1855 I lectured on this subject in Ohio, Indiana, Illinois, Iowa, Missouri, Louisiana, Massachusetts, Pennsylvania, and New York, and wrote volumes for the press. Many of the most earnest spirits in Kansas were from Ohio, Indiana, Iowa, and Illinois, and helped to form the public opinion that gave woman, in that State, a right to vote on temperance and education, and laid the foundation for its present advanced position. Excuse my palsied hand and brain. I am still very feeble, and write with difficulty.

"Yours,

"FRANCES D. GAGE."

Under the *nomme de plume* of "Aunt Fanny," Mrs. Gage has written many beautiful stories for children, stanzas, and sketches of social life. She was an early contributor to the "Saturday Visitor," edited by Jane G. Swisshelm, and has lately written for the New York "Independent." A volume of poems, and a temperance tale, "Elsie Magoon," are the last of her published works. By her own efforts, Mrs. Gage has accumulated enough to secure to herself and her children a pleasant home for her old age.

In April, 1850, a convention was held in Salem, Ohio. J. Elizabeth Jones, Mary Ann Johnson, and Josephine Griffing were the leading spirits, — all women of high moral character and intellectual cultivation. Mary Ann Johnson had lectured to large audiences throughout the country on physiology. Mrs. Jones and Mrs. Griffing were both able writers and speakers. These women circulated petitions in that State, and addressed the Legislature demanding woman's right to her property, wages, children, and the elective franchise. In the reports of this convention we find mention made of Maria L. Giddings, daughter of Joshua R. Giddings, who presented an able report on the laws; of Sojourner Truth, Mrs. Stowe's Lybian Sybil, for forty years a slave in New York, and of the Hutchinson family, who enlivened the occasion with their songs.

Among the representative women of the nineteenth century,

ABBY HUTCHINSON

deserves a passing notice. She was born in Milford, New Hampshire, one of a large family of children. Early in the anti-slavery cause, she, with four brothers, began to sing in the conventions. In all those stormy days of mob violence the Hutchinson family was the one harmonizing element. Like oil on the troubled waters, their sweet songs would soothe to silence those savages whom neither appeal nor defiance could awe. Abby made her first appearance in public at an early age. Anti-slavery, woman's rights, temperance, peace, and democracy have been her themes, — singing alike in the Old World and the New. To farmers on New England's granite hills, to pioneers on the far-off prairies, to merchant princes in crowded cities, and to kings, queens, and nobles, in palaces and courts, have those girlish lips sung the republican anthem, "All men are created equal." She was a girl of strong character and a nice sense of propriety in all things. Although until her marriage her life was wholly a public one, yet she never lost the modesty, delicacy, and refinement so peculiarly her own. She was slightly formed, graceful, with a bright, happy face, and most pleasing manners. She had a fair complexion, dark eyes and hair, teeth like rows of pearls, and in fact might be called beautiful. Her voice, though not of great compass and variety, was full, rich, deep, and well modulated.

All admit that "the Hutchinson family" have acted well their part in the cause of reform, and a second generation is singing still. When Abby retired from the stage her mantle fell on her niece Viola, who, having just married, will probably share the fate of her aunt, being according to Blackstone, wholly absorbed in another, and we shall hear from her no more.

The first national convention was held in Brinley Hall, Worcester, Massachusetts, October 23d, and 24th, 1850. This was the first thoroughly organized, and ably sustained convention, for which extensive preparations were made, as the women of the country had learned by that time what was necessary to make a convention a success. Above three hundred persons, men and women, enrolled their names as members. Among them we find William H. Channing, E. D. Draper, Frederick Douglass, Thomas Earle, Wendell Phillips, William Lloyd Garrison, Parker Pillsbury, Charles Burleigh, Hannah Darlington, Sarah Tyndall, Sarah R. May, S. C. Sargent, C. M. Shaw, Ellen and Marion Blackwell, Mary Adams, and Sojourner Truth. The proceedings of this convention were remarkable for their earnestness and ability. The reports, published both in England and America, in all the leading journals, first drew the attention of Mrs. John Stuart Mill to this subject, and prompted her able article in the "Westminster Review" on "The enfranchisement of women."

Paulina Wright Davis was chosen president of the convention. Her opening address, an hour in length, was a very concise, and able presentation of the work to be done, and the manner of doing it.

In this convention every phase of the question was discussed,—work, wages, property, education, and suffrage,—by the ablest men and women in the country. After this, National Women's Rights Conventions were held annually in the different States of New York, Pennsylvania, Massachusetts, and Ohio, and as the result the laws in these States were essentially though slowly modified. This simultaneous movement in every State, the unanimity of thought and feeling among the ablest women in the country, the striking similarity in the appeals, petitions, resolutions, and speeches, all prove this claim for woman to be one of those great ideas that mark an era in human progress, and not the idiosyncrasy of a few unbalanced minds.

ANTOINETTE BROWN

Was born in Henrietta, Monroe County, New York, May 20th, 1825. At the age of nine years she joined the Congregational church, and sometimes spoke and prayed in the meetings. In childhood she often expressed the wish that she might become a preacher. At the age of sixteen, she taught school during the summer, and attended the academy in Henrietta during the winter. In 1844 she went to Oberlin performing alone her first journey by canal and stage, to begin the experience of college life. While there she taught several branches in the seminary, in order to pay the expenses of her collegiate course. In 1846 she taught in the academy in Rochester. There her first lecture was delivered, in accordance with the custom of the *male teachers*, to address the pupils and visitors at the close of the terms. Her vacations at Oberlin had been passed in extra study of

Greek and Hebrew. It was here she and Lucy Stone had first met, and formed a friendship that has strengthened with their years. Here they fought together the battles of woman's rights with the students and professors, and sustained each other under all the peculiar hardships of their position. As they afterwards married brothers, and purchased homes in New Jersey, their lives have moved on harmoniously together.

In 1846 she returned to Oberlin to go through a three years' course in theology. For some time the Bible argument on the ministrations of woman had been with her a subject of serious and prayerful consideration. It was customary for the students to receive a license to preach, and before finishing their course they would often speak in the pulpits of the neighborhood.

When Miss Brown asked this license, the professors were grievously exercised. But after much thought and consultation they decided "that she was a resident graduate, pursuing the theological course, but not a member of the theological department, and, consequently, she needed no license from the institution, but must preach or be silent on her own responsibility."

Like General Jackson, she took the responsibility, and preached often in different parts of Ohio, while pursuing her theological course of studies.

After quitting Oberlin she spent four years in private reading and study, preaching and lecturing on various reforms. In 1850 she attended the convention in Worcester, Massachusetts, and made a speech on the enfranchisement of woman. She preached whenever and wherever opportunity offered, without regard to sect, — alike in the church at Andover, Music Hall, in Boston, or public halls in Worcester, Cincinnati, and New York. In 1853 she was ordained pastor of a Congregational church in South Butler, Wayne County, New York. The Rev. Luther Lee, Wesleyan minister of Syracuse, preached the ordination sermon. Gerrit Smith and Samuel J. May took part in the ceremonies.

"Then," says Mrs. Blackwell, in a note to me recently, "Dr. Cheever openly branded me and my South Butler Church as infidels; and the New York 'Independent' sustained him, and would only publish a crumb of my reply."

We are happy to say that our noble young friend, Theodore Tilton, was not then editor of that journal.

Miss Brown remained in South Butler but one year, owing to ill health from excessive labor, and painful doubts concerning theological doctrines. As soon as she was re-established in health of body and mind she lectured on reformatory subjects in Cincinnati and elsewhere, and investigated the character and causes of vice in New York, with especial reference to its bearing on woman. The year 1855 was spent in this interesting though painful work, and she published in the "New York Tribune" a number of sketches from life, under the title "Shadows of our Social System."

In 1854 she was a delegate from the Wayne County Society to the World's Temperance Convention, at which Neal Dow presided, in New York. But she was denied her seat, simply because she was a woman. Wendell Phillips and William H. Channing made eloquent speeches in favor of her admission, and she took the platform herself and essayed to speak, but such was the noise and confusion with tongues and canes, and the swaying of the audience to and fro, that all attempts on her part were unavailable.

From the liberal state of public sentiment to-day one can hardly believe it possible that, thirteen years ago, men claiming to be Christian ministers could have so rudely treated a beautiful, highly-educated young girl, a member of the same church with themselves, because she asked that her name might be enrolled with theirs in a World's Temperance Convention, — that she, too, might raise her voice in the metropolis of the nation against the vice of drunkenness.

In January, 1856, Miss Brown married Samuel Blackwell. Though she occasionally speaks, still most of her time is passed at home in the care of a family of daughters. It is said she is writing on theological questions for future publication. Mrs. Blackwell is a close, untiring student. She writes and speaks with ease, has a logical and well-stored mind, and is a woman of pleasing manners and address.

LUCY STONE

Was the first speaker who really stirred the nation's heart on the subject of woman's wrongs. Young, magnetic, eloquent, her soul filled with the new idea, she drew immense audiences, and was eulogized everywhere by the press. She spoke extemporaneously, having no special talent as a writer. Her style of speaking was earnest, fluent, impassioned appeal rather than argument. She excelled in telling touching incidents and amusing anecdotes. I well remember my pleasure the first time I heard her. It was at a Temperance Convention in Rochester, in 1853. A resolution was before the convention, asking of the Legislature a law granting divorce for drunkenness. Lucy took the affirmative; and, although the question was ably debated in the negative by Mrs. C. H. I. Nichols and Antoinette Brown, yet Lucy carried the audience with her.

She was born in West Brookfield, Massachusetts. Her parents were rigid Presbyterians, and trained up their children in an austere manner. She, however, early queried with herself as to the wisdom of existing laws, customs, and opinions. She could not see the justice of her brother's being sent to college to enjoy all the advantages of education, while she and her sisters remained at home to work on the farm. The yoke on her own neck galled her to action. She decided that she, too, would go to college and have a liberal education. The question was thoroughly pondered and debated, and at last decided. She borrowed the money and went to Oberlin, where, with great economy, management, self-denial, and untiring application to her studies, she graduated with high honors. Having discovered her talent for oratory in the debating society at Oberlin, she decided to fit herself for a public speaker.

On her return to New England she became an agent of the American Anti-slavery Society, lecturing alternately for the slave and woman. She travelled through the Western and some of the Southern States, speaking in all the large cities.

In 1855 she was married to Henry B. Blackwell. Thomas W. Higginson performed the ceremony. She accepted the usual marriage under protest,—her husband renouncing all those rights of authority and ownership which were his in law, and she retaining her own name. Although this has been to her a source of great annoyance and persecution, from friends as well as enemies, yet, feeling that the principle of woman's individualism was involved in a lifelong name, she has steadily adhered to her decision. I honor her for her steadfast principle.

The first thing the slave does in freedom is to take to himself a name. Having been Cuffy Lee, or Cuffy Davis, just whose Cuffy he might chance to be, as soon as he is his own master he takes a new name that is henceforth to represent his individual existence. Why wonder that a woman, believing in her own individual existence, who had distinguished her name the world over, should refuse to be so entirely swallowed up in another as to lose even the name to which she had answered for thirty years? I remember I had the same feelings when I was married, though young and unknown, and, although I took my husband's name, I retained my own also.

The name of Lucy Stone is prominent in all the early National Conventions, as she was Secretary of the Woman's Rights organization for many years. Mrs. Stone is small, with dark-brown hair, gray eyes, fine teeth, florid complexion, and has a sparkling, intellectual face. Her voice is soft, clear, and musical; her manner in speaking is quiet, making but few gestures, and usually standing in one place. Gerrit Smith told me once, with great glee, that sitting on the platform when Lucy was speaking, he saw her several times gently stamp her foot!

Mrs. Stone has one daughter, and since her marriage her life has been spent in retirement, until the news that Kansas was to submit the proposition to strike the words "white male" from her Constitution to a vote of the people, roused her again to public duty. She spent two months in the spring of 1867 travelling through that State, speaking to large audiences. She attended the Topeka Convention, at the formation of the "Kansas Impartial Suffrage Association," and has lectured during the past winter on suffrage for woman in Connecticut, Massachusetts, New Jersey, and New York.

MRS. CAROLINE H. DALL.

Born in Beacon Street, Boston. She is more distinguished as a writer than speaker, though she has lectured on various subjects in many parts of the country. Her addresses are uniformly well written, and show great research, and untiring industry. Mrs. Dall is a highly educated woman, a close student, an encyclopedia of historical facts and statistics. Her reports, read in the annual Woman's Rights Conventions, of the progress of the movement, are most valuable and interesting papers. She has published several books under the title, "Woman under the Law," "Woman's Right to Labor," "The Court, the College, and the Market." All her productions have been extensively reviewed and complimented by the press. In speaking of her last work, "The New York Evening Post" says: —

"Mrs. Caroline H. Dall's well-known book, 'The College, the Market, and the Court,' has been issued in a new edition, which contains important additions, some corrections, an index, and some notes on the unfortunate Dr. Todd, who was lately so shockingly mangled by Miss Gail Hamilton. Mrs. Dall's book has been very well spoken of abroad, as indeed it deserves, — for it is the most eloquent and forcible statement of the Woman's Question which has been made."

Many persons, now writing and speaking on this subject, glean their facts from her books, and without always giving credit where it is due. Mrs. Dall has been an active member in the Social Science Association, and read many valuable papers in their public meetings, both in Boston and New York. She was associated with Paulina Wright Davis, in "The Una," — a woman's rights paper, published at Boston in 1854, — and has taken a prominent part in some of the Massachusetts Conventions. She married a Unitarian clergyman, who has been a missionary for many years in Calcutta. Mrs. Dall's department of thought is in the region of facts. Not capable of generalization, her mind does not deal in principles, hence the conclusions she draws from her facts are sometimes neither legitimate nor philosophical.

MRS. C. I. H. NICHOLS.

In Kansas, I had the pleasure of meeting Mrs. Nichols in 1867. She is a native of Vermont, but went to the West several years ago. She has been in Kansas through all the troubles in that State, and to her influence, in a measure, is due its liberal laws for woman. She was in the first constitutional convention, and pressed woman's claims on its consideration. Mrs. Nichols is an able writer and speaker, and is as thoroughly conversant with the laws of her State as any judge or lawyer in it. She has taken a prominent part in all reforms for the last twenty years. She is a noble woman, and has borne the hardships of her pioneer life with a heroism that commands admiration. For many years, Mrs. Nichols ably edited the "Windham County Democrat,"— a whig paper, published at Brattleboro', Vermont. Though her articles were widely copied, it was not then known that they were written by a woman.

SUSAN B. ANTHONY

Was born at the foot of the Green Mountains, South Adams, Massachusetts, February 15th, 1820. Her father, Daniel Anthony, was a stern Quaker, her mother, Lucy Read, a Baptist; but being liberal and progressive in their tendencies, they were soon one in their religion.

Her father was a cotton manufacturer, and the first dollar she ever earned was in his factory. Though a man of wealth, the idea of self-support was early impressed on all the daughters of the family. In 1826 they moved into Washington County, New York, and in 1846 to Rochester. She was educated in a small select school, in her father's house, until the age of seventeen, when she went to a boarding-school in Philadelphia. Fifteen years of her life were passed in teaching school in different parts of the State of New York.

Although superintendents gave her credit for the best-disciplined school, and the most thoroughly taught scholars in the county, yet they paid her but eight dollars a month, while men received from twenty-four to thirty dollars. After fifteen years of faithful labor, and the closest economy, she had saved but three hundred dollars.

This experience taught her the lesson of woman's rights, and when she read the reports of the first conventions, her whole soul responded to the new demand. Her earliest public work was in the temperance movement, where I first met her in 1851, although she had lectured on that subject, and formed temperance societies as early as 1848, while teaching in Canajoharie, N. Y. In the winter of this year, she called a State Temperance Convention in Albany. Mrs. Lydia Fowler, Mrs. Mary Vaughan, and Mrs. Amelia Bloomer all spoke on that occasion. In May following, she called a Woman's Temperance Convention in Rochester. Corinthian Hall was packed during the proceedings. A State society was formed, and three delegates — Miss Anthony, Mrs. Bloomer, and Mrs. Mary Hallowell — were appointed to attend the Men's State Temperance Convention at Syracuse, in June. But these delegates were denied a right in the convention. The very idea of a woman's society, or a woman delegate, quite upset the gentlemen of the convention. The clergy, as usual, were especially denunciatory.

William H. Burleigh, corresponding secretary, in making out his annual report, hailed the formation of a woman's society as a powerful auxiliary to the temperance movement, and he accordingly advocated the recognition of the delegates; but he was scouted, voted down, and that part of his report blotted out. Rev. Mr. Lee, of the Wesleyan Church, invited the ladies to speak in his house in the evening. The consequence was, while they had an immense audience, the men's convention was almost deserted. Similar attempts were made by women all over the country, in the temperance associations; but they were uniformly thrust aside, and the result is, those old organizations have died out, giving place to the orders of Good Templars, Rechabites, etc., etc., that gladly affiliate with woman, in carrying on this important reform. At this time, Miss Anthony's life and mine became nearly one. From my retreat, which I seldom left, being surrounded with a large family of young children, she and I surveyed, year after year, the State and the nation.

Wherever we saw a work to be done, we would together forge our thunderbolts, in the form of resolutions, petitions, appeals, and speeches, on every subject, — temperance, anti-slavery, woman's rights, agriculture, education, and religion, — uniformly accepting every invitation to go everywhere, and do everything. Through all those years, Miss Anthony was the connecting link between me and the outer world, — the reform scout, who went to see what was going on in the enemy's camp, and returning with maps and observations to plan the mode of attack. Wherever we saw an annual convention of men, quietly meeting year after year, filled with *brotherly* love, we bethought ourselves how we could throw a bombshell into their midst, in the form of a resolution, to open their doors to the sisters outside, who had an equal interest with themselves in the subjects under consideration. In this way, we assailed, in turn, the temperance, educational, and church conventions, agricultural fairs, and halls of legislation. We persecuted the educational convention for a whole decade of years, to the infinite chagrin of Professors Davies, Buckley, and Hazeltine, whose feathers always ruffled the moment Miss Anthony, with her staid Quaker face and firm step, walked up the aisle, always taking a conspicuous seat, as if to say, Gentlemen, here I am again, to demand that you recognize as your equals, the hundreds of women before you, — teachers, who sit in these conventions, without a voice or vote in your proceedings. With the aid of such chivalrous men as Superintendents Randall and Rice, we at last triumphed; women were permitted to speak and vote in the conventions, appointed on committees, and to make reports on various subjects. Miss Anthony herself was invited to prepare a report on educating the sexes together, which she read to an immense audience in Troy, in 1858. At the close of her able report, Mr. Hazeltine came to her and said, "While I must admit the talent and power of your report, I would rather see a daughter of mine buried beneath the sod, than that she should stand before a promiscuous audience and utter such sentiments."

Superintendent Randall, standing by, replied, "And I should be proud if I had a daughter able to do it." In October of the same year Miss Anthony delivered the annual address at the Yates County Agricultural Fair, held at Dundee. She was to have spoken in the church, but the crowd was so great, that, with a lumber-wagon for her rostrum, she spoke an hour and a half in the open air. Hers is the one voice among our speakers that never fails to fill the ears of her audience. Her address was pronounced the ablest that had ever been delivered in that county. Miss Anthony's style of speaking is rapid, vehement, concise, and in her best moods she is sometimes eloquent. In late years she speaks extemporaneously, retaining enough of the Quaker to make a failure, except when strongly moved by the spirit. But the spirit is always sure to move when she sees the rights of any human being outraged. From 1852 she has been one of the leading spirits in every Woman's Rights Convention, and has been the acting secretary and general agent through all these years; and when in 1866 we reorganized under the name of "The American Equal Rights Association," she was reappointed to both these offices. From 1857 to 1866, Miss Anthony was also an agent and faithful worker in the anti-slavery cause until the emancipation edict proclaimed freedom throughout the land. She has been untiring in her labors in securing the liberal legislation we now have for women in the State of New York. The property rights of married women were secured by the bills of 1848 and 1849. From that time to the present scarce a year has passed without petitions, appeals, and addresses before our legislature. In the winter of 1854 and 1855 Miss Anthony held fifty-four conventions in different counties of the State, with two petitions in hand,—one demanding equal property rights, the other the ballot,—and rolled up ten thousand names. She performed these fatiguing journeys mostly in stage-coaches in the depth of the winter. Miss Anthony, though not beautiful, has a fine figure and a large, well-shaped head. The world calls her sharp, angular, cross-grained. She has, indeed, her faults and angles, but they are all outside. She has a broad and generous nature, and a depth of tenderness that few women possess. She does not faint, or weep, or sentimentalize; but she has genuine feeling, a tender love for all true men and women, a reverence for noble acts and words, and an active pity for those who come to her in the hour of sorrow and trial. She is earnest, unselfish, and true to principle as the needle to the pole. In an intimate friendship of eighteen years, I can truly say, I have never known her to do or say a mean or narrow thing. She is above that petty envy and jealousy that mar the character of so many otherwise good women. She is always full of the work before her, and does it, going through and over whatever stands in her way. She never sees lions in her path, but does what she is convinced is right, whether it seems feasible to others or not. Hence she is impatient and imperious with those who, not seeing the goal she does, stand in her way. The legislators of this State can testify to her pertinacity and perseverance. Those who have complained of Miss Anthony's impatience, in pushing our cause to a speedy success, must remember that without the cares of husband, children, and home, all her time, thought, force, and affection have centred in this work for nearly twenty years. She has raised and spent thousands of dollars, in printing and postage, having scattered documents without number all over this country and England. No one knows, as I do, the untiring labors of this noble woman in our cause.

What people call cross-grained in her is her quickness in seeing the right, and her promptness in maintaining it, no matter who her opposers may be. An anecdote will serve to illustrate the strong principle, independence, and self-reliance of her character. A lady of superior education, the wife and sister of distinguished men, was placed in an insane asylum to be quietly disposed of, that some domestic difficulties might not be made known. After a two years' incarceration she was released; but, insisting on separation, and the possession of her children, she was again threatened, when she appealed to Miss Anthony for protection. She promptly gave her the necessary assistance, and found a safe retreat for her and her daughter. No threats or persecutions could move her to reveal the hiding-place of her clients. Anti-slavery friends on all sides wrote to her, begging her to have nothing to do with the matter,—that it would injure the reforms she advocated. Leading men in the State wrote to her that she was legally liable for abducting a child from its father, and that she would be arrested some day on the platform in the midst of a speech. Telegrams and letters of threats and persuasion were poured on her thick and fast; among others, Mr. Garrison and Mr. Phillips wrote to her saying, "Do you not know that you are guilty of a violation of law?" "Yes!" she replied; "and I know when I feed and shelter a panting fugitive from slavery I violate law; and yet you would uphold me for violating the law in one case; why not the other? Is a refined, educated, noble woman, flying from the contamination of an unfaithful husband, less worthy of my protection than a black man flying from the tyranny of his master?" Of the threats of arrest from the presiding officer of the Massachusetts Legislature, and an honorable senator of New York, she had no fears, knowing that, in thus doing, they would make public exactly what they desired to conceal.

In the autumn of 1867 Miss Anthony went to Kansas, where she remained during the campaign, which closed so triumphantly, giving nine thousand votes for woman's suffrage.

In Kansas she met for the first time George Francis Train, who had been invited to go there, and stump the State for woman's suffrage, by the "Woman's Suffrage Association" of St. Louis. She travelled with him in Kansas, addressing large audiences, until the day of election, when I joined her at her brother's house, Mayor D. R. Anthony, of Leavenworth. We then went to Omaha, to meet Mr. Train, where we held two meetings, and from that point we came to New York, speaking in all the large cities of nine States. Through the influence of this new and noble champion of woman's rights with Wall Street brokers, she was able to establish "The Revolution,"—the first woman's rights paper in this country, with a name representing the magnitude of the work, — on a financial basis that ensures success.

Some odium has been cast on Miss Anthony for this affiliation with these Liberal Democrats; but time will prove her judgment as sound in this matter as it has been in so many other points where she has differed from her friends.

OLYMPIA BROWN.

Chief among the women who labored in Kansas in 1867, are Olympia Brown and Viola Hutchinson, — the one speaking and preaching, the other singing her sweet songs of freedom, in churches, school-houses, depots, barns, and the open air. Olympia Brown was born in Ohio; she was a graduate of Antioch college, and went through a theological course at

Canton, New York. She is the most promising young woman now speaking in this cause. She is small, delicately organized, and has a most pleasing personnel. She is a graceful, fluent speaker, with wonderful powers of continuity and concentration, and is oblivious to everything but the idea she wishes to utter. While in Kansas she spoke every day for four months, twice and three times, Sundays not excepted.

She is a close, clear reasoner and able debater. The Kansas politicians all feared to meet her. One prominent judge in the State encountered her in debate, on one occasion, to the utter discomfiture of himself and his compeers. By some mistake their appointments were in the same place. She, through courtesy, yielded to him the first hour. He made an argument to show the importance of suffrage for the negro, with an occasional slur on woman. She followed him, using his own words, illustrations, and arguments, to show the importance of suffrage for woman, much to his chagrin, and the amusement of the audience, who cheered her from beginning to end. At the close of the meeting a rising vote was taken, of those in favor of woman's suffrage. All the audience arose, except the judge, and he looked as if he would have given anything if consistence would have permitted him to rise also.

Miss Brown is now an ordained pastor of a Universalist church in Weymouth, Massachusetts, where she receives a liberal salary, and is honored and beloved by her people.

The space assigned me in this volume is too small for more than a brief sketch of this cause and its leaders. As much odium has been cast on these noble women, I cannot close without saying, what I feel to be just and true, of all alike. It is no exaggeration to state, that the women identified with this question are distinguished for intellectual power, moral probity, and religious earnestness. Most of them are able speakers and writers, as their published speeches, letters, novels, and poems fully show; those who have seen them in social life can testify that they are good house-keepers, true mothers, and faithful wives. I have known women in many countries and classes of society, and I know none more noble, delicate, and refined, in word and action, than those I have met on the woman's rights platform. True, they do not possess the voluptuous grace and soft manners of the petted children of luxury; they are not clothed in purple and fine linen, faring sumptuously every day,—for most of them are self-made women, who, through hardships and sacrifice, have smoothed the rugged paths for multitudes about them, and earned a virtuous independence for themselves. All praise to those, who, through ridicule and scorn, have changed the barbarous laws for woman in many of the States, and brought them into harmony with the higher civilization in which we live.

Eng^d by G.E. Perine & Co N.Y.

VICTORIA.

VICTORIA, QUEEN OF ENGLAND.

BY JAMES PARTON.

Great Britain wanted a monarch.

James the Second had abandoned his throne, and had been driven from his country. William and Mary, who succeeded him were childless, and without hope of offspring. Anne, seventeen times in her life, gave the kingdom hopes of an heir, and then disappointed those hopes. She was childless, and it was well known to her household that she was destined to die childless. As it was part of the fundamental law of the kingdom that the sovereign must be a Protestant, the son of the exiled king was excluded from the succession. The English are such slaves to habit and precedent, and the wars of the Commonwealth were so fresh in the recollection of the country, that it does not appear to have occurred to a single individual that the realm of England could be governed unless it could find a person to play sovereign on certain days of the year, in the show-rooms of St. James' Palace. America had not yet taught the world the art of nominating, electing, and deposing chief magistrates. There had once been kings in England, and the shadow of one was felt to be necessary still.

Wanted a monarch. No Roman Catholic need apply.

This was the problem for the "Heralds" of that day. In all the world there was but one person who could rightfully succeed Queen Anne, and that was an elderly lady known to the people of England as the Princess Sophia, and to the people of Hanover as the wife of their sovereign, the elector, Ernest Augustus. King James the First left but two children of the seven who had been born to him. One of these was the unfortunate Charles the First, who lost his crown and his head; the other was the Princess Elizabeth, who in due time married Frederick the Fifth, Elector Palatine, one of the hundred petty sovereigns of Germany. The Princess Sophia was the daughter of this pair, and she was married to Ernest Augustus of Hanover. Being thus the grand-daughter of James the First, and the wife of a Protestant prince, her right to the English throne, in case Queen Anne died without issue, was unquestionable; and hence, in the act of settlement of 1701, she was declared the heiress presumptive.

She had become a widow, and was living in retirement in Hanover as Electoress Dowager, — an elderly lady of excellent character, but as little fitted to govern an empire as a child. The English, however, did not want any one to govern an empire. They meant to do that themselves. They wanted some benevolent and good-looking person to wear the robes, inhabit the palace, and play the part of monarch, in a serene and dignified manner. For such purpose the good old dowager of Hanover might have answered as well as another. This destiny, however, was not in reserve for her; for, seventeen days before the death of Queen Anne, she died, leaving her son George, the Elector of Hanover, heir to the British crown. George Lewis was his name, but he is known in English history as George the First.

Thus it was that the present reigning family came to the English throne. Queen Victoria reigns to-day because of her direct descent, through James the First, from Mary, Queen of Scots, the mother of that pedantic king. On the Hanover side, she can claim an ancestry far more ancient, and far more illustrious than this.

The respect which many persons feel for an old family is perhaps not quite so unreasonable as some of us republicans suppose. Time tries all. As a rule, whatever endures long is excellent of its kind. In families which have long maintained a certain position in the world, we need not look for brilliant genius, nor splendid courage; but if we inquire closely into their history, we shall generally find a full development of what may be termed the preservative virtues, — prudence and family pride. A family which produces a genius appears to exhaust itself in the effort, — it passes away and disappears in the crowd; but where there is robustness of bodily health with a high degree of prudence and family feeling, a race may endure for centuries without producing a single individual of striking merit, or performing any valuable service for mankind. Nevertheless, there must be in such a family real worth and real wisdom. One of the most admirable provisions among the laws of nature is that one which dooms a family of incurable fools to certain and swift extinction.

The family now upon the English throne is one of the oldest in Europe. Among the mountains which divide Italy from Germany a powerful house named Welf held great possessions as long ago as the year 1100. Extending its conquests southward, it ruled some of the finest provinces of Italy, where the name was changed into Guelph, by which it has ever since been known. The Guelphs, with their impregnable castles among the mountains, drawing tribute from the fertile provinces of northern Italy and southern Germany, appear to have been for a time as wealthy and powerful a family as any in Europe of less than imperial or royal rank. It became too powerful. The Guelphs quarrelled among themselves. They divided into two factions, one of which retained the name of Guelph, and the other acquired that of Ghibeline, and each of them was powerful enough to maintain an army in the field. The bloody contest was waged a while among the German mountains. The family quarrel, as was usually the case in those days, absorbed into itself public questions of great pith and moment, until the whole south of Europe were drawn into the interminable strife. It was this famous contest between the Guelphs and the Ghibelines which saddened the existence of the poet Dante, and made him for twenty years an exile from his native city.

When mortals fight, it rarely happens that one party is wholly in the right, and the other wholly in the wrong. Both the Guelphs and the Ghibelines committed enormous outrages. Neither of them was strong enough to hold the other in subjection, and neither was great enough to forgive a fallen foe. When the Guelphs conquered a province or captured a city, they banished the powerful Ghibelines, and confiscated their estates. The Ghibelines, when they were victors, pursued the same policy. Consequently there were always a great number of persons, both within and without the conquered place, whose only hope of regaining their rights and property was in overturning the government. Hence three centuries of fruitless, desolating war.

But although in this cardinal error of the contest there was not a pin to choose between the hostile factions, it is nevertheless evident that the Guelphs were, upon the whole, fighting the battle of mankind. Dante was upon their side, — a great fact in itself. Closely allied with the pope, then the chief civilizing power of Europe, the sole protector of the people against the tyranny of their lords, the Guelphs, were greatly instrumental in limiting the power of the emperors, and preventing all the fairest countries of Europe from lapsing under the dominion of a single dynasty.

It was from these warlike Guelphs of the middle ages that

the present royal house of England descended. Gibbon, indeed, traces the family of Guelph up to Charlemagne; but we need not follow him so far in the labyrinth of heraldry. Let it suffice us to know that a powerful prince of the Guelphian race, six hundred years ago or more, acquired by marriage extensive possessions in the north of Germany. This prince is known in the history of Germany as Henry the Black. Other Henries succeeded, — Henry the Proud, Henry the Lion, and a long line of Henries, Williams, Othos, Georges, and Ernests, until at length we find a branch of the family established in Hanover, and ruling that province with the title of elector.

Not much can be said in commendation of the more recent ancestors of Queen Victoria. George the First was fifty-four years of age when he stepped ashore at Greenwich, and walked to the royal palace in its park, hailed and saluted as King of England. He was an honest, hearty man, brave and resolute; but he had an incurable narrowness of mind, and he was as ignorant of all that a king ought to know as the kings of that period generally were.

"My maxim is," he used to say, "never to abandon my friends; to do justice to all the world, and to fear no man."

The saying does him honor. He was a man of punctual and business-like habits, diligent in performing the duties appertaining to his place, so far as he understood them. But, unhappily, when he left his native country, he left his heart behind him. He loved Hanover, and a man can no more *love* two countries than two women. He understood Hanover; he never understood England; and the thing which he had at heart, during his whole reign, was the aggrandizement of Hanover. He had the satisfaction of dying in his native land, which he was accustomed frequently to visit, and his dust still reposes there in the electoral mausoleum.

His son, George the Second, with all his narrowness and

ignorance, was not without his good and strong points. Like most of his ancestors, he was honest, well-intentioned, and brave; and, like most of his ancestors, he was singularly unfitted to have anything to do with the government of a great nation. The ornament of his court was Queen Caroline, a patron of art and literature, whom the king loved truly, and scolded incessantly, whom he sincerely respected and continually dishonored. The scenes which took place at the death-bed of this queen show us something of the character of both of the ill-assorted pair.

"The king," says a recent writer, "was heart-broken, but he was himself. He could not leave her in peace at that last moment. By way of watching over her, 'he lay on the queen's bed all night in his nightgown, where he could not sleep nor she turn about easily.' He went out and in continually, telling everybody, with tears, of her great qualities. But he could not restrain the old habit of scolding when he was by her side. 'How the devil should you sleep when you will never lie still a moment!' he cried with an impatience which those who have watched by a death-bed will at least understand. 'You want to rest, and the doctors tell you nothing can do you so much good, and yet you always move about. Nobody can sleep in that manner, and that is always your way; you never take the proper method to get what you want, and then you wonder you have it not.' When her weary eyes, weary of watching the troubled comings and goings about her, fixed upon one spot, the alarmed, excited, hasty spectator cried out, with a loud and quick voice, '*Mon Dieu! qu'est ce que vous regardez? Comment peut-on fixer ces yeux comme ca?*' he cried. He tortured her to eat, as many a healthful watcher does with cruel kindness. 'How is it possible you should know whether you like a thing or not?' he said. He was half-crazed with sorrow and love, and a kind of panic. And he was garrulous, and talked without intermission of her and of himself, with a vague historical sense, as if talking of a life that had come to an end.

"One incident of this death-bed scene is probably without a parallel in the history of the human race: She counselled him to marry again, as he sat sobbing by her bedside. Poor man! he was hysterical, too, with grief and excitement. Wiping his eyes and sobbing between every word, with much ado, he got out this answer: '*Non — j'aurai des maîtresses.*' To which the queen made no other reply than, '*Ah, mon Dieu! cela n'empeche pas!*' Criticism stands confounded before such an incident."

Such was George the Second, the great-great-grandfather of the present virtuous sovereign of England. Such was the British Court a little more than a hundred years ago.

The eldest son of George the Second, Prince Frederick, or the Prince of Wales, was stupid even for a prince. He passed his brief existence in political intrigues with his father's enemies, and in debauchery with the worst of the young nobility. No good or even graceful action relieves the tedious record of his life. We need only say of him — for little else is known — that he embittered his father's days, and that England was well rid of him before it came his turn to play the part of king. George the Third, the grandfather of Queen Victoria, was the son of this Prince Frederick.

George the Third, who plays so important a part in the history of the United States, was one of the most virtuous and most mischievous of kings. He was honest, charitable, and temperate; he was as good a father as an ignorant man can ever hope to be; he was an attentive and affectionate husband; he was a considerate and liberal master and patron. If he had been born to the inheritance of a small farm, — if he had been a huntsman in Windsor Park, instead of lord of the castle, — he would have lived happily and wisely, and all his native parish would have followed him mourning to the tomb. But alas for England, tax-paying England! it was his destiny to be *styled* king, and to indulge all his life the fond delusion that he really *was* a king.

With such a father as he had, it is not necessary to say that his early education was most grossly and shamefully neglected; and after his father's death, he fell under the influence of men and women who starved his intellect and fed his pride. Coming to the throne in his twenty-second year, ignorant of history, ignorant of the English people, totally unacquainted with the spirit of a constitutional government, equally obstinate and conscientious, the whole policy of his reign was erroneous. He displaced William Pitt, and promoted Bute. It was he, and only he, who exasperated into rebellion the most loyal of his subjects, — the people of the American colonies. Instead of hailing with joy the accession of Napoleon to supreme power in distracted France, instead of aiding him to bring order once more out of the chaos of that kingdom, instead of being his hearty friend and ally, as he ought to have been for England's sake, as well as for that of France and mankind, he squandered and mortgaged deep the resources of the wealthiest empire on earth, in waging and inciting war against the only man who had it in him to rescue France and prepare her for a nobler future. He drove Napoleon mad; he prepared for him the long series of victories which wasted his time, wasted his strength, and destroyed the balance between his reason and his passions.

When George the Third came to the throne in 1760, the national debt of England was one hundred and thirty millions of pounds. The American war raised it to two hundred and sixty millions. The insensate warfare against the French Revolution made it five hundred and seventy millions; and by the time Napoleon was safely landed in Saint Helena, the debt amounted to the inconceivable sum of eight hundred and sixty-five millions of pounds. It may be safely asserted, that every guinea of this debt was unnecessary, and all except a few millions of it may be considered the price which Great Britain has paid, or is to pay, for allowing four such men as the four Georges of Hanover to occupy the first place in the government,—a place in which a wise and able man could do no very radical good, but one in which an incompetent man may work prodigious harm.

George the Third had fifteen children, of whom all but two survived him. Five of these children were sons, and all of them were robust and vigorous men. Down to a late period in the life of George the Third, no throne in Europe seemed so well provided as his with lineal heirs; and nothing was more improbable than that it should descend to a daughter of the fourth son,—the Duke of Kent. The Prince of Wales, however, had but one legitimate child, the Princess Charlotte, and when she died, in 1817, there was no probability of her father having other legitimate issue. The Duke of York, the second son, a shameless debauchee, also died without legitimate children. The Duke of Clarence, the third son, who afterwards reigned as William the Fourth, had a large family; but, unfortunately, his wife, Queen Adelaide, was not the mother of them.

Edward, Duke of Kent, the fourth of the king's sons, had the reputation, in his lifetime, of being the only one of them who observed the ordinary rules of morality. He is even spoken of as "austerely virtuous;" an accusation which I am inclined to believe was groundless; for, if he was so austerely virtuous, he would hardly have left so many debts behind him for his widow and daughter to pay. Some allowance must be made, however, for those unfortunate princes who held the highest rank in the kingdom, without having the income of a country gentleman. This poor Duke of Kent, although he enjoyed a revenue about as large as that of the President of the United States, was the feudal superior of men who had ten and twenty times that income. What is wealth in one country is poverty in another. An English prince with four thousand pounds a year is a very poor man, unless he is a very great man.

To economize his slender resources, the Duke of Kent resided, for many years, in Germany. He was living there in 1817, when the sudden death of the Princess Charlotte, and her newly born child, made it apparent that, if he lived to the ordinary age of man, he would one day succeed to the throne. This unexpected change in his prospects, it is supposed, led to his marriage, in the following year, with a German princess, Victoria, the widow of the Prince of Leiningen, and a daughter of the Duke of Saxe-Coburg. We now know enough of this lady to have a right to believe that she was a very sensible as well as exemplary woman.

Ere many months, it became evident that the Duchess of Kent was about to become a mother, and the duke was desirous that the child should be born upon the soil of the country of which it might be the the sovereign. One of the elements in the popularity of George the Third, which none of his errors ever sensibly diminished, was the fact that he had been born in England, — a circumstance to which he so aptly alluded, in a speech at the beginning of his reign, that it made an indelible impression upon the country. It was natural that the Duke of Kent should desire to secure this advantage for his unborn child.

Strange to say, this prince of the blood royal actually had not money enough for the journey home, and he wrote to his family for a remittance. They refused it, and he was obliged to borrow the requisite sum from friends in humbler life. At Kensington Palace, in London, on the 24th of May, 1819, the Princess Victoria was born. As she saw the light in the pleasant month of May, they named her the May-flower, and so she was called in the family during her infancy. We have the note, recently published, which the mother of the Duchess of Kent despatched to her daughter, when she heard the joyful intelligence.

"I cannot express," wrote the Duchess of Saxe-Coburg, "how happy I am to know you are, dearest, dearest Vickel, safe in your bed with a little one, and that all went off so happily. May God's best blessings rest on the little stranger and the beloved mother! Again a Charlotte, — destined, perhaps, to play a great part one day, if a brother is not born to take it out of her hands. The English like queens, and the niece of the ever-lamented, beloved Charlotte will be most dear to them. I need not tell you how delighted everybody is here in hearing of your safe confinement. You know that you are much beloved in this your little home."

Three months after, the Duchess of Saxe-Coburg sent to her daughter in England the intelligence of the birth of her grandson, — the Prince Albert of happy memory, whose untimely death the Queen of England still laments.

When the Princess Victoria was but eight months old, her father died, leaving his widow and her infant child nothing but an inheritance of debt, and a rank in the realm of Britain which is an inconvenience and a manifest absurdity unless accompanied with great wealth. Queen Victoria can doubtless well remember the time when her mother was pestered with duns, and when her own allowance of playthings was limited by her mother's poverty. Nor, indeed, considering her rank, was she ever in very affluent circumstances until she ascended the throne, — her mother's allowance being only eight thousand pounds a year, and part of this was expended in discharging the debts of the Duke of Kent.

The little princess was as well educated and trained as a child so unnaturally circumstanced could well be.

"Do not tease your little puss with learning," wrote her

grandmother to the Duchess of Kent, when the child was four years of age. "She is so young still."

And again, when she was seven: —

"I see by the English newspapers that his Majesty and her Royal Highness the Duchess of Kent went on Virginia water. The little monkey must have pleased and amused him. She is such a pretty, clever child."

We also have a very pleasing glimpse of the princess and her mother in the following passage by an anonymous writer: —

"When first I saw the pretty and pale daughter of the Duke of Kent, she was fatherless. Her fair, light form was sporting, in all the redolence of youth and health, on the noble sands of old Ramsgate. It was a fine summer day, not so warm as to induce languor, but yet warm enough to render the fanning breezes from the laughing tides, as they broke gently on the sands, agreeable and refreshing. Her dress was simple, — a plain straw bonnet, with a white ribbon round the crown; a colored muslin frock, looking gay and cheerful, and as pretty a pair of shoes on as pretty a pair of feet as I ever remember to have seen from China to Kamschatka. Her mother was her companion, and a venerable man — whose name is graven on every human heart that loves its species, and whose undying fame is recorded in that eternal book where the actions of men are written with the pen of truth — walked by her parent's side, and doubtless gave that counsel and offered that advice which none were more able to offer than himself, — for it was William Wilberforce. His kindly eyes followed, with parental interest, every footstep of the young creature, as she advanced to, and retreated from, the coming tide; and it was evident that his mind and his heart were full of the future, whilst they were interested in the present."

The death of George the Fourth, in 1830, and the accession of William the Fourth, sixty-five years of age, and without an heir, though twelve years married, rendered it all but certain that the Princess Victoria, a graceful girl of eleven, would one day be called to the throne. Until then, we are told, she was not herself aware of the destiny before her; but had been reared in every respect like any other child of an intelligent family of respectable but limited fortune. She became a highly interesting object both to her family and the people of England. The queen has lately published the cordial letter which her grandmother wrote to congratulate her mother upon the eleventh birthday of the princess:—

"My blessings and good wishes for the day which gave you the sweet blossom of May! May God preserve and protect the valuable life of that lovely flower from all the dangers that will beset her mind and heart! The rays of the sun are scorching at the height to which she may one day attain. It is only by the blessing of God that all the fine qualities he has put into that young soul can be kept pure and untarnished. How well I can sympathize with the feelings of anxiety that must possess you when that time comes! God, who has helped you through so many bitter hours of grief, will be your help still. Put your trust in him."

A few months later, when Parliament had named the Duchess of Kent to the regency of the kingdom, in case the king should die before the princess came of age, the same kind grandmother wrote:—

"I should have been very sorry if the regency had been given into other hands than yours. It would not have been a just return for your constant devotion and care to your child if this had not been done. May God give you wisdom and strength to do your duty, if called upon to undertake it. May God bless and protect our little darling! If I could but once see her again! The print you sent me of her is not like the dear picture I have. The quantity of curls hide the well-shaped head, and make it look too large for the lovely little figure."

And so her childhood passed away. She had, of course, the usual retinue of instructors, and went the usual round of lessons and recreation. The mighty Lablache gave her instruction in singing; and the queen says of him that he was not only one of the best actors and singers ever seen in England, "but a remarkably clever, gentleman-like man, full of anecdotes and knowledge, and most kind and warm-hearted. The prince and queen had a sincere regard for him." That she should acquire a familiarity with the three languages, English, German, and French, was scarcely to be avoided, since German was the native language of her mother, English the language of her country, and French the language of courts. In the volumes which she has recently given us, there are several specimens of the queen's drawing, from which we may infer that she acquired enough of this art for the occasional illustration of a private diary.

The most interesting event, perhaps, of her minority, — at least, the most interesting to herself, — was her first interview with her cousin of Coburg, Prince Albert. From the very birth of these children, their marriage by and by was distinctly contemplated; and, as time went on, it became the favorite project of the grandmother of the cousins, the Duchess of Saxe-Gotha, whose affectionate letters have been quoted above. William the Fourth, it appears, had other views for his niece, and did his best to prevent the meeting of the cousins. But a grandmother and a mother, in affairs of this kind, are more than a match for an uncle, even though that uncle wears a crown. So when Prince Albert and the Princess Victoria were seventeen years of age, the prince came to England, accompanied by his father and brother. Both the young people were aware of the benevolent intentions of all the German members of their family, and each had been in the habit of dreaming of the future in accordance with those intentions. They were well pleased with one another on this occasion. Prince Albert, accustomed to the quiet routine of a German duke's younger son, was equally amazed and fatigued by the gorgeous life of the English court. The late hours were particularly disagreeable to him, — as well they might be.

"My first appearance," he wrote, "was at a levee of the king's, which was long and fatiguing, but very interesting. The same evening we dined at court, and at night there was a beautiful concert, at which we had to stand till two o'clock. The next day the king's birthday was kept. We went, in the middle of the day, to a drawing-room at St. James' Palace, at which about three thousand eight hundred people passed before the king and queen, and the other high dignitaries, to offer their congratulations. There was again a great dinner in the evening, and then a concert which lasted till one o'clock. You can well imagine I had many hard battles to fight against sleepiness during these late entertainments.

"The day before yesterday, Monday, our aunt gave a brilliant ball here at Kensington Palace, at which the gentlemen appeared in uniform, and the ladies in so-called fancy dresses. We remained till four o'clock. Duke William of Brunswick, the Prince of Orange and his two sons, and the Duke of Wellington were the only guests that you will care to hear about.

"Yesterday we spent with the Duke of Northumberland,

at Sion, and now we are going to Claremont. From this account you will see how constantly engaged we are, and that we must make the most of our time to see at least some of the sights in London. Dear aunt is very kind to us, and does everything she can to please us; *and our cousin also is very amiable.* We have not a great deal of room in our apartments, but are nevertheless very comfortably lodged."

The queen has since recorded her recollections of the prince at the time of this visit: —

"The prince was at that time much shorter than his brother, already very handsome, but very stout, which he entirely grew out of afterward. He was most amiable, natural, unaffected, and merry; full of interest in everything; playing on the piano with the princess, his cousin; drawing; in short, constantly occupied. He always paid the greatest attention to all he saw, and the queen remembers well how intently he listened to the sermon preached in St. Paul's, when he and his father and brother accompanied the Duchess of Kent and the princess there, on the occasion of the service attended by the children of the different charity schools. It is indeed rare to see a prince, not yet seventeen years of age, bestowing such earnest attention on a sermon."

After a stay in England of some weeks, Prince Albert returned home, and resumed his studies. Each of the cousins was highly prepossessed in favor of the other. Indeed, the princess seems to have made up her mind, on this occasion, that, if public policy forbade her marrying her cousin Albert, she would never marry at all.

The eighteenth birthday of Princess Victoria, which was May the 24th, 1837, when she attained her legal majority, was celebrated throughout the British Empire as a national festival, and her health was toasted by a million merry circles of loyal Englishmen. Almost on that very day, King William the Fourth, then in the seventy-second year of his age, was stricken with mortal sickness. He lingered four weeks, and then expired. It was on a fine morning in June, as early as five o'clock, that the Archbishop of Canterbury communicated the intelligence to Victoria, and saluted her as Queen of England. Later in the day, the Ministry, the Privy Councillors, and a hundred of the principal nobility, assembled in Kensington Palace to witness the formal proclamation of the youthful queen.

"We publish and proclaim," shouted the herald, "that the high and mighty Princess Alexandrina Victoria is the only lawful and liege Lady, and, by the grace of God, Queen of the United Kingdom of Great Britain and Ireland, Defender of the Faith."

Until this moment, it is said, the young queen had maintained her self-possession; but on hearing these tremendous words, the realization of so many hopes and fond imaginings, she threw her arms about her mother's neck and sobbed. She recovered herself in a few moments, and then the Duke of Sussex, the youngest son of George the Third, and the head of the English nobility, advanced to pay his homage by bending the knee. Her good sense and good feeling revolted against an absurdity so extreme.

"Do not kneel, uncle," she said, "for I am still Victoria, your niece."

Her bearing on this most trying occasion was eminently becoming; and, a few weeks later, when she prorogued Parliament in person, and spoke the royal speech from the throne of the House of Lords, she conciliated every heart by her modesty and self-possession.

There was a circle of relations in Germany for whom these events possessed the deepest interest. The letter which

Prince Albert wrote to congratulate his cousin upon her accession was creditable to his taste and feeling. He was then a student at the University of Bonn, from which he wrote, June 26th, 1837: —

"MY DEAREST COUSIN, — I must write you a few lines to present you my sincerest felicitations on that great change which has taken place in your life.

"Now you are queen of the mightiest land of Europe, in your hand lies the happiness of millions. May Heaven assist you, and strengthen you with its strength, in that high but difficult task!

"I hope that your reign may be long, happy, and glorious, and that your efforts may be rewarded by the thankfulness and love of your subjects.

"May I pray you to think likewise sometimes of your cousins in Bonn, and to continue to them that kindness you favored them with till now. Be assured that our minds are always with you.

"I will not be indiscreet and abuse your time. Believe me always your Majesty's most obedient and faithful servant, ALBERT."

Queen Victoria was crowned at Westminster Abbey about a year after her accession, — June the 28th, 1838. It would be easy to fill many of these pages with accounts of a ceremonial which has increased in splendor as it has diminished in significance. The whole ceremony was founded upon the belief that the Sovereign represented the Majesty, and wielded the power, of the great God of heaven and earth. So long as this belief was real and universal, the ceremony of the coronation, and all the complicated state and etiquette of royal life, was not altogether wanting in propriety. It was the attempt of rude and barbarous men to express their rude and barbarous conceptions of the divine government, and the sacredness and awfulness of even its poor human representative. But people no longer believe that any special divinity resides in, or is represented by, the convenient ducal houses of Germany, from which England borrows a monarch upon occasion. We need not dwell therefore upon the extremely laborious and expensive way in which the English of modern times get the crown placed for a few seconds upon a sovereign's head.

She was queen, then, at length. She was the central figure of a fiction as splendid as the Kenilworth of Sir Walter Scott, and all the world looked with interest upon its gorgeous illusions. In those years of her blooming youth she seemed to the imaginations of men the most brilliant and most enviable of human beings. Nevertheless, she has recently told us, that she was far from happy at that time. She could not, at first, quite reconcile her mind to *be* a fiction. Inheriting something of the obstinacy of her race, she desired to have her own way in some matters in which a constitutional monarch must be submissive. She had a particular prejudice against the tories, — not merely against their principles, but against their persons, — and this prejudice an unhackneyed girl of nineteen was not likely to conceal. On the other hand, she was excessively fond of the whigs, and particularly of the good-natured premier, Lord Melbourne, who had advised and guided her during the first anxious moments of her reign. She carried these prejudices so far, that Lord Melbourne himself, although at the head of the favored party, remonstrated with her upon the subject, and advised her to forgive and conciliate the tories. Then again, being warm in her friendships, she could not endure the idea of parting with some of the ladies about her person, when the tories came into power. She was very restive in this affair, and it was long before she could bend her will to the hard necessity of losing the society of her friends for reasons purely political, over which she had no control.

The strangest part of her conduct was, that, as soon as she became her own mistress, she ceased to correspond with her handsome cousin in Germany. With reference to this subject the queen has written: —

"The only excuse the queen can make for herself is in the fact that the change from the secluded life at Kensington to the independence of her position as Queen Regnant, at the age of eighteen, put all ideas of marriage out of her mind, which she now most bitterly repents. A worse school for a young girl, or one more detrimental to all natural feelings and affections, cannot well be imagined than the position of a queen at eighteen, without experience and without a husband to guide and support her. This the queen can state from painful experience, and she thanks God that none of her dear daughters are exposed to such danger."

Prince Albert was naturally uneasy at her silence. A young man of twenty-one must not long delay to choose a career. So far, his life had been shaped by a secret but confident expectation that he would one day be the consort of his cousin Victoria, and if this was not to be his destiny, it was necessary to seek another. Impatient to know his fate, he came to England in October, 1839, resolved to bring the matter to a conclusion. Three years had passed since the cousins had seen one another.

When last they had met, she was a girl of seventeen, living a retired life at Kensington Palace, with her mother and her tutors, with little retinue and less ostentation. He was but a lively lad, not grown to his full stature, and unbecomingly fat. But now how different were they both!

It was half-past seven in the evening of October the 10th,

1839, when Prince Albert and his brother alighted at the principal entrance of Windsor Castle, one of the grandest-looking royal residences in Europe. At the top of the staircase, the queen herself met them in evening attire, and invested with the dignity which the very title of queen seems to carry with it. Nor was the change in him less striking in a maiden's eyes. The prince had grown tall, symmetrical, and handsome. That down upon his upper lip of three years before was now an elegant mustache. He had become a man. There was also in his countenance, we are told, a gentleness of expression, and a smile of peculiar sweetness, with a look of thought and intelligence in his clear blue eye, and fair, broad forehead, which conciliated every one who looked upon him. He was the very prince of romance,—just the hero wanted for the dazzling fiction of which Victoria was the gentle heroine.

His fate was decided promptly enough. The queen was delighted with his appearance and bearing. She conducted him herself to her mother. It was about dinner-time when they arrived, and yet they could not dine with the queen that night, for a reason which the queen herself explains: "Their clothes not having arrived, they could not appear at dinner, but came in after it in spite of their morning dresses." There was a large company of lords and ministers staying at the castle then, and the etiquette of the dinner could not be dispensed with, even in favor of these young princes.

Four days sufficed! On the fourth day after the arrival of the prince, the queen told Lord Melbourne that she had made up her mind to marry him. The minister said he was very glad to hear it, and that he thought the news would be well received.

"You will be much more comfortable," added Lord Melbourne, in his simple, fatherly manner; "for a woman cannot stand alone for any time in whatever position she may be."

Accordingly, on the following day Prince Albert came in from hunting at the unusually early hour of twelve, for he had received an intimation the evening before that the queen had something particular to say to him. On being summoned to the queen's presence he found her alone. Precisely what occurred on the occasion will never be known. It seems, however, that it devolved upon the queen to propose the momentous question. The following is the prince's version of what passed, as given in a letter to his grandmother: —

"The subject which has occupied us so much of late is at last settled. The queen sent for me alone to her room a few days ago, and declared to me in a genuine outburst of love and affection that I had gained her whole heart, and would make her intensely happy if I would make her the sacrifice of sharing her life with her, for she said she looked on it as a sacrifice. The only thing which troubled her was that she did not think that she was worthy of me. The joyous openness of manner in which she told me this quite enchanted me, and I was quite carried away by it. She is really most good and amiable, and I am quite sure Heaven has not given me into evil hands, and that we shall be happy together. Since that moment Victoria does whatever she fancies I should wish or like, and we talk together a great deal about our future life, which she promises me to make as happy as possible. Oh, the future! does it not bring with it the moment when I shall have to take leave of my dear, dear home, and of you? I cannot think of that without deep melancholy taking possession of me."

As soon as the interview was over, the queen, according to her custom, recorded her feelings in her diary.

"How I will strive," she wrote, in the first gush of tender emotion, "to make him feel as little as possible the great sacrifice he has made! I told him it *was* a great sacrifice on his part, but he would not allow it. I then told him to fetch Ernest (his brother), who congratulated us both and seemed very happy. Ernest told me how perfect his brother was."

The same afternoon, she wrote to her Uncle Leopold, King of the Belgians, who had from the first favored the match most warmly. This letter is highly creditable to the good, simple heart of the maiden queen: —

"My mind is quite made up, and I told Albert this morning of it. The warm affection he showed me on learning this gave me great pleasure. He seems perfection, and I think that I have the prospect of very great happiness before me. I love him MORE than I can say, and shall do everything in my power to render this sacrifice (for such in my opinion it is) as small as I can. He seems to have great tact, — a very necessary thing in his position. These last few days have passed like a dream to me, and I am so much bewildered by it all that I know hardly how to write; but I do feel very happy. It is absolutely necessary that this determination of mine should be known to no one but yourself and to Uncle Ernest until after the meeting of Parliament, as it would be considered, otherwise, neglectful on my part not to have assembled Parliament at once to inform them of it."

To which the good old king replied, very sensibly and happily: —

"In your position . . . you could not EXIST without having a happy and agreeable 'intérieur.' And I am much deceived (which I think I am not), or you will find in Albert just the qualities and disposition which are indispensable for your happiness, and which will suit your own character, temper, and mode of life. You say most amiably that you consider it a sacrifice on the part of Albert. This is true in many points, because his position will be a difficult one; but much, I may say *all*, will depend on your affection for him. If YOU *love* him, and are *kind* to him, he will easily bear the bothers of his position, and there is a steadiness, and, at the same time, a cheerfulness in his character which will facilitate this."

Nothing remained but to announce the intended marriage to the Privy Council, and through the council to the country. The council met, November 23d, to the number of eighty, in one of the large rooms of Buckingham Palace, the queen's London residence. It devolved upon the queen herself to make the announcement to this formidable company.

"Precisely at two," the queen wrote in her diary, "I went in. The room was full, but I hardly knew who was there. Lord Melbourne I saw looking kindly at me with tears in his eyes, but he was not near me. I then read my short declaration. I felt my hands shook, but I did not make one mistake. I felt most happy and thankful when it was over. Lord Lansdowne then rose, and, in the name of the Privy Council, asked that 'this most gracious and most welcome communication might be printed.' I then left the room, the whole thing not lasting above two or three minutes. The Duke of Cambridge came into the small library where I was standing and wished me joy."

The queen wore a bracelet in which there was a portrait of Prince Albert, and she says in her journal, "It seemed to give me courage at the council."

On the 11th of February, 1840, at the royal chapel of St. James, in London, in the presence of all that was most distinguished and splendid in the life of Great Britain, the marriage was solemnized. The queen, as brides generally do, looked pale and anxious. Her dress was a rich white satin, trimmed with orange blossoms, and upon her head she wore a wreath of the same beautiful flowers. Over her head, but not so as to conceal her face, a veil of Honiton lace was thrown. She was sparingly decorated with diamonds. She wore, however, a pair of very large diamond ear-rings, and a diamond necklace. Her twelve bridesmaids were attired in similar taste, and they were all young ladies of remarkable beauty. Prince Albert was dressed in the uniform of a British field-marshal, and was decorated with the collar and star of the Order of the Garter. At the moment when the queen and prince advanced to the communion-table, and stood before the Archbishop of Canterbury, the scene was in the highest degree splendid and interesting. But its splendors seemed to fade away before the majestic simplicity of the marriage service. There was really a kind of sublimity in the plainness and directness of the language employed:—

"Albert, wilt thou have this woman to be thy wedded wife?" and "Victoria, wilt thou have Albert to be thy wedded husband?" and "Who giveth this woman to be married to this man?"

To this last question the Duke of Sussex replied by taking the queen's hand and saying, "I do." Perhaps some in the assembly may have smiled when the Queen of England promised to *obey* this younger son of a German Duke, and when he said, "With all my worldly goods I thee endow." The queen tells us, however, that she pronounced the word *obey* with a deliberate intent to keep her vow, and that she kept it.

There was, of course, the wedding breakfast at Buckingham Palace, which was attended by the royal family, the ministry, the maids of honor, and other personal attendants of the queen and prince. Soon after seven o'clock in the evening, the royal chariot dashed into Windsor with its escort of life-guards, amid the cheers of the whole population of the town. The honeymoon was spent at Windsor Castle.

Prince Albert gave himself entirely up to the duties of his position and gradually relieved the queen from the burdens of royalty. At first, he was not present at the interviews between the queen and her ministers, unless specially invited, but after a year or two he was present as a matter of course, and the queen invariably acted in accordance with his advice. He was, in fact, as much King of England as though he had been born to the title. He said himself, in a letter to the Duke of Wellington, declining the command of the army, that his principle of action was "to sink his own individual existence in that of his wife, — to aim at no power by himself or for himself, — to shun all ostentation, — to assume no separate responsibility before the public." Desiring, he added, to make his position a part of the queen's, he considered it his duty "continually and anxiously to watch every part of the public business, in order to be able to advise and assist her at any moment in any of the multifarious and difficult questions brought before her, — sometimes political, or social, or personal, — as the natural head of her family, superintendent of her household, manager of her private affairs; her sole confidential adviser in politics, and only assistant in her communications with the officers of the government."

To his father, he wrote, a few months after his marriage: "Victoria allows me to take much part in foreign affairs, and I think I have already done some good. I always commit my views to paper, and then communicate them to Lord Melbourne. He seldom answers me, but I have often had the satisfaction of seeing him act entirely in accordance with what I have said."

And again, in the following year: "I study the politics of the day with great industry, and resolutely hold myself aloof from all parties. I take active interest in all national institutions and associations. I speak quite openly with the ministers on all subjects, so as to obtain information, and meet on all sides with much kindness. . . . . I endeavor quietly to be of as much use to Victoria in her position as I can."

Provided thus with a mate so suitable and so efficient, the life of Queen Victoria did not essentially differ from that of any other wife and mother of rank in England, except that it was a thousand times happier than married life usually is in any rank. Happiness in married life depends upon several things; but its fundamental condition is, the hearty acceptance and patient, cheerful discharge of the *duties* of the position. This condition was nobly complied with by this fortunate pair. When the queen was urged to assert her authority as head of the house and nation, since her husband was but one of her subjects, she was not for an instant deceived by such sophistry. She would reply, that she had solemnly promised at the altar to *obey* her husband, and that she would never consent to limit or refine away the obligation. Both of them thus accepting the duties which nature and circumstances had assigned them, and each having for the other a genuine respect and affection, they were as happy as people can rationally expect to be in this world.

November 21st, 1840, the princess royal was born. Two days after, the prince wrote to his father: "Victoria is as well as if nothing had happened. She sleeps well, has a good appetite, and is extremely quiet and cheerful." The queen was soon able to record in her diary, which she did with a full heart, that during the time of her confinement "his care and devotion were quite beyond expression." And again: "No one but himself ever lifted her from her bed to her sofa, and he always helped to wheel her on her bed or sofa into the next room. For this purpose he would come instantly when sent for from any part of the house. As years went on, and he became overwhelmed with work (for his attentions were the same in all the queen's subsequent confinements), this was often done at much inconvenience to himself; but he ever came with a sweet smile on his face. In short," the queen adds, "his care of her was like that of a mother, nor could there be a kinder, wiser, or more judicious nurse."

Both the parents were for a moment disappointed that their first-born was not an heir to the throne. They had not long to wait for consolation. The following is a list of their children: —

1. Victoria, the Princess Royal, — now the wife of the heir-apparent to the throne of Prussia, — born November 21st, 1840.

2. Albert Edward, Prince of Wales, heir-apparent, born November 9th, 1841.

3. Princess Alice Maude Mary, born April 25th, 1843.

4. Prince Albert Ernest Albert, born August 6th, 1844.

5. Princess Helena Augusta Victoria, born May 25th, 1846.

6. Princess Louisa Caroline Alberta, born May 18th, 1848.

7. Prince Arthur William Patrick Albert, born May 1st, 1850.

8. Prince Leopold George Duncan Albert, born April 7th, 1853.

9. Princess Beatrice Mary Victoria Feodore, born April 15th, 1857.

All of these children are still living, — the eldest twenty-eight, the youngest eleven. They appear to have been brought up in the most simple and sensible manner. The queen records several times, in her Highland Diary, that when the family chanced to be separated from their attendants, she heard her children say their lessons herself. Thus on board the yacht, she writes, "I contrived to give Vicky (Victoria, the princess royal) a little lesson by making her read in her English history." On this subject our own gifted and excellent Grace Greenwood has recently related some extremely pleasing anecdotes.

"When I was in England," writes Grace Greenwood, in the "Advance" "I heard several pleasant anecdotes of the queen and her family, from a lady who received them of her friend, the governess of the royal children. This governess, a very interesting young lady, was the orphan daughter of a Scottish clergyman. During the first year of her residence at Windsor, her mother died. When she first received news of her serious illness, she applied to the queen for permission to resign her situation, feeling that to her mother she owed a more sacred duty than even to her sovereign. The queen, who had been much pleased with her, would not hear of her making this sacrifice, but said, in a tone of the most gentle sympathy, —

"'Go at once to your mother, child; stay with her as long as she needs you, and then come back to us. I will keep your place for you. Prince Albert and I will hear the children's lessons; so in any event let your mind be at rest in regard to your pupils.'

"The governess went, and had several weeks of sweet, mournful communion with her dying mother; then, when she had seen that dear form laid to sleep under the daisies in the kirk-yard, she returned to the palace, where the loneliness of royal grandeur would have oppressed her sorrowing heart beyond endurance, had it not been for the gracious, womanly sympathy of the queen, who came, every day, to her school-room, — and the considerate kindness of her young pupils.

"A year went by; the first anniversary of her great loss dawned upon her, and she was overwhelmed as never before by the utter loneliness of her grief. She felt that no one in all that great household knew how much goodness and sweetness passed out of mortal life, that day, a year ago, or could give with her, one tear, one thought, to that grave under the Scottish daisies. Every morning, before breakfast, — which the elder children took with their father and mother, in the pleasant crimson parlor looking out on the terrace at Windsor, — her pupils came to the school-room, for a brief religious exercise. This morning the voice of the governess trembled in reading the Scripture for the day; some words of divine tenderness were too much for her poor, lonely, grieving heart; her strength gave way, and, laying her head on the desk before her, she burst into tears, murmuring, —

"'O mother! mother!'

"One after another the children stole out of the room, and went to their mother, to tell her how sadly their governess was feeling; and that soft-hearted monarch exclaiming, — "'O poor girl! it is the anniversary of her mother's death,' hurried to the school-room, where she found Miss ———, struggling to regain her composure.

"'My poor child!' she said. 'I am sorry the children disturbed you this morning. I meant to have given orders that you should have this day entirely to yourself; take it as a sad and sacred holiday. I will hear the lessons of the children.' And then she added, 'To show you that I have not forgotten this mournful anniversary, I bring you this gift,' clasping on her arm a beautiful mourning bracelet, attached to which was a locket for her mother's hair, marked with the date of that mother's death.

"What wonder that the orphan kissed, with tears, this gift, and the more than royal hand that bestowed it! This was Victoria, fifteen years ago; and I don't believe she has morally 'advanced backward' since then.

"Another anecdote illustrating Victoria's admirable good sense and strict domestic discipline, came to me directly from one who witnessed the occurrence.

"One day, when the queen was present in her carriage, at a military review, the princess royal, then rather a wilful girl of about thirteen, sitting on the front seat, seemed disposed to be rather familiar and coquettish with some young officers of the escort. Her Majesty gave several reproving looks, without avail; 'winked at her, but she wouldn't stay winked.' At length, in flirting her handkerchief over the side of the carriage, she dropped it, — too evidently *not* accidentally. Instantly two or three young heroes sprang from their saddles to return it to her fair hand; but the awful voice of royalty stayed them.

"'Stop, gentlemen!' exclaimed the queen; 'leave it just where it lies. Now, my daughter, get down from the carriage and pick up your handkerchief.'

"There was no help for it. The royal footmen let down the steps for the little, royal lady, who proceeded to lift from the dust the pretty piece of cambric and lace. She blushed a good deal, though she tossed her head saucily, and she was doubtless angry enough. But the mortifying lesson may have nipped in the bud her first impulse towards coquetry. It was hard, but it was wholesome. How many American mothers would be equal to such a piece of Spartan discipline?"

I will venture to borrow another pretty story from Grace Greenwood's budget. The following anecdote was related to her by the hero of it.

"My friend, Mr. W——, is a person of very artistic tastes,— a passionate picture lover. He had seen all the great paintings in the public galleries of London, and had a strong desire to see those of Buckingham Palace, which, that not being a 'show-house,' were inaccessible to an ordinary *connoisseur*. Fortune favored him at last. He was the brother of a London carpet merchant, who had orders to put down new carpets in the state apartments of the palace. And so it chanced that the temptation came to my friend to put on a workman's blouse, and thus enter the royal precincts, while the flag indicating the presence of the august family floated defiantly over the roof.

"So he effected an entrance; and, when once within the royal halls, dropped his assumed character, and devoted himself to the pictures. It happened that he remained in one of the apartments after the workmen had left, and while quite alone, the queen came tripping in, wearing a plain white morning dress, and followed by two or three of her younger children, dressed with like simplicity. She approached the supposed workman, and said, —

"'Pray, can you tell me when the new carpet will be put down in the Privy Council Chamber?'

"And he, thinking he had no right to recognize the queen under the circumstances, replied, —

"'Really, madam, I cannot tell, but I will inquire.'

"'Stay,' she said, abruptly, but not unkindly; 'who are you? I perceive that you are not one of the workmen.'

"Mr. W——, blushing and stammering somewhat, yet made a clean breast of it and told the simple truth. The queen seemed much amused with his *ruse*, and for the sake of his love for the art forgave it; then added, smiling, —

"'I knew for all your dress that you were a gentleman, because you did not "Your Majesty" me. Pray look at the pictures as long as you will. Good-morning! Come chicks, we must go.'"

These are but trifles; but they serve to show the queen's simple and kindly character. Her Highland Diary, recently published, abounds in similar trifles, and exhibits to us the picture of a happy family, always delighted to escape from the trammelling etiquette and absurd splendors of their rank, and capable of being pleased with those natural pleasures which are accessible to most of mankind.

"I told Albert," wrote the queen once, "that formerly I was too happy to go to London and wretched to leave it, and how, since the blessed hour of my marriage, and still more since the summer, I dislike and am unhappy to leave the country, and could be content and happy never to go to town. This pleased him. The solid pleasures of a peaceful, quiet, yet merry life in the country, with my inestimable husband and friend, my all in all, are far more durable than the amusements of London, though we don't despise or dislike these sometimes."

Alas! that a union productive of so much happiness and so much good should have been prematurely sundered by death. In the spring of 1862 the Prince was attacked at Windsor Castle by a disease which the physicians pronounced to be gastric fever. After a short illness the patient sank into a kind of stupor, from which he roused himself with ever-increasing difficulty. Americans will never forget that the last act of this truly wise and noble prince was to review the draft of the letter which the ministry proposed to send to the American government, demanding the return of the confederate commissioners taken from a British Mail Steamer by Captain Wilkes, of the United States Navy. Every tory mind in the universe desired that letter to be couched in such language as would preclude the possibility of a peaceful issue. But Prince Albert had not a tory mind.
Collecting, with a great effort, his benumbing faculties, he read the letter carefully over, and suggested changes which softened its tone, and made far easier a compliance with its just demands. Soon after the performance of this duty, so honorable to his memory, he relapsed into a lethargy from

which death alone released him. The queen was heart-broken. Ever since that lamentable day, she has been a mourner. Her own pathetic words touchingly express the sense she had of his value to her, and of the irreparable nature of her loss.

"It will now be, in fact," she said, "the beginning of a new reign."

I have spoken of the sovereignty of this lady as a "fiction," and compared it with one of the romantic creations of Sir Walter Scott. It is not, however, wholly fictitious. In one respect, it has been a solid and precious reality.

The time has not yet come when nations can safely dispense with imposing and venerable fictions; and until they can, it is highly desirable that those fictions should not be too closely inspected, nor too frankly criticised. If the sailor-king, William the Fourth, had been succeeded by another male creature so devoid of all human worth and dignity as George the Fourth, so licentious, so extravagant, so ignorant, and so vain, could he have reigned over England for thirty peaceful years? Probably not. Long ere this, the sensible people of Great Britain would have begun to ask themselves, "Why maintáin this costly pageant, since it is but a pageant?" The reign of this virtuous and amiable queen has postponed this question for thirty years, during which the people of England have been gaining political knowledge and experience, and drawing nearer the time when it will be safe and expedient to let that man have the name of governing England who does actually bear the chief part in governing. History will, perhaps, decide that this was the chief service which Queen Victoria rendered her country.

EMINENT WOMEN OF THE DRAMA.

BY WILLIAM WINTER.

No record of Eminent Women would be complete without some reference to representative actresses. In these the his tory of the stage, especially within the last two hundred years, is abundantly rich. Since the theatre was re-established in England, at the restoration of the monarchy, in 1660, many brilliant women have practised its art and won its laurels. Many bright names, therefore, appear in the catalogue of famous actresses, from the time of Eleanor Gwynn and Mrs. Sanderson to the time of Helen Faucit and Mrs. Lander. Each successive generation has had its favorite theatrical heroines. Mrs. Pritchard, Mrs. Oldfield, Peg Woffington, Anne Bracegirdle, Kitty Clive, Miss Farren, Mrs. Siddons, Mrs. Yates, Mrs. Jordan, Eliza O'Neill, Louisa Brunton, Sally Booth, Maria Foote, Mrs. Nisbett, Ellen Tree, Adelaide and Fanny Kemble, — these names, and many more, sparkle with fadeless lustre on that ample and storied page of dramatic history. Nor are they merely names. The triumphs of genius outlast all other triumphs. Kings and warriors may be remembered as shadows; but the fair conquerors of the stage inspire a warmer interest and live in a more vivid remembrance. Painting immortalizes their dead and gone beauty. Tradition preserves the memory of their achievements. Literature cherishes the lustrous record of their lives and deeds. That record, from the days of Gerard Langbaine to the days of Thomas Campbell, Leigh Hunt, William Hazlitt, and Charles Lamb, has instructed and charmed a vast multitude of readers. No story, in truth, can be more impressive or more affecting. Genius, beauty, renown, the pageantry of public careers, the wild tumult of popular applause, lives of stainless integrity and heroic self-sacrifice, and lives of glittering infamy, lawless revel, and lamentable anguish, — such are the elements of a narrative that no sympathetic mind can contemplate without emotion or without improvement. To add one brief page to that story — a leaf from the present time — is the purpose of this sketch. Its group of actresses must, necessarily, be a small one, since its scope is restricted within narrow limits. The artists herein described, however, are typical of different nationalities and different orders of talent. As such — and not in negligence of the signal ability and reputation of many of their contemporaries — they have been selected for present description.

I.

ADELAIDE RISTORI.

To all votaries of the stage, Adelaide Ristori is a familiar and an honored name. On the 20th of September, 1866, the great Italian actress made her first professional appearance in America. Since then she has acted in nearly all the important cities in the United States. The way had been smoothed for her coming. Long before she came, portions of her story had been widely circulated in the Press, and her name had become known in almost every household. The record of her life illustrates the development of an original nature and the progress of singular genius. It commences

RISTORI.

in 1826, when Adelaide Ristori was born, in the obscure Venetian city of Cividale del Friuli, Her parents, Antonio Ristori and Maddelena Pomatelli, his wife, were players, members of a strolling theatrical company, and very poor. The little Adelaide made her first appearance on the stage when she was only two months old, being carried on in a basket, in the representation of a comedy called "The New Year's Gift." When four years old, she began to enact juvenile parts, in which, as she was a bright and pretty child, she speedily became a favorite. Her first teacher was her paternal grandmother; and very hard work that teacher had to do, — since the pupil evinced far more partiality for music than for acting, and was not, without great difficulty, diverted from the former to the latter. Perseverance, though, bent the twig, and so gave the desired inclination to the tree. As the child grew, her sphere of employment began to broaden. From juvenile parts she passed to the line of "chambermaids," in which, at the age of twelve, she was notably proficient. Her labor at this time mainly supported her parents, and her six brothers and sisters — younger than herself. Change of place was, of course, frequent, in this nomadic period of her career. The first fixed dramatic company with which she became connected was that of the King of Sardinia, established at Turin. In this city she found her second teacher, Carlotta Marchioni, a famous actress in her day, and not less generous than eminent. To this artist the young Ristori was indebted for sound teaching and judicious encouragement. At times the eccentric old actress would call her "an imbecile," and bid her "go and wash dishes." At other times, when the girl's acting justified approval, she would feign severity and fondly murmur, "I'll have no more to do with you! you act too much as I would have you." In brief, Marchioni had discovered the germ of genius in this bud of womanhood, and she lovingly and faithfully labored to develop it into the perfect flower. With the Turin company Ristori remained until 1841, when she accepted an engagement in the Ducal company of Parma. The next five years of her life were full of labor, variety, and advancement. Her best successes were won in comedy; but she also attained distinction as an interpreter of the romantic drama. That she was surpassingly beautiful in those days can easily be imagined by all who remember the superb charms of her mature womanhood. But she conquered not less by virtue and genius than by personal beauty. In 1846, Guliano del Grillo, son and heir to the wealthy Marchese Capranica, saw Adelaide Ristori, loved her, and won her heart. The parents of the young nobleman, however, sternly forbade him to marry a woman who was not only sprung of humble origin but was an actress. The consequence of this parental opposition was a stolen marriage between these lovers. Not without great difficulty, though, were bride and bridegroom united. Some time after their marriage, which was hastily contracted at a little church near Cesena (Ristori being then on her way from Rome to Florence, to fulfil a professional engagement in the latter city), del Grillo had to make his escape from potent and dreaded parental vigilance, disguised as a peasant and mounted on a mule-wagon, — in which trim he passed safely through many perils, and came at last to Florence and to his wife. Finding their opposition vain, the parents presently relented, and a general reconciliation was attained. In the meanwhile the marriage of Ristori and del Grillo, originally one of public proclamation, — a valid ceremony in the Romagna, in default of the usual rite, — had been solemnly ratified, at Rome, by Cardinal Pacca. Thus, in honor and eminence, closed the first chapter in the brilliant life of the actress. In deference to the wish of her husband's family, she now retired from the stage. A brief period of domestic repose succeeded. But the genius of Ristori, not yet fully satisfied by expression, fretted in retirement and longed for its wonted field of labor. The fetters were soon broken. Hearing that one of her former managers had been imprisoned for debt, the actress determined to give three performances for his benefit. In pursuance of this resolve, she returned to the stage. Her reappearance was made at Rome, in 1849; and so great was her success that the populace stormed the theatre, and wildly demanded her formal and permanent resumption of her legitimate pursuit. Upon all hands her greatness was acknowledged. Even the noble relatives bent to the spell of this victorious hour. Aristocratic scruples were laid aside; a beneficent genius was left free to pursue its natural course; and, from that day to this, Adelaide Ristori has labored almost constantly in the service of the drama. Nor, in so laboring, has she neglected even the least of the duties of private life. Cherished as a wife, reverenced as a mother, and extolled throughout the civilized world as an actress, she is a living rebuke to the idle and petty theory that woman cannot devote herself to an independent pursuit without sacrificing the sanctities of her home.

Ristori's first efforts in tragedy were made after her reappearance at Rome. It was then, indeed, that she determined to dedicate herself to this branch of her art. A renowned Italian actress, Caroline Internari, advised her to this intent; and experience has shown the wisdom of that advice. Step by step, in the course of nineteen years, Ristori has risen to the first eminence among the tragic actresses of her time. Upon the Italian stage her rank was attained with comparative ease. She played many parts; but the culmination of her national success was marked by her performance of Alfieri's *Myrrha*, in 1850. It is a terribly painful impersonation, but it is wonderfully strong. Outside of Italy and France, though, it has never been regarded with much enthusiasm — save that of horror; and there seems no especial need of pausing upon it here. From Italy Ristori turned her eyes to France. To conquer Paris would be to conquer Europe; for Paris was the art-capital of the continent. Taking all the risks, therefore, Ristori selected an Italian company and made her way to the renowned metropolis. It was during the season of the first Universal Exposition, on the 22d of May, 1855, that she made her first appearance in Paris. Silvio Pellico's "Francesca da Rimini" — embodying that sweet, sad story which readers of English poetry have learned by heart in the tenderly musical and delicately colored poem of Leigh Hunt — was the opening piece in this important season. Ristori played *Francesca.* It is a character that reveals her sweetness more than her strength; but her personation of it was a perfect success. Seven nights afterwards she played *Myrrha.* All Paris was at her feet. "Ristori," wrote Jules Janin, then the representative dramatic critic — "she is tragedy itself; she is comedy; she is the drama." "Our language is too poor," said Lamartine, "to express the worth of that woman." Her first season in Paris extended to the 10th of September. At its close she had given three representations of *Francesca*, seventeen of *Myrrha*, twenty-two of *Mary Stuart*, and seven of *Pia da Tolomei;* and she had earned half a million francs. More than that — she had conquered the capital. All the intellect and culture of Paris honored the artist; Ary Scheffer painted her portrait; the Italian residents of Paris gave her a medal; and a diamond bracelet, presented by the Emperor of the French, testified to the imperial homage of "Napoleon III. to Adelaide Ristori." Her second season in Paris was like the first; nor did less success attend her in the other great cities of Europe. At the subsequent incidents of her European career it is only needful to glance in brief and rapid review. In 1857 she visited Spain; and it is recorded, in illustration of her marvellous personal magnetism, that, on one occasion during this visit, she so wrought upon the feelings of Queen Isabella, as to procure the pardon of a poor soldier, condemned to death for a breach of martial discipline. In 1858 she was in Berlin, and was decorated, by the King of Prussia, with the "Order of Merit," — never before attained by a woman, — in honorable recognition of her acting as *Deborah* (the "Leah" of the American stage). In 1860 she played a brilliant engagement at St. Petersburg. So far in Italian. Now, however, she was persuaded to achieve renown in French. Her first venture in this language was made at the Odeon, in Paris, in 1861, in the character of *Beatrix*, in a drama expressly written for her by Legouvé. It proved a hit. The piece was played eighty nights in that year, and afterwards, in 1865, was prosperously revived, both in the capital and in the provincial cities of France. At one time Ristori travelled with two distinct dramatic companies, one Italian and the other French. To London she went in 1863. *Mary Stuart* and *Queen Elizabeth* were there accounted her best impersonations; and, as every theatrical community in America can now testify, they are entirely superb and peerless works of art. In 1864 Ristori went to Egypt and gave thirty-seven performances at Alexandria. Still later she played at Constantinople, at Athens, and at Smyrna. In 1865 she visited Holland, by invitation of the University of Utrecht. By this time she had attained all possible professional honors in the old world, and it was only natural that she should turn her eyes across the sea.

Ristori's American career, as already mentioned, began on the 20th of September, 1866, — her appearance being made under the direction of Mr. J. Grau. The event is remembered as one of the most interesting and exciting that have, of late years, marked the history of the stage. The place was the French Theatre, in New York city. The house was densely crowded. Ristori's entrance, in the first act of "Medea," was awaited with almost breathless suspense, and was greeted with a tumult of joyful enthusiasm. No artist, indeed, could wish for a heartier welcome than American audiences habitually accord to a stranger. Nor, in the case of Ristori, did this spontaneous cordiality abate, as the performance proceeded; for the actress was recalled at the end of each act, and three times at the end of the play. Every heart felt the presence of an extraordinary woman. Her majesty of person and demeanor; her gracious dignity; her powerful and perfectly melodious voice, — the grandest voice that has been heard on the stage in modern times; her stately, Roman head; dark, flashing gray eyes; wonderful mobility of feature; luxuriant freedom and massive grace of gesture; and, above all, the sense that hung about her of exhaustless reserve power, — could not fail, in truth, to thrill the sensitive, sympathetic American temperament. Then, too, her personation of *Medea* disclosed, as in a comprehensive picture, all the chief faculties and qualities of her genius. After-performances did, of course, make them more fully and definitely known; but this performance seemed to crystallize them all. In the tragedy of "Medea" an irresistible appeal is made to sympathy with both passionate and maternal love, — each of which is seen to be scorned and outraged, — and also to admiration for a brilliant personality. *Medea*, a barbaric princess, has not only been deserted by her husband, whom she loves with an intense and wild ardor that is frightful and almost impious, but her children are taken from her, even at the supreme moment of agony when her recreant husband has cast her off in scorn, and announced his design to wed another woman. To be wronged as a wife was a sufficiently miserable disaster. To be wronged as a mother is an overwhelming calamity. The double blow breaks *Medea's* heart and crazes her brain, that is predisposed to madness. Then, in the poisoning of her rival and the slaughter of her children before the altar of Saturn, the climax of her life is attained simultaneously with the crisis of her anguish. Excepting *King Lear*, — the most awful and the most pathetic creation in dramatic literature, — *Medea* is, perhaps, the fullest embodiment known to the stage of pitiable desolation and passionate delirium. Love that bears fruit in wickedness, cruel desertion, long and wretched wanderings, penury, hunger, cold, the gradual wasting of mind and body, gleams of hope extinguished by scornful insult, then fury overleaping love, then a few faint flutterings of natural tenderness, then chaos, — such is the hard and heart-breaking story of *Medea*. The beginning, classic beauty, innocence, pastoral tranquillity; the end, a broken heart and a shattered brain. Few women have succeeded in playing the part at all. Most actresses who have essayed it have merely swamped themselves in vehemence and noise. Only one personation of it, in our day, can justly be compared with Ristori's, and that is the work of the great German actress, Fanny Janauschek. It is, indeed, no light matter to satisfy the requirements of this part, in even the single requisite of maternal love. Not every actress can personate a mother. Ristori, however, at all points throughout her personation of *Medea*, showed great genius and great capacities for its expression. In appearance, she was a perfect type of classic beauty. In spirit, she was a perfect type of fiery vitality. Her subtle knowledge of the human heart, her profound pathos, her extraordinary capacity for the utterance of vehement passion, her glowing imagination, her stateliness of intellect, and her thorough culture in dramatic art, all found utterance in this superb dramatic effort. Thus, at the outset, she conquered American admiration. The victory thus begun by her *Medea*, was finished by her *Mary Stuart* and her *Queen Elizabeth*. With these three characters her name will forever be identified, in the history of the stage. Her

Elizabeth, in particular, was pre-eminently great. Seeing Ristori in that assumption, you saw a woman who was manifestly born to rule; who swayed everything around her with an iron will; who had never even dreamed of doubting her divine right of monarchy; but who, nevertheless, was the victim of human passions, human weakness, and that sorrow which is Heaven's discipline for all mankind. Pride was never depicted better than in her arrogant scorn of rival genius and aspiration, and in her martial defiance of a dangerous enemy, — Philip II., of Spain. Valor found its most chivalric utterance, when she drew the sword of her father, King Henry VIII. Love — the dangerous gentleness and glittering passion of the tigress — was fully portrayed in her fatal dalliance with the brave Earl of Essex. For the rest: vanity, spite, spleen, malignant cruelty, and hypocrisy — all that composed the imperial weakness of the "virgin queen" — were minutely painted in her atrocious conduct toward the captive Queen of Scots. How massive was the nature of the great monarch you could easily comprehend, in contemplating the splendid art of the actress, — her struggles between duty and passion, her terrific remorse, and her lonely, desolate death. Ristori interpreted many other characters while she was in America; but never one that so captivated the popular heart. Time may impair the recollection of the actress in other parts; but it can never dim in memory her lustrous image of England's grandest queen. Analysis of all her personations is, of course, impossible here; but mention of all may usefully be made. She appeared here, during her first engagement, as *Medea*, *Mary Stuart*, *Queen Elizabeth*, *Phædra*, *Judith*, *Pia de Tolomei*, *Francesca da Rimini*, *Adrienne Lecouvreur*, *Thisbe*, *Camma*, *Myrrha*, *Deborah*, *Norma*, and *Lady Macbeth*. That engagement, including her tour outside of New York, extended over a period of eight months, in the course of which time she gave one hundred and sixty-eight performances. The last of these occurred at the French Theatre, in New York, on the night of the 17th of May, 1867, when she took a farewell benefit, appearing as *Medea*. Her first speech in English was made on this occasion, when, at the end of the performance, she came forward, in response to the call of the audience, and spoke the following words: —

"LADIES AND GENTLEMEN, — This is the first moment of profound sorrow I have known in this country. To bid adieu to New York, the birthplace of my success, — to say farewell to the United States, that have everywhere received me with open arms, — awakens emotions too deep for any words my poor tongue can utter. My visit to America is the grand event of my life; — grand in its temerity, grander yet in its triumphs. Your enthusiasm, your munificence, your goodness, I shall remember long and gratefully; remember till memory decays and my heart ceases to throb. Adieu!"

On the following day Ristori sailed for Europe; but in the autumn of 1867 she returned to New York, and commenced, on the 18th of September, her second, and last, American engagement. This was signalized by the production, on the 7th of October, of a new drama, then acted for the first time, Signor Giacommetti's "Marie Antoinette." The play is so constructed that it depicts the queen at various chief periods in her career. Its action commences in 1786, and terminates in 1793. Comedy and tragedy blend in it, and exact from the actress the utmost versatility and the deepest emotion. Ristori amply satisfied the demand. By all who saw the personation, her *Marie Antoinette* will ever be remembered as a stately image of majesty and sorrow. In the drama, as in history, *Marie Antoinette* is seen to have been subjected to bitter injustice and insult: ruthlessly separated from her hus-

29

band; harrowed by the knowledge of his death upon the guillotine; torn from her children; plunged into the deeps of agony and despair; and, finally, led forth to die amid the jeers of the brutal, infernal mob of the French revolution. Her experience, indeed, was the epitome of all miseries; but, over all miseries her indomitable constancy remained the victor. Ristori realized this ideal of suffering and fortitude. Her *Marie Antoinette* was a beautiful, brilliant woman, a loving wife, a fond mother, a proud-spirited queen, a profound sufferer, an exalted conqueror of all the ills of a most wretched fate. In two of the scenes, the pathos of her acting was such as no words can express. One scene, at the end of the fourth act, represented the parting betwixt Louis XVI. and his wife and children. Overcome by his emotions, the king, who knows himself condemned to die, rushes away into his oratory, and closes and fastens the door behind him. The queen and children pursue him: and then it was that Ristori, bursting into a delirium, beat upon the door with both her hands, and cried out upon his name, "Ah! Luigi, una parola — una sola!" and wrung every heart with grief and pity. The other scene represented the wife and children, kneeling in prayer for the husband and father, at that moment on his way to the guillotine. The roll of drums and the wail of the dead-march sounds in their ears, even while they pray, but continually grows fainter and fainter until it dies away in the distance. Ristori's face was a perfect picture of convulsive agony. A stupendous sorrow struggled in it with a vain, despairing effort at resignation. These scenes always produced an extraordinary effect upon the spectators. Historically accurate in every detail, and literally true to nature in every phase of emotion, Ristori's *Marie Antoinette* lives, indeed, in many memories, as the best of all her impersonations. To have seen this piece of acting is to have apprehended every aspect of the French Revolution, — its horror, its pathos, its hideous details, its retributive justice, and its full social significance.

Ristori's second American engagement lasted nine months. Her last appearance in New York was made on the 26th of June, 1868, as *Queen Elizabeth*. The chief new part that she played during her final season was *Isabella Suarez*, in a five-act drama, of a religious character, entitled "Sor Teresa," the work of Signor Luigi Camoletti. The entire number of performances given during her second engagement was one hundred and eighty-one, of which fifty-six were given in the island of Cuba. Her prosperity in America was very great. Personally as well as professionally she made the most pleasing impression throughout this country. "Away from the theatre," wrote one of her most earnest critics and devoted students, — Kate Field, — "she is the most human (and humane), the most simple, the most unaffected, the most sympathetic of women. So strongly is the line drawn between reality and fiction, that, in Ristori's presence, it requires a mental effort to recall her histrionic greatness." . . . That greatness, however, must forever survive in the history of the stage. Putting aside all differences of critical opinion, one thought is held in common by all who have watched her career and studied her achievements. That thought is, that she possesses a great intellect, a good heart, and a pure nature, and that she has exercised the best possible influence upon the drama. True to herself as well as to her profession, by her personal worth and private virtues she has attained a social station commensurate in eminence with that which her genius and aspiring energy have won for her in the world of art. The woman is as great as the actress; and the best minds and purest lives of our time have proudly and gladly recognized a fellowship with Adelaide Ristori.

II.

EUPHROSYNE PAREPA ROSA.

In the autumn of 1866 the musical public of America welcomed to these shores a richly-gifted and very remarkable musical artist,—Euphrosyne Parepa Rosa. At the beginning of her American career she awakened a lively interest. Her talents were seen to be extraordinary, and her temperament was recognized as uncommonly genial. Time has confirmed that first impression, and lively interest has deepened into an affectionate esteem. The story of the artist's life is brief and simple. She was born at Edinburgh, Scotland, in 1839. Her father was a Wallachian nobleman, Baron Georgiades de Boyesku, of Bucharest. Her mother, Miss Seguin, was a sister to the once eminent basso of that name. Their married life lasted but a little while, being terminated by the sudden death of the Baron, whereby his widow, only twenty-one years of age at the time, was left in poverty. To support herself and her infant child, Euphrosyne, the bereaved Baroness shortly afterward adopted the lyric stage as a profession, and presently began the education of her daughter for the same pursuit. This proved a labor of ease as well as of love. In her musical studies the child made rapid progress; and she also acquired, with rare facility, five modern languages,—English, Italian, French, German, and Spanish. At the age of sixteen—in 1855—she made her first public appearance in opera, in the city of Malta. *Amina*, in "Sonnambula,"—a customary rôle of operatic *débutantes*,—was the character she then assumed; and therein she made a marked and promising success. The unusual power and compass of her voice, and the felicitous method of her execution, speedily became themes of praise with European connoisseurs of music. At Naples, Genoa,

Rome, Florence, Madrid, and Lisbon, her first success was repeated and increased. So, for two years, she prospered, on the continent of Europe, receiving the applause of the people, the cordial favor of musical criticism, and the compliments and honorary gifts of nobles and of monarchs. In 1857 she made her début in London, in the same company with Ronconi, Gardoni, and Tagliafico, in "Il Puritani," and thereafter took a high place in the favor of the British public. Her career in England lasted nine years; in the course of which period she became the wife of a British officer, whose death, however, left her in widowhood, at the end of sixteen months. The autumn of 1866, as has already been stated, found her in the United States. The company with which she came included the well-known cornet player, Levy, and the violinist, Carl Rosa, and was directed by Mr. H. L. Bateman. Her début here, September 11, was made in concert, in the city of New York; but she has since achieved honors in oratorio and opera, in most of the principal cities of the Republic. In 1867 she became the wife of Carl Rosa, with whom she has happily lived and labored. Her rank in the musical world is high and honorable, and rests upon solid merits. Nature has endowed her with rich and remarkable gifts. Her voice, a pure soprano, is very powerful, is even in the register, and is thoroughly well balanced. Her method is entirely correct; and, in view of the great volume of her voice, her fineness of execution is unusual and surprising. Perfect in the technical part of music, and thoroughly acquainted with the nature and the scope of her own powers, she does every thing well that she undertakes, and she never undertakes a task that she is not fully able to perform. Her intonation and enunciation are faultless. In oratorio and in the concert room she has no equal. On the stage, however, she somewhat lacks, in acting, the intensity of passionate emotion, the soulful expression, which characterize and denote a great lyric artist. If, however, she have not a dramatic genius, she certainly possesses commanding talents. Her operatic performances in this country have evinced the steady growth of decided dramatic faculty. Great vocal powers have seldom found more ample or more touching expression than those of Parepa Rosa, in the first act of "Norma." To add that one of her very best successes here has been made as *Rosina*, in "The Barber of Seville," is to indicate alike the versatility of her talents and the scope and thoroughness of her culture. There is not, at present, on the American stage, a sounder practical musician than Euphrosyne Parepa Rosa. In social intercourse the lady is agreeable and winning, by virtue of her simple kindness and constant, sunny good-humor.

A New York journalist thus thoroughly sums up the distinguishing merits of this gifted and excellent artist: —

"Madam Parepa-Rosa's rare versatility and conspicuous artistic merit were never fairly appraised until she appeared in the United States, although she had sung in English opera in London, and on the Italian stage in the chief cities of the continent. The story of her American tours during the past two or three seasons would form instructive reading for foreigners. It is within bounds to say that, during a year, she has sung before a quarter of a million of people residing in about twenty-five cities scattered over an area of fifteen hundred miles long by seven or eight hundred wide. On her return home this most indefatigable prima donna will be able to testify to the receptions everywhere accorded her, and to the amount of 'appreciation' that real vocal worth finds, even in the young cities of the new west. We have no record of a singer having accomplished the task that Madam Rosa has so far brilliantly fulfilled. At home in every province of her art, — opera, concert, and oratorio; blessed with a voice that even this trying climate cannot impair, and gifted with a musical memory most wonderful, — she permits her manager to announce her at twenty places in a less number of days; and a two years' experience of her energetic character has taught the public to know that her engagements, though remotely placed, are sure of being fulfilled. It is not unusual for her to sing, in one week, two or three times at the opera, take the lead in an oratorio performance two hundred and fifty miles from the Academy, and appear in concert at two or three different places. This is an average instance of her untiring diligence, and the consequence is that, go where and when she will, she is sure to find a couple of thousand persons assembled to do honor to her talents."

III.

ELLEN TREE (MRS. CHARLES KEAN).

No one thinks of Ellen Tree without kindness and pleasure. By that name rather than her married name she is remembered by play-goers, and will be celebrated in dramatic annals. She is one of the women who have truly adorned the stage, — a good woman, in every relation of life, and a brilliant actress. For forty-five years she has been a member of the dramatic profession. Her first appearance on the regular stage, after a little amateur practice at a private theatre, was made at Covent Garden, London, in 1823, when she enacted *Olivia*, in Shakspeare's "Twelfth Night." By the critics of that period the performance was regarded as "promising;" but that was all; so the young actress went into the provinces, and acted there for the next four years. None of the difficulties that usually attend young theatrical aspirants beset her early career. Two of her sisters were already in the profession, — one, Mrs. Maria Bradshaw, as a singer, at Covent Garden, and the other, Mrs. Quin, as a dancer, at Drury Lane. Their influence, of course, favored their young relative, and an affectionate mother protected, cheered, and encouraged her. In 1827 she was engaged as a member of the Drury Lane company, and in that theatre she made her first conspicuous successes. Her range of characters, even then, was wide. She played *Lady Teazle*, and she also played *Jane Shore*, —— thus touching the antipodes of comedy and tragedy. In that same year, and at that same theatre, Charles Kean made his first professional appearance; and it is probable that the acquaintance then and there commenced, which was afterwards to ripen into love and marriage between these two distinguished artists. At that time, and for several subsequent years, theatrical business appears to have been uncertain and unprofitable in London; and, as a matter of prudence no less than enterprise, Ellen Tree varied her metropolitan engagements with various provincial tours, visiting and playing in the principal cities of England, Ireland, and Scotland. Success, in every respect, continually attended her footsteps. She played by turns all the accepted leading parts in the legitimate drama, and her professional reputation was steadily augmented. One of her eminent successes was her personation of *Clemanthe*, in Talfourd's classic and beautiful tragedy, which was first acted at Covent Garden, May 26th, 1836. With *Ion*, too, one of the purest and brightest of all the denizens of the world of fancy, her name is identified. In 1836, she visited the United States, and made a starring tour of this country, which lasted three years. Her success here was very great, and she found the warmest favor, not merely with the general multitude of theatre-goers, but with the best educated and most refined classes in American society. Years afterwards, in 1865, when, after a long absence, she reappeared in New

York, as Mrs. Charles Kean, it was remarked that many gray-haired men and women appeared among her audiences, lured to unfamiliar footlights by the desire to renew their intellectual association with the brilliant stage heroine of younger and brighter days. In 1839 she returned to England, with £10,000 as the fruit of her professional labors in America. Her first English reappearance was made at the Haymarket, where she was welcomed home almost rapturously by the English public. On the 4th of November, 1839, she appeared at Covent Garden, then under the management of Madame Vestris (afterwards Mrs. Charles Matthews, and since deceased), as the *Countess*, in Sheridan Knowles's drama of "Love," then acted for the first time, but repeated fifty times in the course of that season. In January, 1842, at Dublin, she was married to Charles Kean, with whom for twenty-six years she lived in perfect sympathy and happiness. Three months after their marriage they played a joint engagement, extending over a period of fifty-three nights, at the London Haymarket. "As You Like It," "The Gamester," and "The Lady of Lyons," may be mentioned as typical of the character of the pieces in which they performed. In August, 1845, they came to the United States, bringing with them Lovell's now well-known drama of "The Wife's Secret," written expressly for them, and in which they acted with singular excellence. In this piece, and in Shakspearean plays, Mr. and Mrs. Kean fulfilled a round of engagements in the principal cities of the Republic, with equal fame and profit. In the summer of 1847 they returned to England. Thenceforward, as before, Ellen Tree shared the labors and the fortunes of her husband. She had no separate career, nor did she desire it. In 1848 Mr. Kean was appointed by the Queen of England to be conductor of the Christmas theatrical performances at Windsor Castle, instituted by that sovereign and her lamented consort, the late Prince Albert, with the double design of benefiting the drama and relieving the court of the care and ceremony incident to state visits to the public theatres. This very difficult office Mr. Kean filled for ten years; and, as he was wont to consult his wife on every important matter, it is fair to discern in his signal success some traces of Ellen Tree's prudence, tact, knowledge of human nature, and ripe professional cultivation. At the end of his first season, the queen denoted her appreciation of his services by giving him a diamond ring. In 1850 Mr. Kean became joint lessee of the Princess's Theatre, in London, of which he was left sole lessee and manager in the following year. Here began the most brilliant period of his own and his wife's theatrical career. What Charles Kemble commenced, and Macready continued, Charles Kean triumphantly finished, — the grand and noble work of doing entire justice, in their representation, to Shakspeare's plays. Strangely enough, accuracy on the stage is a modern virtue. *Hamlet*, as played by Garrick, wore the wig and the knee-breeches of Garrick's time. Charles Kemble was the first to make a stand for literal correctness of costume. Macready, who took Covent Garden Theatre for his field of enterprise, in 1837, went further, and made a stand for greater correctness of scenery. But it remained for Charles Kean to do more than had ever before been attempted, by every possible auxiliary of art, skill, learning, labor, and money, to place the plays of Shakspeare on the stage in a thoroughly correct and splendid manner. That work he accomplished; and he is said to have remarked, very late in his life, doubtless in a moment of despondency, that he had wasted the best working years of his career, in endeavoring to sustain the dignity and purity of the British drama. He retired from the management of the Princess's in 1860, having, within his term of nine years, made the most elaborate and brilliant revivals, not alone of Shakspearean, but of divers other dramas. The series commenced in February, 1852, with "The Merry Wives of Windsor." This was followed, in due succession, by "King John," "The Corsican Brothers," "Macbeth," "Sardanapalus," "Richard III.," "Faust and Marguerite," "King Henry VIII.," "The Winter's Tale," "Louis XI.," "A Midsummer Night's Dream," "King Richard II.," "The Tempest," "King Lear," "Pizarro," "The Merchant of Venice," and "Much Ado About Nothing." Each of these pieces had a very long run, and in each Mr. and Mrs. Kean played the principal parts. A public dinner was given to Mr. Kean, on his retirement from the direction of the Princess's Theatre. Mr. Gladstone presided; and, on behalf of the committee and subscribers, presented the retiring manager with a silver vase, valued at two thousand guineas. In the speech that he delivered on this interesting occasion, Mr. Kean made the following significant allusion to the cherished partner of his fortunes: "Mind and body require rest, after such active exertions for nine years, during the best period of my life; and it could not be a matter of surprise if I sank under a continuance of the combined duties of actor and manager, in a theatre where everything has grown into gigantic proportions. Indeed, I should long since have succumbed, had I not been sustained and seconded by the indomitable energy and devoted affection of my wife. You have only seen her in the fulfilment of her professional pursuits, and are therefore unable to estimate the value of her assistance and counsel. She was ever by my side in the hour of need, ready to revive my drooping spirits, and to stimulate me to fresh exertion." In July, 1863, Mr. and Mrs. Kean set out from London, with a small, selected company, including their niece, Miss E. Chapman, Mr. J. F. Cathcart, and Mr. G. Everett, to make a professional tour around the world. They went first to Australia; thence to California; thence to the West Indies; and thence to New York. In the latter city they arrived in April, 1865, and made their first appearance there, at the Broadway Theatre, when it, together with the other theatres, was reopened, subsequent to the assassination of President Lincoln. In the opening pieces, "Henry VIII.," and "The Jealous Wife," Mrs. Kean played *Queen Catherine* and *Mrs. Oakley*. Majesty of mien, fervor of feeling, remarkable variety of intonation and of facial expression, accuracy of method, and charming vivacity betokened in those personations the gifted and cultured actress. She was seen, however, to be altogether unlike the Ellen Tree of former days, the slight; graceful, elegant, laughing lady, who had blazed upon the stage as the radiant *Rosalind*, and dazzled every eye with her beauty and her wit.

> "For beauty, wit,
> High birth, vigor of bone, desert in service,
> Love, friendship, charity, are subject all
> To envious and caluminating time."

The final sojourn of the Keans in the United States lasted a year. On the 16th of April, 1866, at the Academy of Music, in New York, after having appeared in the chief theatres of the United States and Canada, they took a farewell benefit, playing in "Louis XI.," and "The Jealous Wife." There was a very great multitude present, and the occasion lingers in memory as one of the brightest and saddest in the record of the stage. The fine art of acting never received a more fervent, conscientious, and touching illustration than was afforded in this performance. Mr. Kean played with all the energy and fire of his nature, and, at the close of the representation of "Louis XI.," made a most affecting farewell speech to the public. Mrs. Kean's part in "Louis XI." was *Martel*, the peasant's wife. She was very genial and simple in it; and thus, even in a trifle, revealed the es sential charm of her temperament. A sweet, kind, unpretending, helpful, affectionate woman, such Ellen Tree always was; and very naturally, therefore, she has always borne her rare mental gifts and distinguished worldly honors with native modesty, ease, and grace, winning on all sides affection not less than esteem. At the close of their engagement here, Mr. and Mrs. Kean returned to England, there to commence a series of farewell performances, by way of final retirement from public life. This was abruptly terminated by the sudden and serious illness of Mr. Kean, on the 29th of May, 1867, when, at Liverpool, he was playing "Louis XI." He never played again. On the 22d of January, 1868, at Bayswater, near London, he died. His grave is in the village of Catherington, in Hampshire, close by that of his mother. Ellen Tree, of course, will act no more. Sorrow saddens the autumn of her brilliant life. From all quarters, though, she is the recipient of the kindest and sincerest sympathy. The Queen of England, herself a widow, has sent a letter of condolence to the widow of the actor. Better than royal courtesy, however, and better than all the consolations of friendship and fortune, is the consciousness of duty well and truly done toward him whom she loves and mourns, and toward all the world. With that consciousness warm at her heart, Ellen Tree can look back upon a well-ordered, an honorable, a distinguished, and a successful life. Her rank as a dramatic artist is with the best representatives of English comedy.

IV.

CLARA LOUISA KELLOGG.

America's favorite vocalist, Clara Louisa Kellogg, was born in Sumter, South Carolina, in 1842. She is, however, of New England parentage. Her early years were passed in Connecticut. She was educated at the free schools, and in them she used to sing with her little school-mates; but she does not appear to have attracted attention as a child, by either proficiency in vocal exercises or especial beauty of voice. At one time in her girlhood she sang in a church-choir, in the town of Lyme, where she was thought to possess a pretty voice, but one that could easily be shouted down by more vigorous organs. In 1858 her parents were residents of New York city, her mother being what is called "a healing medium,"—in other words, a clairvoyant doctor. Many visitors were attracted to this lady—who is, indeed, described as a singularly gifted and interesting person—by the fame of her success as a physician. One of these visitors, on conversing with Mrs. Kellogg, learned that her "medium" powers had first been exercised in restoring to health her own daughter, a slender, delicate girl, who, at the moment of this conversation, was singing, behind a curtain that divided the room in twain, to the accompanying jingle of a cracked piano. One confidence succeeding another, Mrs. Kellogg said that her daughter's ambition impelled her toward the operatic stage. Reference was hereupon made, by the visitor, to Miss Eliza Logan, the once distinguished actress, — now in retirement, as Mrs. George Wood. At a later period mother and daughter called on this lady, and consulted her as to the expediency of Miss Kellogg's adopting a professional career. The incident is interesting and significant, as indicative of the troubles that beset, at the outset, every aspirant for the artistic life, and of the courageous energy that is needful to meet and overcome them: —

"My sister," writes Miss Olive Logan, in one of her lively, off-hand sketches, "spoke in a disinterested manner to this young girl, — told her of all the haps and mishaps of stage life, — spoke, also, of that unnecessary and unjust obloquy which is attached to the name of every actress, and then bade her go back and ponder seriously. She went back with her mother, and both pondered seriously. They pondered on the fact that the young girl must do something for self-sustenance. They pondered on the limited field of employment which is open to women. They pondered on the emoluments and the delights of being a seamstress, or a shop-girl, or a worker on a sewing-machine. They pondered on the scope afforded the daughter's genius by these employments; and, pondering, they decided. The young girl went upon the stage. She made a failure, — a dire, desperate, seemingly hopeless failure. But she remembered that many a great genius has failed at first, only to triumph at last. There was a plucky spirit in the girl's heart, and she did *not* turn to the sewing-machine as a last resort. Retiring again to private life, she began to labor at art as no galley-slave ever labored at the work to which he was sentenced. Her days and her nights were given to the worship of the goddess she loved; and, on her reappearance on the stage, she was tolerably, if not brilliantly, successful. Her great virtue was that she did not consider herself perfect; but day after day, and night after night, she kept up that unceasing toil which has now made her one of the most celebrated women of the age and the only pure-blood prima donna assoluta of whom America can boast."*

Surmounting all obstacles, Miss Kellogg at last made her

* P. F. Nicholson's "Town and Country."

début at the Academy of Music. This event took place under Mr. J. Grau's management, in 1860, in "Rigoletto." The attempt was a failure. In fact, it was only after her third début that the young vocalist succeeded. Since then her progress has been very rapid to that fame and fortune rightfully due to exalted merit and steadfast energy of character. Very early in her career she had the happiness to attract the attention of a munificent friend of art, — one of those wealthy men, found here and there throughout society, who practically consider that riches are given to them in order that they may promote the general welfare of mankind. That friend was Col. H. G. Stebbins, of New York, who formed so high an estimate of Miss Kellogg's musical gifts, conceived so deep an interest in her singularly delicate, refined, and gentle nature, and foresaw such a bright future for her in art, that he offered to charge himself with the care and cost of her musical education. The offer was accepted by the parents of the singer, and Col. Stebbins faithfully performed his chosen work. In truth, Miss Kellogg was, in a measure, adopted into the family of this sterling gentleman and generous friend, who has been to her a second father. Among the music-teachers then employed for her cultivation were Professor Milet, M. Riznire, and M. Muzio. One of her earliest personations that attracted critical attention and inspired hope for her future, was her *Gilda*, in "Rigoletto," which she played at the Academy of Music, in 1861. Her first really great success, though, was made as *Margherita*, in Gounod's "Faust," which was first produced in New York, in the season of 1864–65. Personal adaptability to the character was, doubtless, one of the chief sources of this success. *Margherita* is a pure, delicate, gentle, loving, simple-hearted, and simple-minded maiden; and Miss Kellogg filled this ideal, not less in spirit than in outward seeming. Another of her successes was made as *Linda di Chamounix*, in May, 1867.

Her acting and singing, in the malediction scene, in act second of this opera, are still remembered, with lively emotions of astonishment and admiration, because of their extraordinary vitality, tragic force, and glittering precision of method, in which art concealed every trace of art and wielded the magical wand of nature. In addition to these, Miss Kellogg has made signal successes in "Crispino e la Comare," "Fra Diavola," "Il Barbiere di Seviglia," "I Puritani," "L'Etoile du Nord," "La Sonnambula," "Martha," "Don Giovanni," "Lucia di Lammermoor," and "La Traviata." Her début in London was made on the 2d of November, 1867, as *Margherita*. Few triumphs so genuine and so brilliant as hers have ever been won upon the London stage, and no American musical artist has hitherto attained a reputation at all commensurate with that which Miss Kellogg now enjoys abroad. Her impersonations, indeed, and her delightful vocal powers have in a surprising manner affected both the mind and the heart of the English people. Many pages might easily be filled with thoughtful and ardent praises of the singer, from the soundest critical journals in London. A single quotation from one of these will not here be misplaced, as representative of the tone of European opinion respecting the prima donna of whom the art-public of her native America is so justly proud.

"Miss Kellogg," said the London "Review," on the Saturday subsequent to her début, "has for four or five years past enjoyed the highest renown in her own land, reports of which have long reached us here; and now we are able to bear testimony to the truth of the praise which has been bestowed on her by American critics. No ordeal could have been found more severe than a first appearance as *Margherita* in Gounod's 'Faust,' a part in which the London public has seen and heard some eight or more artists, — some excellent, all more or less good. Besides others, Madame Miolan-Carvalho (the original *Margherita* in Paris), Mademoiselle Lucca, Mademoiselle Patti, Mademoiselle Titiens, Mademoiselle Artot, and, last of all, Mademoiselle Christine Nilsson, have all been heard here in this part, and have left impressions which render it extremely difficult for any newcomer to succeed in the same character. The great success, therefore, of Miss Kellogg is decisive proof of her merits and accomplishments. Her voice is a soprano of pure and even quality, sufficiently brilliant in its upper portion, and intensely sympathetic in its middle and lower range. She has perfect command over a compass of two octaves, — her execution and intonation evidencing that complete course of student training, the necessary drudgery of which is so frequently shirked by vocal aspirants, and more especially when gifted with naturally fine voices, which are too generally considered by their possessors to be the chief requisites for success; whereas, in point of fact, the voice is but as an instrument apart from the trained skill and art requisite to wield it. Miss Kellogg is one of those exceptional singers who, blessed with a fine voice, have yet not presumed, on the strength thereof, to neglect those minute and laborious details of vocal exercise which form the requisite training for an executive artist. These qualities are apparent in the certainty and precision with which she intonates distant intervals, the note being at once perfectly reached without that wavering which is sometimes perceptible in singers of great pretensions, whose practice of scales and *solfeggi* has not been sufficiently diligent. Miss Kellogg's power, too, of sustaining a note with a prolonged *diminuendo*, finishing with an almost imperceptible *pianissimo*, unfalteringly in tune, is another proof of thorough training. Then her bravura-singing in florid ornamental passages has that distinctness and completeness of style so seldom realized; while her shake is irreproachable in closeness, evenness, and intonation. Beyond these technical merits, Miss Kellogg possesses a refinement and sensibility of style, and a power of expression, aided by a voice of naturally sympathetic quality, which impart a charm to her performance not to be found in mere mechanical excellence. Moreover, Miss Kellogg is an excellent actress, — with an intelligent and expressive face, a graceful figure, and that propriety of gesture, action, and by-play, which denote that the study of acting, apart from singing, has occupied more of her attention than is usual with vocalists."

These views have the double merit of impartiality and truthfulness. In their estimate of the singer there is no extravagance. Miss Kellogg is gifted with extraordinary powers, by which, and by great and continual labor, she has fairly earned her eminence. Nor can her victory be too highly esteemed. Success such as hers in the great art of musical acting implies a rare union of splendid qualities of person, mind, and character. Exquisite sensibility, keen intuitions, an unerring sense of symmetry, a wide grasp of emotions, reason and imagination, sadness and glee, the power to fill as well as the power to conceive an ideal, — all these must the singer possess, who would interpret the human heart and the immortal soul through the most heavenly medium of utterance that God has vouchsafed to his creatures.

V.

KATE BATEMAN (MRS. GEORGE CROWE).

In the career of Kate Bateman — who, at the age of twenty-six years, shares the distinction of the most popular actresses of her time — is seen a conspicuous illustration of the force that is exercised in public life by purity of character and integrity of purpose. She possesses uncommon talents and sterling accomplishments, and these she has employed with a noble energy and singleness of purpose, and in a pure, sweet, womanly spirit, that could not fail, and have not failed, to win unbounded appreciation and sympathy. The most important period in her professional life comprises the last eight years. Within that time she has won both fame and fortune. Her experience of the stage, however, dates back to childhood; and much of her more mature facility is of course to be attributed to early professional training. She was born at Baltimore, Maryland, on the 7th of October, 1842, being the second child of H. L. Bateman and Frances Bateman, — the former well and widely known as a theatrical manager, and the latter reputed as an actress and a dramatic author. Shortly after the birth of Kate, her father, then in mercantile business, returned to the stage, playing, in the domestic drama, such parts as *Martin Heywood* in "The Rent Day," and *Walter* in "The Babes in the Wood." On the 14th of December, 1847, at one of the theatres in Louisville, Kentucky, the latter piece having been cast, and the children who usually played the juvenile parts in it being unable to appear, the Bateman children, Kate and Ellen, — one five years old and the other three, — made their first appearance on any stage. Their début was an accident, but their success was signal. They were very pretty and interesting little girls, and their brightness and cleverness won all the more appreciation because of their extreme youth. Then, too, parental sympathy was touched by the spectacle of father and children playing upon the stage together, in such relations as are sustained by Walter and the Babes. In brief, all the favorable influences combined to make a career and open a brilliant future for these children. Season after season they starred the country under their father's management. New parts were found for them from time to time. Kate used to be especially fine as *Richard the Third*, which she was first cast in at the suggestion of Moses Kimball, in the old days of the Boston Museum, which institution he originated. Her best part, though, was *Henriette de Vigny*, in "The Young Couple." In 1850 the Bateman Children were taken to England, where, in all the great cities of the British Isles, they found even more favor than they had found at home. In August, 1852, they returned to America, and in 1856 they retired from the stage. Ellen was subsequently married and is now Mrs. Claude Greppo. Kate remained in retirement and studied acting. At length, in 1860, she reappeared on the stage, in the character of *Evangeline*, in a drama, by her mother, based on Longfellow's poem. The performance, though very pretty and pleasing, did not, however, make a deep impression upon the public mind. It was seen in many American cities, during the season of 1860–61, but was nowhere greeted with much enthusiasm. In fact, since the chief quality of the character of *Evangeline* is silent fortitude, its delineation affords but little scope for the vivid display of dramatic powers. The most that was possible for the actress was to look like a saintly sufferer and to be picturesque in tableaux. Two years afterwards Miss Bateman again appeared in New York — at the Winter Garden, in April, 1862 — as *Julia*, in "The Hunchback," and this time she made a prodigious popular sensation. Following up this success with a great deal of characteristic energy, she appeared as *Lady Gay Spanker*, in "London Assurance;" *Lady Teazle*, in "The School for Scandal;" *Juliana*, in "The Honeymoon;" *Juliet; Bianca*, in "Fazio;" *Geraldine*, in her mother's tragedy of that name, — originally written for Matilda Heron, — and *Rosa Gregorio*, in a new drama, written for her, by Mr. T. B. DeWalden. Later in the same year, in August, at the same theatre, she played an other engagement, which was signalized by the presentation of her *Lady Macbeth.* Her best successes this year were made in *Julia*, *Bianca*, *Lady Gay*, and *Geraldine.* In all her personations, however, the chief charm was the innate purity of womanhood that shone through them. Very often her art was defective. In some parts (*Juliet* and *Lady Macbeth*, for instance) she seemed utterly at sea. But no person of sensibility could witness her acting without being conscious of contact with an earnest, delicate, womanly nature, that was as refreshing to the mind, jaded by the all too prevalent artifice of the stage, as is the cool, delicious fragrance of trees and flowers and grass, after a light shower in a spring day. And not only did her nature charm by its ingenuous sweetness and win by its purity: a certain fiery force of intellect was perceptible in it, now and then, — shown in the fourth act of "The Hunchback," and in certain scenes of "Geraldine," — that vitalized a style of acting which might otherwise have sometimes seemed insipid. This fiery force, combined with an acute perception of simple pathos, was afterwards to find more abundant scope and more vivid expression. In December, 1862, Miss Bateman made her first appearance as *Leah*, — a character with which her name is now identified; and herein these qualities of her nature were displayed with ample breadth. Few single passages in modern acting are more touching than is her simple, natural, tender scene with Rudolph's child, in the last act of "Leah;" and few kindred efforts have electrified the multitude so much as has her delivery of *Leah's* curse, in the churchyard scene in that drama. These, however, are facts of such common knowledge, that it were needless to dwell upon them. It should be mentioned, though, that the play of "Leah" is an American adaptation of the German drama of "Deborah," by Dr. Mosenthal, made by Mr. Augustin Daly. Miss Bateman's first appearance as *Leah* was made in

Boston; but subsequently, for nearly a year, she starred the country in that character, and everywhere attained new popularity. Her first representation of it in New York was given at Niblo's Garden, in January, 1863. Mr. J. W. Wallack, Jr., and Mr. Edwin Adams appeared in the cast, as *Nathan*, the apostate Jew, and *Rudolph*, the lover. In the autumn of that year, Miss Bateman, accompanied by her father as manager, proceeded to London, where "Leah" was produced in October, having just been revised and revamped by Mr. John Oxenford, dramatic critic of the London "Times." That the performance was a success may readily be seen in the remarkable fact that it was repeated for two hundred and eleven nights in succession, before crowded houses, and greeted with every possible manifestation of public and critical approval. Writers were not wanting, indeed, to point out, truthfully and frankly, the defects of Miss Bateman's acting; yet its force, and its winning charm of fresh, young, gentle personality were none the less recognized.

In the last three months of 1864 Miss Bateman fulfilled prosperous and brilliant engagements in Liverpool, Manchester, Birmingham, Dublin, and Glasgow. The theatres overflowed nightly, and the star of the young actress rose still higher in the skies of fame. Returning to London in the spring of 1865, she reappeared as *Leah*, and also played *Julia*, *Bianca*, *Pauline*, and *Geraldine*, concluding her engagement, at the Adelphi, in July of that year. When autumn came, she made another tour of the principal British provincial cities, in all of which she played, with abundant success, a round of her favorite characters. On her next return to London, she received a complimentary benefit, at Her Majesty's Theatre (since destroyed by fire), given to signalize her farewell to England. The occasion is recorded as one of the most delightful of its kind in recent stage life. Miss Bateman played *Juliet*. Shortly afterwards she sailed for New York, arriving there on the 12th of January, 1866. On the 15th of January, at Niblo's Garden, she reappeared as *Leah;* and here she acted, for the next six weeks, before crowded audiences. She then proceeded to Boston, where she found her popularity unabated. Thence returning, she reappeared at Niblo's; but was forced, by sudden and severe illness, to relinquish her engagement, and to remain for several months in retirement.

In October, 1866, Miss Bateman became the wife of Dr. George Crowe, an English gentleman, son of Eyre Evans Crowe, author of a "History of France," and other works, and for several years editor of the London "Daily News." During the year following her marriage, she did not appear in public life; but, at length, having been entirely restored to health, she accepted an engagement, offered by an English manager, and, on the 7th of October, 1867, she reappeared in Liverpool, as *Leah*, creating a still greater popular excitement than before, — which also attended her professional progress, at Brighton, Manchester, Bath, Bristol, Cheltenham, Dublin, and Edinburgh. She is now in retirement, at her husband's residence, near the city of Bristol, England; but she will return to the stage in October, 1868, and commence the season at the London Haymarket Theatre, where she is engaged for a period of three months.

Her present is full of success, and her future is full of promise. Young, beautiful, distinguished, — a happy wife, an affectionate and cherished daughter, a simple-minded woman, — she moves forward, beneath a sunny summer sky, on a pathway that is strewn with roses. Such women honor the stage by their presence upon it; and their personal assertion of the dignity of the dramatic art is more eloquent and more practically effective than words can possibly be.

VI.

HELEN FAUCIT (MRS. THEODORE MARTIN).

For thirty years Helen Faucit has been a favorite actress on the English stage. For thirty years she has amused and instructed the British public, winning with ease, and wearing with grace, the golden crown of success. In both of the chief branches of dramatic art, as a tragic and as a comic actress, she has attained lofty eminence; nor has she been less esteemed as a woman than admired as an artist. It seems proper, therefore, to select her as the representative English actress of her time. The portraits of Helen Faucit — portraits that, of course, were made long ago — represent a tall, elegant figure; a frank, sweet, expressive, good face; large dark-brown eyes, full of eager intelligence; and a stately head, finely poised upon a swan-like neck, and crowned with luxuriant dark hair that falls in abundant curls on her snowy, sloping shoulders. Such, doubtless, was the fair girl who charmed an earlier generation of the lovers of art, in the brighter days of the British drama. Helen Faucit comes of a theatrical family. Her father and mother, and her three brothers and two sisters, were all members of the dramatic profession. Her early education for the stage was superintended by Mr. Percival Farren, of the Haymarket Theatre. Her first public appearance was made at a theatre in Richmond, near London, in the autumn of 1833, in the character of *Juliet*. The announcement of her *début* ran thus: "A young lady — her first appearance on any stage." The public received her kindly, and she seems to have played very well. But no novice can adequately personate Shakspeare's *Juliet*. The character taxes the art of a thoroughly trained actress; and, in general, it is much more truthfully interpreted by women of fifty, who have passed years upon the stage, than by the freshest beauties of eighteen or twenty-five. Helen Faucit's first appearance in London was made on the 5th of January, 1836, at Covent Garden Theatre, as *Julia*, in the well-known "Hunchback." One extremely interesting incident marked the occasion, showing that imperial firmness of mind, under the most trying circumstances, is not incompatible with the utmost gentleness of womanly temperament. There was a very large audience present in the theatre; and being brought, for the first time, to the test of such tremendous physical magnetism, the nervous power of the young actress faltered, and she succumbed to the icy spell of stage-fright. Her performance, as a matter of course, came very near to being a dead failure. At length, as the second act was drawing heavily to a close, she caught sight, in the orchestra, of the white head and tear-dimmed eyes of her oldest and dearest friend, — a venerable gentleman, whose paternal love and fostering care had cheered and encouraged all her young ambitions. "That white head," she afterwards remarked, "seemed to fill the theatre." Fired by the thought of this friend's past confidence in her talents, and present anguish in prospect of her failure, the actress made a great effort, suddenly recalled her will to its sovereign seat, and so turned the current of her fortune from defeat to victory. Her voice rose loud and clear, and all the fervor of her spirit came into play. As a matter of course, her audience quickly recognized the change, and felt the spell of genuine talent; and their hearty plaudits ratified her success. That success has known "no retiring ebb," but has steadily increased into such eminence as is only won and kept by commanding talents and unsullied integrity. Helen Faucit's next appearance was made as the heroine of "Venice Preserved." After that she played *Mrs. Haller*, and acted the chief part in Joanna Baillie's new drama of "Separation," which had, however, only a short life. But her chief success that season was *Clemanthe*, in Talfourd's "Ion,"—(of which Ellen Tree was the original). For her benefit, on the 20th of June, 1836, she played *Mrs. Beverley*, in the "Gamester," and very deeply touched the hearts of her audience, by her affecting picture of the poor wife's anguish and devotion. Even thus early she seems to have excelled in characters requiring for their portrayal deep feeling and exquisite tenderness. In the following season, she personated the chief female part in Bulwer Lytton's drama of "The Duchess de la Vallière,"—a piece of French extraction, then produced for the first time. It failed, though, and it is never heard of now. On the 18th of April, 1837, Helen Faucit made a hit as *Portia*. Mr. Macready took the lease of Covent Garden Theatre in that year, and made haste at once to engage her in his dramatic company. It will be seen that, from the outset, she faithfully and strenuously worked in the stock companies, which was the secret of her sure progress. Macready kept Covent Garden two years; and, in the course of that time, Helen Faucit played many important parts. Bulwer Lytton's "Lady of Lyons" was, for the first time, acted, during this term of management,—early in 1838,—and Helen Faucit was the original *Pauline*, to the *Claude Melnotte* of Macready. On the 10th of October, 1839, the tragedian abandoned Covent Garden, and accepted an engagement, under Mr. Webster at the Haymarket, Helen Faucit and Mrs. Warner being elected to second him in a round of his chief performances. On the 26th of October, 1841, when Macready again assumed the reins of management, in taking the lease of Drury Lane, Helen Faucit was again engaged as leading lady: and certainly it is no slight testimony to the ability and culture of the actress, that she was thus thrice chosen, to fill a position of the first importance, by an actor so exacting, so coldly intellectual, and so hard to please, as the famous tragedian is well known to have been. Many new pieces were tried, under the new administration of Drury Lane, and in most of them Helen Faucit had to study — and, as the stage-phrase is, "create"— new parts. "Plighted Troth," "The Blot in the Scutcheon," "Gysippus," and "The Patrician's Daughter," may be mentioned among the new dramas, that then, for the first time, saw the light. In all of these Helen Faucit appeared, and she also sustained leading parts in Macready's Shakspearean and other revivals; thus participating in the honors of one of the most brilliant periods of enterprise that are recorded in the history of the British drama. She was the original *Julie*, in Bulwer Lytton's "Richelieu," and the original *Josephine*, in Byron's "Werner." When Macready finally abandoned management, Helen Faucit betook herself to the "star" system, and went into the provinces. Engagements were numerously offered, and successes were numerously achieved. This portion of her career need not detain minute attention. The actress who has once become a popular favorite, has but to fulfil, under the starring system, the usual routine of travelling from city to city, and playing at theatre after theatre, with various business, it is true, but generally with prosperous results, and almost always with increase of fame. For some years past, Helen Faucit has played irregularly, only accepting engagements here and there, under entirely agreeable and advantageous circumstances. She is the wife of Theodore Martin, whose repute in literature, as an able, versatile, and brilliant writer, assuredly needs no bush, and whose rank in the world of English letters is sufficiently indicated by the fact that the Queen of England has selected him to write the Life of the deceased Prince Consort. She has never visited the United States; nor, as she is now upwards of fifty years of age, is it likely that she ever will come to this country, on a professional expedition. American knowledge of her acting, therefore, must depend on the study of English stage records and English criticism. Those authorities bear ample testimony to the brilliancy of her past career and the sterling worth of her talents and character. Adverse opinion has contented itself with calling her "Macready in white muslin." It is not unnatural that her temperament and her style of acting should have been influenced by the strong individuality of that remarkable actor. Few players who have yielded to the enchantment of Macready's art have ever been able entirely to discard his mannerisms in their own playing. Helen Faucit's native merits, however, are such as far outweigh her borrowed defects. A recent critic, Mrs. S. C. Hall, describes her, as follows, in words that clearly depict a true artist and gifted woman: —

"She bears home to the imagination one great harmonious impression of whatever character she is impersonating; but when we look back and analyze that impression, we feel what a wealth of subtle details has gone towards producing it, with what exquisite graduations it has been worked up to its crowning climax. . . . All she says and does seems to grow out of the situation as if it were seen and heard for the first time. . . . . With the ever-wakeful conscientiousness of a real artist, Helen Faucit is continually striving after a higher completeness in all she does. Her characters seem to be to her living things, ever fresh, ever full of interest, and on which her imagination is ever at work. They must mingle with her life, even as the thick-coming fancies of the poet mingle with his. As, therefore, her rare womanly nature deepens and expands, so do they take a richer tone and become interfused with a more accomplished grace. . . . I have often, in former days, seen her, by her intense power of shaping imagination, make characters harmonious which were mere tissues of shreds and patches, and personages 'moving-natural, and full of life,' which, as the author drew them, were hollow phantasms. Conspicuously has she done so with the 'Lady of Lyons.' I saw her when this play was first produced, and memory is sufficiently strong to compare the actress of that time with the actress of to-day. She can be compared with none other than herself; for no actress, since Helen Faucit made the character so essentially her own, has approached her in its delineation. It was then acting of rare grace, and truth, and power; it is now all that, but much more. Time, and study, and refined judgment have enabled her to perfect that which was admirable in its earliest conception. I recall the sensation that moved a crowded house after the curtain fell on the first representation of the 'Lady of Lyons.' There was a rumor that it was the production of Lytton Bulwer, — a rumor only, which, so carefully was the secret kept, some of his most intimate friends emphatically denied. The play, it is needless to say, made an immediate success. It has retained its place as one of the stock pieces of the stage ever since. There is now, indeed, no *Claude Melnotte* to be compared with Macready, although he was by no means young when he performed that youthful part; nor has any one ever approached him in it. But Helen Faucit is far nearer the ideal *Pauline* now than she was in those days; and it is easy to imagine the delight of Lord Lytton in witnessing that which it is not too much to say surpasses, in refined grace and intellectual power, the part as he created it.

"Her *Pauline* is in truth a perfect performance. It has that charm which comes only from the inspiration of genius; for at the root of all art lies the passion, which, as the great French actor Baron said, sees farther than art. But it is also the perfection of art where art is never, even for a moment, seen; the result of careful and continuous study, but with the ease and force of nature in every word, look, and motion. So is the character worked out from the beginning to the end."

Engd by G. E. Perine & Co N.Y.

ANNA E. DICKINSON.

ANNA ELIZABETH DICKINSON.

BY MRS. ELIZABETH CADY STANTON.

In listening to the many interesting incidents of this young girl's life, not all entrusted to me for publication, my feelings have vacillated between pity and admiration, — pity, for all the trials of her childhood and youth, in loneliness, poverty, and disappointment; and admiration for the indomitable will, courage, and rare genius, by which she has carved her way, with her own right hand, to fame and independence. While so many truly great women, of other times and countries, have marred their fair names, and thrown suspicion on their sex by their vices and follies, this noble girl, through all temptations and discouragements, has maintained a purity, dignity, and moral probity of character, that reflect honor on herself, and glory on her whole sex.

Anna Elizabeth Dickinson was born in Philadelphia the 28th of October, 1842. Her father, John Dickinson, was a merchant of sound intellect, and moral principle, a clear, concise reasoner, an earnest abolitionist, and took an active part in the anti-slavery discussions of that time. He was a benevolent, trusting man, and through the noblest traits of his character became involved in his business relations, and was reduced to poverty. His misfortunes preyed upon his mind and health; and he died soon after with a disease of the heart, leaving a wife and five children, Anna, the young est, but two years old. The last night of his life was passed in an anti-slavery meeting, where he spoke earnestly; and on his way home, not feeling well, he stopped at a druggist's to get some medicine, and died there without a struggle.

Her mother, Mary Edmundson, was born in Delaware, of an aristocratic family. She is a woman of refinement and cultivation, and was carefully reared in conditions of ease and luxury.

Both were descendants of the early Quaker settlers, and rigid adherents to the orthodox Friends. Their courtship lasted thirteen years, showing the persistency and fidelity of the father on one side, and the calm deliberation of the mother on the other. As a baby, Anna was cross, sleepless, restless, and crying continually with a loud voice, thus preparing her lungs for future action. She was a wayward, wilful, intensely earnest, imaginative child, causing herself and her elders much trouble and unhappiness. They, seeing her impatience of control, endeavored to "break her will," — a saying that has worked as much cruelty in the world as the proverb of Solomon, "Spare the rod and spoil the child." Fortunately they did not succeed, and through the triumph of that indomitable will we boast to-day that the most popular American orator is a woman. She was considered an incorrigible child at school as well as at home. Though she always knew her lessons, the absurd and arbitrary discipline so chafed her free spirit that she was generally in a state of rebellion.

With courageous defiance she would submit to punishment rather than rules she thought foolish and unnecessary. She had an intuitive knowledge of character, and early saw the hypocrisy, deceit, and sham of the world, — the hollowness of its ceremonies, forms, and opinions; and with wonderful powers of sarcasm she could lay bare the faults and follies of those about her. Hence she was a terror to timid, designing teachers and scholars; and *good* children were warned against her influence. Yet, as she was ever the champion of those who suffered wrong and injustice, she had warm friends and admirers among her schoolmates.

She says she always felt herself an Ishmaelite among children, fighting not only her own battles, but for those too timid and shrinking to fight for themselves. Her school-days were days of darkness and trial. Owing to her mother's limited means, she was educated in the free schools of the Society of Friends. Meeting there the children of wealthy Quakers, they would laugh at her poverty, and thoughtlessly ask her "why she wore such common clothes." She would promptly reply, "My mother is poor, and we work for all we have." Although she accepted her condition with bravery, she determined to better it as fast as she could; yet such taunts were alike galling to her and cruel in those who uttered them. Nevertheless, they were not without their power in developing the future woman; so far from depressing her youthful energies, they stung her into a nobler life. In her hours of solitude she would resolve to lift herself above their shafts, to make a home for her mother, and surround her with every comfort. Thus great souls feed and grow on what humbles smaller ones to dust.

Her love for her mother was the strongest feeling in her nature, and it was to relieve her from constant toil that she early desired some profitable employment that she might earn money for her own support. It was the sorrow of her childhood to see her mother pale and worn, struggling with all her multiplied cares, — for, in addition to her own family, she kept boarders and taught a private school. Thus, with ceaseless love and care and industry, that noble woman fed and clothed and educated her fatherless children, and to-day has the satisfaction of seeing them all noble men and women; and mid peace and plenty she remembers the long days of darkness, poverty, and self-denial no more. For the encouragement of those parents who have wayward, wilful children, I would mention the fact that Anna, who was a greater trial to her mother than all her other children and cares put together, is now her pride, her comfort, and her support.

When about twelve years old she entered "Westown Boarding-School of Friends," in Chester County, and remained there two years; from this she went to "Friends' Select School" in Philadelphia, where she applied herself so diligently to her studies, that, although she pursued over a dozen branches at one time, she seldom failed in a recitation.

During all her school-days, she read with the greatest avidity every book that she could obtain. Newspapers, speeches, tracts, history, biography, poetry, novels, and fairy tales were all alike read and relished. For weeks and months together her average hours for sleep were not five in the twenty-four. She would often read until one o'clock in the morning, and then seize her school-books and learn her lessons for the next day. She did not study her lessons, for, with her retentive memory, what she read once was hers forever. The rhymes and compositions she wrote in her young days bear evident marks of genius. When fourteen years old she published an article headed "Slavery" in the "Liberator." She early determined that she would be a public speaker. One of her greatest pleasures was to get a troop of children about her and tell them stories; if she could fix their attention and alternately convulse them with laughter, and melt them to tears, she was perfectly happy. She loved to wander all over the city alone, to think her own thoughts, and see what was going on in the outer world. One of her favorite rendezvous was the Anti-slavery Office in Fifth Street; where she would stay for hours to hear people talk about the horrors of slavery, or to read papers, tracts, and books on that subject. At seventeen she left school.

She was skilful in all kinds of housework, and orderly in

her arrangements. She was willing to do any kind of work to make an honest living. No service however hard, or humble, seemed menial to her. Being a born queen, she felt she dignified whatever she touched; even the broom became a sceptre of royalty in her hand.

When about thirteen years old she visited a lawyer's office one day, on her way from school, and asked for some copying. He, pleased with the appearance of the bright child, asked her if she intended to do it herself; she said, Yes. He gave her some, which she did so well that he interested himself at once in her behalf, and secured her work from other offices as well as his own. How she could get money to buy books was the one thought; next to helping her mother, that occupied her mind. To this end she would do anything, — run errands, carry bundles, sweep walks, — and as soon as she had obtained the desired sum, she would buy a book, read it with the greatest avidity, then take it to a second-hand book-store and sell it for a fraction of its cost and get another. When seven years old she would take Byron's works, secrete herself under the bed that she might not be disturbed, and read for hours. There was something in the style, spirit, and rhythm, that she enjoyed, even before the thought was fully understood. She had a passion for oratory, and when Curtis, Phillips, or Beecher lectured in Philadelphia, she would perform any service to get money enough to go. On one occasion she scrubbed a sidewalk for twenty-five cents, to hear Wendell Phillips lecture on "The Lost Arts." There are many very interesting anecdotes of her life during this period, illustrating her fortitude under most trying circumstances and her strong faith in a promising future. Through her magnetism and self-confidence she went forward and did many things gracefully and unchallenged, that others of her sex and age would not have had the courage or presumption to attempt. There was something so irresistible in her face and manner that entire strangers would yield her privileges, which others would not dare to ask. In her fourteenth year while with relatives in the country, during the holidays, she attended a Methodist protracted meeting, and was deeply moved on the subject of religion, was converted and joined the church. Her mind, however, was much disturbed on theological questions for several years, but after great distress and uncertainty, with the opposing doctrines and opinions she heard on all sides, she found rest at last in the liberal views of those who taught that religion was life, — faith in the goodness, and wisdom of God's laws, and love to man. She disliked the silent Quaker meetings, and made every excuse to avoid them. Her repudiation of that faith was a source of unhappiness both to her family and herself. About this time she spent a few months as a pupil and assistant teacher in a school at New Brighton, Beaver County; but as her situation there was not pleasant, she applied for a district school that was vacant in that town. About to make the final arrangements with the committee, she asked what salary they gave. One gentleman remarked " A man has taught this school heretofore, and we gave him twenty-eight dollars a month; but we should not give a girl more than sixteen." There was something in his manner and tone so insulting that her pride compelled her to scorn the place she needed, and, drawing herself up to her full proportions, she said with great vehemence, " Sir, are you a fool, or do you take me for one? Though I am too poor to-day to buy a pair of cotton gloves, I would rather go in rags, than degrade my womanhood by accepting anything at your hands.' And she shook the dust of that place from her feet, and went home to struggle on with poverty, firm in the faith of future success. Young, inexperienced, penniless, with but few friends, and none knowing her greatest trials, she passed weeks looking for a situation, in vain. At last she was offered a place as saleswoman in a store, which she accepted;

but finding that it was her duty to misrepresent goods to customers, she left at once, because she would not violate her conscience with the tricks of trade.

The distinctions she saw everywhere between boys and girls, men and women, giving all the opportunities and advantages of life to one sex, early filled her with indignation, and she determined to resist this tyranny wherever she found it. Sitting at home one Sunday in January, 1860, she read a notice that the "Association of Progressive Friends" would hold a meeting that afternoon, to discuss "woman's rights and wrongs." She resolved to go, and, in company with another young girl, was there at the appointed hour. Ten minutes were allowed the speakers to present their opposing views. "It was my good fortune," says Dr. Longshore, "to be there, and to announce at the opening of the meeting, that ladies were particularly invited to speak, as the subject was one in which they were interested. In response to this invitation, after several persons had spoken, Anna arose near the centre of the hall. Her youthful face, black curls, and bright eyes, her musical voice, subdued and impressive manner, commanded at once the attention of the audience. She spoke twice, her allotted time, and right to the point. These were her first speeches in public, and her auditors will long remember that day." She gave a new impulse to the meetings and a fresh interest in the association for months afterward.

The next Sunday she spoke again, and on the same subject. An attempt was made, by an opponent, by interruptions, foolish questions, sneers, and ridicule to put her down. This was a tall, nervous, bilious man, who spoke with the arrogance and assumption usual in that type of manhood,— as if he were a partner of the Most High in giving law to the universe; as if it were his special mission to map out the sphere of woman, the paths wherein she might with safety walk. By some magnetic law he fixed his eyes on this strange girl, into whose soul the floods of indignation were pouring thick and fast; and when he finished, the scene that followed was almost tragic. She rose, her feelings at white heat, and, with flashing eye and crimson cheek, she turned upon her antagonist, looking him square in the face, and poured out the vials of her pent-up wrath,—the sum of all the wrongs she had felt through struggling girlhood; the insults to womanhood she had read and heard; the barbarisms of law, of custom, and of daily life, that but for the strong will God had given her to resist, would have ground her, with the multitudes of her sex, to powder. She poured out such volleys of invective, sarcasm, and denunciation, painted the helplessness of women with such pathos and power, giving touching incidents of her own hard experience, that her antagonist sunk lower and lower into his seat and bowed his head in silence and humiliation, while those who witnessed the scene were melted to tears. Never was an audience more electrified and amazed than were they with the eloquence and power of that young girl. No one knew who she was, or whence she came; but all alike felt her burning words, and withering scorn of him who had dared to be the mouth-piece of such time-honored insolence and cant about the sphere of woman. Pointing straight at him, and, with each step approaching nearer where he sat, saying, You, sir, said thus and so, she swept away his arguments, one by one, like cobwebs before a whirlwind, and left him not one foot of ground whereon to stand. When she finished, he took his hat and sneaked out of the meeting like a whipped spaniel, to the great amusement of the audience, leaving the sympathies of the audience with the brave young girl.

From this hour Elwood and Hannah Longshore became Anna's most faithful and trusted friends and advisers. They appreciated her genius, comprehended the difficulties of her position, and gave her a helping hand in securing means of support. They encouraged her ambition to become a public speaker. So intense and earnest was she in all her desires, that she easily surmounted every difficulty to secure her ends. No lions ever crouched in her path; it was the real, not the imaginary, that blocked her way.

Soon after the scene in the Sunday meeting, two gentlemen called at her home one day and inquired for Anna Dickinson. They had heard her speak, and were so much pleased that they desired to know something of her family and surroundings. As soon as they inquired for Anna, the mother's heart stood still, supposing that these men had come to complain of some of her pranks in the neighborhood; and she was by no means relieved, when she heard that her daughter had made a speech in a public meeting on Sunday, and they had come to congratulate her on her success.

Her public career was at first a great mortification to her mother, who felt that by this erratic course she was bringing shame and humiliation on her family, never dreaming that she was so soon to occupy one of the proudest positions before the American people, to distinguish her family, and place them in conditions of ease and luxury. But she shared the common fate of genius, — persecution in the house of its friends. At this time she became a constant visitor at the house of Dr. Longshore, and found there the affection and wisdom, the warm and sympathizing friendship, her generous and impulsive nature most needed for its development and control. They took her to their hearts, cared for her in every way, and to this day she calls their house her home.

"We felt towards her," says Dr. Longshore, "as if she were our own child, and she lingered with us in her visits with filial devotion. We were the first strangers to manifest an interest in her welfare and future plans, and she reciprocated our friendship with confidence and love. She was always so happy, so full of hope and life, that her presence seemed like that of an angel. Hour after hour, in the evening, when all was still, she would entertain us with her varied experiences, at home, in school, in church, in company, with her teachers, playmates, and strangers, with her efforts to get books, clothes, comforts, laughing and crying by turn. Her recitals were so full, glowing, and eloquent, that we took no note of the passing time, and the midnight hours would often find us lingering still, pleased and patient listeners of this strange child's life."

After reading some thrilling account of the slave system, one night, she had a remarkable dream. She thought she was herself a slave-girl, the victim of all the terrible experiences of that condition. The toil, the lash, the starvation and nakedness, the auction-block, the brutality of driver and owner, were all so vividly painted on her imagination that she could not rid herself of the horrid realities of that system. She could never speak on that subject in public or private, but this terrible memory would come vividly back to her, intensifying her feelings, and giving an added power to her words.

After attending the meeting of Progressive Friends for several weeks, she was invited to speak in Mullica Hill, New Jersey, and on the first Sunday in April, 1860, she made the first speech to which she had given any previous thought. The large school-house was crowded; her subject was "Woman's Work." Speaking from the depths of her own experience, she held the audience in breathless silence for over an hour. There was an indescribable pathos in her full, rich voice, that, aside from what she said, touched the hearts of her hearers, and moved many to tears. Her power seemed miraculous to the people, and they would not disperse until she promised to speak again in the evening. Some one remarked at the adjournment, "If Lucretia Mott had made that speech, it would be thought a great one." In the evening she spoke on the subject of slavery, for the first time, and with equal effect. A collection of several dollars was taken up for her, the first she ever received for giving an address.

Failing to find employment in Philadelphia, she accepted, as a last resort, a district school in Buck s County, with a salary of twenty-five dollars a month. She came home once in two weeks to take part in the Sunday meetings. On her eighteenth birthday she went to Kennett Square, — a small village thirty-two miles from Philadelphia, — to attend an anti-slavery meeting that remained in session two days. She spoke on slavery and non-resistance. In that doctrine of Friends she had no faith. A discussion arose as to the right and duty of slaves to forcible resistance. She and Robert Purvis, who was in the chair, spoke in the affirmative, and, in a protracted discussion, maintained their opinion, against the majority, "that resistance to tyranny is obedience to God." Anna wound up one of her glowing periods with the words of Lovejoy: "If I were a slave, and had the power, I would bridge over the chasm which yawns between the hell of slavery and the heaven of freedom, with carcasses of the slain." The effect of her speech was startling, and thrilled the whole audience. Robert Purvis unconsciously rose from his chair, and bent forward, electrified with a new hope of liberty for his race, looking as if their fate rested on her lips.

During her summer vacation she spoke several times to large audiences in New Jersey. On one occasion, in the open air in a beautiful grove, where hundreds had assembled to hear her, she spoke both morning and afternoon on temperance and anti-slavery, producing a profound sensation. At another time several Methodist clergymen had assembled to lay the corner-stone of a new church in a village where she was announced to speak. They went to hear her, from mere curiosity, in rather a sneering frame of mind; she, knowing that fact, was moved to speak with more than usual pathos and power. They made themselves quite merry in the beginning, but before she closed they were serious, subdued, and in tears. The next day one of them introduced himself to her, and said, "I have always ridiculed 'Woman's Rights,' but, so help me God, I never shall again." At all these meetings contributions were taken up for her benefit, and she began to think that this might prove to be her means of support. On the evening of the day that she closed her school, she advertised a meeting to be held in the school-house, but the crowd was so great that they adjourned to a church near by. She spoke on "Woman's Work;" and with the novelty of the subject and the whole proceeding, she quite startled that stolid community.

Shortly after this she attended another anti-slavery meeting at Kennett Square. This meeting, held just in the beginning of the war, was rather an exciting one, and prolonged discussions arose on the duties of abolitionists to existing laws and constitutions. In the report from "Forney's Press" we find the following notice: —

"The next speaker was a Miss Anna E. Dickinson, of Philadelphia, aged seventeen years, — handsome, of an expressive countenance, plainly dressed, and eloquent beyond her years. After the listless, monotonous harangues of the previous part of the day, the distinct, earnest tones of this juvenile Joan of Arc were very sweet and charming. During her discourse, which was frequently interrupted, Miss Dickinson maintained her presence of mind, and uttered her radical sentiments with augmented resolution and plainness. Those who did not sympathize with her remarks were softened by her simplicity and solemnity. Her speech was decidedly the feature of the evening, provocative as it was of numerous, unmanly interruptions, and followed by discussion of prolonged and diversified interest. Miss Dickinson, we understand, is a member of the Society of Friends, and had been solicited, several times during the day, to address the audience, but waited for the inspiration of the evening, which came in the shape of Mrs. Grew's remarks. They were told, said Miss Dickinson, to maintain constitutions because they were constitutions, and compromises because they were compromises.

But what were compromises, and what was laid down in those constitutions? Eminent lawgivers have said that certain great fundamental ideas of right were common to the world, and that all laws of man's making which trampled upon those ideas were null and void, — wrong to obey, but right to disobey. The Constitution of the United States sat upon the neck of those rights, recognizes human slavery, and makes the souls of men articles of purchase and of sale."

There is not space to give her admirable speech on the higher law, nor the discussion that followed, in which Miss Dickinson maintained her position with remarkable clearness and coolness for one of her years. The flattering reports of this meeting in several of the Philadelphia journals introduced her to the public.

On the evening of the 27th of February she addressed an audience of about eight hundred persons in Concert Hall, Philadelphia. She spoke full two hours extemporaneously, and the lecture was pronounced a success. Many notables and professional men were present; and, although it was considered a marvellous performance for a young girl, Miss Dickinson herself was mortified, as she said, with the length of her speech, and its lack of point, order, and arrangement. She felt that she was not equal to the occasion; instead of being flattered with the praises bestowed upon her, she was filled with regret that she had not made a more careful and thoughtful preparation. But she learned an important lesson from what she considered a failure, worth more than it cost her.

Spring was opening, and her fresh young spirit and strong will demanded some new avenues to labor, some active, profitable work. In her searches for something to do, says a friend, "I met her one day in the street; said she, 'I must work. I dislike the confinement and poor pay of school-teaching; but I shall go crazy unless I have work of some kind. Why can't I get into the Mint?' After considering the possibilities of securing a place there, for some time, our plans were made, and, after many persistent efforts, we succeeded." In April she entered the United States Mint, to labor from seven o'clock in the morning to six at night for twenty-eight dollars a month. She sat on a stool all those long hours, in a close, impure atmosphere, the windows and doors being always closed in the adjusting room, as the least draft of air would vary the scales. She soon became very skilful in her new business, and did twice the amount of work of most other girls. She was the fastest adjuster in the Mint; but she could not endure the confinement, and soon changed to the coining-room. But this dull routine of labor did not satisfy her higher nature. After the day's work was done, she would go to the hospitals to write letters for the sick soldiers, to read to them, and talk over the incidents of the war. Many things conspired to make her situation in the Mint undesirable. The character and conversation of the inmates were disagreeable to her; hence she kept them at a distance, while, her opinions on slavery and woman's rights being known, she was treated with reserve and suspicion in return. In November she made a speech in Westchester on the events of the war, which increased this state of feeling towards her, and culminated in her discharge from the Mint, in the Christmas holidays. This meeting was held just after the battle of Ball's Bluff. In summing up the record of this battle, after exonerating Stone and Baker, she said, "History will record that this battle was lost, not through ignorance and incompetence, but through the treason of the commanding general, George B. McClellan, and time will vindicate the truth of my assertion." She was hissed all over the house, though some cried, "Go on," "Go on." She repeated this startling assertion three times, and each time was hissed. Years after, when McClellan was running against Lincoln in 1864, when she had achieved a world-wide reputation, she was sent by the Republican committee of Pennsylvania, to this same town, to speak to the same people, in the same hall. In again summing up the incidents of the war, when she came to Ball's Bluff, she said, "I say now, as I said three years ago, history will record that this battle was lost, not through ignorance or incompetence, but through the treason of the commanding general, George B. McClellan." "And time has vindicated your assertion," was shouted all over the house. It was this speech, made in 1861, that cost her place in the Mint. Ex-Governor Pollock dismissed her, and owned that his reason was the Westchester speech, for at that time McClellan was the idol of the nation. She says that was the best service the Governor could have rendered her, as it forced her to the decision to labor no longer with her hands for bread, but to open some new path for herself.

She continued speaking, during the winter, in many of the neighboring towns, on the political aspects of the war. As the popular thought was centring everywhere on national questions, she began to think less of the special wrongs of women and negroes, and more of the causes of revolutions, and the true basis of government. These broader views secured her popularity, and made her available in party politics at once. In the mean time Mr. Garrison, having heard Anna Dickinson speak at Westchester and Longwood, and being both charmed and surprised with her oratorical power, invited her to visit Boston, and make his house her home. Before going to Boston some friends desired that she should make the same speech in Philadelphia that had occasioned her dismissal from the Mint. Accordingly, Concert Hall was engaged. Judge Pierce, an early friend of woman's rights, presided at the meeting, and introduced her to the audience. She had a full house, at ten cents admission, was received with great enthusiasm, and acquitted herself to her own satisfaction, as well as that of her friends. After all expenses were paid she found herself the happy possessor of a larger sum of money than she had ever had before; and now, in consultation with good Dr. Hannah Longshore, it was decided that she should have her first silk dress. With this friend's advice and blessing, she went to New England to endure fresh trials and disappointments before securing that unquestioned reputation and pecuniary independence she enjoys to-day. Through the influence and friendship of Mr. Garrison she was invited to speak in Theodoré Parker's pulpit on Sunday morning, as leading reformers were then doing. Accordingly she spoke, in Music Hall, on the "National Crisis." Her first lecture in Boston was the greatest trial she ever experienced. Her veneration for the character of a Boston audience almost overmatched her courage and confidence in her ability to sustain herself through such an ordeal. Her friends also had misgivings, and feared a failure, as they noticed that Anna could neither sleep nor eat for forty-eight hours previous to the lecture. Some were so confident that she would fail to meet the expectations of the immense audience, that they refused to sit on the platform. Mr. Garrison opened the meeting. He read a chapter of the Bible, and consumed some time in remarks in order to make the best of the dilemma, which, in common with many, he, too, apprehended, while Anna waited behind him to be "presented," in an agony of suspense she struggled to conceal. At last she was introduced, and began in some broken, hesitating sentences; but, gradually becoming absorbed in her subject, she forgot herself and her new surroundings, and so completely held the attention and interest of the audience for over an hour that the fears of her friends were turned to rejoicings, the anticipations of the few were more than realized, and her own long anxious hours of prayers and tears were forgotten in the proud triumph of that day. At the close she was overpowered with thanks, praises, and salutations of love and gratitude. As she delivered this lecture in several of the New England cities I give the following notice: —

"The New Star. — If to have an audience remain quiet, attentive, and sympathizing during the delivery of a long lecture, is any indication of the ability, tact, and success of the speaker, we think it may be claimed for Miss Dickinson that she is a compeer worthy to be admitted as a particular star in the large and brilliant constellation of genius and talent now endeavoring to direct the country to the goal of negro emancipation.

"Music Hall was filled to overflowing; hundreds of the audience went early, and must have sat there more than an hour before the lecture began; and, yet, we do not remember to have seen less signs of weariness and inattention at any lecture we ever attended in this city. Her voice is clear and penetrating, without being harsh; her enunciation is very distinct, and at times somewhat rhythmic in its character, with enough of a peculiar accent to indicate that her home has not been in Massachusetts. Her whole appearance and manner are decidedly attractive, earnest, and expressive. Her lecture was well-arranged, logical, and occasionally eloquent, persuasive, and pathetic.

"She traced the demands and usurpations of the Slave Power from the commencement of our government till the present time, and proved that, because it could not hope to control the country in the future as it had in the past, it raised the standard of rebellion, — an act long since determined upon when such an exigency should arise. Slavery being thus proved to be the cause of the war, the justice, necessity, and propriety of its abolition, as a means of present defence and future security and peace, was forcibly illustrated.

"That the slave was prepared for freedom was proved by the thousands who have passed through so much danger and suffering to obtain it. The inhuman character of the fugitive slave enactment was most beautifully referred to, bringing tears to many eyes which are not accustomed to weep over the wrongs of the colored race.

"She spoke in eloquent terms of Fremont, which met with a hearty response from the audience, as did other parts of her address. On the whole, we think her friends here must be greatly delighted with her first effort, on her first visit to our old Commonwealth.

"Previous to the delivery of the lecture, the 'Negro Boatman's Song,' by Whittier, was sung by a quartette, accompanied by the organ, and the exercises were closed by singing 'America,' in which the audience joined." — *Fall River Press.*

She spent the following summer in reading and study, collecting materials for other lectures. She continued, as she had time, to visit the government hospitals, and made herself a most welcome guest among our soldiers. In her long conversations with them, she learned their individual histories, experiences, hardships, and sufferings; the motives that prompted them to go into the army; what they saw there, and what they thought of war in their hours of solitude, away from the excitement of the camp and the battle-field. Thus she got an insight into the soldier's life and feelings, and from these narratives drew her materials for that deeply interesting lecture on Hospital Life, which she delivered in many parts of the country.

In October, 1862, she spoke before the Boston Fraternity Lyceum, for which she received many flattering notices and one hundred dollars. She had hoped, through the influence of friends, to make a series of appointments for the winter, and thus secure a means of support. But the military reverses and discouragements left but little spirit among the people for lectures of any kind, and she travelled from place to place until her funds were exhausted. Her lecture at Concord, New Hampshire, was her last engagement for the season, and the ten dollars promised there was all she had in prospect for future need until something else might offer.

This was a trying experience, for she had just begun to hope that her days of darkness had passed and triumph was near. In speaking of it she says, "No one knows how I felt and suffered that winter, penniless and alone, with a scanty wardrobe, suffering with cold, weariness, and disappointment. I wandered about on the trains day after day, among strangers, seeking employment for an honest living, and failed to find it. I would have gone home, but had not the means. I had borrowed money to commence my journey, promising to remit soon; failing to do so, I could not ask again. Beyond my Concord meeting all was darkness; I had no further plans." But her lecture there on Hospital Life was the turning-point in her fortunes. In this speech she proved slavery to be the cause of the war, and that its continuance would result in prolonged suffering to our soldiers, defeat to our armies, and the downfall of the republic. She related many touching incidents of her experiences in hospital life, and drew such vivid pictures of the horrors of both war and slavery, that, by her pathos and logic, she melted her audience to tears, and forced the most prejudiced minds to accept her conclusions.

It was on this occasion that the secretary of the State Central Committee heard her for the first time. He remarked to a friend, at the close of the lecture, "If we can get this girl to make that speech all through New Hampshire, we can carry the Republican ticket in this State in the coming election." Fully appreciating her magnetic power over an audience, he resolved at once, that, if the State Committee refused to invite her, he should do so on his own responsibility.

But, through his influence, she was invited by the Republican committee, and on the first of March commenced her regular campaign speeches. In the four weeks before election, she spoke twenty times, — everywhere to crowded, enthusiastic audiences. Her march through the State was a succession of triumphs, and ended in a Republican victory. The member in the first district, having no faith that a woman could influence politics, sent word to the secretary, "Don't send that d—— woman down here to defeat my election." The secretary replied, "We have work enough for her to do in other districts, without interfering with you." But when the would-be honorable gentleman saw the furor she created, he changed his mind, and inundated the secretary with letters to have her sent there. But the secretary replied, "It is too late; the programme is arranged, and published throughout the State. You would not have her when you could, and now you cannot have her when you will." It is pleasant to record that this man, who had the moral hardihood to use a profane adjective in speaking of a woman, lost his election; and thus our congressional halls were saved from so demoralizing an influence. His district was lost by a large majority, while the other districts went strongly Republican. When the news came that the Republicans had carried the State, due credit was awarded to Anna Dickinson for her faithful labors in securing the victory. The governor-elect made personal acknowledgments that her eloquent speeches had secured his election. She was serenaded, feasted, and eulogized by the press and the people.

New Hampshire safe, all eyes were now turned to Connecticut. The contest there was between Seymour and Buckingham. It was generally conceded that, if Seymour was elected, Connecticut would give no more money or troops for the war. The Republicans were completely disheartened. They said nothing could prevent the Democrats from carrying the State by four thousand, while the Democrats boasted that they would carry it by ten thousand. Though the issue was one of such vital importance, there seemed so little hope of success, that the Republicans were disposed to give it up without making an effort. And no resistance to this impending calamity was made until Anna Dickinson went into the State, and galvanized the desponding loyalists to life. She spent two weeks there, addressing large and enthusiastic audiences all over the State, and completely turned the tide of popular sentiment. Even the Democrats, in spite of the scurrilous attacks on her by some of their leaders and editors, received her everywhere with the warmest welcome, tore off their party badges, and substituted her likeness, and applauded whatever she said. The halls where she spoke were so densely packed, that Republicans stayed away to make room for the Democrats, and the women were *shut out* to give place to those who could vote. There never was such a furor about an orator in this country. The period of her advent, the excited condition of the people, her youth, beauty, and remarkable voice, all heightened the effect of her genius, and helped to produce this result. Her name was on every lip. Ministers preached about her, prayed for her as a second Joan of Arc, raised up by God to save that State to the loyal party, and through it the nation to freedom and humanity. As the election day approached, the excitement was intense; and when at last it was announced that the State was saved by a few hundred votes, the joy and gratitude of the crowds knew no bounds. They shouted and hurrahed for Anna Dickinson, serenaded her with full bands of music, sent her presents of flowers, ornaments, and books, manifesting in every way their love and loyalty to this gifted girl, who, through so many years, had bravely struggled with poverty to this proud moment of success in her country's cause.

Some leading men in Connecticut presented her a gold watch and chain as a memento for her valuable services in the State, paid her a hundred dollars for every night she had spoken there, and for the last night before election, in Hartford, four hundred dollars. From the following comments of the press, the reader may form some idea of the enthusiasm of the people: —

"MISS DICKINSON AT ALLYN HALL.

"The highest compliment that the Union men of this city could pay Miss Anna E. Dickinson was to invite her to make the closing and most important speech in this campaign. They were willing to rest their case upon her efforts. She may go far and speak much; she will have no more flattering proof of the popular confidence in her eloquence, tact, power, than this. Her business being to obtain votes for the right side, she addressed herself to that end with singular adaptation. But when we add to this lawyer-like comprehension of the necessities of the case, her earnestness, enthusiasm, and personal magnetism, we account for the effect she produced on the vast audience Saturday night.

Allyn Hall was packed as it never was before. Every seat was crowded. The aisles were full of men who stood patiently for more than three hours, the window-sills had their occupants, every foot of standing-room was taken, and in the rear of the galleries men seemed to hang in swarms like bees. Such was the view from the stage. The stage itself and the boxes were filled with ladies, giving the speaker an audience of at least two hundred who could not see her face.

To such an audience Miss Dickinson spoke for two hours and twenty minutes, and hardly a listener left the hall during that time. Her power over the audience was marvellous. She seemed to have that absolute mastery of it which Joan of Arc is reported to have had of the French troops. They followed her with that deep attention which is unwilling to lose a word, but greeted her, every few moments, with the most wild applause, which continued often for several minutes, breaking forth afresh with irrepressible enthusiasm. We find no occasion to abate a word from the very high estimate given of her as an orator from her first speech in this city. And she added vastly, on Saturday night, to the estimate of her by her versatility and ability as an advocate. The speech, in itself, and its effect was magnificent, — this strong adjective is the proper one. If the campaign were not closed, we should give a full sketch of the speech, for its pertinent effect. But the work of the campaign is done. And it only remains, in the name, we are sure, of all loyal men in this district, to express to Miss Dickinson most heartfelt thanks for her splendid, inspiring aid. She has aroused everywhere respect, enthusiasm, and devotion, let us not say to herself alone, but to the country. While such women are possible in the United States, there isn't a spot big enough for her to stand on, that won't be fought for so long as there is a man left."

Fresh from the victories in New Hampshire and Connecticut, she was announced to speak in Cooper Institute, New York. That meeting in May, 1862, was the most splendid ovation to a woman's genius since Fanny Kemble, in all the wealth of her youth and beauty, appeared on the American stage for the first time. On no two occasions of my life have I been so deeply moved, so exalted, so lost in overflowing gratitude, that woman had revealed her power in oratory, — that highest art to touch the deepest feelings of the human soul, — and verified at last her right to fame and immortality. There never was such excitement over any meeting in New York. Although the hall was densely crowded long before the hour announced, yet the people outside were determined to get in at all hazards, — ushers were beaten down, those without tickets rushed in, and those with tickets were pushed aside, and thousands went home unable to get standing-places even in the lobbies and outer halls.

The platform was graced with the most distinguished men and women in the country, and so crowded that the young orator had scarce room to stand. There were clergymen, generals, admirals, judges, lawyers, editors, the literati and leaders of fashion, and all alike ready to do homage to this simple girl, who moved them alternately to laughter and tears, to bursts of applause and the most profound silence. Mr. Beecher, who was president of the meeting, introduced the speaker in his happiest manner. For more than an hour she held that large audience with deep interest and enthusiasm, and, when she finished with a beautiful peroration, the people seemed to take a long breath, as if to find relief from the intensity of their emotions.

Loud cries followed for Mr. Beecher; but he arose, and, with great feeling and solemnity, said, "Let no man open his lips here to-night; music is the only fitting accompaniment to the eloquent utterances we have heard." So the Hutchinsons closed the meeting with one of their soul-stirring ballads, and the audience dispersed.

As none of the materials furnished for this sketch have interested me more than the comments of the press, I give the following. Knowing that Anna Dickinson will be as great a wonder to another generation as Joan of Arc is to this, the testimony of our leading journals to her eloquence and power furnishes an important page in future history: —

"MISS DICKINSON AT THE COOPER INSTITUTE.

"The crowd at the Cooper Institute last evening must be truly called immense, no other word being adequate to the emergency. The attraction was an address by Miss Anna E. Dickinson, of Philadelphia, upon the subject of 'The Day — the Cause.'

"She is of the medium height, slight in form, graceful in movement; her head, well-poised, is adorned with full and heavy dark hair, displaying to advantage a pleasant face, which has the signs of nervous force and of vigorous mental life. In manner she is unembarrassed, without a shade of boldness; her gesticulation is simple, drawing to itself no remark; her voice is of wonderful power, penetrating rather than loud, as clear as the tone of metal, and yet with a reed-like softness. Her vocabulary is simple, and in no instance can there be seen a straining after effective expressions; yet her skill in using the ordinary stores of our daily language is so great, that with a single phrase she presents a picture, and delivers a poem in a sentence.

"Miss Dickinson shows in her oratorical method the feminine peculiarities which lead her sex to prefer results to preliminaries, the sharply defined success of conclusions to the regularly progressing course of previous argument. Her lecture was consequently very effective to the ear, and difficult to report with justice to the speaker. She defined the contest with the South as the struggle between liberty and slavery in the broadest sense of the words, extending to the moral, mental, and social world, and illustrated her position with rapid allusions to the political history of the last ten years. She then drew a variety of comparisons between the loyalty of the two parties at the North, and, in answer to the question what sort of generals each had given to the country, made some hits of great force at many well-known officers, and paid a tribute of praise to others.

"It was in this part of her address that the brightness of her wit and the power of condensed expression already alluded to was seen most clearly. A single stroke of the pencil placed not only a name but a character distinctly before the audience, who took quickly, and fully enjoyed every point. The enrolment act, the threats of the Northwest to compromise for themselves and leave New England out in the cold, and the present splendid revival of patriotic confidence in the North, were treated with surprising power. The applause which burst from the audience at almost every sentence was more hearty and enthusiastic than even in the excited political gatherings of an election season, and was, moreover, applause born of the deepest and best feelings of loyalty. At the conclusion of the lecture, which came to a close with a truly beautiful peroration, the Hutchinson family sang one of their best pieces, and then, by request, followed it with the John Brown song, in the chorus of which the audience joined with a thrilling effect." — *New York Evening Post.*

Her profits from this meeting were nearly a thousand dollars. After her remarkable success in New York, the Philadelphia "Union League," one of the greatest political organizations in the country, invited her to speak in that city. The invitation was signed by leading Republicans. She accepted it; had a most enthusiastic and appreciative audience, Judge Kelley presiding, and, after all expenses were paid, she had seven hundred dollars. In this address, reviewing the incidents of the war, she criticised General McClellan, as usual, with great severity. Many of his personal friends were present, and some, filled with indignation, left the house, while a derisive laugh followed them to the door. The Philadelphia journals vied with each other in their eulogiums of her grace, beauty, and eloquence. The marked attention she has always received in her native city is alike most grateful to her and honorable to her fellow-citizens.

July came, and the first move was made to enlist colored troops in Pennsylvania. A meeting was called in Philadelphia. Judge Kelley, Frederick Douglass, and Anna Dickinson were there, and made most eloquent appeals to the people of that State to grant to the colored man the honor of bearing arms in defence of his country. The effort was successful. A splendid regiment was raised, and their first duty was to serenade the young orator who had spoken so eloquently for their race all through the war. The summer passed in rest and study.

In September, a field-day was announced at Camp William Penn. General Pleasanton reviewed the troops. It was a very brilliant and interesting occasion, as many were about to leave for the seat of war. As the day closed and the people began to disperse, it was noised round that Miss Dickinson was there; a cry was heard at once on all sides,— "A speech! A speech!" The moon was just rising, mingling its pale rays with those of the setting sun, throwing a soft, mysterious light over the whole scene. The troops gathered round with bristling bayonets and flags flying, the band was hushed to silence, and, when all was still, mounted on a gun wagon, with General Pleasanton and his staff on one side, and General Wagner and his staff on the other, this beautiful girl addressed "our boys in blue." She urged that justice and equality might be secured to every citizen in the republic; that slavery and war might end forever, and peace be restored; that our country might indeed be the land of the free, and the home of the brave.

As she stood there uttering words of warning and prophecy, it seemed as if her lips had been touched with a live coal from the altar of heaven. Her inspired words moved the hearts of our young soldiers to deeds of daring, and gave fresh courage to those about to bid their loved ones go, and die, if need be, for freedom and their country. The hour, the mysterious light, the stillness, the novel surroundings, the youth of the speaker, all gave a peculiar power to her words, and made the scene one of the most thrilling and beautiful on the page of history.

In the autumn of 1862, she was engaged to go to Ohio, to speak for a few weeks before election, and a large sum of money was pledged for her services. But some Pennsylvania politicians, appreciating her power, and desiring her help at home, decided to outbid Ohio and keep her in her own State. Accordingly she accepted their proposals, and threw her whole energy and enthusiasm into that campaign. She endured all manner of discomforts and dangers in travelling through the benighted mining districts of the State. She met with scorn, ridicule, threats of violence, and more than once was pelted with rotten eggs and stones, in the midst of a speech. But she went through it all with the calmness and coolness of an experienced warrior. One of the committee admitted afterward that Miss Dickinson was sent through that district because no man dared to go. She returned home after weeks of hard labor and intense excitement, weary and exhausted, and though all agreed that the Republican victory in that State was largely due to her influence, the committee forgot their promises, and, to this hour, have never paid her one cent for her valuable services. Their excuse was, that the fund had been used up in paying other speakers. As if a dozen honorable men could not have raised something in an hour of victory to reward this brave and faithful girl. During the winters of 1863 and 1864, she received invitations, from the State Legislatures of Ohio and Pennsylvania, to speak in their capitals at Columbus and Harrisburg. In January, 1864, she made her first address in Washington. Though she now believed that her success as an orator was established, yet she hesitated long before accepting this invitation. To speak before the President, Chief Justice, Senators, Congressmen, Foreign Diplomats, all the dignitaries and honorables of the government, was one of the most trying ordeals in her experience. She had one of the largest and most brilliant audiences ever assembled in the capitol, and was fully equal to the occasion. She made a profound impression, and was the topic of conversation for days afterwards. At the close of the meeting, she was presented to the President and other dignitaries, and, the next day, had a pleasant interview with the President at the White House.

As this was one of the greatest occasions of her life, and as she was honored as no man in the nation ever had been, it may be satisfactory to all American women to know by whom she was invited and how she acquitted herself. Accordingly, I give the invitation and some comments of the press.

CORRESPONDENCE.

" *To Miss Anna E. Dickinson, Philadelphia, Pa.:*

" MISS DICKINSON, — Heartily appreciating the value of your services in the campaigns in New Hampshire, Connecticut, Pennsylvania, and New York, and the qualities that have combined to give you the deservedly high reputation you enjoy; and desiring as well to testify that appreciation as to secure ourselves the pleasure of hearing you, we unite in cordially inviting you to deliver an address this winter at the capital, at some time suited to your own convenience.

WASHINGTON, D. C., December 16, 1863.

H. HAMLIN,	SCHUYLER COLFAX,
J. H. LANE,	A. C. WILDER,
JAMES DIXON,	THADDEUS STEVENS,
CHARLES SUMNER,	HENRY C. DEMING,
H. B. ANTHONY,	WILLIAM D. KELLEY,
HENRY WILSON,	ROBERT C. SCHENCK,
JOHN SHERMAN,	J. A. GARFIELD,
IRA HARRIS,	R. B. VAN VALKENBURG,
BEN. F. WADE,	and seventy other Representatives.
and sixteen other Senators.	

" *Hon. Hannibal Hamlin, Vice-President of the United States; Hon. Schuyler Colfax, Speaker of the House of Representatives; Hons. J. H. Lane, James Dixon, Charles Sumner, H. B. Anthony, Henry Wilson, John Sherman, A. C. Wilder, Thaddeus Stevens, Henry C. Deming, William D. Kelley. Robert C. Schenck, J. A. Garfield, and others:*

" GENTLEMEN, — I thank you sincerely for the great and most unexpected honor which you have conferred upon me by your kind invitation to speak in Washington.

" Accepting it, I would suggest the 16th of January, as the time; desiring the proceeds to be devoted to the help of the suffering freedmen.

" Truly yours, ANNA E. DICKINSON.

" 1710 Locust St., Philadelphia, Jan. 7, 1864."

"The House of Representatives, by a remarkably large vote, have tendered Miss Dickinson the use of their hall for the occasion.

"Admission to the floor of the House, $1 00; to the galleries, 50 cents. Tickets for sale at the principal hotels and bookstores."

"MISS ANNA DICKINSON'S LECTURE IN WASHINGTON.

"[From the Regular Correspondent of the Evening Post.]

"WASHINGTON, Jan. 17, 1864.

"Miss Dickinson's lecture in the Hall of the House of Representatives, last night, was a gratifying success and a splendid personal triumph. She can hardly fail to regard it as the most flattering ovation — for such it was — of her life. Long before the hour designated in the newspapers for the commencement of the lecture the hall was filled, the capacious galleries as well as the floor. Seats for five hundred persons had been arranged upon the floor, and the tickets — one dollar each — were sold by noon of Saturday.

"A large number of Congressmen were present with their wives and daughters, and many of the leading men of the departments. Here and there an opposition member was visible, but so few in number as to make those who were present unpleasantly conspicuous. At precisely half-past seven Miss Dickinson came in, escorted by Vice-President Hamlin and Speaker Colfax. A platform had been built directly over the desk of the official reporters, and in front of the clerk's desk, from which the lecturer spoke. Mr. Hamlin sat upon her right and Mr. Colfax upon her left. She was greeted with loud cheers as she came in, and Mr. Hamlin introduced her to the select audience in a neat speech, in which he very happily compared her to the Maid of Orleans.

"This scene was one which would evidently test severely the powers of a most accomplished orator, for the audience was not composed of the enthusiastic masses of the people, but rather of loungers, office-holders, orators, critics, and men of the world. But the fair speaker did not seem to be embarrassed in the least, — not even by the movements of a crazy man in the galleries, who carried a flag, which he waved over her head when she uttered any sentiment particularly stirring or eloquent.

"At eight o'clock Mr. and Mrs. Lincoln came in, and not even the utterance of a fervid passage in the lecture could repress the enthusiasm of the audience. It was a somewhat amusing fact that just as the president entered the hall, she was criticising, with some sharpness, his Amnesty Proclamation and the Supreme Court; and the audience, as if feeling it to be their duty to applaud a just sentiment, even at the expense of courtesy, sustained the criticism with a round of deafening cheers. The crazy man in the gallery, as if electrified by the courage of the young woman, waved his flag to and fro with frantic delight. Mr. Lincoln sat meekly through it, not in the least displeased. Perhaps he knew that sweets were to come, but whether he did or not, they did come, for Miss Dickinson soon alluded to him and his course as president, and nominated him as his own successor in 1865. The popularity of the president in Washington was duly attested by volleys of cheers.

"The lecture itself was an eloquent one, and it was delivered very finely. Miss Dickinson has evidently made a most favorable impression upon Congress and the people of Washington. After the lecture was finished the audience called lustily for Mr. Lincoln to speak, but he edged his way out of the crowd to a side door, telling the vice-president on his way out that he was too much embarrassed to speak; which statement, made known to the people present by Mr. Hamlin, caused much laughter. The 'freedmen' will obtain over one thousand dollars as the solid result of the lecture; those present as hearers were delighted; and Miss Dickinson has the consolation of feeling not only that she has aided a good cause, but that she has achieved a fine personal triumph. B."

"MISS DICKINSON'S LECTURE IN WASHINGTON

"At a meeting of the Executive Committee of the National Freedmen's Relief Society of the District of Columbia held on the 26th of January, 1864, the following letter was read: —

"WASHINGTON, January 23, 1864.

"*Rev. W. H. Channing:*

"SIR, — We have the honor to enclose herewith a draft for ten hundred and thirty dollars, being the proceeds of the lecture delivered by Miss Anna E. Dickinson, in the House of Representatives, on Saturday evening, the 16th inst.

"It is the special request of Miss Dickinson that this fund be appropriated for the benefit of the National Freedmen's Relief Society of the District of Columbia, of which you are the vice-president.

"It was in response to an invitation of members of Congress that Miss Dickinson delivered her lecture at the capitol. Her benevolence and patriotism evinced in this gift entitle her to the gratitude not only of those who are the recipients of her munificence, but of every lover of his country.

"Very respectfully, your obedient servants,

"H. HAMLIN,
"SCHUYLER COLFAX."

Immediately upon her return from Washington, she was invited by a large number of the leading citizens of Philadelphia to repeat her Washington address in the Academy of Music, to which she replied: —

"*Messrs. Arch. Getty, Alex. G. Cattell, Thos. Allman, Edmund A. Souder, and others:*

"GENTLEMEN, — I thank you heartily for the honor conferred on me by your most kind invitation, and for the added pleasure of receiving it from my own city of Philadelphia. I would name Wednesday, the 27th inst., as the time.

"Truly yours, ANNA E. DICKINSON.

"WASHINGTON, D. C., January 20, 1864."

The profound impression she made at Washington greatly heightened her rapidly increasing reputation, and she was urged to deliver that address both in New York and Boston.

In Boston, George Thompson, the eloquent English orator and member of Parliament, paid this beautiful tribute to her genius: —

"MY FRIENDS, — If one unaccustomed to public speaking is ever placed in an embarrassing position, it is when he is called upon, as I am now, to address an audience that has been so charmed and highly excited by such eloquence as that which it has been your privilege and my privilege to listen to to-night. Shakespeare says, 'As when some actor who has crossed the stage retires, the eye looks listlessly to see who follows next;' and so I come before you to-night. I have nothing to address to you to-night, nothing. I have been spellbound. America, be proud of your daughter! Were she my countrywoman, I should be proud of my country for her sake. Appreciate her, reward her by following her counsels. I must confess, long accustomed as I have been to public meetings, and hearing the best eloquence on either side of the Atlantic, and to hearing those who are esteemed our most gifted men in Parliament, I have listened to no speech which, for its pathos, its argument, its satire, its eloquence, its humor, its sarcasm, and its well-directed denunciations, has ever been surpassed by any I have heard before. I pray God that the life of this lady may be spared, that she may see the desire of her heart in the unanimous adoption by her fellow-citizens of the great principles she has enunciated to-night. Give me America free from slavery. Give me America in which shall be established universally, as your lecturer has said to-night, without distinction of clime, color, class, or condition, liberty for all, government by all and for all."

Her reputation was now thoroughly established, and during that winter she addressed lyceums nearly every night at a hundred dollars. "Chicago; or, the Last Ditch," was the title of the lecture she delivered in all our Northern cities. In the spring she made a few campaign speeches in Connecticut. She used what influence she had to prevent the renomination of Mr. Lincoln; for she distrusted his plan of reconstruction, after an interview with him, in which he read to her his correspondence with General Banks, then military commander at New Orleans. She was convinced in that interview that in his policy he was looking to a re-election instead of maturing sound measures for reconstruction. During that presidential campaign, though she continually laid bare the record of the Democratic party, the treason of its leaders and generals, and its want of loyalty during the war, yet she had no word of praise for Mr. Lincoln. She never took his name upon her lips, except to state facts of history, after the Baltimore Convention, until his death. She was invited to go to California during that campaign, and offered thousands of dollars, if she would go there and speak for Mr. Lincoln; which she declined. At the opening of the lyceum course that fall, in consequence of her position with reference to the Republican nominee, she had not a dozen invitations for the winter; but, as the season advanced, they began to come in as usual, showing that the committees had withheld them during the months preceding the election, hoping, no doubt, to awe her to silence on Mr. Lincoln. In 1865, she spoke in Philadelphia on the Lincoln monument, and cleared a thousand dollars, which she gave to Alexander Henry, the mayor, to be appropriated for that purpose. On this occasion, she paid a beautiful tribute to the many virtues of our martyred president, delicately making no mention of his faults.

One of the most powerful and impressive appeals that she ever made was in the Convention of Southern Loyalists, held in Philadelphia in September, 1866. In this convention there was a division of opinion between the Border and the Gulf States. The latter wanted to incorporate "negro suffrage" in their platform, as that was the only means of success for the liberal party at the South. The former, manipulated by Northern politicians, opposed that measure, lest it should defeat the Republican party in the pending elections at the North. This stultification of principle, of radical public sentiment, stirred the soul of Anna, and she desired to speak in the convention. But a rule that none but delegates should be allowed that privilege prevented her. However, as the Southern men had never heard a woman in public, and felt great curiosity to hear her, they adjourned the convention, resolved themselves into a committee of the whole, and invited her to address them. The following sketch from an eye-witness will give some idea of the effect she produced on Southern men: —

"A GOOD-NATURED VIEW

Of some matters in and about the Convention is given in the following spicy letter of James Redpath to the Boston 'Traveller:' —

"PHILADELPHIA, Sept. 7.

"THE ADDRESS OF ANNA E. DICKINSON.

"My last despatch from the Convention predicted that the border statesmen would receive a lecture from Anna Dickinson, and stated that they acted as if they anticipated it. This prediction was formed from the appearance of the Maryland delegation, and a knowledge of the character of the orator; and it was fulfilled.

"It was curious to note the audience. There sat, directly in front of the platform, three or four hundred Southern men, few of whom had ever heard a woman speak, — few of whom could debate, when antagonistic views were advanced, without the grossest personal vituperation.

"Their ideal of controversial oratory was with them, and sitting at the right hand of the young maiden as she stepped forward to deliver a speech as denunciatory as ever he uttered, but as free from offensive personal allusions as any oration can be. It was Brownlow, the bitterest and foulest-tongued man in the South. On her left sat John Minor Botts, with his lips tightly compressed, and his face telling plainly that he remained there from courtesy, but would remain a patient listener to the speech.

"She began; and, for the first time since it met, the Convention was so still that the faintest whisper could be heard. She had not spoken long before she declared that Maryland had no business in the Convention, but ought to have been with the delegates who came to welcome. There was vehement applause from the border States.

"'That is a direct insult!' shouted a delegate from Maryland.

"She went on without regarding these coarse interruptions, reviewing the conduct of the border States with scorn, and talking, with an eloquence I never heard equalled in any previous effort, in favor of an open, hearty, manly declaration of the real opinion of the Convention for justice to the colored loyalist, not in the courts only, but at the ballot-box.

"There was none of the flippancy or pertness which sometimes disfigures her public speeches. It was her noblest style throughout, — bold but tender, and often so pathetic that she brought tears to every eye. Every word came through her heart, and it went right to the hearts of all. Kentucky and Maryland now listened as eagerly as Georgia and Alabama.

"Brownlow's iron features and Botts' rigid face soon relaxed, and tears stood in the old Virginian's eyes more than once, while the noble Tennesseean moved his place, and gazed at the inspired girl with an interest and wonderment which no other orator had brought to the fanatic's hard face.

"She had the audience in hand as easily as a mother holds her child; and, like the child, this audience heard her heart beat. It was ennobled thereby. It was really a marvellous speech. The fullest report of it would not do it justice, because the greatness lay in its manner and its effect, as well as in its argument.

"When she finished, one after another Southern delegate came forward, and pinned on her dress the badges of their States, until she wore the gifts of Alabama, Missouri, Tennessee, Texas, Florida, Louisiana, and Maryland."

There have been many speculations in public and private as to the authorship of Anna Dickinson's speeches. They have been attributed to Wendell Phillips, Charles Sumner, George W. Curtis, and Judge Kelley. Those who know Anna's conversational power, who have felt the magnetism of her words and manners, and the pulsations of her generous heart, who have heard her impromptu replies when assailed, see at once that her speeches are the natural outgrowth of herself, her own experience and philosophy, inspired by the eventful times in which she lived.

As well ask if Joan of Arc drew her inspiration from the warriors of her day. It was no man's wish or will that Anna Dickinson uttered the highest thought in American politics in this crisis of our nation's history; that she pointed out the cause and remedy of the war, and unveiled treason in the army and the White House. While, in the camp and hospital, she spoke words of tenderness and love to the sick and dying, she did not hesitate to rebuke the incapacity and iniquity of those in high places. She was among the first to distrust McClellan and Lincoln, and in a lecture entitled "My Policy" to unveil his successor, Andrew Johnson, to the people. She saw the sceptre of power grasped by the party of freedom, and the first gun fired at Sumter, in defence of slavery. She saw the dawn of the glorious day of emancipation, when four million American slaves were set free, and that night of gloom, when the darkest page in American history was written in the blood of its chief. She saw our armies go forth to battle, the youth, the promise, the hope of the nation,—two million strong,—and saw them return, with their ranks thinned and broken, their flags tattered and stained, the maimed, halt, and blind, the weary and worn; and this, she said, is the price of liberty. Through the nation's agony was this girl born into a knowledge of her power; and she drew her inspiration from the great events of her day. Her heroic courage, indomitable will, brilliant imagination, religious earnestness, and prophetic forecast, gave her an utterance that no man's thought could paint or inspire.

WOMAN AS PHYSICIAN.

BY REV. H. B. ELLIOT.

THE care of the sick has from earliest ages devolved on woman. A group by one of our sculptors, representing Eve with the body of Abel stretched upon her lap, bending over it in bewildered grief, and striving to cherish or restore the vital spirit which she can hardly believe to have departed, is a type of the province of the sex ever since pain and death entered the world. To be first the vehicle for human life, and then its devoted guardian, to remove or alleviate the physical evils which afflict the race, or to patiently watch their wasting course, and tenderly care for all that remains when they have wrought their result, — this is her divinely appointed and universally conceded mission. Were she to refuse it, to forsake her station beside the suffering, the office of medicine and the efforts of the physician would be more than half baffled. And yet, where her post is avowedly so important, she has generally been denied the liberty of understanding much that is involved in its intelligent occupancy. With the human body so largely in her charge from birth to death, she has not been allowed to inquire into its marvellous mechanism. With the administering of remedies entrusted to her vigilance and faithfulness, she has not been allowed to investigate the qualities, or to know even the names of the substances committed to her use, or to ascertain the methods of their operation. With the mind to guide at the stages where its tutelage is of incomparable importance, she has not been allowed to learn the delicate lines of its dependence upon the body, or the subtle but invincible influences which they mutually exert. To be a student of these things, with scientific thoroughness, and then to practise independently with what she has thus acquired, has been regarded as unseemly, or as beyond her capacity, or as an invasion of prerogatives claimed exclusively for men. Indeed, the whole domain of medicine has been "pre-empted" by men, and in their "squatter sovereignty" (for no law divine or human has yet deeded it to them) they have sturdily warned off the gentler sex. But they will not be kept off. By quiet approaches they have long been gaining foothold upon the outskirts of the territory. Of late years they have ventured into its very centre, claiming equal rights, or erecting their own edifices and laying foundations for enduring institutions. Under manifold disadvantages and with imperfect appliances, it has yet come to be a fixed fact that, in this realm, as in those of literature and art, there shall be no factitious distinctions from such cause.

To our own country belongs the credit of being foremost in this change, first to admit, and most liberal in fostering it. In England a "female medical society" has existed several years, and offers facilities for instruction by means of lectures upon some branches, sufficient to qualify for a diploma from "Apothecaries' Hall." In connection with it there is now a "Ladies' Medical College," which recently announced fifty students. But the aim of the whole movement is at present only to furnish well trained midwives. In Paris the "Maternity" Hospital affords opportunity for observation in the department which its name indicates, with whatever forms of disease may be collateral or incidental, and receives women nominally as students, but they are not allowed to prescribe in the wards, nor instructed in regard to the remedies used. Indeed, they can hardly rise above the position of proficient nurses. In both countries, the way to the entrance of women upon general practice among their own sex has scarcely yet begun to open.

In the United States, there are three regularly organized institutions for their education, with all the ordinary appliances of Medical Colleges,—at New York, Boston, and Philadelphia. There are hospitals and dispensaries connected with them, and their students and graduates have now, also, the usual privileges in many of the long-established hospitals. Boston, with characteristic forwardness in accepting whatever tends to the promotion of science or philanthropy, was in advance of the other cities in this movement, though outstripped by them in results. As early as 1845 and 1846 Dr. Samuel Gregory, in connection with his brother, Mr. George Gregory, published pamphlets advocating the education and employment of female physicians. In 1847 he delivered a series of public lectures upon the subject, and proposed the opening of a school for the purpose. In 1848 a class of twelve ladies was formed, under the instruction of Dr. Enoch C. Rolfe and Dr. William M. Cornell. An association styled the "American Female Medical Education Society" was organized the same year, and afterward merged in the New England Female Medical College, chartered in 1856, which has been liberally sustained by legislative grants, as well as individual donations. It owns a valuable property, and has many facilities for its work. It has graduated seventy-two women, many of whom are occupying positions of great influence among their sex, both as practitioners of medicine, and as teachers of physiology and hygiene in schools, and has also furnished valuable information upon the laws of health to a large number who have attended partial courses of lectures by its professors. At

Philadelphia the college has quietly pursued its work, through the past eighteen years, with steadily increasing success, notwithstanding the unfriendly attitude of the ordinary professional organizations, and has sent forth a goodly number of skilful physicians. Its corporators assert that "its curriculum of study and requirements for graduation are in all respects as high as those of the best medical schools in this country" and present a catalogue of thirty-eight regular students for the year 1867. At the college in New York, chartered in 1863, one hundred intelligent ladies have already received instruction from a competent corps of professors. Many of these have not designed to practise as physicians; but have availed themselves of this method for obtaining knowledge invaluable to them in their own homes. Twenty-nine have completed the course, and received the legal diploma; and there are now thirty students in regular attendance. The New York Infirmary also, now in its fourteenth year, originated and still chiefly managed by Drs. Elizabeth and Emily Blackwell, has well earned an honorable position and done noble service. It has furnished advice and medicine gratuitously to more than seven thousand women and children during the past year. These ladies have in view the organization of a college, for which a considerable fund has already been collected and a preparatory class formed. In various other directions preliminary steps have been taken toward the same end; and there are estimated to be as many as three hundred women, in full practice, scattered through the land. These institutions are yet in their infancy, and the opposition to their object has been such, on the part of male members of the profession, that they have found difficulty in securing instructors of the highest grade and facilities for thorough clinical or anatomical study. This, however, they are gradually overcoming, and, we doubt not, will soon occupy a position, fully equal at least to that of

C. S. LOZIER, M.D.

the average of similar schools. We have deemed it appropriate to make these introductory statements, in view of the fact that this field for female action is one so little trodden, as yet, that its claims are but vaguely apprehended; and to many of our readers the subject is perhaps entirely new. The few individuals, the outline of whose history we are to give, have been leaders in the whole movement, and are still recognized by their associates as its most prominent advocates. They are also among the ripest and most honorable examples of what it is fitted to accomplish.

MRS. CLEMENCE S. LOZIER, M.D.

It is deeply interesting to trace the causes which have led any one to depart from the ordinary paths of life. In those causes there is often much that is palpably providential, — the impelling of divine influences through extraordinary arrangements, — and there is much of natural operations in accordance with the recognized fitness of things. Both these facts will be apparent in the instance we are now to consider. Why should Mrs. Lozier, a gentle, modest, unambitious, home-loving woman, have chosen the calling of a physician? We shall see as we sketch her biography. She was born Dec. 11, 1813, at Plainfield, New Jersey, the youngest of thirteen children. Her father was a farmer, David Harned, — a name well known at that period in the Methodist Church, of which he was a faithful member, and in which his brothers were successful preachers. Her mother was Hannah Walker. Previous to their residence in New Jersey, they spent some years in Virginia, where Indian tribes, noted for their sagacity, were then numerous. Mrs. Harned, a devout Quakeress, and with much missionary spirit, mingled freely with them. From them she gained valuable information, which, added to reading and close observation, with strong natural predilection, qualified her to act efficiently in the neighborhood as an attendant upon the sick. Subsequently she spent seven years in New York city, engaged in general practice, with the advice and co-operation of her cousins, Drs. Dunham and Kissam, by whom she was highly esteemed. William Harned, an elder brother of Clemence, was also a physician of good reputation in New York, and for some time partner of Dr. Doane, formerly quarantine physician, in an extensive chemical laboratory. Clemence was early left an orphan, and was educated at the Plainfield Academy. In 1830 she was married at New York to Mr. A. W. Lozier. Her husband's health soon failing, she opened a select school at their house in West Tenth Street, which she continued eleven years, averaging sixty pupils from families whose social position indicates the character of the teacher whom they would sustain. Many of those pupils and their children are now her patients. Mrs. Lozier was one of the first teachers in the city to introduce the study of Physiology, Anatomy, and Hygiene as branches of female education. During this period, she read medical works, under the direction of her brother. When her scholars were ill, she would generally be called before the physician, and her advice would be the sole reliance in ordinary diseases. She also at that time, for seven years, was associated with Mrs. Margaret Pryor in visiting the poor and abandoned, in connection with the Moral Reform Society, and often prescribed for them in sickness. Subsequently, while residing in Albany, she visited in the same connection in that city. Her opportunities for observing diseases in their worst forms among women and children were thus unusually extensive. In 1837 Mr. Lozier died; but she continued for some time the occupations to which his invalid condition had led her, though constantly looking forward to the medical profession as that to which she desired to devote herself. In 1849 she attended her first course of lectures at the Central New York College, in Rochester, and graduated at the Syracuse Eclectic College in 1853, having previously applied for admission to several other institutions, and been refused on the ground that no female student could be received. Returning to New York, she entered at once upon regular practice, which she has continued with remarkable success to the present time. Resorting to no means for attracting attention, generous to excess, giving her services gratuitously in numerous instances where fees would usually be exacted, yet her professional income is equalled by only a few of the most prominent practitioners in the city. She never hesitates to treat the most critical cases, and in the surgery required by the diseases of her sex has shown peculiar skill, having performed more than a hundred and twenty "capital operations" in the removal of vital tumors, besides nearly a thousand of a minor character. Many leading physicians now readily meet her in consultation, and she is frequently called out of town for the purpose. In 1867 she visited Europe, where every facility was afforded her for the inspection of hospitals, and eminent men received her, and introduced her to their associates with most gratifying courtesy.

In 1860 Mrs. Lozier commenced a course of familiar lectures in her own parlors, given gratuitously to her patients and their female friends, and attended by many of them with much interest and profit. These continued three years, during which a "Medical Library Association" was formed, for the purpose of promoting reading upon such subjects on the part of ladies. Her own mind, however, was, from the beginning, fixed upon the organization of a Medical College. In her parlor listeners, to whom she was giving only the simplest instruction upon sanitary principles, she foresaw the nucleus of college classes. In her patients and the men of wealth or benevolence to whose families she thus gained access, she anticipated contributors to its funds. All her professional and social intercourse was made to bend to this result with untiring zeal and unwavering confidence. Her own experience, and that of the few others who had met the ordeal, convinced her that by no other means could a thorough training be given to those who desired it, without such sacrifice of personal feeling as no woman should be required to endure. She denied both the expediency and practicability of mingling the sexes in such education, and therefore refrained from co-operating in the measures proposed by others to that end. Many meetings of ladies, for conference, were held at her house; but the disturbed condition of the country prevented the maturing of their plans. Some were wearied or discouraged in the effort, and forsook her; but she never for a moment doubted the success of the movement. At length, in 1863, it was determined to organize. The Library Association was merged in a College Association, a Board of Trustees chosen, a charter obtained, professors engaged, rooms secured, and the enterprise fairly inaugurated. Mrs. Lozier pledged herself, beyond her own subscription, to meet all pecuniary deficiencies for the first year. Her satisfaction and gratitude for the fulfilment of her hopes were complete. Since then she has devoted as much as possible of her time, and a considerable portion of her property, to its advancement. In all her efforts, from their inception to their present results, she has been ably seconded by her son, Dr. A. W. Lozier, whose indefatigable labors were invaluable to the cause. Of him it is fitting to say here that he is an esteemed physician, married to a highly educated lady (who is also a graduate of the Medical College), and is well-established as a practitioner in New York.

Mrs. Lozier's marked characteristic, both personally and professionally, is gentleness, — carried in demeanor, perhaps, to an extreme of quietness, which sometimes detracts from a just impression of her ability, decision, and confidence. Her influence upon her patients is always soothing; and she thus places them in the best mood for the action of remedies, while by her tenderness she wins many hearts, which will affectionately cherish her when time and space shall widely separate them. Not naturally systematic,— not so strict and regular as many might wish in her arrangements and modes of practice,— never making impression by technical phraseology,— much of her success arises from her sympathetic penetration of a case, ready access to the entire state of those seeking her advice, and the use of mild forms of treatment adapted to the susceptible female organism. In her aims she is singularly unselfish. Her simple remark to a friend, in view of one of the most difficult operations, which she had not before performed, but had then decided to undertake, in the presence of one of our first surgeons, instead of entrusting it to his hands, was indicative of her habitual spirit: "I desire to do this for the sake of the cause, for the credit of woman." It is her absorbing idea, and in it her own personal aspirations are merged. At the basis of her whole character, however, and the source from which spring all its movements, is a spiritual faith. Years ago, amid trials known only to a limited circle, she grasped the unseen hand of the Great Physician, upon which she has never ceased to lean, and which has never failed to lead her. In a private letter (which we must be pardoned for quoting) she says, "I am so much indebted to my religious teachings, to an unwavering faith in a present Saviour, and his constant inspiring love, that I want to tell all the world about that, and how I feel the gift of healing to be the talent committed to me by him, and then how I feel indebted to Mr. L. N. Fowler and his excellent wife, Dr. Lydia F. Fowler, to Mrs. C. F. Wells, and many other helps which God has raised up for me." We mention this, not for the purpose of eulogy, but because our sketch would be incomplete without the distinct acknowledgment of that which is most radical, and upon which Mrs. Lozier herself places her utmost dependence.

MISS ELIZABETH BLACKWELL, M. D.

In the subject of the previous sketch, our attention was directed to one whom native tendencies and favoring circumstances so combined to lead to the chosen pursuit, that her engagement in it was, from childhood, almost a foregone conclusion; and it would have required a strong compulsion to divert her from it. In the lady whose name we now present, we observe very different elements of character, and different influences prompting to a similar course. Miss Blackwell is of English parentage, and was born at Bristol, England, in the year 1821. Her father moved to the United States in 1831, and first established himself in business at New York. In accordance with his circumstances and views, his children had at that time every advantage for a liberal education. Proving unsuccessful in his enterprises, he removed to Cincinnati, hoping there to retrieve his fortunes, but died in 1837, leaving his family among strangers, to depend entirely upon their own efforts for support. Elizabeth, with well-matured mind, and already developing the energy which has since so thoroughly characterized her, though but seventeen years of age, opened a school, which she sustained satisfactorily several years.

An apparently slight occurrence directed her attention to the study of medicine. A female friend, afflicted with a distressing disease, expressed her keen regret that there was no one of her own sex to whom she and other like sufferers could resort for treatment. There were women who had assumed the medical title, but without authority, and with little claim to confidence. Most of them, also, were of disreputable character, and their practice not only unreliable, but largely criminal. Her friend, appreciating Miss Blackwell's abilities, and knowing that she had yet no settled aim in life, urged upon her the duty of devoting herself to this object, rescuing the title as applied to women from reproach, and meeting a want which multitudes painfully felt. The suggestion was immediately repelled, as utterly repugnant to her tastes and habits. She had a peculiar and extreme aversion to anything connected with the sick-room, or with the human body in its infirmities. Even the ordinary physical sciences were uncongenial to her. Metaphysics and moral philosophy, the abstract sciences, accorded far more with her inclinations. Pressed upon her, however, as a question for conscientious consideration, and, with characteristic firmness, setting aside personal preferences, she soon decided that the call upon her was providential, and her duty plain. The opprobrium to be encountered and the difficulties to be surmounted only deepened her determination. Writing for advice to six different physicians in different parts of the country, their invariable reply was, that the object, though desirable, was impracticable; "utterly impossible for a woman to obtain a medical education. The idea eccentric and utopian." Her reasoning from such counsel was brief, and her conclusion peculiar. "A desirable object, a good thing to be done, said to be impossible. I will do it." She at once commenced medical reading, under the direction of Dr. John Dixon, of Ashville, N. C., in whose family she was residing as governess. Removing the next year to Charleston, S. C., she supported herself by giving lessons in music, but continued to study, with regular instruction from Dr. S. H. Dixon, afterwards professor in the medical department of the New York University, and pursued it further under Drs. Allen and Warrington, of Philadelphia. She found the study deeply interesting, and followed it with ardor and thoroughness, while benevolence and singleness of purpose speedily overcame her aversion to the associations of disease. Upon applying for admission to the medical schools of New York, Philadelphia, and Boston, she was uniformly refused. From ten others the same answer was returned, until at Geneva the faculty submitted the question to the students, who unanimously voted for her reception, at the same time assuring her that nothing on their part should ever occur to wound her feelings while in attendance, — a pledge which they nobly kept. Entering in 1846, she graduated in 1848, — the first woman who received the medical degree in the United States. So violent, and so ignorant, too, was the opposition of her own sex, that during those two years no lady in Geneva would make her acquaintance; common civilities, even at the table, were denied her, and in the street she was deemed unworthy of recognition. Within the college walls she found nothing but friendliness and decorum; and on the evening of public graduation the cordiality of the students in making way for her to receive her diploma, and pleasantly indicating their congratulations, was marked and respectful. The next morning (she was to leave town in the afternoon) her parlor was filled with ladies. Success had turned the tide. Doubtless, also, many, moved by the evident approval of her associates in study, were satisfied at last that her motives were honorable, and her abilities adequate to her work.

The same year, Miss Blackwell went to Europe, and entered as a student "La Maternité," at Paris, with special reference to obstetrics. She also studied in 1850 and 1851 at St. Bartholomew's Hospital, in London. In the autumn of 1851 she returned, and commenced practice in New York city. Here again she experienced difficulties which only an indomitable will and the consciousness of a lofty aim enabled her to meet. With no such facilities from extended acquaintance and gradual entrance upon the work as subsequently favored Mrs. Lozier, she found a "blank wall of social and professional antagonism facing the woman physician which formed a situation of singular loneliness, leaving her without support, respect, or counsel." The title had been appropriated by such a class, that the sign was too generally supposed to indicate either a charlatan or an agent of infamy, and it was almost impossible to find a respectable boarding-house upon which her name would be allowed to appear. Notwithstanding all the hindrances, however, her testimonials and soon-proved qualifications gradually gained for her the confidence of all classes, the co-operation of physicians, and an extent of practice entirely satisfactory. The Quakers were first to receive her; and among them she has ever since maintained a most desirable position. Contrary to her own expectation, and to the usual impression also, her services have not been limited to, nor even chiefly required for, diseases peculiar to her own sex, but she is called and relied upon generally as the regular family physician; and in that capacity her relation to a wide circle of families is permanent.

In 1859 she again visited Europe, gave a course of lectures in London on the connection of women with medicine, and was registered as a member of the British Medical profession.

At about the time when Miss Blackwell established herself in New York, her sister Emily commenced the study, under Dr. John Davis, demonstrator at the Medical College of Cincinnati. In 1852 she entered the Rush Medical College, at Chicago, reading also with Dr. Daniel Brainerd, of that city, and spending the summer vacations in such attendance as was permitted her at Bellevue Hospital, New York, and graduated at the Cleveland College in February, 1854. That year and the two following she spent abroad, — one year in Edinburgh, one in Paris, one in London; and returning in December, 1856, located in New York. We regret that our limits forbid a more extended reference to this lady, whose abilities, attainments, and personal excellences cause her to share the respect of the public and the calls of private practice equally with her sister. It has seemed necessary to make Elizabeth Blackwell, as the elder physician, and for some reasons the more prominent, the special subject of our notice. In our further statements, however, we shall find them so thoroughly identified in their professional sphere, that they must necessarily be named together.

The "New York Infirmary for Women and Children," was the product of their united thought and effort. It was incorporated in the winter of 1853, and opened in the spring of 1854 as a dispensary, regulated and attended by Dr. Elizabeth. In 1856, on the return of Dr. Emily from Europe, they associated with them temporarily, Dr. M. E. Zakrzewska, a Polish lady, enlarged their plans, took a house, and opened it as a hospital, as well as a dispensary. The object was threefold, — a charity for the poor, a resort for respectable patients desiring special treatment, and particularly a centre to female students for practical clinical study. The Boston and Philadelphia colleges had already been chartered, and sent forth a number of graduates; but there was then no hospital which their students could freely visit, nor was there any designed exclusively for female patients. The New York Infirmary was therefore, for some years, the only woman's hospital in both these senses, and supplied an essential element in any full scheme of instruction. About thirty students have availed themselves of its advantages, by spending a year in daily attendance at its bedsides, and accompanying its visiting assistants into the homes of the poor. With an honorable list of consulting physicians, the treatment is yet entirely conducted by the Drs. Blackwell and their female associates. Up to the present time over fifty thousand patients have received prescriptions and personal care by this means; and nearly a thousand have been inmates of its wards. Every variety of operation connected with midwifery (except the Cesarean), has there been successfully performed by Dr. Emily Blackwell, as attending surgeon. Both the sisters took an active part in the organization and work of the "Ladies Central Relief Association," during the war; and their parlor lectures to nurses about to enter the service of the army were highly valued.

In the personal qualities as well as professional methods of the Drs. Blackwell, the intellectual element decidedly predominates. Clear judgment, close analysis, and steady purpose mark their treatment of cases which come under their charge. They are strenuous advocates of thorough scientific attainments on the part of women who would engage in the profession; and enter continual protests against short courses of study, and low standards of acquirement in institutions for that purpose. On this account, they have refused to co-operate with any which have been organized, perhaps exacting too much from those which are confessedly imperfect at the beginning, and laboring under unavoidable disadvantages. Their influence, however, has thus been stimulating to all who are engaged in such efforts, "provoking them to good works." A paragraph in one of their lectures expresses their spirit. "It is observation and comprehension, not sympathy, which will discover the kind of disease. It is knowledge, not sympathy, which can administer the right medicine; and though warm sympathetic natures, with knowledge, would make the best of all physicians, without sound scientific knowledge, they would be most unreliable and dangerous guides." They are also firm in their conviction of the expediency of mingling the sexes in all scholastic training, and have very reluctantly relinquished for the present, the hope of opening the ordinary colleges to female applicants. In their mode of practice they adopt the main features of the "regular" system, while refusing to be absolutely bound by any such limitations in their examination and use of remedies. On the whole, they furnish each as complete an instance as has come under our observation among women, of cool, dignified, self-poised character, scorning shams and artifices, resolutely, with disinterested motive, set on the attainment of worthy ends. In religious connection, they are Episcopalians, though, in theology as well as medicine, they seem to be independent searchers for truth.

MISS HARRIOT K. HUNT, M. D.

Perhaps no American woman of our time has made herself heard and felt in so many directions and amid such diverse circumstances as Harriot K. Hunt. Many have achieved more eminence in some one department, and the world of fashion or literature or art recognize them where she is unknown. But the parlor and the platform, the sick-room and the court-room, asylums and churches, wretched hovels and mansions of elegance, East and West, have been the scenes of her animated speech and determined work. By the lovers of truth and goodness, the radical philanthropists of various orders, she is widely known. Many causes have been promoted by her public advocacy. In private relations many a crushed, despairing woman has risen to new life under her stirring appeals, many a bold, profligate man has shrunk abashed before her pungent rebukes. It is difficult, therefore, to eliminate the professional part of her history from the social and reformatory, as our design obliges us to do, and to condense it into our brief limits.

She is a genuine Bostonian (a title which has significance,

both favorable and unfavorable), pedigreed, born, bred, and habituated as such. Her father, Joab Hunt, lived many years in the street in which his parents and grandparents had lived and died. He was of a strong stock, full of vitality physical and mental. Her mother, Kezia Wentworth, was of an equally vigorous ancestry, and possessed a mind of remarkable qualities, argumentative, practical, independent, and withal abounding in tenderness and genial brightness, as did also her father, in whom humor and earnestness seem to have been happily combined. He was a shipping merchant, and through energy and prudence came into easy circumstances, amid which, Harriot and her sister Sarah, the only children, were reared. Harriot was born in 1805, the first child, fourteen years after her parents' marriage, and was joyfully welcomed and carefully trained. Her home was a happy one, and everything which affection could devise to foster her constitutional buoyancy of character was lavished upon her. Nothing occurred to shade the steady brightness of her life until 1827, when the sudden death of her father changed all her prospects. His estate was found to be encumbered and the settlement difficult. A few months previous, with some intimations of his embarrassed affairs, the sisters had opened a school, which became now the chief dependence of the family, beyond the small income from the property. It was also a means of discipline to themselves, qualifying them for their future work, brought them more into contact with the domestic lives of others, and acquainted them with those private underlying facts in regard to the condition of young girls and their home management, upon which so largely depends their health in maturer years. Harriot says of it, "My school was flourishing and I loved it. Yet I never felt it my true vocation. It seemed to be preparing me for something higher and more permanent. It was but transitional." In 1830 her sister was prostrated by severe illness. This, with the experience of medical treatment in connection with it, formed the turning-point in the history of both. It was a distressing, complicated disease, and the prescriptions were after the severest forms of the old school of practice. After ten months' sickness without improvement, the sisters were roused to consider and study. They procured medical books and read, and arrived at the conclusion that the case had been misunderstood. Then came a change of physicians, with some advantage; but the interest awakened in the study of medicine and the conviction that much of the ordinary practice was blind and merely experimental, led them to pursue the investigation further for themselves and for the benefit of similar sufferers. In 1833, Mrs. Mott, an English woman, established herself in Boston. Her husband was a physician, but the care of female patients devolved chiefly upon her. She made extravagant claims to medical skill in the treatment of cases regarded as hopeless; yet her general success was too evident to be denied. She attracted their attention, and, in spite of friendly protests and the displeasure of former attendants, the invalid was placed under her care. The result was favorable. After more than three years' confinement, she was soon able to walk the streets and to attend church. Relations of intimacy and affection were created between the physician and her patient's family. After a time they changed their residence, leasing their own house, and taking rooms in Mrs. Mott's. Then the school was given up, and Harriot accepted the position of secretary to Mrs. Mott, conducting an extensive correspondence with patients. She entered upon it with her usual ardor. It enlarged the sphere of her observation, intensified her sympathy especially for those afflicted with hidden ailments, and "deepened the instinct which pointed her to the medical profession." Meanwhile she read with avidity everything which bore upon it. She was fascinated by it, eager for knowledge in each department and delighted with the results of research. Her mind, however, biased by her experience in her sister's case, turned most readily in the direction of inquiry after the laws of health. She "endeavored to trace diseases to violated laws, and learn the science of prevention. That word, prevention, seemed a great word to me," she says; "curative was small beside it." The death of Dr. Mott caused Mrs. Mott to return to England and broke up the household. Still the studies were pursued, with an increasingly clear persuasion of what the purpose of her life was to be, and a very distinct recognition of providential guidance in it. The period spent thus, nearly three years (including her attendance in Mrs. Mott's office), in addition to the more private reading in the sick-room during the intervals of relief from school duties, was one of extreme application. Few students after the regular modes, with all the facilities of tuition afforded them, have ranged over a wider field of knowledge or searched it more thoroughly, so far as it can be exhibited in books. The opportunities for more practical examination by the bedside, or in contact otherwise with the subjects of maladies, came subsequently, and were pursued with an eagerness sharpened by the consciousness of deficiency resulting from the previous lack. In 1835 an office was opened, the two names, Harriot and Sarah, associated. They studied and practised together. Often in the late night hours they recited to each other lessons from medical works, or compared views upon cases presented during the day. Each new case was a fresh revelation to them, or gave them a deeper insight into what they had already learned. There is a singular charm about this part of their biography, as we have obtained glimpses of it. Harriot evidently took the lead in everything. She was thirty years of age,—the very acme of human life,—in vigorous health, every faculty fully developed and toned to its highest point, of indomitable will and overflowing with enthusiasm. With no professional support, no conferred title as guaranty of capacity or attainment, no advertising resorts for attraction, she launched from the safe harbor of domestic privacy and social protection upon an untried sea of responsibility and public scrutiny, with suitable discretion, and yet with unflinching confidence that she was on the track to which the Divine Hand had brought her. Her practice was not after any established formulas. She was bound by the regulations of no school, as none had endorsed her. She valued the ordinary medicines, so far as she perceived their restorative effects, but received and used freely any remedial agency whether moral or physical. She writes, "I was particularly attracted to mental diseases and often found physical maladies growing out of concealed sorrows. We were frequently surprised by the successful termination of many of our cases through prescription for mental states; and the causes of diseases, with the quality of remedies for them, became a deeper study. Love for our calling gave life to the calling. Every fact we gathered had its use, and while the perceptive faculties were stimulated, the reflective were educated for guidance." And again, "Medication alone is not to be relied on. In one-half the cases medicine is not needed and is worse than useless. Obedience to spiritual and physical laws — hygiene of the body and hygiene of the spirit — is the surest warrant for health and happiness. It is only the quacks of the profession, emulous of the quacks ostracized by the faculty, who put their trust in dosing. The true physician knows better."

Patients gathered slowly at first, but with steady increase. Many were declined conscientiously, because beyond her present knowledge or ability, and without any false pride of reputation. Obstetrics and other surgery she never practised. We pass over a few years, during which she was gaining experience, position, influence, and property. Her sister married and removed, and she was left alone in her professional work, which began to grow rapidly in its demands upon her. In 1843 a "Ladies' Physiological Society" was organized in Charlestown, at her suggestion. The members met twice a month, to read and converse upon topics which the name indicates, while industriously occupied for some benevolent object. Within the year it increased in numbers from a dozen to fifty, and was long sustained with spirit and benefit, and, for aught we know, is still in active existence. Its formation was eventful to Miss Hunt, as giving her the first hint of the possibility of lecturing to her own sex. At many of their meetings she addressed them, and acquired thus the freedom and facility of speech which she has since exercised abundantly, before larger and more general audiences, upon a variety of subjects. In 1847, at the suggestion of friends, as well as the prompting of an earnest wish for information through every avenue, she applied to the faculty of Harvard College for permission to attend a course of lectures in the medical department, stating that, at the age of forty-two, after twelve years' practice, which had become extensive, and ranking among her friends many of the most intelligent citizens, it would be evident to them that the request must proceed from no want of patronage, but simply from a desire for such scientific light as could be imparted by their professors, and as would make her more worthy of the trusts committed to her. The application was refused, simply upon the ground of expediency, without assigning reasons. Three years afterward she repeated it, accompanying it with an able letter, hoping that the favor with which Miss Blackwell had been received elsewhere, and the full discussion of the matter on several occasions, might induce a different decision. It proved so; and permission was granted by the proper officers. The students, however, waxed indignant at the prospect of such an associate in their studies (or, perhaps, such a witness of their manners), and vehemently protested. Unwilling to create disturbance, where her object had been entirely disinterested, she generously declined to avail herself of the long-coveted opportunity. The medical class of 1851, at Harvard, so unlike that of 1846, at Geneva, in the case of Miss Blackwell, gained for themselves an unenviable notoriety. In 1853 the Female Medical College, at Philadelphia, conferred upon Miss Hunt the honorary degree of M. D. She had well earned it, and, whatever may be her technical irregularities, has conferred as much honor upon the title as it has upon her.

In 1850 Miss Hunt began to attend conventions held with reference to the interests and rights of woman. Every aspect of that movement profoundly affected her, and she gave her influence earnestly to it. Her special part in it, however, and her public speech, when opportunity offered, was concerning the sanitary reforms needed among women, and their right and duty to take care of themselves and each other and their offspring in that respect. "Woman as physician to her sex" was her theme. The conventions furnished her fitting occasions for urging it. They brought her also more prominently before the public, and prepared the way for numerous meetings, called for the purpose exclusively of listening to her appeals upon the subject. At intervals, through several summers, as convenience served, and she could be spared from professional charge at home, she made tours through New England, New York State, and Ohio, delivering addresses, organizing associations, visiting colleges and schools. That she spoke well and effectively may be inferred from the character of her audiences, composed of the most intelligent classes, and the practical results in societies formed, and new impulse given to measures for the education of women in every department. During the last few years her life has not been marked by any events which could appropriately be noticed in our sketch. She has continued her residence in Boston, and pursued her practice in a steadily increasing circle. Her example has encouraged others to enter the field; and she has now some able co-laborers in the city, whom she thankfully welcomes and assists, declaring, "All women-workers have my benediction." At the end of twenty-five years she celebrated her silver wedding to her profession. Her house was crowded with cordial friends, who decorated it with flowers, and testified their esteem by abundant tokens. Advanced in years, her spirit is still buoyant as ever. She writes, "Knowing that all life is from the Lord, mine, professionally, has been radiant, and I have enjoyed so much in it!" "My hair is white, but my life is precious to me." "As year after year has glided away, I have gathered flowers and fruits, which have cheered and beautified the approach of age. Signal blessings, providential interpositions, interior guidance in emergencies, religious thankfulness for strength in times of need, distrust, and sin, mark the periods of my life, rather than days and months." Sorrowing much over suffering, with burning indignation against vices and oppressions, her habitual mood is yet joyful; and few who come into her presence can resist its magnetic power, or fail to go from it stirred to higher and purer endeavors. She has cured many, enlightened, cheered, and elevated multitudes.

In religious faith Miss Hunt is Swedenborgian, — attracted to it, perhaps, by her imaginative and soulful temperament; by her affinity with its subtile metaphysics, with which it penetrates and illuminates the physical sciences; by its ethereal spirituality, and by the magic words, "truth, good, and love," with which it plays upon the fervent mind, yearning for harmony and peace, like evening bell-chimes upon the ear weary of the world's clamor. Whatever may be its doctrinal soundness, its influence has been to invest her character and experience with a peculiar glow deeply satisfactory to herself, and impressive to those who know her.

We have endeavored, thus, to represent impartially, three of the most advanced, most trusted, and most successful female physicians of our country. They were pioneers in a movement which has already resulted in the introduction of hundreds to the same position. They prepared themselves for it with fewer facilities than any who have followed them; bending circumstances to their will, rather than shaped in their course by the suggestion of circumstances; compelling advantages, commanding helps, forcing open (but never rudely) avenues long closed to the sex. It would be difficult to find more complete contrasts than they present, both physically and mentally; and yet, like the geometric problem of the triangle described within the circle, they are, from their distinct points of departure, perfectly included within the same circle of aim and influence. The world owes a debt of gratitude and honor beyond computation to those who, at the sacrifice of much that was dear to them, in the face of opprobrium or misjudgment, aware of the immense responsibilities involved, in the spirit of a true Christian ministry, neither anticipating nor seeking the large emoluments which have come to them, have led the way into such a sphere. As we have more fully pondered the subject, the persuasion deepens that no more flagrant wrong to humanity could be committed, than that of hindering the entrance into it of any who, with so pure intention and intelligent fitness, seek admission.

We could readily now extend much further our record of worthy compeers in this work. Diplomas are multiplying year by year, and among the recipients are "honorable women not a few." Every large city, and many of the smaller towns, would furnish names to add to our roll of honor; and a multitude of voices would unite in urging the claims of one and another for a place upon it. Our desire to express the cordial appreciation which we have of all such must, however, be restrained. We limit ourselves to the notice of two, one as illustrating the possibilities of large success in general practice, the other the influences to be quietly exerted in the department of professional instruction. We draw both instances from Philadelphia, partly because they well represent the college established there, and partly because that city is probably the best field in which this branch of woman's labors can fairly exhibit its fruits.

MRS. HANNAH E. LONGSHORE, M. D.

Mrs. Longshore is the daughter of Samuel and Paulian Myers, born May 30th, 1819, in Montgomery County, Maryland. Her parents were natives of Burks County, Pennsylvania, and members of the "Society of Friends." When she was two years old, they moved into the District of Columbia, where she received her early education, attending a private school in Washington City. In the year 1832, unwilling to remain longer under the demoralizing influence of a slave-holding community, they again changed their residence, and settled on a farm in Columbiana County, Ohio. Here the whole household co-operated in industry and the most rigid economy, to secure for themselves a quiet and happy home. Samuel Myers was evidently a man of practical religious character, and strong individuality,—one whom unwearying diligence, careful reading, and meditation had developed into a good reasoner and a sound philosopher. Having had experience in teaching, and taking a deep interest in his children, it was his daily practice to aid them in their studies as well as to use every opportunity for familiarizing their minds with the principles of science. His aim was to make study a pleasure, to quicken their perceptions and strengthen their reflective powers. The "divinity of labor" was also with him a cherished sentiment, part of his religious creed. In his family and elsewhere he dwelt on it with emphasis. He maintained that every child had a right to the best possible advantages for intellectual culture, and, equally, that it was the interest and duty of society to train them in habits of intelligent industry; that every one should contribute in some way to the common product; no sinecure posts, no drones, no consumers who should not be either directly producers, or so actively helpful to the producers that they could claim a share of the benefit, on the apostolic principle that "if any would not work neither should he eat." His children grew up deeply imbued with this principle, and with it a feeling of individual responsibility and self-reliance. There were six children, one brother and five sisters. The older sisters passed much time in the open air, in the society of their father on the farm, aiding him in the various branches of labor adapted to their capacity. During the busiest seasons in the field, however, a portion of the day was devoted to reading and to conversations between parents and children. All the branches of natural science were more or less considered during these periods, while at labor as well as in the intervals of rest. It was beautiful and instructive to witness the family group in these discussions, and note the thoughtfulness and enthusiasm exhibited, — frequently the utmost eagerness and exhilaration of spirit. In the same connection religion, morality, social reforms, politics, and whatever interested or agitated society, received such share of their attention as other duties permitted, and the mental development of each child seemed to demand. In these respects they were different from most of their acquaintances. Independent, united, satisfied with their domestic resources for enjoyment, they became somewhat isolated. They were respected in the neighborhood, yet feared and shunned by many as eccentric. Summer after summer, in rural simplicity, was thus occupied. When not working in the field, Hannah was assisting a delicate, feeble mother in household duties, and caring for the younger children. These physical toils, combined with mental activity, imparted discipline and courage to accomplish whatever task was undertaken. The comparative leisure of winter was more fully devoted to study, occupied as pupil or teacher in the district school. She attended one term at the New Lisbon Academy, about two miles from her home. This distance she walked at morning and evening, regularly braving the storms, the bitter cold, and drifting snow. Neither the long walk, nor domestic duties, nor other trifling reasons, were ever offered or needed as an excuse for imperfectly prepared lessons. Beside the milking-pail, the churn, the wash-tub, the ironing-table, somewhere would the book be placed, that study might progress while the hands were busy. She joined the literary society connected with the academy, prepared essays, and gave lectures on scientific subjects.

At a very early period an interest in anatomy was developed. When ten years of age she was often occupied in the examination of insects, and the dissection of small animals, pursuing it with the same nicety and accuracy with which she would also analyze flowers, to gratify a craving for knowledge in these departments. Very soon her attention was turned to the study of medicine, with a view to practise, by the family physician, whose prescriptions it had been her part to administer in the family. Arrangements were made to commence regular reading; but untoward events frustrated the plan, and it was postponed. At the age of twenty-two she married, and the subsequent six years were chiefly devoted to domestic duties, partly on a farm, and partly in a quiet village. This, though apparently a blank portion of her history, was not blank in useful experience. It was here that her well-developed, but comparatively unregulated forces of mind and heart, and indomitable energy, were concentrated and directed into a practical channel. She was put upon her own resources, and her innate executive qualities were brought into requisition. Never entirely satisfied that she was occupying her whole sphere, she nevertheless resolved that she would fill that portion of it well. The proficiency she acquired in the performance of every service connected with house-keeping, and the charge of a family in sickness and health, she often refers to with thankfulness. Without this skill and experience she would not feel qualified to meet the emergencies often occurring in her relations to other families, nor to practise her profession with thoroughness. At the end of these six years events favored a change in her circumstances, and the busy cares of a farmer's wife were exchanged for the quiet village home, with only her own family, consisting of husband and two children, to occupy her. It was then, when her youngest child was four years old, and some leisure offered, that she resumed her favorite study. The books and maps, skeletons, and preparations of her brother-in-law, Prof. J. S. Longshore, who was also her preceptor, were at her service. She proceeded with the usual course, and at the end of two years entered as a student the "Female Medical College of Pennsylvania," located in Philadelphia. It was the first session of that institution. At the close of the second session, in 1850, she was one of the ten members who composed the first graduating class. As an indication of regard for her qualifications, the faculty immediately elected her "Demonstrator of Anatomy," and she acceptably served the college in that capacity. Her "sign" was the first one exhibited in Philadelphia by any female graduate in medicine. The calls of patients were at first few, and principally of the poorer classes. It was found no easy matter for an entire stranger, unheralded, to obtain practice. Ignorance, prejudice, and petty persecution were to be encountered. Sneers and ridicule were the staple arguments against her. Some *gentlemen* of the profession took special pains to array public sentiment against the movement. "A woman's intellectual incapacity and her physical weaknesses will ever disqualify her for the duties." "She will either kill her patients or let them die." "It would be evidence of insanity or idiocy to employ her." "If you call in a woman you will have to call a man afterward, and no man will meet a woman in consultation." These expressions were heard on every side. With unwavering purpose and confidence in ultimate success, she was not discouraged, but availed herself of this enforced leisure, to prepare and deliver a course of "Lectures to Ladies on Medical Subjects." She also delivered a carefully written lecture, on the "Medical Education of Women," to a large and appreciative audience, in one of the largest halls of the city, and repeated it, as well as the course to ladies, in other halls and churches. These lectures, besides inducing consideration and right views upon the general subject, introduced her more fully to the public, and enabled her hearers to form some judgment of her qualifications for the duties she had assumed. The result was, that, one by one, many of those who heard her called on her for advice and aid. By the third year her practice had increased so that she was obliged to abandon all idea of further lectures, and also to resign her position as demonstrator in the college. Since then it has steadily extended, until few physicians of either sex, and among women perhaps none, except Mrs. Lozier, can equal it. As many as three hundred families in the city rely upon her exclusively for medical care, and it is no uncommon thing for her to prescribe for forty patients in a day. Her practice is legitimate and general, that is, it includes all forms of disease, acute and chronic, in respectable family treatment, with surgery among women and children. Of the latter, she has had occasion to perform many extremely delicate and dangerous operations, — with what success, the best testimony that can be desired, is the growing confidence with which she is called upon by the most intelligent class of citizens. The objection often urged against the introduction of female physicians, — that they cannot endure the inevitable fatigues and exposures, — has met a practical answer in the instance of Mrs. Longshore. Inheriting from her mother a delicate constitution, her early childhood was one of sensitiveness and suffering, notwithstanding the benefit derived from the mode of life which we have described, judiciously regulated. At the age of fifteen she very narrowly escaped from a prostrating and protracted attack, requiring many months for recovery. At the time of graduation, the faculty predicted an early death from consumption. Since then her weight has greatly increased, and she gives every token of vigor. It is her conviction that her continued life and present degree of health are due to the active habits of the profession.

Mrs. Longshore is constitutionally extremely diffident. For many years she was so easily embarrassed that she dreaded and shunned society, beyond the limited circle of a few friends. To appear in public as a lecturer, and to visit strangers professionally, always required a struggle against this timidity and the habit of reserve; yet she has so far subdued it, by absorption in her objects, that it would hardly be detected in her deportment. In appearance she is characterized by entire simplicity, equally removed from coarseness and from affectation; not adopting the Quaker costume and language, but plain in her mode of speech and dress, with an openness of countenance expressive of a truthful spirit. Direct, unhesitating, and informal in her approach to a case; unpretending, and yet evidently assured in the exercise of her judgment; with a peculiar mingling of personal modesty and professional positiveness, she inspires patients with immediate trust, which is rarely forfeited. Cool, cheerful, rapid in her manner as physician, almost seeming to make light of their ailments, she leaves them refreshed by her visit, scarcely conscious of their need of condolence, and yet often before leaving the houses of those endeared to her by long acquaintance or dependence upon her care, she sheds the tears of a true woman and a sympathizing mother. Her mind acts with the quickness of intuition or of keen perceptions, and a brief interview, with a few questions, usually suffices to guide her in the choice of remedies. In her selection of these, she is not governed by any routine, nor limited to one school of medicine, but considers that she is at liberty to avail herself of any means which her experience has proved useful or the peculiarities of the case suggest. For some time past, the prejudices which she at first encountered from the "fraternity," especially under the pressure of resolutions early adopted by the county society and some other organizations, have yielded to the evidences of her ability; and now some of the leading physicians of the city freely meet her in consultation, while others, too much trammelled by regulations, or personal fears, to act openly, have recommended her to their female patients, and, in several instances, while publicly uniting in measures of opposition to women as practitioners, have privately sent to her for treatment their own wives and daughters.

In the midst of these exacting and exhausting claims upon her time, Mrs. Longshore is, in her domestic relations, affectionate and faithful. Her husband and children are preferred above all other objects of interest. Without them, she often declares that life would lose its chief charm to her, — a declaration the sincerity of which they and her intimate friends fully credit and abundantly testify, and which is confirmed by the order of her household, and by her readiness at any time to consult their comfort at the sacrifice of her own. Her warm and active sympathy, also, with every movement promising benefit for the wronged, the oppressed, and suffering, especially to those of her own sex, is well known among her friends. Her gratuitous labors among the poor she has always felt to be a duty, and congenial to her disposition. She never knowingly accepts a fee from the needy, while she is constantly distributing food, clothing, and other comforts, gathered from every source within her reach. Not so much marked by the devotional element, or uplifting spirituality, as some whom we have already noticed, she is certainly abundant in those fruits of pure and undefiled religion, which consist in visiting the widow and the fatherless in their affliction, and keeping unspotted from the world, and we trust is actuated in it by the divine precept "to do good and to communicate; for with such sacrifices God is well pleased."

A younger sister, Miss Jane V. Myers, M. D., resides in her family, and has a large and lucrative independent practice.

An older half-sister, Mrs. Mary F. Thomas, M. D., now living at Camden, Indiana, has been actively engaged in that State several years. For two years she was editor, and for a longer time contributor to a semi-monthly journal devoted mainly to the cause of women, published in Richmond, Indiana. During the rebellion she was occupied much in collecting and distributing supplies, and a portion of the time her husband, O. Thomas, M. D., and herself had charge of a hospital in Tennessee.

MISS ANN PRESTON, M. D.

If we were seeking a subject for an attractive biography merely, there are many women whom we might have chosen in preference to Miss Preston, for the striking characteristics or stirring incidents which their lives would have furnished; yet there are few whose lives are more worthy of record, or their qualities of imitation, or whose work has been more effective for the cause we are advocating. Indeed, the few facts which we are allowed to use are given us for their bearings upon the cause, rather than for personal representation. Identified with the college and the hospital, she prefers to be known chiefly through them, and to have her reputation merged in whatever good they may accomplish. Yet the public, who witness and honor these results of unobtrusive labor, have right to know more of the personality of one who is so clearly a workman that needeth not to be ashamed.

She was born December, 1830, at West Grove, Pennsylvania, in the old homestead of her grandfather, where her father was born and died, and where she lived until constrained to leave it for a wider sphere of action. Her father was Amos Preston, a devoted Quaker. An obituary notice of him, by one who had known him from childhood, speaks of him as a man of unusual intellectual gifts, "enthusiastic in the pursuit of truth, particularly on those subjects which most nearly affect the present and everlasting welfare of the race, and inflexibly faithful to his convictions of duty; possessed of a warm social nature and a rare faculty for entering into sympathy with the wants and interests of others, which, together with his acknowledged disinterestedness, inspired confidence, so that he was trusted and loved by his personal friends as few men have been. In the domestic relations the beauty of his character shone conspicuous. The family government was that of perfect love, while frankness and mutual confidence marked his intercourse with his children." Her mother also is mentioned as "fond of literature and having an intense love of nature, with a sensitive nervous organization. "Miss Preston evidently combines in herself the constitutional traits of both parents. Her only sister dying in infancy, the delicate health of her mother brought the chief care of a large family upon her, making her early life one of close occupation and grave responsibilities. Her opportunities for education were therefore limited to the country school (which, however, was of high order), and a period spent at boarding-school in West Chester, the county town. But the neighborhood of their residence was one of remarkable intellectual activity and culture, and of moral excellence. A valuable public library, with a Lyceum and Literary Association, gave tone to society, diffused intelligence and promoted discussion upon all current questions. She regards her connection with these as one of the richest blessings of her youth, and as having important bearing upon her subsequent life. During that period, also, she shared largely with true-hearted men and women in earnest efforts of general philanthropy. Her influence in these directions was distinctly marked, while in the genial domestic circle, amid all her practical duties, she was cultivating a refined taste, often evinced in poetic effusions, whose pure sentiments have been appreciated by many readers.

To a mind like hers, uniting keen sensibilities with energy of purpose and breadth of aim, the charms of such a home must have been great, while the impulse to pass beyond its limitations was equally strong.

The years, however, passed on profitably and happily, until she reached maturity. She would long before have entered some wider and less secluded path, had not her mother's continued need of assistance, while six brothers were reaching manhood, seemed an imperative claim. But the aspiration to more fully "labor for God's suffering ones" was pressing. The time had come when she felt the necessity for a broader field of satisfying work, and a fuller independence than was possible with her surroundings. She loved study, and medical subjects were peculiarly interesting to her, yet she had not shaped for herself the course which she should permanently take. At this midway point, when the ties which had so long bound her to the ordinary routine of woman's cares were loosened, and the remaining half of probable life required definite direction, in 1850 the "Woman's Medical College of Pennsylvania" was opened at Philadelphia. Information of proposals preliminary to it had reached her and engaged her thoughtful attention, and when they developed into practical form it commended itself to her as meeting a vital want in society. It satisfied the desires of her own mind. Without hesitation she turned toward it as settling the question of what her future should be, and became one of the first applicants for admission as a student. The college opened favorably, with a faculty of six professors, regular practitioners, and graduates of regular schools; though encountering, as was anticipated, the opposition of a large portion of the profession. It was the first in the world chartered, for the purpose, with the usual appliances for the instruction of women in all the departments of medical learning. Imperfections were unavoidable at the outset of such an enterprise, pecuniary means inadequate, a self-sacrificing disposition needed on the part of all engaged in it. But, "sustained by the profound conviction that the cause was right and must succeed, that the study and practice of medicine are adapted to woman's nature, that the profession and the world need her, and that her entrance into this enlarged sphere of virtuous activity is the harbinger of increased happiness and health for her and the race,"— they patiently continued their work. Miss Preston, with thorough enthusiasm, and yet with the calm steadiness of a ripened mind, entered into the whole movement, while on her own part pursuing faithfully every branch of allotted study. It was a great change from the rural scenes in which her unruffled life had been spent, uncongenial to her temperament and habits; but no personal considerations could turn her from her course. Firm-willed and deeply conscientious, she devoted every energy to preparation for the new responsiblities which she was to assume. Her attainments were as complete as her opportunities rendered possible. She commenced practice in the city without ostentation or undue eagerness for occupation, true to the principles which she has often since urged upon students: "None can sustain others who are not themselves self-sustained;" "Nothing but strict inward rectitude can give that repose and strength to the spirit which will enable it to bear up safely through every difficulty;" "Those who are admitted into the very sanctuaries of society, and entrusted with the most sacred confidences, should indeed be strong and wise, and pure and good;" "If you prove yourselves capable and worthy, society is ready to receive you, but solid superstructures are the work of time, and slowly, carefully, woman must work her way." Conforming to the general rule expressed in this last sentence (to which instances like Mrs. Longshore are exceptional), she deliberately felt her way into her true position. Friends who perceived her abilities aided her advancement. Arrangements were made for her to lecture to classes in Philadelphia, Baltimore, New York, and other places. Meanwhile changes occurred in the college faculty, and in 1854 Miss Preston was elected to the chair of "Physiology and Hygiene," which, as well as the position of "Dean," she still occupies. It is well adapted to her taste, and gives full scope to her capabilities. She fills it with dignity and acceptance. The annual announcements of the college prepared by her, are models of clear, sound, and forcible statement, while her introductory lectures and valedictory addresses, delivered by appointment of the faculty, are replete with striking thoughts. In 1861 "The Woman's Hospital of Philadelphia" was incorporated, an essential auxiliary to the college and an invaluable charity. It has attained already a position which commands for it the highest respect of the community, has received liberal contributions for its endowment, and possesses a handsome property in buildings and grounds. Nearly three thousand patients were treated through its means, and at the dispensary connected with it, during the past year. Miss Preston was at the outset appointed one of its board of managers, corresponding secretary, and consulting physician, and still acts in those capacities. During this period her private practice has become sufficiently established and remunerative to meet all her wishes, though her frail health, requiring constant vigilance against over-exertion, has obliged her to limit it, — refusing night calls and obstetrical cases. In 1867 the Philadelphia County Medical Society adopted a preamble and resolutions setting forth in plain terms their objections to the practice of medicine by women, and declining to meet them in consultation,— a conclusion, however, by which many of their most reliable members refused to be bound. Miss Preston immediately published a reply, so admirable in temper and argument as to turn the tide of opinion, both in the profession and outside of it, among intelligent observers, very much in favor of those in whose behalf she wrote. No rejoinder, so far as we are informed, was attempted; but the restraints upon consultation have been relaxed instead of confirmed, and a better understanding of the whole subject now prevails. Of course we do not ascribe the improvement entirely to this cause, yet we cannot doubt that the adjustment of these difficulties, as well as the advanced ground occupied by the medical work for women in that vicinity, is owing as much to her well-regulated, judicious, but intelligent, firm and persistent efforts as to any other that can be named. Personally her position in the esteem of the public, and more intimately of a large circle of friends, is beyond dispute or possible change, and tranquilly though busily she occupies it. With the care which she has learned to exercise over hereditary susceptibilities, many years more of usefulness appear probable for her, within which she can hardly fail to see her utmost aims accomplished for the institutions and objects to which she has dedicated herself with a true consecration, while many who go out from her instructions will bear the permanent impress of her serene, unwavering character.

CAMILLA URSO.

BY MARY A. BETTS.

"The violin is the violet," says the Chevalier Seraphael in that most imaginative and fantastic of musical novels, "Charles Auchester." How came the fancy to the writer's brain? Was it because the violet, with its trembling blue petal and its evanescent fragrance, reminds one of the woods, the mingling harmonies of brook and bird-voice, of wind-swept trees and restless wind? Or, was it because to the artist the violet was the most perfect of flowers and the violin of instruments?

An instrument it certainly is of torture and delight. How we have all groaned at the melancholy squeaks of a poor fiddle in the street! With what a rapture have we followed the violins in the orchestra, as their penetrating and aerial tones completed for us the harmonic pictures or the wordless songs! And in the hands of a genius whose thoughtful brain and ardent heart have comprehended and mastered its powers, what a magical shell is this crooked, stringed, sonorous thing of wood!

The brain and heart of a true violinist came into the world one summer-day in the city of Nantes, France. This beautiful old Huguenot city was then the residence of Salvator Urso, a musician from Palermo, Sicily, and his Portuguese wife, whose maiden name was Emilie Girouard. Signor Urso was an organist and flutist of rare merit, educated thoroughly in all the principles of his art by his father, who had done hearty service to music in younger days. On the 13th of June, 1842, Camilla Urso was born,—the first child of a happy union. Though four brothers followed her, the little daughter was most passionately beloved by her father, who gloried in her inheritance of that gift which had been his resource and constant pleasure. The warm Southern sky never looked upon a more attractive child than the little Camilla. Young geniuses are not always charming. Precocity is often accompanied by conceit and nervous irritability. But Camilla's bright cheerfulness was even more fascinating than her talent.

She was alive to all the subtle mysteries of sound at an age when the "Cradle Song" is the favorite melody of most children. Her father was first flutist in the orchestra of the opera, and carried her to the theatre almost every night. Through the long performances she sat, rapt in childish happiness, never growing tired, never weary of repetition. Madame Urso now declares that she heard more operas then than she has listened to ever since.

At the age of six she found and proved her vocation. Her father was organist at the Church of the Holy Cross. One day she stood listening at his side while the choir performed the mass of St. Cecilia. Solemnly, slowly, the organ tones swelled and died. Clear voices of soprano and tenor rose upon the air with the saddening plaint of *Kyrie Eleison.* The orchestral harmonies interwove their pathetic or triumphant music. The dark-haired child, with the broad brow and sweet, parted lips, listened,—not awed by the under-wave of the mighty organ, not following with curious, imitative mouth the soaring voices and melodious words,—but enchanted for life by the inarticulate passion and sorrow of the violin's changing vibrations. The last note of the mass floated into silence, but the little Camilla did not mingle in the crowd of departing worshippers. Her father's hand aroused her, and she walked home announcing in a firm tone, which was most amusing, coming from that tiny figure: "I wish to learn the violin."

Her studies were immediately begun, and her progress was most rapid. In a year she appeared at a concert given for the benefit of a widow, whose husband had been one of Signor Urso's friends.

The announcement of the concert astonished the citizens of Nantes. It was considered the height of absurdity for a child to attempt to play on so difficult an instrument. Friends came to applaud, enemies to laugh, but all were amazed and delighted. Little Camilla had no timidity, no anxiety for success. Her new white satin shoes, the first she had ever put on, were much more engrossing for the time than the violin she was to handle. The principal journal of Nantes spoke thus of the performance: —

"Never had violinist a *pose* more exact, firmer, and at the same time perfectly easy; never was bow guided with greater precision than by this little Urso, whose delivery made all the mothers smile. Listen, now, to the Air Variée of the celebrated De Beriot; under these fingers, which are yet often busied with dressing a doll, the instrument gives out a purity and sweetness of tone, with an expression most remarkable. Every light and shade is observed, and all the intentions of the composer are faithfully rendered. Here come more energetic passages: the feeble child will find strength necessary, and the voice of the instrument assumes a fulness which one could not look for in the diminutive violin. Effects of double stopping, staccato, rapid arpeggios, — everything is executed with the same precision, the same purity, the same grace. It is impossible to describe the ovation that the child received. Repeatedly interrupted by applause and acclamations, she was saluted at the end by salvos of bravos and a shower of bouquets."

Soon after this Signor Urso went to Paris, resigning his position at Nantes for the purpose of giving the most thorough musical education to the daughter of whose genius he was so proud. He proposed that she should be received into the Conservatoire.

The professors met the proposition with incredulity and amazement. "Absurd, indeed!" they said; "she is too young, and a woman cannot be a pupil of the Conservatoire." But Signor Urso persisted. "Only hear her," he said, "before deciding." So the little sprite appeared before the most exacting, the most critical of juries. Auber, Rossini, Meyerbeer, and Massart were among the judges.

They retired for a decision, and at the door the little appli cant and the trembling father waited. At last the answer came. The new pupil was accepted unanimously. The father's hat went into the air with triumph.

For three years Camilla studied almost incessantly. No advantages were wanting to the young aspirant for musical honors. Simon was her first teacher, but her chief instructor was Massart, who took an extraordinary interest in the development of her powers. He received her into his class, and gave her, in addition, private lessons. All this instruction was gratuitous.

From this time she had no opportunity for the amusements other children enjoy. She practised ten and twelve hours a day, learning harmony, solfeggi, and mastering difficulties far beyond her years. To acquire that steadiness of position for which she is now so remarkable, she placed one foot in a saucer while playing. Fear of breaking the dish was a sufficient motive to keep her feet motionless; and to this simple contrivance we are indebted, in part, for Madame Urso's wonderful accuracy and agreeable repose of manner.

The years of training were interrupted by a series of concerts in the departments and a three months' tour in Germany. This was a special indulgence, as pupils of the Conservatoire are not allowed to play in public. Camilla performed at Heidelberg, Baden-Baden, and Mayence, receiving everywhere the recognition due to an artist, not to a prodigy. That German public, so devoted to music in its highest forms, led by masters of such varied genius, took the child to its heart. Nobles and princes paid her compliments and bestowed beautiful presents upon her. A countess, who took the most affectionate interest in her, insisted on giving her an ornament she had worn at her own confirmation,—a large cross of pearls attached to a long chain of red coral.

From these triumphs she returned to Paris and her studies with Massart.

In a few months she appeared at the public concerts of Paris, at the Salle Herz, the Société Polytechnique, the Conservatoire, and the Association of Musical Artists. Her success was great. A critic, speaking of her at this time, says:—

"She is walking in the steps of the greatest *virtuosi*. She plays the violin, not as a well-organized child might play after a certain period devoted to study, but, indeed, with a skill truly prodigious. Her *pose*, her energy, her bowing, reveal the consummate artist. But what is most surprising is the sentiment of her execution; she excels in that essential expression which comes wholly from the soul, and which the composer, from lack of means to note and write out, abandons to the discretion and intelligence of the executant."

At the age of nine she performed before Louis Napoleon, then President of the National Convention. He was greatly delighted with her playing, and promised that, if he should ever advance in position and influence, she might claim his protection, and he would be happy to do her any favor in his power. The wily "Man of Destiny," whose ambition was even then planning the renewal of the empire, and an attempted mastership of Europe, has probably forgotten the pledge. Camilla has never reminded him of it, preferring to depend on her own powers for all place she may hold in the world's esteem.

In 1852 the little Urso received propositions from a Mr. Faugas, of North Carolina, to come to America. He offered her a salary of twenty thousand dollars a year; and, as the family was in need of the assistance the child's violin could give, the offer was gladly accepted.

Preparations were made for an extensive tour, and a concert-troupe of eight was engaged. Auber, hearing of her intended departure, presented her with the following testimonial, which she justly regards as one of her dearest treasures: —

"NATIONAL CONSERVATORY OF MUSIC AND OF DECLAMATION.

"PARIS, *August* 12, 1852.

"Mademoiselle Camilla Urso is a young pupil of the National Conservatory of Music. Although still at a very tender age, she has obtained brilliant success in several concerts in Paris, and above all at the Conservatory, where the jury have decreed to her by election the first prize at the competition for the prizes of the year.

"Learning that she is soon to depart for the United States, I am delighted to state the happy qualities which ought to ensure her a noble artistic career.

"The Americans have already nobly proved that they are not only just appreciators of the fine arts, especially of music, but that they know as well how to recompense with generosity the merits of the celebrated artists who are heard in the hospitable towns of their rich and beautiful country.

"AUBER,
"Member of the Institute,
"Director of the Conservatory."

The child-artist came to this country with her father, but they soon discovered the insinuating Faugas to be a swindler. The moneys for Camilla's services were not forthcoming, and the engagement was hastily broken.

The Germania Society now offered an engagement, and the little Urso played for them a year, meeting everywhere with great applause and admiration. At the end of the year she joined Madame Alboni, who was then singing in this country, and performed at six concerts with her in Trippler Hall, New York.

In 1852 Madame Henriette Sontag, Countess Rossi, came to this country to make a trial of the public which had received Jenny Lind with such enthusiasm and generosity. She won honors everywhere by her dramatic talent and marvellous voice.

Hearing of Camilla Urso's success, she proposed to add her to her own concert-troupe. At the conclusion of his daughter's engagement with Alboni, Signor Urso accepted the overtures of Sontag, and Camilla joined her at Cincinnati, in December, 1853.

Brief as was their connection, the most tender relations were established between them. Nothing could be more beautiful than the sight of this magnificent woman, who was then the imperial mistress of song, surrounding with truly maternal kindness the lonely little novice whom chance had brought to her arms.

The generous affection of Madame Sontag was never forgotten by the child, and the now famous violinist speaks of her benefactress with a devotion which years cannot diminish.

"She was perfection—an angel, in talents, temper, and goodness. At fifty-two one would kneel to her,—what must she have been at twenty? She herself took the place of my mother, who was not in America. She plaited my hair, attended to my dresses, and cared for me in everything."

Camilla accompanied Madame Sontag to New Orleans, where they gave eighteen concerts, followed by six weeks of opera, in which Madame Sontag was the star. The two artists created a genuine *furore*, exciting their Southern audiences to the highest pitch of enthusiasm. Bouquets came in showers, and the applause was incessant. One night Madame Sontag carried eighty-six bouquets from the stage, and the fairy violinist often received fifteen or twenty.

From New Orleans Madame Sontag went to Mexico, and Camilla never saw her again. They parted in March, 1854, and Signor Urso took his daughter to Savannah, and subsequently gave concerts in different cities of Georgia and some other Southern States. They then returned to New York, where, in May, they heard of the sudden death of Madame Sontag by cholera.

The news of this loss prostrated the sensitive child with grief. She refused to appear at concerts, and seemed to lose all animation and vivacity. A change of scene was at last imperatively necessary, and she went with her father to Canada in 1856.

This trip was very successful, though not entirely professional. She travelled through the country, giving some concerts, and winning admiration from crowded houses.

One incident of her trip was very enjoyable,—her reception on board of a French corvette. The officers desired to do honor to their gifted little compatriot, and invited her to visit them. She was then a charming young lady of fourteen. She appeared before her admiring friends in a costume combining the three national colors of France. The gallant marines showed her a hundred graceful attentions, presented her with bouquets, and she, in return, bewitched them with the music of her violin.

While in Canada she met with a serious loss. Her collection of presents, containing a magnificent bracelet presented by the Germania Society; her cross of pearls with its chain of coral, and other ornaments of great value, prized as the souvenirs of her childhood's triumphs, and her European residence, were in New York. On the 22d of February, 1859, when the people of the house where she had left her property had gone to see the annual parade in honor of Washington's birthday, some one entered and possessed himself of her jewels. Search was unavailing, nothing was ever again heard of them.

On her return from Canada her mother met her in New York. The joy of mother and daughter, reunited after so long a separation, may easily be imagined. They spent some time together, and then professional duties called the child away. She had received overtures from a Mrs. McCready, a reader of some celebrity at that time, to accompany her in a tour through the West. They proceeded as far as Nashville, Signor Urso remaining in New York, when Camilla discovered that the contract was not to be fulfilled, the readings not to be continued, — in short, that she had fallen once more into the hands of swindlers. The McCreadys, after treating her with great injustice and unkindness, left her penniless in Nashville. A pitiful position for a young girl scarcely fifteen years old! But Camilla's courage and resources were fully equal to the occasion. This timid creature, who had always relied entirely on her father's advice and direction, — who had not been educated into that habit of self-reliance so frequently a characteristic of American girls, — determined to give a concert herself. She wrote to her friends giving information of the state of affairs, and then applied to a musician of the city for some counsel as to time and place. She enlisted the sympathy of the citizens of Nashville. The result was a full house, and four hundred dollars for the empty pocket.

Soon after this she retired from public life. For five years she did not appear in a professional character except for charitable purposes. But the cherished violin did not lose its power in these years of quiet. She learned more of life, and through varied experience her genius grew.

When she returned to the concert hall, on the 16th of March, 1863, at a Philharmonic concert in New York, she won instantly her old place, and "rained influence" upon us with those calm wavings of her enchanted bow. She was soon engaged to play at the Philharmonic concerts in Boston. In the autumn of 1863 she received a beautiful gift from some of the modern Athenians in the form of a watch and chain, —the watch decorated with green enamel, and a diamond of great value. On one side of the watch was engraved,—

"CAMILLA URSO.
FROM HER BOSTON FRIENDS.
NOV. 8th, 1863."

The gift was enclosed in a velvet box, bearing upon the cover her initials in gold within a laurel wreath.

Engagements now crowded upon her, and she visited in succession most of the cities that had known her as a child, spending much time in Boston, New York, and Chicago.

In 1864 she went to Europe, sailing in the "China," on the 26th of August. Reaching Liverpool she prepared at once to go to Paris,—her home for some years, and the scene of some of her earliest triumphs. She was wonderfully successful in this centre of art, and became the "lioness of the saloons."

Pasdeloup's monster orchestra was then performing in the Cirque Napoleon. Paris, with all its superb theatres has no large music hall. Camilla Urso was invited to play with this orchestra, and played, at one of their concerts, Mendelssohn's great concerto.

The minister of fine arts, Count Newerkerque, sent for her to play at the palace of the Louvre. Never had she performed before so distinguished an assembly as there in the beautiful cabinet of the minister. Two hundred and fifty gentlemen were present. Diplomatists, princes, and soldiers, with their hard-won crosses, rendered homage to the fair violinist, who saw with delight the faces of Alexander Dumas, Lord Cowley, and Professor Alard. Her finest morceau on this occasion was a Fantasie-Caprice of Vieuxtemps.

From Paris she went to Arras, Boulogne, Valenciennes, and Cambray. At Boulogne she appeared at two successive concerts given by the Musical Society of that town, — a circumstance almost unknown in the records of the society.

After spending fourteen months abroad, she returned to America, where she has remained ever since. Her life since then has been the same story of travel, study, and concerts. She has become a great favorite both in the East and West.

What Boston thinks of her may be understood from the fact that she has given more than one hundred concerts in that city. There she feels herself entirely at home, surrounded by sympathetic and appreciative friends. One of the sincerest and most highly prized of all tributes to her musical accomplishments is a letter, which was addressed to her, after a concert in Music Hall, by the musicians of the orchestra of the "Harvard Association:" —

"We, the undersigned, members of the musical profession in Boston, who have been recently witnesses of the extraordinary musical talent displayed by Camilla Urso, in her performances on the violin, deem it our pleasure and duty as brethren (who, it may be admitted, are the more thoroughly capable of recognizing skill in this department of the art) to offer some fitting testimonial to her. In no way, perhaps, can we express our regard so beneficially as by giving to the public a professional estimate of her ability.

"We would especially record her performance of the violin concerto by Mendelssohn, — one of the most difficult works for that instrument; her playing of which was so marvellously fine and near perfection itself as to excite our highest admiration. It is not enough to say that it was a wonderful performance for a woman; it was a consummate rendering, which probably few men living could improve upon.

"It may seem needless to characterize her playing, but a few traits may be pointed out, namely, her complete repose of manner; largeness of style; broad, full, and vigorous attacking of difficulties; utmost delicacy of sentiment and feeling; wonderful staccato; remarkable finish in trills, with an intonation as nearly perfect as the human ear will allow. When to these are added a comprehensive mind, with a warm musical soul vibrating to its work, we have an artist who may be nearly called a phenomenon in the womanly form of Camilla Urso.

"Signed by the whole orchestra, namely, Carl Zerrahn, William Schultze, William Wieser, Stephen A. Emery, Carl Meisel, Otto Dresel, Thomas Ryan, Wulf C. J. Fries, B. J. Lang, Ernst Perabo," etc.

The outside world of mere lovers of music sometimes give their opinions of Camilla's playing in remarks equally earnest, though hardly scientific. One auditor, after listening to her in wide-mouthed amazement, declared with a most emphatic gesture, that she was "woman enough to vote." At a concert in Chicago, an admirer, who was asked whether there had been any flowers on the stage that night, answered, "None but Camelia Urso."

In the spring of 1865, soon after her return from Europe, Madame Urso played at a concert in New Haven. The hall was crowded with a noisy audience, composed mainly of students, irrepressible and critical, and young ladies who were deeply occupied with them and their criticisms. The unhappy pianist of the occasion met with hearty contempt. The talking went on as gayly as ever. But when the violinist entered, with her simple, natural manner, and stood quietly a moment waiting, the house was hushed. First she played a brilliant Fantaisie of Vieuxtemps, displaying all her skill in the execution of musical difficulties. Every one followed her with the most eager attention. At the end came hearty applause, and an imperative recall. "The Last Rose of Summer" was her answer to the waiting crowd. Tenderly, wearily, the notes of the familiar air breathed to us of regret far beyond the sentimental lament of Moore's song. Not a movement disturbed the flow of the melody. The quiet of sadness seemed to hold the listeners. The music ceased, she bowed once more, but the audience would not permit a withdrawal. She seemed unwilling, at first, to respond to this *encore*, — this tribute often more tiresome than flattering. But, after a minute's indecision, the violin went up to her shoulder again, and the very genius of fun seemed to possess it. She played "Yankee Doodle," but the spirit of the monotonous old tune was surely transmigrated into a robin, drunk with the intoxicating air of some June morning. It was surely a bird who took up the quaint refrain, and repeated it again and again with mocking variations in frolicsome abandonment. The audience, a few minutes ago half ready to weep, laughed and applauded by turns, in full sympathy with the versatile artist. Players often execute tricks with the strings that are laughter-provoking, mere legerdemain, as meretricious as it is inartistic, but seldom has such an airy spirit of humor expressed itself through the violin.

A little story found its way into the "Musical Gazette" recently, which is so characteristic that it ought to be quoted entire.

Ole Bull, Camilla Urso, and Miss Alida Topp met at a party, a few evenings since.

"You play beautifully, my child," said the Norwegian to Miss Topp, "but you can't do the greatest music. No *woman* can; it takes the biceps of a man."

"*My* arm is strong enough," answered the brilliant young pianist, laughing; "I break *my* pianos as well as a man could, and Steinway has to send me a new one every week."

"You see," responded Ole Bull, turning to Madame Urso, "you see how these people treat their pianos. They bang them, they beat them, they kick them, they smash them to pieces; but our fiddles! *how we love them!*"

"Oh, yes, indeed," was Camilla's earnest answer, with a flash of her most expressive eyes.

Her fiddles are three, her favorite one being a Guiseppe Guamarius, made in 1737. For this she has a standing offer of $2000 in gold. An Amati is also in her little collection, and the prize violin of the Exposition of 1867, made by C. A. Miremont, which was sent her at the close of the Exposition. Her bow was made in 1812.

The grave, and frequently sad expression of Madame Urso's face, during her performances, has given rise to many anecdotes of her life which are absurdly untrue.

All who love the charming artist will be glad to know that family sufferings do not add to the pathos of her "Elegies," and that beatings are not reserved for the patient mistress of the bow.

Those who have the pleasure of her acquaintance know that a more genial, sunny enthusiast does not exist than the supposed victim of marital cruelty. Simple in her tastes, single-minded in her devotion to her art, she denies herself society, and lives for her violin and her few cherished friends. She is no idler, satisfied with the attainments of the past, but steadily works her way to new laurels. Seven and eight hours a day is her usual time of practice, and in the long summer days, when other artists seek change or diversion, she finds her recreation in her beloved instrument.

On being asked whether she composed for her violin, she answered, "Yes, some little pieces, — the Mother's Prayer, the Dream, — but they are nothing. It is enough for me to render the works of the great masters."

In her childlike devotion to the genius of Beethoven, Chopin, and Mendelssohn, she reminds one of Hilda, the girl-artist of Hawthorne's "Marble Faun," whose life was spent in study of Raphael and Michael Angelo. It is better, thinks this earnest woman, to render vocal the great conceptions of the past, than to win a cheap reputation by fleeting musical mediocrities.

Her remarkable memory retains all the music she plays, the orchestral parts as well as her own.

Madame Urso's stay in this country is now uncertain. Her latest performances have been in the New England cities, and in New York. She has accepted an engagement in California, and will probably leave for San Francisco in July. Her ardent desire is to return to Paris, and make that city her home. If she leaves us, it will be with the possibility of coming again to America, at some time in the distant future. She will take with her a thousand good wishes, and leave behind her memories of delight.

HARRIET G. HOSMER.

BY REV. R. B. THURSTON.

THE number of women who have acquired celebrity in the art of painting is large; but half a score would probably include all the names of those who have achieved greatness in sculpture. Without raising the question whether women are intellectually the equals of men, or the other question, which some affirm and some deny, whether there is "sex of the soul," they differ; and there are manifest reasons of the hand, the eye, and the taste, for which it should be anticipated that they would generally neglect the one department of æsthetic pursuits, and cultivate the other with distinguished success. The palette, the pencil, and colors fall naturally to their hands; but mallets and chisels are weighty and painful implements, and masses of wet clay, blocks of marble, and castings of bronze are rude and intractable materials for feminine labors. Sculpture has special hindrances for woman, — though not for any lack of power in her conception and invention, yet in the manual difficulties of the art itself. But genius and earnestness overcome all obstacles, and supply untiring strength; and the world give honorable recognition to those women who have, with a spirit of vigor and heroism, challenged a place by the side of their brothers as statuaries, and have with real success brought out the form of beauty and the expression of life and passion which sleep in the shapeless and silent stone.

Engd. by Augustus Robin. N.Y.

HARRIET G. HOSMER.

One of the most remarkable examples is found in the subject of the following sketch. The materials from which it is composed are derived from much correspondence, for which we are under special obligations to Wayman Crow, Esq., of St. Louis, the early friend of the artist, and to Dr. Alfred Hosmer, her kinsman, now of Watertown, Mass.; from notices and descriptions of her works in various periodicals, and from narratives published several years ago by Mrs. L. Maria Child, in a Western magazine, and Mrs. Ellet, in her volume of the "Artist Women of all Ages and Countries." The latter gives a consistent portraiture of Miss Hosmer, but has been led into inaccuracies in regard to several of the alleged facts. The notice of Tuckerman, in his book of "American Artist Life," is quite too meagre to be just and valuable. Mrs. Child, who was a family friend, and at one time nearest neighbor of Dr. Hosmer, and who wrote in his house, furnished a very pleasing and reliable sketch. Great care has been taken to preserve in these pages everything which is valuable, and to exclude whatever is not authentic.

Harriet G. Hosmer was born in Watertown, Mass., October 9, 1830. Undoubtedly she was endowed with rare genius by nature; and the incidents of her early life evidently conduced much to its development in her chosen pursuit, and to the bold and unique traits of character for which she is distinguished.

Her father was an eminent physician, whose wife and elder daughter died of consumption while she was yet a child, leaving her the only domestic solace of his afflictions, and hope of his heart. She inherited a delicate constitution, and, as if he saw the same spectral hand which had desolated his home reaching out for her, he made the preservation of her health the first consideration in his system of juvenile training. It was a maxim with him, "There is a whole lifetime for the education of the mind; but the body develops in a few years, and, during that time, nothing should be allowed to interfere with its free and healthy growth."

In her early childhood Harriet was much abroad, usually accompanied by a little dog, which she tricked out with gay ribbons and small, tinkling bells; while her fearless ways and bright, pleasant features often drew the attention of strangers. Dr. Hosmer's house stood near the bank of the Charles River, and her youth was inured to skating, rowing, and swimming, as well as archery, shooting, and riding. Horse, boat, and weapons were supplied, and diligently she improved them. She became remarkable for dashing boldness, skill, and grace. She could tramp with a hunter, manage her steed like an Arabian, rival the most fearless in the chase, and the best marksmen with gun and pistol, and astonish and alarm her friends by her feats upon and in the water, as agile and varied as those of a sea-nymph.

Machinery very early excited her interest. Her questions elicited information, and her ingenuity appeared in little contrivances for her own amusement. A clay-pit near home afforded materials, and there she spent many hours in modelling horses, dogs, and other objects which attracted her attention.

The fruits of her tastes and her prowess gradually found their place in the house. Her own room became a cabinet of natural history, and the curious works of her youthful genius. Game, furred and feathered, which her gun had brought down, dissected and stuffed by her own hands, butterflies and beetles in glass cases, and reptiles preserved in spirits covered the walls. An inkstand was made of a sea-gull's egg and the body of a kingfisher. Among her trophies a crow's nest, which she climbed a lofty tree to obtain during her school-days at Lenox, rested, after she had gained fame in Italy, on the stand which she had made for it.

While she was thus securing physical health and power of endurance, her mind was growing as well; but not without certain incidental disadvantages from the free, wild, and even rude manner of its development. Books did not suit her active temperament and her taste for concrete things. Of education and culture in the sense of the schools, during the years of childhood, she had little. In this respect she resembles Rosa Bonheur, who found her early education chiefly in the lessons of nature learned out of doors. Her sports and the prophetic labors of the clay-pit beguiled many of the hours of study; and, very naturally, through her unrestrained liberty and occupations usually regarded as suitable only for boys, she acquired much of the character and manners of a brave, roguish boy. She was an intractable pupil, and if the report is correct was "expelled from one school, and given over as incorrigible at another." Nevertheless it is said, "Those who knew her well loved her dearly," and defended her from criticism with the testimony, "There is never any immodesty in her fearlessness, nor any malice in her fun." Yet at this period she was a mystery to her friends. There is good testimony at hand that "her own father confessed again and again his ignorance" of her.

It is little matter, so long as there is no moral damage, when outrage is done to mere conventionalities; and great gain to health, enjoyment, enterprise, and genius may well raise inquiry whether a public sentiment in regard to the education of girls has not prevailed quite too much to the effect that they should be

> "Ground down enough
> To flatten and bake into a wholesome crust
> For household uses and proprieties."

Anecdotes abound in illustration of Miss Hosmer's untamed frolicsomeness and disposition to practical jokes. In one of those moods of unlicensed humor she caused to be published in the Boston papers a notice of the death of an aged and retired physician then residing in her native village. His friends, moved by the intelligence, came from the city to make inquiries concerning the sudden event, and to offer their condolence.

This incident led to the first important transition in her life; for it convinced her father that some new measures were essential in her education; and, after careful inquiry, in her sixteenth year, Miss Hosmer was placed in the celebrated school of Mrs. Sedgwick, in Lenox, Berkshire County, Massachusetts. Dr. Hosmer frankly informed Mrs. Sedgwick of his daughter's history and peculiar traits, and that teachers had found her difficult to manage. The pupil was received with the remark, "I have a reputation for training wild colts, and I will try this one."

With the old anxiety, and in accordance with his fixed principle of securing the physical development first, and the mental afterwards, Dr. Hosmer had stipulated that her athletic exercises should be continued. They were, indeed, included in the training of the school; but in all the feats of strength, courage, and agility, Harriet was the wonder of her companions.

Mrs. Fanny Kemble was accustomed to spend summers at Lenox, and was an intimate friend of the Sedgwicks. Surprising anecdotes are related by eye-witnesses of her strength and her equestrian feats. Miss Hosmer enjoyed opportunities of hearing her reading and conversation, and received from her friendly encouragement in her art-career, which was afterwards gratefully acknowledged. Her passion for sculpture found exercise in making plaster casts of the hands of her mates. Her room was decorated, as before at home, with the trophies of the hunt and the spoils of the woods.

She remained three years under the judicious care of Mrs. Sedgwick, forming permanent friendships in the school, becoming acquainted with many persons of eminence, moulded by society of the first order, and inspired by the romantic mountain scenery, — a combination of influences of nature and of life, which, in her father's judgment, were highly conducive to the success she so early attained. When in her nineteenth year she returned to Watertown, much improved by the wise direction given to her energies, her early predilections ripened into a purpose to make sculpture her pursuit. She had a thought, — she must make it a thing.

Having this end in view, she entered the studio of Mr. Stephenson, in Boston, for lessons in drawing and modelling, frequently walking the distance from home and back of fourteen miles, besides performing her æsthetic tasks. Under his instruction she completed a beautiful portrait-bust of a child, and a spirited head of Byron in wax.

To perfect herself in anatomy, so essential to the sculptor, Miss Hosmer desired, in addition to all she could learn from books and her father, the knowledge which can be obtained only in the dissecting-room. The Boston Medical School had refused a request for the admission of a woman, but the Medical College of St. Louis afforded the required facilities. Prof. McDowell gave her efficient aid, and sometimes private lectures, when she was present while he prepared for his public demonstrations. She acknowledged her obligations to him "with great affection and gratitude, as being a most thorough and patient teacher, as well as at all times a good, kind friend;" and afterwards confirmed her words by presenting to him a medallion likeness, cut in marble from a bust by Clevenger. She received a diploma for her attainments.

Friendship added charms to the pursuit of science in St. Louis. At Lenox she had formed an affectionate intimacy with a school-mate, the daughter of Mr. Wayman Crow, an eminent citizen of that city. An invitation to visit there had incidentally opened way to the scientific privileges she sought; while in his family she found her residence, and in him, she says, "the best friend I ever had."

In that Western city, as aforetime, Miss Hosmer set at defiance the conventional rules which ordinarily govern, and perhaps too much afflict, young women, both by entering the classes for instruction, and by her transits by day or evening from the dwelling to the college, as well as by her customary exercises. The tongue of animadversion could not, perhaps, be entirely silent, even though, in that new region, with its fresh social freedom, she might be less exposed to censure than in the older and more staid New England; but it is asserted to the credit of the members of the college that she suffered no annoyance from them. Some may believe that a knowledge of her prowess in the use of deadly weapons was her security, — for it would be little honor to fall by a woman's shot, — and others may hold that blamelessness without affectation, integrity, and earnestness of character in a high pursuit are their own best protection, — safer than any rules of a suspicious and prudish propriety. She justified herself to her friends, gained their hearts by her vivacious and genial qualities in the domestic circle, and preserved unsullied honor.

Before her final departure from St. Louis for her native place, she resolved to see as much of the West as possible. It was the dry and warm season of the year, and the navigation of the Father of waters was uncertain and difficult. She embarked for New Orleans; spent several days in that city, making herself acquainted with its objects of interest, sleeping on board of the steamer, and returned, attended all the way by her usual good fortune. Without stopping so long as to greet her friends, she ascended the river to the Falls of St. Anthony, on a challenge from the captain of the boat, scaling a lofty cliff, which had been regarded as inaccessible, with the courage and agility of an Alpine hunter, and which according to his promise, received the name of Hosmer's

Height; visited the Dacotah Indians, smoking the pipe of peace with the chief, which was afterwards preserved in "the old house at home;" and explored the lead mines at Dubuque, narrowly escaping a fatal accident there, which would have left her friends in ignorance of her fate; for they did not know where the spirit of adventure had led her; and her arrival at St. Louis again was the relief of their anxiety.

These happy months over, she returned to her father's house and her art. Ever ready to indulge and facilitate her purpose, Dr. Hosmer fitted up a small studio for her convenience in his garden, which she called facetiously her shop. There she wrought out various contrivances of mechanical ingenuity, and produced her first work in marble, — a reduced copy of Canova's bust of Napoleon, for her father. The labor was performed by her own hands, that she might be practically familiar with every part of the process. The likeness and workmanship are both good.

Soon afterwards she commenced Hesper, — her first original and ideal work. Mrs. Child, who saw it in the garden studio in the summer of 1852, by Dr. Hosmer's invitation, gives the following account of its execution and description, which were published in the "New York Tribune," under the caption, "A New Star in the Arts:" —

"She did every stroke of the work with her own small hands, except knocking off the corners of the block of marble. She employed a man to do that; but as he was unused to work for sculptors, she did not venture to have him approach within several inches of the surface she intended to cut. Slight girl as she was, she wielded for eight or ten hours a day, a leaden mallet weighing four pounds and a half. Had it not been for the strength and flexibility of muscle acquired by rowing and other athletic exercises, such arduous labor would have been impossible.

"I expected to see skilful workmanship; but I was not

prepared for such a poetic conception. This beautiful production of Miss Hosmer's hand and soul has the face of a lovely maiden, gently falling asleep to the sound of distant music. Her hair is gracefully arranged, and intertwined with capsules of the poppy. A polished star gleams on her forehead, and under her breast lies the crescent moon. The hush of evening breathes from the serene countenance and the heavily drooping eyelids. I felt tranquillized while looking at it, as I do when the rosy clouds are fading into gray twilight, and the pale moon-sickle descends slowly behind the dim woods. The mechanical execution of this bust seemed to me worthy of its lovely and lifelike expression. The swell of cheek and breast is like pure, young, healthy flesh; and the muscles of the beautiful mouth are so delicately cut, that it seems like a thing that breathes."

Hesper was presented by the artist to her friend, Miss Coolidge, of Boston.

When it was completed she said to her father, "Now I am ready to go to Rome." Rome is the Mecca of artists. The tomb of the prophet is not more attractive to devout Mussulmen than its æsthetic treasures to all the children of genius. They flow thither from every cultivated nation, for the study of the noblest models, the inheritance of ancient and modern ages, for the sympathy and encouragement of companions in aspirations and toils, for the exhilaration and joy of artistic fellowship,—perhaps, also, for the indispensable end of more favorable opportunities for making known their works and of obtaining remuneration for their life-labors; and they often encounter as well the trials which spring from our poor nature, and allow no paradise on earth,—the envy, jealousy, bitter criticism, and aspersion of partakers and competitors in the same pursuits and the same glories.

About this time Miss Hosmer formed acquaintance with

Miss Charlotte Cushman, who recognized her ability, and kindled her desire to study at Rome to a flame. It was arranged that her father, whose affection and devotion to his daughter seemed to equal her energy and enthusiasm, should accompany her there, and leave her, returning himself to his profession.

She rode on horseback to Wayland to bid farewell to her friend, Mrs. Child, and said, in reply to the questions, "Shall you never be homesick for your museum parlor in Watertown? Can you be contented in a foreign land?" "I can be happy anywhere with good health and a bit of marble."

Lingering only a week in England, in her eager haste, she arrived at "the Eternal City" November 12, 1852. John Gibson, the most renowned of English sculptors of this century, was then in the zenith of his fame. It was the young artist's strong desire to become his pupil, — a desire clouded with much apprehension, because it had been intimated that want of persistency in overcoming difficulties on the part of ladies had brought disappointment upon instructors; and the success of her application was extremely doubtful. But two days after the arrival a friendly sculptor laid before him, as he sat at breakfast at the Café Gréco, two daguerreotypes, the one presenting a front, the other a profile view of Hesper, and stated briefly Miss Hosmer's history and desire. Mr. Gibson contemplated them silently for a few moments and then said, "Send the young lady to me, — whatever I can teach her, she shall learn." The "London Art Journal" asserts that she was received by Mr. Gibson, "not as a professed pupil, but as the artist friend of our countryman." Mrs. Ellet writes, "Ere long a truly paternal and filial affection sprung up between the master and the pupil, a source of great happiness to themselves, and of pleasure and amusement to all who know and value them, from the curious likeness, yet unlikeness, which existed from the first in Miss Hosmer to Mr. Gibson, and which daily intercourse has not tended to lessen." She expressed her joy in the new relation in a letter. "The dearest wish of my heart is gratified in that I am acknowledged by Gibson as a pupil. He has been resident in Rome thirty-four years, and leads the van. I am greatly in luck. He has just finished the model of the statue of the queen; and, as his room is vacant, he permits me to use it, and I am now in his own studio. I have also a little room for work which was formerly occupied by Canova, and perhaps inspiration may be drawn from the walls."

The approach to the apartment she occupied was from the Via Fontanella through a large room containing numerous productions of Mr. Gibson's genius, a garden filled with orange and lemon trees and various flowers, a fountain trickling in a shady recess, then the master's studio, and from this by a flight of stairs within a curtain, — nature, imagination, and labor, all at one. She remained seven years in the studio of her teacher and friend.

The first winter in Rome was spent in modelling from the antique. The Venus of Milo, the Cupid of Praxiteles, and Tasso of the British Museum, were copied, in which the pupil proved the correctness of her eye, the soundness of her knowledge, and power of imitating the roundness and softness of flesh, which Mr. Gibson on one occasion stated he had never seen surpassed and rarely equalled. Her faculty of original conception had been evinced before in Hesper.

Her first design was the bust of Daphne, the beautiful maiden changed into a laurel when fleeing from Apollo, after the god had slain her lover, beseeching the earth to swallow her up. It is now in the possession of her liberal patron and friend of St. Louis, W. Crow.

It was speedily followed by the Medusa, represented as she was before she was transformed into a gorgon. The hair, retreating in waves from the forehead, changes into serpents. It is described as a "lovely thing, faultless in form, and intense in its expression of horror and agony, without trenching on the physically painful." It is owned by Mrs. Appleton, of Boston.

"These busts," wrote Mr. Gibson, "do her great honor." They were publicly exhibited in Boston in 1853. The next year Mr. Gibson wrote to Dr. Hosmer, to give him assurance of his daughter's unabated industry and success in her profession, relating also the favorable judgment of the Prussian Rauch, then very aged and one of the greatest of living sculptors.

In the summer of 1855 Miss Hosmer completed Œnone, her first full-length figure in marble. Œnone was a nymph of mount Ida, who became the wife of Paris, the beautiful shepherd, to whom Venus had promised the fairest woman in the world. The statue represents her as a shepherdess, bending with grief for her husband's desertion. Her crook lies on the ground. It was sent to Mr. Crow, who had given her, at her departure from America, an order for her first statue, to be filled in her own time by a subject of her own selection. It is a very beautiful production, and afforded such satisfaction that she was commissioned to execute another, on the same terms, for the Mercantile Library of St. Louis.

This order was answered after two years by the life-size statue of Beatrice Cenci, sleeping in her cell, after having been subjected to extreme torture, the morning before her execution.

Her father, a monster who deserved double death, but had escaped public justice by his wealth, had been assassinated. The daughter was accused of parricide, and, though guiltless, condemned. The marble expresses the sleep of innocence.

This was a very fine work. It was exhibited in London, and several American cities, where it received high encomiums. A beautiful engraving of it was published in the "London Art Journal" with honorable criticism. Mr. Gibson is said to have remarked, on viewing it completed, "I can teach her nothing." It was a gift to the library, of an unknown friend to the artist.

The insalubrity of the Campagna, the level country surrounding Rome, is well known. Southward is the region of the Pontine marshes, of ancient malarious fame, on which consuls, emperors, and popes have made vast expenditures, without subduing the malignity of nature. The pestilential air still spreads pallor over the features of the poor people who are compelled to live there, and even invades the city. It was the wish of Dr. Hosmer that his daughter should take refuge in some healthy place during the sickly season, and the first summer was passed at Sorrento, on the bay of Naples. The next year her zeal prevailed against all considerations of prudence; she would not leave the shadow of St. Peter's and the art treasures in the midst of which she wrought. The third summer, 1855, came, and she prepared for a journey to England. But the course of true art, like that of love, does not always run smoothly. The resources of Dr. Hosmer were not inexhaustible; the expenses of the artist's residence and pursuits in Rome were large; financial embarrassments were encountered; and retrenchment was urged with emphasis from home. In these circumstances she remained to prosecute her labors with the aim to produce some work of such attractive character as should secure immediate returns. The result was Puck, described by Shakespeare's fairy: —

"Either I mistake your shape and making quite,
Or else you are that shrewd and knavish sprite
Called Robin Good-fellow; are you not he
That fright the maidens of the villagery;
Skim milk; and sometimes labor in the quern,
And bootless make the breathless housewife churn;
And sometimes make the drink to bear no barm;
Mislead night-wanderers laughing at their harm?
Those that Hobgoblin call you, and sweet Puck,
You do their work; and they shall have good luck."

It is about the size of a child four years of age, seated on a toadstool which splits beneath its weight. The lips are pouting; a muscle-shell cleaves to the forehead at the parting of the hair; the left hand rests, confining under it a lizard; the right hand holds a beetle, and is raised in the act of throwing; the legs are crossed, and the great toe of the right foot turns pertly up; — the whole composing a figure of so much drollery and fun, that those who have seen it, when describing it, are wont to break into a gleeful laugh. This unique impersonation of humor in marble, conceived, perhaps like some gems of humorous poetry and romance in the hour of adversity, has been very popular. Twenty-five or thirty copies have been made. One is in the collection of the Prince of Wales.

Puck was followed by a companion figure named Will-o'-the-Wisp.

At this time was resident in Rome Madame Falconnet, an English lady, whose daughter, a lovely girl of sixteen years, had recently died. Being a Catholic, she was permitted to erect a mortuary monument in the church of San Andrea del Fratte. The design was entrusted to Miss Hosmer. It was modelled in clay in the winter of 1857, and executed in marble a year later. It is a portrait statue of the daughter, the figure of a beautiful maiden, resting upon a sarcophagus, in the sleep that has no waking. In this production the still repose of death is finely contrasted with the breathing slumber of life, which even the stone expresses in Beatrice Cenci. Mr. Layard, distinguished for his explorations in Nineveh, thus speaks of it in a letter addressed to Madame Falconnet: "I think you may rest fully satisfied with Miss Hosmer's success. It exceeds any expectations I had formed. The unaffected simplicity and tender feeling displayed in the treatment is all that could be desired for such a subject, and cannot fail to touch the most casual observer. I scarcely remember ever to have seen a monument which more completely commanded my sympathy and more deeply interested me. I really know of none, of modern days, which I would rather have placed over the remains of one who had been dear to me. Do not believe this is exaggerated praise. I faithfully convey to you the impression made on me. I attribute this impression, not more to the artistic merit of the work than to the complete absence of all affectation, to the simple truthfulness and genuine feeling of the monument itself." Mr. Gibson concurred in this commendation.

This was the first instance of the work of a foreign sculptor finding a permanent place in Rome. It was a tribute of the high appreciation in which the artist was then held and was regarded as a great honor.

About the same period was modelled the fountain of Hylas In mythological story, Hylas, the adopted son of Hercules, when the Argonautic expedition stopped at Mysia, went to a well for water. The naiads of the fountain, enraptured with his beauty, drew him in, and he was drowned.

The design of the sculptor consists of a basin in which dolphins are spouting jets, and an upper basin supported by swans; from this rises a pyramid, on which the fair boy stands, while the nymphs reach up their hands to draw him into the waters at his feet. The conception is classically just and highly poetical.

Before the two works last described were executed in marble, in the summer of 1857, Miss Hosmer returned to America,—five years from her departure. She had become a daughter of fame, but was still a child of nature. Her vivacity remained; she was modest and unpretentious in her enthusiasm; and her aspirations were kindled for yet higher achievements in the realms of art.

During this visit her mind was much occupied with the design of a statue of Zenobia, Queen of Palmyra, as she appeared when led in chains in the triumphal procession of Aurelian. She searched libraries and read everything that could be found relating to that illustrious and unfortunate sovereign. Subsequently she labored upon it with so much assiduity and anxiety that her health was impaired, and she was ordered into Switzerland by her physician to save her life.

The statue is of colossal size, seven feet in height, a very noble figure, the commanding effect of which grows upon the mind,—a triumph of patient study, of genius, and of mechanical skill. Zenobia is represented walking. The movement has blended lightness, vigor, and grace. The left arm supports the drapery, which is elaborately cut; the right, without a purpose, for it can neither bless her people nor inspirit her troops, descends naturally as living muscle. The wrists bear the chains,—not heavy and galling,—perhaps Roman severity made them weightier. The head, crowned, is slightly bowed; the lips express disdain of the surrounding pageant of victorious foes; the eyes, downcast, and the features of oriental beauty reveal a soul self-sustained and absent, far away in memories of her magnificent empire of the East. She is still a queen in spirit, undethroned by calamity.

In this production Miss Hosmer made a bold, and, on the part of woman, an almost unexampled, adventure into the regions of the highest historic art; and she returned wearing the laurels of success. The statue received the highest praise. Critics pronounced its vindication in the light of the noblest models of Grecian art, and ascribed to it legitimate claims to a place in the front rank of works of sculpture. We well remember the impression it made in Boston, where we were scarcely more interested in the fascinating form itself, than in observing the effect it produced on the minds of visitors who, with quiet demeanor, speaking low, appeared like persons coming unwontedly under the influence of a spiritual power which arrested their steps and excited profound emotions. The poet Whittier says, "It very fully expresses my conception of what historical sculpture should be. It tells its whole proud and melancholy story. The shadowy outlines of the majestic limbs, which charmed us in the romance of Ware are here fixed and permanent: —

'A joy forever.'

In looking at it I felt that the artist had been as truly serving her country while working out her magnificent design abroad, as our soldiers in the field, and our public officers in their departments."

In another sense besides what those words convey the artist served her country. The marble was purchased by A. W. Griswold, Esq., of New York, and is now in his possession. By his generous consent after the time agreed upon for its delivery, it was exhibited for the benefit of the soldiers in the famous Sanitary Fair at Chicago; and there the stately queen, who for her grasp at power trod the dust of captivity in chains sixteen centuries ago, ministered relief to the sufferers of the war for the republic and liberty. It is an instance of the reproach, from which human nature is not always exempt, even in a good cause, that a part of the proceeds on that occasion was retained by the exhibitors.

Very few productions of the modern chisel have excited so much remark as Zenobia. There is an almost romantic story connected with its exhibition in London. The critics recognized its merits, but denied that such a statue ever was the work of a woman, charging Miss Hosmer with artistic plagiarism, and ascribing the real authorship to Mr. Gibson, or an Italian sculptor. An article making such assertions appeared in the "London Art Journal" and "The Queen." For this Miss Hosmer commenced a suit for libel; but soon after, the author of the libellous communication died; the suit was withdrawn on the condition that the editors should publish a retraction in those periodicals, and, also, in the "London Times" and "Galignani's Messenger," which was done. The retraction of the editor in the "Art Journal" was prefaced by a vigorous letter from the artist, in which the assertion occurs that Mr. Gibson would not allow any statue to go out of his studio, as the work of another, on which more assistance had been bestowed than was considered legitimate by every sculptor.

A large price was offered for Zenobia by the Prince of Wales; but the author said, "It must go to America." She received five thousand dollars from the proceeds, besides all expenses, of its exhibition for her benefit.

In the year 1860 Miss Hosmer revisited her native town, called there by the serious illness of her father. While tarrying once more at home she received a commission to design a bronze portrait statue of Col. Thomas Hart Benton, the distinguished senator and most eminent citizen of Missouri. Her former residence in St. Louis was remembered; and a degree of local pride was mingled with admiration for her success. Her friends knew her ability to express in marble beauty, tenderness, grace, and dignity; but thus far her works had been chiefly in the range of feminine characters. Could she depart from this sphere of art, and with equal skill set forth the strong, rugged, massive qualities of the famous statesman, and thus create for herself a reputation which need not bow before any difficulties, nor shrink from an enterprise requiring the most masculine capacity? The commissioners to the fullest extent trusted in the breadth and power of her genius. We append her reply to their communication, because it was so pertinent and characteristic of herself:—

"WATERTOWN, *June* 22, 1860.

"GENTLEMEN:—I have had the honor to receive your letter

of the 15th inst., informing me that the execution of the bronze statue, in memory of the late Col. Benton, for the city of St. Louis, is entrusted to me. Such a tribute to his merit would demand the best acknowledgment of any artist; but in the present instance my most cordial thanks will but insufficiently convey to you a sense of the obligation under which I feel you have placed me.

"I have reason to be grateful to you for this distinction, because I am a young artist; and, though I may have given some evidence of skill in those of my statues which are now in your city, I could scarcely have hoped that their merit, whatever it may be, should have inspired the citizens of St. Louis to entrust me with a work whose chief characteristic must be the union of great intellectual power with manly strength.

"But I have, also, reason to be grateful to you because I am a woman; and, knowing what barriers must in the outset oppose all womanly efforts, I am indebted to the chivalry of the West, which has first overleaped them. I am not unmindful of the kind indulgence with which my works have been received; but I have sometimes thought that the critics might be more courteous than just, remembering from what hand they proceeded; but your kindness will now afford me an ample opportunity of proving to what rank I am really entitled as an artist unsheltered by the broad wings of compassion for the sex; for this work must be, as we understand the term, a *manly* work; and hence its merit alone must be my defence against the attacks of those who stand ready to resist any encroachment upon their self-appropriated sphere.

"I utter these sentiments only to assure you that I am fully aware of the important results which to me as an artist wait on the issue of my labors, and hence, that I shall spare no pains to produce a monument worthy of your city, and worthy of the statesman who, though dead, still speaks to you in language more eloquent and enduring than the happiest efforts in marble and bronze of ever so cunning a workman.

"It only remains for me to add that as I shall visit St. Louis before my departure to Europe, further details may be then arranged. I have the honor to remain, gentlemen,

"Respectfully yours,

"H. G. HOSMER."

In accordance with her purpose, Miss Hosmer visited St. Louis, Jefferson City, and other places, examining portraits and mementos of Col. Benton to supply herself with materials for the work. The next year she submitted photographs of her model to the commissioners and to his relatives, by whom they were unanimously approved. The plaster cast was sent from Rome to Munich to be cast at the royal foundry, the most celebrated in the world. In due time the statue arrived at the city of its destination; but partly on account of the war, more especially on account of hesitation in regard to the site, it remained three years or more boxed as it came from Europe. The location was at last fixed in Lafayette Park; and on the 27th day of May, 1868, the inauguration of the statue took place with imposing religious and patriotic ceremonies, in presence of a vast concourse of citizens and strangers.

By an appropriate selection Mrs. Fremont, the daughter of Col. Benton, unveiled the features of her father in bronze to the eyes of the multitude. The figure is ten feet in height, and weighs three and a half tons. A foundation was laid for it forty feet square, which rises two feet above the ground. On that rests a pedestal of New England granite ten feet square, so that the entire elevation is twenty-two feet. The upper drapery is a cloak of the kind which Col. Benton was fond of wearing. The hands appear unrolling a map. John

Gibson expressed his opinion in a letter to the commissioners in the following terms: —

"The general effect of the figure is grand and simple. The ample cloak, which covers considerably the odious modern dress, is rich and broad, and the folds are managed with great skill, producing graceful lines. The head, a fine subject, is reflective and well modelled; also the position of the hands holding the paper, or plan, is very natural and well composed. In fact, I consider the work does the authoress great honor; and I feel it will give satisfaction to the gentlemen of the committee who had the penetration to entrust the execution of such a work to their countrywoman; and I may add, that the Americans may now boast of possessing what no nation in Europe possesses, — a public statue by a woman, — a little woman, — young, with great talent and love of her art."

A letter of W. Crow, written the day after the inauguration, states that the general expression of the thousands who saw it was favorable. Critics pronounced it a success as a work of art. Friends of Col. Benton declared it to be a good likeness. His relatives were more than gratified, — they were delighted.

On the east side of the pedestal, the name BENTON is deeply cut. On the west side, the words: —

"THERE IS THE EAST —
THERE IS INDIA."

This motto was selected by the artist with excellent judgment. It associates this memorial of a great man with no transient political questions, but with a vast enterprise of national utility and honor, a triumphant work of civilization, the grandeur of which will be revealed more and more in successive ages, in regard to which the forecasting views of the statesman will be held in honored remembrance, when the party struggles of his time will be forgotten, when majestic journeys across the continent will be incidents of common life. Our readers will be glad to see the peroration of the speech on the Pacific Railroad which suggested the motto: —

"Let us complete the grand design of Columbus, by putting Europe and Asia into communication, and that to our advantage, through the heart of our own country. Let us give to his ships, converted into cars, a continued course unknown to all former times. Let us make the iron road — and make it from sea to sea — . . . . the line which will find on our continent the Bay of San Francisco at one end, St. Louis in the middle, the national metropolis and great commercial emporiums at the other, and which shall be adorned with its crowning honor, the colossal statue of the great Columbus, whose design it accomplishes, hewn from the granite mass of a peak of the Rocky Mountains overlooking the road, — the mountain itself the pedestal, and the statue a part of the mountain, — pointing with outstretched arm to the western horizon, and saying to the flying passenger, "There is the East — there is India."

The contract price of the statue to be paid to the artist was ten thousand dollars; the entire expense of the monument about thirty thousand dollars.

In the Dublin Exhibition of 1865, Miss Hosmer offered to the public the Sleeping Faun, in marble of life size, which was sold on the day it was opened for five thousand dollars. Sir Charles Eastlake said, "If it had been discovered among the ruins of Rome or Pompeii, it would have been pronounced one of the best of Grecian statues." It was exhibited again in the Universal Exposition of Paris, 1867, where, with the great paintings of Church, Bierstadt, Huntington, and others, it gave to the most æsthetic nations new apprehensions of the progress and honors of American art. "Among the many pieces of marble statuary of modern artists," says the United States Commissioner, E. C. Cowdin, Esq., "none was more admired than the Sleeping Faun, a figure of antique grace finely conceived and admirably executed."

The Waking Faun, a companion piece, at a recent date was only clay. It is owned, with a second copy of the former, by Lady Ashburton, of England.

Another classic and beautiful work was a fountain designed for Lady Maria Alford. A figure of a woman, a siren, sits above the centre of the basin, which holds the water, singing. Below are three pleasing little figures, mounted on dolphins, which lie on the broad leaves of aquatic plants, enchanted by the music.

A writer in Rome, after describing this fountain, says, "Miss Hosmer has a peculiar mode of tinting the marble. I think she must have caught the better part of Gibson's idea; for she does not give it a flesh color, but a light creamy tint, which adds greatly to the expression of the statue and seems like the true color of old marble." Pointing to the fountain she said, "All those babies have got to be washed before they go away." This is the only reference we have obtained to her practice in regard to coloring statuary, — a novelty, introduced by Gibson, which encounters much opposition on the ground that it turns a statue into a doll, — that the office of sculpture is the expression of form, and should not in color, which belongs to another art, assume to be the counterpart of nature.

Several works of a varied character have been recently completed or are still in progress. Among them is a gateway for the entrance to an art-gallery at Ashridge Hall, England, ordered by Earl Brownlow. It is eight feet by sixteen, of very elaborate design. The price paid to the artist is twenty-five thousand dollars.

Another is a chimney-piece for Lady Ashburton, illustrating the death of the Dryads. It also is to be sixteen feet high. The figures are of life size in alto relievo. The cost is twelve thousand five hundred dollars.

The Bridge of Sighs, so named, was ordered two years ago by a literary gentleman of London. It illustrates in marble Hood's popular poem descriptive of a drowned woman.

In 1860 Miss Hosmer sent to her friend, Mr. Crow, at his request, the drawing of a monument for a cemetery. The cross as a symbol has been virtually surrendered to the Catholics, though Protestants may employ it with perfect right and propriety; and we trust the use of it will return. Like others, Mr. Crow had felt the incongruity with Christian faith of the heathen symbols, — the inverted torch, the Egyptian gateway, the Grecian temple, — which occur so frequently in our burial-places, and desired something new and appropriate, which should express a Christian's hopes.

The design consists of a marble pedestal, of elaborate and beautiful construction, surmounted by a group of statuary, — Christ restoring to life the daughter of Jairus. The prostrate form and the countenance of the dead maiden vividly present the fact of our mortality. The noble figure of the Saviour is full of tenderness, but without sorrow: he is doing a work of joy. On the entablature of the pedestal are the inscriptions, on the one side, "I AM THE RESURRECTION AND THE LIFE:" on the opposite side, "HE THAT BELIEVETH IN ME, THOUGH HE WERE DEAD, YET SHALL HE LIVE." On the broad spaces beneath, the family names are to be carved.

This design has not yet been put into marble; but it is eminently desirable that the conception should be realized. The subject is not hackneyed; it is sculpturesque, appropriate, and Christian. When adequately accomplished it will be a noble testimony, not only to the artist, but also to the friend whose Christian sentiments called for it; and the community of Christians have reason for deep interest in it. The symbols of faith should transcend the lower conceptions of sense, sorrow, disappointment, and darkness, giving to our cemeteries instead a characteristic expression of chastened confidence and joyful hope.

A very few days after the death of President Lincoln, a poor colored woman of Marietta, Ohio, made free by his proclamation, proposed that a monument should be erected, by the colored people of the United States, to their dead friend; and she handed to a citizen of that place five dollars as her contribution for the purpose. Twenty-three thousand dollars were raised and deposited in the hands of a committee, with the request that they would take measures for the erection of a monument in Washington.

Miss Hosmer heard of the proposed "Memorial to Freedom," and, prompted by her friends, designed a monument, a plaster cast of which has been exhibited in Boston. The structure consists, first, of a base sixty feet square, to which seven steps ascend. Four *bas reliefs* in bronze surround this base, representing incidents in the life of the president, his early occupations, his career as a member of the Legislature, his inauguration at Washington, memorable events of the war, his assassination and funeral obsequies. On the corners of this base are four short, round columns, on which stand four statues of the negro, finely idealized, showing him in four conditions, — sold as a slave, laboring on a plantation, a guide to our troops, and finally a freeman and soldier.

An octagonal base rests on the lower, on four sides of which are the inscriptions: —

"ABRAHAM LINCOLN;
MARTYR PRESIDENT OF THE UNITED STATES;
EMANCIPATOR OF FOUR MILLIONS OF MEN;
PRESERVER OF THE AMERICAN UNION."

Upon this is a circular base, around which is a *bas relief* of thirty-six female figures, hand in hand, symbolical of the Union of the States. From this rises a pillared temple, within which stands the statue of the president, holding in the left hand a broken chain, in the right the proclamation of emancipation. Upon the cornice of the temple are inscribed the concluding words of that instrument: "And upon this, sincerely believed to be an act of justice, I invoke the considerate judgment of mankind, and the gracious favor of Almighty God." Four mourning Victories standing around the central figure with trumpets reversed express the sorrow of the nation.

In this design, the description of which is given chiefly in the author's words, she endeavored to express the idea that the Temple of Fame which we rear to the memory of Lincoln rests upon the two great acts of his administration, — the Emancipation of the Slave, and the Preservation of the American Union; and with beautiful fitness the end is accomplished. The work itself is sufficient evidence of her convictions as a pronounced and stanch friend of freedom and the Union. It must have been a labor of love; she must have fashioned it with her heart as well as with artistic genius.

The "London Art Journal" published an engraving and description, modified by presenting four female figures near the columns of the temple bearing wreaths to the freedmen, from which we extract the following sentences: "With the exception of the great monument to Frederick the Great, at Berlin, by Rauch, the Lincoln Monument is the grandest recognition of the art of sculpture that has been offered to our age. Bearing in mind that this is to be called the Freedmen's Monument, it was necessary that the circumstances attending the act of emancipation should form, as they do, the principal features of the design. It will stand a simple, comparatively unadorned, yet most imposing, memorial of the dead, and a lasting witness to the lady sculptor who has had the honor to be selected for its execution."

The committee adopted the design, "deeming it the greatest achievement of modern art," and confident that every one who loves his country, and loves art, and honors Abraham Lincoln, will aid in the completion of this great work. It will cost two hundred and fifty thousand dollars; but this should not prevent its erection. There are now commenced or proposed three memorial structures, which the nation may well hasten to complete, even in times of political and financial difficulty, — the monuments to the Pilgrims, to Washington, and to Lincoln.

It will be observed that Miss Hosmer has wrought on ideal subjects. She would have enjoyed abundant patronage working on busts, but has preferred to give the creations of her own imagination a solid, enduring form. She thus makes a higher challenge for immortal fame.

These pages convey to our readers materials for forming their own judgment of the estimation in which she should be held as an artist. If compared with women, she has very few rivals. We do not know whether the name of Sabina Von Steinbach, who adorned the famous cathedral of Strasburg, and whose sculptured groups are the objects of admiration to this day, is more illustrious. If compared with men, there are many who compete for the palm; and the opinions of critics, no doubt, will differ, at least for a period. Time is necessary to establish the position of a genius of the highest rank. We think Miss Hosmer can afford to wait, and that she needs no indulgence of criticism on the score of her sex. She has not gained the elevation on which she now stands, unchallenged and unopposed. The sketch of Mrs. Child gives a paragraph to the fact. She herself, in the pithy and pointed words of the letter to the "London Art Journal," before adverted to, seems to say from her own experience: "Few artists who have been in any degree successful enjoy the truly friendly regard of their professional brothers; but a woman artist who has been honored by frequent commissions is an object of peculiar odium." That journal, after the impeachment which has been related, said, in connection with the Freedmen's Monument: "Of her power to fulfil the trust reposed in her there can be no doubt; her genius is of the highest order, and she has proved her capacity by producing some of the greatest works in sculpture of our age." And again: "The works of Miss Hosmer, Hiram Powers, and others we might name, have placed American on a level with the best modern sculptors of Europe. There are examples from the studios of the artists we have named specially that have not been surpassed by any contemporary sculptor of any nation; while there is no doubt that already the foundation has been laid for a school of sculpture in the Western World, which will ennoble the people who have sprung from the same loins as ourselves, who speak the same language, and read our literature, and, in spite of what some say, are proud of the old country from which they have descended." This is not the judgment of partial friends nor incompetent critics.

Miss Hosmer's diligence and enterprise have gained this crown for her genius. She has her days for the reception of visitors and her seasons for recreation and athletic exercise; but her hours of study are sacred, and she spares no effort to attain perfection in her art. "She studies from life and from death."

She received the commission for the "Bridge of Sighs" in Paris. Desiring to observe for herself the peculiar effects on the body, of death by drowning, in company with her friend, Mr. Crow, she visited the Morgue several times, till she found the required subject. When working upon the Cenci she had models go to sleep on a bench, till she had fixed the attitude of the girl sleeping in the prison. When she executed the Medusa, the hair of which changes into serpents, she found no good casts of a snake in Rome,—her knowledge of anatomy teaching her that they were taken from dead, not living specimens. She employed a herdman near the city to procure one alive, tied it to a piece of marble in her studio till she was ready, then gave it chloroform and made her cast, keeping it in the plaster three and a half hours. The reptile came out alive and well, was sent back by Goviona, turned loose in its old haunt; and she had the best model of a snake in the capital of art, of which other artists avail themselves.

Her studio in the Via Margutta is said to be itself a work of art, and the most beautiful in Rome, if not in Italy. The entrance is made attractive with flowers and birds. In the centre of the first room stands the Fountain of the Siren. Each room of the series contains some work of art, hanging baskets, and floral decorations. Her own apartment, in which she herself works, displays her early tastes in flowers and broken relics of art, with collections of minerals, drawings, and rare books. A lady writes for the use of this sketch: "She superintends her work herself, and will wield the chisel more adroitly than any practised workman. In this she has the advantage; for many artists can only design, and ignore the practical working of their ideas, which, left to a mechanical taste, often leave us an inexpressible dissatisfaction, while admiring the conception."

In the process of sculpture, the sculptor first works out carefully his own ideal in a small image of clay. The rude and mechanical labor of enlarging this image into the clay model of full size (which often requires a frame of iron and a blacksmith's forge), taking the plaster cast, and finally transferring it to marble, is done by hired workmen. "Still," in the words of Miss Hosmer, "their position in the studio is a subordinate one. They translate the original thought of the sculptor, written in clay, into the language of marble. The translator may do his work well or ill, — he may appreciate and preserve the delicacy of sentiment and grace which were stamped upon the clay, or he may render the artist's meaning coarsely and unintelligibly. Then it is that the sculptor himself must reproduce his ideal in the marble, and breathe into it that vitality which, many contend, only the artist can inspire. But, whether skilful or not, the relation of these workmen to the artist is precisely the same as that of the mere linguist to the author who, in another tongue, has given to the world some striking fancy or original thought."

Miss Hosmer's genius is not limited to sculpture. There are those who believe that, had she chosen the pursuit of letters, she would have excelled as much in literature as she does in art, — that she would have wielded the pen with as much skill and power as she does the chisel of the statuary. Evidences of this are found in her correspondence. She has published a beautiful poem, dedicated to Lady Maria Alford of England, and a well-written article, in the "Atlantic Monthly," on the Process of Sculpture, perspicuous and philosophical in its treatment of the subject. In it she defends women-artists against the impeachments of their jealous brothers.

Becoming a resident of Rome, Miss Hosmer preserved many of the habits of independence and freedom of exercise which she had formed in her native land. The latter was an indispensable condition of health: accordingly she rode about the city and its environs without restraint; and after a while people ceased to wonder.

About six years ago three persons established a pack of hounds in Rome for the purpose of fox-hunting. Our artist, as one of them, contributed two hundred and fifty dollars, and procured the services of a huntsman, whom she mounted at her own expense. This grew into a society of Italians and foreigners. Americans gave their money liberally, and with English residents entered warmly into the sport. Miss Hosmer, it is related, rode with astonishing ease and fearlessness. "None of the English officers excelled her in leaping ditches and fences. With her friend, Miss Cushman, she often led the chase, returning with quite as just claims for the fox as gentlemen could present." By the rules of the hunt the tail of the fox, called the brush, is given to the best and boldest rider as a trophy; but the Italians, having a majority of the members, managed everything in their own way, and, whatever might be his feats of horsemanship, never did an American receive the coveted honor. At length an act of injustice done to the American consul brought to pass a serious imbroglio in the association of hunters for recreation — and a fox. Hitherto Miss Hosmer had borne the absence of courtesy to herself in silence; but on that occasion she withdrew from the society, and addressed a spirited and spicy letter to the master of the Roman hounds, which was sent to this country for general publication, that it might be well understood with what readiness American money was received, and with what facility the honors passed to other hands.

In stature Miss Hosmer is rather under the medium height. The engraving which accompanies this sketch is from a drawing by her friend, Emily Stebbins, executed quite a number of years ago. It presents her as much resembling a fair and brilliant boy; and this agrees well with the description given by Mrs. Child of her appearance when she first returned to this country: "Her face is more genial and pleasant than her likenesses indicate; especially when engaged in conversation its resolute earnestness lights up with gleams of humor. She looks as she *is*, — lively, frank, and reliable. In dress and manners she seemed to me a charming hybrid between an energetic young lady and a modest lad. . . . She carried her spirited head with a manly air. Her broad forehead was partially shaded with short, thick, brown curls, which she often tossed aside with her fingers, as lads do." A recent photograph shows the same style of wearing the hair, and shape of the forehead, with changes of time. The eyes are more deeply set beneath the brows; and the mouth and chin with bolder curve give the expression of maturity and force.

In manner Miss Hosmer is prompt and decided. Her conversation is original, humorous, and animated; her voice clear and ringing; and her laugh, which frequently occurs, musical. She is fond of puns, and inclined to facetiousness. A common signature of letters to her friends is a hat. One of her English friends named her Berritina, — in Italian, small hat. An anecdote related to the writer by the gentleman concerned exhibits her self-reliant and almost defiant spirit. He had dined with her at the house of the American consul. When the company separated, after dark, he proposed to accompany her home. "No gentleman," was the reply, "goes home with me at night in Rome." It is needless to say she is a prominent figure in American society there.

It has already sufficiently appeared that her character is strongly marked, positive, piquant, and unique. Some would call her masculine and strong-minded. She certainly defies conventionalities, and is self-sustained, bold, and dashing to a degree which must offend those who believe it is scarcely less than a sin that a woman should trespass on the ancient rules of occupation, and the borders of that gentleness and delicacy which they have regarded as special properties and ornaments of her sex. But the defence of her youth may be repeated; her boldness is not immodest, and her humor is not malicious. No trace appears of corrupt principles and evil sentiments; and if "spirits are not finely touched but for fine uses," then her works prove that she must have been sculptured by nature as one among the noblest forms of the human soul.

By the ordinances of the Creator, and by characteristic endowments, most women must find their wisest, happiest, and most exalted life in the circle of domestic love and duty, but they are not all called to reign in the sacred dominion of the family; and, without involving themselves in questions agitated on many platforms concerning the rights and sphere of woman, not a few of their best spirits are quietly working out those problems by enterprising and honorable endeavors with triumphant results. If legislation, from whatever cause, in the past has been unjust, and if sad instances are recorded of calumny which has foamed out against the daughters of learning and art, it is still true that men generally have shown themselves disposed to honor those who have performed lofty achievements. From the time when "the women that were wise-hearted" wrought for the construction and decoration of the Tabernacle in the wilderness, and the time when Hypatia taught philosophy in Alexandria with inspiring eloquence, to the present, facts show that true and great-hearted women can find sufficient encouragement, from age to age, in the justice, admiration, and substantial rewards of brothers who are brothers; and bright on the pages that shall preserve the history of those noble sisters will stand the name of Harriet G. Hosmer.

ROSA BONHEUR.

BY PROF. JAMES M. HOPPIN.

The happy and beautiful name which heads this article is befitting the career of one of the most famed and brilliant of women; but, apt as it is, it fails to give us an idea of the remarkable energy and brave persistency of character by which its possessor has fairly acquired her fame.

About ten years ago, a gallery of French paintings of some of the most noted modern artists was opened for exhibition in the city of New York, in which, notwithstanding two vigorous pictures by Dubufe, senior, and one or two landscapes by Isabey, and some other works of well-known painters, by far the most interesting picture in the collection, which drew all eyes to it, was the portrait of Rosa Bonheur, by Dubufe, junior, which is now classical.

The face of Mademoiselle Bonheur, in this portrait, is full of fire. The bright, black eyes have great intensity of expression. The features, by no means beautiful, are yet noble, and convey the impression of concentrated force, as if sharpened by thought. The hair, cut short, is parted like a man's on one side of the head; and the costume, also, gives the suspicion of something like masculine attire. The keen and ardent intellectuality of the countenance contrasts strongly with the placid, "sonsie" expression, the stubbed horns, and gentle eyes of the well-fed, amiable yearling, whose portrait is by Mademoiselle Bonheur's own pencil, and on which she is represented as carelessly and confidently leaning.

At the same time that this gallery was opened, there was also on exhibition in the city Rosa Bonheur's picture of the "Horse-Fair,"—*Marché aux Chevaux*. This magnificent painting fairly introduced Rosa Bonheur to the American public; although, I believe, it was not the first of her pictures which had been brought to this country. It is pure life and movement. It is full of hurrying power. The horses seem to be detached from the canvas, and one almost feels, at first sight, like getting out of the way quickly, lest some of those big-boned steeds, not apparently under the entire control of their grooms, should trample him down in their fury. The dust, lit up by the sunshine of a hot summer's day, pervades with its powdery cloud the lower line of the picture. The horses are a natural breed of useful and powerful animals, in fine condition, and excited by the emulation and rush of numbers. Their necks are clothed with thunder, and the noise and shouting have brought out all their mettle and fire. The closest and most patient study is shown in marking the typical individualities of the animal, and in the production of such living power without the slightest particle of exaggeration. One can see the great masses of muscle quiver, and the very hair of the horses' coats flying about. Yet, with this absolute truth to nature, there is no servile imitation; but there is that creative touch which makes the horses alive, and bids them, as Michael Angelo said to the bronze steed of the Emperor Aurelius, "March!"

Undoubtedly this is Rosa Bonheur's greatest picture, on which her fame chiefly rests; but, in our estimation, one or two others of her paintings—especially of her cattle-scenes—are not only more pleasing, but are equally characteristic of her peculiar genius. "The Ploughing Scene in the Nivernais,"—*Labourage Nivernais*,—now in the Luxembourg gallery, is a charming pastoral landscape in the heart of sunny France, breathing the tranquil repose of nature, which softens and refines the manifestations of rough animal force. Yet how admirable the hearty strain and tug of the great oxen under the encouraging voice of their driver, as the ploughshare mounts a little rising slope of the furrowed field! One powerful white bull in the team, less tractable to the yoke than his fellows, still hangs back with a sullen light in his eye. A long, flowering shrub has been laid over upon its side by the cruel share; while, on the very edge of the ploughed ground, another little flower, untouched, lifts up its pretty, fearless head. But it is not often that our artist indulges in such delicate feminine touches as this; for her genius is bold and strong, and vies with that of man, despising the appeal to the mere poetic sensibility.

Such rural groups as "The Cantal Oxen," "Hay-making," "Morning in the Highlands," "Denizens of the Mountains," and others, are grand pastoral pictures, in which the animals seem to be, as they should, but parts of the wide and open nature.

One of her cattle-scenes tells its story at a glance. A majestic bull stands in the centre of the group, in the full perfection of his strength, the monarch of the fields. An older bull and cows lie around on the grass of a high table-land, intermixed with heather, with a wide horizon of craggy mountains in the distance.

A little way off from the central group stands, somewhat foreshortened, and as if cast in iron, a massive young bull, with a lowering and jealous expression of countenance, looking toward his companions, his horns like short daggers, and his tail brandished in air, as if he were already measuring in his rude breast the strength of his antagonist, which ere long is to be tested in deadly combat.

But there is no forcing of such a meaning on the beholder.

The idea of the piece may be this, or it may be something else equally in accordance with nature. The animal painting of the day, developed in England by Sir Edwin Landseer and others, while wonderfully true and beautiful, and in the case of the first-named artist highly poetic, contains that, as it appears to us, which is predicated upon a false principle. While there is doubtless harmony in creation, and something of typical human nature in all the lower orders of being, yet this truth may be so exaggerated as to become absolutely untrue and degrading. We are touched by the pathos of "The Shepherd's Chief Mourner" and the poetry of "Coming Events cast their Shadows before," and we laugh at "Dignity and Impudence," taking home the latent lesson on humankind so exquisitely conveyed; yet to work upon this idea altogether, to press this sentiment or fancy of moral resemblance between man and the brute creation too far, and to attribute human qualities to animals, surely takes from the truth of nature, lowers art itself, and produces often but a well-painted fable or burlesque. Rosa Bonheur at least never sins in this way. You may call it a want of the poetic element, but her animals are true to nature, and are not human beings; they are only simple oxen, sheep, horses, and dogs, subordinate parts of the animal world, keeping their own place, exhibiting the well-known traits and instincts of man's irrational servants, claiming to be nothing higher than they are, beautiful as manifesting the nature God gave them, belonging solely to the sphere of rural life, and framed in by the mountains, fields, woods, and streams, by the homely features or the sweet tranquil beauty of pastoral scenery. She is thus, as one has said, as true a daughter of Paul Potter, as of Raymond Bonheur.

Rosalie Bonheur was born in Bordeaux, France, March 23d, 1822.* Her father, Raymond Bonheur, was an artist

* The following sketch of Mademoiselle Bonheur's life is, for the most part, drawn directly from French sources.

of some original power, but was compelled by poverty to renounce his higher studies and his dreams of artistic fame, and to devote himself to giving lessons in drawing. He was thus all his life kept in the humbler walks of his profession, though he found his reward at last in living to see the fame of his daughter Rosa.

Day and night this worthy man toiled at his occupation of drawing-master, aided by his young wife Sophie, who gave lessons in music, walking daily from one end of the city to the other. Through the incessant labors of these devoted parents, the prospects of their little family, already increased to four children, became at length brighter, and Raymond set about preparing two large pictures for the Paris exhibition, when he was called upon to suffer the sudden bereavement of his wife's death. This blow crushed his hopes. Bordeaux became insupportable to him, and he removed to Paris when Rosa, his eldest child, was seven years old.

She was placed with her two little brothers under the care of a worthy matron named Catherine, who lived in the Champs Elysées; and the children were daily sent to the school of the Sisters Chaillot.

But sturdy little Rosa liked sunshine better than school, and played truant on pleasant days. Her wandering steps were drawn irresistibly toward the neighboring Bois de Boulogne, which, at that time, bore very little resemblance to the present beautiful park.

Then it was but a rough young forest or copse-wood, untrimmed and uncared for, that had sprung up in the place of the fine old oaks and beeches cut down by the Cossacks in 1815.

Great dusty avenues ran through this wood at right angles, which was very rarely visited excepting by the duellist and suicide. Sometimes the people of the villages around came to the wood to find a shady place in the heat of dog-days; and here and there might be met a stray, solitary rider. But, in spite of the shadows and solitude, the Bois de Boulogne had an unconquerable attraction for Rosa.

To her, a ten-years-old child, there was nothing so magnificent in the whole world as this forest walk. With her independent manners, brisk gait, her hair cut close, and her round, chubby face, she might have been taken for one of the truant boy-heroes of the Chaillot school, if the little petticoat coming down to her knee had not shown her sex.

She might often have been seen bounding like a kid along the forest walks, while the good Catherine supposed she was snug and safe at school.

Making excursions to the rivers and the hills, she plucked big bouquets of daisies and marigolds, or she broke her way into the thick copse, throwing herself on the grass and passing whole hours listening to the songs of the linnets, watching the magical effects of the sunlight struggling through the wood, and gazing dreamily at the great white clouds that floated through the summer sky.

At another time, stopping on the side of the road, she drew with a stick, on the sand, the objects that met her eye, horses and riders, animals and people, framing in her personages with a fanciful landscape, dotted with windmills and cottages.

Her drawing sometimes so absorbed her, that she did not notice the odd group that, after a while, gathered about her, down on their knees, too, in admiration, at the precision of the figures which the little artist had traced on the dusty road-side.

One of them said to her one day: —

"You draw well, my little girl!"

"Yes, indeed," replied the child, with a decided air. "Papa draws well too. He gave me lessons."

But these erratic ways were after a while found out, and, for better oversight, Rosa was apprenticed to a seamstress.

The spirited child felt this change bitterly; and it was very soon seen that the monotonous bondage of needle-work was wearing upon her sadly; and her pale face and meagre features caused her father to take her away, and place her in a *pension*, or young ladies' school, where, for her board and education, he gave drawing-lessons three times a week.

Rosa soon began to show her bold, self-willed nature, that brooked no control, and turned the school upside down with her pranks.

Nothing could exceed the fun and ingenuity of her extravagant madcap tricks. Cutting out grotesque caricatures of the older scholars and the teachers, especially of the English master, she fastened these by threads to balls of chewed paper, and then flinging them to the ceiling, there they dangled and grimaced, to the infinite amusement of the younger scholars.

There was no search for the offender. Rosa was at once sentenced to a dry crust and water.

But, in the mean while, her extraordinary talent was recognized, and madame, who kept the school, was very careful to gather up these cuttings and caricatures for her album, forming thus an amusing collection.

In her other studies Rosa made poor progress. Drawing absorbed her. You might punish her and deprive her of food, and shut her up, but she would sketch landscapes with charcoal on the walls of her closet prison.

At the year's end, to the embarrassment of her father and the envious admiration of the other pupils, she never failed to bear away the first prize for drawing.

Rosa would have been even happy at this school, were it not that her school-mates, by their mean jealousy and spite, deeply wounded her self-esteem.

Most of the girls belonged to aristocratic and wealthy families, and the daughter of a poor drawing-master was looked upon by them as a kind of mendicant, admitted by an act of special charity into their company.

Twenty times a day, and especially at meal-times, these young simpletons humiliated and martyrized their fellow-pupil by making comparisons of her plain gown with their silk dresses, or their silver goblet with her pewter tankard.

These needle-points stung Rosa's proud young spirit. She grew morbid and sombre. She avoided the society of her companions. She had long crying fits, and at times was violently irascible and demonstratively contemptuous of the whole establishment.

M. Bonheur found it necessary to take his daughter home under his own humble roof, and here her troubled spirit found rest. She threw herself at once wholly into artistic pursuits. All day long she never quitted her father's study, drawing and painting incessantly. When it grew too late to draw, she betook herself to modelling in wax or clay; for she early developed a remarkable genius for sculpture, and for some time the struggle was hard as to which branch of art she should follow, but finally the charms of color prevailed over those of form.

When she had decided to pursue painting as a vocation, she spent her mornings at the Louvre Gallery, studying and copying the pictures of the great masters of the Italian school, and of Poussin and Lesueur, rather slighting the Flemish painters. The director of the Louvre Gallery, M. Mousseline, said of her at this time, "*Je n'ai pas vu jusqu'ici d'exemple, d'une telle application, et d'une telle ardeur au travail.*"

When she had finished her day's work at the Louvre, she began her studies with her father. He was her only teacher; and he did not permit her to do anything for public exhibition until he thought her genius was sufficiently matured.

Four years were thus passed in the study of the old masters.

But at length she was forced to answer the question, to what particular aim were her efforts to be directed? Should she become an historical painter? That would be to forget that she was a woman. Should she be a *genre* painter? That was something which did not meet the inmost bent and quality of her mind.

Then it was that the remembrance of her early wanderings in the "Bois de Boulogne" came freshly to her. She recalled the long delights and delicious dreams that she had, as a child, in communion with open nature in the fields and woods, and she awoke to the fact that she was to be a painter of pastoral nature.

Immediately, with the energy of will which she put into everything that she undertook, and which Goethe says makes the difference between the great and small mind, she began to study, not the painted classical landscapes, with their eternal mountains like mill-stones, and their Arcadian fountains covered with Greek inscriptions, but the streams, woods, fields, and mountains near at hand, of God's making, and covered with their living flocks and herds.

Every morning Rosa departed with her painting apparatus, and some simple provision for her noontide meal, crossing the city barriers, and straying, wherever her fancy led her, in the green fields around Paris.

After having walked a long distance into the country, she rested at the border of some stream, prepared the colors of her palette, and made a rapid sketch of the scene where she happened to be.

She returned home worn out with fatigue, and often with her garments drenched and covered with mud; but this did not prevent her from doing the same thing the next day.

Her attention was even then given to animated nature,

drawing the animals that she came across in the fields, and studying their habits; but she longed to have a farm-yard and stable at home, and, in fact, a couple of all the animals that were in the ark. As she could not quite realize this wish, she came as near it as possible.

They lived in the sixth story of a house in the Rue Rumfort. Their lodging consisted of four very small rooms, opening out upon a little terrace. Rosa managed to make this terrace into a hanging garden, with flowers, rope-weeds, and other climbing plants, — a kind of oasis flourishing amid an endless desert of roofs and chimneys. And here was installed a pretty sheep of Beauvais, with fine, long silken wool, and which for two years served as a model for our young artist.

But this was not enough. With a courage above her sex, the young girl went three times a week to visit the *abattoir* of the Roule. There she passed whole days braving the disgusting features of the place, and working and taking sketches amid a crowd of butchers and flayers.

At last she made her début in the *Salon* exhibition of 1841, with two pictures, entitled "Goats and Sheep," and "Two Rabbits."

The next year she followed with "Animals in a Field," "A Cow lying in a Meadow," and "A Horse Sale." In 1844 she exhibited "Horses out to Pasture," and "Horses going to Water."

She kept her pictures in her study until she was satisfied with them, never compromising her reputation with a hasty production; so that in the exhibition of 1844 she had but three little paintings and the clay model of a bull; but, in 1845, she sent in twelve pictures of marked merit with the true stamp of genius.

Mademoiselle Bonheur did not have to struggle through long years of obscurity. She rose at once into fame. Her works, though at first a little timid, showed unexampled accuracy, purity, and a vigorous sentiment of nature.

The purchase of her noble picture of "Cantal Oxen," by England, set the seal to her reputation; and at the same time the French committee of award decreed her a medal of the first class. Horace Vernet, president of the commission, proclaimed her triumph before a brilliant assembly, and presented her in the government's name, a superb Sévres vase.

In 1849 Rosa Bonheur sent to the Exhibition a number of remarkable paintings, among them the famous "Ploughing Scene in the Nivernais," and a "Morning Scene" ordered by the government. In eight years she had exhibited thirty-one pictures, and many more were painted for private individuals. Her reputation had now become European, indeed world-wide; she could not fulfil half her orders from rich amateurs, and wealth began to flow in upon her.

But she was still the same simple Rosa Bonheur that she is to-day, absorbed in her art, and never showing any extravagance or excess of display in her pictures. She never attempted the sensational or impossible. She did not try any novel methods of effect, and was true to nature.

All her pictures are truly felt and thoroughly executed. There is no need of searching for any other cause of success. Simplicity has done more for her than artifice for others. In looking at her pictures people were surprised to find an impression of a serious character in the faces of the great white and red oxen, the limpid eye, and the muzzle dripping with foam; the peaceable look of sheep browsing on the savory grass of the hills and mountains, and the landscape breathing the pensive charm and filled with the perfume of the summer fields; it was in fact art which simply reproduced the charm of nature.

"The mission of Rosa Bonheur," says M. Lepelle, of Bois Gallais, "is to decipher the sublime poetry of rural nature, and to translate to us the works of God. It is in the fields, the woods, the most rugged and solitary mountains, that she finds the inspiration for her pictures, and her pencil teaches us to read deeper lessons in the book of creation."

Perhaps the highest quality of Rosa Bonheur as an artist, and that is saying a great deal, is her truth to nature, — what the French call "the probity of her pencil." Here she wins our inmost sympathy.

Physically, Rosa Bonheur is of medium, or rather small, stature. Her features are a little hard and masculine, but regular. Her forehead is broad and beautiful. All the lines of her face indicate immense force of character. Her black or dark-brown eyes are full of brilliancy; her hands are small and finely shaped.

Owing to the peculiar demands of her department of art, leading her to traverse fields, to visit farm-yards and markets, to mingle among shepherds, laboring men, and horse-dealers, she is accustomed, on such excursions, to wear a man's dress, and looks very much in it like a young farmer. It is impossible to recognize her sex. But she never appears in this garb excepting in the country.

Her dress at all times is simple to carelessness. Greedy of time alone, she cannot afford to spend it upon herself.

Wearing a great slouched hat, coming over her face and neck, she walks quickly with a firm step, her head down, observing no one, and preoccupied with thought. She is invariably accompanied in her rambles by two great dogs, of one of which she has made a portrait.

Her masculine dress has sometimes led her into some odd adventures, that are related by her biographers, but which we do not think is worth the while to repeat.

She lives in the Rue d'Assas, near the corner of the Rue Vagiraud, in the only quarter of Paris where one still finds gardens which have not given way to modern improvements and to an avalanche of stones. Her little cottage, standing back from the street a short distance, is literally embowered in foliage.

The ground floor contains a dining-room and three sleeping apartments quite modestly furnished. On the first floor, ascending to it by a carefully carpeted staircase, you come to Mademoiselle Bonheur's atelier. This is hung with green velvet, and is filled with exquisite and bizarre objects of art; and, with its tapestry, inlaid floors, pictures, bronzes, pieces of armor, skins of wild animals for rugs, and branching horns of deer and oxen upon the walls, it forms a curious and brilliant *salon*. It is open for receptions on Fridays. While courteously entertaining her guests Mademoiselle Bonheur still continues working. "Allow me to resume my brush; we can talk just as well together," she says, after the first salutation.

She rises at six, and when the day closes she is still found at her easel, not leaving it until an hour after midnight. During this long period of work she is refreshed by now and then hearing reading and music.

It is said that George Sand is her favorite author, though it is difficult to understand how a character of such perfect simplicity and purity as Rosa Bonheur's could find the slightest satisfaction of mind or heart from such an author. Evidently she yields to the irresistible charm of the style, feeling that the poison of the ideas has no danger for her.

She early decided not to marry, wedding herself to her art. During her visit in England, it was half jocosely and half seriously talked of, that Sir Edwin Landseer should marry her; but perhaps the fact of her vigorous rivalship in the same line of art daunted the amiable old bachelor. It is said that when he first saw her "Horse Fair," he magnanimously and humorously exclaimed, "It surpasses me, though it's a little hard to be beaten by a woman."

Mademoiselle Bonheur has made many journeys. She has visited the picturesque portions of France, and roamed over the Pyrenees into Spain. Her delight is in the mountains, — the more solitary and wild the better; and she seldom fails to bring home from these excursions a number of exquisite sketches. Her companion in these journeys is a Mademoiselle Micas, who resides with her in Paris. This is a middle-aged lady, herself an artist, who, besides being gifted with many mental accomplishments, is said to have a remarkable power of subduing vicious animals by the magnetism of her eye. She thus approaches the most dangerous bulls roaming the mountain pastures, who are induced to stand quietly for their portraits.

Rosa has partially realized the dream of her youth in becoming the possessor, at her home in the Rue d'Assas, of quite a number of animals, — two horses, four goats, an ox, a cow, donkeys, sheep, and dogs, without naming many smaller animals, and rare fowls and birds.

She studies the individual traits of animals. She loves to give their natural history, which she does with piquant originality. She grows poetical and enthusiastic in setting forth the characters and dispositions of her favorites. In conversation, she has vivacity joined with depth of judgment and exquisite delicacy of ideas. She knows how to be very sarcastic, but her generous nature does not allow her to exercise her talent often in this direction. She is abrupt and independent, but kindly, noble, and self-sacrificing.

In 1849 she lost her father, whom she loved with all the devotion of her strong nature.

Her father had been made the director of the Communal School of Design for girls, in the Rue Dupuytren. Rosa assisted him in his duties, and after his death took his place nominally, although her sister Juliette, now Madame Peyrol, really carries on the school.

Rosa makes a weekly visit to the institution, and this is

the great day of the week for the school, — a day of mingled laughter and tears.

The moment her quick, firm step is heard in the hall of the building, there is a solemn silence.

She passes rapidly round in review, giving to each pupil's work a penetrating glance and word.

Above all she cannot endure bad drawing, and where a scholar repeats her mistakes she is sometimes very severe, telling her that she had better go home to her mother and learn to make bread, or some cutting remark of the kind; which, however, a moment after is followed by some excessively droll and good-natured speech, that dries up the tears of the poor girl, and sets her laughing with the rest.

Upon her great picture of the "Horse-Fair," Rosa Bonheur spent eighteen months of the most conscientious and exhausting labor. Dressed in a blouse, she went twice a week to the horse-market, studying the animals, and, in fact, their Normandy owners and grooms, the portraits of some of whom she has spiritedly painted. This picture was bought by the French government, but afterwards fell again into Mademoiselle Bonheur's hands, and she sold it to M. Gambart for forty thousand francs. It was purchased by William P. Wright of New Jersey, and is now owned by A. T. Stewart.

Rosa Bonheur has received immense sums for her pictures, and has, indeed, but to offer her paintings and her portfolio of sketches to the public, to become wealthy; but she is not greedy of money, and is so generous in her gifts to relatives and charitable objects, that she does not accumulate property. She has been known to send to the *Mont de Pieté* the valuable gold medals that she has received in order to raise funds to assist fellow-artists.

She supports two aged females, who were formerly her servants. Among many stories of her liberality we mention two. A poor lady artist, who had been coldly repulsed by several rich men of her own profession, to whom, in her extreme distress, she had reluctantly applied for assistance, went at last to Rosa Bonheur, who immediately took down a small but valuable painting from her study wall, and insisted upon her accepting it, by which a very considerable sum of money was raised.

A young sculptor, who was an ardent admirer of her genius, addressed her a modest note enclosing a bill for a hundred francs, which, he said, was all he possessed, asking her if she would send him a little drawing of the value of the bill. The same evening she returned to him his bill accompanied by an exquisite sketch estimated to be worth at least a thousand francs.

We would close this brief account of her life, by quoting from a graphic description, recently written by a Paris newspaper correspondent, of Rosa Bonheur and her country home: —

"Rosa Bonheur's workshop is far away from the breweries of Mont Breda, or the chestnuts of the Luxembourg. You must take the Lyons line; get out at Fontainebleau, and ask the first individual you meet the road to Chateau By. After an hour's walk, in a thick wood, you perceive at an opening of the Thourmery woods an airy-looking building, in which the architect has combined iron, brick, and wood with rare artistic taste. From the cellar to the roof everything is graceful and coquettish in this miniature castle. Its irregularity is its greatest charm, and your eyes could feast all day on the turrets hung with ivy and the balconies entwined with honeysuckle, if your ears did not ring with a peculiar harmony which detracts from your admiration. You imagine that in the barn near by an Orpheus transformed into an animal is chanting forth a chorus of Richard Wagner's; but, after listening attentively, this strange concert is found to proceed from the bleating of sheep, the lowing of cows, the neighing of horses, and the yelping of dogs.

"The servant pointed out to me a funny-looking little man, coming towards me knitting his eyebrows. He had on an enormous straw hat. Looking under it I perceived a soft, beardless face, browned by the sun and lighted up by two moderate-sized chestnut-colored eyes. The small nose rather exaggerated the size of the large mouth, showing two rows of superb teeth. Long hair flowed from under her large peasant hat in great negligence.

"'Who are you?' 'Where do you come from?' and 'What do you want?' said she to me sharply. She stopped in front of me, and thrust her hands in the pockets of a pair of gray-ribbed velvet pants. I had been struck with the minuteness of those hands, and looked at her feet, which were equally microscopic, in spite of their thick covering of calfskin undressed, with pegged soles.

"This Cæsar-like apostrophe disconcerted me a little, but recovering my coolness, I answered, 'I am a journalist, and I wish to see Miss Bonheur.'

"'Well, look at her,' said the little peasant, taking off his head-gear.

"She continued in a milder tone, 'You must excuse me; you understand that I am obliged to keep intruders away. If talent makes a wild beast of a person, it is scarcely worth desiring. You know, also, the loss of time occasioned by the visits of strangers; the weariness caused by their questions. Come now with me; I am going to show you my sheep; if it tires you I can't help it; hurry, because I left one half shorn, and if the fleece is not taken off at once the poor beast burns on one side and freezes on the other. I was born to be a farmer, but fate decided otherwise. I am a painter, and out of my element.'"

We should be glad, were we able, to make a detailed criticism of Mademoiselle Bonheur's works and artistic genius. We will offer a few words, setting forth as best we can her relative rank as an artist, and, in the phrase of that philosophic French critic, M. Taine, the "*milieu*" to which her character and style of art-production belongs.

Rosa Bonheur is acknowledged to be, beyond all gainsaying, a master. She is one of the few painters of the day of any country, who deserve that title. She has attained that proud eminence, which many a man of decided power, but who still walks in stereotyped paths, has not been able to win. It implies that in her own special field of art she has exhibited an original genius, and has become a leading, if not the leading, representative. She is, undoubtedly, the greatest *female* artist who has ever lived.

Of the two principal departments of art comprehended in the idealistic and naturalistic schools, Rosa Bonheur belongs decidedly to the latter. Nature has been her inspirer. We have seen how, by the sole force of her youthful genius, she broke away from the classical school, like a young horse that throws his rider, leaps the roadside fence, and gallops, with fiery eye and streaming mane, into the wide green fields, rejoicing in his new-found liberty. She has taken the real facts of nature for the basis of her art. She loves nature. One must love the little violet before he can paint it. By a patient, self-forgetting study of nature, by winding herself into her inmost confidence, by following those deep principles of beauty and life that are so hidden and evasive, she has grasped the secret of power. She is not beholden to the Louvre Gallery, nor to Poussin. She does not look at the clear and open face of nature "through a glass darkly" of the older school of pastoral painters, who, while men of genius, have followed some preconceived theory, some solemn artificiality, or some symbolic idea, which came between the truth of nature and the eye and soul of the artist; but in her brave and simple faith she goes away from pictures and crowds out into the pure country, lonely and still, and smelling of the fresh-broken earth and new-mown hay; she traverses rough clayey roads through the fields; she sits in the bare cottages of peasants; she chats with ploughmen in their broad-brimmed hats and blouses; she talks, too, with the patient beasts as they stand panting in the furrows, or with dreamy eye ruminate their cud under the tree-shadows in the sultry noontide; she comprehends the language of their voices, looks, and motions, and spells out, with a child-like docility, the broad page made by the hand of the Great Artist, and pictured over with flocks of sheep, — the earliest type of innocence and purity.

She goes to maternal earth for her nourishment, from whose ample breast is drawn the support of man. A healthful, ruddy child of earth, not of heaven, is her art, — playmate of the herds and flocks, baptized by the morning dew, and sleeping amid the spicy heather of the mountains. Rosa Bonheur belongs to the Dutch or Flemish school of pastoral painters, with a far finer and more earnest spirit, and with the more thorough and scientific training of the modern French school.

She is a perfectly accomplished artist in drawing, anatomy, and all the more technical and mechanical portion of her art. She skilfully uses the palette knife on her landscapes for the production of harmonious effects, which, it is said, few artists are able to do. As a colorist, or tonist, Troyon, her most formidable rival as an animal painter, is said to somewhat excel her, but in no other respect. Yet, after all, it is not in these things that the great artist is seen, but in the quality of the mind, its vigor and fineness, its capacity to produce. Here, Rosa Bonheur, deeply musing, striking out a new path for herself, going to the unfrequented but ever fresh sources of nature, having confidence in her own powers, and producing original and splendid results, shows her true greatness.

She has been called an imitator of nature, and no idealist, or without poetry and imagination; and she has been, in this regard, unfavorably compared with Sir Edwin Landseer. But all art is in one sense imitation. It is not nature itself, but it is only a representation of natural objects. It is an illusion, whose perfection is to awaken the same feelings that nature does, to grasp the essential idea which gives life and interest to the object, and forms its real subject in the mind. Rosa Bonheur does this. Her pictures are vital with the true spirit of the scene, or of an animal, and where there is poetry in the subject, there is poetry in her picture; but it is of an unobtrusive, unsentimental, every-day, naturalistic sort. It does not say, "See, here is a poem;" but its truth and beauty steal upon one unconsciously, like the beauty of simple rural scenery and country life. She does not seek the unknown, but takes the commonest and most familiar objects. She speaks to the popular heart and the common mind. While her pictures are full of almost unapproached genius in her peculiar field, yet they are comprehensible by all. Take her picture of the "Muleteers crossing the Pyrenees." They are but three common Spanish peasants, working for their daily bread; but they have come to the top of the mountain pass, among the mists and clouds, and are now beginning to descend. The way grows easier. The prospect of getting to their journey's end, of the safe termination of their wearisome march, and of the good wages that await them, fills their minds with careless happiness, which, joined to rude physical strength and spirits, makes them sing and exult. And the animals, how full of character! They evidently sympathize with their masters' content; they know very well, too, that their labors have culminated. What solemn trustworthiness and official respectability in the richly caparisoned and belled mule that cads! — what amusing knowingness in the multitude of long ears all pointed forwards! — what awkward obstinate-headedness, expecting cudgel blows, in the young rebel straying from line to pluck thistles! — what a mingling of sagaciousness and *insouciance* in the long heads and soft, almost human, eyes! There is nothing sensational, nothing highly wrought and imaginative, but there is exquisite truth, insight, thoroughness, sincerity, healthful atmosphere, power, and beauty.

Rosa Bonheur's pencil will yet produce, it is hoped, still more perfect works, bringing out undeveloped powers. She has been strongly urged to come to this country and visit our western regions, and to paint the buffalo and his Indian hunter on their boundless native prairies; but this she will never do; and her forte is not wild nature; for the fine spirit of the woman shows itself, even in the bold vigor of her genius, by her choice of domestic nature, and her preference, in the animal creation, of the noble and gentle friends of man, rather than of his foes and victims of his deadly skill. The ox rather than the lion is the symbol of her artistic inspiration. While she loves to seek the wild solitudes of mountain nature, it would seem to be for the sake of their healthful repose, and in order to find her favorite animals in their native haunts and their free modes of life.

In this quiet domain of art the feminine mind, with its truth, purity, and love of beauty, finds a fit field; though not, perhaps, in the province of what is called high art, or ideal art, but rather in the simpler province of naturalistic art. Nature is woman's field,—the study of the fresh, pure works of God, filled with his goodness and love; and yet any field, or any branch of art, for which her genius best disposes her, should be open to her freely, even if she cannot hope to become an Angelica Kauffmann or a Rosa Bonheur.

Rosa Bonheur has shown what woman can do. She has

asserted her right to follow the free bent of her own genius. She has dared to pursue the path which she felt God marked out for her; and she has thereby said to other women, if you can, do the same. Through much that seemed to be totally opposed to her sex, and impossible for a woman to achieve, she has steadily made her way, with a pure, bright purpose, and a strong, constant heart, until now the foremost men in the world recognize her equal claim to greatness. She asks no favor to be yielded her on account of her sex. She claims to be judged by her works on her essential merits, and she stands proudly, but unambitiously, the full, intellectual peer of man.

Genius has no sex. The qualities of the masculine and feminine minds, while profoundly harmonious, even in their contrasts, and together forming the perfect man, are, doubtless, as a general thing, differently "made up" in their relative proportions and dispositions, according to the varied needs of their life-work. In the masculine mind, perhaps, the constructive and philosophic elements are more prominently controlling, and in the feminine mind the intuitive and sympathetic; yet there is the same mind in both, the same "fiery particle," the same imperial and divine faculty, whether it is shown in the ruling ability of a Henry IV. of France, or an Elizabeth of England; in the philanthropic capacity of a John Howard, or a Florence Nightingale; in the literary scope and depth of an Alfred Tennyson, or a Mrs. Browning; in the creative artistic power of an Edwin Landseer, or a Rosa Bonheur.

MRS. JULIA WARD HOWE.

BY MRS. LUCIA GILBERT CALHOUN.

FOURTEEN years ago there came from the famous press of Ticknor & Company, a small volume of Poems, whose first page, beside the imprint of the publishers, bore only the simple title-line

PASSION FLOWERS.

An anonymous book of poetry does not commend itself to the reading mob, and not many copies were sold. But the critics read it, and the scholars, and that small public which had heard that it was Mrs. Howe's book, and desired to know what sort of verses a woman of society, a wit, a housewife, and a mother of children would write. It was a book that invited, and received, and defied criticism; a book powerful, pungent, and unripe. Its personalism was terrible. In every page it said, "Lo, this thing that God has made and called by my name! What is it? Why is it? Behold its passions and temptations; its triumphs and its agonies; its fervors and its doubts; its love and its scorn; its disappointment and its acquiescence!" Here at last, in America, was a woman-poet; not an echo, nor a shadow, nor a sweet singer of nothings. Another Sidney, chivalrous, gracious, and eager for her part in the battles of life; to whom, also, the muse said, "Look into thy *heart*, and write!" She was not an artist, for her song had mastered her, but it must needs have been strong-winged, and bold to do that. Clearly she was a many-sided woman, whom heart and imagination alone would have made a devotee, and her keen intellection alone a free lance, and who thus alternately believed much and nothing, alternately accepted and defied destiny. So much one might read of her history in this book.

Society knew also that she was born and reared in New York, her father being a wealthy banker, well-bred, and scholarly. Determined that this pet daughter — a wise little atom even in her babyhood — should not be merely a fashionable girl, he gave her teachers and books, appealed to her ambition, aroused her artistic instinct, and kindled her religious nature. The quick spirit responded to every touch. A wise and loving man meant only to mould a wise and loving woman; but day by day the steady eyes grew more intent in their questioning; day by day the broad brow wore lines of deeper thought; day by day the elder mind caught glimpses in the younger of that strange, ineffable gift which men call genius. The brilliant girl had written verses almost as soon as she could write at all. French and Italian she readily mastered, and in time, leaving behind her the waste and weary land of German grammar, she came into such a shining inheritance of German literature as seemed to create in her new faculties of comprehension. Goethe and Schiller were her prophets and kings, and she received with large welcome the subtile philosophers of their speculative nation. While a school-girl she published first, a review of Lamartine's Jocelyn, with translations in English verse, and afterwards a more thoughtful review of Dwight's translation of the minor poems of Goethe and Schiller.

So she grew to ripe girlhood, — reading, writing, dreaming; fiery within, as her warm tints and rich bright hair declared her, but cold without, under the repression of her education. To this day it is plain that she cannot easily reconcile her antagonisms. That her reason accepts the strictest formulas of life, her energetic intellect works well and thoroughly in the harness of existing laws and limits, while her "red temperament" sometimes besets her to set all bonds at naught, and scatter heresies of thought and conduct like firebrands.

At twenty, sentimental, romantic, longing for the actual vivacity of life, and finding only the dulness of routine, she was subject to seasons of passionate and profound melancholy. Her German studies had made her indifferent to the formal worship in which she had been bred, and no vital belief offered itself to her. Into this vague, hungry, and dark mood of hers came the awful kindness of death. The idol of her heart—her father—died, and within a brief time a dear brother also, and the questioning heretic became a religious and spiritual enthusiast. This exaltation lasted for two years. During that time the young devotee read little else than the Bible, which she undertook as a meritorious religious exercise.

One day a friend put into her hand "Guizot's History of Civilization," and then her new life began. She studied it with all the force of her vigorous mind, and its large thought aroused her from her dream of holiness to a life of use, while it lent wings to her self-centred imagination. She was now a liberal in politics, — in religion a thoughtful inquirer. She studied Paradise Lost, and felt its gloomy grandeur, while it nevertheless compelled her reason to reject an eternal hell as impossible. At twenty-three she married Dr. Samuel G. Howe, of Boston, — a man whose heroic labors for Greece in her struggle for independence, whose beautiful devotion to the blind, and whose anti-slavery crusades made men speak of him as the new Bayard. They went abroad immediately. In England the petted child, the young heiress, the idol of her own circle, the haughty belle, found that her only claim to social distinction was her husband's fame, which the recent publication of Dickens's "American Notes" had made dear to all noble English hearts. To a woman of her strong, self-centred nature, of her conscious power, and stately pride, this acceptance of her as the appendage of another, this carelessness of what sovereignty might be in herself, was an abasement as bitter as salutary. She had dreamed of literary fame; but this sudden humiliation, the new cares, the alien interests that crowded upon her, postponed her career for years. She came to the Old World as a queen comes to her own. Its beauty, its maturity, its solemn antiquity seemed her inheritance. Rome, magnificent and desolate, made her life a rapture. There her first child was born, and her passion of mother-love was hardly deeper than her passion of sad tenderness for the supreme city. Now for the first time her firmament was high enough to let her stand upright. She lived in this divine atmosphere for months, and then came back to the cold clearness of New England days, settled into the prosaic round of house-keeping, and gave herself much to society.

In spite of household cares and baby hands tugging at her priceless hours, she saved time for the hard study which was the breath of her life. She read Swedenborg, and the tough difficulties she encountered only stimulated her. She toiled at Comte, and made new resolves of thoroughness and breadth of culture. In 1850 she again went abroad, returning to her beloved home, where she wrote most of the poems included in "Passion Flowers," and where art, and books, and her precious children made that winter her golden prime. Coming back to Boston, Dr. Howe undertook the charge of "The Commonwealth,"—a newspaper dedicated to free thought, and zealous for the liberty of the slave.

And now Mrs. Howe's opportunity was come. She wrote editorials, literary articles, and verses, contributing, also, those brilliant paragraphs for which the paper was famous in its day. This success opened the way for the publication of "Passion Flowers," so overblamed and overpraised. Two years after came "Words for the Hour," — a book that palpitated, such red heart's blood coursed through the lines. These poems, like the first, were wayward, inartistic, obscure, defiant, but they were riper, and even more full of promise. In each the thought was strong, and deep, and true. The stately rhythm that now and then broke on the ear, the full and passionate expression, the terrible sarcasm, the sudden lyric glimpses, lavished by this intense soul dowered with the love of love, the hate of hate, the scorn of scorn, revealed a power which no woman but Mrs. Browning had exceeded. The critics decided to accept the new poet; but a nature so intense, a personality so strong as hers, is rarely understood or estimated at its worth. On the one hand she was assaulted with flattery, and on the other with abuse. She went steadily on her way, saying such wittily sharp things of her detractors that it argued no small courage in a man to couch a lance at her, — still studying like an undergraduate, still writing with the industry of a country parson, — and in 1857 publishing "The World's Own," — a play produced at Wallack's Theatre, in New York. It was brilliant, full of dramatic feeling, and well managed, but lacked a certain theatrical suppleness, a stage-effectiveness, without which it could not succeed.

In 1859 Dr. and Mrs. Howe accompanied the dying Theodore Parker to Cuba. A charming book of travels, witty, brilliant, airy, and graceful, was her account of this journey, published first in the "Atlantic Monthly," and then, with additions, in a volume which she called "A Trip to Cuba." Fun is very near feeling, in fine souls, and all through the book, under the ring of the laugh one catches the breathing of a sigh, as the shadows of the glittering island-life, and the shadows of a parting friendship fell on the bright observer. About these days, or earlier, readers of the "New York Tribune" were charmed with occasional letters from Boston, from New York, or Washington, about the gay world and people and places of note, about summer days and autumn glories, about art and poetry and religion. Eagerly asking whose they were, such readers came for the first time into glad relations with Mrs. Howe, and felt her to be a benefactor, for the true thoughts and bright pictures she had given them. Since 1860 her studies have been principally philosophical, including Swedenborg, Spinoza, Kant, Fichte, and Hegel. "I am afraid," she said, naively, to a friend, "I am afraid I believe in each one till I read the next."

During the last eight years she has written many admirable social and philosophic papers, which she herself values far above her poems. Six lectures on Ethics were cordially received in the drawing-room, where she read them to an audience of critical listeners. And at Northampton, at the time of the meeting of the American Society of Arts and Sciences, she read, before many of the academicians, a remarkable lecture on "Man *a priori*, and *a posteriori*." She has written, also, thoughtful essays, entitled "Polarity," "Limitation," and "The Fact Accomplished." She gave last year, to the "Christian Examiner," three able papers on "The Idea and Name of God," on "The Ideal Church," and "The Ideal State."

In 1866 she was daring enough to publish "Later Lyrics," — a third volume of miscellaneous verses, and was justified of her courage by the worth of her work. Her splendid "Battle Hymn of the Republic," set to the ringing tramp of the "John Brown Song," was the Marseillaise of the war. Who will forget, —

"Mine eyes have seen the glory of the coming of the Lord:
He is trampling out the vintage where his grapes of wrath are stored:
He hath loosed the fateful lightning of his terrible swift sword;
His truth is marching on.

"I have seen him in the watch-fires of a hundred circling camps;
They have builded him an altar in the evening dews and damps;
I can read his righteous sentence by the dim and flaring lamps;
His day is marching on.

"I have read a fiery gospel writ in burnished rows of steel;
'As ye deal with my contemners, so with you my grace shall deal;
Let the Hero, born of woman, crush the serpent with his heel,
Since God is marching on.'

"He hath sounded forth the trumpet that shall never call retreat;
He is sifting out the hearts of men before his judgment-seat;
Oh, be swift, my soul, to answer him, be jubilant, my feet!
Our God is marching on.

"In the beauty of the lilies Christ was born across the sea,
With a glory in his bosom that transfigures you and me;
As he died to make men holy, let us die to make men free,
While God is marching on."

In this third volume there is much less of the obscure, the fantastic, the forced. A lyrical series called "Her Verses," says a fine critic, "are so charged with wild passion, that they recall Mrs. Browning's 'Sonnets from the Portuguese,' with more of the Sappho, and less of the saint." Mrs. Howe has not yet mastered her splendid powers. When she has fully possessed herself America will be yet prouder of her one great woman-poet; for Harriet Prescott writes too few verses for her fame's sake, and all other women too many.

Mrs. Howe's last book is just published. It is called "From the Oak to the Olive; a Plain Record of a Pleasant Journey," and is the story of a trip from London to Athens, by way of Paris, Marseilles, Rome, Naples, and Venice. This journey was undertaken in 1867, to assist in distributing American supplies to the destitute and heroic Cretans. The road is old enough, but the traveller had new eyes. Her book is filled with lovely pictures of scenery and people, of high life, and low life, of clear character-drawing, and quaint fancies. More than this, it is profoundly thoughtful, and goes straight to the heart of institutions, manners, and habits of thinking.

With the private life of an author, or a queen, the public has no business at all. Whether Mrs. Howe stands in the kitchen eating bread and honey, or sits in the parlor counting out her money, may not be told in these pages. But certain things that any person in society may know are the property of the gentle reader. She has auburn hair, and large, sad eyes, "where soul seems concentrate in sight." Her mouth is her fine and expressive feature, though her whole face is mobile. Her bell-like voice and her pure enunciation have a charm like music, and the eloquence of her fine hands is irresistible; her wit is brilliant, ready, merciless, and her sarcasm polished and swift as the axe of the headsman Rudolph. Her friends know that music is her passion, swaying her whole being; that the drama is to her the Beautiful Art, as she has written of it in a noble poem called "Hamlet at the Boston;" that she found the infancy of her children a constant miracle of beauty, and that now, they pet and rule her as if she were the child; that the dignity of her nature, forcing her to accept simplicity as the best good, makes all luxurious and showy living distasteful to her, while her sense of symmetry and harmony delights in order and elegance.

For the rest, in the winter she dwells in Boston, abode of the blest, and in summer she lives in an enchanted glade, the loveliest place on the earth, which nobody can enter without the magic password, and about which all that the world will ever know is written in tinted lines, and called "In my Valley." The lesson of her life is earnest work, and more than any one of her sex in America, perhaps, she has demonstrated that it *is* wisdom for Women to learn the Alphabet.

TESTIMONIALS

OF THE

PHILOSOPHY OF HOUSE-KEEPING,

BY MR. & MRS. JOSEPH B. LYMAN.

Opinion of S. Edwards Todd, Esq., Agricultural Editor of the New York Daily Times.

I can heartily recommend your treatise, as it tells every one who reads its pages what to do and how to do it, in the most feasible and philosophic manner. It is exactly such a work as almost every house-keeper in the country can take into the kitchen and dining-room, and learn, from the plain, simple, practical details recorded in its pages, how to engineer every department of house-keeping with as much skill and efficiency as a joiner working from his diagrams in his Illustrated Architect.

Your book ought to be carefully studied by every house-keeper in the city and country. I heartily recommend it to all farmers and mechanics, to husbands and wives, to young men and young women. Could I have had such a book when I exchanged my state of single blessedness for that of married felicity, the practical instructions which I then needed, and which are contained in THE PHILOSOPHY OF HOUSE-KEEPING, would have been of more pecuniary value to me than the cost of a thousand books.

The Hartford Courant says:

THE PHILOSOPHY OF HOUSE-KEEPING really sets forth a philosophy of living which is sensible and practical. There is in most families abundance of material for health and comfort, if it was not misused by ignorant and incompetent house-keepers. The health depends so much upon the diet, and the observance of certain simple rules, that there is more need of information in the home department of life than in any other.

The book before us is comprehensive in its design, but simple and methodical in its plan. Cooking assumes the dignity of an art, and properly so. The book is clearly and agreeably written. We know of no one of its class that will be so useful to house-keepers.

The Soldiers' Friend, New York, says:

The volume is printed in good, clear type, on good paper, and presents to the eye, in an attractive form, a great amount of valuable information, hints, and rules, worthy of study by every house-keeper. And we advise all who want an excellent manual, to supply themselves with it, as it is placed within their reach by the publishers.

Opinion of the Rev. Samuel Seelye, D.D., of East Hampton, Mass.

The style in which it is written is elegant and chaste, showing a high degree of literary culture.

The Boston Daily Traveller says:

This is a book that is needed in every family; and it contains a vast amount of useful information, brought together in small compass, and well arranged. It is the most valuable work upon the subjects treated that we have seen.

The Springfield Republican says:

THE PHILOSOPHY OF HOUSE-KEEPING is a book which should be in the hands of every house-keeper; the good sense and thorough understanding of all the matters of which it treats, that characterize it, render it an invaluable companion for the mistress of a family. We commend it to all our readers, hoping that in their hands it may do much to inaugurate the era of hygienic house-keeping.

www.ingramcontent.com/pod-product-compliance
Lightning Source LLC
LaVergne TN
LVHW021054110826
845150LV00001B/70

* 9 7 8 1 4 2 5 5 6 7 1 7 0 *